Private Health Insurance

Can private health insurance fill gaps in publicly financed coverage? Does it enhance access to health care or improve efficiency in health service delivery? Will it provide fiscal relief for governments struggling to raise public revenue for health? This book examines the successes, failures and challenges of private health insurance globally through country case studies written by leading national experts. Each case study considers the role of history and politics in shaping private health insurance and determining its impact on health system performance. Despite great diversity in the size and functioning of markets for private health insurance, the book identifies clear patterns across countries, drawing out valuable lessons for policymakers while showing how history and politics have proved a persistent barrier to effective public policy.

This title is also available as Open Access on Cambridge Core.

SARAH THOMSON is a Senior Health Financing Specialist at the WHO Barcelona Office for Health Systems Strengthening.

ANNA SAGAN is a Research Fellow at the European Observatory on Health Systems and Policies.

ELIAS MOSSIALOS is Brian Abel-Smith Professor of Health Policy, Head of the Department of Health Policy and Director of LSE Health at the London School of Economics and Political Science.

European Observatory on Health Systems and Policies

The volumes in this series focus on topical issues around the transformation of health systems in Europe, a process being driven by a changing environment, increasing pressures and evolving needs.

Drawing on available evidence, existing experience and conceptual thinking, these studies aim to provide both practical and policy-relevant information and lessons on how to implement change to make health systems more equitable, effective and efficient. They are designed to promote and support evidence-informed policy-making in the health sector and will be a valuable resource for all those involved in developing, assessing or analysing health systems and policies.

In addition to policy-makers, stakeholders and researchers in the field of health policy, key audiences outside the health sector will also find this series invaluable for understanding the complex choices and challenges that health systems face today.

Series Editors

JOSEP FIGUERAS Director, European Observatory on Health Systems and Policies

MARTIN MCKEE Co-Director, European Observatory on Health Systems and Policies, and Professor of European Public Health at the London School of Hygiene & Tropical Medicine

ELIAS MOSSIALOS Co-Director, European Observatory on Health Systems and Policies, and Brian Abel-Smith Professor of Health Policy, London School of Economics and Political Science

REINHARD BUSSE Co-Director, European Observatory on Health Systems and Policies, and Head of the Department of Health Care Management, Berlin University of Technology

Private Health Insurance

History, Politics and Performance

Edited by

SARAH THOMSON
WHO Barcelona Office for Health Systems Strengthening

ANNA SAGAN
European Observatory on Health Systems and Policies,
London School of Economics and Political Science, London
School of Hygiene and Tropical Medicine

ELIAS MOSSIALOS
London School of Economics and Political Science

CAMBRIDGE
UNIVERSITY PRESS

University Printing House, Cambridge CB2 8BS, United Kingdom

One Liberty Plaza, 20th Floor, New York, NY 10006, USA

477 Williamstown Road, Port Melbourne, VIC 3207, Australia

314–321, 3rd Floor, Plot 3, Splendor Forum, Jasola District Centre,
New Delhi – 110025, India

79 Anson Road, #06–04/06, Singapore 079906

Cambridge University Press is part of the University of Cambridge.

It furthers the University's mission by disseminating knowledge in the pursuit of
education, learning, and research at the highest international levels of excellence.

www.cambridge.org
Information on this title: www.cambridge.org/9780521125826
DOI: 10.1017/9781139026468

First published 2020

A catalogue record for this publication is available from the British Library

ISBN 978-0-521-12582-6 Paperback

European Observatory on Health Systems and Policies

The European Observatory on Health Systems and Policies supports and promotes evidence-based health policy-making through comprehensive and rigorous analysis of health systems in Europe. It brings together a wide range of policy-makers, academics and practitioners to analyse trends in health reform, drawing on experience from across Europe to illuminate policy issues.

The European Observatory on Health Systems and Policies is a partnership hosted by the World Health Organization Regional Office for Europe, which includes the Governments of Austria, Belgium, Finland, Ireland, Norway, Slovenia, Spain, Sweden, Switzerland, the United Kingdom, and the Veneto Region of Italy; the European Commission; the World Bank; UNCAM (French National Union of Health Insurance Funds); the Health Foundation; the London School of Economics and Political Science; and the London School of Hygiene & Tropical Medicine. The Observatory has a secretariat in Brussels and it has hubs in London (at LSE and LSHTM) and at the Berlin University of Technology.

Contents

Figures

Tables

Boxes

Acknowledgements

The editors are indebted to the many national experts who contributed to writing and reviewing the chapters in this volume. They are listed below. We thank them for their patience in seeing the book through to publication. We are also grateful to Bob Evans (University of British Columbia) for his contribution to the planning of the book, Joe Kutzin (WHO headquarters) for his feedback on the overview chapter and Camilo Cid (Pan American Health Organization), Valeria de Oliveira Cruz (WHO Regional Office for South-East Asia), Awad Mataria (WHO Regional Office for the Eastern Mediterranean), Grace Kabaniha (WHO Regional Office for Africa) and Peter Cowley (WHO Western Pacific Region) for their comments on selected country-based chapters and Jonathan North and Caroline White (European Observatory on Health Systems and Policies) for preparing the manuscript for publication. The editors alone are responsible for any mistakes.

We dedicate this book to the memory of Revital Gross and Alan Maynard, who contributed to an early draft. Revital Gross was Associate Professor at the School of Social Work, Bar-Ilan University and a Senior Researcher at the Smokler Center for Health Policy Research, Myers-JDC-Brookdale Research Institute. Alan Maynard was Professor of Health Economics at the University of York and the founding director of the Centre for Health Economics.

Contributors

Shuli Brammli-Greenberg: Faculty member, Department of Health Administration and Economics, Braun School of Public Health, Faculty of Medicine, the Hebrew University of Jerusalem, and Senior Research Scholar, Smokler Center for Health Policy Research, Myers-JDC-Brookdale Institute, Jerusalem, Israel.

Lawrence D. Brown: Professor of Health Policy and Management, Mailman School of Public Health, Columbia University, New York, New York, United States.

Agnès Couffinhal: Senior Economist, The World Bank, Washington DC, United States.

Luca Crivelli: Head, Department of Business Economics, Health and Social Care, University of Applied Sciences and Arts of Southern Switzerland, Manno, Switzerland, and Vice-Director Swiss School of Public Health, Professor at Università della Svizzera italiana, Lugano, Italy.

Maria Dolores Montoya Diaz: Professor, School of Economics, Business and Accounting, University of São Paulo, São Paulo, Brazil.

Stefanie Ettelt: Associate Professor in Health Policy, Department of Health Services Research and Policy, London School of Hygiene and Tropical Medicine, London, United Kingdom.

Denzil G. Fiebig: Professor, School of Economics, University of New South Wales, Sydney, Australia.

Carine Franc: Senior Health Economist Research, INSERM, National Institute for Biomedical and Human Health Research, and Associate xvi *List of Contributors*

Researcher, Institute for Research and Information in Health Economics (IRDES), Paris, France.

Sherry A. Glied: Dean, Professor of Public Service, Robert F. Wagner Graduate School of Public Service, New York University, New York, New York, USA.

Kees van Gool: Deputy Director and Professor, Centre for Health Economics Research and Evaluation, University of Technology Sydney, Australia.

G. Emmanuel Guindon: Centre for Health Economics and Policy Analysis (CHEPA)/Ontario Ministry of Health and Long-Term Care Chair in Health Equity, Associate Professor in the Department of Health Research Methods, Evidence, and Impact (HEI), associate member of the Department of Economics, McMaster University, Hamilton, Ontario, Canada.

Noah Haber: Postdoctoral fellow, Meta-research Innovation Center at Stanford (METRICS), Stanford University, Stanford, California, USA.

Jane Hall: Distinguished Professor of Health Economics, University of Technology Business School, and Director of Strategy, Centre for Health Economics Research and Evaluation, University of Technology, Sydney, Australia.

Jeremiah Hurley: Dean of Social Sciences, Professor at the Department of Economics and the Centre for Health Economics and Policy Analysis, McMaster University, Hamilton, Ontario, Canada.

Naoki Ikegami: Professor Emeritus, Keio University, and adjunct researcher, Japan Medical Association Research Institute, Tokyo, Japan.

Patrick Jeurissen: Professor in Fiscal Sustainability of Health Care Systems, Radboud University Medical Centre, Nijmegen, the Netherlands.

Soonman Kwon: Professor of Health Economics and Policy, School of Public Health, Seoul National University, Seoul, South Korea.

Yue-Chune Lee: Professor, Institute of Health and Welfare Policy and Masters program on Trans-disciplinary Long-Term Care and Management, National Yang-Ming University, Taipei, Taiwan, China.

Dan P. Ly: PhD candidate in Health Policy, Harvard University, Cambridge, Massachussetts, USA.

Hans Maarse: Emeritus Professor of Health Policy Science, University of Maastricht, Maastricht, Netherlands.

Di McIntyre: Emeritus Professor, Health Economics Unit, University of Cape Town, Cape Town, South Africa.

Heather McLeod: Extraordinary Professor, Department of Statistics and Actuarial Science, University of Stellenbosch, Stellenbosch, South Africa, and Honorary Senior Research Fellow, School of Nursing, University of Auckland, Auckland, New Zealand.

Philipa Mladovsky: Assistant Professor, Department of International Development, London School of Economics and Political Science, London, United Kingdom.

Elias Mossialos: Co-Director, European Observatory on Health Systems and Policies, and Brian Abel-Smith Professor of Health Policy, London School of Economics and Political Science, London, United Kingdom.

David Muthaka: Economic Policy Analyst, Kenya and Research Associate at Kenya Institute for Public Policy Research and Analysis (KIPPRA), Nairobi, Kenya.

Emma Pitchforth: Senior Lecturer and Senior Research Fellow in Primary Care, University of Exeter, Exeter, United Kingdom.

Andres Roman-Urrestarazu: Assistant Professor, International Health Department, Maastricht University, Maastricht, the Netherlands, and Harkness Fellow 2020–2021, University of Cambridge, Cambridge, United Kingdom.

Anna Sagan: Research Fellow, European Observatory on Health Systems and Policies, London School of Economics and Political Science, London School of Hygiene and Tropical Medicine, London, United Kingdom.

Wael Fayek Saleh: Assistant Professor, Faculty of Medicine, Cairo University, Cairo, Egypt.

Flavia Mori Sarti: Professor, School of Arts, Sciences and Humanities, University of São Paulo, São Paulo, Brazil.

Samantha Smith: Research Fellow, Centre for Health Policy and Management, Trinity College, Dublin, Ireland.

Sarah Thomson: Senior Health Financing Specialist, WHO Barcelona Office for Health Systems Strengthening, Barcelona, Spain.

Brian Turner: Lecturer, Department of Economics, Cork University Business School, University College Cork, Cork, Ireland.

Ruth Waitzberg: Research Scholar, Smokler Center for Health Policy Research, Myers-JDC-Brookdale Institute, Jerusalem, Israel; PhD Fellow, Department of Health Systems Management, School of Public Health, Faculty of Health Sciences, Ben-Gurion University of the Negev, Beer-Sheva, Israel; and Fellow researcher, Department of Health Care Management, Faculty of Economics and Management, Technical University Berlin, Berlin, Germany.

1 | *Why private health insurance?*

SARAH THOMSON, ANNA SAGAN, ELIAS MOSSIALOS

A disproportionate impact on health system performance

Private health insurance makes a small contribution to spending on health in most countries around the world, but its effect on health system performance can be surprisingly large owing to market failures and weaknesses in public policy. Because private health insurance can have a disproportionate impact, leading to risk segmentation, inequality and inefficiency, it should be considered and monitored with care.

Proponents of private health insurance fall into two camps. Some see private health insurance as attractive in its own right: in their view, a permanently mixed system of health financing will enhance efficiency and consumer choice. Others regard private health insurance as a second-best option in the context of fiscal constraints: not as desirable as public spending on health, but preferable to out-of-pocket payments. In richer countries, it is argued, encouraging the wealthy to pay more for health care or allowing public resources to focus on essential services will relieve pressure on government budgets (Chollet & Lewis, 1997). In poorer countries, private health insurance can play a transitional role, helping to boost pre-paid revenue and paving the way for public insurance institutions (Sekhri & Savedoff, 2005). A key assumption in both contexts is that private health insurance will fill gaps in publicly financed health coverage, even though economic theory indicates that gaps may be filled for some people, but not for others. Analysts who acknowledge this tension suggest that it can be addressed through regulation (Sekhri & Savedoff, 2005).

Evidence of international interest in private health insurance first emerged in the early 1990s, in work funded by the European Commission. Studies systematically analysing private health insurance in the European Union (Schneider, 1995; Mossialos & Thomson, 2002; Thomson & Mossialos, 2009) were later extended to cover other countries in Europe (Thomson, 2010; Sagan & Thomson, 2016a, 2016b). Comparative analysis of experience outside Europe began to appear from the late 1990s, with publications focusing on high-income countries (Jost, 2000; Maynard & Dixon, 2002; OECD, 2004; Wasem, Greß & Okma, 2004; Gechert, 2010) as well as low- and middle-income countries (Chollet & Lewis, 1997; Sekhri & Savedoff, 2005; Drechsler & Jütting, 2005; Preker, Scheffler & Bassett, 2007).

This volume adds to comparative research by offering an analysis of private health insurance in 18 high- and middle-income countries globally, which together account for one third of the world's population. It focuses on several of the world's largest markets, both in terms of population coverage and contribution to spending on health; covers a range of different market roles; and includes countries in which private health insurance is the only form of health coverage for some people.

The chapters that follow are mainly single-country case studies based on a standard format to enable international comparison. Each case study examines the origins of a particular market for private health insurance, considers its development in the light of stakeholder interests and discusses its impact on the performance of the health system as a whole. Country case studies reflect national developments up to 2017.

By examining national successes, failures and challenges with private health insurance, the volume aims to:

- identify contextual factors underpinning the emergence, evolution and regulation of private health insurance, including the role of internal and external stakeholders in influencing market development and public policy;
- assess the performance of private health insurance against evaluative criteria such as financial protection, equity in access and use, efficiency and quality in service delivery, and contribution to relieving fiscal and other pressures on the health system; and
- inform policy development in countries in different income groups.

The following sections of this chapter define private health insurance; outline market failures in voluntary health insurance and their consequences; summarize the history of and politics around the development of private health insurance, to understand how we got to where we are today; review data on the size of contemporary private health insurance markets; consider evidence on how well private health insurance performs; and draw policy lessons for countries seeking to introduce or extend the role of private health insurance or to minimize its adverse effects on health system performance.

No two markets for private health insurance are the same

Private health insurance is often defined as insurance that is taken up voluntarily and paid for privately, either by individuals or by employers on behalf of employees (Mossialos & Thomson, 2002). This definition recognizes that private health insurance may be sold by a wide range of entities, both public and private in nature. It distinguishes voluntary from compulsory health insurance, which is important analytically because many of the market failures associated with health insurance only occur, or are much more likely to occur, when coverage is voluntary (Barr, 2004). The reference to private payment signals a further defining characteristic: private health insurance premiums are typically linked to a person's risk of ill health or set as a flat rate, whereas pre-payment for publicly financed coverage is almost always linked to income.

The main focus of this volume is on voluntary private health insurance, defined in terms of the role it plays in relation to publicly financed coverage. Table 1.1 highlights four distinct roles and shows the countries in this volume in which they are present. Understanding the role private health insurance plays in a given context matters because role often influences the nature of public policy towards a market.

People buy **supplementary** private health insurance as a way of obtaining pre-paid access to private facilities, avoiding waiting times for publicly financed specialist treatment or benefiting from enhanced amenities in public facilities. **Complementary** private health insurance fills gaps that occur when the publicly financed benefits package is not comprehensive in scope or involves user charges (co-payments). In contrast to supplementary private health insurance and complementary private health insurance covering services, which can be found in many countries, complementary private health insurance covering user charges is much less widespread. People buy **substitutive** private health insurance because they are excluded from publicly financed coverage on grounds of age or income, or are allowed to choose between public and private coverage.

Three chapters in this volume focus on what the System of Health Accounts (OECD, Eurostat, WHO, 2017) refers to as compulsory private health insurance in the Netherlands, Switzerland and the United

Table 1.1 *Private health insurance (PHI) roles*

PHI role	Driver of demand for PHI	Main reason for having PHI	Country examples in this volume
Supplementary	Perceptions about the quality and timeliness of publicly financed health services	Offers faster access to services, greater choice of health care provider or enhanced amenities	Australia, Brazil, Egypt, India, Ireland, Israel, Japan, Kenya, Republic of Korea, South Africa, Switzerland, Taiwan, China
Complementary (services)	The scope of the publicly financed benefits package	Cover of services excluded from the publicly financed benefits package	Canada, Germany, Israel, the Netherlands, Switzerland
Complementary (user charges)	The existence of user charges (co-payments) for publicly financed health services	Cover of user charges (co-payments) for goods and services in the publicly financed benefits package	France
Substitutive	Rules around entitlement to publicly financed coverage	Covers people excluded from publicly financed coverage or allowed to choose between publicly and privately financed coverage	Chile; Egypt; Germany; the Netherlands before 2006; the United States

Source: Adapted from Foubister et al. (2006).

Note: Markets often combine elements of the first two roles; some combine elements of the first three.

States, included here as examples of the transition from voluntary to compulsory private health insurance. Parts of the private health insurance market in Chile, France and Germany are also classified as compulsory private health insurance in the System of Health Accounts. With the exception of Chile, private health insurance in these countries initially operated on a voluntary basis, played a significant role in the health system and became compulsory as part of a drive to extend coverage to the whole population, as described in Box 1.1. Chile has allowed the whole population to choose between public and private coverage since 1981; it is compulsory to be covered and everyone must contribute the same minimum share of their income towards coverage, regardless of which option they choose. Although the decision to opt for private rather than public coverage is voluntary in Chile and for higher earners aged under 55 years in Germany, substitutive private health insurance in these countries is classified as compulsory pre-payment in the System of Health Accounts.

Box 1.1 From voluntary to compulsory private health insurance in five countries

Health insurance in **Switzerland** has always been provided by private entities. In 1996, it became compulsory for the whole population for the first time. People pay premiums related to their risk of ill health to non-profit private insurers. People with low incomes receive subsidies from local government.

Publicly financed coverage became compulsory for lower earners in **the Netherlands** in 1941. Between 1941 and 1986, higher earners were allowed to choose between public and private coverage. In 1986, the richest third of the population was excluded from public coverage and relied on substitutive private health insurance. A national health insurance scheme was introduced in 2006. It is compulsory for all residents, operated by a mix of for-profit and non-profit private entities (former sickness funds and private insurers), governed under private law, extensively regulated by government and financed through a combination of flat-rate premiums, income-related contributions and subsidies for poor people.

In 1970, **Germany** allowed higher-earning employees to choose between public, private and no coverage; previously they had been excluded from publicly financed coverage. Since 1994, those who opt for substitutive private health insurance can no longer return to public coverage after the age of 65 years, lowered to 55 years in 2000, even if their earnings fall below the income threshold. In

---

Box 1.1 (cont.)

2009, health insurance became compulsory for all residents. Those over 55 years old who had already opted for private coverage were no longer entitled to public coverage. Substitutive private health insurance is now their only source of coverage.

The Affordable Care Act introduced in the **United States** in 2014 made health insurance compulsory for people under the age of 65 years for the first time. Compulsory coverage provided by private insurers in return for risk-rated premiums now operates alongside publicly financed coverage for older people (Medicare) and poor people (Medicaid) introduced in 1965.

France allows private entities to cover user charges (co-payments) for publicly financed health services. By 2015, over 90% of the population was covered by complementary private health insurance covering co-payments. In 2016, it became compulsory for employers to provide this form of private health insurance for their employees. Employees now have compulsory private health insurance covering co-payments, while those who are not employed may have voluntary private health insurance covering co-payments.

Source: Chapters in this volume.

Table 1.2 presents information on health spending in the 18 countries in 2017, the most recent year for which internationally comparable data are available.

Market failures lead to risk segmentation, inequality and inefficiency

Market failures in health insurance are well established (Barr, 1992). Economic theory posits that voluntary forms of health insurance will only result in an optimally efficient allocation of health care resources if certain assumptions hold: the probabilities of becoming ill are less than one (no pre-existing conditions), independent of each other (no endemic communicable diseases) and known or estimable (insurers are able to estimate future claims and adjust premiums for risk); and there

Table 1.2 *Overview of spending on health in the countries in this volume, 2017*

Countries	Public spending on health as a share of GDP (%)	Public spending on health as a share of current spending on health (%)	Other compulsory spending on health as a share of current spending on health (%)	Voluntary PHI as a share of current spending on health (%)	Out-of-pocket payments as a share of current spending on health (%)
High-income countries					
Australia	6.3	69	0	10	18
Canada	7.8	74	0	10	14
Chile	4.5	50	10	6	34
France	8.7	77	6	7	9
Germany	8.7	78	7	1	13
Ireland	5.3	73	0	13	12
Israel	4.7	64	0	11	22
Japan	9.2	84	0	2	13
Netherlands	6.5	64	17	6	11
Republic of Korea	4.4	57	1	7	34
Switzerland	3.8	30	33	7	29
United States of America	8.6	50	34	0	11

Table 1.2 *(cont.)*

Countries	Public spending on health as a share of GDP (%)	Public spending on health as a share of current spending on health (%)	Other compulsory spending on health as a share of current spending on health (%)	Voluntary PHI as a share of current spending on health (%)	Out-of-pocket payments as a share of current spending on health (%)
Upper middle-income countries					
Brazil	4.0	42	0	29	27
South Africa	4.4	54	0	36	8
Lower middle-income countries					
Egypt	1.8	33	0	1	60
India	1.0	27	0	5	62
Kenya	2.4	49	0	10	24

Source: WHO (2020).

Notes: GDP: gross domestic product. 'Public spending on health' comprises government budget allocations and social insurance contributions. In Chile, this includes income-based contributions for substitutive PHI. 'Other compulsory spending on health' comprises the following non-income-based contributions: for substitutive PHI above the income-based contribution (Chile); for complementary PHI covering co-payments among employees, which has been compulsory for employees since 2016 (France); for substitutive PHI, which has been compulsory for people who opt out of national health insurance since 2009 (Germany); for national health insurance above the income-based contributions (the Netherlands); for national health insurance (Switzerland); for compulsory and voluntary cover offered by private insurers (United States of America). In Taiwan, China, PHI accounts for 9.5% and out-of-pocket payments for 34.7% of current spending on health (Kwon, Ikegami & Lee, this volume). If tax subsidies for voluntary PHI are included, then the share of current spending on health channelled through voluntary PHI rises from 36% to 47% in South Africa and from 10% to 13% in Australia and Canada.

are no major problems with adverse selection, risk selection, moral hazard and monopoly (Barr, 2004).

Moral hazard and monopoly issues can be problematic for both compulsory and voluntary health insurance and researchers have questioned whether moral hazard poses a genuine threat to efficiency in health insurance (Nyman, 2004; Einav & Finkelstein, 2018). This leaves probabilities, adverse selection and risk selection as the most likely sources of failure in markets for voluntary health insurance.

Insurance premiums are a function of the probability of illness and the expected costs of treating ill health. They are considered to be actuarially fair when they reflect the health risk of the pool of people being covered, allowing the insurer to meet its obligations to members of the pool and avoid financial losses for the firm.

Actuarial fairness is challenging to achieve for several reasons. First, it is difficult to sustain a voluntary health insurance market among people who are already ill or at high risk of becoming ill and in the context of epidemics (Barr, 2004). Second, if people conceal information and buy insurance for a premium that does not accurately reflect their health risk, the financial viability of the pool will be jeopardized: premiums will rise over time and those with a lower risk of ill health will leave to buy cheaper insurance from other firms (Akerlof, 1970). So-called adverse selection can lead to the collapse of a market. Ensuring stability is the main reason why private health insurance markets require financial regulation in the form of standards for insurer entry, operation, exit and reporting, although adverse selection is most effectively addressed by making health insurance compulsory. Third, to prevent adverse selection, insurers will engage in risk selection, attempting to attract low-risk people to the pool and deter high-risk people from enrolling.

Owing to risk selection, some people may not be able to obtain insurance if insurers reject applications for coverage; some may not be able to obtain sufficient insurance if pre-existing conditions or certain types of treatment are excluded from coverage; and some may not be able to obtain insurance at a price they can afford to pay. Private health insurance will therefore segment risk among enrollees as well as between those with and without private health insurance. This in turn limits redistribution between rich, poor, healthy and sick; violates the equity principle of access to health care based on need rather than ability to pay (Culyer, 1989); and exacerbates inequality in the health system. Some of these consequences can be avoided through material regulation involving rules around premiums, benefits and other contractual conditions (Hsiao, 1995).

Risk selection has other unwanted side-effects. It is a pure cost from a health system perspective, because it fails to produce any social benefit, and it may lower incentives for efficiency in the organization and delivery of health insurance and health services if insurers maintain margins by selecting low-risk people rather than by streamlining operations and exerting leverage over providers (Evans, 1984; Rice, 2001; Rice, 2003).

While risk segmentation is primarily the outcome of market failures, it is sometimes compounded by public policy regarding the boundary between publicly and privately financed coverage and the nature and extent of regulation.

How we got to where we are now: the importance of history and politics

Economic theory clearly indicates some of the likely outcomes of fostering private health insurance. To understand how private health insurance affects health system performance also requires context-specific analysis. The diversity that makes private health insurance difficult to define means its impact will vary depending, to a large extent, on public policy. Two markets that play the same role can have divergent outcomes because of differences in public policy, which in turn may reflect the way in which public policy has been shaped by history (past events) and politics (stakeholder interests).

Each case study in this volume reviews the origins of private health insurance and developments over time. Taken together, the case studies reveal a number of patterns in how markets were established, their evolution and the role that private health insurance has played in national debates about moving towards universal health coverage.

As the precursor to publicly financed coverage, private schemes were usually organized around employment

Private health insurance generally predates national health insurance. In its earliest forms, before the rise of modern medicine, its primary purpose was to compensate people for earnings lost through illness. For this reason it was exclusively linked to employment. Over time, loss-of-income schemes, first established by guilds of skilled workers in Europe in the Middle Ages, gave way to occupation-based mutual aid associations serving industrial workers, laying the foundation for contemporary welfare states (Abel-Smith, 1988).

By the mid-19th century, employment-based private health insurance offered by mutual associations had become the norm across much of Europe (Saltman, Busse & Figueras, 2004). In South Africa, private schemes were introduced at the turn of the 20th century, under British rule, for white mine workers; they remained the preserve of white South Africans until the 1970s (McIntyre & McLeod, this volume). The non-profit health plans operating in Israel today emerged from the trade union movement of the early 1900s and came under government regulation following the creation of the state of Israel in 1948 (Brammli-Greenberg & Waitzberg, this volume).

As medical care progressed and treatment became more costly, health care providers began to develop health insurance themselves, to enable patients to pay for their services. From the beginning of the 20th century, physicians in the Netherlands and hospitals and physicians in Australia, Canada and the United States were active in setting up schemes, some of which are still in operation. Provider-initiated schemes were usually linked to hospitals run by the voluntary (charitable) sector. Consequently, many were non-profit-making entities operating according to social principles such as open enrolment (accepting all applicants) and community rating (basing premiums on average risk rather than individual risk).

In a third stage of development, schemes organized around employment or initiated by health care providers were joined by insurers operating on a commercial basis.

The middle-income countries in this volume have tended to follow a different path. In Chile, Brazil, Kenya and India, private health insurance emerged following government decisions to enhance private involvement in the health system after some form of national health insurance had already been established. These decisions took place in 1976 in Brazil, 1980 in Chile, the 1980s and 1990s in Kenya and 1999 in India. Something similar occurred in central and eastern Europe in the 1990s, after the collapse of the Soviet Union, when new laws allowed private health insurance to operate alongside publicly financed coverage (Kornai & Eggleston, 2001; Thomson, 2010).

In Japan, the Republic of Korea and Taiwan, China, private health insurance has its origins in accident or life insurance and continues to be linked to life insurance and other types of financial investment vehicle, often offering cash benefits in case of illness.

Compulsory publicly financed coverage was a response to the failure of voluntary schemes to cover the whole population

Very few of these early forms of private health insurance succeeded in covering more than a minority of the population, partly due to their roots in employment and their voluntary nature, but also because they were unaffordable for many people, including those most in need of protection from health care costs.

In some countries, access to employment-based health insurance was enhanced through schemes organized by charitable entities (most often linked to the Church) and local authorities, but even these were not enough to achieve universal population coverage. A census of the Swiss population held in 1903 found that only 14% belonged to any type of scheme, including those run by the Catholic Church, cantons and municipalities (Crivelli, this volume).

Following the example set by Germany in 1883 (Ettelt & Roman-Urrestarazu, this volume), governments began to think about setting up some form of national system that would extend coverage to more people. Private schemes were uniquely placed to play a major role in these new arrangements. Non-profit actors adhering to social principles formed the basis for what would eventually become national health insurance in Germany, the Netherlands and Israel, leaving other private actors to cover any remaining gaps. France proved to be the exception: when publicly financed coverage was established in 1945, the government chose to introduce new institutions rather than build on the tradition established by mutual associations known as *mutuelles*, even though the *mutuelles* covered around two thirds of the population by 1939.

It was at the point of instituting national health insurance that the key distinction between schemes shifted from type of actor to compulsory versus voluntary.

Private interests consistently tried to block the expansion of publicly financed coverage

In many countries a variety of stakeholders (health care providers, private insurers, people with private health insurance and political parties) have taken steps to prevent the development of national health insurance, most often by arguing that it should be limited to poorer people.

For example, the Blue Cross and Blue Shield plans created by health care providers in the United States in the 1920s and 1930s were part of a deliberate and ultimately successful attempt by the medical profession to construct an alternative to publicly financed coverage (Brown & Glied, this volume). To this day, the publicly financed schemes that were eventually implemented in 1965 are limited to covering older people (Medicare) and poor people (Medicaid), together accounting for only one third of the population.

In Germany, proposals to extend publicly financed health coverage to the whole population, which would effectively abolish substitutive private health insurance, have always been opposed not just by private insurers and health care providers (who benefit from charging higher fees when treating privately insured people), but also by the relatively rich households who rely on private coverage and fear having to accept a lower standard of access to health care under a universal scheme (Ettelt & Roman-Urrestarazu, this volume).

With the exception of Germany and the United States, private insurers have generally failed to prevent the implementation of a fully universal scheme. Nevertheless, in several instances they have delayed it and, by being part of the health system landscape, they have been able to influence the parameters for reform.

In Switzerland, the government's first choice for national health insurance was to establish a system run by public entities, but opponents launched a referendum against it, and it was rejected by popular ballot in 1900 (Crivelli, this volume). Burnt by this experience, the government's next attempt aimed to overcome opposition by leaving the management of the new system in the hands of private actors and allowing cantons to decide whether health insurance should be mandatory. Although the revised proposal was accepted by referendum in 1912, it paralysed reform efforts for over 80 years; health insurance only became compulsory for the whole population in 1996.

In the Netherlands, the national medical association not only ensured that the earliest attempts to introduce national health insurance, from 1901 onwards, were restricted to poor people so as not to damage physician incomes; they also encouraged physicians to set up their own health insurance schemes, which soon came to dominate the market

(Maarse & Jeurissen, this volume). Lobbying by private insurers subsequently stood in the way of efforts to extend publicly financed coverage to the whole population throughout the 20th century (Maarse & Jeurissen, this volume). As in Germany, insurer resistance to change was bolstered by resistance on the part of those covered by substitutive private health insurance. It is therefore not surprising that when a universal scheme was finally set up in 2006, it compensated private insurers by allowing them to take part in the national scheme, alongside sickness funds, and limited the extent of direct cross subsidies from richer to poorer households.

Australia's first attempt at creating a national scheme (known as Medibank) was achieved in 1974 under a Labour government after years of opposition from a coalition of private insurers, private hospitals, physicians practising privately and the politically conservative Liberal Party (Hall, Fiebig & van Gool, this volume). The scheme did not last long. In 1976, a newly elected conservative coalition turned it into a government-owned insurance company, renaming it Medibank Private, and forced it to compete with private insurers. A genuinely national scheme was not re-introduced until the Labour Party returned to government in 1984. Since then, private schemes have mainly played a supplementary role.

Government intervention in private health insurance markets has intensified

Looking at the development of private health insurance markets indicates minimal change in role. The only significant change has been the abolition of substitutive private health insurance in the Netherlands in 2006. By far the most striking and widespread phenomenon has been the intensification of government intervention over time. Box 1.2 highlights major developments in private health insurance markets across the 18 countries, starting in the second half of the 20th century, after some form of national health insurance had been established in most countries, and going up to the end of 2017.

Some of the need for greater intervention can be linked to changes in market structure leading to changes in market conduct. Initially, markets were often dominated or exclusively run by non-profit organizations offering people relatively easy access to private coverage based on social principles such as open enrolment and community rating. The entry

---

Box 1.2 Major developments in markets for private health insurance in this volume, 1960–2017

1960s
- The **Netherlands** reaffirms compulsory publicly financed coverage for lower-earning workers only, allowing higher earners to choose between public, private or no coverage (1964).

1970s
- **Germany** makes public coverage compulsory for white-collar workers with earnings below a specified threshold and allows higher-earning white-collar workers to choose public, private or no coverage (1970).
- Private insurers are allowed to operate in **Brazil** (1976).

1980s
- **Chile** introduces choice of public or private coverage for the whole population (1981).
- **Australia** introduces tax rebates for private health insurance (1981) and later removes them (1983).
- The **Netherlands** abolishes choice of public or private coverage; those with earnings over a threshold are no longer eligible for publicly financed coverage; regulation of the substitutive private health insurance market intensifies (1986).
- **Germany** extends choice of public, private or no coverage to all higher-earning employees (1989).
- Publicly financed health plans in **Israel** institute compulsory supplemental coverage (mid-1980s); this is later prohibited (1995) but the health plans can offer it on a voluntary basis as separate financial entities.
- Deregulation of the private health insurance market in **South Africa** (1980s, early 1990s).

1990s
- The Third Non-Life Insurance Directive establishes a single European market in health insurance (1992).
- Medical savings accounts established in the private health insurance market in **South Africa** (1994).

Box 1.2 (cont.)

- Liberalization of the private health insurance market in **Ireland,** as required by EU law; the government introduces material regulation of private health insurance, including a risk equalization scheme (1994).
- **Germany** makes the decision to opt for private rather than public coverage irreversible for those aged 65 years and above; introduction of a standard tariff (premium) in substitutive private health insurance (1994).
- National health insurance offered by competing health plans becomes mandatory in **Israel** (1995).
- **Australia** introduces tax penalties for high earners who do not purchase private health insurance (1997).
- **South Africa** introduces material regulation of the private health insurance market (1998, with effect from 2000).
- Tighter material regulation of supplemental plans introduced in **Israel** (1998).
- **Australia** re-introduces tax rebates for private health insurance (1999).
- Legislation liberalizes the insurance sector in **India,** including health insurance (1999).

2000s
- Creation of Superintendencia de ISAPREs as the regulator of private health insurance in **Chile** (2000).
- **Germany** makes the decision to opt for private coverage irreversible for people aged 55 years and over (2000).
- **France** provides free complementary private health insurance covering co-payments to poor households (CMU-C, 2000) and subsidizes private health insurance for poor households not eligible for CMU-C (ACS, 2002).
- Introduction of lifetime community rating in private health insurance in **Australia** (2000).
- All private health insurers in **Brazil** are mandated to offer a reference plan as an option (2000).
- Health savings accounts established in the private health insurance market in the **United States** (2002).

Box 1.2 (cont.)

- Health plans in **Israel** to compensate national health insurance retroactively for the use of infrastructure and staff within supplemental insurance (2002).
- **Chile** introduces minimum benefits for private health insurance (2003).
- The Fillon Law in **France** introduces tax exemptions for employers offering mandatory group private health insurance contracts that comply with certain rules (*contrats solidaires*) (2003) (further strengthened in 2010 and 2013); private health insurance contracts must meet additional criteria (*contrats responsables*) to enable insurers to qualify for exemption from premium income tax (2004).
- Introduction of the Universal Health Insurance scheme in **India** (2004).
- The **Netherlands** establishes a universal scheme, abolishing substitutive private health insurance (2004, with effect from 2006).
- A court ruling against current restrictions on private health insurance in the province of Quebec in **Canada** (2005).
- **Israel** introduces regulation to separate supplemental insurance from national health insurance (2005).
- Proposed expansion of the private health insurance market in the **Republic of Korea** (2005).
- **Ireland** triggers the risk equalization scheme (2005) and is challenged by BUPA in the High Court (2006).
- **Kenya** strengthens the regulatory framework for private health insurance (2006).
- Removal of tariffs from general insurance in **India**, including for private health insurance (2007).
- **South Africa** commits to pursuing a national health insurance system (2007).
- New commercial policies for private surgery in **Israel** are prohibited from covering expenses that are covered by supplemental insurance (2007).
- Health insurance becomes universally compulsory in **Germany**; substitutive private health insurance is subject to extensive new regulations (2009).

Box 1.2 (cont.)

2010s

- Introduction of means testing for the private health insurance tax rebate in **Australia** (2010).
- Tax on responsible contracts re-introduced in **France** but at lower rates than non-responsible contracts (2010).
- Patient Protection and Affordable Care Act (ACA) enacted in the **United States** (2011, with effect from 2014).
- Green Paper on national health insurance in **South Africa** suggests private health insurance could be restricted to so-called top-up insurance (2011; reiterated in a White Paper in 2015).
- Risk equalization scheme implemented in **Ireland** (2012); private bed charges to be levied on the use of any bed in public hospitals by privately insured patients (2014); lifetime community rating introduced (2015).
- **Switzerland** introduces choice of hospital for all (previously only available through voluntary private health insurance) (2012).
- Commercial insurers in **Israel** are prohibited from reimbursing surgeries covered by national health insurance or supplemental private health insurance (2014).
- **France** extends ACS eligibility (2015).
- Employers in **France** are mandated to provide employees with complementary private health insurance (2016).

Source: Chapters in this volume.

---

of commercial insurers operating on different principles (risk rating, exclusion of pre-existing conditions, rejection of applications) threatened this business model in many countries, among them Australia, Canada, France, Ireland, Israel, the Netherlands, Switzerland and the United States. In response, some non-profit entities adopted a more commercial approach, meaning that governments could no longer rely on the presence of mutual associations to ensure access to private health insurance.

Greater intervention has also followed market expansion or growth, which makes problems with private health insurance more visible and less acceptable. In such instances, intervention has been driven by three aims:

- enhancing consumer protection, occasionally in response to insurer fraud (Kenya) or malpractice (Germany), but more commonly to reduce financial and transaction costs for consumers in the face of multiple and potentially confusing coverage options (almost all of the countries in this volume);
- protecting publicly financed coverage from fiscal pressures exacerbated by (mainly) substitutive and supplementary private health insurance; this type of intervention has usually tried to limit the damage associated with allowing people to choose between public and private coverage by restricting (Germany) or abolishing (the Netherlands) access to publicly financed coverage for some people; clarifying and enforcing boundaries between public and private coverage (Ireland, Israel); and reducing tax subsidies for private health insurance; and, overwhelmingly,
- maintaining or enhancing access to private health insurance and financial protection for those with private health insurance; Table 1.3 provides examples of the types of material regulation introduced in the countries in this volume.

The need to secure affordable access to private health insurance is arguably greatest where private health insurance plays a substitutive role or a complementary role covering co-payments. It is no coincidence, therefore, that these are the private health insurance markets in which governments have intervened most heavily and persistently (Chile, France and Germany, and the Netherlands before the introduction of a universal scheme in 2006). Intervention has intensified in the supplementary markets in this volume too, to meet all three of the aims highlighted above (Australia, Brazil, Ireland, Israel, Kenya and South Africa).

Private health insurance today: implications for health system performance

The case studies in this volume provide empirical evidence on the impact of private health insurance on health system performance in three areas (financial protection, access to health services, and efficiency and quality in health service organization and delivery) as well as on the contribution of private health insurance to relieving fiscal and other pressures on health systems. The focus of this section is on voluntary private health insurance rather than compulsory coverage operated by private insurers as in the Netherlands, Switzerland and the United States.

Table 1.3 *Examples of measures to ensure voluntary private health insurance is accessible, affordable and offers quality coverage*

Measures	Countries
Accessibility	
Open enrolment	Australia, Germany, Ireland, Israel, South Africa
Lifetime cover	Brazil, Germany, Ireland
Guaranteeing supply of marketed policies	Australia, Brazil
Prohibiting switching penalties	Netherlands, Switzerland
Rating of plans to facilitate choice	Australia
Other	France[a], Kenya[b]
Affordability	
Community-rated premiums	Australia, Brazil, Chile, Ireland, Israel, South Africa
Risk equalization to support community rating	Chile, Ireland
Ageing reserves	Germany
Premium caps	Brazil, Germany
Premiums subsidized, discounted, waived or fully covered by the government	Australia, France, Germany, Ireland, South Africa
Limits on insurer profits	Australia, Chile
Scope and depth of coverage	
Cover of pre-existing conditions	Brazil, Germany, Ireland, Israel
Minimum or standard benefits	Brazil, Chile, France, Germany, Ireland, Israel, South Africa
Caps on user charges in private health insurance	Chile, Germany, South Africa
Prohibition of benefit ceilings	France, Chile, South Africa
Provisions to encourage cover of gaps in publicly financed coverage	Australia

Sources: Chapters in this volume; Sagan & Thomson (2016a and 2016b).

Notes: [a] Making it mandatory for employers to buy complementary private health insurance for employees (from 2016).

[b] Allowing monthly rather than annual payment of premiums.

Does private health insurance enhance financial protection by filling gaps in publicly financed coverage?

Private health insurance will enhance financial protection for those who buy it by reducing their exposure to out-of-pocket payments. How well it is able to fill gaps in publicly financed coverage at health system level can be assessed by looking at data on private health insurance as a share of total and private spending on health and information on the share of the eligible population covered by private health insurance.

Global spending data show that the contribution of private health insurance to current spending on health is marginal in the vast majority of countries. Across all countries, voluntary private health insurance accounts for only 4.6% on average, ranging from 2.4% in lower middle-income countries to 6.3% in upper middle-income countries (Fig. 1.1). The range in Fig. 1.1 shows there is a great deal of variation at country level, particularly in upper middle-income countries.

Voluntary private health insurance accounts for more than 10% of current spending on health in only 23 countries (Fig. 1.2). Over half of these are middle-income countries, many in Africa, Latin America and

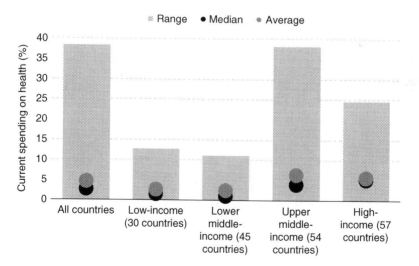

Figure 1.1 Voluntary private health insurance as a share (%) of current spending on health globally by country income group, 2017

Source: WHO (2020).

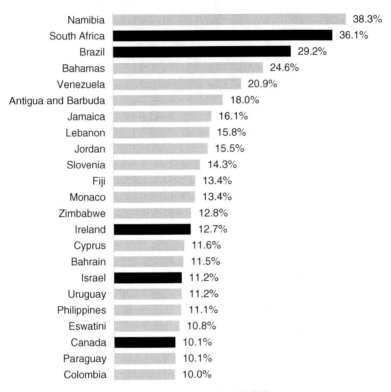

Figure 1.2 Countries globally in which voluntary and compulsory private health insurance accounts for at least 10% of current spending on health, 2017

Source: WHO (2020).

Notes: Countries covered in this volume are marked in black. Voluntary private health insurance accounts for less than 10% of current spending on health in Australia, Chile, Egypt, Germany, India, Kenya, Japan, the Netherlands, the Republic of Korea, Taiwan, China, Switzerland and the United States of America.

the Caribbean. In over 80 countries, voluntary private health insurance accounts for less than 2% of current spending on health. Over time, the voluntary private health insurance share of current spending on health has remained relatively stable.

Globally, the relationship between voluntary private health insurance and the out-of-pocket payment share of current spending on health is very weak (Fig. 1.3, first panel). In spite of significant gaps in coverage in many countries, as demonstrated by high levels of out-of-pocket payments, spending on voluntary private health insurance is low. This indicates that while gaps in publicly financed coverage are a prerequisite for voluntary private health insurance, they are not enough for a private health insurance market to develop and grow. In 2017, out-of-pocket payments were the dominant source of private spending on health in over 95% of countries (WHO, 2020). The voluntary private health insurance share of current spending on health exceeded the out-of-pocket payment share in only 9 out of 186 countries: Namibia, South Africa, Brazil, Slovenia, Monaco, Ireland, Eswatini, Qatar and Botswana. Even among the generally large markets selected for this volume, voluntary private health insurance accounts for over 30% of private spending on health in only eight countries: Australia, Brazil, Canada, France, Ireland, Israel, the Netherlands and South Africa.

Across countries, there is a much stronger association between public spending on health and out-of-pocket payments (Fig. 1.3, second panel), which suggests that increases in public spending on health are much more likely to reduce gaps in coverage than increases in spending through voluntary private health insurance.

Data on voluntary private health insurance spending need to be interpreted alongside information on the role that private health insurance plays and the share of the population covered by private health insurance. In South Africa, for example, private health insurance playing a supplementary role covers around 16% of the population (Fig. 1.4), overwhelmingly people from higher income groups (McIntyre & McLeod, this volume), but voluntary private health insurance premiums account for over a third (36%) of current spending on health (Table 1.2). In contrast, supplementary private health insurance in Ireland accounts for a much smaller share of current spending on health (around 13%) but covers close to half of the population (46%). Similarly, private health insurance playing a complementary role in countries like France, Israel and the Netherlands accounts for a much smaller share of current spending on health than in South Africa, but covers over 80% of the population (Fig. 1.4). If tax subsidies are included in private health insurance spending, the share of current spending on

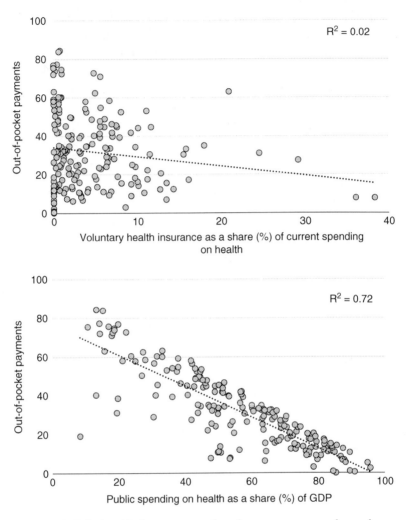

Figure 1.3 Relationship between out-of-pocket payments as a share of current spending on health and voluntary private health insurance and public spending on health globally, 2017

Source: WHO (2020).

Notes: The figure includes 186 countries. GDP: gross domestic product.

health channelled through private health insurance in South Africa rises to 47% (WHO, 2020).

Supplementary private health insurance does not usually achieve high levels of population coverage, as Fig. 1.4 shows. Relatively high demand in Australia and Ireland is fuelled by long waiting times for publicly financed specialist care, substantial tax incentives to buy private health insurance (although these have been reduced over time) and penalties for those who do not buy private health insurance at younger ages (Turner & Smith and Hall, Fiebig & van Gool, this volume). The very high levels of population coverage in Japan, Korea and Taiwan, China are not typical and largely reflect the sale of private health insurance alongside life insurance (Kwon, Ikegami & Lee, this volume).

Rates of population coverage appear to be high where private health insurance plays an explicitly complementary role (Fig. 1.4). Canada, Israel and the Netherlands are, however, outliers in terms of complementary private health insurance covering services; in other countries, this type of market rarely covers more than one third of the population and often much less than that (Sagan & Thomson, 2016a).

In markets for complementary private health insurance covering user charges, globally only Croatia and Slovenia come close to France in terms of population coverage (Sagan & Thomson, 2016a; Vončina & Rubil, 2018; WHO Regional Office for Europe, 2019).

Various mechanisms help to explain high levels of take up in these markets for complementary private health insurance:

- private health insurance being sold by the same entities that provide publicly financed coverage in Croatia, Israel and the Netherlands; this was also the case in Slovenia when the market was first established and high rates of population coverage were achieved;
- easy access to the private health insurance market ensured through open enrolment in Croatia, France, Israel, the Netherlands and Slovenia;
- affordable access to private health insurance ensured through regulation in Croatia, Israel and Slovenia and targeted tax subsidies that make private health insurance free for the poorest households in Croatia and France; and
- linking private health insurance to employment so that it is compulsory for employees (France) or de facto near universal for employees (Canada).

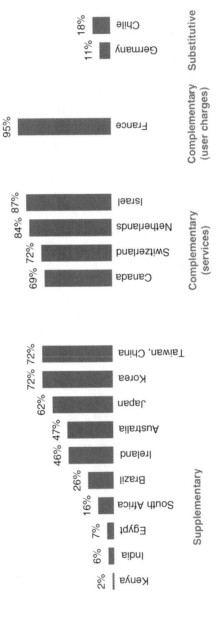

Figure 1.4 Share (%) of the population covered by private health insurance in the countries in this volume by role, latest year available

Source: Authors.

Substitutive private health insurance is the only form of coverage available to some of the population in Germany (people aged over 55 years since 2000, people aged over 65 years since 1994) and the United States (non-poor people under 65 years), as well as in the Netherlands between 1986 and 2005 (richer households). Private health insurance has not been able to fully fill the gap in publicly financed coverage in the United States, even after the passing of the Affordable Care Act in 2014. In Germany and the Netherlands, however, gaps have been filled through extensive and increasing regulation of the private health insurance market involving open enrolment, lifetime cover, minimum benefits, premium controls and, eventually, compulsion.

Just because people have private health insurance does not mean that they do not experience gaps in coverage. In France, for example, the quality of private health insurance coverage (the extent to which it covers all the user charges a person has to pay) varies by socioeconomic status, with better-off people enjoying a greater degree of financial protection (Couffinhal & Franc, this volume). Erosion in the quality of private health insurance coverage over time has been one of the notable features of some markets. It is particularly evident in markets where medical savings accounts have been introduced (South Africa and the United States), but is also documented in France, Germany (through the growing use of deductibles for substitutive private health insurance policies) and Australia.

Does private health insurance enhance access to health services?

Across the countries in this volume, and beyond, voluntary private health insurance is systematically more likely to be bought by people who are relatively wealthy, employed, better educated and living in urban areas with access to private health care providers (Sagan & Thomson, 2016a). The lowest levels of take up are often among people in vulnerable situations: people living in poverty, older people and people who are ill or at high risk of ill health.

This pattern has three negative consequences for health system performance. First, it exacerbates socioeconomic inequality in access to health care in a wide range of countries: in Brazil, for example, fewer than 6% of people in the poorest income quintile had private health insurance in 2013, compared with around 65% of people in the richest (Diaz et al., this volume). Second, it skews the distribution of health care away from need, leading to concerns for efficiency in addition to concerns for equity. And third, it segments risk in the health system, as described in Box 1.3. The examples in Box 1.3 show that risk segmentation can arise by design as well as due to risk selection on the part of private insurers.

Box 1.3 Selected examples of risk segmentation linked to private health insurance

National health insurance in **Germany** was initially only compulsory for blue-collar workers, on the grounds that richer workers did not require protection organized by the state. Later, richer people were permitted to opt into the national scheme. If they chose not to, they could obtain voluntary coverage from private insurers. By design, the option of substitutive private coverage is limited to higher earners, segmenting the population by income. The privately insured are also generally healthier than those in the national scheme thanks to risk selection by private insurers, who are allowed to rate premiums on the basis of individual health risk and can offer subscribers lower premiums in return for higher co-payments in the form of deductibles. This exacerbates population risk segmentation and segments risk among those with private health insurance. Over time, people with private coverage aged, their health deteriorated and their premiums rose, in part owing to miscalculation of lifetime risk by private insurers. Some of them tried to return to the national scheme, adding to financial pressure in the publicly financed part of the health system. The federal government intervened heavily in the private health insurance market in 1994, prohibiting anyone who had opted for private coverage from returning to the national scheme if they were aged over 65 years. In 2000, it lowered the age restriction to 55 years and introduced measures to secure access and financial protection for people now forced to rely on private coverage, including a limit to deductible amounts (Thomson & Mossialos, 2006).

In **France**, private health insurance plays a complementary role, covering user charges for publicly financed health services. Private health insurance coverage rose steadily after 1945, reaching 86% of

---

Box 1.3 (cont.)

the population in 2000. In response to evidence of socioeconomic inequality in access to health care linked to private health insurance, the Government introduced vouchers (CMU-C) for people on low income to purchase private health insurance in 2000 and subsidies (ACS) for those just above the threshold for vouchers in 2005. As a result of these measures, private health insurance coverage exceeded 90% of the population by 2015. Unequal access to private health insurance remains a challenge, however, with financial barriers being the most common reason that people give for not being covered. As in Germany, the population is segmented twice: first, because private health insurance is more affordable for richer people; and second, through subsidies to purchase private health insurance, which only benefit the poorest people. The 2016 requirement for all employers to offer private health insurance to their employees is likely to add another layer of segmentation. It aims to improve access to group contracts, known to be more advantageous than individual contracts. Although this may reduce unequal access to private health insurance among employees, it may increase inequality between salaried employees and other groups of people (students, retirees and unemployed or self-employed people.

The development of supplementary private health insurance in **South Africa** has led to segmentation by race and income. Before the 1970s, private health insurance only covered white workers. Later, take up encompassed other people, encouraged by tax subsidies for government employees. Today, private health insurance offers access to private health care providers to a relatively wealthy minority (16% of the population), while the majority (84%) rely on publicly financed services in public facilities. The magnitude of spending through private health insurance (about 47% of total spending on health) significantly limits the potential for income and risk cross-subsidies in the health system. Medical savings accounts introduced in 1994 and held by about 45% of those with private health insurance segment risk within the market.

Sources: Sagan & Thomson (2016a); Ettelt & Roman-Urrestarazu, Couffinhal & Franc, McIntyre & McLeod, McLeod & McIntyre, this volume.

Does private health insurance enhance efficiency and quality in health service organization and delivery?

The premise underlying this question is that private entities are more likely than public bodies to improve some aspects of health system performance because of incentives created by the pursuit of profit (or margins) in a competitive environment (Gilbert & Tang, 1995; Johnson, 1995; Chollet & Lewis, 1997). In health insurance markets this would be achieved through strategic purchasing leading to greater efficiency and quality in health service delivery and through efforts to minimize administrative costs.

In practice, however, striving for efficiency gains through strategic purchasing has not been the driving force behind private health insurance markets. Historically, it was common for health insurance markets to operate on a retrospective reimbursement basis, simply offering people compensation for health care costs that they had already incurred. Markets for private health insurance often kept this model, even after purchasers operating under national health insurance had switched to the provision of in-kind benefits, either because of their need to provide customers with enhanced choice of provider in substitutive and supplementary markets or because their role was to cover the costs not covered by national health insurance in complementary markets.

As a result, outside the United States, insurers in most private health insurance markets have not engaged in strategic purchasing. Very few have been able to exercise leverage over health care providers through selective contracting, prospective payment, performance monitoring or vertical integration. Instead, many have maintained margins by selecting risks, especially when competing with national health insurance (as in Chile, Germany and the Netherlands before 1986), and by shifting costs onto households through the use of co-payments, benefit ceilings, deductibles and medical savings accounts.

The failure of private insurers to carry out strategic purchasing can push up prices throughout the health system, undermining overall performance. In South Africa, for example, private insurers have had limited purchasing power over health care providers and the introduction of medical savings accounts in the 1990s further weakened their leverage (McLeod & McIntyre, this volume). As a result, private hospital prices in South Africa are similar to prices in countries with much higher levels of GDP, such as France, Germany and the United Kingdom, making it more expensive for the public sector to recruit and retain medical specialists (Lorenzoni & Roubal, 2016).

Where data are available, they suggest that administrative costs are almost always higher in private health insurance markets than under publicly financed coverage (OECD, 2018; Sagan & Thomson, 2016a). Higher administrative costs in private health insurance markets may be attributed to the bureaucracy required to assess risk, rate premiums, design products and review claims, as well as the duplication of tasks necessitated by fragmented pooling.

Does private health insurance relieve fiscal and other pressures on health systems?

Private health insurance may relieve fiscal pressure if it covers a significant share of the population. It is difficult to think of private health insurance as providing genuine fiscal relief when it draws financial and other resources away from those who need them most, however: in other words, when the relief for the government of not having to pay for the things private health insurance covers is offset by a reduction in the performance of the publicly financed part of the health system.

The experience of the countries in this volume highlights different ways in which private health insurance affects the magnitude and allocation of public resources and can therefore add to fiscal pressure. These effects are often most evident in substitutive private health insurance markets and large supplementary private health insurance markets promoting faster access to health care and enhanced choice of health care provider.

Loss of financial contributions to public coverage: In Chile and Germany (and in the Netherlands before 2006), publicly financed coverage loses higher than average income-related contributions when people opt for private health insurance, in Germany because only richer people are given this choice and in Chile because those opting out are more likely to come from richer groups. This leaves the publicly financed scheme with a lower level of funding per person than it would have if it covered the whole population. The loss of contributions from richer people is compounded by the fact that public funds cover a pool with a higher than average risk of ill health than the private health insurance pool (Box 1.3; Ettelt & Roman-Urrestarazu, this volume; Maarse & Jeurissen, this volume). In the Netherlands, this led the government to introduce a levy on those with private health insurance, to compensate the publicly financed scheme for the additional cost of covering older people.

Porous borders between public and private coverage: In Germany, private health insurance premiums rose rapidly with age in the 1980s and early 1990s (in part due to miscalculation on the part of private insurers), causing some older and sicker people to take early retirement so that they could return to public coverage. The influx of older people added to the fiscal pressure faced by the publicly financed scheme and led the government to prohibit people aged over 55 years from returning to public coverage once they had made the decision to opt for private health insurance. In turn, the government was then compelled to introduce a wide range of regulations to ensure that private health insurance would remain accessible and affordable for these older people.

The Netherlands faced a similar situation in the 1970s and early 1980s, which was why choice of public or private coverage was abolished in 1986 in favour of excluding richer people from public coverage. As in Germany, this move required the government to intervene heavily in the market to ensure access and affordability for those reliant on private health insurance.

Porous borders between public and private coverage are also an issue in Chile.

Inadequate compensation for use of public facilities by people with private health insurance: In Brazil, Chile and Ireland, a significant share of people covered by private health insurance continue to use public facilities. The use of public facilities by those with private health insurance is permitted by law, but in Brazil and Chile the compensation that private insurers are supposed to pay public facilities has been difficult to enforce (Diaz et al. and Ettelt & Roman-Urrestarazu, this volume), and is now being sought through the courts in Brazil. In Ireland, private insurers have never been charged the full economic cost of the use of public hospital beds by privately insured patients, although this anomaly is beginning to be addressed (Turner & Smith, this volume).

Migration of health professionals from public to private facilities where demand for private facilities is sustained by private health insurance: In Kenya, the vast majority of doctors work in private facilities. In South Africa, the rate of doctors per 100 000 people is more than five times higher in the private sector than the public sector (McIntyre & McLeod, this volume). This drain on human resources can have major implications for the quality of care in public facilities.

Without private health insurance, the demand for private facilities would be hugely diminished in both countries. In spite of this, a fragmented private health insurance market has not been able to exert leverage over private health care providers. As a result, private insurers have responded to having to pay the very high prices charged by private hospitals in South Africa (Lorenzoni & Roubal, 2016) by shifting costs onto subscribers through medical savings accounts, eroding the quality of private health insurance coverage and adding to fragmentation (McLeod & McIntyre, this volume).

Another consequence of the growth and power of private facilities in South Africa and the associated imbalance in human resources and inflation in health care prices has been to make a genuinely national system of health insurance seem unduly expensive if it must purchase services from private facilities or attract staff to work in public facilities (McIntyre & McLeod, this volume).

Failure to align provider incentives leads to increased waiting times for publicly financed treatment: In countries like Germany, Ireland and Israel, doctors permitted to work in both sectors face strong financial incentives to prioritize private health insurance-financed patients, for example, being paid more to treat people with private health insurance or when working in private facilities, which has increased waiting times for publicly financed patients. Although this has not been such an issue in Germany, where waiting times are not significant, it has been problematic in Ireland, where waiting times are the main reason for purchasing supplementary private health insurance, and in Israel.

The problems in Ireland stem from the fact that nearly half of the population has supplementary private health insurance, which is high by international standards. The large size of this market, encouraged not only by long waiting times for specialist treatment but also by extensive tax subsidies and (more recently) financial penalties for those who fail to buy private health insurance before the age of 35 years, exacerbates inequality in timely access to health care.

Indiscriminate tax subsidies for private health insurance: Inequality in access to health care and fiscal pressure are intensified by indiscriminate use of tax subsidies to encourage take up of private health insurance, especially tax subsidies applied to marginal tax rates, as in Canada, Ireland before 1995 and the United States, which increase as people pay higher rates of tax, meaning wealthier people receive the highest tax subsidies and the poorest people may not receive any tax subsidy at all. France is the only country covered in this volume to target tax subsidies for voluntary private health insurance at poor people.

The use of tax subsidies has had a particularly marked effect on the availability of public funds for health care in Brazil and South Africa, where tax subsidies for private health insurance amount to around 30% of federal government spending on health (Brazil) and around 30% of all government spending on health (South Africa), even though private health insurance covers only a fraction of the population (24% in Brazil and 16% in South Africa) and is heavily skewed in favour of the richest people in both countries.

In Australia and Ireland, tax subsidies for private health insurance have also been substantial in relation to public spending on health, and analysis has shown that these subsidies are not only inequitable but also an ineffective and therefore inefficient means of relieving pressure on public hospitals and reducing waiting times for publicly financed patients (Hall, Fiebig & van Gool and Turner & Smith, this volume).

Tax subsidies are shown to be particularly inappropriate in markets for supplementary private health insurance. To the extent that tax subsidies encourage the growth of such markets, they also ensure that negative spill-over effects are more pronounced.

Finally, markets for private health insurance often result in other spill-over effects, which may be less tangible or quantifiable than the skewing of public resources but can have important and lasting consequences. These include the following outcomes.

- Limited transparency and the associated increase in transaction costs for governing bodies and people facing multiple health insurance options. In the Netherlands, a dual system of public and private coverage was deemed to be cumbersome and was eventually abandoned, but Chile, Germany and the United States have not yet managed to make the transition to a unified universal scheme. In Egypt and Israel, some households have triple coverage.
- Significant capacity and resources deployed to oversee and regulate market actors who are often recalcitrant, sometimes fraudulent and

frequently litigious. Government efforts to regulate private health insurance have encountered legal challenges in many countries, including Chile, France, Germany, Ireland, the Netherlands and the United States.

- Time and energy spent debating issues that would not arise in the absence of powerful private interests. One of the most frequently raised questions is whether private insurers should play a role in providing publicly financed coverage in addition to private health insurance, which has dogged policy debates about moving towards universal health coverage in almost every country in this volume (most recently in Chile, Egypt, Germany, India, Ireland, the Netherlands, South Africa and the United States).

Lessons from international experience

The countries in this volume show great diversity in the role that private health insurance plays in health systems and in the size and functioning of different markets. In spite of such diversity, it is possible to identify patterns across countries and lessons for policy-makers thinking about establishing, expanding or addressing problems in a market for private health insurance.

Private health insurance rarely lives up to the expectations set out at the beginning of this chapter: in essence, that it can be used to relieve pressure on government budgets and enhance health system performance. An overview of the history, politics and performance of some of the world's largest markets for private health insurance reveals a disappointing picture. While private health insurance benefits some people – generally those who are already relatively advantaged – it often has negative consequences for the performance of the health system as a whole, even when its contribution to spending on health is small.

Common problems with private health insurance include:

- an inability to fill gaps in publicly financed coverage and reduce out-of-pocket payments in the vast majority of countries globally, demonstrating limited potential to improve financial protection at the level of the health system;
- inequality in access to health services between people with and without private health insurance as well as between those with private health insurance; because voluntary private health insurance

is systematically more likely to be bought by people in higher socioeconomic groups, the larger the market, the more visible and less acceptable this inequality is likely to be;

- the absence of incentives for private health insurance to enhance efficiency and quality in organization and health service delivery in most countries, combined with fragmented purchasing power, means very few private insurers engage in strategic purchasing; in some instances, this pushes up prices in the wider health system;

- a tendency to add to fiscal pressure, particularly where boundaries between public and private coverage are not clearly defined or enforced, incentives are not aligned across the health system and tax subsidies for PHI are indiscriminate; as a result, financial and human resources are drawn away from publicly financed coverage to the benefit of people with private health insurance; and

- other less obvious effects such as an increase in transaction costs due to limited transparency; the capacity and resources required to oversee the market; and the time and energy spent debating issues that would not arise in the absence of private health insurance.

Many of the problems associated with private health insurance can be attributed to failure on the part of policy-makers to recognize and manage what are essentially predictable risks; predictable because they are clearly set out in economic theory on market failures in health insurance. History and politics have also posed a challenge to effective public policy towards private health insurance, resulting in struggles to ensure adequate oversight of the market and mitigate negative spill-over effects.

Learning from international experience, policy-makers can try to ensure that private health insurance contributes to attaining policy goals through:

- clarity in national health financing policy frameworks about the role of private health insurance in the health system;

- better understanding of the way in which private health insurance affects health system performance: anticipating predictable risks and likely problems should result in a lowering of expectations about what private health insurance can achieve at health system level; and

- better oversight of private health insurance: this requires willingness and capacity to set and enforce clear boundaries between public and private coverage, align incentives across the health system, regulate for financial and consumer protection, and carefully monitor the market.

Policy-makers will benefit from acknowledging from the outset the very limited extent to which a poorly regulated market can enhance health system performance; paying attention to the risks inherent in creating new actors and institutions that may be difficult to direct and impossible to dismantle; and recognizing where a particular policy design reflects history and politics more than informed choice. For example, the countries that opted to establish national health insurance using employment-based private schemes did so for historical and political reasons rather than technical considerations. In today's context, taking this route would not be an optimal pathway to universal health coverage. Similarly, giving people the ability to choose between public and private coverage – perhaps the most egregious policy design of all – was not the outcome of a desire to foster choice and competition in Germany or the Netherlands but of historical decisions reflecting the needs and circumstances of a very different time. In both countries, the difficulty of mitigating negative effects has been exacerbated by politics, as seen in strong and effective opposition to change from health care providers, private insurers and people with private health insurance. Chile's decision to opt for a policy design that was already causing problems elsewhere (and soon to be abandoned in the Netherlands) reflected politics too: an ideological belief in the value of choice and competition.

The experience of these and other countries suggests that it is challenging to address negative effects once they have begun to be visible. Even when there is clear evidence of public policies that create or perpetuate inequality and inefficiency (indiscriminate tax subsidies, for instance, or incentives encouraging providers to prioritize people with private health insurance) some governments have been reluctant to take corrective action due to lobbying on the part of private insurers and health care providers or for fear of antagonizing the relatively wealthy and influential people most likely to benefit from private health insurance.

Finally, it is important to be aware of how frequently the interests created by private health insurance have obstructed the expansion of publicly financed coverage. Having to give thought to whether private insurers should play a role in providing publicly financed coverage has not only complicated policy debates about universal health coverage in many countries, it has also slowed national progress towards this goal.

References

Abel-Smith B (1988). The rise and decline of the early HMOs: some international experiences. *Milbank Quarterly*, 66(4):694–719.

Akerlof GA (1970). The Market for 'Lemons': Quality Uncertainty and the Market Mechanism. *The Quarterly Journal of Economics*, 84(3):488–500. http://doi.org/10.2307/1879431.

Barr N (1992). Economic theory and the welfare state: a survey and interpretation. *Journal of Economic Literature*, 30:741–803.

Barr N (2004). *The economics of the welfare state*, 4th edition. Oxford, Oxford University Press.

Chollet D, Lewis M (1997). *Private insurance: principles and practice. Innovations in health care financing: proceedings of a World Bank conference, March 10–11, 1997*, World Bank Discussion Paper No 365. Washington DC, World Bank.

Culyer AJ (1989). The normative economics of health care finance and provision. *Oxford Review of Economic Policy*, 5(1):34–58.

Drechsler D, Jütting J (2005). *Private health insurance for the poor in developing countries?* OECD Development Centre, Policy Insights 11. Paris, OECD publishing.

Einav L, Finkelstein A (2018). Moral hazard in health insurance: what we know and how we know it. *Journal of the European Economic Association*, 16(4):957–82.

Evans RG (1984). *Strained mercy: the economics of Canadian health care.* Toronto, Butterworths.

Foubister T et al. (2006). *Private medical insurance in the United Kingdom.* Copenhagen, WHO Regional Office for Europe on behalf of the European Observatory on Health Systems and Policies.

Gechert S (2010). Supplementary private health insurance in selected countries: lessons for EU governments? *CESifo Economic Studies* 56(3):444–64.

Gilbert N, Tang KL (1995). *The United States. Private markets in health and welfare: an international perspective.* Oxford, Berg Publishers Limited.

Hsiao WC (1995). Abnormal economics in the health sector. *Health Policy*, 32(1-3):125–39.

Johnson N (1995). *Introduction. Private markets in health and welfare: an international perspective.* Oxford, Berg Publishers Limited.

Jost TS (2000). Private or public approaches to insuring the uninsured: lessons from international experience with private insurance. *New York University Law Review*, 76(2):419–92.

Kornai J, Eggleston K (2001). *Welfare, choice and solidarity in transition.* Cambridge, Cambridge University Press.

Lorenzoni L, Roubal T (2016). *International comparison of South African private hospital price levels.* OECD Health Working Papers, No. 85. Paris, OECD Publishing, available at: https://doi.org/10.1787/5jrrxrzn24wl-en.

Maynard A, Dixon A (2002). Private health insurance and medical savings account: theory and experience. In: Mossialos E, et al. *Funding health care: options for Europe.* Buckingham, Open University Press.

Mossialos E, Thomson S (2002). Voluntary health insurance in the European Union: a critical assessment. *International Journal of Health Services,* 32(1):19–88.

Nyman JA (2004). Is 'moral hazard' inefficient? The policy implications of a new theory. *Health Affairs (Millwood),* 2004;23(5):194–9.

OECD (2004). *Private health insurance in OECD countries.* Paris, OECD Publishing.

OECD, Eurostat, WHO (2017). A System of Health Accounts 2011: revised edition. Paris: OECD Publishing.

OECD (2018). OECD iLibrary [online database].

Preker A, Scheffler R, Bassett M (2007). *Private voluntary health insurance in development: friend or foe?* Washington DC, World Bank.

Rice T (2001). Individual autonomy and state involvement in health care. *J Medical Ethics,* 27(4):240–4.

Rice T (2003). *The economics of health reconsidered,* 2nd edition Chicago, Health Administration Press.

Sagan A, Thomson S (2016a). *Voluntary health insurance in Europe: role and regulation.* Copenhagen, WHO Regional office for Europe on behalf of the European Observatory on Health Systems and Policies. Observatory study series (43), available at: http://www.euro.who.int/en/about-us/partners/ observatory/publications/studies/voluntary-health-insurance-in-europe- role-and-regulation-2016.

Sagan A, Thomson S (2016b). *Voluntary health insurance in Europe: country experience.* Copenhagen, WHO Regional office for Europe on behalf of the European Observatory on Health Systems and Policies. Observatory study series (42), available at: http://www.euro.who.int/en/about-us/partners/ observatory/publications/studies/voluntary-health-insurance-in-europe- country-experience-2016.

Saltman RB, Busse R, Figueras J (2004). *Social health insurance systems in western Europe.* Maidenhead, Open University Press.

Schneider M (1995). *Complementary health schemes in the European Union, European Commission seminar*, Prien am Chiemsee, Bavaria 14–16 October 1992. Augsburg, BASYS.

Sekhri N, Savedoff W (2005). Private health insurance: implications for developing countries. *Bulletin of the World Health Organization*, 83(2):127–34.

Thomson S (2010). What role for voluntary health insurance? In: Kutzin J et al., eds. *Implementing health financing reform: lessons from countries in transition*. Copenhagen, WHO Regional Office for Europe on behalf of the European Observatory on Health Systems and Policies.

Thomson S, Mossialos E (2006). Choice of public or private health insurance: learning from the experience of Germany and the Netherlands. *Journal of European Social Policy*, 16(4):315–27.

Thomson S, Mossialos E (2009). *Private health insurance in the European Union. Final report prepared for the European Commission, Directorate General for Employment, Social Affairs and Equal Opportunities*. Brussels, European Commission.

Vončina L, Rubil I (2018). Can people afford to pay for health care? New evidence on financial protection in Croatia. Copenhagen, WHO Regional Office for Europe, available at: www.euro.who.int/en/health-topics/Health-systems/health-systems-financing/publications/2018/can-people-afford-to-pay-for-health-care-new-evidence-on-financial-protection-in-croatia-2018.

Wasem J, Greß S, Okma K (2004). The role of private health insurance in social health insurance countries. In: Saltman R et al., eds. *Social health insurance systems in western Europe*. Maidenhead, Open University Press.

WHO (2020). Global Health Expenditure Database [online database]. Geneva, World Health Organization, available at: http://apps.who.int/nha/database/Select/Indicators/en.

WHO Regional Office for Europe (2019). Can people afford to pay for health care? New evidence on financial protection in Europe. Copenhagen, WHO Regional Office for Europe, available at: www.euro.who.int/en/health-topics/Health-systems/health-systems-financing/publications/2019/can-people-afford-to-pay-for-health-care-new-evidence-on-financial-protection-in-europe-2019.

2 | Private finance publicly subsidized: the case of Australian health insurance

JANE HALL, DENZIL G. FIEBIG AND KEES VAN GOOL

Australia's Medicare is a universal, publicly funded comprehensive insurance scheme that provides all its citizens with free treatment in public hospitals, and subsidizes out-of-hospital medical services and pharmaceuticals. Yet alongside this public insurance there exists a strong private health insurance sector that covers private in-hospital treatment or general (largely dental and other) ancillary services. Policy initiatives implemented since 1997 have provided both incentives and penalties to encourage the uptake of private insurance. The proportion of the population with insurance for hospital treatment grew from around 33% in December 1996 to a high of 45% in 2000; it then declined slightly until 2007 and has increased since then to 47% in December 2015 (APRA, 2016). Consequently, significant public funds have been directed to support the private health insurance industry and, by extension, the private health care sector. Current policies reflect the ambiguities of the electoral popularity of Medicare alongside the push to restrain public spending.

This apparently anomalous situation can only be understood in the context of the contested ground between public and private interests in health care financing. In less than 40 years, from 1970 to 2010, Australia moved through the following approaches to health care financing: voluntary private insurance with public subsidies (pre-1974); publicly financed national universal health insurance (Medibank, 1974–1976); a series of policy changes that returned the system to voluntary, predominantly private, insurance with public subsidies (1976–1984); publicly financed national universal health insurance (Medicare, 1984–1996); publicly financed national universal health insurance with publicly subsidized private health insurance (1996–2006); and publicly financed national universal health insurance with an expanded role for publicly subsidized private health insurance (2006 until time of publication). Following a change of government in 2007, a new direction in health care financing was sought. Interestingly, given the previous focus on the roles of public and private financing, the 2007 election was focused on public hospitals and how financing should be shared between Commonwealth (the national government is officially the Commonwealth of Australia) and states, but did not directly address insurance. A further change of government (led by the Liberal-National Party in 2013) reversed much of the agreed reform strategy, leaving the future direction, including the future for private health insurance, uncertain.

The economic rationale for such massive government subsidies in the private health insurance market is far from clear. Certainly, in the lead-up to the 1996 election, there was widespread concern about the affordability of private health insurance; and the Prime Minister of the day suggested that premiums would actually fall. Not surprisingly, this has not happened and premiums have continued to rise faster than general inflation. If anything, dissatisfaction with the value for money of private insurance has grown, in spite of the high level of population coverage. The Minister for Health established a community consultation at the end of 2015. Over 40 000 Australians responded to the open consultation (online), which showed that the cost of private health insurance was of greatest concern overall (Department of Health, 2015/2016).

Financing the health system

Australian health care is primarily financed by governments (both at the national and state levels). The structure of government – Australia is a federation formed from six independent colonies, each of which has retained its own government – and the revenue base affect the responsibilities and financial flows. At federation, the state governments retained their responsibilities and functions unless these were specifically ceded to the national government. The national government has had the power to raise income taxes since the 1940s, which gives it a stronger revenue base. The taxing powers of states are limited and states rely on transfers from national government through both general and special-purpose grants.

Within the health system, around two thirds of total spending is contributed by governments, mostly from general revenue. There is a small specific income tax levy, which was introduced in 1984 to raise the additional funds required to finance universal free public hospital treatment. The original Medicare levy taxed individuals 1% of their income, with exemptions for low income households. Over time the levy has been increased several times including a half a percentage point increase from July 2014 to fund the National Disability Insurance Scheme. The levy currently stands at 2% and raised around 17% of Australian Government health spending (AIHW, 2016a).

Special-purpose grants for health were introduced (in 1945) to assist states with the funding of hospitals. Hospitals had been established primarily by charitable and religious organizations; by the early 20th century state governments had a major role in funding them and gradually took control, assuming ownership. These 5-yearly agreements on hospital funding between the Australian government and the states and territories continue as the basis for the funding of state health services, primarily public hospitals, but these agreements also provide the opportunity to establish other national health policies. Also in the 1940s, the Australian government established a national Pharmaceutical Benefits Scheme, initially providing a limited range of drugs at no charge; over time the formulary has grown and co-payments have been introduced.

Nongovernment finance (33% of total finance) comprises primarily individual out-of-pocket expenses (18.8%); only 8.4% of total funds, or about a quarter of the nongovernment share, is raised from private insurance (AIHW, 2016a). The private insurance contribution has been growing steadily over the last decade whereas the relative government share has declined. Private health insurance is highly regulated under a policy whose features were established in the period after the Second World War. Insurance was to be voluntary with no compulsion; medical care would be provided on a fee-for-service basis; there would and should be patient co-payments – hence government could not set or limit medical fees. Further, insurance premiums were to be community rated, with open enrolment (although a few small specialized funds were exempt from this last provision). Further, insurance could only be provided by non-profit organizations, so managing to avoid "unhealthy competition".

These developments occurred against a background of alternative proposals for some form of national health insurance with salaried or capitated payments for medical care, all of which were treated with hostility by the medical profession. This ended in a constitutional challenge to the government powers and the amendment of the Australian Constitution that forbade civil conscription of doctors and dentists. In this way, the architecture of the Australian health care system was established, with public support for private voluntary insurance for both hospitals and medical care, and the protection of fee-for-service payments.

There were 36 registered insurance funds in 2016 (APRA, 2016). The larger funds include the organizations initially developed by the hospitals and the doctors as mutual organizations, and the government-owned insurer (Medicare). Smaller funds are often the descendants of earlier friendly societies and workers' cooperatives. Private health insurance policy is the responsibility of the national government; responsibility for monitoring and regulation was transferred in mid-2015 from an independent statutory authority, the Private Health Insurance Administration Council, to the Australian Prudential Regulatory Authority which oversees the financial services sector.

The current mix of health service provision

Australia spent 10.03% of its gross domestic product on health in 2014–2015, an increase from 8.6% of gross domestic product a decade earlier (AIHW, 2016a). The three major spending components are hospitals, accounting for 44% of recurrent spending; primary care accounts for 38%, which includes general practitioner consultations, dental services and pharmaceuticals; and the remaining 22% is categorized as other medical goods and services. Almost 50% of the "other" category consists of referred medical services such as specialist consultations, pathology and imaging. Although private health insurers contribute to all three sectors, their biggest contribution is in the hospital sector (AIHW, 2015).

Most medical services are provided by independent private practitioners on a fee-for-service basis. General practitioners play an important gatekeeping role in the system, as referral is essential for any reimbursement of specialist services, including diagnostic tests, and therefore most hospital admissions. People are able to choose their own medical provider. Medicare provides subsidies for privately provided medical services. Where practitioners charge above the Medicare reimbursement rate, the patient faces out-of-pocket payments. The levels of co-payments vary by area of residence and specialty (rural and remote-area residents and patients requiring specialist surgical, medical, or obstetric care and anaesthetics tend to face higher co-payments).

The Pharmaceutical Benefits Scheme is universal and covers a comprehensive range of drugs – around 90% of all prescriptions written are covered by the Pharmaceutical Benefits Scheme. Since its introduction, co-payments have been progressively introduced and stand at (as of July 2016) Aus$38.30[1] for each prescription item for general beneficiaries and Aus$6.20 for those receiving social security benefits, with safety net measures to limit total out-of-pocket exposure. Dental services are almost entirely privately provided, under fee-for-service private practice arrangements. However, there are some public dental services with an emphasis on emergency care for low-income groups.

Public and private hospitals account for 59% and 41% of admissions, respectively (AIHW, 2016b). Public hospitals generally have a more complex case-mix and the major teaching and research-intensive hospitals are public. Public hospitals can also admit private patients who, though housed in the same facilities, and treated by the same medical and nursing staff, face charges for hospital and medical services. In 2014–2015, 17% of public hospital admissions were for private patients, with 79% of those covered by private health insurance (AIHW, 2016b). Other private admissions are covered by insurance for motor vehicle accidents, workers' compensation, benefits provided to military veterans or through out-of-pocket payments.

The (national) Commonwealth government has the responsibility for providing medical services (Medicare Benefits Scheme) and pharmaceutical benefits (the Pharmaceutical Benefits Scheme). Both programmes are based on the government setting fee rebates or negotiating pharmaceutical prices, but with few, if any, controls on service/prescribing levels. Therefore, both programmes represent open-ended spending commitments. Public hospitals are owned and operated by the six state and two territory governments, which are able to apply constraints to total spending. Costs are met by states and territories with a similar level of Commonwealth contribution, negotiated through 5-yearly agreements between each state government and the Commonwealth Government (now known as the Australian Health Care Agreements).

Private health insurance has been limited to covering private hospital treatment (a supplementary role) and ancillary services, now called general insurance, which typically covers out-of-hospital provision of dental, optical, physiotherapy and other allied health services, which are poorly provided in the public system or are not covered by Medicare (a complementary role). Around 85% of Australians with private health insurance hold a combined hospital and ancillary services product

[1] Australian dollars are used throughout the chapter.

(PHIAC, 2015a). The type of ancillary services covered and the extent of coverage, usually specified as a spending limit, are detailed according to each policy. Insurers are free to design their own packages; however, once a policy type is on the market it cannot be removed while there are still purchasers of that policy. Private insurance is not allowed for pharmaceuticals as these are covered by the Pharmaceutical Benefits Scheme. However, insurers can make some drugs available before Pharmaceutical Benefits Scheme approval, for example Herceptin for breast cancer treatment, but this is done on a case-by-case basis and not explicitly covered in the policy (Pearce et al., 2012). The idea of a "broader health cover" was developed and enacted in legislation in early 2007. This was intended to enable private health insurance to cover services that are extensions of hospital care (such as providing care following early discharge), substitutes for hospitalization (such as hospital-at-home schemes), or programmes that prevent hospitalization (PHIAC, 2016).

Developments before 1974

Medical services are provided by independent private practitioners primarily on a fee-for-service basis. The first doctors to arrive in the British colony in 1788 were naval surgeons employed to care for the military and convicts. As the number of free settlers grew, the doctors sought the right of private practice and by 1820 they were able to leave government service and establish full-time private practices. Hospitals began as charitable institutions, which operated nursing facilities for the care of the poor, in which medical practitioners provided their services for free. These Honorary Medical Officers worked otherwise in private, fee-for-service practices and had the highest standing among the medical professionals. Meanwhile, developments in the effectiveness of medical and nursing care had two effects: growth in costs prompted the charities to turn to the government for assistance; and growth in demand spurred the introduction of charges. An intermediate level of care (private medical care with accommodation in a small, multi-bedded room) was available for the respectable working and middle class, and private medical care in a single room for those who could afford (relative) luxury (Crichton, 1990).

Private insurance was established first by the hospitals, in 1932, and then by doctors, in 1946, as a means of reducing the problem of bad debts. Government involvement in health insurance was established in the 1950s with the national government introducing subsidies for medical services; these were not paid directly but rather through the private insurance funds, so entrenching private health insurance. Those without insurance could be seen at hospital outpatient clinics free of charge. Patients generally had to queue to access these services and the clinics were often attended by doctors in training and offered limited amenities. Hospitals admitted inpatients under a three-tier system. Free treatment was available but was means-tested, and accommodation for these public patients was in large, multi-bedded (Nightingale-style) wards, where they were regarded as teaching material for students and junior medical staff. Senior doctors donated their services in return for the right to treat their private patients. Private patients were offered two standards of accommodation: intermediate in small, multi-bedded rooms; or private in single rooms. Insurance could be bought for either type of amenity. Those without insurance were required to pay out of pocket. Individuals and families were pursued, through the courts if necessary, to repay their debts. Consequently, people would avoid seeking care until their condition was severe, and many would give false names and addresses if admitted, giving rise to problems with continuity of care. Developments and reforms, even the introduction of Medicare, have not changed these arrangements substantially.

The contest between public and private financing: 1975–1996

By this time, there were two major political parties in Australia. The Liberal Party, politically conservative, traditionally aligned with business interests, had governed in coalition with the National Party, which represented the interests of the rural sector. The alternative, the Labor Party, was supported by the trade union movement. A change in government in 1972, after 23 years of the conservative coalition in power, ushered in a time of major social change, including the introduction of publicly financed universal health care. Medibank, as the new programme was known, was financed from general taxation, provided universal access to public hospitals at no charge, and a rebate on medical fees of 85% of the scheduled fee (Duckett, 2007). The organized medical profession resisted the advent of "socialized medicine" and the political conflict delayed the introduction of Medibank until 1975 (Crichton, 1990; Scotton, 2001). Private health insurance funds continued to operate with community-rated premiums and open enrolment, although their membership base was steadily declining. Soon after Medibank became operational there was a further change in government, amid intense political instability. The conservative coalition returned to power, promising the retention of Medibank, although following various changes, which gradually reversed the universality of the scheme, it became Medibank Private operating as a health insurance fund owned by the government in competition with other private insurers. The major changes were: October 1976, a levy of 2.5% of taxable income was introduced on those without private insurance; May 1978, bulk-billing was restricted to pensioners and the socially disadvantaged, and the medical rebate was reduced to 75% of the scheduled fee; November 1978, the levy which penalized those without private insurance was abolished, and the rebate was reduced to 40% of the scheduled fee; May 1979, payment of rebates was restricted to services for which the scheduled fee exceeded Aus$20; September 1981, rebates were reduced to 30% of the scheduled fee and were only paid to those with private medical insurance, and means-testing was introduced for free treatment in public hospitals (Duckett, 2007). Hence, by 1983, health care financing had returned to arrangements very similar to the pre-1974 situation. Free medical treatment was limited and often available at the discretion of the provider; public hospital treatment was only free to those with limited means. The privately insured were favoured through tax deductibility of premiums and a subsidy for rebates. Not surprisingly, private health insurance became a major source of finance, with around 70% of the population having both medical and hospital cover. Nonetheless, around 14% of the population had no insurance coverage or public entitlement, and were exposed to potentially major medical bills. The public were ill-informed and confused by the frequent changes to financing arrangements; their entitlements were altered not just by changes in Commonwealth policy but also by state-level changes in eligibility for public hospital treatment. By this time, Medibank and universal tax-financed hospital care had ceased. Medibank Private continued as the government-owned private insurer, operating under an independent but government-appointed board, and today it is the largest health insurance fund in Australia.

Medicare was introduced under another Labor government in 1984 and was very similar in design to the original Medibank (Duckett, 2007). Again, the introduction of a universal tax-financed scheme was accompanied by strong opposition from the medical profession

(Crichton, 1990). This time there was much greater political stability and the structure of Medicare has remained intact. The coincidence of private insurance, private medicine and private hospital interests produced a strong coalition that found a political alliance. The Liberal Party retained its opposition to Medicare from 1984 until 1996, going into each election with a platform of repealing the universality and public financing of Medicare, limiting public financing to the disadvantaged, and encouraging private insurance. This was despite the clear strong public support for Medicare. It was not until 1996, after promising to continue Medicare, albeit with a complementary role for private insurance, that the conservative parties once again won a national election.

The original design of Medicare had not been explicit about the role of private insurance and private hospitals. There were those who argued for a *laissez-faire* approach, postulating that, if left alone, private insurance would decline until it reached a natural plateau, covering those who wished to buy the higher amenity of private hospital treatment. If this was the rationale, it is hard to see what the basis was for retaining community rating. However, community rating remained, with little or no discussion, let alone criticism, as part of making insurance affordable – perhaps a symbol of the Australian commitment to fairness. The alternative view was that the financial viability of Medicare required the coexistence of a strong private hospital sector, as the public system had never been intended to cope with the growing demands of the entire population. But if this rationale is accepted, there is no clear case for the universality of Medicare, which is considered to be a critical feature of the scheme.

The private health insurance incentives strategy: 1996–2006

At the time of the return of a Liberal government in 1996, private insurance was restricted to offering cover for private hospital treatment (it comprised both care in private hospitals and private care in public hospitals; it also covered day-only admissions in free-standing day-surgery facilities and a range of ancillary services, such as dentistry, optometry and physiotherapy) (Hall & Savage, 2005). As noted above, premiums were community-rated and almost all insurers were required to accept all customers. The 1996 to 2007 era was marked by consolidation of registered insurance funds operating in Australia (PHIAC, 2016). In the period between 1995 and 2010, the number of insurance funds fell from 49 to 37. However, despite the large number of funds, the market was (and remains) highly concentrated with the largest four holding 85% market share; with Medibank Private and the British United Provident Association (BUPA) Group having market shares in excess of 25% each.

Private health insurance coverage had reached a low of 32% of the population in 1996. Although this coverage was low in historical terms for Australia, it was nonetheless high compared with, for example, the United Kingdom, where fewer than 10% chose to buy private insurance rather than rely solely on the National Health Service. The private health insurance incentives strategy commenced in 1997 with the introduction of a subsidy for low-income earners to purchase insurance and a tax surcharge (1% of taxable income) for high-income individuals without private insurance. Hence it was termed the "carrots and sticks" policy. The estimated cost to government was Aus$600 million per annum [or 11.5% of the Australian government's outlay on public hospitals at that time (Hall, 2001)]. This measure, however, seemed to have no impact on the trend of falling coverage.

The second step was introduced in January 1999. The "carrot" was extended to a 30% rebate on insurance premiums without any means test. It was initially estimated to cost Aus$1.5 billion per annum but this figure was then revised to Aus$2.1 billion in the second year. The second stage of the policy – the 30% rebate – was associated with a flattening of the downward trend and the level of insurance coverage stabilized. Lifetime Health Cover, the third step introduced in July 2000 in addition to the rebate and the tax surcharge, involved modifying community rating to allow for age-related premiums to be charged to those taking out insurance after the age of 30. The base premium was increased by 2% for each year beyond 30, but the rate was locked in at the rate at which people first purchased insurance. The aim of the scheme was to encourage the young, with relatively good risk profiles, to buy private insurance and maintain it for life. Although this measure constituted a major change in the structure of health insurance, it involved little or no cost to the government. Community-rated premiums had been accepted as a permanent feature of insurance regulation over the previous 50 years, despite other changes in policy. At the same time, provisions were made to encourage private insurance to offer "no-gap" or "known-gap" policies to limit unforeseen out-of-pocket costs, essentially introducing complementary insurance for the co-payment component of in-hospital medical fees. Insurance coverage increased following Lifetime Health Cover so that by the end of 2000, insurance coverage had reached 45%, almost a 50% increase on its 1996 low. In 2005, the rebate was increased for older people, to 35% and 40% for people aged over 65 and over 70, respectively. An obvious consequence of this increase in coverage plus more generous support for older people was an increase in the cost of the rebate to Aus$3.6 billion or 10% of Australian Government spending on health (AIHW, 2009).

There is one more avenue of health-insurance-related government spending that warrants a brief comment. The increasing concern with the growing level of co-payments, particularly in general practice, was the impetus for the introduction of the Medicare Safety Net in March 2004. The Safety Net covers out-of-hospital medical services for which medical benefits are paid (that is, services covered by Medicare). Once a specified level of co-payments has been reached, all further co-payments are reimbursed at 80%, leaving individuals and families with 20% in out-of-pocket expenses. This represents a major change to the previous health insurance arrangements, as public funding is no longer restricted to the scheduled (that is, government-determined) fee but will apply to whatever fee the doctor will actually charge. Following the introduction of the Safety Net, there has been little change in patient co-payments but major changes in fee levels. This resulted in a far higher liability for spending than had been predicted; for every Safety Net dollar spent, around 70 cents went to providers in higher fees. Further, the changes in fee levels have been most marked for specialist providers, in particular for private obstetrics and assisted reproductive services (Van Gool et al., 2009). Indeed, the Safety Net has made out-of-hospital practice more lucrative for some providers than in-hospital services. As a result, there is clear evidence among some specialist groups that they are switching fees and services away from the inpatient sector covered by private health insurance and towards the out of-hospital sector that is covered by public funding. As technologies develop and enable more procedures to be delivered in the out-of-hospital sector, this practice may become more widespread and, as a result, will place additional strain on public financing.

The effectiveness of the private health insurance strategy

The question of whether the incentives achieved their intended objective is not clear-cut, simply because there was never an agreed and clear statement of the objective. At the time the strategy was developed, the government argued that increasing private insurance coverage would reduce public hospital use (Australian Government, 2007); and that this would be the case was reinforced by the popular media (Haas et al., 2001; Hall, 2001). However, over time, the objective was transformed into providing additional choice for private insurance (Australian Government, 2007). Whether Australians do in fact value this form of improved choice is hard to assess. Nonetheless, the introduction of the incentives was followed by a dramatic increase in the proportion of the population with private insurance. Private health (hospital) insurance coverage reached its lowest level in 1998, with 30.2% of the population holding hospital insurance in December 1998. By December 2000, population coverage reached 45.4%. This was a major increase in the number of people with private health insurance. Hence, on the simplest measure (and the one used by the government in assessing its performance), the strategy was extremely successful. A more interesting question is which component of the strategy was effective. The private health insurance rebate has been one of the most controversial pieces of legislation due to the large costs. The most recent AIHW (2016a) data reveals that the rebate costs the Australian Government around Aus$5.7 billion annually (representing around 9% of its total spending on health) yet it apparently had little effect on insurance coverage. It was the third stage, Lifetime Health Cover, that was accompanied by the jump in coverage; indeed the cut-off date for insurance enrolment without the age-related premium had to be extended as the insurance companies simply could not handle the number of new customers. Lifetime Health Cover was simply a regulatory change, whereas the 30% rebate was costly because it required a substantial and ongoing windfall gain to the 30% of the population already holding private insurance. Lifetime Health Cover was accompanied by a very aggressive advertising campaign, under the slogan "Run for Cover", so there was both a price impact (expected future increases above the base premium) and a non-price impact. It is likely that some were frightened into buying insurance, some believed that they were buying in at a premium that would remain stable for the rest of their lives, while many were just confused.

The timing of the introduction of the rebate and Lifetime Health Cover – both were introduced over a 12-month period – is such that it is very difficult to disentangle their effects. Butler (2002) argued, on the basis of the aggregate data, that the 30% rebate was costly and largely ineffective while Lifetime Health Cover was inexpensive and effective. Frech, Hopkins & Macdonald (2003), using aggregate data, concluded that the regulatory change had more impact than the rebate, but that the rebate was still significant in increasing demand for private health insurance. In contrast, Palangkaraya & Yong (2005), modelling individual decision-making using data from the National Health Survey and simulating the effects of policy change, concluded that Lifetime Health Cover was responsible for around 42% of the increase in private health insurance. Ellis & Savage (2008), using a similar approach and the same data set, noting that Lifetime Health Cover in fact changes the future price of private health insurance, find an effect of the non-price aspects of the policy, particularly for younger age groups. They attribute this effect to the advertising campaign. They concluded that the rebate reinforced the effect of Lifetime Health Cover for single people, but it weakened its effect for families in that it also reduced the future price of insurance.

Adverse selection, hospital use, cost to government

The design of Lifetime Health Cover was aimed at reversing adverse selection, which was widely perceived to be a key and critical feature of the Australian health care system (see in particular, Industry Commission, 1997). As the evidence for adverse selection was based strongly on the changing age profile of the insured, the solution was to provide an incentive for people to buy insurance before the age of 30 and then maintain it. The majority of new entrants to the private insurance pool following the incentives were under 65 years of age. The proportion of people aged 65 years and over in the insured population decreased from 14.9% in December 1998 to 10.4% in December 2000, although it had increased again to 14.0% in 2008 (PHIAC, 2010).

Barrett & Conlon (2003) investigated the extent of adverse selection in health insurance and concluded that, measuring the health risk by the number of chronic conditions, adverse selection had increased over the 6 years before the introduction of the insurance incentives strategy. However, they also found evidence of better health risks selecting into insurance. This selection was based on self-assessed health status and risky behaviours (such as smoking or alcohol consumption); a finding confirmed by Doiron, Jones & Savage (2008) using more recent data. Vaithianathan (2004) argued that community rating in Australia could in fact be circumvented, as insurers market different insurance plans with coverage designed to appeal to different risk groups, for example by offering plans excluding cataract surgery and joint replacement.

More insight into why people buy health insurance is provided in an analysis by Fiebig, Savage & Viney (2006) using data collected since the introduction of the incentives. Insurance purchasers were categorized according to their reasons for purchasing health insurance. Security and peace of mind were identified as the only reasons for buying insurance by 24% of purchasers. For 13% of purchasers, choice of private hospital and doctor was key, 15% of purchasers were driven by financial reasons and the other categories comprised people who valued various combinations of the above factors. It should be noted that the combination of the rebate on insurance premiums and the income tax surcharge meant that many above-average income earners faced a negative price for insurance. In other words, they saved money by buying insurance and thereby avoided the additional income tax levy. Those driven by "security" reasons were likely to have held their insurance for 5 years or more before the introduction of the incentives, whereas those motivated by financial reasons were much more likely to buy insurance only after the incentives were introduced (Fiebig, Savage & Viney, 2006).

Having private insurance does not necessarily equate with the use of the private system. All residents are entitled to free public hospital care. Fiebig, Savage & Viney (2006) showed that those who bought insurance for financial reasons were less likely to choose the private system when admitted to hospital than those who valued choice and had held insurance since before the recent introduction of incentives. Vaithianathan (2002) stressed the importance of individuals who have been historically self-insured. They have a preference for private care but have felt that private health insurance has not offered them good value, presumably because they tend to be younger, healthier and wealthier than the average population. These individuals may be enticed into purchasing private health insurance by policy changes but their choice of hospital treatment may not change because they would have used the private health system irrespective of their insurance status.

Private hospital use did indeed rise following the expansion of private insurance. This has been taken as a measure of policy success by the government, which had set a goal of increasing private admissions as a proportion of total (public and private) hospital admissions. Some analysts have argued that this represents a welfare improvement, based on the assumption that every private admission has replaced a public admission (see for example Hopkins & Frech, 2001; Frech, Hopkins & Macdonald, 2003; Harper, 2003). However, it is not clear whether the share of private admissions would have actually remained unchanged if private insurance had not expanded, as private hospital use had also been rising throughout the period in which private health insurance coverage was falling. Private and public hospitals are not perfect substitutes. The highly specialized and university teaching hospitals are public hospitals; almost all emergency departments are located in public hospitals. Although there has been a concomitant change in the nature of private hospitals with increasing ownership by for-profit corporations, increasing case-mix severity and the availability of more sophisticated facilities, elective admissions are still the main focus of private hospital activity. Further, there is a moral hazard effect; that is, the purchase of private insurance encourages the over-use of the services covered by insurance. Several studies have shown that the insured are much more likely to be high users, though this is difficult to disentangle from adverse selection. The study by Savage & Wright (2003) using data from the National Health Survey showed a substantial effect on increased length of hospital stay due to moral hazard associated with insurance whereas Doiron, Fiebig & Suziedelyte (2014), using detailed administrative data, found large moral hazard effects but only for elective procedures.

The cost of subsidizing private health insurance continued to grow, from Aus$2 billion in 2000–2001 to almost Aus$5.7 billion in 2014–2015 (AIHW, 2006, 2016a). However, there was no evidence of reduced pressure on public hospitals, as demonstrated by increasing workloads. It has been argued that, given there were already substantial waiting lists particularly for elective surgery, a decrease in public hospital activity should not have been expected and that the increased throughput of the total hospital system, in terms of shorter waiting times, represents a real welfare gain (Frech & Hopkins, 2004). It is then necessary to ask whether the insurance subsidies represent the most efficient means of achieving those gains. Lu & Savage (2006), using the estimated reductions in Medicare admissions and hospital days, find that the average cost of a private admission produced by the private insurance incentives amounted to Aus$28 606 in 2001–2002. The actual average cost of a public hospital admission in that year was Aus$28 61 (Lu & Savage 2006). As private hospitals appear to be at best as efficient in producing episodes of hospital care as public hospitals, at least the same expansion of capacity could have been managed through the public system (Duckett & Jackson 2000). This would have avoided the moral hazard problem associated with private insurance as shown by longer hospitalizations, more intensive resource use and possibly higher admission rates (Robertson & Richardson, 2000; Savage & Wright, 2003). More recent work by Cheng (2014) simulates the impact of reducing the subsidies and finds that any resulting increase in public spending on hospital care would be substantially less than the cost savings associated with lower subsidies.

New directions, stalled reform and policy uncertainty (2007 onwards)

Since 2007, there have been four national elections and six changes of Prime Minister. The 2007 election resulted in a change of government (from Liberal to Labor). The Government changed again in 2013. In the intervening period, the Global Financial Crisis of 2007–2008 struck. Although Australia was much less affected than many other countries (Australian Bureau of Statistics, 2010), the aftermath has increased concerns about government budget deficits and increasing government spending.

The health issue in the 2007 election was funding for public hospitals, in contrast to the previous elections, where the policy distinction between the two parties was drawn around the role of private financing of health care and health insurance. The new Labor government embarked on a structural reform process, establishing an inquiry (the National Health and Hospitals Reform Commission) to develop a long-term plan for Australia's health system (National Health and Hospitals Reform Commission, 2009). However, the terms of reference excluded any change to the status quo of private insurance. After a long process of negotiation with state and territory governments a reform package was agreed some 18 months and a change of Prime Minister later (Council of Australian Governments, 2011).

The main features of the National Health Reform Agreement were: (i) an agreed level of national government funding for public hospital care which, for the first time tied Commonwealth government funding to the volume of hospital services delivered; (ii) public reporting of hospital performance; (iii) new local organizations called Medicare Locals, to take responsibility for filling gaps in and co-ordinating the primary care of a geographically defined population base. Arrangements for private health insurance, the Pharmaceutical Benefits Scheme and the Medicare Benefits Scheme remained unchanged. Although this did not represent a comprehensive plan for reform, it did provide a basis for further development to which all governments were committed (not generally easily accomplished in a federal system) (Hall, 2010). At the same time, the new Labor Government looked to the insurance rebates for savings. Over the 2010 and 2014 period, the Commonwealth Government introduced several measures including: (i) means-testing with four different tiers based on income and family composition; and (ii) restricting increases in the rebate (enacted under Labor but not effective until 2014). This latter measure has meant that the rebate is no longer tied directly to private health insurance premium rises, which have been increasing in excess of 5.5% per year since 2010. The rebate is now calculated on the basis of a weighted average to changes in the consumer price index and private health insurance premiums. These measures have meant that the rebate has moved from a standard 30% subsidy to a more complex set of arrangements where any individual's private health insurance rebate entitlement is dependent on their income, family composition, age and inflation. Rebates currently range from 0% to 35.72%; those with zero entitlement fall into income brackets which attract the financial penalty for not holding private health insurance.

This period also marks the start of serious change in the operating status of private health insurance funds. In 1995, 96% of policies were issued by not-for-profit funds; by 2010 this share had fallen to 30% (PHIAC, 2016). This dramatic change reflects the ownership status changes of a number of large funds including: Medibank Private, which was converted to for-profit and then privatized by the Australian Government; MBF, which was purchased by BUPA in 2008; and NIB, which was publicly listed in 2007. These changes have meant that government subsidies for private health insurance have a direct bearing on private investment returns.

After the change in government in 2013, the national sense of direction embodied in the National Health Reform Agreement did not last long. Many aspects of the Agreement and several new agencies were reversed and disbanded (Hall, 2015). The public hospital funding agreement was reversed, with the Commonwealth contribution to be much more limited in the future. For the Commonwealth Government, this reflects a need to improve the budgetary position by moving back to surplus. It had the effect of highlighting the imbalance between revenue bases of states and territories and their expected service provision, which although it affects many sectors of service delivery, is most stark for hospital services.

In response, the Commonwealth Government initiated a process to develop a white paper on reforming federal and state relationships with a major emphasis on health care reform. The Department of the Prime Minister and Cabinet released a draft issues paper which outlined a set of reform options that to some extent represented innovative ideas about future directions affecting federal, state and private health insurance funding arrangements. One option was a proposal for the Commonwealth Government to contribute to all hospital services regardless of whether they occurred in a public or private hospital (Prime Minister and Cabinet, 2015). However, these proposals have not progressed over the last 18 months and have been taken off the Council of Australian Governments' agenda. Similarly, proposed changes to the Medicare safety net have been "paused" (the word of Prime Minister at the time) while the Government considers wider aspects of health reform. These include a number of reviews that are generally very focused and specific. For example, the MBS review is a detailed investigation of the classification and scheduled fee for out-of-hospital services provided under Medicare without addressing the underlying issue of the incentives generated by fee for service provision (Hall et al., 2015).

Although the 2013 Liberal election promises included restoring the levels of the private health insurance rebate, this has not been implemented. Initially the income tiers that determined the level of insurance rebate were indexed annually. Indexation has been paused since 2015 until 2021, so further reducing the value of the rebate. Meanwhile, there has been an expansion of the products and range of services offered under private health insurance. New provisions from 2007 allowed private health insurance to cover hospital substitute services (such as hospital in the home) and chronic disease management programmes. Initial enthusiasm for chronic disease management appears to have peaked with the number of participants and value of benefits paid falling since 2012–2013. Insurers have also established or acquired other health businesses, with the provision of dental and optical centres and more recently primary care. Medibank Private was involved in a more controversial scheme whereby it entered into an arrangement with a primary care group to provide same-day access at bulk-billed rates for Medibank Private clients by paying an "administration fee" to the clinics.

Controversy focused on whether such payments could be considered as private insurance cover for Medicare-funded primary care services and hence illegal. This pilot scheme has been discontinued but BUPA is progressing with opening its own primary care clinics, open to insured and non-insured patients.

The replacement of Medicare Locals with new regional organizations, Primary Health Networks, was designed to allow private health insurers to become operators of the Networks or to join consortia that would operate Networks. There are some partnerships involving insurers, but it seems that insurers are playing a minor role.

At this stage it is difficult to ascertain the impact of these latest private health insurance reforms. However, membership has fallen slightly from 47.4% to 47% of the population in the year to June 2016, which is the first drop in membership numbers in 15 years. The fall is higher at younger ages (APRA, 2016). There have also been widespread reports that private health insurance members are downgrading their insurance policies, implying that they are switching to cheaper products with higher deductibles and greater restrictions. The extent to which patients admitted to public hospitals use their insurance (that is, choose to be admitted as private patients) is increasing, apparently encouraged by hospital policies. As a result the payout in benefits by private insurers is increasing at a faster rate than revenue; in 2012–2013 benefits increased by 9.1% while membership increased by only 2.2% (PHIAC, 2015b). This, plus the fact that the rebate is no longer directly linked to private health insurance premium increases, also appears to have put additional pressure on insurance funds to contain their costs.

Private health insurance continued to be unpopular with voters due to rising premiums and difficulty in understanding what was covered by different insurance products. In October 2015 the Commonwealth Minister for Health announced a review and called for public submissions. Although the consultation period was just 1 month, over 40 000 responses were received. At the end of 2016, the Commonwealth Minister for Health affirmed that the review was proceeding and would deliver an insurance rating system of gold, silver and bronze products to inform consumers and deliver value for money (Minister for Health, 2016).

Another issue that is likely to affect the Government's capacity and political will to change insurance arrangements arose during the 2016 election campaign. The Government had determined to outsource the processing of Medicare claims, an administrative change rather than a significant policy change. At the end of the campaign, the Opposition used this to target voters with a message about the privatization of Medicare. Although inaccurate, the "Mediscare" was credited with being a major contributor to the closeness of the election result. Suggestions of privatization are now a potent political weapon. Not surprisingly, the new Commonwealth Minister for Health was quick to emphasize that the Government's long term health plan was based on a "rock-solid" commitment to Medicare (Minister for Health, 4 Feb 2017). It includes a commitment to a hospital system comprising public and private sectors. In another interview, the Minister provided a view of the Australian health system as consisting of the three pillars of the Pharmaceutical Benefits Scheme, Medicare, and private health insurance (*The Australian* 4 Feb 2017). This suggests that support for private health insurance will remain a political priority for the government.

Conclusions

Sax, a well-respected bureaucrat and commentator on the Australian health system, described the evolution of health policy in Australia as "a strife of interests masquerading as a contest of principles" (Sax, 1984); and this is no more so than in the confusing and often ambiguous interplay around private health insurance. The focus on insurance since the 1980s has taken place at the expense of other aspects of the health system. When Medicare was established, there was a much clearer separation between hospital care and care in the community and the financial structure underlying them. This structure is not well designed for the coordination of care across hospitals and out-of-hospital services, for coordination across multiple providers, for the long-term management of chronic diseases, or for treatments that require complementary procedures, aids or prostheses and pharmaceuticals. Rather than have a substantial re-design of the system, each problem has been dealt with separately. For example, dental care has been traditionally excluded from Medicare. It is provided privately but private health insurance offers limited cover. There has been a range of very limited public subsidies or public programmes for dental care aimed at the most disadvantaged. Services provided by professionals other than medical practitioners have been excluded from Medicare. Hence, in primary care, employment of nurses has been very limited compared with many other countries.

Services such as physiotherapy, speech therapy and other related health care are partially covered by insurance, depending on the policy type. The uninsured must either pay out of pocket or wait for limited public services. Consequently there has been a piecemeal approach to introduce small fixes and new spending programmes. As the Industry Commission had previously commented:

> In undertaking reforms, governments have had a number of objectives, some of which are incompatible. Ad hoc and piecemeal reforms to a complex, interactive system can have some beneficial effects, but also can create further tensions and the need for additional government interventions. The outcome is a system that, despite numerous policy changes, has inherent and unresolved tensions (Industry Commission, 1997).

As a result, Australia has so far failed to address the fundamental pressures of the health system. Whether a new coherent vision will develop to guide further reform remains to be seen. The strife between public and private interests is as yet far from resolved and the contest of principles is likely to continue.

References

Australian Bureau of Statistics (2010). *The global financial crisis and its impact on Australia. Year Book Australia, 2009–10*: www.abs.gov.au/AUSSTATS/abs@.nsf/Lookup/1301.0Chapter27092009%E2%80%9310, accessed on 13/01/2017.

Australian Government (2007). *Budget 2007–08, Budget Papers No. 1–4*. Canberra, Commonwealth of Australia.

AIHW (Australian Institute of Health and Welfare) (2006). *Health expenditure Australia 2004–05*. Health and welfare expenditure series No. 28, Cat. no. HWE 35. Canberra, AIHW.

AIHW (2009). *Health expenditure Australia 2007–08*. Health and welfare expenditure series no. 37. Cat. no. HWE 46. Canberra, AIHW.

AIHW (2015). *Health expenditure Australia 2013–14: analysis by sector*. Health and welfare expenditure series no. 55. Cat. no. HWE 65. Canberra, AIHW.

AIHW (2016a). *Health expenditure Australia 2014–15*. Health and welfare expenditure series no. 57. Cat. no. HWE 67. Canberra, AIHW.

AIHW (2016b). *Admitted patient care 2014–15: Australian hospital statistics.* Health and welfare expenditure series no. 68. Cat. no. HSE 172. Canberra, AIHW.

APRA (Australian Prudential Regulatory Authority) (2016). *Private Health Insurance Annual Coverage Survey*: www.apra.gov.au/AboutAPRA/Pages/ Default.aspx, accessed on 19/12/2016.

Barrett GF, Conlon R (2003). Adverse selection and the decline in private health insurance coverage in Australia: 1989–95. *The Economic Record*, 79(246):279–96.

Butler JR (2002). Policy change and private health insurance: did the cheapest policy do the trick? *Australian Health Review*, 25(6):33–41.

Cheng TC (2014). Measuring the effects of reducing subsidies for private health insurance on public expenditure for health care, *Journal of Health Economics*, 33:159–79.

Council of Australian Governments (2011). National Health Reform Agreement 2011: www.yourhealth.gov.au/internet/yourhealth/publishing .nsf/Content/nhra-agreement; accessed on 19/12/2016.

Crichton A (1990). *Slowly taking control? Australian governments and health care provision, 1788–1988.* Sydney, Allen and Unwin.

Department of Health (2015/2016). www.health.gov.au/internet/main/ publishing.nsf/Content/phiconsultations2015-16, accessed on 04/01/2017.

Doiron D, Fiebig DG, Suziedelyte A (2014). Hips and hearts: the variation in incentive effects across hospital procedures. *Journal of Health Economics*, 37:81–97.

Doiron D, Jones G, Savage E (2008). Healthy, wealthy and insured? The role of self-assessed health in the demand for private health insurance. *Health Economics*, 17(3):317–34.

Duckett SJ (2007). *The Australian health care system*, 3rd edition. Melbourne, Oxford University Press.

Duckett SJ, Jackson TJ (2000). The new health insurance rebate: an inefficient way of assisting public hospitals. *Medical Journal of Australia*, 172:439–42.

Ellis RP, Savage E (2008). Run for cover now or later? The impact of premiums, threats and deadlines on private health insurance in Australia. *International Journal of Health Care Finance*, 8(4):257–77.

Fiebig D, Savage E, Viney R (2006). *Does the reason for buying insurance influence behaviour?* CHERE Working Paper 2006/1. Sydney, CHERE.

Frech HE, Hopkins S (2004). Why subsidise private health insurance? *Australian Economic Review*, 37(3):243–56.

Frech HE, Hopkins S, Macdonald G (2003). The Australian private health insurance boom: was it subsidies or liberalised regulation? *Economic Papers*, 22(1):58–64.

Haas M et al. (2001). The news on health care costs: a study of reporting in the Australian print media for 1996. *Journal of Health Services Research and Policy*, 6(2):78–84.

Hall J (2001). *The public view of private health insurance*. CHERE Discussion Paper 45. Sydney, CHERE.

Hall J (2010). Health care reform in Australia: Advancing or side-stepping? *Health Economics*, 19(11):1259–63.

Hall J (2015). Australian health care – the challenge of reform in a fragmented system. *New England Journal of Medicine*, 373:493–7.

Hall J, Savage E (2005). The role of the private sector in the Australian health care system. In: Maynard A, ed. *The public–private mix for health*. London, Nuffield Provincial Hospitals Trust.

Hall J et al. (2015). Medicare review must deal with 'elephant in room'. *The Conversation*: https://theconversation.com/medicare-review-must-deal-with-elephant-in-the-room-incentives-40819; accessed on 19/12/2016.

Harper I (2003). *Preserving choice: a defence of public support for private health care funding in Australia*. Commissioned by Medibank Private Limited. Melbourne, Harper Associates.

Hopkins S, Frech HE (2001). The rise of private health insurance in Australia: early effects on insurance and hospital markets. *Economic and Labour Relations Review*, 12(2):225–38.

Industry Commission (1997). *Private health insurance*. Canberra, AGPS.

Lu M, Savage E (2006). *Do financial incentives for supplementary private health insurance reduce pressure on the public system? Evidence from Australia*. CHERE Working Paper 2006/11. Sydney, CHERE.

Minister for Health (2016). *Transcript of doorstop Parliament House*. 19 October 2016 www.health.gov.au/internet/ministers/publishing.nsf/Content/health-mediarel-yr2016-ley161019.htm; accessed on 20/12/2016.

Minister for Health (2017). *Transcript of doorstop Melbourne*. 4 February 2017 www.greghunt.com.au/Media/MediaReleases/tabid/86/ID/4145/Doorstop--Melbourne.aspx; accessed on 5/07/2017.

National Health and Hospitals Reform Commission (2009). *Final Report. A Healthier Future for All Australians*. Canberra, Commonwealth of Australia.

Palangkaraya A, Yong J (2005). Effects of recent carrot-and-stick policy initiatives on private health insurance coverage in Australia. *Economic Record*, 81(254):262–72.

Pearce AM et al. (2012). Delays in access to affordable medicines: putting policy into perspective. *Australian Health Review,* 36(4):412–18.

PHIAC (2010). *Operations of Private Insurers Annual Report 2009–10.* Canberra, Private Health Insurance Administration Council.

PHIAC (2015a). Report March 2015: www.apra.gov.au/PHI/PHIAC-Archive/Documents/PHIACAust-Mar15.pdf; accessed on 03/01/2017.

PHIAC (2015b). *Operations of the Private Health Insurers. Annual Report 2013–14:* www.apra.gov.au/PHI/PHIAC-Archive/Documents/Operations-of-PHI-Annual-Report-2013-141.pdf; accessed on 19/12/2016.

PHIAC (2016). Competition in the Australian Private Health Insurance Market: www.apra.gov.au/PHI/PHIAC-Archive/Documents/Competition-in-the-Australian-PHI-market_June-2015.pdf; accessed on 03/01/2017.

Prime Minister and Cabinet (2015). Reform of the Federation: discussion paper 2015; https://federation.dpmc.gov.au/publications/discussion-paper; accessed on 19/12/2016.

Robertson IK, Richardson JR (2000). Coronary angiography and coronary artery revascularisation rates in public and private hospital patients after acute myocardial infarction. *Medical Journal of Australia,* 173(6):291–5.

Savage E, Wright DJ (2003). Moral hazard and adverse selection in Australian private hospitals: 1989–90. *Journal of Health Economics,* 22(3):331–59.

Sax S (1984). *A strife of interests: politics and policies in Australian health services.* Sydney, Allen and Unwin.

Scotton RB (2001). The making of Medibank. In: Mooney G, Plant A, eds. *Daring to dream: the future of Australian health care – essays in honour of John Deeble.* Bentley, Black Swan Press.

The Australian. Hunt's priority: clear direction to save health. 4 February 2017.

Vaithianathan R (2002). Will subsidising private health insurance help the public health system? *Economic Record,* 78:277–84.

Vaithianathan R (2004). A critique of the private health insurance regulations. *Australian Economic Review,* 37(3):257–70.

Van Gool KC et al. (2009). Who's getting caught? An analysis of the Australian Medicare Safety Net. *The Australian Economic Review,* 42(2):143–54.

3 Private health insurance in Brazil, Egypt and India

MARIA DOLORES MONTOYA DIAZ, NOAH HABER,
PHILIPA MLADOVSKY, EMMA PITCHFORTH, WAEL
FAYEK SALEH AND FLAVIA MORI SARTI[1]

The case studies presented in this chapter provide evidence of varied experience with private health insurance in three middle-income country settings – Brazil, Egypt and India – where there are large and persisting socioeconomic differentials and where private spending accounts for more than half of health care financing. Brazil is a very large private health insurance market with a recently introduced system of regulation whereas Egypt and India are very small markets with minimal regulation. In all three countries private health insurance plays a supplementary role and overwhelmingly covers richer people employed in the formal sector. All three countries are struggling with regulation of the market to enhance transparency, protect consumers and minimize negative effects on the publicly financed part of the health system.

This chapter presents an overview of the three markets and their development, including the existing regulatory frameworks. It also attempts to provide some evidence on how private health insurance contributes to meeting health financing policy goals in these countries and its future viability.

Brazil[2]

MARIA DOLORES MONTOYA DIAZ AND FLAVIA MORI SARTI

The current configuration of the Brazilian health system is the result of extensive social policies implemented during the 1980s and 1990s,

---

[1] In alphabetical order.
[2] The original version of the Brazil case study was based on a summary by Philipa Mladovsky of an OECD report prepared by Stéphane Jacobzone and Vivian Figer OECD (2008). Chapter 3. The Private Health Insurance Sector Review of Regulatory Reform. Brazil: Strengthening Governance for Growth Paris, OECD. The authors thank the following people for providing additional information for the case studies: Silvana Pereira and Maria Inês S. Silvério (Brazil), Sameh El-Saharty (Egypt) and Harshad Thakur (India).

determining a predominant role of the public sector in health coverage and a supplementary role for the private health sector. The public sector within the Brazilian health system, known as the Unified Health System (*Sistema Unico de Saude*, SUS), provides health care for approximately 75% of the Brazilian population and maintains a structure of health assistance mainly based on public organizations under direct public management. Promotion of equity through provision of universal, comprehensive health care cover is a major concern in Brazil. Yet, there are major challenges regarding financing, management and infrastructure of the Brazilian health system, generating substantial gaps between supply and demand in public and private health care. Supplementary private health insurance and out-of-pocket payments provide alternative means of financing access to health care for some population groups, mainly in private hospitals and through private diagnostic and therapeutic support services (Santos et al., 2008). Tax incentives are available for those who purchase private health insurance, and studies have found that these have expanded both the private health insurance market and the supply of private hospitals (Ocké-Reis, 1995). Health care providers play a significant role in the provision of private health insurance through Group Medicine and Dentistry schemes and Medical and Dental Co-operatives.

Brazil's private health insurance market is one of the largest internationally, accounting for over a quarter of all spending on health and covering a quarter of the population – mainly richer and better educated households living in urban areas in the south-east who are covered by group plans. In September 2015, the private health insurance market reached a new high of 71.4 million beneficiaries (see Fig. 3.1), dropping to 70.5 million in September 2016 due to the economic crisis. In terms of per person spending on private health insurance, at 373 in current purchasing power parity in 2015, Brazil is more similar to countries such as Australia and Ireland than to countries with a similar level of gross domestic product, such as Mexico (WHO, 2018).

Before 2000 the market was largely unregulated, which allowed distortion and abuse (Preker et al., 2010). Since then, a regulatory framework has been progressively implemented, attempting to correct market failures, protect consumers and ensure financial solvency of organizations offering health plans. A new authority, the National Supplementary Health Agency (*Agência Nacional de Saúde Suplementar*, ANS), was created to oversee this market. In addition, private health insurers were required to reimburse the SUS for care delivered by SUS providers to patients with private health insurance plans.

Market origins

According to ANS[3], a milestone in the history of social security and health plans in Brazil was the establishment in 1923 "(...) for each of the existing railway companies in the country, a Pension Fund for its respective employees." These funds, based on the Eloy Chaves Law, were managed and financed by the employers and employees and were meant to provide comprehensive health assistance for workers and their dependants. Although this is not commonly seen as the origin of the private health insurance market in Brazil, similarities between these funds and the current operators of health insurance self-management schemes are apparent. In fact, the general welfare fund for the employees of the Bank of Brazil (CASSI) established in 1994 is the oldest health plan in Brazil that is still in operation.

The arrival of major foreign companies in the 1960s, particularly in the automobile industry, generated the need to provide medical insurance cover for industrial and private sector workers. In 1966 health insurance was established in the law, but private health insurers were not allowed to operate until 1976. During this period, compulsory health insurance was provided through a system of social insurance that was financed from taxes levied on wages and that progressively spread among workers in different sectors of the economy. Provision of certain health care services in this system was assured through government contracts with both public and private providers. Political changes that occurred in Brazil during the 1980s promoted the establishment of publicly funded health assistance through the Brazilian Unified Health System (SUS), based on universal population coverage. Nevertheless, dissatisfaction with the SUS pushed middle- and high-income individuals to seek care in the private sector. This, together with private health sector regulation and economic growth, led to a growing demand for private health insurance, which developed rapidly over the 1990s (Fernandes et al., 2007).

---

[3] See ANS website (www.ans.gov.br/aans/quem-somos/historico) (in Portuguese).

Market overview and development

The main types of entities offering private health insurance are Group Medicine and Group Dentistry and Medical and Dental Co-operatives. According to Decree 3,232/86 of the Ministry of Labour, Group Medicine and Group Dentistry are for-profit private entities that provide hospital and dental services through their own facilities or through a network of accredited providers. In mid-2016, 35 million people were covered by Group Medicine or Group Dentistry schemes, which is equivalent to 49% of those with private health insurance (Fig. 3.1). The Medical and Dental Co-operatives are non-profit organizations that operate under the Law of Co-operatives (Law 5,764/71). They account for 31% of private health insurance beneficiaries. Together, Group Medicine and Group Dentistry and Medical and Dental Co-operatives cover 80% of private health insurance beneficiaries, pointing to a strong role of health care providers (health professionals and facilities) in the private health insurance market. The remainder of private health insurance beneficiaries purchase cover from commercial for-profit insurers specialized in health (11%); self-management schemes that are used by major companies and are similar to employer-based insurance in the US context[4] (7%); and not-for-profit entities certified by the National Council for Social Care (*Conselho Nacional de Assistencia Social*) as philanthropic organizations of public interest (2%). Commercial for-profit health insurance plans and Group Medicine and Group Dentistry schemes have been the most dynamic arrangements recently in terms of the number of beneficiaries, growing by, respectively, 27% and 21% between 2011 and 2016 (Fig. 3.1).

The majority of private health insurance providers (69% of the total number) are very small, with 7000 beneficiaries on average. Jointly, they cover only 8.4% of the total number of private health insurance beneficiaries. The largest 18 insurers (1.5% of the total number) have more than 700 000 beneficiaries, on average, and cover 43.4% of the total number of private health insurance beneficiaries (ANS, 2016).

Table 3.1 shows that private health insurance is a profitable business in Brazil. Between 2009 and 2016 claims ratios and monthly revenues increased for all sizes of medical and hospital private health insurance

---

[4] The self-management schemes are also used by public entities, in which case they are not subject to oversight by the ANS.

Table 3.1 *Private health insurance claims ratios and average monthly revenues in Brazil according to insurer size, 2009 and 2016*

Operator size	2009		2016	
	Claims ratio (%)	Average monthly revenue (in real US$[c])	Claims ratio (%)	Average monthly revenue (in real US$[c])
Total	82.3%	45.39	84.9%	57.40
Medical and hospital private health insurance operators[a]	83.0%	54.17	85.6%	72.36
Small	80.5%	45.28	84.7%	77.39
Medium	84.0%	48.96	86.1%	63.77
Large	83.0%	57.49	85.5%	74.42
Dental private health insurance operators[b]	48.5%	5.16	48.5%	4.99
Small	51.0%	6.10	47.9%	5.99
Medium	54.8%	6.06	57.0%	5.23
Large	45.4%	4.69	46.7%	4.83

Sources: ANS (2010); ANS Presentation (2017).

Notes: small: up to 20 000 beneficiaries; medium: 20 000–100 000 beneficiaries; large: over 100 000 beneficiaries. The shares of small, medium and large operators in the total number of medical and hospital private health insurance operators and in the total number of dental private health insurance operators are unknown.

[a] Group Medicine, Medical Co-operatives, commercial for-profit insurers specialized in health, self-management schemes and philanthropic schemes.

[b] Group Dentistry or Dental Co-operatives.

[c] As of June 2016. Hence, the 2009 data were corrected for 2016 prices and, subsequently, all R$ values were converted into US dollars at the average exchange rate for the month of June 2016, 1 US$ = R$3.42.

providers, with the average monthly revenues increasing by as much as 71%[5] for small operators. Small operators achieved higher average monthly revenues than both medium and large operators. Baldassare (2014) explains this trend by the fact that small operators tend to

[5] This was higher than the rate of inflation in the same period (59.4%).

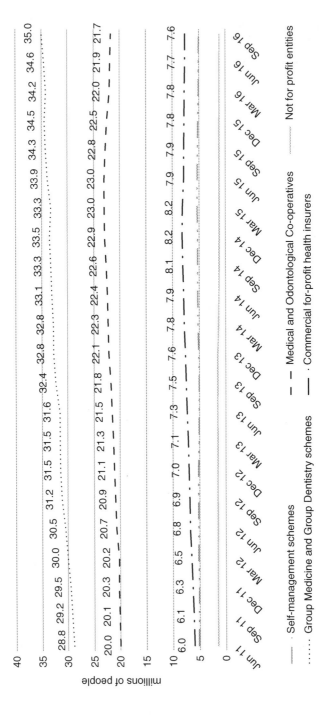

Figure 3.1 Number of beneficiaries of private health insurance plans in Brazil by type of insurance provider, 2011–2016

Source: ANS (2016).

serve beneficiaries in small towns and provide health services of lower complexity. The study analysed data from 2001 to 2012 and concluded that "small operators (up to 20 thousand beneficiaries) presented better results in all measures, with higher rates of profitability, liquidity and lower loss ratio" (p.64). Small operators are also subject to normative resolution RN 274 issued by the ANS in 2011, which established differentiated treatment for small and medium-sized operators and aimed to reduce administrative expenses of such operators.

Private health insurance is generally voluntary and contracts can be taken out on an individual, family or group (collective) basis. The latter may be "sponsored", with premiums at least partially paid by a third party, usually an employer, or "nonsponsored", with premiums wholly paid by the beneficiaries and with "membership" defined by affiliation with a council, union or professional association that contracts with the insurer on behalf of its members. A third-party administrator (TPA) is usually used to represent the beneficiaries in periodic negotiations of insurance premiums with the insurer and for administering claims. The insurer is responsible for guaranteeing provision of health care benefits. Both insurers and TPAs are required to register with the ANS. Between

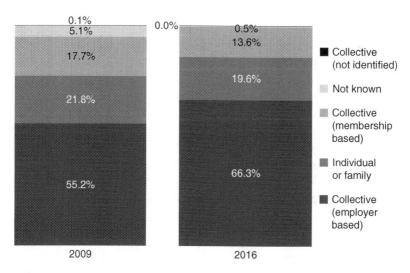

Figure 3.2 Beneficiaries of health care plans in Brazil by type of contract, 2009–2016

Source: ANS (2010, 2016).

2009 and 2016, the number of beneficiaries of group contracts increased by 28.6%, reflecting a long-term trend. In 2016, approximately 80% of private health insurance beneficiaries had collective private health insurance cover (Fig. 3.2).

Public policy towards private health insurance

The current regulatory framework for private health insurance is set out in two laws; one from 1998, which defined the market; and another from 2000, which established the ANS and defined its competencies. The 1998 legislation (Law 9,656) was the first comprehensive effort at regulating the private health insurance sector. It attempted to correct market failures such as information asymmetry, risk selection and abusive benefits exclusions; to protect consumers; and to ensure financial solvency of organizations offering health plans (Preker et al., 2010). It also required health plans to reimburse the SUS for care delivered by SUS providers to patients with private health plans (this was implemented after the ANS was established in 2000). Contracts that were issued before 1999 (so called "old" contracts) cover 10.5% of private health insurance beneficiaries (ANS, 2016). They are not convertible into "new" contracts and are not subject to the new legislation: what was settled by the original contract prevails. The rights and obligations established by the Law 9,656 apply to all contracts issued after 1999 ("new") and to the plans that were issued before 1999 but were adapted to the norms of this Law ("adapted").

The ANS is linked to the Ministry of Health but has administrative and financial autonomy. Its main tasks are to issue licenses to insurers operating in the market; set conditions for market entry, operation and exit; and, if necessary, demand fiscal and/or technical recovery plans from insurers, closure of plans and in some cases liquidation of the insurer. Although these regulations are intended to ensure financial stability, they are also alleged to serve as barriers to entry (Macera & Saintive, 2004). The ANS does not specifically aim to attract foreign investment in the sector and private health insurers must be incorporated in Brazil to obtain a license.

The new regulatory framework established three possible types of contracts: (i) a *reference plan* has to be offered as an option by all private health insurers (to reduce information asymmetry); it offers outpatient and hospital care and obstetrics; it cannot exclude pre-existing conditions; but it may impose co-payments; (ii) *segmented plans* cover either outpatient care, or inpatient care, or dental care; and (iii) *amplified plans* cover additional services compared to the reference plan.

Under the new rules, insurers must renew contracts or provide an equivalent substitute; cannot reject applications based on age or health status; and cannot increase the premiums of individuals aged over 60 who have had the same contract for more than 10 years (for contracts issued before 2003) or exclude pre-existing conditions for individual, family or nonsponsored group contracts with fewer than 50 members. Since 2004, individuals over 59 years have been included in the last age band for health insurance premiums increases[6] (there are 10 specific age bands allowed for premium rates). Financial incentives are provided to insurers who offer health promotion and prevention. With the exception of individual contracts for people aged less than 60 years old, premiums must be community rated. However, operators can segment consumers into different risk groups through the content of the products on offer. The ANS reviews premiums for new individual and family contracts and self-insurance schemes but does not control premiums for group contracts on the grounds that groups have sufficient bargaining power, although consumer groups claim that this is not the case (IDEC and CREMESP, 2007).

The new regulatory framework indirectly covers health service providers by requiring contracts between them and the insurers. The ANS authorizes providers that may be contracted and has established an ombudsman to monitor consumer claims. These steps are considered to have improved oversight, but there is still a long way to go. In general, there is little information on the insurers and providers and the relationship between them, although there have been initiatives to improve it, such as the Information Exchange in Supplementary Health (*Troca de Informacoes em Saude Suplementar*) set up in 2006 or a web-based tool named Performance Index of Supplementary Health (*Indice de Desempenho da Saude Suplementar*) set up by the ANS in 2004 to enable evaluation of insurer quality. Private health insurers also have to follow protocols of the Private Insurance Superintendence

[6] ANS Normative Resolution 63.

(*Superintendencia de Seguros Privados*), which establishes financial regulations for the **private health insurance** market in Brazil.

Assessment of market impact on health system goals

Equitable access to health care and financial protection

The private health insurance market in Brazil is unusual, even compared with OECD countries, because it accounts for a relatively high share of private spending. In 2015, this share stood at around 47% of private spending on health, compared with about 35% in 2000 (WHO, 2018). This suggests that private health insurance may have contributed to lowering out-of-pocket payments: the share of out-of-pocket payments decreased from 36% to 28% of total spending on health over the same period (WHO, 2018). However, any reduction in out-of-pocket payments is likely to have been concentrated among the richer households who can afford to purchase private health insurance cover, and this in turn has probably exacerbated inequalities in access to health care and to financial protection against impoverishing health spending. Some analysts have argued that the government has allowed population preferences and financial resources to determine access to health care (rather than need), which has also fuelled an expansion in private health care provision (Fernandes et al., 2007). Regulations enhancing access to private health insurance policies and the requirement on all private health insurance operators to offer a low-cost basic health plan (that is, reference plan) have contributed to this trend.

Access to private health insurance is highly uneven, with less than 6% of the individuals in the poorest income quintile having private health insurance cover in 2013 compared to around 65% of individuals in the richest quintile (Table 3.2). The share of individuals with private health insurance cover increased across all income quintiles between 1998 and 2008, probably as a result of growing incomes and the increasing formalization in the labour market.

There are also large geographical differences in private health insurance coverage (Fig. 3.3). At the end of 2016, the share of population covered ranged from 6% in Acre (AC) in the north region to 43% in the State of São Paulo (SP) in the south-east region.

Although private health insurance cover increased considerably in the north between 2000 and 2016, only 11% of people living in this region had private health insurance cover in 2016, compared with

Table 3.2 *Private health insurance coverage among Brazilian population by income quintile, 1998–2013*

Quintile of per person income	1998	2003	2008	2013
Q1 (poorest)	2.7%	2.8%	3.5%	5.5%
Q2	7.4%	7.5%	10.1%	12.2%
Q3	16.4%	16.0%	18.4%	21.5%
Q4	31.9%	31.7%	32.7%	36.2%
Q5 (richest)	63.0%	63.5%	62.7%	64.7%
Total	24.2%	24.2%	25.4%	27.9%

Source: Authors' elaboration with microdata data from the National Household Sample Survey (*Pesquisa Nacional por Amostra de Domicílios*, PNAD) (IBGE 1999, 2004, 2009) and the National Health Survey (*Pesquisa Nacional de Saúde*, PNS) (IBGE 2014).

Figure 3.3 Private health insurance coverage rates in Brazil, by state (% of population), September 2016

Source: Authors based on data from from ANS (2016).

Table 3.3 *Regional private health insurance coverage rates in Brazil (% of regional population), 2000–2016 (selected years)*

Year[a]	North	Northeast	Southeast	South	Middle-West	Total
2000	4.8	8.3	30.1	13.9	11.9	18.4
2005	6.6	8.0	30.1	17.0	13.3	19.0
2010	9.5	10.5	36.0	23.4	15.5	23.4
2015	11.5	12.5	37.9	25.7	21.9	25.7
2016	10.7	12.4	36.5	25.1	21.5	24.9

Source: Authors' calculations based on ANS (2017a) and IBGE (2013).

Note: [a] Measured in September of each year.

36.5% in the south-east (Table 3.3). Coverage rates have been found to be related to the regional Human Development Index: the lower the Human Development Index, the lower the level of private health insurance coverage (Fernandes et al., 2007).

A 1998 national survey performed by the Brazilian Institute of Public Opinion and Statistics showed that 44% of the population used both the SUS and the private system, while 16% did not use SUS services at all (Medici, 2004). Even among people with only elementary schooling or less (7% of the population), 12% did not use the SUS, probably because of limited geographical access to public services, while 48% of those who had completed college never used it, perhaps because they rely on private health insurance instead (Medici, 2004).

Private health insurance take-up does not directly affect the funding of the public system. However, the picture is complicated. First, tax relief on private health insurance premiums constitutes an indirect form of public subsidy. According to Ocké-Reis & Gama (2016), in 2013 tax relief accounted for 30.5% of annual health spending of the federal government, with this proportion remaining relatively stable since 2003. "Considering the financing needs of the SUS, this fact deserves to be highlighted, since (...) in 11 years, at average prices of 2013, the government subsidized the sector by approximately R$230 billion. In the last year (2013), subsidies reached R$25.4 billion" (p.22).

Second, a significant number of people with private health insurance cover continue to use publicly financed health services (ANS map, 2017). Law 9,656 states that private health insurers should compensate the SUS for the use of public services if these were delivered to private health plan patients. These provisions have been progressively implemented by the ANS. Between 2000 and 2017, the ANS demanded around R$6.6 billion in compensation. About R$1.6 billion of this amount (24.2%) has been collected and remitted to the National Health Fund[7]. This corresponds to 43% of the total value of publicly reimbursable care[8] and to less than 2% of the annual health spending of the federal government. A further R$2.1 billion (32.1% of total ANS claims) is being pursued through the judicial system (ANS, 2017b: p.33).

Incentives for efficiency and quality in service organization and delivery

Analysis has found that most operators did not operate efficiently at the beginning of the 2000s, perhaps because of insufficient regulation and lack of expertise in financial management (Fernandes et al., 2007). Leal (2014) states that one of the results of the new regulations was "the adoption of strategies for reducing the risk of client portfolios by the operators, through [strategies for] higher growth in [health care] segments [that were] less intensively regulated such as dental plans and collective medical plans. In this context, there has been an increase in financial incomes and stability (in real terms) of monthly premium revenues (of private health insurance operators), though in the case of individual medical plans subject to specific regulation of the ANS premium increases were higher than inflation. Regarding the use of resources, there has been an increase in accident rate and an increase of efficiency of the market by way of selling and administrative expenses could not be unequivocally demonstrated. Furthermore, analysis of the median operator in a sample of operators showed increased profitability, mainly due to the increase in number of contracts, as the increase in the profit margin was small." (p.11). There are no data or studies on quality of health care service organization and delivery in Brazil.

---

[7] The National Health Fund provides financial administration of the SUS at the federal level.

[8] Notifications not contested by the operators or whose objections were rejected by ANS, R$3.7 billion.

Egypt
WAEL FAYEK SALEH

Health financing in Egypt is highly fragmented. Several financing agencies cover different population groups, with no risk pooling or equalization between them. The whole population is entitled to services offered by the Ministry of Health and around half of the population is covered by a publicly financed scheme for formal sector public and private employees, their dependants and retired people. This scheme is operated by the Health Insurance Organization (HIO). Public spending on health is low, accounting for 30.2% of current spending on health in 2015 (WHO, 2018). Private spending is largely financed through out-of-pocket payments.

Private health insurance plays a mainly supplementary role, financing access to care in the private sector. It also provides substitutive cover for formal sector workers who have chosen to opt out of the HIO coverage. Private health insurance covers around 5% of the population (Nassar & El-Saharty, 2010). However, as many policy-holders are not registered with any regulatory body, their actual number may be higher than what is officially reported.[9] The actual share of private health insurance in total spending on health and in private spending on health, officially estimated at, respectively, 1% and 2%, is also likely to be higher – at least triple these numbers according to some sources. Most of those with "registered" private health insurance cover obtain it through closed-membership schemes organized by trade unions (syndicates) on a non-profit basis. The remainder are mainly wealthier employees of large state-owned or private entities and corporations.

Market origins

The insurance industry was established in the second half of the 19th century by foreign firms insuring cotton production and export. In 1939, the first laws governing the industry were enacted and by the 1950s there were more than 200 private insurance companies in Egypt. In 1961 the industry was consolidated into three state-owned insurance companies and one state-owned reinsurance company (Nassar & El-Saharty, 2006). The monopoly of the nationalized companies was relaxed in the late 1970s, leading to the establishment of three

---

[9] Around 7–10% of the population, according to some informal sources.

bank-owned insurance companies. Further reforms introduced in the 1980s and 1990s encouraged private and international players to enter the market (Insurance Federation of Egypt, 2006).

In 1988 the Medical Union became the first professional organization to establish a health insurance scheme for its members. The following year the Middle East Medicare Plan (commonly known as Medicare) became the first managed care organization. The first commercial health insurers were established in the late 1990s and in 2000 the relaxation of foreign ownership rules allowed several multinational insurance firms to set up local non-life operations.[10] The Egyptian Bankers Takaful Insurance Company introduced Islamic insurance operations in 2007 (AXCO, 2007).

Very high out-of-pocket spending on health, rising income levels and reforms in the insurance industry have created a potential market for private health insurance. Alongside this, growing demand for private health care has been driven by the perceived lower quality and responsiveness of public sector provision (Rafeh, 1997; Rannan-Eliya et al., 1998; Gericke, 2004; Partners for Health Reformplus, 2004).

Private health insurance premiums increased steadily between 2002 and 2007 from LE (Egyptian Pound) 38.4[11] in 2002 to LE241.3 million in 2007 (EISA, 2007). By 2016, private health insurance premiums in Egypt rose to LE1.1 billion (US$60.3 million) (Middle East Insurance Review, 2017). However, the contribution of private health insurance to current spending on health continues to be marginal (El-Saharty & Maeda, 2006); in 2015, it accounted for only 1% of current spending on health (WHO, 2018). In the same year, out-of-pocket payments amounted to 89% of private spending on health (which is less than the 95% seen in 2000, according to WHO data) and to 62% of current health spending (unchanged compared with 2000). The share of private prepaid plans increased from 0.4% in 2000 to 1.7% in 2011 (Oxford Business Group, 2017).

Market overview and development

The main types of private health insurers are: trade unions (syndicates) and private or state-owned companies. Private companies can be further

---

[10] AIG, Allianz, ACE, Royal & Sun Alliance and BUPA.
[11] The average exchange rate in 2016 was 1US$ = 10.1 LE.

divided into commercial (for-profit) insurers and health maintenance organizations (HMOs). People are encouraged to take-up private health insurance through tax subsidies in the form of tax relief on premiums. In 2002 it was estimated that 3.3 million Egyptians, or about 4.9% of the population, had some form of private health insurance cover. The majority of people with private health insurance cover (about 97%) were covered by syndicates, with the remaining 2.6% being covered by private companies (commercial insurers and HMOs) and 0.6% by state-owned companies (Nassar & El-Saharty, 2006). Since then, it is estimated that the number covered by private companies has doubled or tripled.[12]

Detailed information on private health insurance schemes is limited, particularly on schemes that were not overseen by the Egyptian Insurance Supervisory Authority (EISA), the regulatory authority that governed the insurance industry under the Ministry of Investment until 2009. In July 2009, the Egyptian Financial Supervisory Authority (EFSA) took over this role, as well as that of the Capital Market Authority and the Mortgage Finance Authority.

Syndicate ("nikabat") schemes

These organizations promote the social welfare of various professions such as doctors, engineers and lawyers. Around 70% of syndicate scheme members live in the two largest cities, Cairo and Alexandria. The annual premium charged by syndicate schemes is generally around LE250 per enrollee, with premiums increasing with duration of enrolment on the assumption that senior members have higher incomes. Other family members, including parents, can enrol in return for higher premiums and higher cost sharing. No medical examination is required before enrolment. Annual subscriptions can be renewed for life.

Scheme benefits vary but are usually provided up to an annual spending ceiling of about LE10 000 per enrollee for a basic package of ambulatory care and up to an additional LE3000–5000 for more specialized services. Members are entitled to a capped number of outpatient consultations per year, although they can buy coupons for additional outpatient visits.[13] Inpatient and major outpatient services require prior

---

[12] These figures are supported by the author's own estimations.

[13] The price of a consultation paid with a coupon is lower than what it would

approval. Cost sharing (set as a coinsurance rate of about 20–30%) applies to inpatient and most outpatient services. Services excluded from cover commonly include dental, optical and maternity care. Prescription drugs are not covered except as part of inpatient treatment. Very few schemes reimburse the use of services from providers outside their accredited provider networks. Providers are paid on a fee-for-service basis but the schemes are able to set relatively low fees because of the large volume of services they guarantee. Utilization reviews are occasionally conducted, mainly by the Medical Union scheme.

The schemes keep costs down through low spending on marketing and by sharing costs with the syndicates' administration. They are also subsidized from other sources of income generated by the syndicates (for example, stamp tax revenues for the lawyers' syndicate). As the schemes are non-profit they are exempt from corporation tax. They are self-regulated by the elected representatives of the syndicates rather than by EFSA, which means that they are not subject to minimum capital or solvency requirements and do not need to register their insured subscribers (unlike the HMOs, see below).

Private and state-owned companies

When it started, this served less than 0.2% of the population – mainly employees of private, well-financed companies, a few high-income individuals and the international community (Rafeh, 1997). By 2016, the number of subscribers had grown substantially.[14] Demand seems to have increased rapidly in recent years from a very low base. Premiums from commercial insurers (not including HMOs) and state-owned companies totalled LE241.3 million in 2007 (EISA, 2007). This represented a 400% increase from 2002, although it is not clear to what extent the increase was caused by growing numbers of subscribers or rising premiums.

(1) **Commercial (for-profit) insurers:** Most plans charge annual premiums ranging from LE1000 to LE1800 per enrollee. The annual benefit limit is typically around LE20 000 but it can go up to LE50 000

---

have been if paid out of pocket, which means that the syndicates partly subsidize the cost of outpatient consultations.

[14] To around 750 000 people covered (that is, roughly tripled), according to the author's own estimations.

per beneficiary with sublimits for most service categories. Similar to syndicate schemes, most insurers use preferred-provider networks and provider payment is based on fees per service or disease category. To increase choice, reimbursement of services rendered outside these networks is generally possible up to a ceiling. In terms of benefits, with the exception of group policies covering more than 100 members, most plans have long exclusion lists. Unlike syndicate schemes, however, coverage usually includes optical, dental and maternity care, up to a ceiling. Expensive interventions require prior authorization. Over 70% of policies are held on a group basis by employees of large public or private entities and companies that have opted out of HIO coverage. Premiums are revised annually to adjust for high-risk individuals, are usually paid by employers and generally depend on the number of subscribers, their age and the level of cover chosen. Further, cover is commonly offered at below cost and partially subsidized by other more profitable lines of business, typically life insurance.[15]

Under the former EISA regulations, commercial insurers were required to have a minimum capital requirement of about LE30 million (this was considered as high in relation to the volume of premiums generated in the market); hold funds in Egypt with a value at least equal to the value of their technical reserves; and abide by solvency requirements. To what extent this will be revisited is still not clear.

(2) **Health maintenance organizations:** The HMOs[16] are entities comprising networks of doctors and providers that provide managed care in return for an annual premium. Established as general incorporations, HMOs are not supervised by EISA, and can avoid registration of insured subscribers and minimum capital or solvency requirements. Annual premiums are usually marginally lower than those of commercial insurers. HMOs offer a wide range of services including comprehensive outpatient and inpatient services and emergency

---

[15] Many commercial (for-profit) insurers are in fact TPAs. This allows them to (i) avoid any actuarial insurance risk; (ii) act as an intermediary for a life insurance company; and (iii) avoid minimum capital requirements demanded from health insurance companies.

[16] The number of HMOs is not known but it has been decreasing in recent years. It is therefore likely to be lower than the number (15–30) reported by Nassar & El-Saharty (2010).

care. In general, they do not cover dental care, maternity care, home visits, regular check-ups or optical care, require prior authorization for more expensive treatments and charge co-payments. A medical examination is usually required before enrolment and premiums are risk rated. As they are not under EISA supervision, HMOs have been in a position to exclude high-risk individuals. Recently, many HMOs have been struggling due to rising health costs and many have transformed into TPAs to avoid managing actuarial risk.

(3) **State-owned companies:** State-owned companies are under the regulation of EFSA. Among them, three (Al Chark, National Insurance and Misr Insurance) have 50% of the state-owned market share. In 2006, these three insurers and the state reinsurance company merged, forming the Insurances Holding Company. State-owned companies offer group cover at below cost due to cross subsidization from more profitable lines of business. Most of the plans are community rated.

The overall market share of the state-owned insurers has been steadily declining.[17] This is because the government has been decreasing its budgets and the quality of care offered by state-owned companies is generally perceived to be lower than that offered by the private companies. State-owned companies also tend to incure more losses than private companies as their subscriber base is generally older (though the losses are ultimately covered by the government).

Assessment of market impact on health system goals

Equitable access to health care and financial protection

A study using data from the Household Health Service Utilization and Expenditure Survey suggested that, controlling for various socioeconomic and demographic variables, access to private health insurance (private companies and syndicates) is unequal, with factors such as higher income levels, higher education and urbanization increasing the probability of enrolment (Nassar & El-Saharty, 2006). Low demand for private health insurance may be explained by survey data from 2002, which showed that 54% of uninsured households preferred to remain uninsured, whereas the average household was willing to spend

[17] For all insurance categories, including health care insurance.

LE83–180 on premiums per household per year (MOHP Government of Egypt, 2002). This is substantially lower than the premiums charged by commercial insurers, but is within the range of premiums charged by syndicate schemes.The scope of the benefits package and the price of premiums are not regulated, so private health insurance is largely unavailable to poorer people and people with high levels of morbidity. Premiums are exempt from income tax, which constitutes an indirect and regressive form of public subsidy.

The effect of these inequalities in access to private health insurance on equity in the use of health services is difficult to estimate. A study that attempted to measure the impact of private health insurance on health financing by comparing the effects of total private health insurance coverage, HIO coverage or no insurance coverage was not able to draw firm conclusions due to the small number of private health insurance enrollees in the sample (Nassar & El-Saharty, 2006). However, it identified equity concerns associated with the much larger HIO scheme, which enables the wealthier, formally employed population to use health services at a higher rate than the poorer, uninsured informal sector. Three quarters of those covered by private health insurance were also covered by the HIO (Nassar & El-Saharty, 2006). In addition, these individuals have access to services offered by the Ministry of Health (offered to the whole population), meaning that they effectively have triple coverage.

Incentives for efficiency and quality in service organization and delivery

The regulatory system is to be reformed[18] to enhance its supervisory role and increase transparency and the dissemination of information. The creation of EFSA is thought to be a step in that direction. In the past, the weaknesses of the EISA regulatory framework and reporting mechanisms contributed to a lack of detailed information on insurers and available plans and prevented consumers from easily comparing the benefits and value for money of different private health insurance plans. This, together with the absence of one regulator for all types of private health insurance, has limited competition between various subsectors and plans in the market, which may have lowered efficiency.

---

[18] A health insurance bill has been on the government's agenda for many years.

Private health insurance schemes are not required to publish data on client satisfaction or quality of care and quality of care was not regulated by EISA or EFSA. Although private providers may in many cases provide better quality care than the HIO or the Ministry of Health, there is little to suggest that private health insurance has improved the quality and efficiency of private or public health care provision due to the weakness of its contracting mechanisms, which do not create appropriate incentives for providers.

India

NOAH HABER, EMMA PITCHFORTH AND PHILIPA MLADOVSKY

The health system in India is financed from a number of sources: state and central government budgets; the private sector, including the not-for-profit sector targeting populations directly and through insurance; households through out-of-pocket payments; social and community-based insurance; and external financing (Rao et al., 2005). Out-of-pocket payments are the dominant source of funding, accounting for 65% of total spending on health and 93% of private spending on health in 2015 (WHO, 2018). Private health insurance accounts for 5% of current spending on health (WHO, 2018), but it is rapidly becoming the primary source of health financing through public–private partnerships, with recent political focus on achieving universal access to health care by 2022 (Patel et al., 2015). These public–private partnerships have led to large increases in private health insurance coverage in India over the past decade, with the proportion of people covered growing from 3–4% of the population in 2005 (Prinja et al. 2012) to 22% in 2014 (IRDA, 2015; WHO, 2018).

Public spending on health is among the lowest in countries in the region or of similar income, making up only 3.9% of gross domestic product in 2015 (WHO, 2018). Government-sponsored schemes cover 74% of all people with private health insurance, but they account for only 13% of the total value of claims filed[19] (IRDA, 2015). Private providers make up the majority of both outpatient (70%) and inpatient (60%) care (Patel et al., 2015). Private health care is generally considered to be of much higher quality than public care (Rao et al., 2014), though

---

[19] Estimated from the value of premiums collected and the claims ratios reported by the Insurance Regulatory and Development Authority (IRDA).

there is very large variation in the type and quality of care provided (Mackintosh et al. 2016). This has motivated the government to provide public financing of public–private partnerships such as the Rashtriya Swasthya Bima Yojana (RSBY) scheme (see below), which enables access to higher-quality private health care for those who could otherwise not afford it (Devadasan et al., 2013; Virk & Atun, 2015). However, private health care is generally unregulated (Garg & Nagpal, 2014), leading to continuing concerns over quality and access to care (Patel et al., 2015). There are large disparities in both financing and provider coverage between urban/rural areas as well as between income groups. Health insurance schemes in India typically only cover inpatient care. This leaves very large gaps in financial protection (Selvaraj & Karan, 2012) and poorly incentivizes more cost-effective preventive care in outpatient settings (Ahlin et al., 2016; Devadasan et al., 2013; Prinja et al., 2012).

Market origins

The history of private health insurance in India is extremely short. Before 1999, the Government of India maintained a legal monopoly on all forms of insurance, using a nationalized insurance organization and its subsidiaries for all insurance provision (Sinha, 2002). The first private health insurance scheme in India, Mediclaim, was introduced in 1986[20] as a hospitalization indemnity scheme administered by government-owned non-life insurance firms (USAID, 2008), on which modern Indian health insurance schemes are still based. TPAs, which constitute another feature of the health insurance market in India, were introduced in 1996. The TPAs serve as the intermediaries between the insurers, providers and policy-holders (Bhat & Babu, 2004; Gupta et al., 2004; USAID, 2008), handling the majority of insurance transactions to this day.

Market overview and development

As part of wider economic reforms and liberalization of markets, the Indian parliament passed the Insurance Regulatory and Development Authority (IRDA) Act in 1999, which allowed the private sector and foreign firms to participate in the private health insurance market under

[20] "Mediclaim" is now a generic term that describes health-related indemnity insurance in India, and is offered by most major insurers.

the regulation of the IRDA (USAID, 2008). The General Insurance Corporation became the national reinsurance organization as part of this reform, with four subsidiary insurance companies (Gupta et al., 2004). These four companies are now independent but publicly owned insurance companies, blurring the line between private and public health insurance. Market liberalization resulted in around two thirds of for-profit private health insurance companies having foreign partners and the first stand alone private health insurance company launching by 2006 (USAID, 2008). In January 2007 the IRDA removed tariffs from general insurance with the aim of driving additional growth of the private insurance market, better risk management and risk rating, and the development of new, consumer-oriented policies (PricewaterhouseCoopers, 2007; USAID, 2008).

The number of persons covered by voluntary private health insurance has grown from 0.69 million in 1991–1992 to 3.5 million in 1998–1999 and around 17 million in 2005–2006, reaching 1.56% of the population by 2006 (USAID, 2008). In 2015, 74 million individuals were insured under either group or individual insurance schemes (6% of the population), with an additional 214 million (17% of the population) covered by government-sponsored schemes (IRDA, 2015). The publicly owned insurers currently control 64% of the health insurance market, with private general non-life insurance companies making up 22%, and insurance companies that exclusively offer health insurance controlling the remaining 14% of the market. Life insurers can also offer private health insurance in the form of additional optional health benefits; however, health coverage offered through these riders is marginal.

In 2004, the national government introduced the Universal Health Insurance (UHI) scheme, a public–private partnership that attempted to extend private health insurance to those living below the poverty level through central government premium subsidies. The only annual premium to be paid by the individual was Rs365[21] per person (UHI is also referred to as the "Government Rupee-a-Day" scheme). The scheme was implemented through the four public sector insurance companies but it was largely unsuccessful, partly because it was loss-making for the insurance companies due to adverse selection and because the families below the poverty level were unwilling or unable to prepay the annual premium in a lump sum (USAID, 2008).

[21] The average exchange rate in 2016 was US$1 = Rs67.2.

Recognizing the weaknesses of UHI, in 2007 the Indian government launched RSBY – a national scheme for people living below the poverty line. RSBY provides annual hospitalization coverage up to Rs30 000 for a family of five and some coverage for transportation. All pre-existing diseases are covered from day one and there is no age limit for beneficiaries (Jain, 2010).

As with UHI, RSBY is government funded but relies on private health insurance operators for its implementation. However, in the case of RSBY each state government selects the implementing insurance company (public or private) through an open tendering process. In addition to their normal role of providing insurance, the contracted operators are responsible for enrolling a predefined list of households below the poverty level; contracting nongovernmental organizations to conduct information and awareness campaigns; setting up a kiosk in each village to manage the scheme; and providing a toll-free call centre. Other innovative features are: a one-off registration fee of Rs30; a paper-less system that uses biometric-enabled smart cards; portability of insurance across India; private health insurance operators that contract both public and private government accredited hospitals, creating competition between the two sectors because beneficiaries can choose the provider; direct reimbursement of providers by the implementing insurance company or TPA (Jain, 2010). In 2016, RSBY covered over 41 million persons (around 3% of the population) (RSBY, 2016).

Types of policies

Almost all insurance products in the Indian market cover hospitalization expenses. The main sources of out-of-pocket expenses (dental services, ophthalmology, preventive care, long-term care and expenses associated with outpatient services) are typically not covered.

Insurance policies are typically based on the Mediclaim programme from 1986 (Rao et al., 2005; USAID, 2008). Policies cover people aged 5–80 years old although children aged from 3 months to 5 years may be covered if a parent is covered at the same time. Additionally, it is possible to increase coverage to 85 years if policy coverage continued without any breaks. There is no patient cost-sharing up to the ceiling of the sum insured. Coverage includes expenses incurred during hospitalization and/or domiciliary hospitalization due to illness, disease or injury (such as room and board at the hospital; nursing expenses; surgeon, anaesthetist, medical practitioner, consultant, specialist fees; anaesthesia, blood, oxygen, operation theatre charges, surgical appliances, medicines and drugs, diagnostic material, X-ray; dialysis, chemotherapy, radiotherapy, cost of pacemaker, artificial limbs and cost of organs and similar expenses) and relevant medical expenses up to 30 days before and 60 days after hospitalization. Exclusions include pre-existing conditions, diseases contracted within the first 30 days from the commencement of the policy, expenses of treatment for certain diseases (during the first year), preventive treatment, plastic surgery, cost of spectacles, contact lenses, hearing aids, dental treatment, AIDS, maternity, naturopathy. The benefit limit varies widely across plans and the premiums are calculated from a matrix of sum insured and age of the person (USAID, 2008).

Other types of private health insurance policies offered in India are critical illness policies and hospital cash policies (USAID, 2008).

Pricing

Average annual premiums per person covered have more than tripled in the past 5 years for the individual market, from Rs928 in 2010 to Rs3454 in 2015, while group rates have remained relatively stable at around Rs2000 rupees per person per year (IRDA, 2015).

Between 1995 and 2005, claims grew at a faster rate than premiums, indicating a decreasing profitability of private health insurance (USAID, 2008). Claim ratios for government-sponsored schemes rose rapidly from 93% in 2013/2014 to 108% in 2014/2015 and currently only the individual insurance policy market remains profitable, with both group and government-sponsored insurance plans being sold at a loss (on average) (IRDA, 2015). One possible reason is that the four main private health insurance operators have not had the actuarial capacity for pricing or analysing health services costs and utilization increases and have used "intuitive pricing", prioritizing premium affordability to the insuring public. Another reason is that private health insurance premiums have not increased in line with medical inflation (USAID, 2008). A third reason is that non-life private health insurance operators have tended to absorb losses from health insurance products by cross-subsidizing from other more profitable areas of insurance. Previously, under the Insurance Act, operators in the non-life insurance market had to adhere to the tariffs set by the Tariff Advisory Committee, or face punitive action. However, the nonseparation and categorization of health insurance under "miscellaneous" insurance meant that health insurance was not tariffed. As tariffs in the other non-life insurance segments were set high in comparison with private health insurance premiums,[22] profits in these other lines of insurance were greater than in private health insurance (USAID, 2008).

The cost of health insurance policies, group and individual, has varied considerably between companies. In general, premiums are determined by age of the insured and level of coverage. National pricing has been maintained with non-urban areas subsidizing urban areas where medical costs are far higher. However, differential geographical pricing is permitted and may become more common in response to high hospitalization costs in some areas (USAID, 2008).

Public policy towards the market

The IRDA, in place since 1999, has a dual function to both regulate and develop the insurance market. In terms of regulation, it covers:

- consumer protection through licensing of insurers, regulation of advertising and regulation of TPAs
- solvency of health insurers through minimum capital and surplus laws and regulations and auditing
- grievance and dispute resolution through an insurance ombudsman system established in 1998 following recognition that the civil courts and consumer protection were ineffective for insurance-related claims because of delays and high expense (USAID, 2008).

Recognizing the limitations of a retrospective reimbursement system where the burden for maintaining receipts and filing claims lies with the policy-holder, TPAs first emerged in 1996. TPAs came under the regulation of IRDA in 2002, partly to help increase uptake of private health insurance. TPAs have the following responsibilities (Bhat et al., 2005; USAID, 2008):

- enrolment services including the enrolment of policy-holders and dependants into its system and issuing photo-ID cards to both

---

[22]   Some claimed that insurance companies offered miscellaneous class products to purchasers of insurance at prices below cost to compensate for historically overpriced tariffed insurance (USAID, 2008).

- call-centre services including pre-authorization of hospital expenses and deposit waiver for admission to the network hospital
- managing access to hospital network, which allows policy-holder-negotiated services and rates, including admission deposit waiver and direct settlement of bills
- claims administration including adjudication, processing and settlement of claims for in-network and out-of-network claims
- information reporting including generating predefined reports for enrolment, claim related statistics and operations performance statistics to the insurer and generating periodic financial information and operating performance reports to the IRDA.

Although TPAs are not mandatory, they handle over half of all cashless health insurance claims transactions (IRDA, 2015). However, it is not clear whether TPAs have increased demand for private health insurance. Furthermore, the introduction of TPAs and direct settlement has led to uncontrolled price increases by hospitals who charge higher rates to the insured than uninsured (policies such as Mediclaim have a maximum annual sum assured, and it is thought that hospitals target this figure). TPAs have limited criteria on which to base hospital selection and do not require hospitals to demonstrate or sustain quality of care.

Another step to encourage private health insurance uptake was the introduction of tax incentives. Since 2002, the government has allowed a deduction from taxable pay of premiums up to Rs15 000 (Rs20 000 for senior citizens). This may have contributed to growth in demand (USAID, 2008) but analysis of the value and effectiveness of this tax subsidy for private health insurance is lacking.

Assessment of market impact on health system goals

Equitable access to health care and financial protection

A system based on risk-rated premiums, determined by health status and age has implications for equitable access, because typically those most in need pay higher premiums. Stringent exclusions based on pre-existing conditions mean that currently those most in need of insurance, the sick, are excluded. There is often ambiguity over what constitutes a pre-existing condition, allowing companies to apply exclusion retrospectively and not cover claims made by policy-holders (USAID, 2008).

Historically, private health insurance coverage has been more common in urban than rural areas and almost entirely restricted to the wealthiest two quintiles of the population (Arokiasamy et al., 2006). There were also geographic differences in private health insurance take-up, with states such as Assam having negligible share of population covered and Maharashtra having higher private health insurance coverage, and differences according to the religion of household head (higher among Jain households than any other) (International Institute for Population Sciences, 2007). However, it is unclear how the recent increase in private health insurance coverage has changed the equity landscape in India, particularly as health insurance coverage continues to move towards universal levels.

Tax incentives have led to public subsidization of the private health insurance premiums of this population. As such, the development of private health insurance has not supported national health policy. The current Five Year Plan (2012–2017), which aims to ensure access to health care for all, calls specifically for expansion of public–private partnerships, in particular expansion of RSBY (Government of India, 2013). Unfortunately, these types of public–private partnerships lack strong incentives and provisions for outpatient and preventive care.

Incentives for efficiency and quality in service organization and delivery

There is no incentive for providers to limit care, other than the limits of sums covered by policies. Related to this, there is no obligation for providers to provide quality care and providers bear no risk for the prices they charge. Medical costs have therefore increased without any guarantee of quality of care. The lack of regulations in this area is a major concern. Administrative costs are high and have not been improved by poor coordination between TPAs and insurance companies.

Conclusions

Private health insurance has failed to address the problem of high out-of-pocket payments on health care in the three countries studied here. It is unable to do so because it is beyond the financial reach of those most in need of access to health care and financial protection, even where there is regulation to ensure open enrolment and a minimum package of benefits (Brazil), and because it is mainly targeted at formal sector employees or at professionals (Egypt). Depending on how they are structured, tax subsidies for private health insurance do not always reach the poor or those who are denied access to the market due to age or pre-existing conditions and therefore end up paying for the health care costs of those who are already better off, both financially and in terms of health status.

In Brazil, private health insurance is an important component of health financing policy. Brazilian government has responded to the manifold negative effects of private health insurance growth by introducing measures to expand access to the market, and improve the efficiency and quality of the care provided under private health insurance. So far, expanding access to private health insurance has had the presumably unintended effect of exacerbating inequalities in access to health care and financial protection.

This offers important lessons to Egypt and India, where private health insurance penetration levels are low and where the private health insurance regulatory framework remains weak. Addressing this weakness is particularly pressing for the Indian government as it increasingly finances health care for the poor through private health insurance, via schemes like RSBY and UHI. Potentially the government is in a good position to shape the future market, with IRDA being already in place as a regulatory authority with responsibility for market development. However, health insurance needs to be identified and regulated as a separate insurance commodity. The growth in the number of individuals covered by private health insurance has stagnated in recent years, with the exception of government-sponsored plans. It is plausible that this is due to a relatively low value proposition of private health insurance to the consumer, due in part to lack of control over medical costs or quality of care. Second, inefficiencies remain in the processing of claims and relationships between TPAs and insurance companies. This in turn adversely affects consumer experience. Finally, there has been little marketing effort on the part of health insurers, which may have led to a poor understanding of private health insurance in the population.

In Egypt the expansion of private health insurance is not envisaged as a key policy for meeting health system goals. Efforts to introduce an insurance law seem to have stalled in recent years, hampered, among others, by the 2011 uprising and subsequent economic situation, lack of workers skilled in key insurance functions, including premium rating and underwriting, limited development of the reinsurance market and lack of general insurance data. Capital requirements for a private health insurance business are very high, which results in private health insurance being sold with other insurance products for cross-subsidization. The attractiveness of operating as a TPA compared with a health insurance company further impedes the development of the private health insurance market. All that, along with the weak economic situation, will probably make it challenging for the sector to grow formally over the foreseen future.

References

Ahlin T et al. (2016). Health insurance in India: what do we know and why is ethnographic research needed. *Anthropology & Medicine*, 23(1):102–24.

ANS (2010, 2011, 2016). Caderno de Informação da Saúde Suplementar (Information Notebook on the Supplementary Health): www.ans.gov.br/perfil-do-setor/dados-e-indicadores-do-setor; accessed on 15/12/2017.

ANS (2017a). Beneficiários de planos privados de saúde – Beneficiários por UF, região metropolitana e capital (Beneficiaries of private health insurance – Beneficiaries per state, region and capital): www.ans.gov.br/anstabnet/cgi-bin/dh?dados/tabnet_br.def; accessed on 15/12/2017.

ANS (2017b). Boletim Informativo: Utilização do Sistema Público por Beneficiários de Planos de Saúde e Ressarcimento ao SUS (Newsletter: Use of the Public System by Beneficiaries of Health Plans and Reimbursement to SUS): www.ans.gov.br/images/stories/Materiais_para_pesquisa/Materiais_por_assunto/boletim_ressarcimento_julho_2017.pdf; accessed on 15/12/2017.

ANS map (2017). Mapa da utilização do SUS por beneficiários de planos privados de saúde (Map of SUS use by beneficiaries of private health insurance): www.ans.gov.br/images/stories/Materiais_para_pesquisa/Materiais_por_assunto/beneficiarios_sus_2017.pdf; accessed on 15/12/2017.

ANS Presentation (2016, 2017). [in Power Point format, available for download, which consolidates, in tables and graphs, the main numbers related to beneficiaries and operators. The information is standardized and updated quarterly]: www.ans.gov.br/images/stories/Materiais_para_pesquisa/Perfil_setor/Dados_e_indicadores_do_setor/dados_consolidados_da_saude_suplementar_dez-16.ppt and www.ans.gov.br/images/stories/Materiais_para_pesquisa/Perfil_setor/Dados_e_indicadores_do_setor/DadosConsolidados-da-Saude-Suplementar.ppt; accessed on 15/12/2017.

Arokiasamy P et al. (2006). *Health System Performance Assessment – World Health Survey, 2003. New Delhi, Internationals Institute for Population Sciences (IIPS)* Delhi, India, WHO-India.

AXCO (2007). *Insurance Market Reports.* London, Egypt Life and Benefits London.

Baldassare RM (2014). Análise do desempenho econômico-financeiro de operadoras de planos de saúde no mercado de saúde suplementar brasileiro; master dissertation in Portuguese. (Analysis of the economic-financial performance of health plan operators in the Brazilian supplementary healthcare market): http://bibliotecadigital.fgv.br/dspace/handle/10438/11790; accessed on 15/12/2017.

Bhat R (2005). *Third Party Administrators and health insurance in India: Perceptions of providers and policyholders.* Ahmedabad, Indian Institute of Management Ahamedabad.

Bhat R, Babu SK (2004). Health insurance and third party administrators: issues and challenges. *Economic and Political Weekly,* 39(28):3149–59.

Devadasan N et al. (2013). Promoting universal financial protection: evidence from the Rashtriya Swasthya Bima Yojana (RSBY) in Gujarat, India. *Health Research Policy and Systems,* 11:29.

EISA (2007). Egyptian Insurance Supervisory Authority 2006/2007 Annual Report.

El-Saharty S, Maeda A (2006). *Egypt health policy note. Egypt Public Expenditure Review.* Washington, DC, World Bank.

Fernandes E et al. (2007). An analysis of the supplementary health sector in Brazil. *Health Policy,* 81(2–3):242–57.

Garg P, Nagpal J (2014). A review of literature to understand the complexity of equity, ethics and management for achieving public health goals in India. *Journal of Clinical and Diagnostic Research,* 8(2):1–6.

Gericke C (2004). Financing health care in Egypt: current issues and options for reform: www.wm.tu-berlin.de/fileadmin/f8/wiwidok/diskussionspapiere_wiwidok/dp05-2004.pdf; accessed on 15/12/2017.

Government of India. (2013). *Twelfth Five-Year Plan.* New Delhi: SAGE Publications India Pvt Ltd. http://planningcommission.nic.in/plans/planrel/fiveyr/12th/pdf/12fyp_vol3.pdf; accessed on 15/12/2017.

Gupta I et al. (2004). Third party administrators: theory and practice. *Economic and Political Weekly,* 39(28):3160–4.

IBGE (Instituto Brasileiro de Geografia e Estatística [Brazilian Institute for Geography and Statistics]) (1999). *Pesquisa Nacional por Amostra de Domicílios 1998 [National Household Sample Survey 1998].* Rio de Janeiro, IBGE (text and database in Portuguese).

IBGE (2003). *Pesquisa Nacional por Amostra de Domicílios 2003 [National Household Sample Survey 2003]*. Rio de Janeiro, IBGE (text and database in Portuguese).

IBGE (2008). *Pesquisa Nacional por Amostra de Domicílios 2008 [National Household Sample Survey 2008]*. Rio de Janeiro, IBGE (text and database in Portuguese).

IBGE (2013). Estimativas de população (Population estimates): www .ibge.gov.br/home/cstatistica/populacao/estimativa2013/default.shtm; accessed on 15/12/2017.

IBGE (2014). *Pesquisa Nacional de Saude 2013 [National Health Survey 2013]*. Rio de Janeiro, IBGE (text and database in Portuguese).

IDEC and CREMESP (2007). Planos de Saude, nove anos apos a Law 9 656/98. As falhas da regulamentação, A omissão da Agência Nacional de Saude Suplementar, (ANS), O comportamento do mercado, Conselho Regional de Medicina do Estado de São Paulo (CREMESP) and Instituto Brasileiro de Defesa do Consumidor (IDEC).

Insurance Federation of Egypt (2006). *Annual Report*. Giza, Insurance Federation of Egypt.

International Institute for Population Sciences (2007) *National family health survey (NFHS-3), 2005–06: India*: Volume 1. Mumbai, IIPS.

IRDA (2015). *Annual Report 2014–2015*: www.irda.gov.in/; accessed on 15/12/2017.

Jain N (2010). *56 million steps towards universal coverage: RSBY Health Insurance for the Poor in India*. Eschborn, Deutsche Gesellschaft für Technische Zusammenarbeit (GTZ) GmbH.

Leal RM (2014). O mercado de saúde suplementar no Brasil: regulação e resultados econômicos dos planos privados de saúde (The supplementary health market in Brazil: regulation and economic results of private health plans) [thesis]; Institute of Economics – UFRJ: www.ie.ufrj.br/images/pos-graduacao/ppge/Tese_RodrigoMendesLeal-v-25ago2014.pdf.

Macera AP, Saintive MB (2004). *O Mercado de Saúde Suplementar no Brasil* (The Supplementary Health Market in Brazil). SEAE Working Paper 31.

Mackintosh M et al. (2016). What is the private sector? Understanding private provision in the health systems of low-income and middle-income countries. *Lancet*, 388(10044):596–605.

Medici AC (2004). Financing and decentralizing health policies in Brazil. Achievements, problems, challenges and proposals. Paper presented at the World Bank international conference on Governance and Accountability in Social Sector Decentralization, Washington DC, 18 and 19 February

2004: www1.worldbank.org/publicsector/decentralization/Feb2004Course/ Background per cent20materials/Medici.doc; accessed on 04/10/2008.

Middle East Insurance Review (2017). Egypt: Health insurance premiums exceed EGP1 bn in 2016. Middle East Insurance Review [Online] 30 March 2017: www.meinsurancereview.com/News/View-NewsLetter-Article?id=38704&Type=MiddleEast, accessed on 24/08/2017.

MOHP Government of Egypt (2002). *Egypt household health service utilization and expenditure survey Cairo, MOHP Health Sector Reform Program.* Cairo, MOHP.

Nassar H, El-Saharty S (2006). *Egypt: Voluntary Health Insurance – Case Study.* Washington DC, World Bank.

Nassar H, El-Saharty S (2010). Chapter 5 Egypt. In: Preker AS, Zweifel P, Schellekens O, eds. *Global marketplace for private health insurance: strength in numbers.* Washington D.C, World Bank.

Ocké-Reis CO (1995). *O setor privado de saúde no Brasil: os limites da autonomia, Tese de mestrado em Saúde Coletiva.* Rio de Janeiro, IMS/UERJ.

Ocké-Reis CO (2004). Challenges of the Private Health Plans Regulation in Brazil. IPEAWorking Paper 1 013, Rio de Janeiro, IPEA.

Ocké-Reis CO, Gama FND (2016). Radiografia do gasto tributário em saúde, 2003–2013 (Radiography of tax expenditure on health, 2003–2013). Technical Note IPEA. n. 19 (Diest); http://repositorio.ipea.gov.br/handle/11058/6528; accessed 15/12/2017.

OECD (2008). Chapter 3. *The Private Health Insurance Sector Review of Regulatory Reform. Brazil: Strengthening Governance for Growth.* Paris, OECD.

Oxford Business Group (2017). Great progress for Egyptian Public Health. Oxford Business Group 2017. https://oxfordbusinessgroup.com/overview/under-strain-while-public-health-has-seen-significant-progress-greater-investments-are-required, accessed on 24/08/2017.

Partners for Health Reformplus (2004). *Health care utilization, expenditures, and insurance: household survey findings from Suez Governorate, Egypt.* Bethesda, MD, The Partners for Health Reformplus Project, Abt Associates Inc.

Patel V et al. (2015). Assuring health coverage for all in India. *Lancet,* 386(10011):2422–35.

Preker AS et al. (2010). *Introduction: Strength in numbers. Global Marketplace for Private Health Insurance: Strength in Numbers.* Washington DC, World Bank.

PricewaterhouseCoopers (2007). *Healthcare in India: emerging market report.* London, PricewaterhouseCoopers.

Prinja S et al. (2012). Universal Health Insurance in India: Ensuring Equity, Efficiency, and Quality. *Indian Journal of Community Medicine: Official Publication of Indian Association of Preventive & Social Medicine*, 37(3):142–9.

Rafeh N (1997). *Private Health Insurance in Egypt. Innovations in Health Care Financing*. World Bank Discussion Paper No. 365. Washington DC, World Bank.

Rannan-Eliya RP et al. (1998). *Egypt National Health Accounts 1994/95*. Cairo and Boston, Department of Planning, Ministry of Health and Population, Arab Republic of Egypt, and Data for Decision Making Project, Harvard School of Public Health.

Rao KD et al. (2014). Progress towards universal health coverage in BRICS: translating economic growth into better health. *Bulletin of the World Health Organization*, 92(6):429–35.

Rao KS et al. (2005). *Financing of Health in India. Financing and Delivery of Health Care Services in India, Background Papers of the National Commission on Macroeconomics and Health*. New Delhi, National Commission on Macroeconomics and Health. Ministry of Health & Family Welfare, Government of India.

RSBY (2016). National Summary. www.rsby.gov.in/Overview.aspx; accessed on 15/12/2017.

Santos IS et al. (2008). O mix público-privado no Sistema de Saúde Brasileiro: financiamento, oferta e utilização de serviços de saúde. *Ciências saúde coletiva* [online] 13(5):1431–40.

Selvaraj S, Karan AK (2012). Why publicly financed health insurance schemes are ineffective in providing financial risk protection. *Economic & Political Weekly*, XLVII(11):60–8.

Sinha T (2002). Privatization of the insurance market in India: from the British Raj to monopoly Raj to Swaraj. Nottingham, Centre for Risk & Insurance Studies, The University of Nottingham.

USAID (2008). *Private health insurance in India: promise & reality*. Washington, Bearing Point Inc for USAID.

van Doorslaer E et al. (2006). Effect of payments for health care on poverty estimates in 11 countries in Asia: an analysis of household survey data. *Lancet*, 368(9544):1357–64.

Virk AK, Atun R (2015). Towards universal health coverage in India: a historical examination of the genesis of Rashtriya Swasthya Bima Yojana – the health insurance scheme for low-income groups. *Public Health*, 129(6):810–17.

WHO (2018). *Global Health Expenditure Database*. Geneva, WHO.

4 | Private health insurance in Canada

JEREMIAH HURLEY AND G. EMMANUEL GUINDON

A majority of Canadians hold some form of private health care insurance, most commonly obtained as an employment benefit. Private insurance accounts for around 13% of spending on health and its financing role is essentially limited to complementary coverage for services not covered by public insurance programmes. Private supplementary insurance for services covered by the public insurance system effectively does not exist in Canada (the exception is a negligible role in the Province of Québec). This limited role for private insurance in health care reflects the core policy vision for health care financing in Canada, which emphasizes equal access to medically necessary health care, especially physician and hospital services. Compared with many other countries, Canada's private health insurance market is relatively uncomplicated, viewed in terms of either the products offered or the regulations imposed. Although Canadians regularly debate the relative split between public and private finance overall, and a small set of advocates have persistently pressed for a greater role for private insurance, private insurance has not figured prominently in Canada's health care policy debates, which since the late 1960s have focused on the publicly funded health care system.

Three Canadian health care policy challenges, however, are drawing the role of private health insurance into the centre of policy debate. The first was the emergence in the mid-1990s of long waiting times for some common, high-profile services such as orthopaedic surgery, eye surgery, diagnostic imaging and cancer treatments. These waiting times have fuelled advocates for parallel private financing alongside public insurance and for loosening restrictions on supplementary private insurance. Such advocates were emboldened by a landmark ruling of the Supreme Court of Canada in 2005 (Chaoulli v. Government of Québec) that, in the presence of excessive waiting times in the public system, Québec's statute prohibiting private insurance for publicly insured services violated Québec's Charter of Rights. Though the ruling applied only to Québec, the judgement galvanized those advocating for a fundamental change in the role of private insurance in Canadian health care. Similar legal challenges to provincial restrictions on supplementary private insurance are making their way through the courts in Alberta, British Columbia and Ontario (Mertl, 2016; McCreith v. Ontario, 2007; Murray v. Alberta, 2007; Cohn, 2015; Thomas & Flood, 2015).[1]

The second element drawing private insurance into the centre of policy debate is the growing importance of pharmaceuticals in the modern pantheon of medically necessary therapies. Prescription drugs are excluded from the core services covered by Canadian Medicare, so the majority of pharmaceutical costs are privately financed. Many Canadians, however, are either uninsured or underinsured for prescription drugs (Canadian Institute for Health Information 2015). This has prompted many to call for an expansion of public financing for prescription drugs [National Forum on Health, 1997; Commission on the Future of Health Care in Canada, 2002; Senate of Canada, 2002; Advisory Panel on Healthcare Innovation, 2015; Morgan et al., 2015]. Some proposals call for full public coverage that would supplant the large role of private insurance in this sector; others call for various types of public–private partnerships to ensure universal coverage. All of them bring to the fore the question of the desired role for private insurance in this important and expensive sector of health care.

Finally, policy-makers and system analysts increasingly appreciate the interactions between the publicly and privately financed components of the overall health care system. Unequal access to privately insured services can lead to unequal access to and use of publicly insured services. Stabile (2001), Allin & Hurley (2009) and Devlin, Sarma & Zhang (2011), for instance, found that other things being equal, those with private drug insurance used more publicly financed physician services (an effect unlikely to be driven by selection). This type of evidence

---

[1] In *Allen v Alberta*, Darcy Allen, who underwent surgery in the United States, argued that the Alberta Health Care Insurance Act stopped him from obtaining private health care insurance that would have allowed more timely access to the surgery he required and covered the cost of that operation. As a result, he argued, the Alberta Health Care Insurance Act had infringed on his Constitutional rights to life, liberty and security of the person based on the decision in Chaoulli. Allen's case was dismissed by Court of Queen's Bench of Alberta in 2014, by the Court of Appeal of Alberta in 2015 and by the Supreme Court of Canada in 2016 (Allen v. Alberta, 2014, 2015; Darcy Allen v. Her Majesty the Queen in Right of Alberta, 2016).

prompts hard questions regarding the scope of policies necessary to achieve objectives set for the publicly financed health system.

This chapter reviews the role of private health insurance in Canada. It begins with a brief overview of the Canadian health care system; considers the historical path that led to the current role for private health insurance; examines the current market for private health insurance; assesses the evidence for how private insurance contributes to or detracts from health financing goals; and offers some concluding comments on private health insurance in Canada.

Canada's health care system

Canada is a federation, so the design of the Canadian health care system derives from the allocation of responsibilities in Canada's constitutional documents between the federal government and the provincial governments. The British North America Act of 1867 and the 1982 Constitution assign responsibility for health care to provincial governments and provide the federal government with extensive revenue-raising power. Consequently, Canada's health care system comprises 13 distinct provincial/territorial[2] health care systems. Each provincial system, however, conforms to national standards embodied in the 1984 Canada Health Act, which the federal government enforces through a system of conditional federal transfers (the Canada Health Transfer) to the provinces (Box 4.1).

By international standards, Canada spends an above-average amount on health care. Per person spending on health in 2016 was Can$5900, which placed it 12th among OECD countries behind the United States, Switzerland, the Netherlands and Norway, among others (OECD, 2017).[3] Health care spending in Canada represented 10.6% of gross domestic product in 2016 (OECD, 2017). After slowing in the mid-1990s during a period of unprecedented fiscal restraint in the public sector, real (inflation-adjusted) total health care spending rose at an annual rate of 4.6% between 1996 and 2008 (Canadian Institute for Health Information, 2010) but has decreased by an average of 0.6%

---

[2] Canada includes ten provinces and three territories. We refer to them generically as provinces.

[3] Unless explicitly noted, all dollar figures quoted in this chapter refer to Canadian dollars (Can$).

Box 4.1 Canada Health Act national standards for full federal transfer

To be eligible for the full federal transfer, a provincial public insurance plan must conform to each of the following five Canada Health Act principles:

Accessibility: the plan must not impede, either directly or indirectly, whether by charges made to insured persons or otherwise, reasonable access to insured health services.

Comprehensiveness: the plan must cover medically necessary physician and hospital services, including surgical–dental services that require a hospital setting.[a]

Universality: the plan must cover all provincial residents on uniform terms and conditions.[b]

Portability: the plan must not impose a minimum period of residence in excess of 3 months for new residents, it must cover its own residents when temporarily in another province (or country in the case of non-elective services) and during the waiting period in another province for residents who have moved permanently.

Public administration: the provincial plan must be administered and operated on a non-profit basis by a public authority.

Sources: Government of Canada (1984), Marchildon (2005, 2013).

Notes: [a] Insured services exclude services covered by the workers' compensation system, which are financed through employer contributions to the workers' compensation fund.

[b] The insured population excludes certain subgroups such as members of the military, Royal Canadian Mounted Police, prisoners and aboriginals, who are covered by the federal government.

---

per year between 2010 and 2015 (Canadian Institute for Health Information 2015).

Health care in Canada is predominantly publicly financed (Table 4.1). In 2014, 71% of health care was financed publicly, a level that is a bit lower than the peak of 77% in 1976 but which has remained relatively constant since the late 1990s. The Canada Health Act's focus on physician and hospital services, however, leads to a unique pattern of

Table 4.1 *Health care spending in Canada by source of funds, 2013*

Provider type	Total health care spending	Public health care spending	% of total spending	Private health care spending	% of total spending
Total	209 457	148 143	70.7%	61 314	29.3%
Physician services	31 683	31 288	98.8%	395	1.2%
Hospital services	62 381	56 487	90.6%	5 894	9.4%
Drugs	33 397	12 044	36.1%	21 353	63.9%
Dental care	12 878	791	6.1%	12 087	93.9%
Other health professionals	7 897	1 069	13.5%	6 828	86.5%
Other institutions	21 938	15 537	70.8%	6 402	29.2%
Other[a]	39 283	30 928	78.7%	8 354	21.3%

Source: CIHI (2015).

Notes: All figures in Can$ millions; figures may not add due to rounding.

[a] For example, expenditure on capital, public health, administration, health research.

public financing across health care sectors. Public financing for physician and hospital services, commonly referred to as Canada's Medicare programme, constituted 99% and 91% of spending in these sectors in 2013. Outside these two sectors the role of public insurance is markedly smaller and more variable. Public finance is next most important for other institutions, such as long-term care facilities, and least important for dental care (for which the only universally publicly insured dental care is inpatient oral surgery and the public sector finances about 6% of all services). In between is the drug sector, for which the public sector financed 36% of all drugs (and 43% of prescription drugs) in 2013. De facto, therefore, Canada's "single-payer, universal" system of public finance accurately applies only to physician and hospital services. Unsurprisingly, Canada has one of the lowest levels of public spending on pharmaceuticals among OECD countries (OECD, 2017).

The public insurance programmes are financed primarily through personal income and consumption taxes levied by both the federal and provincial governments. Two provinces – British Columbia and Ontario – retain national health care premiums for the core Medicare services. The premiums vary according to income in both of these provinces and in addition by household composition in British Columbia; none of the provinces risk-adjust the premiums. An individual cannot be denied service for failure to pay the premium, so they are, de facto, simply taxes.[4] Three provinces (Québec, Alberta and Nova Scotia) charge premiums to some beneficiaries of their public drug insurance programmes. The premiums depend on income and beneficiary status: Québec and Nova Scotia exempt those on social assistance; Alberta exempts seniors and those on social assistance (Canadian Institute for Health Information, 2012). Four provinces (Newfoundland, Québec, Ontario and Manitoba) collect a health-specific payroll tax (rates up to 4% depending on the size of a firm's payroll), but in general, neither local taxes nor payroll taxes contribute meaningfully to health care finance.

Private finance encompasses a mixture of direct, out-of-pocket payments for care (48%), private insurance coverage (41%) and "non-consumption" spending (11%), which includes non-patient revenue to hospitals (ancillary operations, donations and investment income), spending on research and capital expenditure in the private sector (Table 4.2).[5] Overall, private out-of-pocket spending is a larger source of finance than is private insurance, though again, this varies by sector. Private insurance plays an important role only outside the physician and hospital sectors. In 2012, for instance, although 12% of health care was financed through private insurance, this proportion ranged from a low of effectively 0% for physician services and 2.6% for hospital care to over 56% for dental services (Table 4.2). Dental care is the only sector for which private insurance finances a majority of care. Private insurance is next most important for drugs, for which it finances about 30% of spending. Insurance for dental care and drugs are the largest sources

---

[4] In British Columbia, many employers pay the premium on behalf of employees as one component of health care-related benefits provided to employees. Just under half of British Columbia residents have their premium paid by an employer (CLHIA, 2016).

[5] Private insurance does not, in general, cover cost-sharing requirements within public insurance programmes. One exception to this is large deductibles that apply for higher-income, working-age populations within some provincial public drug insurance programmes. A person's private insurance obtained as a retirement benefit from their previous employer may also cover such cost-sharing. It is also possible for an individual to hold supplementary private insurance in parallel with public drug coverage (a person's private insurance obtained as a retirement benefit from their previous employer may cover drugs also covered by the public plan), though such insurance is relatively rare.

Table 4.2 *Private health spending in Canada, 2012*

Provider type	Out-of-pocket	% total health care spending	% private health care spending	Private insurance	% total health care spending	% private health care spending	Non-consumption	% total health care spending	% private health care spending
Total	29 197	14.1	48.4	24 616	11.9	40.8	6 514	3.1	10.8
Physician services	442	1.5	97.8	9.7	0.0	2.2	0.0	0.0	0.0
Hospital services	933	1.6	16.8	1 508	2.6	27.1	3 119	5.5	56.1
Drugs	9 328[a]	29.8	18.7	9 815	31.4	51.3	0.0	0.0	0.0
Dental care	4 723	37.9	40.4	6 977	56.0	59.6	0.0	0.0	0.0
Other health professionals	4 546	57.5	66.9	2 246	28.4	33.1	0.0	0.0	0.0
Other institutions	5 979	27.7	100.0	0.0	0.0	0.0	0.0	0.0	0.0
Other[b]	3 246	10.0	30.3	4 060	12.5	37.9	3 396	10.5	31.7

Source: CIHI (2014).

Notes: All figures in Can$ millions; figures may not add due to rounding.

[a] This includes out-of-pocket spending on both prescription drugs and over-the-counter medications. Out-of-pocket costs for prescription drugs constitute approximately 70% of this total.

[b] For example, expenditure on capital, public health, administration, health research, personal health supplies, and other health care goods and services.

of revenue for the private insurance industry: private insurers derived 40% of premium revenue from drug insurance and 28% from dental insurance in 2012 (Canadian Institute for Health Information 2014).

Although most provinces decentralized governance in the 1990s, beginning in the early 2000s a number of provinces have recentralized health system governance. Regionalized health authorities generally control institutional care (acute hospital and long-term care), community care (home care services), public health and a variety of smaller programmes. In no instance does their authority extend to public, community-based drug programmes or physician services, which in all provinces are administered by the provincial ministry of health. Provincial governments allocate budget envelopes to regional health authorities based on a mixture of historical funding levels and need criteria, and each regional health authority allocates its budget among the services, programmes and providers over which it has authority. Although regional health authorities increasingly use contractual approaches in their relationships with providers of services, nowhere is the relationship between the regional authorities and providers in their region formally structured as a purchaser–provider split designed to foster an internal market.

Hospitals in Canada are most commonly funded through annual global budgets. The basis for the global budget varies across the provinces and regions. In most settings a hospital's budget includes a large purely historical component, but hospital funding methods increasingly incorporate factors based on a hospital's case-mix adjusted volume. Physician services are funded predominantly by fee-for-service, though the role of alternative payment methods – including capitation, salary, programmatic funding and incentive-based payments – has been increasing, especially within the primary care sector. Long-term care is funded either through global budgets for public facilities or, for private facilities, through per diem public subsidies to facilities based, in many cases, on standardized assessments of the severity of the condition of residents in a facility (Marchildon, 2013).

All provinces offer a public drug-benefit plan for community-based drug purchases.[6] Public drug coverage is concentrated among older people and individuals on social assistance, but all residents

---

[6] All prescription drugs obtained while an inpatient in a hospital are free (such costs are included in hospital budgets).

are potentially eligible for coverage in British Columbia, Alberta, Saskatchewan, Manitoba, Ontario and Québec, albeit with greater cost-sharing for working-age and/or high-income individuals (Canadian Institute for Health Information, 2012). British Columbia and Manitoba changed from age-based coverage criteria to income-based criteria in 2003 and 1996, respectively. In 1996–1997, Québec introduced a novel public and private financing arrangement for its universal drug coverage scheme, Canada's only explicit public–private insurance partnership (see Box 4.2). Public expenditure on drugs varies across the provinces, ranging from a low of 33–37% of prescription drug expenses in Atlantic provinces (Newfoundland, Prince Edward Island, Nova Scotia and New Brunswick) to nearly 50% in Saskatchewan (Canadian Institute for Health Information 2015).

Box 4.2 Québec's mixed public–private universal drug plan

In 1997, the province of Québec implemented a compulsory prescription drug insurance plan for all its residents designed on a social insurance basis. Universal coverage is achieved through a coordinated mixture of private insurance plans, most often available through employment, and a public plan, administered by the *Régie de l'assurance maladie du Québec*. The *Régie* was established in 1969 with the objective to develop the public health insurance plan in the province of Québec. All residents under the age of 65 who are eligible for a private plan must obtain at least its prescription drug coverage component for themselves, their spouse and children, provided their spouse and children are not already covered by another private plan. Insurance plans provided by employers may have eligibility requirements (for example, exclude part-time, temporary or contractual employees) and may not provide coverage to all employees. However, risk selection based on age, sex or health status is not permitted. The premium is negotiated between the policy-holder (that is, typically a group plan sponsor such as an employer, union or association) and the insurer, but is paid by the persons insured.[a] The *Régie* sets the maximum annual individual contribution to the cost of such insurance (Can$1046 effective from

---

Box 4.2 (cont.)

July 2016 to June 2017). The *Régie*, in collaboration with *Revenu Québec*, conducts eligibility verifications to ensure that those who have access to a private plan do not obtain coverage from the public plan. When turning 65, those who have access to a private plan with basic prescription drug coverage can choose to retain their private plan coverage or join the public plan.

The public prescription drug insurance plan provides coverage to persons aged 65 and over, social assistance recipients, persons who do not have access to a private plan, and children of persons covered by the public plan. The public plan charges a premium collected through income tax; the premium is capped at Can\$660 per adult per year (effective from July 2016 to June 2017), depending on net family income.[b] The public plan covers prescription drugs listed on a formulary published by the *Régie*. Individuals must register for the public plan. Failure to register does not exempt individuals from paying the premium and payment of the premium is not a substitute for registration. Individuals who fail to register receive no drug coverage. See Pomey et al. (2007) for additional details on the introduction and design of Québec's programme.

Notes: [a] As of 1 January 2007, an employer is obliged to deduct premiums for private prescription drug insurance from employee remuneration unless the employee is covered under another private insurance plan.

[b] The following individuals are exempt from paying the premium: children of insured persons, social assistance recipients, low-income seniors, seniors who have a private prescription drug plan whose benefits exceed those contained in the public plan. (Seniors who have private coverage more limited than that of the public plan must pay the premium.)

Canadian health care, like health care systems around the world, faces a number of difficult challenges. Some of the prominent current policy challenges include long waiting times for selected services, shortages and a maldistribution of some health professionals, an outmoded primary care delivery system dominated by physicians in solo or small group practice, a drug sector with ever-rising costs and increasing access problems for some Canadians, and dated information systems that impede information sharing and the creation of an electronic health record.

The development of private health insurance in Canada

Canada's current financing and delivery arrangements largely derive from a series of policy decisions made in the 1950s and 1960s, which themselves reflected an assessment at that time of the contribution that private insurance could make to achieving key policy goals. The 1930s witnessed both the emergence of private health care insurance as a marketed commodity and some of the first initiatives to provide public insurance. A survey conducted by the Canadian Medical Association in 1934 identified 27 hospital prepayment plans operating in six provinces (Hall, 1964). Under prepayment plans (akin to modern health maintenance organizations in the United States), the hospital was both the insurer and provider: an individual paid a fixed premium to a hospital in return for the provision of specified services should they be needed during the period covered. The first "Blue Cross" prepaid plan for hospital services was established in Manitoba in 1937 (Hall, 1964).[7] This was quickly followed by Blue Cross plans in Ontario in 1941, Québec in 1942, the Maritimes and British Columbia in 1943 and Alberta Blue Cross in 1948. Profession-sponsored (and controlled) prepayment plans for medical services developed in parallel with the spread of hospital insurance. The first such plan was offered in Toronto in 1937, followed by plans in Windsor, Ontario and Regina, Saskatchewan in 1939, and then a series of plans across Canada during the 1940s. The Medical Services Association of British Columbia, established in 1940, was the first province-wide medical plan. Life insurance companies and casualty insurance companies (which insure all risks other than life) also began offering various types of health care and disability insurance during this period, with life insurance companies tending to focus on the group market while casualty insurers concentrated on the individual market. Finally, insurance cooperatives played an important role, especially in the early part of this period and in the west of Canada.

During the same period, calls for public insurance programmes grew as well, especially in the western provinces that were particularly hard hit by the depression. These initiatives often found considerable support

---

[7] Blue Cross is an association of independent, regionally operating health insurance plans that conform to defined plan criteria. Blue Cross began as an association of hospital prepayment plans in the USA. Blue Cross Canada is organizationally distinct from its US counterpart, though they operate on the same model.

within the medical profession, in part for purely economic reasons: many patients could not pay for care privately, making it difficult for a physician to maintain a practice. The public efforts included municipally based initiatives, such as the municipal doctor programme and the creation of hospital districts to finance and oversee hospitals, and provincial initiatives to introduce public insurance. Both Alberta and British Columbia passed public health insurance plans in the 1930s, though neither plan was implemented. National health care insurance was a central element in the federal government's vision for post-war social programmes. The federal plan, however, was scuttled in the breakdown of the federal–provincial Dominion talks in 1945, leaving provinces to act alone. In 1946 Saskatchewan became the first province to implement a provincial hospital insurance plan. Saskatchewan was followed in 1949 by British Columbia and Alberta.

By the 1950s voluntary insurance had made considerable in-roads into the Canadian middle class. This had a number of important impacts vis-à-vis public and private financing. It reduced the pressure for large-scale public action because a substantial proportion of the population had access to at least some insurance. It also weakened physician support for public insurance, especially public medical insurance. The medical profession strongly advocated for private plans, particularly physician-sponsored plans, which retained control and power for the profession. These developments altered the nature of the debate regarding public health insurance. Rather than public insurance, many analysts now advocated limiting the public role to public subsidy for low-income individuals that would enable them to purchase private insurance. The success of both the voluntary private insurance plans and the few then-existing provincial public plans demonstrated the soundness of such insurance plans and the value people placed on insurance. The gaps in private coverage (even in urban Ontario) suggested, however, that private insurance could never provide universal coverage, and the increasing demands on provincial and local resources and on hospitals themselves provided an opportunity for the federal government to act on its national vision. The result was the Hospital Insurance and Diagnostic Services Act of 1957. This legislation provided universal public insurance for inpatient hospital services financed through a combination of provincial revenue (raised through a variety of specific instruments across the provinces) and matching federal grants. The provincial hospital insurance plans supplanted private insurance for medically necessary inpatient services. Hospital benefits offered by private insurance shrank to supplementary, mostly nonmedical, services associated with a hospitalization (for example, room upgrade from ward to semi-private).

The huge success of public hospital insurance, the growing importance to Canadians of access to a wide range of health care services and, ironically, concern by the medical profession over growing support for public universal insurance (rather than public subsidy to private insurance) prompted the establishment in 1961 of the Royal Commission on Health Services led by Justice Emmett Hall (hereafter the "Hall Commission"). The Hall Commission was given a broad mandate with respect to the planning, delivery and financing of health care in Canada. The starting point for the Commission's assessment of private and public insurance options was the principle that all Canadians should have access to necessary health care, a principle agreed to by all major stakeholders such as the medical profession, private insurers, business and consumer groups. Major stakeholders, however, differed on the best policies for achieving this objective. The medical profession, private insurers and private industry argued that this could best be achieved through private insurance supplemented with public subsidies to those who otherwise could not afford such insurance; others argued for a system of universal public insurance. The Commission judged three issues as central to the policy choice: the ability of voluntary insurance to provide universal comprehensive insurance; the costs associated with means-testing to determine eligibility for a public subsidy; and the legitimacy of compelling individuals to participate in such a public insurance scheme. In the end, the Commission recommended, in addition to the then-existing system of universal hospital insurance, a system of universal public insurance for medical services, dental services, drugs and home care. This recommendation was based on the judgement that a system of private insurance, even accompanied by public subsidies, could not achieve universal coverage and access;[8] that the number of persons requiring subsidy under a private system would be large and that means-testing would require a large, expensive and unnecessary administrative infrastructure; and that compulsory membership of

---

[8] This conclusion was based on the observation that private insurance had left a substantial portion of Canadians uncovered at that time and the experience of Australia, which since 1953 had been unable to achieve universal coverage through a system of private voluntary insurance and public subsidy.

a universal public plan would not violate fundamental rights. The Commission viewed universal public insurance as a less costly way to achieve universal coverage than a system based on private insurance (Hall, 1964).[9]

Based on the Commission's recommendations, the federal government passed the Medical Care Act of 1966 which, like the 1957 Hospital Insurance and Diagnostic Services Act, provided for a system of matching federal grants to provincial medical care insurance plans that met defined criteria of universality, comprehensiveness, public administration and portability. By 1972, all provinces had public plans that complied with these principles. Because of fiscal concerns, the legislation excluded drugs, dental care and home care services. The 1957 Hospital Insurance and Diagnostic Services Act and the 1966 Medical Care Act, later consolidated in the 1984 Canada Health Act, defined the basic roles of public and private insurance in Canada that exist to this day.

The current market for private health insurance

Who has private health insurance coverage?

No single source summarizes the number and characteristics of Canadians who hold private health insurance. Figures regarding various aspects of private insurance coverage demonstrate that a large majority of Canadians hold some type of private health insurance. The majority of those covered obtain insurance as a benefit of employment (of themselves, a spouse or a parent). The data are most comprehensive for private drug coverage. Self-reported data from the 2014 Canadian Community Health Survey indicate, for instance, that 54% of Ontarians held employer-based prescription drug coverage and 5% held individually purchased drug insurance (Statistics Canada, 2014).[10] These self-reported data suggest somewhat lower coverage than other sources. The Canadian Life and Health Insurance Association (CLHIA), for example,

---

[9] With regard to the administrative costs of means-testing, it observed that: "The health services will make enough demand on our resources. We must not waste them" (Hall, 1964: 743). It also noted that the administrative costs of private voluntary insurers would exceed those of a public insurer (such costs were estimated to be 22% higher), again wasting valuable resources better allocated to health care itself.

[10] An additional 16% reported government-provided coverage.

estimates that about 24 million Canadians (or about two thirds) were covered by private extended health care insurance (that is, insurance schemes that reimburse expenses such as prescription drugs, dental, hospital and medical expenses, not covered by provincial government plans) in 2015 (CLHIA, 2016).

In 2005, among those who were employed, the rates of coverage for health-related benefits varied substantially according to the sector of employment, workplace size (employers with over 500 employees were three times more likely to offer such benefits than those with fewer than 20), part-time/full-time status (full-time employees were three times more likely to receive benefits), earnings (those earning Can $20 per hour or more were 2.9 times more likely to receive benefits than those earning less than Can$12 per hour) and union status (unionized employees were about 30% more likely to receive benefits than non-unionized employees) (Statistics Canada, 2008).

Insurance organizations

Three types of insurers in Canada sell private health care insurance: for-profit health and life insurance companies, non-profit insurance organizations whose primary business is health coverage, and for-profit property and casualty insurers whose primary business is not health-related. The market is dominated by for-profit life and health insurers, which nationally account for approximately 80% of the private health insurance market; non-profit health insurers rank next; property and casualty insurers constitute less than 5% of the market.[11] The relative market shares of these different types of insurance organizations vary by province, and the non-profit insurers in particular have a strong regional structure. The most recent available data indicate that in the early 2000s just over 80% of insurers operated in more than one province and were subject to both federal and provincial regulations; the

---

[11] Estimates vary by source and time period; good, comprehensive data are not readily available. A publication from the Department of Finance suggests that for-profit life and health organizations account for up to 90% of private health insurance sold in Canada (Department of Finance, 2002). The Director of Statistical Services at the Canadian Life and Health Insurance Association estimated that the large non-profit insurers account for about 20% of the market, though she noted that this was based on limited data available (A. Freeburn, personal communication).

remainder operated in a single province and were subject to provincial regulation only (Vella & Faubert, 2001).

The primary source of information on private insurers comes from an annual factbook published by an industry trade organization, the CLHIA. Although the CLHIA membership is made up of life and health insurance companies, and does not include property and casualty insurers, some of the data reported in the annual CLHIA factbook includes property and casualty insurers. Consequently, the data reported represents over 99% of the for-profit insurance organizations (I. Klatt, personal communication).[12]

The CLHIA reported that in 2014, 127 insurance organizations sold health insurance products in Canada (CLHIA, 2015). Nearly all were incorporated in Canada (93) or the United States (23). The sector has been subject to a number of mergers and acquisitions since the mid-1990s, which has increased market concentration in the industry. Among the 127 insurance organizations, 64 life and health insurance companies and 16 not-for-profit health care benefit providers sold over 99% of all private complementary health care and disability insurance products and 47 property and casualty companies sold the balance. The vast majority of the 64 life and health insurance companies were incorporated as publicly traded stock companies; the remaining were mutual companies formally owned by the policy-holders. Since 1997 many insurance organizations have changed status from mutual companies to for-profit stock companies traded on stock exchanges. This transformation was allowed by regulatory changes in 1997 and 1998 and has been motivated by the companies' desire to gain access to equity capital (Vella & Faubert, 2001). The non-profit sector has only a few

---

[12] CLHIA factbooks include data from all life and health insurers and nearly all of the health insurance business of property and casualty insurers, regardless of whether they are members of CLHIA. Recent editions of the CLHIA factbooks report data about the health insurance business of federally registered and provincially incorporated insurance providers in Canada. This includes insurance companies (life and property and casualty), fraternal benefit societies, provincial Blue Cross organizations and other not-for-profit health care benefit providers. Casualty insurers, such as automobile insurers, also finance health care needed as a result of accidents covered by auto insurance policies. Such coverage is excluded from data reported by the CLHIA; we also exclude such coverage from consideration because it is not associated with health insurance policies (Klatt, 2008; CLHIA, 2014, 2015, 2016).

firms that operate nationally, and is dominated by regional Blue Cross organizations, which are associated with the Blue Cross and Blue Shield Association in the United States (Blue Cross, 2016).[13]

Insurance products

Private insurers in Canada offer nine basic types of health-related insurance (Table 4.3). Extended health care plans insure a range of hospital and other health care expenses not covered by a provincial public insurance plan, including hospital amenities, prescription drugs, non-physician providers, vision care, medical devices, travel insurance and ambulance service. Policies normally include deductibles and coinsurance provisions as well as annual and/or lifetime maxima for specific types of services. The details vary by plan, and cost-sharing is in general increasing, but cost-sharing provisions are usually relatively minor for hospital services and prescription drugs. Private prescription drug coverage, for example, typically has an annual individual or family deductible of Can$25 per individual or Can$50 per family; requires 20% cost-sharing above the deductible; and might have an out-of-pocket payment limit of approximately Can$2000. The coverage may be more limited for other services in the plan, depending on the coverage purchased by the plan sponsor. Coverage for nonphysician services such as physiotherapy, chiropractic care or counselling may be limited to a specific number of visits annually or a maximum dollar amount (for example, Can$500–600), depending on the plan sponsor's selection (I. Klatt, personal communication).

The market for extended health care insurance is heavily dominated by group contracts provided by employers to employees or purchased through professional orders, associations and unions for their members. Group contracts dominate for the usual reasons: for workers, the value of such an employment benefit is tax exempt (more on this below); for others, access to a group policy through an association (for example, a farm cooperative) offers substantially lower premiums than those available in the individual market; and, for insurers, group contracts incur

[13] This regional structure is beginning to blur. Medavie Blue Cross, for instance, sells both individual and group policies in New Brunswick, Nova Scotia, Prince Edward Island and Newfoundland, but also sells group policies only in Québec and Ontario.

Table 4.3 *Private health insurance products in Canada, 2014*

Insurance product	Description	Population covered in 2014 in 000s	
		Group policies[a]	Individual policies
Extended health care insurance[b]	Covers the following services where they are not publicly insured: hospital services, prescription drugs, non-physician providers, vision care, travel insurance and other miscellaneous services	39 100 (110.0%) 25 000 insured policies 14 100 uninsured policies (provide administrative services only)	1 900 (5.3%)
Hospital insurance only	Covers only nonmedically necessary hospital ancillary services	618 (1.7%)	106 (0.3%)
Prescription-drug insurance only	Covers community-based prescription drugs	772 (2.2%)	not reported
Dental insurance	Covers community-based dental services	15 200 (42.8%)	444 (1.2%)
Critical illness insurance	Provides a lump-sum cash payment on the first diagnosis of one of several contractually specified conditions	1 700 (4.8%)	
Long-term care insurance	Provides contractually specified payments for those who can no longer function independently due to physical or cognitive impairment and/or ageing	261 (0.7%)	87 (0.2%)

Long-term disability insurance	Provides income replacement at a contractually specified rate in the event of long-term disability	11 037 (31.1%) 10 100 insured policies 937 uninsured policies	970 (2.7%)
Short-term disability insurance	Provides income replacement at a contractually specified rate in the event of short-term disability	500 (127%) 2 600 insured policies 1 900 uninsured policies	not reported
Accidental death and dismemberment insurance	Provides contractually specified cash payment in the event of death or loss of one or more body parts as a result of an accident	18 800 (52.9%)	2 200 (6.2%)
Travel insurance only	Covers the costs of emergency medical services (that are not publicly insured) required when travelling outside Canada	9 700 (27.3%) As a separate benefit included with some extended health care plans[c]	

Source: Coverage figures obtained from CLHIA (2015)

Notes: Figures in parentheses indicate the number covered as a proportion of the Canadian population.

[a] Includes an unknown amount of double-counting when two (or more) members of a household each obtain coverage for themselves and their dependants from different group policies. Hence, the figures overestimate the extent of private insurance coverage. The CLHIA estimates that adjusting for double-counting reduces the number of Canadians covered through these plans to about 24 million for private complementary health benefits and 20 million for dental care benefits.

[b] The set of included services varies across policies. The defining feature is that a single policy covers multiple types of services that are not publicly insured. All policies include hospital services; most include prescription drugs; the variation is largest for other services.

[c] Most group coverage is obtained as part of extended health policies. Most individual policies are sold at time of travel on a trip-by-trip basis. 9.9 million individual policies sold in 2009.

lower overhead costs and reduce the potential for adverse selection. In 2015, revenue from group contracts constituted 90% of total premium revenue (CLHIA, 2016).

Most complementary hospital and prescription drugs are obtained through extended health care benefits, so the markets are considerably smaller for policies that provide only complementary hospital coverage or only prescription drug coverage (I. Klatt, personal communication; CLHIA, 2015, 2016). Dental plans cover community-based dental services only. Dental coverage is normally obtained through stand-alone policies and is not included in an extended health care policy. Dental policies also normally include modest deductibles and cost-sharing in the range of 20% above the deductible.

Disability income insurance plans insure against lost income if one is unable to work due to accident or ill health.[14] Both accidental death and dismemberment insurance and critical illness insurance are indemnity policies that pay a pre-specified amount of money when a specified health-related event occurs. Accidental death and dismemberment insurance pays the predetermined amount, which varies according to the injury, to those who die or are dismembered in an accident. Critical illness insurance provides a predetermined payment if any of a pre-specified set of critical illnesses occur, such as heart attack, stroke and cancer. In recent years it has been one of the fastest-growing types of private insurance in Canada because it avoids restrictions on private insurance for publicly insured services (it does not cover any services per se) while providing resources to purchase private care if necessary in the event of a serious illness. Nearly all of its coverage is through individual polices, although it is increasingly included in extended health care policies provided to employees by employers. The number of Canadians covered under critical illness plans on either a group or an individual basis increased from 1.1 million to 1.7 million between 2009 and 2014 (CLHIA, 2010, 2015).

From the early 2000s, long-term care insurance has emerged as a new private insurance product in Canada but the market for such a product remains underdeveloped (Colombo et al., 2011; SCOR, 2003). Fewer than 350 000 Canadians were covered under long-term care insurance plans in 2014 (a lower number than in 2010) (CLHIA, 2014, 2015).

---

[14] Disability income insurance typically supplements income provided by the Canada or Québec Pension Plans, Workers' Compensation and/or Employment Insurance.

Travel insurance covers costs associated with emergency medical services required while travelling outside Canada.[15] It is most commonly obtained as part of an extended health care policy, but can also be purchased on a trip-by-trip basis from travel-related agencies.

In addition to standard group insurance plans, some employers offer a type of defined contribution plan called Health Spending Accounts. Such accounts can either substitute for or complement standard insurance benefits depending on the overall set of benefits provided by an employer. Under a Health Spending Accounts plan, each year an employer makes a predetermined contribution to an employee's health spending account (the amount must be specified before the start of the year). These funds are then available to an employee to fund eligible health-related services, defined as the services that would qualify for the medical expense tax credit in the tax code. Unspent balances at the end of the first year can be rolled over into the second year, but at the end of the second year after which a contribution is made, tax regulations require that the employee forfeit unspent balances (which revert to the employer). The employer's contributions are tax deductible for the employer and non-taxable to the employee. The market for Health Spending Accounts is very small.

Finally, private insurers in Canada also sell administrative services to governments and to private sector organizations that self-insure their members. Medavie Blue Cross, the Atlantic Canada Blue Cross organization, for example, provides administrative services to a number of public insurance programmes.[16] It also offers, on contract with the Ministry of Health, nongroup, individual complementary health insurance plans (Alberta Blue Cross and Alberta Health and Wellness, 2007). Plans that

[15] Provincial coverage must be portable within Canada, and most provincial public plans provide some coverage for emergency care required while travelling. But the provincial plans usually reimburse at Canadian rates, which are considerably lower than charges incurred in other countries, especially the United States, which is a popular destination for Canadians.

[16] Under contract with the federal government Medavie Blue Cross administers health claims for veterans, members of the Canadian Forces and members of the Royal Canadian Mounted Police. In Nova Scotia, it administers the Nova Scotia Medical Services Insurance, the province's public insurance plan for physician services, and Nova Scotia's Senior's Pharmacare and Family Benefits Pharmacare programmes. In New Brunswick, it has since 1975 administered the province's Prescription Drug Program. Similarly, Alberta Blue Cross administers the province's Palliative Care Drug Coverage, Prescription Drug Benefits and Dental Assistance for Seniors programmes.

private insurers administer on behalf of private companies are called "uninsured plans", for which employers accept the financial risk but contract out the administration of the benefits. At the end of 2014 such plans covered more than 14 million individuals (5.7 million workers and 8.4 million dependants) with extended health care insurance, 13 million (5.5 million workers and 5.1 million dependants) with dental care coverage, and 2.4 million workers with long-term and 970 000 workers with short-term disability income insurance. Premium income from uninsured plans constituted 41% of all premium income for group insurance plans (CLHIA, 2016).

Private health insurance regulation

Private health care insurers in Canada are subject to two types of government regulation: regulation intended to ensure the financial solvency of insurers and regulation of the types of policies offered by private insurers and the terms and conditions under which the policies are sold.

Financial regulation

Financial regulation is conducted by the Office of the Superintendent of Financial Institutions at the federal level and, in the province of Québec, by the Financial Markets Authority (*Autorité des marchés financiers*). The Office of the Superintendent of Financial Institutions and the Financial Markets Authority conduct regular inspections and insurers are required to submit annual returns to document solvency. All insurers (for-profit and non-profit) are required by federal government regulations to be a member of Assuris, an industry-funded non-profit organization that protects policy-holders in the event that an insurer becomes insolvent. Assuris guarantees policy-holders recovery of 100% of the promised benefits for health expenses below Can$60 000 and 85% of health expenses above Can$60 000.

Regulation of insurance products

Provincial governments regulate the market for private health insurance both directly, by regulating the provision of private health insurance, and indirectly, by regulating the provision of private health care services. Canadian regulation of the design of insurance products, their pricing and their sale are for two reasons relatively weak by international standards. First, as has been emphasized, private insurance has for 50 years played a minor role in health care financing, and no role for core hospital and physician services. Second, most people obtain private insurance through group contracts in which they face little or no choice. Hence, the private insurance sector in Canada has not been subject to the kinds of policy focus found in settings in which people rely on private health insurance as a major source of financial protection and people must obtain such insurance through individual policies. Undoubtedly some negative effects of market failure, discrimination, strategic policy design and other phenomena exist in some Canadian markets, but to date they have been rare enough or small enough to escape policy concern.

The most important product regulation is that which prohibits private insurers from covering publicly insured medical and hospital services. Five provinces (British Columbia, Alberta, Manitoba, Ontario and Prince Edward Island) prohibit private insurers from covering publicly insured physician and hospital services. In the province of Québec, private insurers are only permitted to cover publicly insured services for very few selected services, including total hip or knee replacements and cataract extractions with intraocular lens implantations.[17] Provincial governments have indirectly limited the growth of private insurance through regulation of physicians and the fees they charge for private services, which has made the provision of privately financed services also covered by the public plan financially non-lucrative. For publicly insured physician services, most provinces require that a physician either fully opt into the provincial plan or fully opt out; a physician cannot choose to charge privately for some patients but publicly for others.[18]

---

[17] For more details, see Québec Health Insurance Act, Section 15. (www .legisquebec.gouv.qc.ca/en/ShowDoc/cs/A-29)

[18] Since September 2004 physicians in Ontario have been prohibited from opting out of the public plan and receiving payment from a private third party, though physicians who opted out before September 2004 were exempt. Four provinces (Alberta, Saskatchewan, New Brunswick and Prince Edward Island) do allow physicians to opt out for specific patients and bill the patients directly rather than bill the provincial plan. In Alberta and Saskatchewan, physicians billing patients directly cannot charge a fee higher than the fee in the public plan (so there is no incentive to bill directly); patients can also seek reimbursement from the provincial plan. New Brunswick and Prince

A physician would therefore have to support an entire practice through private, out-of-pocket payment by patients, which is not feasible for most physicians. In addition, many provinces also regulate the fees that can be charged by physicians who opt out of the public plan (Flood & Archibald, 2001). Manitoba, Ontario and Nova Scotia prohibit opted-out physicians from charging private fees greater than the fees paid by the public plan. Other provinces permit opted-out physicians to charge fees higher than those in the public plan; however, all but Newfoundland and Prince Edward Island prohibit such patients from receiving any public subsidy. Newfoundland is the only province that currently allows private health insurance coverage for publicly insured physician and hospital services, allows opted-out physicians to charge more than the public fee and allows patients to receive public coverage for a service even when the fees charged are higher than those of the public plan. In such cases, the physician must bill the patient directly and the patient must subsequently obtain reimbursement from the province as is applicable. As noted above, few physicians have opted out of the public plan: in 2013 no physicians were opted out in seven of the ten provinces – Alberta, Saskatchewan, Manitoba, New Brunswick, Nova Scotia, Prince Edward Island and Newfoundland – while two were opted out in British Columbia and 24 in Ontario (Health Canada, 2015). In 2016, 339 physicians were opted out in Québec (71 specialists and 261 general practitioners) (RAMQ, 2016).

Regulation of premiums and the terms of sale

Neither the federal government nor any provincial government regulates the premiums that private insurers can charge for health insurance.

Tax regulations

A number of regulations within the federal and provincial tax codes support private health insurance in Canada. Currently, both the federal government and all provincial governments allow firms to deduct the

---

Edward Island allow physicians to charge a higher fee, but if the physician does so, the patient cannot seek reimbursement from the province. Prince Edward Island does not allow private insurance to cover such services; private insurance could cover such costs in New Brunswick (Boychuk, 2006).

cost of health benefits provided to employees. The federal government and all provinces except Québec exclude the value of such benefits from the employee's taxable income. The exclusion of health insurance benefits from taxable income dates from 1948, and the current value of this tax expenditure is estimated to be Can$2.5 billion in 2013 for the federal government alone (Department of Finance, 2016). Public spending on health in Canada was estimated to be Can$145 billion in 2013 (Canadian Institute for Health Information 2015), suggesting that combined federal and provincial tax expenditures associated with private health insurance constitute about 3% of public health care spending in Canada. A number of provincial governments have attempted to remove this tax provision, and the federal government last debated removing it in 1994. Only the government of Québec succeeded in doing so: since 1993 Québec has included the value of employer-provided health insurance in taxable income.

Both the federal government and provincial governments also provide a set of health-related tax credits. The two most important are the medical expense tax credit (value of approximately Can$1.3 billion in 2013) and the disability tax credit (value of Can$770 million in 2013) (Department of Finance, 2016). The medical expense tax credit allows individuals to claim a tax credit for eligible medical expenses greater than 3% of their income, or Can$2228 (in 2015), whichever is greater.[19] Premiums paid by individuals for private insurance qualify as a medical expense under this provision.[20] This provision affects private insurance in three ways: it reduces the net cost of out-of-pocket payment, dampening demand for private insurance; it subsidizes insurance by making an insurance premium an eligible expense; and the set of services eligible for the tax credit also defines the services eligible to be paid from a health spending account. The disability tax credit applies to individuals with a severe and prolonged mental or physical impairment. In 2016 it equalled Can$7889 for qualifying individuals.

[19] The list of eligible expenses is varied, ranging from the expected ones such as eyeglasses, ambulance expenses, dental and drug expenditures to, under defined circumstances, air conditioners and furnaces for those with respiratory problems, vehicle and home modifications, the incremental cost of gluten-free products for those with coeliac disease and note-taking services for the disabled.

[20] In Québec, a premium paid by an employer, which counts toward taxable income, is also eligible to count toward the tax credit.

Assessment of market performance

Because private health insurance plays a relatively limited, complementary role in financing health care in Canada, with the exception of a few sectors, its overall effects on market performance are correspondingly small. As has been emphasized, by policy design, private insurance plays no meaningful role for medically necessary physician and hospital services; its role in these sectors is limited to inpatient amenities and a small set of non-publicly covered services. It has also played no meaningful role for long-term care and home care services because market penetration for insurance products is so low.

Private insurance has had the largest impact on system performance through its operations in the drug and dental sectors. But even here its impact on overall performance has historically been limited by the small size of these sectors and, in the case of dental care, the absence of a strong substitute or complementary relationship between dental services and other health care services, and a lack of public concern regarding access to dental care beyond a small set of specific services such as serious oral surgery or specific groups such as children. Drug financing, however, emerged as a central policy concern during the 1990s as drugs became both a growing component of overall health expenditure and an essential therapeutic agent for an expanding set of medical conditions. In 1996–1997 Québec established its universal drug coverage through its mixed public–private approach; in 1997 the National Forum on Health recommended national universal publicly financed drug coverage (National Forum on Health, 1997), and in 2002 both the Romanow and the Kirby Commissions recommended publicly financed national catastrophic drug coverage (Commission on the Future of Health Care in Canada, 2002; Senate of Canada, 2002). More recently, calls for a national pharmacare have intensified (Morgan et al., 2015).

The limited role of private insurance in financing health care means that the private insurance sector in Canada has been little studied.[21] Policy and research attention have focused overwhelmingly for the last 35 years on the publicly financed system. We know surprisingly little

---

[21] A relatively small group of strong advocates of a greater role for private insurance, however, has ensured that it has remained part of the policy debate, and the iconic and media value of private insurance – conveyed primarily through anecdote and story – is disproportionately large given its limited role in financing health care in Canada.

about either the operation of the private insurance sector or the effects of its activities. This is changing because the role of private insurance is central to some of the current policy challenges facing Canadian health care, but there remains a relative dearth of publicly available data and information upon which to base studying the private insurance sector.

Financial protection

Private insurance in Canada contributes in only a minor way to universal protection against financial costs. Public insurance fully covers medically necessary physician and hospital services. Private insurance coverage is a trivial source of finance for long-term care and home care. Extended health care insurance generally covers at least some non-physician providers, but such coverage is often restricted to a small number of visits annually or to low limits on maximum annual coverage. Indeed, the policies are structured so as to provide minimal financial protection: they cover occasional use of such providers for routine services while doing little to help those who may need regular, ongoing, more intensive care. Although private insurance finances a majority of community-based dental care, such services are generally not a large source of financial risk. The bulk of insurance payments cover routine visits and minor procedures that are both modest and quite predictable. Private insurance contributes the most toward financial protection in the drug sector, where it covers a large number of individuals not covered by public insurance programmes. Drug spending is becoming an increasing source of financial risk to individuals as the use of drugs in treatment expands and the costs of new drugs marches ever upward. Private drug insurance policies generally include small deductibles and cost-sharing provisions (though they are increasing), maximum out-of-pocket spending limits and relatively high maximum coverage limits, so the plans provide important financial protection.

Equity in financing

Canadian health policy is strongly committed to equity in health care financing. Policy documents explicitly interpret equity in finance as horizontal equity, which requires equal contributions by those with equal ability to pay, and vertical equity, which requires contributions to be directly related to ability to pay. Policy statements are less clear as to whether vertical equity implies progressivity in finance, whereby contributions increase as a proportion of income. The Romanow Commission offered one of the few explicit judgements on this in positing that vertical equity implies progressivity (Commission on the Future of Health Care in Canada, 2002).

Only a limited number of studies have empirically assessed equity in health care financing in Canada. Fewer still have examined private finance. Nonetheless, findings across studies are generally consistent and it is possible to draw a few conclusions from existing evidence.

Public finance to support health care appears to be essentially proportional or perhaps mildly progressive. The two largest sources of public revenue are income and consumption taxes, which have counteracting effects: income taxes are progressive but consumption taxes are regressive. McGrail (2007) estimated that public financing for physician and hospital services in British Columbia in both 1992 and 2002 was effectively proportional (Kakwani indices of progressivity of 0.021 and 0.026, respectively). Hanley et al. (2007) found that public finance for prescription drugs in British Columbia over the period 2000–2005 was proportional (annual Kakwani indices of –0.002 to –0.008 over the period). Mustard et al. (1998) similarly found that public finance in Manitoba in both 1986 and 1994 was essentially proportional. Smythe (2002), however, found public financing in Alberta to be more strongly progressive. Provincial public contributions as a proportion of income, for example, rose from 4% to 8% between the lowest and highest income deciles.

Two studies (Mustard et al., 1998; McGrail, 2007) conducted net fiscal incidence analyses for the health sector that considered both tax payments to finance health care and benefits received in the form of publicly financed health care services. Utilization of health care services is highly regressive – the value of services received by low-income individuals is a much higher proportion of their income than it is for high-income individuals (both because absolute levels of utilization by low-income individuals are greater than for high-income individuals and because any given amount of utilization is a larger share of income for a low-income individual than for a high-income individual). Hence, both found that, because contributions are roughly proportional to income but use is highly regressive, the incidence of net benefits is highly progressive: on net, for low-income groups in Canada the value of publicly financed services received far exceeds their contribution, so the health care system redistributes economic resources from high-income groups to low-income groups.

Studies of the incidence of private insurance financing are more limited. Private insurance coverage is strongly related to income, causing contributions for private insurance to increase with income. Smythe (2001), for instance, estimated that in 1994 only 4% of households with incomes less than Can$5000 had access to employer-sponsored private insurance; the proportion rose to 54% for those with incomes between Can$20 000 and Can$30 000, and was over 90% for households with incomes greater than Can$60 000. Bhatti, Rana & Grootendorst (2007) found a substantial positive income gradient with respect to holding private dental insurance. Controlling for a range of demographic and health factors, the probability that those with an income of over Can$80 000 held private dental insurance was 34 percentage points greater than those with an income of less than Can$15 000. Hanley et al. (2007), however, estimated that prescription drug financing through private insurance in British Columbia was mildly regressive (Kakwani index –0.10) in both 2000 and 2005. Smythe (2002) estimated that private financing (including both out-of-pocket and private insurance payments) in Alberta was regressive (Kakwani index –0.12). We are not aware of any net incidence studies for private health insurance in Canada.

The exclusion of the value of employer-provided health insurance from employees' taxable income generates substantial tax expenditures. This tax exclusion reduces a person's income tax payment in proportion to their marginal tax rate; for middle- and low-income individuals its exclusion from income reduces payroll taxes for the Canadian Pension Plan and Employment Insurance; and for low-income workers it increases eligibility for rebates of the General Services Tax. Smythe (2001) estimated that the value of these tax expenditures in 1994 was less than Can$0.50 per household for households with incomes below Can$5000 and Can$250 for households with incomes over Can$100 000. Hence, the tax treatment of private insurance generates a strongly regressive element in health care finance.

Corscadden et al. (2014) examined how health care affected the distribution of income by estimating the tax contributions and the value of benefits received from physician services, drugs and hospital services over a person's lifetime and found that benefits received from publicly funded health care in Canada reduce the income gap between the highest and lowest income groups by about 16%.

Equity of utilization

Both federal and provincial governments in Canada identify allocation according to need as the explicit distributional health policy goal for health care services. The primary, though not exclusive, policy designed to achieve this goal is removal of financial barriers at the point of service, especially for physician and hospital services. Equity of utilization of health care has been extensively studied in Canada, reflecting both a strong concern for equity and the availability of population health survey data upon which to assess equity. Here we emphasize recent work that employs the concentration index approach pioneered by the ECuity group (Wagstaff & van Doorslaer, 2000) to estimate income-related equity of utilization. Most of this work has focused on physician and hospital services, although studies of other sectors are increasingly available. A general finding consistent with the international literature is that greater reliance on private finance, including private insurance, is associated with less equity in the utilization of health care services.

Overall, the pattern of findings suggests that, controlling for need, use of general practitioner (GP) services is not strongly related to income in Canada. A first generation of studies that tested for an income gradient using regression methods consistently found that, controlling for need, the coefficient on income was not statistically significant (Birch & Eyles, 1992; Birch, Eyles & Newbold, 1993). More recent studies based on concentration indices obtain a mixture of point estimates that, although statistically different from zero (due in part to large sample sizes), are small in absolute magnitude, suggesting little income-related inequity. van Doorslaer et al. (2005), Jimenez-Rubio, Smith & van Doorslaer (2007) and Marsden & Xu (2009), for instance, obtain slightly pro-poor horizontal equity indices, while Allin (2008) obtains a slightly pro-rich horizontal equity index. Studies consistently found offsetting effects for the likelihood of any visit and the conditional number of visits: the likelihood of any visit to a GP was generally estimated to be pro-rich, but conditional on seeing a GP, the number of visits was distributed pro-poor (that is, low-income individuals had more visits than high-income individuals even after controlling for need).

In contrast, controlling for need, analyses consistently found a pro-rich income-related gradient in the use of specialist services in Canada (Alter, Austin & Tu, 1999; van Doorslaer et al., 2005; Alter et al., 2006; van Doorslaer, 2007; Allin, 2008; Grignon, Hurley & Wang, 2015).

The income-related gradient is modest by international standards, but it nonetheless clearly exists. We do not have a good understanding of what causes this gradient.

Hospital services are distributed in a strongly pro-poor manner even after controlling for need (Jimenez-Rubio, Smith & van Doorslaer, 2007; van Doorslaer, 2007; Allin, 2008). By international standards, the gradient is large. Once again, we do not have a good understanding of what drives this income-related gradient.

Sectors that rely heavily on private finance, including private insurance, tend to exhibit strong income-related gradients in use. Dental care, which is almost entirely privately financed, exhibits the largest income-related gradient (van Doorslaer, 2007; Grignon et al., 2010; Grignon, Hurley & Wang, 2015). Access to drugs has been less studied, but Zhong (2008) found a large impact of drug financing arrangements in Ontario on income-related equity: income-related use of drugs was pro-poor among older people, who are covered by the public insurance programme, but pro-rich among working-age individuals, who must finance drugs privately; furthermore, the introduction of coinsurance provisions in the public programme was associated with a reduction in equity among older people. Allin & Laporte (2011) found that in the Ontario public drug benefit programme for seniors, after adjusting for need, the mean number of drugs claimed was modestly pro-poor and there was little difference in spending on medications between income groups. Kratzer et al. (2015) found that Ontarians with chronic conditions who held private drug insurance were more likely to use prescription drugs than those without.

Rewarding good-quality care and providing incentives for efficiency in the organization and delivery of services

To the best of our knowledge, the private insurance industry has undertaken almost no efforts to improve the quality and efficiency of health care services in Canada. On the contrary, there is some evidence that the private health insurance industry may have become more inefficient. Law, Kratzer & Dhalla (2014) found that the percentage of private health insurance premiums paid out as benefits had decreased markedly in the 1990s and 2000s, leading to a gap between premiums collected and benefits paid of Can$6.8 billion in 2011. The private insurance industry continues to function largely as bill payers. Increasing costs for privately insured services (especially drug costs) is a growing concern for employers, but the most prevalent response has been demand-side cost-sharing. In addition, employers increasingly rely on benefit managers to advise them on how to control such costs.

Administrative costs

Private insurers in Canada incur greater administrative costs than do the public insurers. Woolhandler, Campbell & Himmelstein (2003) estimated that administrative overhead costs for Canadian private insurers were 13.2% of expenditures whereas those of the public system were 1.3%. Indeed, administrative costs for Canadian private insurers slightly exceeded those of US private insurers.

Interactions between the publicly and privately financed health systems

Wherever private insurance and public insurance systems coexist, they inevitably interact. Policy debate has centred mostly on interactions when public and private insurance cover the same services and providers are able to work in both systems. Such a situation can lead to privileged access to those with private insurance, providers playing each system to their advantage, and potentially longer waiting times in the public system as the private system draws scarce resources away.

By prohibiting or making unprofitable private insurance (and private finance more generally) for publicly insured physician and hospital services Canada has successfully minimized such interactions. Canada, however, faces increasing pressure to relax its insurance prohibitions. As noted earlier, in June 2005 the Supreme Court ruled that, in the presence of "unreasonable" waiting times (though it did not define "unreasonable"), Québec's prohibition on private insurance for publicly insured services violated the Québec Charter of Rights and Freedoms. The long-term implications of this decision are not clear. The ruling applied only to Québec. The government of Québec responded by passing legislation that guarantees maximum waiting times for three procedures that in recent years have had long waiting times: hip replacement, knee replacement and cataract removal; enables the creation of private, for-profit clinics; and allows private insurance for only the three above-noted procedures when they are provided by a physician who has opted out of the public plan (Québec National Assembly, 2006); this list was subsequently expanded to include approximately 50 procedures (Contandriopoulos et al., 2012; Government of Québec, 2016). Similar lawsuits are under way in three other provinces, raising the chances of additional decisions against laws prohibiting private insurance and, eventually, a ruling with respect to the Canadian Charter of Rights with national implications (Allen v. Alberta, 2014; Cohn, 2015; Thomas & Flood, 2015; Mertl, 2016). However, the effects on private insurance and private finance remain uncertain even if such bans are struck down nationally because complementary regulations that inhibit the development of private finance would remain in force (Boychuk, 2006). Cohn (2010, 2015) notes that 5 and 10 years after the Chaoulli decision, very few insurance schemes sought to offer coverage for publicly insured services to Canadians. Cohn (2010) was able to document only two small insurance schemes, one of which was more properly characterized as a medical tourism scheme. Similarly, Cohn (2015) was only able to document a few very small niche operators that offered medical tourism coverage. Of note, none of the major insurance companies have sought to capitalize on the Chaoulli v. Québec decision (Cohn, 2015).

The growth of the market for privately financed nonmedically necessary services (paid mostly out of pocket) that fall outside the Canada Health Act increasingly generates interactions with the public system. Such services include traditional cosmetic procedures and an increasing array of "lifestyle" health care services that do not address an underlying health problem but which must be provided by a health professional. Such services constitute one of the fastest-growing components of health care spending. The expansion of such services does not raise equity concerns – they are nonmedically necessary services – but it does generate all of the other potentially negative effects of supplementary private insurance. Specifically, the expansion of such services draws health care inputs (for example, provider time and effort) away from the public system and bids up their prices, compromising the ability of the public system to ensure access to medically necessary services.

The growth of this market in nonmedically necessary services also has more subtle effects. By regulating a physician's ability to opt out and charge fees greater than the public fee, Canada has successfully inhibited the growth of privately financed markets. However, these regulations do not apply to the services, which are not publicly insured. Furthermore, because the financial and physical capital invested to provide such services can often be used to provide both nonmedically necessary and medically necessary publicly insured services, the growth of this sector can make private practice for those doctors who have opted out of the public system increasingly viable through the provision of a mixture of privately financed medically necessary and nonmedically necessary services; and further develop the privately financed sector as this entrepreneurial capital seeks out profitable uses. These forces are still relatively minor in Canada outside a small number of cities, but they are growing.

The heavy reliance on private finance, and private insurance in particular, in the drug sector creates at least three types of policy-relevant interactions between the public and private systems. The first two arise from complementarities between privately financed drugs and publicly insured medical services. Obtaining a prescription drug requires a medical visit and, for many individuals, the expected outcome of a medical visit is a drug prescription. Hence, when a person is ill, if the expected outcome of the visit is a prescription for a drug that must be paid privately, the full cost of the visit is not zero, but rather the free medical visit plus the cost of the prescribed drug. Inability to purchase the resulting prescription may inhibit individuals from making some physician visits. Hence, private finance for drugs distorts the use of publicly financed physician visits toward those with greater ability to pay, either because of higher income or private insurance coverage. Indeed, Stabile (2001) and Devlin, Sarma & Zhang (2011) found that those who have drug insurance were more likely to visit a physician than were those who did not have insurance, while Allin, Law & Laporte (2013) found that Ontario seniors with private prescription drug insurance used more publicly funded medications and incurred more in costs to the public programme (about 16%). Furthermore, Allin & Hurley (2009) found that private insurance contributed to income-related inequity in visits to general/family practitioners in Canada. Wang et al. (2015) evaluated the effects of Québec's mandatory, universal prescription insurance on drug use, and GP and specialist visits, hospitalizations, and health outcomes, and found that it increased prescription use and GP visits, especially among the previously uninsured and those with chronic conditions, while having little effect on specialist visits and hospitalizations. The estimated spillover effect on the number of GP visits was about 10%.

The second interaction rooted in complementarities arises in the cancer sector. The publicly funded cancer system in Ontario (as in other provinces) has chosen not to cover some of the new, very expensive cancer drugs that are judged not to be cost-effective. Because they have been approved for sale, individuals are able to purchase these drugs privately. Such intravenous drugs, however, must be infused in suitable facilities by trained professionals. Such settings are generally found only in the publicly funded hospital facilities that treat cancer patients. In Ontario, for instance, a number of publicly funded hospitals administer privately purchased intravenous cancer drugs and infuse those drugs for private payment, guided by the following recommendations of a Provincial Working Group: (i) the practice does not contravene the Canada Health Act or relevant provincial legislation because the drugs are not publicly funded; (ii) hospitals should administer only drugs for which Cancer Care Ontario's Program in Evidence-Based Care has not issued a recommendation against the use of the drug for the specific indication; (iii) all drugs administered should be prepared by the hospital pharmacy – a hospital is not to infuse a drug purchased elsewhere and brought to the infusion clinic; (iv) patients are to be charged for the costs of the drug only, with no mark-up; and (v) patients are to be charged a fixed infusion fee to cover non-drug costs and, for certain radioimmunotherapies that are more complex to administer, hospitals can charge an additional fixed fee per patient (Provincial Working Group on the Delivery of Oncology Medications for Private Payment in Ontario Hospitals 2006). The working group also recommended that privately funded treatment should not displace publicly funded patients from treatment, though it offered no guidance on policies and practices to ensure this. The recommendations were first implemented at Ontario's 16 regional cancer centres, but ultimately the decision to provide such privately financed services and the precise policies followed rests with individual hospitals.[22]

The third interaction arises when public and private insurers structure benefit plans strategically in an attempt to shift costs on to the other. The Nova Scotia government, for instance, has explicitly made the public Pharmacare programme second payer for seniors who have private drug coverage through their previous employer's retirement benefits. It also requires companies operating in both Nova Scotia and other jurisdictions

---

[22] As far as we are aware, the Ministry has not acted formally on the recommendations of the working group, so they remain as guidance for hospitals.

to offer such retiree benefits to Nova Scotia employees if they are offered to employees in other locations. In Québec, where residents aged 65 or over are automatically covered by the provincial drug insurance plans, businesses have increased the premium they charge retirees for drug coverage to encourage retirees to rely on the public plan rather than the company-provided retirement benefit.

Lastly, arguments about the unsustainability of publicly financed health care in Canada are often based on the observation that health care costs have been rising "too fast" to be sustainable. Ironically, however, one of the fastest-growing components of health care for the last number of years has been drugs, a sector in which private finance and private insurance play a dominant role. Hence, the fast rate of growth for privately financed services can undermine confidence in the long-run sustainability of the overall system, including the public system.

Discussion

Perhaps the most striking aspect of private insurance in Canada has been the virtual policy neglect of the sector since the introduction of public hospital and medical insurance. Public insurance relegated private insurance to a small role on the periphery of policy concern: covering nonmedically necessary physician and hospital services, drugs, dental care and assorted other services. Private insurance was, to a large extent, seen as irrelevant to achieving the core health policy objective of universal access to necessary health care.

This view, however, is changing. Private insurance is back in the Canadian health policy debate, for many different reasons. On one hand, the limited scope of Canada's public insurance programmes fails to ensure access to all medically necessary care, particularly prescription drugs. Ensuring such access will require an expanded role for public finance in the drug sector, with proposals ranging from universal, first-dollar public insurance just as Canadians enjoy for physician and hospital services, to universal public catastrophic coverage, to mixed public–private systems such as in Québec. Neither policy has a clear upper-hand in the debate, so private insurance continues to figure prominently in debates for expanding drug coverage.

Pressure to introduce private supplementary insurance is growing. The pressure emanates from two principal sources: the sustainability debate noted above and waiting times. In Canada, as in nearly all high-income countries, many claim that publicly financed health care is unsustainable and therefore we must inject more private finance. In Canada this is coupled with frustration over the restrictions on private options for publicly financed services, especially where long waits exist for those services, leading to calls for supplementary private insurance as the best particular way to expand private finance. Those who argue that the public health care system is unsustainable as currently financed cite, in particular, the increasing proportion of government programme spending devoted to health care and the implied crowding out of other programmes, such as education (for example, Task Force on the Funding of the Health System, 2008). Opponents argue that conclusions drawn from such trends ignore at least three things: there is much confusion about how to measure programme spending, and the trends differ notably depending on the definition chosen (Béland, 2008); since the late 1990s tax cuts, which presumably represent a policy choice, have had a far larger impact on the ability of governments to fund programme spending than have increases in health care spending (Evans, 2005, 2007; Lahey, 2015; Evans & Smith, 2015); finally, correlation does not imply causation, and more rigorous analysis suggests, for example, that increases in health care spending do not necessarily crowd out other government spending (Landon et al., 2006). There is little evidence that supplementary private insurance decreases waiting times in the public system, and there is evidence that those with private drug coverage use more publicly financed physician services. Good evidence, however, often plays a small role in such debates. Canadians still strongly support the publicly financed health system and its principles, but the power of such superficially compelling arguments among a worried public should not be underestimated in building a popular view that, even if private insurance is second-best, it may nonetheless be the preferred policy among feasible alternatives. Further, given the legal challenges to insurance regulation (for example, in British Columbia), key issues related to the role of private insurance may well be settled through the courts rather than the legislature.

The debate about the role of private insurance in Canada marshals powerful forces on each side and, regardless of the specific ways in which these and related policy debates turn out, two things are certain: Canada can benefit by drawing on the wider international experience with health care finance to craft policies that advance its public policy objectives and minimize the extent to which the development of private insurance detracts from these objectives; and private insurance will figure more prominently in Canadian policy debates in the coming decades than it has since the founding of Medicare.

References

Advisory Panel on Healthcare Innovation (2015). Unleashing Innovation: Excellent Healthcare for Canada. Report of the Advisory Panel on Healthcare Innovation. Ottawa ON: Government of Canada, 2015: http:// healthycanadians.gc.ca/publications/health-system-systeme-sante/report-healthcare-innovation-rapport-soins/alt/report-healthcare-innovation-rapport-soins-eng.pdf; accessed on 18/11/2016.

Alberta Blue Cross and Alberta Health and Wellness (2007). Non-group coverage. Alberta Blue Cross: www.ab.bluecross.ca/government-programs .html; accessed on 23/10/2007.

Allen v Alberta (2014). ABQB 184 (CanLII): http://canlii.ca/t/g6ddt; accessed on 08/11/2016.

Allen v Alberta (2015). ABCA 277 (CanLII): http://canlii.ca/t/gl0z4>; accessed on 09/11/2016.

Allen v Her Majesty the Queen in Right of Alberta (2016). Supreme Court of Canada. Case No. 36715; accessed on18/02/2016.

Allin S (2008). Does Equity in Healthcare Use Vary across Canadian Provinces? *Healthcare Policy*, 3(4):83–99.

Allin S, Hurley J (2009). Inequity in publicly funded physician care: what is the role of private prescription drug insurance? *Health Economist*, 18:1218–32.

Allin S, Laporte A (2011). Socioeconomic status and the use of medicines in the Ontario Public Drug Program. *Canadian Public Policy*, 37:563–76.

Allin S, Law MR, Laporte A (2013). How does complementary private prescription drug insurance coverage affect seniors' use of publicly funded medications? *Health Policy*, 2013;110:147–55.

Alter DA, Austin P, Tu JV (1999). Effects of socio-economic status on access to invasive cardiac procedures and on mortality after acute myocardial infarction. *New England Journal of Medicine*, 341(18):1359–67.

Alter D et al. (2006). Socio-economic status and mortality after acute myocardial infarction. *Annals of Internal Medicine*, 144(2):82–93.

Béland F (2008). Arithmetic failure and the myth of unsustainability of universal health insurance. *Canadian Medical Association Journal*, 1771(1):54–6.

Bhatti T, Rana Z, Grootendorst P. (2007). Dental insurance, income and the use of dental care in Canada. *Journal of the Canadian Dental Association*, 73(1):57a–h.

Birch S, Eyles J (1992). *Equity and efficiency in health-care delivery: the distribution of health-care resources in Canada and its relationships to needs for care.* Prague, Omnipress Publishing.

Birch S, Eyles J, Newbold KB (1993). Equitable access to health care: methodological extensions to the analysis of physician utilization in Canada. *Health Economics*, 2(2):87–101.

Blue Cross (2016). Blue Cross Association – About Us. Blue Cross: www.bluecross.ca/en/about.html; accessed on 01/11/2016.

Boychuk G (2006) Provincial approaches to funding health services in the post-Chaoulli era. Unpublished document.

Canadian Institute for Health Information (2010). *National health expenditure trends, 1975–2010.* Ottawa, Canadian Institute for Health Information.

Canadian Institute for Health Information (2012). *Drug expenditure in Canada, 1985–2012.* Ottawa, Canadian Institute for Health Information.

Canadian Institute for Health Information (2014). *National health expenditure trends, 1975–2014.* Ottawa, Canadian Institute for Health Information.

Canadian Institute for Health Information (2015). *National health expenditure trends, 1975 to 2015.* Ottawa, Canadian Institute for Health Information.

Chaoulli v Quebec (Attorney General) (2005). SCC 35 (CanLII): http://canlii.ca/t/1kxrh; accessed on 08/11/2016.

CLHIA (Canadian Life and Health Insurance Association) (2010). *Canadian life and health insurance facts, 2010 edition.* Toronto, Canadian Life and Health Insurance Association.

CLHIA (2014). *Improving the accessibility, quality and sustainability of long-term care in Canada.* Toronto, Canadian Life and Health Insurance Association.

CLHIA (2015). *Canadian life and health insurance facts, 2015 edition.* Toronto, Canadian Life and Health Insurance Association.

CLHIA (2016). *Canadian life and health insurance facts, 2016 edition.* Toronto, Canadian Life and Health Insurance Association.

Cohn D (2010). Chaoulli five years on: all bark and no bite? A paper presented at the 2010 Annual Meeting of the Canadian Political Science Association Concordia University, Montreal, Québec.

Cohn D (2015). Chaoulli ten years on: still about nothing? The Canadian Political Science Association Annual Meeting, Ottawa, ON: www.assocsrv.ca/cpsa-acsp/2015event/Cohn.pdf

Colombo F et al. (2011). Help wanted? Providing and paying for long-term care. Paris, OECD Publishing.

Commission on the Future of Health Care in Canada (2002). *Building on values: the future of health care in Canada*. Ottawa, National Library of Canada.

Contandriopoulos D et al. (2012). The visible politics of the privatization debate in Québec. *Healthcare Policy*, 8(1):67–79.

Corscadden L et al. (2014). Publicly financed healthcare and income inequality in Canada. *Healthcare Quarterly*, 17(2):7–10.

Department of Finance (2002). *Canada's life and health insurers*. Ottawa, Department of Finance: www.fin.gc.ca/activty/factsheets/health_e .pdf; accessed on 09/11/2016.

Department of Finance (2016). *Report on federal tax expenditures*. Ottawa, Government of Canada: www.fin.gc.ca/taxexp-depfisc/2016/taxexp16-eng. asp; accessed on 09/11/2016.

Devlin RA, Sarma S, Zhang Q (2011). The role of supplemental coverage in a universal health insurance system: some Canadian evidence. *Health Policy*, 100(1):81–90.

Evans B, Smith C, eds. (2015). Transforming provincial politics: the political economy of Canada's Provinces and Territories in the neoliberal era. Toronto, University of Toronto Press.

Evans RG (2005). Political wolves and economic sheep: the sustainability of public health insurance in Canada. In Maynard A, ed. *The public–private mix for health*. London, Nuffield Trust.

Evans RG (2007). *Economic myths and political realities: the inequality agenda and the sustainability of Medicare*. Centre for Health Services and Policy Research, University of British Columbia, Working Paper 07-13W. Vancouver, BC.

Flood C, Archibald T (2001). The illegality of private health care in Canada. *Canadian Medical Association Journal*, 164(6):825–30.

Government of Canada (1984). *Canada Health Act*.

Government of Québec (2016). S-4.2, r. 25 – Regulation respecting the specialized medical treatments provided in a specialized medical centre. Publications Québec: http://legisquebec.gouv.qc.ca/en/ShowDoc/cr/ S-4.2,%20r.%2025/; accessed on 18/11/2016.

Grignon MJ et al. (2010). Inequity in a market-based health system: evidence from Canada's dental sector. *Health Policy*, 98(1):81–90.

Grignon M, Hurley J, Wang L. (2015). Income-related inequity in health and health care utilization in Canada. CHEPA Working Paper Series, Paper 15-02. Hamilton, Centre for Health Economics and Policy Analysis, McMaster University.

Hall E (1964). *Report of the Royal Commission on Health Services*, vol. 1. Ottawa, Queen's Printer.

Hanley G et al. (2007). Distributional consequences of the transition from age-based to income-based prescription drug coverage in British Columbia, Canada. *Health Economics*, 17(12):1379–92.

Health Canada (2015). *Canada Health Act – annual report for 2014–2015.* Ottawa, Health Canada.

Jimenez-Rubio D, Smith PC, van Doorslaer E (2007). Equity in health and health care in a decentralised context: evidence from Canada. *Health Economics*, 17(3):377–92.

Kratzer J et al. (2015). The impact of private insurance coverage on prescription drug use in Ontario, Canada. *Healthcare Policy*, 10:62–74.

Lahey KA (2015). Canada's massive tax cuts 1997–2016 – Federal 'revenue holes' created in 1997–2005 and 2005–2016. Feminist Legal Studies Queen's Working Paper. Kingston, Queen's University: http://femlaw.queensu.ca/sites/webpublish.queensu.ca.flswww/files/files/workingPapers/KLTxCuts199720052016Oc112015.pdf; accessed on 18/11/2016.

Landon S et al. (2006). Does health care spending crowd out other provincial government expenditures? *Canadian Public Policy*, 32(2):121–41.

Law MR, Kratzer J, Dhalla IA (2014). The increasing inefficiency of private health insurance in Canada. *Canadian Medical Association Journal*, 186:E470–4.

Marchildon GP (2005). *Health systems in transition: Canada.* Copenhagen, WHO on behalf of the European Observatory on Health Systems and Policies.

Marchildon GP (2013). *Canada: Health System Review.* Copenhagen, WHO Regional Office for Europe on behalf of the European Observatory on Health Systems and Policies.

Marsden D, Xu SY (2009). Income-related inequity in Ontario GP utilization. McMaster RDC Research Paper No. 17, Hamilton, ON: http://socserv.mcmaster.ca/rdc/RDCwp16.pdf; accessed on 08/11/2016.

McCreith v Ontario (Attorney General) (5 September 2007), No 07-CU-339454PD3 (Ont Sup Ct) Statement of Claim.

McGrail K (2007). Medicare financing and redistribution in British Columbia, 1992–2002. *Health Care Policy*, 2(4):123–37.

Mertl S (2016). BC refutes Charter challenge of medicare. *Canadian Medical Association Journal*, 188(15):E369–70.

Morgan SG et al. (2015). *Pharmacare 2020: The future of drug coverage in Canada.* Vancouver, Pharmaceutical Policy Research Collaboration, University of British Columbia.

Murray v. Alberta (Calgary Health Region), 2007 ABQB 231 (CanLII): http:// canlii.ca/t/1r699>; retrieved on 10/11/2016.

Mustard C et al. (1998). Paying taxes and using health care services: the distributional consequences of tax financed universal health insurance in a Canadian province, paper presented at the Centre for the Study of Living Standards Conference, *The State of Living Standards and the Quality of Life in Canada*, Ottawa, 20–31 October: www.csls.ca/events/oct98/must1 .pdf; accessed on 20/05/2011.

National Forum on Health (1997). *Canada health action: building on the legacy*, vol. 1: *The final report of the National Forum on Health*. Ottawa, Government of Canada Publications, Health Canada.

OECD (2017). Health expenditure and financing: Health expenditure indicators, OECD Health Statistics (database): http://dx.doi.org/10.1787/ data-00349-en; accessed on 30/11/2017.

Pomey M-P et al. (2007). Public/private partnerships for prescription drug coverage: policy formulation and outcomes in Québec's universal drug insurance program, with comparisons to the Medicare prescription drug program in the United States. *Milbank Quarterly*, 85(3):469–98.

Provincial Working Group on the Delivery of Oncology Medications for Private Payment in Ontario Hospitals (2006). *Report of the Provincial Working Group on the Delivery of Oncology Medications for Private Payment in Ontario Hospitals*. Toronto, Cancer Care Ontario, 27 July.

Québec National Assembly (2006). *An Act to Amend the Act Respecting Health Services and Social Services and Other Legislative Provisions, Bill 33*. Québec, Québec Official Publisher.

RAMQ (Régie de l'assurance maladie) (2016). Liste des professionnels de la santé non-participants ou désengagés au régime de l'assurance maladie du Québec avec adresse de pratique au Québec. Québec: Service de l'admissibilité et du paiement: www.ramq.gouv.qc.ca/SiteCollectionDocuments/professionnels/ facturation/desengages.pdf; accessed on 30/11/2017.

SCOR (2003). Private LTC Insurance. International Comparisons. Scor Technical Newsletter No. 9, Scor, Paris: www.actuaries.org/IAAHS/ OnlineJournal/2006-1/scorltc1.pdf; accessed on 30/11/2017.

Senate of Canada (2002). *The health of Canadians – the federal role*, vol. 5: *Principles and recommendations for reform – part 1*. Ottawa, Standing Committee on Social Affairs, Science, and Technology.

Smythe JG (2001). *Tax subsidization of employer-provided health care insurance in Canada: incidence analysis*. Unpublished Working Paper. Edmonton, University of Alberta, Department of Economics.

Smythe J (2002). *The redistributive effect of health care finance in Alberta, 1997. Institute of Health Economics Working Paper 02-07.* Edmonton, University of Alberta, Department of Economics.

Stabile M (2001). Private insurance subsidies and public health care markets: evidence from Canada. *Canadian Journal of Economics,* 34(4):921–42.

Statistics Canada (2008). *Workplace and employee survey compendium, 2005.* Ottawa, Statistics Canada, Catalogue No. 71-585-X.

Statistics Canada (2014). *Canadian Community Health Survey, 2014.* Ontario Share File. Ottawa, Statistics Canada.

Task Force on the Funding of the Health System (2008). *Getting our money's worth: report of the Task Force on the Funding of the Health System.* Québec, Government of Québec.

Thomas B, Flood CM (2015). Putting health to rights: a Canadian view on global trends in litigating health care rights. *Canadian Journal of Comparative and Contemporary Law,* 1(1):49–78.

van Doorslaer E (2007). Equity in health and health care in Canada: an international perspective. In: Lu M, Jonsson E, eds. *Financing health care: new ideas for a changing society.* Weinheim, Wiley-VCH Verlag GmbH and Co. KGaA.

van Doorslaer E, Masseria C, Koolman X and the OECD Health Equity Research Group (2005). Inequalities in access to medical care by income in developed countries. *Canadian Medical Association Journal,* 174(2):177–83.

Vella M, Faubert R (2001). *Adapting to change: the life and health insurance industry amidst a changing financial services landscape.* Ottawa, Statistics Canada, Catalogue No. 63–016.

Wagstaff A, van Doorslaer E (2000). Equity in health care finance and delivery. In: Culyer AJ, Newhouse JP, eds. *Handbook of health economics.* Amsterdam, Elsevier Science.

Wang C et al. (2015). Mandatory universal drug plan, access to health care and health: evidence from Canada. *Journal of Health Economics,* 44:80–96.

Woolhandler S, Campbell T, Himmelstein D (2003). Costs of health care administration in the United States and Canada. *New England Journal of Medicine,* 349(8):768–75.

Zhong H (2008). Equity in pharmaceutical utilization in Ontario: a cross-section and over-time analysis. *Canadian Public Policy,* 33(4):487–507.

5 | Regulating private health insurance: France's attempt at getting it all

AGNÈS COUFFINHAL[1,2] AND CARINE FRANC[3,4]

Publicly financed health coverage in France is universal. Nevertheless, in 2015, private health insurance accounted for 13.3% of total spending on health (French Ministry of Health, 2016),[5] one of the highest shares internationally. According to the most recent survey data available, 95% of the population is covered by a complementary health insurance contract that primarily reimburses statutory user charges. Nine out of ten people insured have a private contract while the rest benefit from publicly funded complementary coverage known as *Couverture maladie universelle complémentaire* (CMUC) due to their low income (Barlet, Beffy & Renaud, 2016; based on the 2012 Health, health care and insurance survey).[6]

The chapter begins by describing the basic features of the statutory health insurance system and the dynamics of its regulation, which explain the role that private health insurance has come to play over time.

[1] The World Bank.
[2] The opinions expressed and arguments employed here are solely those of the authors.
[3] French National Institute of Health and Medical Research (Inserm) – Centre d'Epidémiologie et de Santé des Populations (CESP), Inserm U1018.
[4] The authors are grateful to Christine Meyer from the National Federation of French Mutual Funds (*Fédération Nationale de la Mutualitée Française*) and Michel Grignon from McMaster University for their detailed comments and suggestions. Any errors remain ours.
[5] Throughout the chapter, "total health expenditure" refers to spending on medical goods and services, equal to around 81% of what the OECD counts as total health expenditure (which also includes long-term care for older people, some care for disabled people, population-based prevention, medical education and research, management of the health system and investment) (French Ministry of Health 2016: pp.170–1).
[6] The ESPS survey covers the noninstitutional population (that is, people living in care homes, hospitals, prisons, etc. are excluded).

142

It then provides an overview of the private health insurance market. Historically, the market has been dominated by non-profit mutual associations known as *mutuelles*. The final section distinguishes three themes around which public policy towards the private health insurance sector has emerged since the 1990s. First, harmonization of regulation aims to encourage competition and increase transparency in the market. Because of their grounding in the social economy, *mutuelles* and, to a lesser degree, other non-profit insurers have benefited from specific tax exemptions and other advantages deemed to contradict European Union competition law. Over time, and largely due to pressure from for-profit insurers, regulations have changed to level the competitive playing field and protect activities organized in the "general interest" of solidarity and mutual aid. The second type of regulatory intervention, first introduced in 2000, aims to strengthen equity of access to private health insurance and therefore to health care. The publicly funded CMUC and a more recent voucher scheme for low-income households sought to limit socioeconomic differences in access to private health insurance. Finally, since January 2016, all employers – irrespective of the size of their business – have been required to provide private complementary health insurance to their employees. The third regulatory trend seeks to increase the overall efficiency of the health system by better aligning the incentives of private and public insurers on the one hand, and the providers of care on the other.

Health system context and the role of private health insurance

Universal coverage through statutory health insurance

All legal residents are covered by statutory health insurance, an entitlement of the wider social security system. Set up in 1945, the statutory scheme initially offered coverage based on professional activity and was contingent on contributions. The scheme has always been administered by a number of noncompeting health insurance funds catering to different segments of the labour market. The main fund (*Caisse Nationale d'Assurance Maladie des Travailleurs Salarié*) currently covers 91% of the population (DSS, 2015). The two other sizeable funds cover self-employed people (*Régime Social des travailleurs Indépendants*, RSI) and agricultural workers (*Mutualité Sociale Agricole*). In 2000, the Universal Health Coverage (*Couverture Maladie Universelle*, CMU) Act changed the public insurance entitlement criterion from professional activity to residence. This allowed a small but growing share of the population, that had previously been excluded from the statutory scheme (and was covered through locally funded schemes), to benefit from the same rights as the rest of the population.[7] In 2016, this mechanism was generalized and simplified to become the *Protection Universelle Maladie* and now around 3.8% of the population draw their social health insurance membership from their residency status.[8] The benefits package was harmonized in 2001. In 1991, the funding of the French social security system (and therefore also of statutory health insurance), which initially relied on payroll contributions, was expanded to include taxes on a wider range of income sources. In 2014, payroll contributions represented around 47% of statutory health insurance revenue and other earmarked taxes represented nearly 50% (DSS, 2015).

Cost sharing and choice of provider

The scope of services covered by the publicly funded benefits package has always been broad in France and the preferred public spending control mechanism has been to limit the depth of public coverage, leaving the patient to pay a share of the cost (see Table 5.1). Since 2005, the government has introduced a range of additional flat-rate co-payments.[9] Another source of out-of-pocket payments is the difference between the actual market price of a service and the official tariff based on the statutory health insurance reimbursement rate (Couffinhal & Paris, 2001). This difference is particularly high for products such as dental prostheses and eyewear, and for the services of some physicians ("Sector 2" physicians), mainly specialists, who are allowed to charge more than the official tariff. In order to balance extra-billing, additional provisions were introduced in the global agreement linking the public health insurance system and physicians' unions in October 2012. Sector 2 doctors are incentivized to sign a voluntary 3-year "access to health care" contract, which restrains extra-billing practices (Chevreul et al., 2015). More recently, in December 2015, the National Assembly

---

[7] Since then, entitlement to statutory health insurance has been de-linked from payment of contributions.
[8] Authors' computation based on CNAMTS (2016) and INSEE (2016).
[9] Some of these co-payments are meant not to be reimbursed by private health insurance.

Table 5.1 *User charges for publicly financed health care in France, 2016*

	Statutory coverage rates (%)	Co-insurance rates (%)	Additional insurable co-payment	Additional non-insurable co-payment[a]
Physician visit, GP home visit	70[b]	30	€18 for procedures of €120 or more	€1 per visit (max €4 per day per doctor)
Dental treatment	70[b]	30	None	None[c]
Other health services providers	60	40	None	None
	60	40	€18 on procedures of €120 or more	€0.50 per service (max €2 per day)
Laboratory tests	60 / 70[d]	40 / 30	€18 on procedures of €120 or more	€1 per laboratory test (max €4 per day per laboratory)
Prescription medicines	15 / 30 / 65 / 100[e]	85 / 70 / 35 / 0	If generics are available, the reimbursement is based on the average price of generics	€0.50 per packet
Hospital care	80	20	€18 catering day fee	€1 per outpatient visit

Source: Public Health Insurance website. www.ameli.fr.

Notes: [a] The amount is deducted from public reimbursement and limited to €50 per patient per year.

[b] Falls to 30% if the patient does not obtain a referral to ambulatory specialist care.

[c] €1 deductible applies only to dentists, not dental surgeons.

[d] The rate depends on the type of test and the qualification of the health professional performing the test. The HIV diagnostic test is free of charge.

[e] Depending on the type of medicine.

adopted a government reform (*projet de loi de modernisation de notre système de santé*), which generalizes the third-party payment to all social health insurance beneficiaries. Third-party payment requires physicians to directly bill social health insurers (and, if they so decide, they can also directly bill complementary health insurers) rather than charging patients at the point of service. The measure, strongly opposed by physicians, was implemented in 2017 for some categories of insured exempted from statutory co-payments and will be extended to the entire population.

Patients have traditionally enjoyed free choice of provider and been able to self-refer to specialists. A 2004 reform introduced a voluntary "preferred primary care provider" gatekeeping system. Patients who comply with gatekeeping retain the same coverage rates as before, whereas those who do not are reimbursed at lower rates (for example, 30% rather than 70% for physician services) and providers are allowed to charge them more than the official tariff (Com-Ruel, Dourgnon & Paris, 2006).

In 2015, statutory health insurance funded 78.2% of total spending on health (see Table 5.2), a share that has remained relatively stable since the mid-1980s (Fenina & Geffroy, 2007; Fenina, Le Garrec & Koubi, 2010; French Ministry of Health, 2016). However, while over 90% of hospital spending is publicly financed (92.5% in 2015), a share that has not changed in the last ten years, less than 67% of ambulatory care was publicly financed in 2015, and this share has fallen from 77% in 1980 (Le Garrec, Koubi & Fenina, 2013). But this overall coverage rate of outpatient care masks important differences: for the 83% of the population that does not benefit from statutory exemption of co-payments due to chronic disease (see below), coverage of outpatient care is only 51% (HCAAM, 2013). In other words, public coverage of ambulatory care has become relatively less generous over time and is quite low for the majority of the population.

Cost containment

For many years, health policy has focused on the need to curb public spending on health and to limit the statutory scheme's deficits. The latter has been in deficit for more than 20 years, with an annual deficit that came close to 1% of gross domestic product in 2003 and 2004 and came close to these levels again during the financial crisis. In 2015, the social health insurance deficit was €5.8 billion (down from €6.5 billion in 2014 and €11.6 billion in 2010) representing in 2015 approximately 0.3% of gross domestic product (Comptes de la Sécurité Sociale, 2016). Successive reform plans,[10] typically combining a reduction in the benefits package with increases in contribution rates, have generally managed to keep spending growth in check for a few months, but no structural reform has ever been attempted. A 2004 reform was slightly bolder in this respect. It redefined the statutory health insurance funds' joint role in financial stewardship and significantly increased their capacity to negotiate prices with providers and adjust the benefits package (see Polton & Mousquès, 2004 or Franc & Polton, 2006).

The statutory health insurance deficit decrease of recent years is mainly attributed to a reduced growth in hospital spending and a drop in medicine prices caused by greater use of generic drugs. However, pressure on the system is unlikely to recede in the mid and longer term, particularly due to the price of innovative drugs – cost containment will remain a policy priority in the years to come (HCAAM, 2010; French Ministry of Health, 2016).

Purchaser–provider relations

The statutory health insurance scheme is the main purchaser of services in a system that is traditionally characterized by its limited emphasis on managing care – a system in which providers enjoy substantial autonomy. In 2015, nearly 60% of physicians worked in private practice on a fee-for-service basis, and provided the bulk of outpatient care (Sicart, 2011; Barlet & Marbot, 2016). Global agreements negotiated between the statutory scheme and associations of health professionals set the tariffs for reimbursement of patients. Efforts to cap the overall amount paid to physicians in a given year have always failed due to opposition from the powerful physicians' unions. However, in 2009, the statutory scheme, under the leadership of the main fund (*Caisse Nationale d'Assurance Maladie des Travailleurs Salariés*) and in spite of strong opposition from the physicians' unions, managed to implement a pay-for-performance system for general practitioners (GPs) (the *Contract d'Amélioration des Pratiques Individuelles*). In addition to their fee-for-service income, participating GPs receive additional remuneration,

---

[10] On average, there was a new reform plan every 18 months between 1975 and 1995 (Hassenteufel & Pallier, 2007).

which varies with their number of patients and their level of progress towards or achievement of quality indicators related, among other, to chronic patient care and prevention. GPs who do not achieve the targets are not penalized. In 2011, the pay-for-performance scheme was extended to additional specialties (cardiologists and gastroenterologists) and incorporated into the physicians' collective agreement under the label *"rémunération sur objectifs de santé publique"* (ROSP). The list of indicators was also expanded to 29 indicators. In 2015, 68% of targets were achieved by participating physicians and 72% of them had progressed in their achievement compared with the previous year. Participating physicians received on average €6756 in 2015. The ROSP represented a gross spending of €404 million in that year and was fully provisioned for in the National Health Insurance Expenditure Target,[11] which was met that year.

Open-ended funding of the public hospital sector came to an end during the 1980s, when global budgets based on historical costs were introduced. Private hospitals, which currently provide two thirds of all surgical procedures, were paid on a fee-for-service basis until 2005. A diagnosis-related group payment system was introduced in 2004 and covered all hospitals by 2008. The harmonization of tariffs across public and private hospitals, initially announced for 2012, was postponed till 2016 and is still not fully achieved. On the other hand, diagnosis-related group tariffs are identical across public hospitals. The new payment system works in conjunction with national spending caps for acute care (Busse et al., 2011).

The significant role of private health insurance

Private health insurance complements the statutory scheme by covering statutory user charges. Its size and significance have increased over time. In 1960, the market covered about 30% of the population; this share grew to 50% in 1970, 70% in 1980 and reached 95% in 2013 (Buchmueller & Couffinhal, 2004; Franc, 2005; Barlet, Beffy & Renaud, 2016). France is now one of the OECD countries where private health insurance is the most widespread. In 1960, private health insurance accounted for around 5% of total spending on health, rising

---

[11] This target (ceiling) for social health insurance expenditure has been in place since 1996 (Chevreul et al., 2015).

to 12.1% in 2001 and 13.3% in 2015 (Fenina, Le Garrec & Koubi, 2010; French Ministry of Health, 2016). The share of private insurance in the funding of different types of health care varies, ranging from a low 3.8% for medical transportation and 5.2% for hospital care to 21.7% for outpatient services and 39% for nonpharmaceutical medical goods (see Table 5.2).

There is no systematic analysis of the determinants of this increase in demand for private insurance. In addition to the initial and continuing influence of *mutuelles* in the public policy environment (see below), it is safe to assume that increased demand has been prompted by increases in statutory user charges, deterioration in the extent of statutory coverage for certain types of care (with growing differences between the official tariff and the actual price paid by patients) and an income effect.

As out-of-pocket payments increased (from €217 on average per person and per year in 1980 to €604 in 2010 and €636 in 2015[12]) and private health insurance became more widespread, differences in access to health care between the privately insured and those without voluntary insurance became more significant. Since 2000, additional public schemes have been set up to ensure that low-income households receive adequate financial protection. These have been designed around the concept of complementary insurance rather than targeted increases in the depth of statutory coverage, mainly to avoid stigmatization of households near the poverty line. These measures aim to ensure that poorer households have a dual coverage package comparable to the one available to the rest of the population (statutory plus complementary cover). They are also organized to prevent a household from having to change private insurer if its circumstances change.

The first scheme, the CMUC, was introduced in 2000, at the same time as entitlement to statutory coverage (CMU) became universal. This means-tested complementary insurance scheme can be managed by private insurer or by local statutory health insurance funds (the household chooses). Since 2009, it has been fully financed by a tax on private insurers' turnover. Taking this tax revenue into account (€2.1 billion in 2015), the share of total spending on health actually financed by private insurers in 2015 is 14.4% rather than 13.3% (as reported in Table 5.2).[13] A second scheme, involving a voucher (*l'Aide Complémentaire*

[12] Authors' calculations based on French Ministry of Health (2016).
[13] See the tables in French Ministry of Health (2016: p.97 and p.103).

Table 5.2 *Health care financing by source of funds in France, 2015*

	Total spending on health (%)	Hospital care (%)	Outpatient care (%)	Medical goods (%) Medicines	Medical goods (%) Other[a]	Medical transportation (%)
Statutory health insurance	76.8	91.3	64.7	68.8	43.0	93.1
Other public funds	1.4	1.2	2.0	1.5	0.8	0.9
Private insurance	13.3	5.2	21.7	12.8	39.0	3.8
Households	8.4	2.3	11.7	17.0	17.2	2.2
Total	100.0	100.0	100.0	100.0	100.0	100.0

Source: French Ministry of Health (2016: p.15).

Note: [a] Eyewear, dental prostheses, small medical devices and bandages.

Santé, ACS), was introduced in 2005 to subsidize the purchase of private health insurance by all households with incomes below 135% of the CMUC's threshold (since 2012). In 2014, between 64% and 77% of the target population (between 5.8 million and 7 million) was estimated to be covered by the CMUC, but the ACS, despite consistent efforts to extend take-up, reached only 1.35 million people by the end of 2015 (around 25% of its target population) (CMU Fund, 2016).

Overview of the private health insurance market

Types of insurer

The three types of insurer that operate in the private health insurance market differ in terms of their organizational objectives, the share that health care represents in their overall activity and the way they have been regulated. Their respective lobbies have a distinct influence on debate about the organization of the health system, often supporting differing views about the role that private health insurance should play and the type of regulation needed to facilitate it.

Mutuelles developed during the 19th century to provide voluntary social protection, including protection against health risks. In 1900, roughly 13 000 *mutuelles* covered over 2 million people and by 1939 two thirds of the population had some form of coverage against the financial risk of illness (Sandier, Paris & Polton, 2004). *Mutuelles* also managed mandatory social insurance schemes introduced during the first half of the 20th century (although these were limited in coverage breadth and scope), but in spite of their political and economic importance they were not given a role in managing the social security system created in 1945. Instead, they laid the foundations for the private health insurance market (Buchmueller & Couffinhal, 2004).

Membership of *mutuelles* is now usually open, although it was originally organized along occupational lines or in specific geographic areas. Historically, *mutuelles* emphasized mutual aid and solidarity among members, and broader social responsibility. This is reflected in the way they have traditionally conducted their business; for example, some *mutuelles* define premiums as a percentage of income. Complementary health insurance is now the *mutuelles'* main line of business (see Table 5.3).

Provident institutions developed after 1945 to manage the newly created mandatory retirement schemes for employees. They later diversified their activities to provide other forms of social insurance to employees, including health insurance. Provident institutions operate on a non-profit basis and are jointly managed by representatives of employers and employees.

For-profit insurers entered the market in the 1980s to diversify their product range using health, some suspected, as a loss leader.[14] Health has remained a marginal line of business for them.[15]

The French market is characterized by competition between types of insurance organizations. When commercial insurers entered the market, it was expected that, as they were not bound by solidarity principles, they would differentiate premiums to attract low-risk clients. The question that arose was whether *mutuelles'* way of operating would remain viable in the face of adverse selection or whether they would be forced to adopt more market-oriented strategies in order to survive. The fact that their market share has remained remarkably stable suggests that a pragmatic balance was achieved, partly due to the "complementary" nature of the market, which limits the potential gains from differentiating between high and low risks, and partly due to successful marketing by the *mutuelles* to strengthen collective identity around values that appeal to their clients, such as nondiscrimination and solidarity (Buchmueller & Couffinhal, 2004). However, the *mutuelles'* market share has declined since 2005, to the benefit of commercial insurers, whose market share increased by 33% between 2001 and 2014 (see Table 5.3). Risk profiles also differ across types of insurer: people aged over 60 years constitute 29% of *mutuelles'* clients versus only 24% for commercial insurers, a difference which, if explained by a "cohort effect", might decrease over time (in 2009, the shares were respectively 25% and 17%). Moreover, people aged under 25 years represent almost one third of *mutuelles'* clients (30%), 23% of provident institutions' clients and 28% of insurance companies' clients. Recent changes in regulation (see below) may also explain why the balance between different operators is slowly shifting.

The health insurance market is not highly concentrated, although rapid consolidation has taken place in recent years. The number of insurers has decreased by two thirds since 2001, largely due to consolidation

[14] Before then, commercial insurers provided basic health care insurance for some households that did not benefit from the statutory scheme, notably among the self-employed and, after 1945, in the agricultural sector.

[15] Equivalent to 2.2% of total commercial insurance turnover.

Table 5.3 *Key features of the French private health insurance market, 2014*

	Mutuelles	Provident institutions	Commercial insurers	All
Profit status	Non-profit	Non-profit	For-profit	
Number of institutions	453	26	94	573
Share	79%	5%	16%	100%
Change in share (%) 2001–2014	*–70%*	*–54%*	*–20%*	*–66%*
Number of people covered (million)	38	13	12	63
Share	60%	21%	19%	100%
Turnover (€ million)	18048	6291	9570	33909
Evolution 2001–2014	*+70%*	*+92%*	*+160%*	*+93%*
Share	53%	19%	28%	100%
Change in share (%) 2001–2014	*–12%*	*0%*	*33%*	*n.a.*
Expenditure (€ million)	13647	4994	7041	25682
Change in expenditure (%) 2001–2014	*+53%*	*+81%*	*+140%*	*+76%*
Share	53%	20%	27%	100%
Share of total health expenditure	7.2%	2.6%	3.7%	13.5%
Group policies as a share of total business	29%	85%	44%	44%
Group policies as a share of insured (2013)	31%	88%	28%	54%
Health as a share of total business	84%	47%	5%	15%
Estimated claims ratio	0.76	0.79	0.74	0.76
Percentage point change in the ratio 2001–2014	–9.5%	–6.0%	–6.3%	–8.4%

Sources: Centre Technique des Institutions de Prévoyance (2016), French Ministry of Health (2016), CMU Fund (2016), Barlet, Beffy & Renaud (2016) and authors' calculations.

Notes: An increase in the claims ratio denotes a deterioration in profitability (spending on benefits increases faster than premiums collected). Italics indicate the percentage change.

among *mutuelles* following a change in their regulatory framework in 2002. However, the market remains fragmented: in 2014, the 20 largest insurers accounted for 50% of business (in terms of turnover) while around 68% of insurers had an annual turnover of less than €14 million (less than 0.05% of total). At the other end of the spectrum, the five largest insurers have a turnover of over €1 billion (and the largest one over €2.2 billion, that is, approximately 6% of total) and 30 operators with turnovers of over €250 million (5% of insurers) accounted for 59% of total turnover. In 2014, the 10 largest (1.7% of the total number of insurers: four *mutuelles*, four provident institutions and two commercial insurers) accounted for 34% of premium income.

Overall, private health insurance seems to be a profitable business (see Table 5.3), particularly for commercial insurers. The industry-level claims ratio has deteriorated somewhat since 2001, largely due to the decline in profitability of *mutuelles* (perhaps because the latter are believed to cover a higher share of older people on average).[16,17]

Private health insurance products

In 2014, more than half of the privately insured obtained cover through employment (see Barlet, Beffy & Renaud, 2016). In 2013, 48% of firms (with more than 10 employees), corresponding to 70% of employees in the private sector, offered health insurance to their employees (Barlet, Beffy & Renaud, 2016). Indeed, the probability of an employee being offered health insurance through the workplace varies with the size of the firm: in 2013, 46% of firms with 10 to 49 employees offered insurance compared with 76% of firms with 250 to 499 employees and 90% of firms with 1500 or more employees. The higher the proportion of executives in the company, the more likely the firm is to offer private cover and the more comprehensive this coverage is likely to be. Employers pay an average of 57% of the premium for their employees.

---

[16] Franc, Perronin & Pierre (2008) show that nearly two out of three policy-holders change their private health insurer during the transition to retirement and that a significant proportion of policy-holders originally affiliated with a commercial insurance company chooses a *mutuelle*.

[17] In order to meet the new prudential requirements, more than 100 *mutuelles* transferred a proportion of or their entire portfolio to larger *mutuelles* (this does not affect their members) (Barlet, Beffy & Renaud, 2016: p.34).

The provision of health insurance by employers was incentivized and is now mandatory. In 2009, a 2003 law (known as the Fillon law) came into effect after a transition period designed to allow employers to change the contracts they offer their employees. Under the law, tax exemptions for employers offering cover to employees are restricted to mandatory group contracts and contracts that comply with rules set by the authorities (see below). Over the transition period, companies adapted their supply of complementary health insurance to continue to benefit from tax rebates. In 2009, only 15% of employers offered voluntary contracts and 6% offered mixed contracts (mandatory for some statutory categories of employees and optional for others); these shares were 36% and 5%, respectively, in 2003. A third of the group contracts had been signed for less than 2 years. In January 2013, within the framework of a National Inter-professional Agreement, and in the context of a broader Law aimed at protecting employment (*loi sur la sécurisation de l'emploi*), the French government required all employers (irrespective of the size of their business) to offer private complementary health insurance to their employees from January 2016. This measure is expected to increase access to private health insurance for the employed, but its impact on the risk structure of the individual insurance market could lead to a rise in premiums for those covered (students, retirees, unemployed and civil servants) (Franc & Pierre, 2015).

Surveys of the privately insured (Couffinhal & Perronin, 2004; Célent, Guillaume & Rochereau, 2014), insurers (Garnero & Rattier, 2011; Garnero & Le Palud, 2014) and more rarely of employers (Guillaume & Rochereau, 2010) have led to a better understanding of the products available. They show that there is large variation in the extent of financial coverage among private health insurance contracts. Some only reimburse statutory user charges, including for goods and services for which the official tariff is notoriously lower than the market price (minimal coverage).[18] More comprehensive contracts reimburse patients beyond the official statutory tariff. The most comprehensive ones offer reimbursement that exceeds the average price for the good or service covered. Their beneficiaries can therefore use services that are priced above the market average (which is itself higher than the

---

[18] For example, the statutory tariff for a spectacle lens is less than €3, whereas the average market price is €60.

statutory tariff) and face no out-of-pocket payments beyond the mandatory nonrefundable statutory co-payments.[19]

The distribution of coverage levels for individual contracts depends highly on the type of contract (group or individual). It was roughly as follows in 2013: around 22% of individual contracts offer minimal coverage (compared with only 6% for group contracts), an additional 69% provide limited coverage (compared with 29% for group contracts), 6% offer average coverage (compared with 13% for group contracts) and the remaining 3% are very comprehensive (compared with 53% for group contracts) (Barlet, Beffy & Renaud, 2016). However, the content of insurance contracts is rapidly changing: for instance, the 2013 law mandating group health insurance also defined a minimum basket of benefits. In 2015, the content and the price of complementary health insurance contracts eligible for the ACS voucher were also regulated (see below).

In 2013, the average annual premium in the individual market for a contract covering single individuals aged between 40 and 59 years was €612; this premium was around 49% higher for individuals aged between 60 and 74 years and 85% higher for older individuals (Garnero & Le Palud, 2014). The premium for a contract providing minimal coverage was around 15% lower than the contract offering average coverage for single individuals aged between 40 and 59 years. The average annual premium for a group contract in 2013 was €840 and was 29% higher for a very comprehensive coverage contract, keeping in mind that employers usually pay for around 57% of the premium. The premium for 91% of individual contracts varied with age in 2013 (100% of contracts offered by insurers and 89% of contracts offered by *mutuelles*). Although private insurers typically offer a larger number of contract options than *mutuelles*, there are no systematic differences between types of insurer in terms of coverage depth.

A recent trend towards increased product diversification makes it more difficult for consumers to compare contracts. In the last 15 years, many insurers have started offering "cafeteria plans", in which the insured are invited to select their level of coverage for each type of care.

---

[19] Patients have some choice in the price they pay (for example, choice of provider, material used for a dental prosthesis). The highest coverage contract will always set a limit on reimbursement. Therefore, a contract can never guarantee 100% coverage.

These are being marketed as a way of adapting the contract to individual needs while keeping it affordable. Another trend is for insurers to cover preventive services, irrespective of whether they are publicly covered, or even alternative or complementary medicine (for example, chiropractic services, homeopathic remedies). Some insurers now also offer ex-post premium rebates to policy-holders based on utilization (in effect a no-claims bonus system) (HCAAM, 2007). By purchasing these types of products, households provide insurers with a wealth of information about their utilization patterns and, indirectly, their health status. However, this method of (indirect) risk rating does not yet appear to be much of a concern in policy debates.

The tradition of "managed care" is not strong among private insurers. Complementary benefits are closely based on statutory benefits and, for most services, represent a small portion of the total cost of care (except for optical and dental care). As a result, private insurers have had few incentives and little leverage with which to engage providers and undertake active purchasing – all the more so because the statutory sector has not enjoyed much success in this domain either. *Mutuelles* have a long history of direct service provision through dental clinics, optical centres, pharmacies and even hospitals. In 2015, there were roughly 2600 such facilities open to the general public (including 746 optical shops, 475 dental centres, 54 pharmacies), with a total turnover of €3.7 billion.[20] However, while *mutuelle*-owned facilities are known to provide services at low prices (in particular for dental care), with the exception of a few leading institutions, their reputation for quality is not so good.

Beginning in the mid-1990s, some private insurers initiated more proactive interventions in the health care sector, often involving "call centres". Most of this activity relates to dental care and eyewear and is advertised as customer service rather than risk management or cost control. For example, insurers may evaluate proposed fees or offer to negotiate prices on behalf of patients or set up more formal agreements with provider networks. These agreements may contain elements of quality improvement and price moderation in return for potential increases in service volume, but remain relatively loose because selective contracting is illegal. More recently, some insurers

---

[20] In comparison, benefits paid by the *mutuelles* amounted to €17.7 billion in 2015.

have bypassed this problem by organizing and becoming partners of an independent platform that manages networks of health professionals and contracts directly with patients who choose to join. Another area of intervention by insurers is the provision of advice about health and prevention.

Little information is readily available about these projects, their success or even their number. A rapid analysis of the 10 largest private insurers' websites shows that they all offer the services described above to some extent and use this offer as a marketing argument. Some *mutuelles* promote access to their providers' networks more proactively as part of this strategy. Others have created dedicated structures, sometimes as joint ventures, that openly seek to become service providers to a range of insurers. A significant initiative was launched by the *mutuelles* in 2006: with an initial focus on cancer, cardiovascular diseases and addictions, regional call centres provide guidance, medical advice and support to their members in what could eventually become a "disease management" approach. The consensus seems to be that while call centres and other managed-care activities have not yet been profitable, this type of investment could pay off in the long run, particularly if the scope of private health insurance increases. The most recent initiatives typically rely on communication technologies, with the introduction of telephone applications to monitor reimbursements, locate in-network providers, or advise patients on prevention. The largest insurance company even offers telephone consultations and the possibility of subsequently picking up a prescription at a nearby pharmacy.

Market development and public policy

Until the early 1990s, public authorities had paid little attention to the private health insurance market and its regulation. Although the market had grown steadily, the attitude of the public authorities could have been described as benevolent "laissez-faire", with an implicit encouragement of the market's development. Indeed, as pressure on the public system's finances increased, the government welcomed the fact that private health insurance could neutralize, to an extent, the perceived impact of unpopular cost containment decisions such as increases in user charges. Over time, however, a series of factors contributed to changing the market's operating environment. First, competition grew following the entry of new insurers. Second, it became increasingly obvious that there were socioeconomic differences in access to health care, and that financial barriers, linked to socioeconomic differences in access to private health insurance, were an explanatory factor. Third, as pressure to curb public spending on health persisted, and as both statutory and complementary cover provided similar incentives to patients and providers, there was growing recognition that better coordination among them could enhance efficiency in the health system. Each of these factors has led to the introduction or revision of specific aspects of the regulatory environment for private health insurance.

Policy debates and regulatory dynamics have been influenced by the positions of the two main players in the market – commercial insurers and *mutuelles* – who promote different types of regulation. On the political front, because of their historical role and their specialization in the health sector, *mutuelles* have always played a key role in health system policy debates through their main professional association (*Fédération Nationale de la Mutualitée Française*, FNMF), and have been represented on the boards of the statutory health insurance funds since 1996. As a lobby, FNMF has traditionally taken the view that complementary insurance is critical to accessing health care and market regulation should therefore be conducive to an environment in which no discrimination can take place; redistribution among risk groups and even social classes is encouraged, or at least an environment in which firms that operate on these principles are somewhat shielded from market competition. More broadly, FNMF claims a strong commonality with the statutory scheme and advocates comanagement of the health system to increase its efficiency.

The commercial insurers' lobby (*Fédération Française de l'Assurance*, FFA) has never been as explicitly involved in policy debates as the *mutuelles*. As might be expected, they tend to support proposals that would increase the scope of private health insurance, and have actively lobbied to level the competitive field and eliminate what they argue are anticompetitive and unfair advantages granted to *mutuelles* (and, to a lesser extent, provident institutions). In the late 1990s, one of the bolder commercial insurers put forward a highly controversial proposal to introduce "health management organization-style" management of both statutory and complementary health benefits. The proposal generated heated debate, including among the commercial insurers themselves, and was eventually withdrawn (Buchmueller & Couffinhal, 2004).

Regulatory harmonization to encourage competition and increase transparency

Because their origins and governance models are entirely different, the three types of insurer have always been regulated under different sets of rules: the *mutuelles* by the *Code de la Mutualité*, the foundations of which were laid in the middle of the 19th century; the provident institutions by the Social Security Code; and commercial insurers by the Insurance Code. Two key differences in these rules later became the focus of debate: the *mutuelles* were subject to less stringent financial and prudential requirements than other types of organizations; and both *mutuelles* and provident institutions benefited from specific tax exemptions; in particular they were exempt from a 7% tax on insurance premiums and also enjoyed other exemptions linked to their non-profit status. This preferential treatment of non-profit organizations was intended to acknowledge their contribution to the general interest and their being embedded in the social economy.[21] In addition to being governed by different sets of rules, the activities of the three types of insurer were monitored by different bodies.

The need to transpose EU competition law into French law was the main thrust behind the increasing harmonization of insurer regulation. Favourable taxation of non-profit insurers violates EU policy requiring equal treatment of all insurers, independent of their form of organization. On these grounds, the FFA lodged a complaint with the European Court of Justice in 1993 and obtained a favourable ruling in 1999. In the wake of this, but also in order to fully transpose the EU insurance directives into national law, a series of changes took place.[22] The *Code de la Mutualité* was revised in 2003 to increase compliance with EU requirements, particularly with regard to prudential aspects, initiating a strong process of consolidation among the *mutuelles*. Indeed, the EU's Solvency II Directive, which sets out stronger requirements for insurer capital adequacy and risk management, came into effect on 1 January 2016. This directive intends to ensure uniform and improved

---

[21] The term "social economy" refers to the third sector in the economy, between the private sector and business and the public sector and government. It includes organizations such as cooperatives, nongovernmental organizations and charities.

[22] Coron & Poinsart (2006) provide a detailed analysis of the impact of EU directives on complementary social protection.

protection for insureds in the European Union and bring down the price of contracts. This European harmonization also aims to facilitate the control of international insurance groups and promote a single European insurance market. But this Directive induced a new challenge because *mutuelles* are owned by their policy-holders and are therefore limited in their capacity to raise capital in the financial markets. Due to strong competition in the private health insurance market and the implementation in 2002 of Solvency I and in 2016 of Solvency II Directives, the consolidation process among the *Mutuelles* has been rapid over the past 15 years (Table 5.3).

On the fiscal side, tax exemption criteria have been redesigned and now apply to contracts that fulfil specific criteria rather than contracts provided by a given type of organization. In response to the FFA complaint, from October 2003 exemption from the 7% tax on insurance premiums has been granted to all contracts that adhere to a "solidarity principle". This principle prohibits an insurer from requesting any health information before subscription or charging risk-rated premiums. It automatically applied to *mutuelles*, and commercial insurers were expected to adapt their contracts to benefit from the exemption. The impact in practice may not have been very significant because underwriting was never a common practice in the private health insurance market. The 2004 health insurance reform added new criteria that the contracts must meet to remain exempt from insurance premium tax. So-called "responsible contracts" guarantee minimum levels of coverage and seek to enhance efficiency in the health system (see below).

By 2010, survey data suggested that virtually all private health insurance contracts met the criteria for responsible contracts (Garnero & Le Palud, 2014). Since 2008, all tax exemptions previously only granted to non-profit entities, now apply to the share of any insurer's business that adheres to the principles of a responsible contract (although such contracts also have to represent a significant share of their overall health insurance business).[23] However, to help curb the government deficit, taxes on these contracts were re-introduced, starting at 3.5% in 2010 (compared with 7% for nonresponsible contracts), and reaching 7% in 2014 (compared with 14% for nonresponsible contracts).

[23] Responsible contracts must apply to at least 150 000 voluntary policy-holders or represent between 80% and 90% of all contracts in the insurer's health portfolio. For mandatory group contracts, responsible contracts must have 120 000 subscribers or represent between 90% and 95% of the total portfolio.

The three types of insurers are now supervised by a single authority.[24] Initially focused on insurers' profit status, the debate on how private insurance should be regulated has gradually shifted towards trying to provide advantages to insurers that serve the general interest, regardless of corporate form. The changes brought about by this harmonization process have indirectly contributed to reaffirming the principles that differentiate the social economy from the business sector. For instance, before the 2003 *Code de la Mutualité* reform, *mutuelles*' pricing practices were supposedly less discriminatory than those of commercial insurers, but they were free to decide how to set premiums. The new regimen explicitly bars *mutuelles* from risk rating: their premiums can vary only according to a subscriber's income, length of time since initial subscription, statutory health insurance fund, place of residence and age, and based on the total number of insured. At the EU level, *mutuelles* have been actively involved in lobbying for the creation of a European Mutual Society Status and, by March 2011, a written declaration establishing European statutes for mutual societies, associations and foundations had been signed by most members of the European Parliament.

In an effort to further promote competition and transparency, the 2012 Social Security Financing Act requires all providers of voluntary health insurance to report to consumers the levels and breakdown of administrative costs (premium collection, portfolio administration, claims management, reinsurance), and acquisition costs (commissions, marketing, commercial networks) and the sum of these two amounts as a percentage of premiums.

Ensuring access to private health insurance to favour equity

Over time, and in the wake of cost containment reforms that shifted health care costs to the private sector through increased user charges, out-of-pocket spending on health gradually rose, exacerbating financial barriers not only to health care but also to private health insurance due to higher premiums. In the context of increased recognition of the importance of private health insurance in securing access to health care,

[24] The Supervisory Authority for Insurance Companies and Mutual Societies (*Autorité de Contrôle Assurance et des Mutuelles*), created in 2003 and replaced in 2010 by the Prudential Supervision Authority (*Autorité de Contrôle Prudentiel*) renamed (*Autorité de Contrôle Prudentiel et de Résolution*).

a series of public interventions was introduced to enhance access to complementary cover for those likely to be excluded from the market.

The first major equity-related intervention in the market focused on risk selection and was primarily aimed at limiting underwriting and increasing portability. The 1989 *Loi Evin* defined a set of rules applicable to all insurers. It reinforced the rights of the privately insured by prohibiting: the exclusion of pre-existing medical conditions from group[25] contracts; premium differentiation among employees based on health status; termination of contract or reduction in coverage once someone had been insured for 2 years; premium increases for specific individuals based on health status. It also allowed retirees and other individuals leaving a group to request their complementary coverage to be maintained by the insurer and limited any increase in tariff to 150% of the initial premium;[26] and enforced strict rules regarding information that the insurer had to provide to the insured (details of the benefits package) as well as to the employers (annual financial accounts for the contract). These rules were further strengthened in 2009, when the obligation to offer strictly identical coverage to former employees (except if the dismissal is justified by serious breach of employment contract) was confirmed in court, and in 2010 when an employer was condemned to pay compensation for failing to fully inform employees on the guarantees underwritten. The 2013 employment protection Law, which mandates private insurance for all employees, also enhanced the entitlements to coverage of former employees. Coverage must be maintained for up to 12 months (previously 9 months) free of charge for former employees.

The *Loi Evin* primarily focused on medical underwriting and, although it was implicitly concerned about the affordability of contracts, its measures were not specifically targeted at low-income individuals. The provisions of the CMU Act (2000) were the first to address income-related inequalities in access to complementary insurance. CMUC provides free complementary cover to all legal residents whose income is below a certain threshold, taking into account their household size. As of April 2016, the monthly income threshold was €721 for single

---

[25] Individual contracts could exclude cover of certain pre-existing conditions if these were clearly defined and consumers were made aware of the exclusion before enrolment.

[26] Since the insured lost the benefit of the employer's contribution upon termination of group coverage, the actual premium increase, before the enactment of this law, was usually much higher.

adults and €1082 for two-person households. At the end of 2015, CMUC benefited 5.4 million people (3.5% more than the previous year) corresponding to 8% of the population,[27] including 44% of children and youth under 20 years of age[28] (CMU Fund, 2016). Despite a 7% increase in eligibility thresholds in 2013 (which made up for a previous erosion in real terms), non-take-up remains high: it was estimated to be between 23% and 36% in 2014 (CMU Fund, 2016). No survey data are available on the factors explaining non-take-up, but a 2015 report from the French public audit commission suggested that the administrative burden imposed on eligible populations to obtain or renew their coverage constitutes a major barrier – including for people who are automatically eligible as recipients of other welfare payments (Cour des Comptes, 2015).

CMUC aims to provide poorer households with free access to health care. It covers all statutory co-payments, offers lump-sum reimbursements for eyeglasses and dental prostheses and prevents health professionals from charging beneficiaries more than the statutory tariff or the lump-sum amount. However, health professionals have not universally accepted this unfunded mandate. A situation testing undertaken in 2008 among a representative sample of physicians showed that a quarter of physicians rejected CMUC beneficiaries when they requested a first appointment by phone (Desprès, 2010). The rate was 32% among dentists and 9% among GPs (the latter are seldom allowed to charge more than the official fee).

A wealth of empirical studies has shown how health care use in France is higher among the privately insured than those without complementary cover.[29] When CMUC was introduced, it was argued that the provision of free care would generate abuse. However, the use of services by CMUC beneficiaries has been studied extensively and research shows that the scheme has had the desired impact. The first study showed that, although health care expenditure was much higher for CMUC beneficiaries compared with the rest of the population, this difference could be attributed to their worse health status; in fact, for a given health status, the use of care by CMUC beneficiaries was comparable to that of the privately insured (Raynaud, 2003). These findings have proved consistent (Boisguérin, 2007).

---

[27] Authors' estimate based on CMU Fund (2016) and INSEE (2016).
[28] This age group represents 25% of the population.
[29] See Buchmueller et al. (2003) for a literature review.

Other longitudinal studies confirm that the increase in use pertained to types of care that individuals previously did not use and for which financial barriers were larger (for example, specialists' services) (Grignon, Perronnin & Lavis, 2007). In other words, CMUC appears to have achieved its objective of putting its beneficiaries on a par with the privately insured.

CMUC beneficiaries can decide who will manage their complementary cover: either a private insurer of their choice[30] or their local statutory health insurance fund. Private insurers can choose whether they want to register as CMUC managers and must offer open enrolment if they do. In 2015, 56% of insurers were registered to manage CMUC contracts compared with over two thirds of all insurers in 2013 (CMU Fund, 2016). Registration is more common among larger insurers and also depends on the type of insurers: in 2015, 64% of *mutuelles* were registered, 83% of provident institutions and only a third of insurance companies (35%). At the end of 2015, less than 13% of CMUC beneficiaries chose to have their contracts managed by a private insurer (compared with more than 15% in 2012). This trend may have been established by the government, which automatically gave local statutory health insurance funds responsibility for covering 3.4 million people who benefited from the programmes CMUC replaced.[31] More generally, however, requesting private management increases the administrative burden for beneficiaries and, as a result, many of them prefer to let the local statutory health insurance fund manage both their statutory and complementary health benefits. On the supply side, the non-profitability of managing CMUC (see below) has undoubtedly been a powerful deterrent. CMUC beneficiaries are fairly concentrated among a small number of insurers: in 2015, the 16 insurers reporting more than 10 thousand CMUC beneficiaries managed around two thirds of all privately insured CMUC beneficiaries: 10 *mutuelles* covered 75% of these beneficiaries, five commercial insurers 21% and one provident institution 4%.

[30] This option was included to avoid stigmatizing beneficiaries as recipients of a means-tested benefit by ensuring that households that could not afford complementary cover temporarily might be able to remain covered by the same insurer, albeit under a different regimen.

[31] These 3.4 million people represented nearly 75% of CMUC beneficiaries in September 2000 (Boisguérin, 2001).

The CMU Fund[32] created in 2000 manages CMUC financing but the mix of funding sources has changed over time and overall the scheme appears to be slightly underfunded.[33] Initially, the Fund received around three quarters of its resources from the government budget and the remainder from a tax on private insurers' turnover (CMU Fund, 2011). In 2006, this tax represented around 32% of the Fund's resources, with the rest coming from earmarked taxes on alcohol (26%), taxes on tobacco (14%) and a transfer from the general revenue pool (25%). In 2009, the government stopped financing CMUC and it has since then been exclusively funded from the health insurance turnover tax (the rate rose from 1.75% in 2000 to 2.5% in 2006 and 6.27% in 2014). As of 2016, all taxes on health insurance contracts are administratively merged and a global rate of 13.27% applies to "responsible contracts" turnover (see above) and 20.27% to contracts not meeting these criteria. The 6.27% remains transferred to the CMU fund. In 2015, this tax represented around 85% of the Fund's resources, the other 15% being derived from taxes on tobacco.

From its revenues, the CMU Fund reimburses managing institutions up to a flat amount per beneficiary of €408 in 2015,[34] either as a direct transfer to local statutory health insurance funds or as a rebate per registered beneficiary on the turnover tax for private insurers.[35] The average spending of CMUC beneficiaries managed by statutory health insurance funds tends to be significantly higher than that of those whose benefits are managed by private insurers (€416 vs. €376 in 2015), because the former, although younger, have worse health status on average (CMU Fund, 2016). Overall, the figures show that managing CMUC contracts is not a profitable business.

When beneficiaries lose their CMUC entitlement, provided their contract was previously managed by a private insurer, that company must offer them for at least 1 year a contract whose guarantees are very similar or identical to those under CMUC and whose annual premium is

[32] *Fonds de financement de la protection complémentaire de la couverture universelle du risque maladie.*

[33] Financing of ACS described below is also done by the CMU Fund and organized similarly.

[34] Prior to 2013, the flat amount per beneficiary was given out to all managing entities based on the number of CMUC beneficiaries covered, irrespective of actual expenditure (and whether it was above or below this flat amount).

[35] In reality, only private managing entities are put at risk. Since 2013, public health insurance funds receive additional funding from the CMU fund if the expenditure exceeds the ceiling.

regulated (around €421 inclusive of taxes per adult in 2015). For low-income households with incomes above the CMU threshold, a voucher scheme (ACS) introduced in 2002 supports access to complementary cover. The voucher either creates an incentive for households that otherwise would not be able to afford private health insurance to purchase cover or, if they are already covered, helps them purchase contracts with more generous benefits. As of 2015, the scheme has been extended to all households with incomes below 135% of the CMUC threshold (the percentage was increased over time). Although the resources taken into account to measure monetary poverty are not the same as those used to assess entitlement to the ACS, at this point, the scheme appears to be available to most households who fall below the poverty line (Cour des Comptes, 2015). The amount of the yearly subsidy varies according to household characteristics (size and age); it was increased several times to reach €100 in 2015 for individuals under 16 and €550 for individuals over 60. Since July 2015, the ACS beneficiaries have to obtain their contract from a list of eligible providers selected by a public tender. Each provider's bid had to include three predefined coverage options. Eleven providers (mostly consortia of insurance providers) were selected. By the end of 2015, 227 insurers offered contracts eligible for the ACS. They covered 80% of the ACS beneficiaries before the reform (which means that 20% of beneficiaries have had to change provider). This measure is estimated to have significantly reduced premiums between 2014 and 2015: by 14% for contracts providing the highest levels of guarantees, by 24% for mid-range contracts and by 37% for the contracts with the lowest levels of guarantees (CMU Fund, 2016).

In 2015, additional advantages were provided to ACS beneficiaries: they cannot be balance-billed by Sector 2 providers and they benefit from third-party payment. Further, they are exempted from the non-insurable co-payment at the point of service (see Table 5.1) and can decline mandatory coverage by the employer.

All these measures aim to expand take-up of the voucher, which, by the end of 2015 had only reached 1.35 million people, around a quarter of its target population (CMU Fund, 2016). A 2009 randomized experiment designed to understand why take-up is low showed that an increase in the benefit had a modest impact on take-up, but that targeted information sessions were poorly attended and considered to be a further deterrent by those who chose not to attend them. Among the 17% of the sample who ended up applying for the voucher, only a little more than half eventually received the benefit, and this uncertainty is likely to compound the administrative burden of applying (Guthmuller, Jusot & Wittwer, 2011). The recent measures appear to have slightly improved take-up, which increased by 12.6% in 2015 (compared with 3.9% the previous year).

Analyses continue to show that progress is still needed to ensure better access to health care for low-income households and pensioners. A 2012 survey found that the risk of foregoing a doctor visit was three times as high for people with no complementary cover of any sort compared with those who benefit from non-CMUC private health cover (Célent, Guillaume & Rochereau, 2014). Moreover, at similar levels of income, households that benefit from CMUC have a lower risk of foregoing care for financial reasons than those with non-CMUC complementary cover. In other words, there is still a high degree of heterogeneity in coverage among low-income households and there remain differences between the insured and uninsured which, by 2012, the ACS had not been able to bridge. More recent results confirm that while CMUC goes a long way towards bridging the gap between covered low-income house-holds and "average" households, the uninsured – a significant share of whom could benefit from the ACS – continue to forego care more frequently for financial reasons (Boisguérin, 2009; Célent, Guillaume & Rochereau, 2014).

Most recently, access to insurance for pensioners has become a sub-ject of concern, but actual implementation of recent regulation adopted to address the issue seems unlikely. Households with at least one retired member are as frequently covered as the general population by private insurance but they mostly subscribe to individual insurance contracts (93% compared with 54% for the population, Table 5.3). Their pre-miums are high, as are their remaining out-of-pocket payments. Health spending represents 5.6% of retired households' disposable income (compared with 2.9 for non-retired households). It is as high as 6.6% of disposable income for those 76 years or older and 11% for households in the bottom quintile (versus only 3% for the top quintile) (Barlet, Beffy & Renaud, 2016). The 2016 yearly Social Security Financing Act provided for the introduction of specific contracts for seniors. The measure was heavily criticized by all private insurers (see below) and the decrees laying out implementation details have not been published, considerably reducing the probability that the measure would become effective before the 2017 elections.

Incentives and efficiency in the health insurance system

In the last 10 years, policy-makers have paid increasing attention to the role that private health insurance plays in financing health care and to its complementarity with the statutory sector. Following efforts to improve access to complementary cover, attention has focused on the need to align incentives across statutory and complementary insurance and to better coordinate the two sectors. For many years, public authorities relied on private health insurance to compensate people for increases in statutory user charges. At the same time, it was widely acknowledged that this de facto cancelled any moderating effect that increases in user charges and similar measures might have had. Moreover, the resulting shift from public to private funding probably reduced fairness in financing the health system, as premiums are presumed to be less redistributive across income levels than taxes. Over time, private insurers became increasingly dissatisfied with their lack of involvement in the regulation of a system that they were increasingly expected to fund. The 2004 health insurance reform took steps to correct these problems and paved the way for the emergence of a new relationship between statutory and private insurers.

As mentioned earlier, the reform created a new type of "socially responsible" complementary contract that seeks to align incentives across statutory and private insurance and promote some minimum quality standards.[36] To qualify as responsible, a contract must provide a minimum level of coverage to policy-holders, systematically covering statutory co-payments for physician visits that take place within the gatekeeping system (leaving the patient with only €1 to pay per visit so long as they do not seek care from a physician who charges more than the official tariff); increase the reimbursement rate for most common drugs (from 65% to at least 95%), as long as these are prescribed within the gatekeeping system; and refund statutory user charges for at least two priority preventive services out of those listed by the Ministry of Health. In addition, it must not reimburse the higher statutory co-payments incurred by patients who seek care outside the gatekeeping system or cover nonreimbursable co-payments (see Table 5.1). In other words, the corresponding share of individuals' health care expenditure has become

---

[36] Recall that responsible contracts must also follow the "solidarity principle" of limited underwriting.

explicitly nonrefundable. Since April 2015, responsible contracts must comply with additional obligations including the capping of reimbursements for optical care and for the extra fees of the physicians who have not signed an "access to health care" contract.[37] Further, insurers are not allowed to cap the number of hospital catering day fees covered. In summary, a complementary contract is responsible if it provides a legally defined minimum level of coverage, if it contributes to promoting prevention and, more importantly, if it does not counteract the incentives embedded in the public sector's cost containment measures.

A range of incentives aims to encourage the development of responsible contracts. In addition to the fiscal incentives targeting insurers noted earlier, fiscal incentives targeting employers who purchase group contracts have been in place since 2008 and, between 2005 and 2015, individuals could only use ACS vouchers to purchase responsible contracts (since 2015 the choice was further restricted between three options as discussed in the previous section). Although the impact of the 2015 reforms is not known, the market was not believed to have fundamentally changed between 2005 and 2015 because it was relatively easy for most insurers to adjust their contracts to the new requirements.

There was a sense initially that the reform would give the government a powerful lever to influence the content of complementary contracts and that it would be able to add new conditions over time. But decisions to replace tax exemptions with a tax penalty for nonresponsible contracts (+ 2% in 2011 and + 7% in 2014) – motivated by the need to control public deficits in the wake of the financial crisis – have undermined some of the reform's potential. Moreover, private insurers objected to this measure and raised premiums, penalizing poorer households. In response, the government increased the ACS eligibility ceiling, a measure that was ultimately financed by private insurers. The main concern at this point is that the level of risk in the pool of those individually insured will increase due to the generalization of group insurance,[38] which could raise premiums and lead to further segmentation.

---

[37] As of 2017, a consultation with a Sector 2 physician without a ACS can at most add 100% to the statutory insurance tariff.

[38] Households with employees that previously may have subscribed to individual insurance are removed from the risk pool, which will include relatively more pensioners, unemployed, etc.

As cost-control measures and measures aimed at better aligning incentives for providers and patients were implemented simultaneously, it is impossible to assess how the reform may have affected patients. One thing is clear, however: the combination of all these reforms has made it very difficult for patients to understand and anticipate the net amount that they will ultimately have to pay out of pocket. The generalization of third-party payments for all physician fees partly aims to offset this by reducing how much individuals have to pay at the point of care.

The 2004 reform also created a platform to allow all private insurers to participate in the regulation of the health system and defend their interests. A new institution was set up and the 33 members of the board of the Union of Voluntary Health Insurers (*Union Nationale des Organismes d'Assurance Maladie Complémentaire*, Unocam) represent the three types of private insurer.[39] For the first time, complementary insurers are explicitly and formally involved in national discussions on health care and health insurance. Unocam is mandated to publicly comment on the draft version of the Health Insurance and Social Security Financing Act, which sets the budget for these institutions every year. It is also invited to participate in annual negotiations between the union of statutory health insurance funds and health professional unions, and it can collectively enter into direct negotiations with health professionals. Since 2009, Unocam has been actively involved, along with statutory insurers, in negotiations with surgeons, anaesthetists and obstetricians to define new rules for balance-billing. The rules would re-introduce this option within strictly defined limits while guaranteeing complementary cover of the extra fee to maintain access for all. In addition, Unocam is consulted before changes are made to the statutory benefits package; it can become a member of other health system institutions;[40] and it can act as a lobby for private insurers to promote a common agenda.

[39] There are 17 members from the FNMF, which represents almost all *mutuelles*, eight members from the FFA, representing commercial insurers, seven members from the Technical Centre for Provident Institutions (*Centre Technique des Institutions de Prévoyance*), representing provident institutions and one member representing a special Fund for the Alsace-Moselle territory.

[40] It has representatives on the board of the Economic Committee for Health Products (*Comité Economique des Produits de Santé*), which helps set prescription drug prices. In 2007, it became a member of the new Health Data Institute (*Institut des Données de Santé*), whose mandate is to increase the coherence of information systems and monitor their quality for risk management.

One of its main initiatives has been to lobby for private insurers to be granted access to statutory health insurance databases. Unocam argues that this would enable private insurers to fulfil their mission, particularly in managing responsible contracts, but the demand raises serious concerns about protecting the privacy and the confidentiality of medical information.[41]

In spite of differences in the views of its members, Unocam now routinely contributes to public debate. This is largely the result of its working approach, which relies on technical working groups and studies in which all members participate. Nevertheless, the impact of this new platform is difficult to assess. Unocam is technically an advisory body and neither policy-makers nor insurers are bound to take into account its position. Many of its negative opinions or suggestions for cost savings in the health system have not been acted upon: for instance, Unocam issued a negative opinion on the draft 2016 Social Security Financing Act, which envisaged the introduction of insurance contracts for seniors, arguing that this plan would further segment the market and limit options for risk pooling. Nevertheless, Unocam has given complementary insurers a seat at the table.

Conclusions

Statutory coverage in France is universal and comprehensive, particularly when it comes to hospital care, and people suffering from chronic illnesses or undergoing costly treatments are generally exempt from statutory user charges. Nevertheless, during the 1990s, it became clear that those without private health insurance, especially people with low incomes, had less access to outpatient care. From 2000, the government introduced a series of measures to improve access to complementary cover, which is now recognized as an integral part of the social protection system. Evaluations indicate that the most significant measure, CMUC, has reduced inequalities in access to health care. Still, the take-up of the CMUC, and to a worse extent of the ACS, a subsidy meant to support the near-poor's access to complementary cover, has been limited. Group coverage has been mandated for all employees since 2016. For those still

---

[41] Private insurers and *mutuelles* are not requesting access to the same level of detail. *Mutuelles* are only seeking access to anonymous aggregate data, while private insurers are interested in accessing detailed individual information.

uncovered and increasingly for those covered in the individual market, private spending on health constitutes a high burden and monitoring access to care will continue to be important. Still, among OECD countries, France has achieved the lowest share of out-of-pocket spending in total spending on health (OECD, 2017a).

From an equity perspective, over time, the development of private insurance has changed the extent to which health financing arrangements match financial burden with individual capacity to pay and distribute health care services and resources based on individual need. Indeed, measures aimed at curbing public spending on health care have shifted costs from statutory to complementary insurance, which by nature is less redistributive. However, the funding of CMUC and ACS by private insurers adds a degree of income-related cross-subsidization to the complementary market.

Ultimately, achieving such a high level of prepayment and risk-pooling by relying extensively on private insurance has a cost. Administrative spending on health represents 6% of current expenditure, the second highest proportion among OECD countries, well above the OECD average of 3% (OECD, 2017b). More than 45% of that administrative spending is incurred by private insurance – which covers around 13% of health spending.[42] Whether it might be possible to achieve the same level of coverage at a lower cost overall may be worth a debate.

By reimbursing statutory user charges, complementary cover can offset demand-side incentives put in place by the statutory system to contain costs. However, it has also promoted access and financial protection and has made affordable increases in price beyond statutory fee, for instance for physician services, eyewear and dental prostheses. In 2004 and more recently in 2013, the government introduced strong incentives for private insurers to offer so-called "socially responsible contracts" that support demand-side incentives and cap the rates of coverage for some types of care for which prices have rapidly increased over the past decade, like optical and doctors' extra-fees. Indeed, historically, leaving private insurers to fill in the gaps left by the statutory system has given them little incentive to exert leverage over providers. Even

[42] In 2011, total management costs are estimated at €12.5 billion. The management costs of the Statutory Health Insurance, which accounts for more than three quarters of health expenditure (78.2%), represent slightly more than half (52%) (IGAS, 2013).

if insurers have found themselves increasingly dissatisfied with their role of passive payer and have slowly started to engage providers more actively, it would be difficult to demonstrate that they have curbed the growth rate of these spending categories. There are initial signs – and certainly hopes – that the caps on the amounts insurers are allowed to reimburse through responsible contracts may be more effective in that respect, by curbing the willingness of those who have substantial coverage to pay ever more.

A final issue concerns the contribution of private insurance to the health system being transparent and understandable. On that account, performance is poor and probably declining: statutory user charges have increased many times; rules about what providers can charge patients were made more complex by the introduction of voluntary gatekeeping; complementary contracts are becoming increasingly diversified; and responsible contracts are subject to additional reimbursement rules. All in all, it is difficult to see how patients can anticipate the net amount they will have to pay out of pocket for each contact with the health system. On that account, the standardization of ACS contracts and the intro-duction of responsible contracts probably have contributed to reducing the heterogeneity. Still, overall, the system remains complex and costly.

After decades of *laissez-faire*, regulation of private health insurance has evolved rapidly in the last 15 years, with the authorities trying to strike a balance between equity, efficiency and reducing public deficits. Indeed, a key and persistent underlying tension comes from the need to keep public spending on health in check. Although the current system tries to align incentives across statutory and private insurers, the private insurers could be tempted to offer contracts that are not "socially respon-sible", at least to those who can afford them. Such a shift would once again increase inequalities in access to complementary cover, perhaps not so much between the haves and have-nots as between those who can afford comprehensive but less regulated cover and those who cannot. An alternative scenario would be for statutory and private insurers to intensify cooperation and increase their attempts jointly to manage care and access to care and to influence provider behaviour and expectations. However, the French health system does not have a good track record on either of these fronts. Indeed, the 2004 reform, which paved the way for private insurers to have more say in the design of the health system and to be more closely involved in system-level negotiations between providers and the statutory health insurance scheme, has not fundamentally changed the dynamic of the system. Finally, excluding services from statutory coverage is a more radical option, which could redefine the scope and role of private health insurance but would require explicit and politically difficult discussions about the types of services that must remain funded publicly.

Analyses and debates around possible scenarios to improve the equity and efficiency of health financing have become more prominent in recent years (Dormont, Geoffard & Tirole, 2014; Pierron, 2016). Health was also an important topic of debate in the 2017 presidential election. The Government of President Macron has since confirmed its intention to focus on strengthening public health and prevention, but also reducing out-of-pocket payments for eyewear, dental and auditory prostheses and other measures, which could impact the private health insurance market.

References

Barlet M, Marbot C (2016). Portrait des professionnels de santé – édition 2016. *Collection Panoramas de la DREES – Santé*. April 2016, 160 p. Paris, DREES.

Barlet M, Beffy M, Renaud D (2016). La complémentaire santé : acteurs, bénéficiaires, garanties – édition 2016. *Collection Panoramas de la DREES – Santé*, April 2016, 102 pp. Paris, DREES: http://drees.social-sante.gouv .fr/IMG/pdf/oc2016.pdf.

Boisguérin B (2001). Les bénéficiaires de la Couverture Maladie Universelle au 30 septembre 2000. *Études et résultats* No. 96. Paris, DREES, French Ministry of Health.

Boisguérin B (2007). Les allocataires des minima sociaux: CMU, état de santé et recours aux soins, *Études et résultats* No. 603. Paris, DREES, French Ministry of Health.

Boisguérin B (2009). Caractéristiques sociales et recours aux soins pour les bénéficiaires de la CMU-C en 2006. *Études et résultats* No. 675. Paris, DREES, French Ministry of Health.

Buchmueller T, Couffinhal A (2004). Private health insurance in France. *OECD Health Working Paper* No. 12. Paris, OECD.

Buchmueller T et al. (2003). Access to physician services: does supplemental insurance matter? Evidence from France. *Health Economics*, 13(7):669–87.

Busse R et al., (2011). *Diagnosis-Related Groups in Europe. Moving towards transparency, efficiency and quality in hospitals*. Maidenhead, Open University Press.

Célent C, Guillaume S, Rochereau T (2014). Enquête sur la santé et la protection sociale 2012: www.irdes.fr/recherche/rapports/556-enquete-sur-la-sante-et-la-protection-sociale-2012.pdf; accessed on 19/07/2017.

Centre Technique des Institutions de Prévoyance (2016). *Annual Report 2016*. Centre Technique des Institutions de Prévoyance (CTIP): https://ctip.asso.fr/wp-content/uploads/2016/07/CTIP-livre-30ans.pdf; accessed on 19/07/2017.

Chevreul K et al. (2015). France: Health system review. *Health Systems in Transition*, 17(3):1–218.

CMU Fund (2011). Rapport d'activité 2010. Fonds de financement de la protection complémentaire de la couverture universelle du risque maladie: www.cmu.fr/userdocs/Rapport_activite_2010.pdf; accessed on 14/09/2011.

CMU Fund (2016). Rapport d'activité 2015. Fonds de financement de la protection complémentaire de la couverture universelle du risque maladie: www.cmu.fr/rapports_activite.php; accessed on 19/07/2017.

CNAMTS (2016). Rapport charges et produits, July 2016: www.ameli.fr/fileadmin/user_upload/documents/cnamts_rapport_charges_produits_2017.pdf; accessed on 19/07/2017.

Comptes de la Sécurité sociale (2016). Résultats 2015, prévisions 2016 et 2017: www.securite-sociale.fr/IMG/pdf/rapport-ccss-vol1-20160922-023102-163-40.pdf; accessed on 19/07/2017.

Com-Ruelle L, Dourgnon P, Paris V (2006). Can physician gate-keeping and patient choice be reconciled in France? Analysis of recent reform. *Eurohealth*, 12(1):17–19.

Coron G, Poinsart L (2006). Les mutations de la protection sociale complémentaire sous l'influence des directives européennes: le cas des institutions de prévoyance et des mutuelles. February: www.rt6-afs.org/IMG/doc/Les_mutations_de_la_protection_sociale_comple_mentaire20-07.doc; accessed on 25/08/2011.

Couffinhal A, Paris V (2001). Utilization fees imposed to public health care system users in France. Paris, IRDES: www.irdes.fr/EspaceAnglais/Publications/OtherPubs/UtilisationFeesImposedFrance.pdf; accessed on 25/08/2011.

Couffinhal A, Perronnin M (2004). *Accès à la couverture complémentaire maladie en France: une comparaison des niveaux de remboursement*. Enquête ESPS 2000–2, with Chevalier J and Lengagne P. *Rapport CREDES 1521*. Paris, CREDES.

Cour des Comptes (2015). Le fonds de financement de la protection complémentaire de la couverture universelle du risque maladie:

www.ccomptes.fr/Publications/Publications/Le-fonds-de-financement-de-la-protection-complementaire-de-la-couverture-universelle-du-risque-maladie; accessed on 19/07/2017.

Desprès C (2010). *Le refus de soins à l'égard des bénéficiaires de la Couverture maladie universelle complémentaire à Paris: une étude par testing auprès d'un échantillon représentatif de médecins (omnipraticiens, gynécologues, ophtalmologues, radiologues) et de dentistes parisiens'* (in collaboration with Guillaume S, Couralet PE): www.cmu.fr/site/cmu.php4?Id=3&cat=106; accessed on 20/09/2011.

Dormont B, Geoffard P-Y, Tirole J (2014). *Refonder l'assurance-maladie.* Note du CAE no. 12: www.cae-eco.fr/IMG/pdf/cae-note012-en2.pdf; accessed on 19/07/2017.

DSS (Direction de la Sécurité Sociale) (2015). Les chiffres clés de la Sécurité Sociale 2014: www.securite-sociale.fr/IMG/pdf/chiffres_cles_2015_web.pdf; accessed on 19/07/2017.

Fenina A, Geffroy Y (2007). *Comptes nationaux de la santé 2006. Série Statistiques, Document de travail* No. 114. Paris, DREES, French Ministry of Health.

Fenina A, Le Garrec M-A, Koubi M (2010). *Comptes nationaux de la santé 2009, Série Statistiques, Document de travail* No. 149. Paris, DREES, French Ministry of Health.

Franc C (2005). Quelles perspectives pour l'assurance maladie complémentaire? *Revue Sève,* 6:43–8.

Franc C, Pierre A (2015). Compulsory private complementary health insurance offered by employers in France: Implications and current debate. Health Policy (2015): http://dx.doi.org/10.1016/j.healthpol.2014.12.014; accessed on 19/07/2017.

Franc C, Polton D (2006). New governance arrangements for French health insurance. *Eurohealth,* 12(3):27–9.

Franc C, Perronnin M, Pierre A (2008). Private supplementary health insurance: retirees' demand. *Geneva Papers of Risk and Insurance – Issues and Practice,* 33:610–26.

French Ministry of Health (2016). Les dépenses de santé en 2015 – Résultats des comptes de la santé. September 2016: http://drees.social-sante.gouv.fr/IMG/pdf/cns2016.pdf; accessed on 19/07/2017.

Garnero M, Le Palud V (2014). Les contrats les plus souscrits auprès des organismes complémentaires santé en 2010. *Série Statistiques, Document de travail* No. 191. Paris, DREES.

Garnero M, Rattier M-O (2011). Les contrats les plus souscrits auprès des complémentaires santé en 2008. *Études et résultats, DREES, French Ministry of Health* No. 752. Paris, DREES.

Grignon M, Perronnin M, Lavis JN (2007). Does free complementary health insurance help the poor to access health care? Evidence from France. *Health Economics*, 17(2):203–19.

Guillaume S, Rochereau T (2010). La protection sociale complémentaire collective: des situations diverses selon les entreprises. *Questions d'économie de la santé*, IRDES No. 155. Paris, IRDES.

Guthmuller S, Jusot F, Wittwer J, in collaboration with Després C (2011). Take-up rate of a subsidising scheme for acquiring a complementary health insurance in France: key findings from a social experiment in Lille. *Questions d'économie de la santé*, IRDES No. 162. Paris, IRDES.

Hassenteufel P, Pallier B (2007). Towards Neo-Bismarckian health care states? Comparing health insurance reforms in Bismarckian welfare systems. *Social Policy and Administration*, 41(6):574–96.

HCAAM (Haut Conseil pour l'Avenir de l'Assurance Maladie) (2007). *Rapport du Haut Conseil pour l'Avenir de l'Assurance Maladie Juillet 2007:* www.securite-sociale.fr/IMG/pdf/hcaam_rapport2007.pdf; accessed on 19/07/2017.

HCAAM (2010). *Rapport annuel 2010 – l'assurance maladie face à la crise: eléments d'analyse;* www.securite-sociale.fr/IMG/pdf/hcaam_rapport2010 .pdf; accessed on 19/07/2017.

HCAAM (2013). *Rapport annuel 2013* in Partie 1 : *L'accessibilité financière des soins après assurance maladie obligatoire:* www.securite-sociale .fr/IMG/pdf/rapport_annuel_2013.pdf; accessed on 19/07/2017.

IGAS (Inspection Générale des Affaires Sociales) (2013). *Les coûts de gestion de l'assurance maladie:* www.igas.gouv.fr/IMG/pdf/RM2013-146P_2_ .pdf; accessed on 19/07/2017.

INSEE (2016). *Bilan Démographique 2015.* Insee Première No. 1581. Paris, Institut National de la Statistique et des Études Économiques: www .insee.fr/fr/statistiques/1908103; accessed on 19/07/2017.

Le Garrec MA, Koubi M, Fenina A (2013). 60 années de dépenses de santé, *Études et résultats*, No. 831. Paris, French Ministry of Health (DREES).

OECD (2017a). Health expenditure and financing: Health expenditure indicators, OECD Health Statistics (database): http://dx.doi.org/10.1787/ data-00349-en; accessed on 30/11/2017.

OECD (2017b). *Tackling Wasteful Spending on Health*, Paris, OECD Publishing.

Pierron L (2016). *Complémentaire santé, Sortir de l'incurie*. Paris, Terra Nova.

Polton D, Mousquès J (2004). Sickness funds reform: new governance. *Health Policy Monitor* October. www.hpm.org/survey/fr/a4/3.

Raynaud D (2003). Impact de la CMU sur la consommation individuelle de soins. *Études et résultats* No. 229. Paris, DREES, French Ministry of Health.

Sandier S, Paris V, Polton D (2004). *Health care systems in transition: France*. Copenhagen: WHO Regional Office for Europe on behalf of the European Observatory on Health Systems and Policies.

Sicart D (2011). Les médecins au 1er janvier 2010. *Série Statistiques, Document de travail* No. 152. Paris, DREES, French Ministry of Health.

6 Statutory and private health insurance in Germany and Chile: two stories of coexistence and conflict

STEFANIE ETTELT AND ANDRES ROMAN-URRESTARAZU

In Germany and Chile, the market for private health insurance exists alongside and "within" a statutory health insurance system that covers a large majority of the population. Private cover comes in two forms: substitutive, chosen to replace statutory cover, which means that the privately insured do not contribute to this aspect of the social security system (unless statutory health insurance is partly funded through the government budget); and complementary or supplementary, allowing people to "top up" publicly financed benefits. In both countries, the vast majority of the population is covered by statutory health insurance. However, some parts of the population, mostly those who are able to afford it, have the option of choosing between private and statutory coverage. In Germany, the group of people given this choice is limited by regulation, with those allowed to "opt out" of the statutory system having to demonstrate that they have earnings above a threshold. Once they have chosen the private option, the possibility of returning to statutory cover is limited. In Chile, choice of substitutive private cover is also dependent on earnings as a private plan is significantly more expensive than contributions to the statutory system, but there is no fixed threshold for those who wish to opt out. Also, the privately insured in Chile are allowed to re-enter the statutory system at any time, an option that has been intentionally precluded in the German system to reduce the potential for further risk segmentation.

This chapter describes the origins and development of private health insurance in Germany and Chile, providing a comparative assessment of its effects on consumers and the health financing system as a whole. The chapter provides a detailed overview of the market for private health insurance in both countries, followed by a comparative assessment of the impact of private cover in relation to financial protection, equity and efficiency, as well as the aims and effects of recent health insurance reforms in both countries.

Financing and delivery of health care in Germany

Total spending on health care was 11% of gross domestic product in 2015, of which 84% was from public sources (WHO, 2018). About 87% of the population (2015) are members of sickness funds in the statutory health insurance scheme (*Gesetzliche Krankenversicherungen*, GKV) (GKV Spitzenverband, 2016). GKV contributions currently amount to 14.6% of earned income and are equally split between employers and employees. In addition, the government now allows sickness funds to charge an additional income-adjusted premium per enrollee. The government pays contributions for groups such as the long-term unemployed on benefits. Since 2009, GKV contributions have been centrally pooled in a virtual health fund and distributed to sickness funds based on a relatively sophisticated risk-adjustment formula that includes morbidity. Membership of the GKV is compulsory for most people, but certain groups such as civil servants and the self-employed are formally excluded.[1]

About 11% of the population are covered by substitutive private health insurance (*Vollversicherung* offered by *privaten Krankenversicherung*, PKVs) (PKV, 2015). Almost half of the population with substitutive private health insurance are recipients of "*Beihilfe*" (a subsidy) as civil servants, members of the armed services and recipients of social benefits or a veteran pension. Health insurance was only made universally mandatory in January 2009, although coverage was near universal before then (only about 0.2% were uninsured in 2007; Statistisches Bundesamt, 2008). About 24.3 million people are estimated to have taken out complementary and/or supplementary (*Zusatzversicherung*) private health insurance in 2014 (PKV, 2015); these voluntary plans are substantially more popular in western states than in eastern states (BMG, 2010).

---

[1] Legislation specifies a number of criteria for voluntary GKV membership; eligible people include those previously insured as dependants but who have lost this status; employees who were working abroad and require insurance after their return; and migrants of German ethnic origin from eastern Europe (*Spätaussiedler*).

Health care delivery is organized through a mix of public, private non-profit (typically charitable or church-affiliated) and private for-profit (commercial) providers. Indeed, pluralism of provider ownership is a statutory principle of the health system. In 2015, about 29% of hospitals were publicly owned (for example, by a *Land*, district or city council), 35% were private non-profit and about 36% were private for-profit (compared with 15% in 1991) (DKG, 2016). In spite of the increase in commercial ownership, almost half of all hospital beds are in public hospitals, compared with 18% in commercial hospitals and 34% in private non-profit hospitals (DKG, 2016). About 41% of physicians, both general practitioners and specialists (constituting about half of office-based physicians), work in ambulatory practices, in single or group practices (based on information from Busse & Blümel, 2014). Patients have free choice of provider, irrespective of their insurance status, so that both GKV members and the privately insured can access (almost) any provider.

The history of health insurance in Germany

The origins of private health insurance

Private health insurance has largely developed alongside statutory health insurance. In 1884, statutory health insurance was made mandatory for industrial workers at the national level through legislation passed by the Reichstag in 1883. It was the first national social insurance scheme of its kind. Its origins in voluntary social protection schemes can be traced back to self-help schemes of professional guilds and crafts in the late Middle Ages (Busse & Riesberg, 2004).

From its inception, membership of statutory health insurance was clearly defined and initially limited to industrial workers and their families only. Later in the 20th century, membership was gradually expanded to other occupational groups, including "white-collar" workers (1970) and farmers (1972) (PKV, 2002). All other population groups were formally excluded and could only obtain health cover privately, on a substitutive basis. Private health insurance had existed before the introduction of statutory health insurance legislation, but, in the absence of a legal framework, it is hard to distinguish "social" and "private" initiatives. Arguably, the first "private" insurance scheme was created in 1848 for civil servants of the policing department in Berlin (Prussia) (PKV, 2002).

A first state regulator was created in 1901 to oversee the behaviour of private insurers, the Imperial Supervisory Agency for Private Insurance (*Kaiserliches Aufsichtsamt für die Privatversicherung*). Private health insurance grew in popularity in the mid-1920s (when the middle classes began to recover from the devaluation crisis), leading to an increase in the number of insurance companies and an expansion of the market. In 1934, a revision of the eligibility criteria for statutory cover[2] created an additional influx to private health insurance, because those not legally required or entitled to join the GKV were now formally excluded. The Second World War led to the collapse of private health insurance (all insurance, in fact). After the war, private insurers had to recreate their business from scratch in the western part of Germany, while private insurance was prohibited in the Soviet Occupied Zone. A first association of private health insurers was formed in 1946 in the British Occupied Zone (PKV, 2002).

In 1970, mandatory GKV coverage was extended to white-collar workers. The 1970 Act Relating to Health Insurance for Workers (*Gesetz betreffend der Krankenversicherung der Arbeiter*) also allowed white-collar workers with earnings above a threshold to opt out of GKV or retain membership on a voluntary basis. About 815 000 people switched from private cover to the GKV as a consequence of this change in legislation (PKV, 2002). In 1989, choice of statutory or private cover was extended to all workers with earnings above the threshold (with the exception of civil servants who had always had private cover), a change reflecting the increasingly obsolete distinction between white-collar and blue-collar workers. Private cover was still voluntary for high-income earners, although most of them took out insurance. After the country was (re-)unified in 1990, the "two pillar" health insurance system was expanded to the five eastern states.

Since 1994, individuals over the age of 65 (55 years from 2000) have been legally prevented from returning to the GKV once they have opted for private cover, even if their earnings have fallen below the threshold (€4950 per month in 2018). This measure was introduced to protect

---

[2] The "*Ersatzkassen*", mostly schemes that were organized before the introduction of statutory health insurance, were required to decide whether to join the GKV or exclude insuring "blue-collar" workers and in effect become private. As a result, many *Ersatzkassen* joined the GKV, while members who did not qualify for the GKV had to leave.

sickness funds from further risk segmentation resulting from younger people opting for private cover and rejoining the GKV when they are older and have to pay private premiums in excess of contributions to the GKV. At the same time, private insurers were required to offer a "standard tariff" to ensure that (primarily) older[3] privately insured people who were unable to join the GKV because of their age would be able to pay for private cover. The standard tariff covers the range of services covered by the GKV at a maximum price equivalent to the average maximum GKV contribution, irrespective of individual health risk or age.

Recent policy developments

Substitutive private health insurance has been a source of controversy in Germany since the 1990s. The split between statutory and private cover has frequently been criticized as being unfair, because it allows wealthier individuals to opt out of the statutory scheme and pay lower premiums than they would under the statutory scheme (at least as long as they are young and healthy). This has been regarded by many as incompatible with the principle of social solidarity. At the same time, there have been long-standing concerns about financial pressures on the privately insured, as private premiums have increased substantially over time.

Public debate about the future of private health insurance intensified in 2003, following the publication of a report by the Rürup Commission (*Kommission für Nachhaltigkeit in der Finanzierung der sozialen Sicherungssysteme*). The report discussed options for securing the financial sustainability of the health system and included a proposal to abolish substitutive private health insurance and introduce a universal system of "citizens' insurance". An alternative suggestion was to include private health insurance in the national system of risk adjustment. Both proposals were supported by a majority of Social Democrats and Green Party politicians (then forming the federal government), but did not obtain sufficient political support to pass in both chambers of parliament and were eventually abandoned.

---

[3] Those over 65 years, who were privately insured for at least 10 years, and those over the age of 55 years with an income that had fallen below the threshold that would normally require them to join GKV.

Further sustained debate took place following the election of a new coalition government formed by the (conservative) Christian Democrats and the Social Democrats in September 2005. This led to an agreement on a number of reform proposals in February 2007. While most changes – such as the introduction of cost-effectiveness analysis for pharmaceuticals, the creation of a health fund to virtually pool resources across all sickness funds and the merger of GKV associations at the federal level – were directed at the GKV, the reform also had substantial implications for private health insurance. Following the coming into force of the Act to Promote Competition within the GKV (*GKV-Wettbewerbsstärkungsgesetz*) in January 2009, health insurance, public or private, became mandatory for all residents. The Act stipulated that anyone who was not enrolled in the GKV must take out private health insurance or rejoin the GKV. Private insurers were required to offer a new type of tariff (the so-called basic tariff, which is similar to the standard tariff introduced in 1994) to a wider group of individuals, including people over the age of 55 years, people receiving benefits or a pension, and all those who opted for private cover from January 2009[4] (see below).

Arguably, the outcome of the 2007 reform reflects two dynamics in contemporary German health policy. Although substitutive private health insurance was repeatedly discussed before the reform, there was no political majority in support of the abolition of the dual health insurance system (often dubbed *Zweiklassenmedizin* – two-tier medicine – by its critics). In spite of its acknowledged problems (for example. the increase in premiums for older people and the absence of cost control) private health insurance is still the favoured model in large parts of the conservative and liberal (pro-private/pro-corporate) establishment. The dual insurance system is also fiercely defended by the medical profession. Thus the political costs of change are high, creating a propensity to maintain the status quo.

Any changes have largely been introduced at the margins of the system; for example, making people demonstrate earnings above the threshold for 3 years instead of 1 year (introduced in 2007 and revoked in 2010), or the introduction of *Wahltarife* (optional tariffs) within the GKV, which allow sickness funds to offer a more diversified range of

---

[4] Those with contracts concluded after this date may switch to the basic tariff but no longer to the standard tariff.

insurance plans.[5] These new tariffs were at least in part intended to attract or retain those able to choose between GKV and private cover. In contrast, reforms introduced in 2010 by the federal government (then a coalition of Free Democrats and Christian Democrats) aimed to increase the attractiveness of private cover vis-à-vis statutory cover by allowing sickness funds to charge a premium in addition to wage-based contributions. However, a further reform introduced in 2015 under a coalition of Christian Democrats and Social Democrats reduced the contribution rate for people with GKV insurance to 14.6%. Sickness funds can still charge their members an additional fee, but this fee is calculated as a share of income as opposed to being a flat fee.

The succession of recent reforms has led to increasingly stringent regulation of the substitutive private market, which is not uncontested. The PKVs opposed several aspects of the 2007 and earlier reforms, notably rules around the basic tariff, the transferability of ageing reserves and allowing sickness funds to offer voluntary benefits (limited to pharmaceuticals excluded from the statutory package, such as homeopathic drugs). Several private insurers submitted a joint appeal to the Federal Constitutional Court to review the 2007 Act on the grounds that it disadvantaged private subscribers and infringed on the entrepreneurial freedom of insurers (PKV, 2008). The appeal was rejected in June 2009 (Bundesverfassungsgericht, 2009).

Concerns about the future viability of private health insurance were voiced by a PKV working group in 2008 – "Social Security 2020". In an internal discussion paper (leaked to the press), the group proposed considering the introduction of universal compulsory health insurance, private or public, based on flat-rate premiums independent of age and individual risk. Their concern was that population ageing, in conjunction with regulation, would undermine their ability to attract a sufficient number of young and healthy customers to be able to keep premiums stable. Although the proposal was supported by larger (commercial) insurers, it was fiercely opposed by others (mostly mutual associations) (Fromme, 2008). Some speculated that the days of substitutive private health insurance were numbered, largely due to growing dissatisfaction among the privately insured who faced ever increasing premiums (*Zeit* online, 2012). More recently, private health insurers have come under

---

[5] Plans with deductibles, previously only offered to those with private coverage, or plans with rebates for people who enrol with a dedicated family practitioner.

increased financial pressure due to low interest rates in the capital market and a rising number of defaulters (Greß, 2016).

Overview of the market for private health insurance in Germany

Market structure

Substitutive insurance provides full cover of the costs of health care equivalent (or more) to the benefits covered by statutory health insurance. Complementary or supplementary insurance typically covers the costs of health services that are excluded from the GKV and/or that attract a statutory user charge. In 2014, about 24.3 million people had complementary/supplementary cover, compared with 13.8 million in 2000 (BMG, 2010; PKV, 2015).

Private products are currently offered by 49 insurance companies (PKV, 2015); 24 of these are publicly listed corporations, usually with a wider insurance portfolio; 18 are mutual associations, which specialize in health care; an additional seven insurance companies are listed stock corporations that only offer complementary/supplementary insurance. The market is not highly concentrated – in 2014 the four largest insurance companies had a joint market share of 51% (PKV, 2015). In addition, there are two private funds for railway and postal workers, dating back to the time when both enterprises were (fully) state-owned and their employees were civil servants, and a number of small private insurers operating regionally and only in the complementary market (there were 31 such insurers in 2009 and their combined market share was 0.002%) (PKV, 2010).

Eligibility

Eligibility for substitutive cover is limited to those not mandatorily covered by the GKV, that is, people with earnings above the threshold. Self-employed people are not required to join a sickness fund and usually take out private cover.[6] The health care costs of civil servants (including teachers and police officers) are mostly covered by the state through

---

[6] They would have to pay both the employer's and employee's share of the GKV contribution, which makes GKV membership unattractive to them.

"Beihilfe".[7] Civil servants only have to cover a small proportion, for which they can buy complementary private cover.

Premiums and policy conditions

Private premiums are based on an assessment of an individual's risk profile at the time of purchase and adjusted for age, sex and medical history. For employees, the cost of the premium is typically shared with the employer. The employer's share includes premiums for the insured and any dependants. It is set at 50% of the rate that employers and employees would have to contribute if the employee were in the GKV, and is capped at 50% of the actual insurance premium (PKV, 2009). Dependants are not automatically covered and must pay separate premiums. Some insurers offer group contracts, purchased through employers. Group contracts may offer financial and other advantages, such as lower premiums and waivers of risk assessment and waiting periods (DKV, 2008).

Insurers can reject applications and exclude pre-existing conditions or charge a higher premium to cover them. From 2009, however, they are required to accept any applicant (open enrolment) eligible for the basic tariff and cannot exclude cover of pre-existing conditions for this category of clients. Like the standard tariff, the basic tariff covers services provided under the GKV at a capped premium (€665.29 per month in 2016). If people can demonstrate that they cannot afford the full premium for the basic tariff, the premium will be reduced by 50% and the remainder will be subsidized by the state. If this is still unaffordable, individuals will receive a state subsidy under the social benefits scheme.

Substitutive private cover is for life and operates on a funded basis. Since 2001, insurers have been required to build up ageing reserves to cover age-related increases in costs (and slow the increase of premiums) later in life; reserves are built by charging all clients between the ages of 21 and 60 an additional 10% of all premium payments made.

---

[7] The level of *Beihilfe* varies for federal and state civil servants, as the states and the federal level each have developed different legislation in relation to civil servants in their jurisdiction. Several changes were made to the *Beihilfe* system in the 1990s, partly in response to financial pressures on public employers associated with the rising costs of health care and demographic ageing (Bundestag, 2005).

Benefits

Substitutive private cover typically offers the same comprehensive range of benefits as the GKV. Some specific services may be excluded, such as dental care or treatment in a health resort. From 2009, private plans have had to cover both outpatient (ambulatory) and (non-long-term) inpatient services. Before this, it was possible to choose to be covered for one or the other only. Insurers typically impose a waiting period of 3 months before benefits apply (or 8 months for childbirth, psychotherapy and dental care), but this may be waived if a new customer was previously covered by the GKV (DKV, 2008).

Benefits are mainly provided in cash and may involve cost sharing. Co-insurance is common in dental care and most plans offer deductibles. The deductible amount has been capped at €5000 per year (PKV, 2009). In 2005, about 75% of privately insured individuals (excluding those eligible for *Beihilfe*) opted for a deductible (25% of those eligible for *Beihilfe*) (Grabka, 2006). Older people are likely to opt for higher deductibles than younger people (Grabka, 2006).

The private market offers a wide range of complementary plans, providing reimbursement for services fully or partly excluded from the GKV, such as eyewear, hearing aids and some health checks and diagnostic services (typically excluded or restricted on the grounds of their limited effectiveness or added value). Complementary plans are also available for services that involve statutory user charges, such as dental care, pharmaceuticals. There are also plans offering "top-ups" in hospital, including accommodation in a one- or two-bed ward and treatment by the chief consultant. Despite the enormous variety of plans available, they largely cover combinations of the same services.

Paying providers

Like sickness funds, private insurers are largely bound by collective agreements on provider payment formed by the associations of sickness funds and provider associations (that is, German Hospital Association and Associations of GKV Physicians). In addition, they can form agreements with providers that only treat privately insured patients. Vertical integration with providers is rare and not permitted in some cases (insurers are not allowed to own polyclinics).

Private insurers are generally price takers. In the hospital sector, prices per service are reimbursed based on diagnosis-related groups and prices are identical for statutory and private health insurance. In ambulatory care, prices are based on a list of "basic prices" issued by the Federal Ministry of Health. However, physicians can charge higher fees by multiplying the basic price by a factor set to reflect the level of complexity and time for treatment (for example, a factor of up to 3.5 for personal services rendered by a physician and 1.3 for laboratory services). Physicians are also allowed to bill in excess of these prices, although this requires approval of the insurer before the service is provided (PKV, 2008). Waldendzik et al. (2008) have demonstrated that prices for physician services are more than twice as high for the privately insured as for those covered by the GKV. Prices for high-cost pharmaceuticals are now negotiated with pharmaceutical companies for both sickness funds and private insurers. Given the pressure on premiums in recent years, private insurers have shown increased interest in developing better tools to manage care and contain costs (Genett, 2016). However, this is likely to compromise their ability to attract new members.

Unlike sickness funds, private insurers only form direct contractual relationships with subscribers, not with providers. As a result, they have little leverage over providers, many of whom are allowed to charge higher fees for privately insured patients than for GKV members. While insurers routinely check all medical bills submitted by patients, these procedures mainly aim to uncover exaggerated accounts of delivered services or services not covered by the patient's plan (such as those associated with a pre-existing condition).

Legislation and regulation

Health insurance is heavily regulated through legislation. Social Code Book V (SGB V) regulates all aspect of statutory health insurance, including criteria for eligibility and opting out. It does not regulate private health insurance directly (perhaps with the exception of the basic tariff), but changes in legislation aimed at reforming the GKV often affect private health insurance. Private cover is regulated through a number of laws and ordinances applying to the insurance market in general (for example, insurance contract law) or to private health insurance specifically (for example, provisions for savings). Financial oversight of the private health insurance market is exercised by the Federal Supervisory Office for Financial Services (*Bundesanstalt für Finanzdienstleistungsaufsicht*), an agency of the Ministry of Finance.

Developments in the private health insurance sector are also closely observed by the Ministry of Health, although the latter has little direct control over the market. Indeed, interventions typically require changes in legislation and need to be agreed by parliament.

From 2009, customers have been allowed to take the portion of the ageing reserve attributable to the basic tariff with them if they change private insurer (or the entire reserve if they change plan within the same company). This change was introduced to facilitate consumer mobility and promote competition in the private market. Private cover qualifies for tax subsidies. Until recently, a maximum ceiling for tax subsidies applied to all types of insurance, which meant that tax subsidies did not usually provide an incentive to purchase private health insurance. In January 2010, however, a special tax subsidy was applied exclusively to health insurance, including GKV cover.[8]

Financing and delivery of health care in Chile

Health care in Chile is financed through a dual system of statutory health insurance (*Fondo Nacional de Salud*, FONASA) and private health insurance (*Instituciones de Salud Previsional*, ISAPRE). Health insurance is mandatory for workers, pensioners and the unemployed (unless they are unable to pay). In 2013, about 76.3% of the population were covered by the statutory scheme and 18.2% had voluntary private cover (Sánchez, 2014; Superintendencia de Salud, 2015). About 2.95% of the population have access to health care as members of the army (Sánchez, 2014; Superintendencia de Salud, 2015). Contributions for the statutory scheme are deducted from wages, at a rate of 7% up to a ceiling. People with no or low income are also entitled to join FONASA. Their contributions are covered by the government. Health services funded by FONASA are mainly provided by public providers.

---

[8] The subsidy covers private cover equal to GKV cover and GKV contributions (*Ärztezeitung*, 2009). It was introduced as part of a set of laws aimed at reducing the burden of taxation on citizens (*Bürgerentlastungsgesetz*). The law responded to a ruling of the Federal Constitutional Court (*Bundesverfassungsgericht*) in February 2008, which had challenged the previous practice of a lower tax subsidy for the privately insured on the grounds that health insurance cover (and some other types of insurance) is a basic need and should therefore be tax free (BgBl, 2009).

FONASA membership is organized in two tiers. Members of the first tier (A and B, indicating a monthly income below €280 per person) have access to public providers only, organized through 29 local health authorities. Members of the second tier are divided into categories C with an income between €280 and €400 and D with an income above €400, and can choose between public and (accredited and contracted) private providers if they are willing to make a co-payment and buy a pay-as-you-go voucher for additional benefits (originally introduced under the SERMENA system; see below). This is called *Modalidad de Libre Eleccion*. The privately insured, that is, ISAPRE customers, have access to a wider choice of mainly for-profit private providers. However, some crossover between public and private providers can be observed between both FONASA and ISAPRE members. For example, since 2005, as part of the regimen of Explicit Health Guarantees (*Garantías Explícitas en Salud*, AUGE), which guarantees a certain set of services for all FONASA members (see below), if the guarantees are not met by public providers, FONASA members can use private providers instead. Also, wealthier FONASA members tend to use the *Modalidad de Libre Eleccion* and pay-as-you-go vouchers to expand their choice of and access to outpatient services. On the other hand, some underinsured ISAPRE users tend to use public providers for catastrophic events and pay FONASA fees for these.

In terms of provider payment, ISAPRE schemes generally pay private providers on a fee-for-service basis. They usually accept prices prevailing in the market, but in some cases they use lists of preferred providers and negotiate prices with them in bulk (that is, for all providers on the list). FONASA tends to pay public providers according to a centrally defined list of hospital and physician fees and capitation payments for primary care. These fees are much lower than those paid by the ISAPRE schemes (SERNAC, 2011).

Even though vertical integration has been explicitly forbidden by law since 2005,[9] ISAPRE schemes have increasingly integrated vertically with

---

[9] The reason for this prohibition is the fact that in cases of vertical integration the insurer can manipulate demand for health services and steer patients to the most profitable (integrated) provider, transferring costs and profits from providers to insurers and vice versa.

providers through structures such as health care holdings or integrated care clusters (where the use of certain providers is encouraged through financial hedges). These structures, similar to health care holdings that underlie the health maintenance organizations in the USA (Valencia, 2012), control about 42% of the private provider market (Valencia, 2012; Superintendencia de Salud, 2013). Vertical integration can be viewed as a response to the growing public discontent with escalating health care costs ascribed to the use of fee-for-service as a method of payment in the private subsystem and the resulting excessive profits of private providers (Superintendencia de Salud, 2013). By merging vertically with providers, ISAPRE insurers can shift costs to the the provider level, avoid increasing premiums at the insurer level and maintain high profits at the level of the health care holding or cluster (Superintendencia de Salud, 2013). A recent study from the *Superintendencia de Salud* that compared the prices of four services (caesarean section, normal delivery, cholecystectomy and appendectomy) showed that, in 2016, patients affiliated with vertically integrated private health insurance companies paid on average 19% more for these services than patients with comparably priced plans with similar coverage who were insured in companies that were not vertically integrated (Sandoval & Herrera, 2016).

The history of health insurance in Chile

The first period of statutory health insurance (1880s–1950s)

Throughout most of the 19th century, local authorities and charitable organizations were the main providers of health care, with almost no involvement of the central government in health care delivery. At the end of the century, political pressure to address the health needs of the industrial poor grew, leading, in 1886, to the creation of the Public Relief Commission (*Junta de Beneficiencia*). This public–private body was mandated to develop a first administrative framework, bringing together various forms of providers, supported by a state subsidy, while maintaining their organizational autonomy. In 1917, renewed political and social pressure led to the creation of the Council of Public Relief (*Consejo de Beneficiencia*). The Council initiated a national programme to improve health care infrastructure, introducing, among other things, nationwide quality standards in hospitals. By the late

1920s, this network of state-funded hospitals had become the main health care provider.

In 1924, legislation passed by parliament (Law 4.054) established a system of statutory health insurance (the "*Cajas*" system). Coverage was introduced in three tiers, with separate *Cajas* for blue-collar workers, white-collar workers and civil servants. The schemes were funded through contributions levied on wage income (initially 3%), contributions from employers (equalling 2% of the employee's wage) and support from the state (1%). *Cajas* reimbursed providers on a fee-for-service basis, later changing to a preferred-provider approach, which led to increasing vertical integration of payers and providers.

From 1942, white-collar workers were able to join the National Medical Service for Employees (*Servicio Medico Nacional de Empleados*, SERMENA). This scheme was created under the umbrella of the *Cajas* and allowed its members free choice of health care provider. By 1943, 37 *Cajas* covered around 1.5 million workers and their families (30% of the population) (Alexander, 1949). However, the *Cajas* system left large sections of the population without coverage. Rural peasants and the urban poor in the informal economy (about 33% of the urban labour force in 1952) were excluded (Raczynski, 1994), and dependants were only covered after 1936.

Introduction of the National Health Service (1950s–1970s)

In response to gaps in coverage, in 1952, the populist centre-right administration of President Carlos Ibáñez del Campo merged the *Cajas* with a wide range of religious, municipal and other public or charitable health care providers to create the National Health Service (*Servicio Nacional de Salud*, SNS). Mandatory earmarked contributions to the SNS continued to be based on wages (5% for employees, 10% for employers). However, as historical budget deficits required continuous subsidization, transfers from the general government budget became de facto the main source of funding. By 1955, about 1.6 million workers contributed to the SNS, representing 65% of the active population. Individual benefits in terms of the volume of services consumed had risen by approximately 250% in real terms between 1920 and 1950 (Arellano, 1985).

White-collar workers could still join SERMENA, which had been transformed into a supplementary insurance scheme in 1952. SERMENA members could purchase a pay-as-you-go voucher for additional benefits (including dental, ophthalmological, occupational and mental health services) and choose from a range of providers that were part of the SNS, although not available under the usual arrangement, as well as private providers (*Modalidad de Libre Elección*). The voucher entitled patients to partial reimbursement for additional services, although many services also involved hefty user charges (Vergara-Iturriaga & Martínez-Gutiérrez 2008). SERMENA was popular with doctors, as it allowed them to earn extra income, and with wealthier people (Illanes, 1993; Horwitz et al., 1995). However, it was criticised for undermining the SNS because it relied on SNS capacity and infrastructure, which was not available to people who could not afford to pay extra.

The emergence of private health insurance

Following elections in 1970, incoming president Salvador Allende hoped to build a unified health service (*Servicio Unico de Salud*) that would bring together the public and private components of the system and integrate SERMENA into the public health system. Because this would have limited choice previously available to a privileged group of people, it faced opposition. In 1973, a military coup led by General Augusto Pinochet swept the Allende government out of office. The *Junta*'s social and economic policy was shaped by neoliberal ideas and the following years therefore saw a radically reduced involvement of the state in the delivery of services. In 1975, the *Junta* decentralized the SNS, so that it was organized as 27 regional health trusts. Responsibility for primary care was transferred to municipalities (*Sistema Nacional de Servicios de Salud*). The role of the Ministry of Health was largely limited to national goal-setting and policy-making. In contrast to the previous integrated system, the new approach separated funding, provision and regulation, and allowed the private sector to be involved in both funding and providing health care. Providers were paid on a fee-for-service basis and choice was opened up to anyone who could afford to purchase a voucher. In 1979, the SNS and SERMENA were merged through decree to form FONASA.

These reforms prepared the ground for the entry of private health insurance. A 1980 decree (Law Decree 3.626) created the legal and institutional framework, stipulating that all workers in the formal economy would pay a mandatory 4% of their taxable earnings or pension income into a central health fund, but would then be able to choose to join FONASA or a private insurer (ISAPRE) (in which case the contribution would be transferred to the private insurer). The reform also introduced the tiered system still in use today within FONASA. Category A and B users (unemployed people or informal sector workers) were exempt from making contributions and joined FONASA by default; they usually had no choice of provider and were exempt from user charges. Users in categories C and D, in contrast, enjoyed more choice but were also required to pay user charges (10% of the services tariff in category C, 20% in category D).

Individuals opting for private cover usually also had to pay user charges. Legislation required ISAPREs to cover services covered by FONASA (that is, the "basic plan" for category A and B). However, in contrast to FONASA, ISAPRE user charges were not regulated and could therefore be substantial. To begin with, about 50% of those who were privately insured had previously been covered by one of the more privileged *Cajas* (for workers employed in mining or railroads) that had not been part of the SNS (Scarpaci, 1989). These mostly joined "closed" ISAPREs exclusively available for members of certain companies or unions. Contracts with private insurers were for 1 year and extensions were subject to review, allowing private insurers to increase premiums substantially over time. However, if a contract could not be renewed or an ISAPRE customer wanted to leave the scheme, he or she was allowed to join FONASA unconditionally.

Development of the private health insurance market in the 1980s

Uptake of private health insurance was initially slow in the 1980s, its share only growing from 0.5% of the population in 1981 to 4.5% in 1986 (Raczynski, 1994). This was attributed to the high cost of premiums, the economic recession of 1981–1983 and reluctance among users to enter the market. There were also concerns about coverage limitations for maternity and sick pay, which by law had to be included in both FONASA and ISAPRE plans. Several private plans also refused to enrol married women without a separate income and/or required female applicants to undergo a pregnancy test (Scarpaci, 1989). As a result of the economic crisis and devaluation of the national currency in the early 1980s, many private insurers faced increasing deficits (Scarpaci,

1989). The situation improved after 1986 when legislation was introduced requiring private insurers to make provisions for maternity and sick pay, for which insurers were compensated through tax funding. Low-income earners who had taken out private insurance also became eligible for a tax break of 2% of their gross earnings (this was abolished in 2000). Mandatory contributions for both ISAPRE and FONASA rose from 4% in 1981 to 6% in 1983 and 7% in 1986, an increase of 88% in 6 years (Scarpaci, 1989).

The number of privately insured people increased in the second half of the 1980s, rising from under 500 000 in 1985 to 1.4 million in 1988 (about 11% of the population), mainly in response to the improved economic climate, which increased salaries. The number of private insurers rose from 17 to 31 during the same period, with smaller companies entering the market (Scarpaci, 1989). The market share of the three largest insurers fell from 74% in 1981 to 46% in 1988 (Scarpaci, 1989). Migration of wealthier people from FONASA to ISAPRE meant a loss of income for FONASA. By 1988, the ISAPRE system covered 11% of the population but collected more than half of all mandatory contributions, accounting for 38% of total spending on health (Raczynski, 1994). Raczynski (1994) argues that resources previously collected by the state were increasingly directed to the private sector.

Major health insurance reforms of the 1990s

Following the return to democracy in 1990, health sector reform was a priority for the newly elected government. Between 1990 and 1994, the government tried to rebuild and modernize public health services, largely to compensate for previous structural adjustment programmes and budget cuts. Although health care was a concern throughout the 1990s, reforms to the health insurance system failed to generate the support required for large-scale changes, mainly due to strong opposition in Congress from right wing senators appointed by the army. Between 1994 and 2000, the government tried to circumvent this opposition by promoting the modernization of the public health sector and fostering competition between public and private schemes to improving the efficiency of both parts of the system.

Between 2003 and 2005, led by a centre-left government that had declared health reform a priority, parliament approved comprehensive legislation, including changes aimed at addressing the inequities arising from a dual health insurance system. The Financing Law (Law no. 19.888) introduced in 2003 increased taxes on alcohol and cigarettes and raised the VAT rate from 18% to 19% so that the additional 1% could be allocated to health care. It also increased the level of revenue transferred from the central government to the public health system (Minsal, 2008). Government transfers are still crucial, given the low incomes of the population (the average monthly salary in 2013 was approximately €564) and the low share of wage-related contributions in FONASA's budget. In 2013, only 42.5% of FONASA members made such contributions and the share of these contributions has historically accounted for less than 60% of FONASA's budget (Superintendencia de Salud, 2015).

Further legislation (Law no. 19.895, called the "Short Law for ISAPREs" because of its relatively uncontroversial nature), enacted in 2003, introduced additional requirements to ensure financial solvency and transparency among private insurers. The Health Authority Act was introduced in 2004 to strengthen the supervisory role of the Ministry of Health vis-à-vis insurers. Importantly, legislation passed in 2003 defined a set of medical conditions, referred to as "explicit health guarantees" (*Garantias Explicitas en Salud*, AUGE), that private plans must cover for a premium that is community-rated across insurers. The selection of conditions covered rose from 25 in 2005 to 80 in 2016, reflecting the national burden of disease and disability. User charges for explicit guarantee services were regulated (for both ISAPRE and FONASA) and the privately insured had to access them through a network of preferred providers. FONASA members were allowed to seek care from a private provider if the public sector was not able to deliver the service within a certain period of time. The explicit guarantee system therefore acted as a waiting time guarantee.

The "Long Law for ISAPREs" was introduced in 2005. It applied community rating to ISAPRE premiums and established rules for premium setting. Both these rules and the community rating of premiums were strongly opposed by the association of private health insurers and right-wing politicians in Congress. The law set the rate of annual premium changes for ISAPRE (to be calculated based on a table of risk factors) and created a risk equalization scheme (*Fondo Compensatorio Solidario*) among open ISAPRE schemes to fund explicit guarantees. This was meant to standardize the price of services in both sectors for selected conditions. In addition, plans that covered services beyond those included in the explicit guarantee had to cover the same range of services covered by FONASA for users in category D and guarantee choice of provider. It was hoped that, by regulating premiums, coverage and prices through preferred-provider arrangements within the explicit guarantees system, would encourage providers to standardize services, discontinue the practice of treating patients differently based on their insurance status and improve quality of care, with these positive effects increasing as the AUGE system expanded.

Implementation of the "Long law" in 2005 met with heavy criticism from private insurers because the changes introduced substantially increased their financial risk. At the same time, patient groups regarded some of the indicators included as risk factors, such as sex and age, as discriminatory and challenged their constitutionality in court. The table of risk factors was declared unconstitutional by the Constitutional Tribunal in 2010 (though it is still in effect), a decision that effectively reversed the 2005 law and presented an important setback to the agreements reached in Congress.

Overview of the market for private health insurance in Chile

Market structure

In 2015, private health insurance was offered by 13 insurers, with the three largest holding a market share of almost 60% (Sánchez, 2014). Seven of these insurers were open ISAPRE schemes and the other six were closed ISAPRE schemes covering workers in the mining industry and railroads, and civil servants. There is also a growing market for complementary and supplementary health insurance, with 12.3% of the population having purchased some sort of complementary or supplementary insurance plan in 2010 (Sánchez, 2014).

Complementary or supplementary insurance is offered almost exclusively through group contracts (87% of the complementary market; Departamento de Estudios y Desarrollo 2008) and plans typically provide greater choice of provider, a reduction in user charges and increased cover for catastrophic illness, which is often capped by private plans for conditions not covered by the explicit guarantees, such as trauma.

Before the introduction of the explicit guarantees, about 40 000 different ISAPRE plans were on the market. It is estimated that their number has increased to 64 000, indicating that reforms have not produced the desired convergence of plans (Comisión Asesora Presidencial, 2014).

Eligibility

Health insurance is in principle compulsory for all workers, pensioners and unemployed people, although in practice the latter (as well as those employed in the informal sector) are not required to make contributions. Everyone except miners can choose to join FONASA or an ISAPRE scheme. Traditionally seen as being of strategic importance, miners working under permanent contracts are automatically privately insured, usually in one of the closed plans.

Premiums and policy conditions

Private health insurance in Chile is available to those able to afford the premiums. Financing has been historically based on mandatory wage contributions (7% of wage income up to a ceiling; see above). These contributions are capped at €186 per month, as are contributions made by FONASA members (Superintendencia de Pensiones, 2015). However, if this mandatory contribution does not cover the full price of the private health insurance premium, households must pay the difference themselves. Companies offering private plans are also allowed to negotiate wage-based contributions with customers that exceed the statutory ceiling if they wish to offer additional services not covered by the basic premium or a larger choice of providers (Bastías et al., 2008). Although the cap may in theory increase the financial risk borne by ISAPRE schemes, the risk is in practice small due to cream-skimming practices applied when contracts are renewed (see below). FONASA contributions are very low in comparison. For someone in category C (the second highest income category), assumed to have a monthly income below €380, the monthly FONASA contribution would be about €27.

Private premiums are based on individual risk (age, sex) and characteristics (number of dependants covered), with a proportion of the price calculated as a community rate to cover the explicit guarantee conditions introduced in 2003. Contracts are usually annual and extensions are subject to a review based on individual risk factors. Insurers can reject applications and limit cover of nonguaranteed services. Before 2003, they were also allowed to cap benefits through "stop-loss" clauses for cover of catastrophic events or chronic conditions (Jack, 2002). Stop-loss clauses meant services could be excluded from cover at a time when the insured needed them most, creating a powerful disincentive for higher-risk people to opt for private cover and a strong incentive for the privately insured to switch to FONASA once they had reached the limit of their private plan. They therefore led to further segmentation of the national health insurance "market". The introduction of explicit guarantees and catastrophic cover with a cap on deductibles[10] put an end to this practice; insurers are no longer allowed to limit cover of guaranteed services.

Following earlier attempts to limit financial risk for the privately insured (see footnote 97), the Superintendencia de Salud (an arm's-length regulatory body set up following the merger of the regulator for statutory cover and the ISAPREs regulator) has had greater oversight of premiums since 2003, although many of the original rules were contested by insurers. Insurers must now set premiums within 30% of a basic premium set by the insurer, which limits their ability to differentiate between plans and enrollees. The Superintendencia sets parameters for the risk factors used to calculate premiums, a more controversial change that was fiercely opposed by insurers and deemed unconstitutional in 2010. This policy was combined with the creation of a risk equalization mechanism, extensively elaborated in the Long Law and overseen by the Superintendencia. The mechanism, based on age and gender, virtually redistributes resources between insurers. It was also strongly opposed by insurers and, so far, its impact on risk selection has been negligible, especially given that AUGE (since renamed as Garantías Explícitas de Salud) benefits for ISAPRE users do not allow for a choice of provider (a preferred network of providers has to be used) which for many users was an important factor when choosing private health insurance.

Benefits

The privately insured have access to a wide range of private providers and the private sector is seen as providing more choice and faster access.

---

[10] From 2000, insurers were required to provide additional cover for catastrophic illness (*Cobertura Adicional de Enfermedades Catastróficas*). However, this covered only 85.5% of the costs of care (Superintendencia de Salud, 2008) and insurers had some discretion in determining the threshold beyond which catastrophic cover was initiated.

FONASA members with complementary voluntary health insurance also have access to a wider range of providers (with the scope of entitlement dependent on the contract chosen). ISAPRE benefits are required by law to match FONASA entitlements. Any additional benefits are negotiated with enrollees based on guidelines set by the Superintendencia.

Contracts are typically annual. Enrollees can lose their private cover if they become unemployed, although they can then switch to FONASA. Conversely, they can remain privately insured on a voluntary basis. Since the introduction of explicit guarantees, insurers' ability to increase premiums arbitrarily is much more limited. Cost-sharing requirements for the privately insured are substantial. In 2006, half of all private plans covered only 70% of the costs of ambulatory care and 90% of the costs of inpatient care (Perticara, 2008) and out-of-pocket payments (at 32.4% of total spending on health in 2016 compared with the OECD average of about 20% (2015 data); OECD, 2017) remain a serious barrier to accessing health care services (Pedraza & Toledo, 2012; Cid et al., 2006). Inequalities arising from the way in which ISAPRE benefits are priced and defined have been well documented. Perticara (2008) concluded that both FONASA and ISAPRE schemes imposed a high burden of cost sharing on patients, but that financial risk was substantially higher for the privately insured than the publicly covered. She also showed that user charges paid by the poorest 5% of the population were about 200 times higher, proportionately, than those paid by the wealthiest 5%. ISAPRE users continue to incur larger out-of-pocket payments than FONASA users not only in absolute terms, but also in terms of the share of their incomes – in 2013 out-of-pocket payments accounted to, respectively, 6.1% and 3.8% of the incomes of ISAPRE and FONASA members (Pedraza & Toledo, 2012; Castillo-Laborde & Villalobos Dintrans, 2013).

Paying providers

ISAPREs pay providers on a fee-for-service basis[11] using market prices negotiated with individual providers and, in some cases, negotiating prices in bulk with preferred providers (see above). Most insurers offer

---

[11] Similar to publicly covered wealthier patients (FONASA category C and D) who can opt (and pay extra) for additional choice of provider (*Modalidad Libre Elección*).

a list of preferred providers with whom discounted prices have been negotiated. Fees are also agreed collectively in the case of services covered by the explicit guarantees. To control costs, many insurers have vertically merged with service providers (see above). Nevertheless, fee-for-service at prevailing market prices remains the predominant payment mechanism for most insurers, providing incentives for providers to give preferential treatment to the privately insured (and those opting for provider choice under FONASA) and to over-provide profitable services to them (Vergara-Iturriaga & Martínez-Gutiérrez, 2008). So far, this approach to paying providers has not been challenged.

Legislation and regulation

Since the reforms of the early 2000s, regulation of the private insurance industry has substantially increased (Table 6.1). Much has been done to increase transparency for consumers and limit the financial risk for enrollees associated with catastrophic events, risk selection, stop-loss clauses and user charges. The Superintendencia de Salud oversees market conduct and financial performance and also acts as an advocate for consumers. It regulates both statutory and private cover.

Serious concerns have been raised about potential collusion among private insurers, which would undermine competition (Agostini, Saavedra & Willington, 2008). Agostini, Saavedra & Willington (2008) suggested that the five largest insurers offered plans with identical user charges with coverage below the level prescribed by the Superintendencia (only reimbursing 90% instead of 100% of the cost of inpatient care and 70% instead of 80% of the costs of outpatient care). In 2005, the National Economic Prosecutor (*Fiscalía Nacional Económica*) brought the insurers to court. The insurers were acquitted in the first instance and later also by the Supreme Court of Justice, which established that parallel behaviour was insufficient to prove tacit collusion.

The impact of private health insurance in Germany and Chile

The following paragraphs attempt a comparative assessment of the operation and regulation of private health insurance in both countries and its effects on financial protection; equity in relation to financing and access to health care; and the problems arising from risk selection and market segmentation. The relationship between statutory and private

Table 6.1 *Development and regulation of private health insurance in Germany and Chile, 1970–2016*

Germany	
1970	Expansion of mandatory statutory health insurance to white-collar workers; white-collar workers with earnings above a threshold continued to be allowed to opt for private health insurance
1989	Introduction of choice of statutory or private health insurance for all individuals with higher earnings
1990	German Reunification
1994	Introduction of the PKV standard tariff
1994	Introduction of the age limit for returning to the GKV: individuals aged 65+ cannot return to GKV (lowered to 55+ in 2000)
2001	Introduction of a compulsory ageing reserve surcharge of 10% on all PKV premiums
2004	Statutory health insurance funds allowed to sell voluntary complementary and supplementary policies
2007	Extension of qualifying period during which individuals have to be earning above the threshold in order to be allowed to opt out of the GKV (from 1 year to 3 years)
2009	Health insurance (statutory or private) made mandatory; PKV basic tariff made a legal requirement; introduction of portability of ageing reserves to reduce barriers to switching insurer among the privately insured
2010	Qualifying period extended in 2007 reduced to 1 year; extended to 2 years in 2011
2011	Discounts for medicines negotiated by statutory health insurance funds are valid for PKV also; access to PKV for high-income employees is improved: individuals need to have income above the threshold for 1 year only

Chile	
1973	Military coup bringing the Military Junta to power
1979	Merger of SNS and SERMENA to form FONASA; decentralization of the health system and formation of 27 autonomous regional health trusts
1980	Establishment of private health insurance represented by ISAPRE; FONASA to become the regulator of private health insurance
1986	Introduction of the *Ley de Salud* (Health Act)

Table 6.1 *(cont.)*

Chile	
1989	National referendum and beginning of transition to democracy
1990	Creation of the Superintendencia de ISAPREs as the regulator for private health insurance
2000	Introduction of mandatory catastrophic insurance coverage (CAEC); the aim of this policy was to cap payments at a threshold, to reduce the financial burden experienced in cases of serious illness
2003	Introduction of the system of "explicit health guarantees" (AUGE), standardizing insurance plans; private insurers must provide these explicit guarantees at a community-rated price and within a preferred-provider framework; user charges are regulated for both ISAPRE plans and FONASA
2005	Creation of the *Superintendencia de Salud* as a regulator for the entire health care sector and health insurance market; enactment of the "Long ISAPRE law", which applied community rating to ISAPRE premiums and introduced strict rules for the setting of premiums in the future – annual premium changes for ISAPRE were to be calculated based on a table of risk factors; a risk equalization scheme (*Fondo Compensatorio Solidario*) was created as a mechanism to fund the community-rated explicit guarantees
2010	Constitutional Tribunal declares the table of risk factors unconstitutional, effectively reversing the 2005 law
2010	Establishment of the hospital concession programme (arrangements between public and private health care providers, whereby the private sector designs, builds, finances and maintains hospital infrastructure and the public sector reimburses the delivery of services provided in this setting); the programme ran until 2014
2011	Abolition of the 7% mandatory health care contribution for pensioners over the age of 65
2014	Report of the Presidential Commission for Health Reform (*Comisión Asesora Presidencial Para El Estudio Y Propuesta De Un Nuevo Régimen Jurídico Para El Sistema De Salud Privado*) sets out nonbinding recommendations for private health insurance reform, including the return to a single-payer public insurance system. A minority report proposed introducing a broader minimum health plan, at a single premium, into the private system, with a compensation fund for reducing risk-selection behaviour (which could also eventually be open to FONASA) (Bossert & Leisewitz, 2016); so far none of these recommendations has been implemented

Table 6.1 *(cont.)*

Chile	
2015	The Financing System for Diagnosis and Treatment of High Cost Programmes (*Ley Ricarte Soto*) established to increase financial protection and catastrophic coverage for illnesses not included in the explicit guarantee regimen for both ISAPRE and FONASA users

Source: Authors.

Notes: FONASA: *Fondo Nacional de Salud*; GKV: *gezetzliche Krankenversicherung*; ISAPRE: *Instituciones de Salud Previsional*; PKV: *privaten Krankenversicherung*; SERMENA: *Servicio Medico Nacional de Empleados*; SNS: *Servicio Nacional de Salud*.

health insurance is complex and in both countries both types of cover are heavily regulated. In its origin, the Chilean approach was inspired by Bismarck's reforms, which laid the foundation for statutory health insurance and, in doing so, shaped private health insurance.

Both countries are unusual in offering people a choice of statutory or private health insurance but there is substantial variation in regulating the boundary between statutory and private cover. In Germany, the choice is largely limited to people with earnings above a legally defined threshold; those who choose substitutive private cover face substantial barriers to returning to the statutory scheme (the GKV) and in fact cannot return to it if they are over 55 years old. In Chile, anyone can opt for substitutive private cover and there are no restrictions on switching back to statutory cover; people can freely access publicly provided care should they lose their private cover.

Substitutive private health insurance covers about 11% of the population in Germany and 18.2% in Chile. Private cover is generally taken out by wealthier people, although there are some exceptions in Germany, where civil servants and those who have opted out and are over 55 are privately insured by default, irrespective of income. In Chile, private cover is attractive to those who can afford the premiums because it offers greater choice of provider, particularly access to private providers. FONASA members must pay extra to access privately provided services. Private cover also allows people to avoid the waiting lists that afflict the public sector. In contrast, the additional benefits offered by private cover in Germany are relatively modest, as both the publicly and privately insured draw on more or less the same pool of public and private providers. However, there is some evidence to suggest that those with private cover experience shorter waits in ambulatory care and in hospitals (Schwierz et al., 2011).

The two countries share similar concerns about the interaction between statutory and private health insurance in three areas. First, the payment mechanisms associated with private cover tend to distort priorities in care delivery by creating incentives for providers to treat private patients preferentially. This problem affects all types of health care in Chile, whereas in Germany it is most dominant in the ambulatory sector, where office-based doctors are allowed to charge higher prices for private than for statutory patients. However, incentives to over-provide services arising from fee-for-service payment are not restricted to private insurers in either country. Second, there is evidence of risk segmentation due to the selection of low risks by private insurers (see below). Third, there are substantial concerns about cross-subsidization between statutory and private cover, although the direction of these transfers is not entirely understood.

In both countries, the political costs of reforming (or abolishing) substitutive private health insurance are significant because private health insurance enjoys the support of health professionals and wealthy beneficiaries unwilling to forsake its advantages. Nevertheless, policy-makers have managed to address some concerns over time, although the pace of reform has differed. Chile has been able to achieve major reform in the last 15 years only, resulting in the introduction of a risk equalization mechanism (of limited effectiveness), and increasing cat-astrophic cover, among other things. In Germany, policy-makers have introduced successive reforms since the mid-1990s, but the main driver of risk selection – the option for wealthier people not to contribute to statutory cover – has not been removed.

Perhaps related to the above are differences in socioeconomic context. Public services in Chile still face substantial resource constraints, hence the need to ration care through waiting times. Some governments have promoted private health insurance as a panacea, a means of improving efficiency, reducing public sector bureaucracy and limiting pressure on public budgets. In Germany, high spending on health care (public and private), as well as high consumer expectations, have created a climate where rising costs are a constant concern. In the past, pressure to reform has mostly been felt in the statutory system. However, in recent years hikes in premiums, the rising number of defaulters and low interest rates in the capital markets have put substantial pressure on private insurers to control costs.

Financial protection

Health coverage is universal in both countries, but in Germany all residents are required to be covered and some who have opted for private cover are unable to return to the statutory scheme. In contrast, people in Chile do not have to pay contributions to FONASA and can still access publicly provided health services; additionally, those who opt for private cover can return to FONASA at any time. This difference has important implications. Arguably, ensuring financial protection for those with substitutive private cover ought to be a lower public policy priority in Chile than in Germany. However, in recent years both countries have introduced reforms to enhance financial protection among the privately insured.

Private insurers in Germany are allowed to set premiums reflecting individual risk and to exclude cover of pre-existing conditions, but they must cover both inpatient and outpatient care and match the benefits offered by the GKV. Deductibles are capped. Legislation also limits increases in premiums to what is necessary to maintain the financial viability of the insurer. During the 1990s, substitutive premiums rose sharply for many older people, in part due to previous miscalculation by insurers. To prevent this from happening again, the government requires insurers to impose a permanent surcharge on new subscribers to build up sufficient "ageing reserves". Survey data from 2005 indicate that about 350 000 people (or 5% of those) with substitutive cover paid premiums that were higher than the maximum GKV contribution, and the average age of this group was 61 years (Grabka, 2006).

In Chile, the government introduced "explicit guarantees" for the treatment of selected conditions in 2003, to ensure the provision of minimum benefits for those with private cover. However, the policy has still not been applied consistently, with persistent problems of access and financial protection for patients and increasing hospital debts due to the purchase of guaranteed services from private providers. Reforms have also introduced premium pricing controls (including a community rate for services included in the explicit guarantees), a risk equalization mechanism, the abolition of stop-loss clauses that capped benefits, and regulation of user charges. The table of risk factors used to limit risk rating was declared unconstitutional in 2010 and negotiations in Congress have not resolved this issue. Private premiums are significantly higher than contributions to FONASA, a problem compounded by high user charges.

Equity

Critics of Germany's dual insurance system argue that substitutive private health insurance undermines equity in the health system as a whole. Higher earners, especially when they are young and healthy, benefit from being able to buy private cover for less than they would have to contribute to the GKV. Questions have also been asked about the effect of the substitutive market on the GKV, particularly as the GKV loses the contributions of those who leave it, an issue exacerbated by the fact that those opting out are largely higher-earning low risks. Some argue that the loss of income results in the GKV indirectly subsidizing the privately insured (particularly if it is mainly poorer high-risk individuals that eventually return to the GKV). Preventing older people from returning to the GKV has been one way of addressing this issue, as has increasing the qualifying period for opting out from 1 year to 3 years (although the latter policy was eventually reversed). Conversely, the association of private insurers (PKV) claims that the privately insured indirectly subsidize outpatient care for GKV members because outpatient doctors can (and do) charge higher fees to private patients (Niehaus & Weber, 2005). However, it is not clear whether these additional funds are used by providers to benefit GKV members. Office-based physicians tend to argue that outpatient (specialist) practices depend on the income from privately insured people, but arguably these higher fees contribute to cost inflation in the health sector (Busse & Riesberg, 2004).

Several studies confirm variation by insurance status in waiting times for appointments with outpatient specialists in Germany, with a 2008 study showing GKV members waiting about three times longer than privately insured people (Mielck & Helmert, 2006; Schellhorn, 2007; Lüngen et al., 2008; Schwierz et al., 2011). The difference between the two groups ranged from 24.8 working days for a gastroscopy to 17.6 working days for an allergy test (including pulmonary function test) and 4.6 days for a hearing test (Lüngen et al., 2008). The studies show mixed results in terms of variation in satisfaction levels. Research also shows that the privately insured have faster access to patented and innovative drugs than GKV members (Krobot et al., 2004; Ziegenhagen et al., 2004).

Variation in access to care by insurance status is modest in Germany compared with Chile. Criticisms about the impact of substitutive private cover on equitable access to care have been repeatedly voiced in Chile, where privately insured people typically have significantly faster access to (a wider range of) health services (Zuckerman & de Kadt, 1997; Holst, Laaser & Hohmann, 2004). Access variations are frequently cited as a cause of major inequalities in health care use and health outcomes (Zuckerman & de Kadt, 1997; Jack, 2002; Holst, Laaser & Hohmann, 2004). Household survey data from 2006 show that use of health care was 30% higher in the wealthiest than in the poorest income quintile (Fischer, González & Serra, 2006), while a 2003 study found that people with the lowest incomes had the worst self-rated health (Subramanian et al., 2003). These inequalities in health care utilization and self-rated health appear to have persisted at least up to 2013 (Ministerio de Desarrollo Social, 2013).

Risk segmentation

Substantial segmentation of the national risk pool attributed to allowing people to choose between statutory and private cover has been a major concern in both Germany and Chile. In Germany, the regulatory framework exacerbates risk segmentation, as (with the exception of the standard and basic tariff) private insurers are allowed to reject applications for cover, risk rate premiums, exclude cover of pre-existing conditions, charge extra for dependants and offer discounted premiums in exchange for high deductibles. The ability of private insurers in Chile to select "good" risks has been substantially curtailed by recent reforms, including the introduction of risk equalization, explicit guarantees and premium regulation. However, evidence of the effects of these changes is lacking and some of the measures have not yet been implemented consistently.

The substitutive market in both countries enjoys a high concentration of low risks, while the statutory scheme covers a disproportionate number of high risks, notably women and children, older people and individuals with larger families (see Tables 6.2 and 6.3). In Germany, in 2014, about 50% of the privately insured were men, while women and children accounted for 31% and 18%, respectively (PKV, 2015). Risk selection is highest among those with earnings above the threshold. Differences in health status and health care use are less visible among those who are required to be covered by the GKV and those who are privately insured by default (Leinert, 2006). A similar pattern is seen in Chile, where older and poorer people are less likely to be privately insured than younger and wealthier people. Indeed as of 2013, the oldest

Table 6.2 *Health status and health care use among the publicly and privately insured in Germany, 2006*

Indicators	Mandatory GKV	Voluntary GKV[a]	Mandatory PKV[b]	Voluntary PKV[a]
Been ill during the last 3 months	46%	42%	47%	28%
Chronically ill	47%	33%	45%	23%
Regularly take medication	50%	35%	54%	21%
Number of visits to a doctor in a year	6.6	4.4	6.2	3.2

Source: Leinert (2006).

Notes: GKV: *gezetzliche Krankenversicherung*; PKV: *privaten Krankenversicherung*.

[a] Includes those with earnings above the threshold and self-employed people.

[b] Includes civil servants entitled to *Beihilfe* and non-active people (for example, pensioners).

Table 6.3 *Characteristics, health status and health care use among the publicly and privately insured in Chile, 2006*

Indicators	FONASA (statutory)	ISAPREs (private)
Average monthly income (in €)	292.1	973.4
Risk index [a] (based on the table of risk factors used by the *Superintendencia de Salud*)	5.53	5.02
Average age of the insured	51.1	44.6
Degree of urbanization of the insured (1 = urban; 0 = non-urban)	0.63	0.87
Level of education of the insured (total years in education, average)	7.86	13.51
Health status (composite score indicating the amount of health care received in the last 3 months)	2.32	2.31
Days spent in hospital (1 = hospitalized for more than a week in the last month; 0 = no hospitalization)	0.02	0.01

Source: Dawes Ibáñez (2010).

Notes: FONASA: *Fondo Nacional de Salud*; ISAPRE: *Instituciones de Salud Previsional*.

Differences in averages for all variables are statistically significant ($P < 0.01$).

[a] Although the risk index seems similar across both groups, there are important differences in its components, such as education and income levels.

and poorest quintiles of the population accounted for less than 5% of those covered by ISAPRE schemes (Barrientos & Lloyd-Sherlock, 2000; Ministerio de Desarrollo Social, 2013). Using household survey data from 2000 and 2006, Dawes Ibáñez (2010) showed that the probability of taking out private cover increases with income and decreases with risk of ill health.

Incentives for quality and efficiency in care delivery

One of the assumptions underlying choice of insurer is that competition will create incentives for quality and efficiency in care delivery. In Germany, however, the high costs involved in changing from one private insurer to another – now mainly due to risk-rated premiums and exclusion of pre-existing conditions but previously due to the non-portability of ageing reserves – has meant that there has been almost no competition among insurers for those already part of the substitutive market. Instead, competitive efforts have focused on attracting new entrants. From 2009, ageing reserves have had to be portable, which the government hoped would improve competition between private insurers. Competition between statutory and private health insurance does not seem to be a dominant policy objective in Chile, at least in the current political climate. But previous governments, particularly the military regime of General Pinochet in the 1970s and 1980s, promoted the market by channelling subsidies to private insurers. This was, in part, a response to (perceived) burgeoning bureaucracy in the private provider system.

German private insurers face a major problem in being unable to control provider fees, although this has become increasingly debated. The GKV partly shares this problem, which can be attributed to a general lack of transparency in pricing and reimbursement. An internal paper prepared by the Federal Association of Sickness Funds showed that two in five invoices for hospital care were flawed or inappropriate, adding about €1.5 billion to the costs of hospital care (*Spiegel* online, 2010). Private insurers are particularly weak in challenging the billing practices of office-based physicians because they have little insight into the appropriateness of the services delivered. They may also be reluctant to challenge physicians due to the fact that they market themselves as being able to give enrollees better access to health care.

Private insurers in Chile face similar difficulties in controlling provider behaviour, partly due to fee-for-service payment, which provides strong incentives to over-provide services to (and over-charge) privately insured people. For example, caesarean section rates have been consistently higher among privately insured women than among those who give birth in public hospitals (Murray, 2000; Guzmán, 2012; Guzmán, Ludmir & DeFrancesco, 2015). Market fragmentation may also contribute to private insurers' weakness in negotiating with providers. Even so, private insurers in Chile seem to be more aggressive in purchasing than in Germany because, among other things, there is a more vertical integration of insurers and providers. Spending on administration per enrollee is about twice as high for private insurers as for FONASA (Cid et al., 2006; Comisión Asesora Presidencial, 2014).

What is the future for private health insurance?

Substitutive private health insurance in Germany and Chile has been shaped by the existence and development of statutory health insurance as the dominant payer, occupying a niche carved out by legislators and regulators. Its interactions with the rest of the health system have given rise to difficulties and, in both countries, the issue of risk segmentation is as yet unresolved. The loss of higher earners to the GKV continues to undermine the notion of solidarity on which the German social security system rests. There have also been long-standing concerns about *Zweiklassenmedizin* ("two-tier medicine") and large parts of the population are uncomfortable with the idea that wealthier people can receive better care. Nevertheless, the political barriers to major reform of health care financing in Germany are substantial. Previous efforts to abolish substitutive private health insurance have been consistently opposed by an alliance of medical professionals, the Free Democrats and large parts of the Christian Democratic Party. Increasing dissatisfaction among the privately insured may help trigger reform in the years to come (*Zeit* online, 2012), with current financial pressures making the business model of offering statutory insurance increasingly less attractive for both insurance companies and customers.

Although Chile has had some success in facilitating major health insurance reform, and has been able to improve financial protection for the privately insured, the Constitutional Tribunal's 2010 decision to revoke legislation forcing insurers to use a standardized set of risk factors when determining premiums has meant that the issue is not fully resolved. Also, risk segmentation between ISAPREs and FONASA will continue, because policy-makers have not tried to prevent the privately insured from rejoining the statutory scheme if private insurance becomes unaffordable. However, the German experience shows that prohibiting people from returning to the statutory scheme creates new problems, as some people may lose coverage all together; nor does it prevent risk segmentation. Even more difficult, in the Chilean context, is the issue of differential payment methods for public and private providers. Substantial reform of and investment in public provision would be required for the health system to become more equitable without reducing quality of care for those who are currently benefiting from private provision.

References

Agostini C, Saavedra E, Willington M (2008). Collusion in the private health insurance market: empirical evidence for Chile. *ILADES, Georgetown University Working Papers*. Santiago, Chile, ILADES-Universidad Alberto Hurtado.

Alexander R (1949). Social security in Chile. *Social Forces*, 28(1):53–8.

Arellano JP (1985). Social policies in Chile: a historical review, *Journal of Latin Americal Studies*, 17(2):397–418.

Ärztezeitung (2009). Krankenversicherung: Beiträge sind ab 2010 komplett absetzbar (Health insurance: contributions are fully deductible from 2010). *Ärztezeitung* 22 June.

Barrientos A, Lloyd-Sherlock P (2000). Reforming health insurance in Argentina and Chile. *Health Policy and Planning*, 15(4):417–23.

Bastías G, Pantoja T, Leisewitz T, Zárate V (2008). Health care reform in Chile. *Canadian Medical Association Journal*, 179:1289–92.

BgBl (2009). Gesetz zur verbesserten steuerlichen Berücksichtigung von Vorsorgeaufwendungen (Bürgerentlastungsgesetz Krankenversicherung) (The Act on the improved taxation of preventive expenses (Citizens' Relief Act – Health Insurance)). *Bundesgesetzblatt*, 43:1959–73.

BMG (2010). Daten des Gesundheitswesens 2010 (Health care data 2010): www.bmg.bund.de; accessed on 14/12/2010.

Bossert TJ, Leisewitz T (2016). Innovation and change in the Chilean health system. *New England Journal of Medicine* 2016, 374:1–5.

Bundestag (2005). *Dritter Versorgungsbericht (Third care report), Drucksache 15/5821.* Berlin, Deutscher Bundestag.

Bundesverfassungsgericht (2009). Verfassungsbeschwerden in Sachen Private Krankenversicherung erfolglos (Constitutional grievances in the field of private health insurance are unsuccessful): www.bundesverfassungsgericht .de/pressemitteilungen/bvg09-059.html; accessed on 30/12/2010.

Busse R, Blümel M (2014). Germany: health system review. *Health Systems in Transition* 16(2):1–296.

Busse R, Riesberg A (2004). *Health care systems in transition: Germany.* Copenhagen, WHO Regional Office for Europe on behalf of the European Observatory on Health Systems and Policies.

Castillo-Laborde C, Villalobos Dintrans P (2013). Caracterización del gasto de bolsillo en salud en Chile: una mirada a dos sistemas de protección (Characterization of out of pocket payments in Chile: a look at two systems of protection). *Rev Médica Chile,* 141(11).

Cid C et al. (2006). Equidad en el financiamiento de la salud y protección financiera en Chile: una descripción general (Equity in Chile's health financing and financial protection: a general description). *Cuadernos Médico Sociales,* 46:5–12.

Comisión Asesora Presidencial (2014). *Estudio y Propuesta de un Nuevo Marco Jurídico para el Sistema Privado de Salud (Study and proposal for a new legal framework for the private health system).* Santiago, Chile.

Dawes Ibáñez AV (2010). Health care reform and its effect on the choice between public and private health insurance: evidence from Chile [thesis]. Pontificia Universidad Católica de Chile, Instituto de Economía.

Departamento de Estudios y Desarrollo (2008). *El Mercado de los Seguros Complementarios de Salud (The market for complementary health insurance).* Santiago, Chile, Departamento de Estudios y Desarrollo.

DKG (2016). Eckdaten der Krankenhausstatistik (Basic hospital statistics). Berlin: Deutsche Krankenhausgesellschaft (German Hospital Federation): www.dkgev.de/media/file/27611.Eckdaten_Krankenhausstatistik_Stand_ 2016-06-10_.pdf; accessed on 15/12/2016.

DKV (2008). *Versicherungslexikon der Deutschen Krankenversicherung* (Insurance glossary of the German health insurance): www.dkv.com/ versicherungslexikon_a_bis_z.html; accessed on 13/09/2008.

Fischer R, González P, Serra P (2006). Does competition in privatized social services work? The Chilean Experience. *World Development,* 38(4):647–64.

Fromme H (2008). Zehn Seiten Kriegserklärung an die privaten Krankenversicherungen (Ten pages of war declaration directed at the private health insurance): www.ftd.de/unternehmen/versicherungen/:Zehn%20 Seiten%20Kriegserkl%E 4rung%20Krankenversicherung/370096.html; accessed on 1/08/2008.

Genett T (2016). Entsolidarisierung des Kollektivs? Digitale Gesundheitsdaten und Beitragskalkulation in der PKV (Desolidarization of the collective? Digital health date and calculation of the contribution in the PKV), *Gesellschaftliche Kommentare*, 3–4:1–2.

GKV Spitzenverband (2016). Kennzahlen der gesetzlichen Krankenversicherung (Key figures of the statutory health insurance), National Association of Statutory Health Insurance Funds. Berlin, September 2016: www.gkv-spitzenverband.de/media/grafiken/gkv_kennzahlen/kennzahlen_gkv_2016_q2/GKV_Kennzahlen_Booklet_Q2-2016_300dpi_2016-09-20.pdf; accessed on 15/12/2016.

Grabka MM (2006). Prämienentwicklung in der PKV – eine empirische Untersuchung auf Basis des SOEP (Premium development in the PKV – an empirical investigation based on the Socioeconomic Panel (SOEP)). In Jacobs K, Klauber J, Leinert J, eds. *Fairer Wettbewerb oder Risikoselektion. Analysen zur gesetzlichen und privaten Krankenversicherung (Fair competition or risk assessment. Analyses of statutory and private health insurance)*. Bonn, Wissenschaftsliches Institut der AOK.

Greß S (2016). Germany country profile. In: Sagan A, Thomson S, eds. *Voluntary health insurance in Europe. Country experience*. Copenhagen, WHO Regional Office for Europe on behalf of the European Observatory on Health Systems and Policies.

Guzmán E (2012). Perfil epidemiológico de la cesárea en Chile en la década 2000–2010 (Epidemiological profile of caesarean section in Chile in the decade 2000–2010), *Medwave*, 2012;12.

Guzmán E, Ludmir J, DeFrancesco M (2015). High cesarean section rates in Latin America, a reflection of a different approach to labor? *Open J Obstet Gynecol*, 2015, 5:433–5.

Holst J, Laaser H, Hohmann J (2004). Chilean health insurance system: a source of inequity and selective social insecurity. *Journal of Public Health*, 12(4):271–82.

Horwitz C, Bedregal P, Padilla C, Lamadrid S (1995). *Salud y estado en Chile. Antecedentes de la creación del Servicio Nacional de Salud en Chile. El contexto político y social Chileno*. (Health and State in Chile: Background for the creation of the National Health Service in Chile. The Chilean social and political context). Santiago de Chile, Publicaciones Científicas de la Representación OPS/OMS en Chile.

Illanes M (1993). En el nombre del pueblo, del estado y de la ciencia: historia social de la salud pública (In the name of the people, the State and Science: Social history of public health in Chile). In: *Colectivo de Atención Primaria Chile 1880/1973: hacia una historia social del siglo XX (Primary Care Collective Chile 1880/1973: towards a social history of the XX century)*. Santiago de Chile, Colectivo de Atención Primaria.

Jack W (2002). Public interventions in health insurance markets: theory and four examples from Latin America. *World Bank Research Observer*, 17(1):67–88.

Krobot KJ et al. (2004). The disparity in access to new medication by type of health insurance: lessons from Germany. *Medical Care*, 42(5):487–91.

Leinert J (2006). Morbidität als Selektionskriterium (Morbidity as a selection criterion). In: Jacobs K, Klauber J, Leinert J, eds. *Fairer Wettbewerb oder Risikoselektion. Analysen zur gesetzlichen und privaten Krankenversicherung (Fair competition or risk assessment. Analyses of statutory and private health insurance)*. Bonn, Wissenschaftsliches Institut der AOK.

Lüngen M et al. (2008). Waiting times for elective treatment according to insurance status: a randomized empirical study in Germany. *International Journal for Equity in Health*, 7(1).

Mielck A, Helmert U (2006). Vergleich zwischen GKV- und PKV-Versicherten: Unterschiede bei Morbidität und gesundheitlicher Versorgung (Comparison between GKV and PKV insured persons: differences in morbidity and health care). In: Böcken J et al. eds. *Gesundheitsmonitor 2006 (Health monitor 2006)*. Gütersloh, Bertelsmann Stiftung.

Ministerio de Desarrollo Social (2013). *Encuesta Casen 2013. Salud: "Síntesis de Resultados. (Casen survey 2013: Results synthesis)*. Santiago, Chile, Ministerio de Desarrollo Social.

Minsal (2008). Department of Health Statistics: http://deis.minsal.cl/index .asp; accessed on 26/01/2011.

Murray SF (2000). Relation between private health insurance and high rates of caesarean section in Chile: qualitative and quantitative study. *BMJ*, 321:1501–5.

Niehaus F, Weber C (2005). *Der überproportionale Finanzierungsbeitrag privat versicherter Patienten zum Gesundheitswesen (The disproportionate contribution of privately insured patients to health care)*. Cologne, Wissenschaftliches Institut der PKV.

OECD (2017). Health expenditure and financing: Health expenditure indicators. OECD Health Statistics (database): http://dx.doi.org/10.1787/ data-00349-en; accessed on 30/11/2017.

Pedraza CC, Toledo LP (2012). El gasto de bolsillo en salud: el caso de Chile 1997 y 2007 (Out-of-pocket payments in health: the case of Chile 1997 and 2007). *Pan American Journal of Public Health*, 2012;31.

Perticara M (2008). *Incidencia de los gastos de bolsillo en salud en siete países latinoamericanos (Incidence of out of pocket payments in seven Latin American countries)*. Santiago (Chile), ECLAC.

PKV (2002). *Wissenswertes über die Private Krankenversicherung. Informationen für Lehrer und Schüler (Useful information about private health insurance. Information for teachers and students)*. Cologne, Verband der Privaten Krankenversicherung.

PKV (2008). *Gesundheitsreform 2007, Neuregelungen für die PKV (Health reform 2007, new regulations for the PKV)*. Cologne/Berlin, Verband der Privaten Krankenkassen; www.pkv.de/recht/gesundheitsreform_2007/; accessed on 13/09/2008.

PKV (2009). *Der privaten Krankenversicherungsschutz im Sozialrecht (Private health insurance in social law)*. Cologne, Verband der Privaten Krankenversicherung.

PKV (2010). *Zahlenbericht der privaten Krankenversicherung 2009/2010 (2009/2010 figures for private health insurance*. Cologne, Verband der Privaten Krankenversicherung.

PKV (2015). *Zahlenbericht der Privaten Krankenversicherung 2014 (Financial report for private healthcare insurance 2014I)*, Cologne, Verband der Privaten Krankenversicherung.

Raczynski D (1994). *Social policies in Chile: origin, transformations, and perspectives. Democracy and Social Policy Series, Working Paper* no. 4. Notre Dame IN, University of Notre Dame.

Sánchez M (2014). Análisis de los Planes de Salud del Sistema Isapre (Analysis of ISAPRE health insurance plans). Santiago, Chile, Departamento de Estudios y Desarrollo.

Sandoval G, Herrera J (2016). Estudio revela que integración vertical de clínicas e isapres no favorece a sus afiliados (Study reveals that vertical integration of clinics and isapres does not favor its affiliates), LATERCERA 1 December 2016: www.latercera.com/noticia/estudio-revela-integracion-vertical-clinicas-e-isapres-no-favorece-afiliados/; accessed on 02/06/2017.

Scarpaci JL (1989). Dismantling public health services in authoritarian Chile. In: Scarpaci JL, ed. *Health services privatization in industrial societies*. New Brunswick, NJ, Rutgers University Press.

Schellhorn M (2007). Vergleich der Wartezeiten von gesetzlich und privat Versicherten in der ambulanten ärztlichen Versorgung (Comparison of waiting times of statutorily and privately insured persons in outpatient care). In: Böcken J, Braun B, Amhof R, eds. *Gesundheitsmonitor 2007 (Health monitor 2007)*. Gütersloh, Bertelsmann Stiftung.

Schwierz C et al. (2011). Discrimination in waiting times by insurance type and financial soundness of German acute care hospitals. *European Journal of Health Economics*, 12(5):405–16.

SERNAC (2011). Estudio de precios: Diferencias de más de 2 mil por ciento en precios de exámenes en clínicas privadas (Price study: Differences of more than 2 thousand percent in prices of exams in private clinics), Servicio National del Consumidor. 17 October 2011: www.sernac.cl/26020/; accessed on 02/06/2017.

Spiegel online (2010) Kassen beklagen Millionenverlust durch falsche Rechnungen (Sickness funds complain of loss of millions due to incorrect bills), *Spiegel* online 28 December: www.spiegel.de/wirtschaft/soziales/0,1518,736867,00.html; accessed on 30/12/2010.

Statistisches Bundesamt (2008). *Sozialleistungen. Angaben zur Krankenversicherung (Ergebnisse des Mikrozensus) (Social benefits. Information on health insurance (results of the microcensus)*. Wiesbaden, Statistisches Bundesamt.

Subramanian SV et al. (2003). Income inequality and health: multilevel analysis of Chilean communities. *Journal of Epidemiology and Community Health*, 57:844–8.

Superintendencia de Pensiones (2015). *Aumento de topes imponibles para el cálculo de cotizaciones 2015 – Prensa (Increasing the caps for wage deducted health contributions)*. Santiago, Chile, Superintendencia de Pensiones. Supt Pensiones Informa.

Superintendencia de Salud (2008). *Estadísticas consolidada de cartera del sistema isapre año 2008 (Statistics for the ISAPRE system in 2008)*: www.supersalud.cl/documentacion/569/w3-article-4274.html; accessed on 26/01/2011.

Superintendencia de Salud (2013). Prestadores de Salud, Isapres y Holdings: ¿Relación Estrecha? (Health providers, ISAPRE and health care holdings: a close relationship?): www.supersalud.gob.cl/documentacion/666/articles-8826_recurso_1.pdf; accessed on 15/12/2016.

Superintendencia de Salud (2015). Estadísticas Financieras de las Isapres a marzo de 2015. (Financial statistics for the ISAPRE system up to March 2015). Santiago, Chile, Superintendencia de Salud.

Valencia R (2012). Esta es la concentración de las Isapres que explica altas utilidades (This is the concentration of ISAPRE that explains high revenue). La Nacion.

Vergara-Iturriaga M, Martínez-Gutiérrez MS (2008). The Chilean health system financing. *Salud Publica de Mexico*, 48(6):512–21.

Walendzik A et al. (2008). *Vergütungsunterschiede im ärztlichen Bereich zwischen PKV und GKV auf Basis des standardisierten Leistungsniveaus der GKV und Modelle der Vergütungsangleichung (Differences in the medical compensation between PKV and GKV on the basis of a standardized benefits level and models of remuneration adjustment)*, Report of a project funded by the Hans-Böckler-Stiftung: www.stefan-gress.eu/mediapool/40/403223/data/165.pdf; accessed on 13/08/2008.

WHO (2018). Global health expenditure database (GHED) [online database]. Geneva, WHO: www.who.int/health-accounts/ghed/en/; accessed on 15/01/2018.

Ziegenhagen DJ et al. (2004). Arzneimittelversorgung von PKV-Versicherten im Vergleich zur GKV (Pharmaceutical care of the PKV insured persons compared to GKV). *Gesundheitsökonomie und Qualitätsmanagement* 9:108–15.

Zeit online (2012). Nie mehr zweite Klasse (No more second class), *Zeit* online 3 February 2012.

Zuckermann E, de Kadt E, eds. (1997). *The public–private mix in social services. Health care and education in Chile, Costa Rica and Venezuela.* Washington DC, Interamerican Development Bank.

7 | Uncovering the complex role of private health insurance in Ireland

BRIAN TURNER AND SAMANTHA SMITH

The role of private health insurance in the Irish health system can be assessed from different angles and from all angles it appears complex. Despite universal entitlement to public hospital services, private cover – predominantly for hospital services – is purchased by nearly half of the population. This high level of demand has remained buoyant over time in the face of premium increases, adverse economic conditions, reductions in public subsidies and controversy within the market. Also, while private health insurance accounts for less than 15% of total spending on health, it commands a high profile in media and policy discussions and has substantial leverage over how public and private resources are allocated within the health system, particularly in the acute care sector.

This chapter analyses the structure and development of the market for private health insurance in Ireland and considers its impact on the wider health system. The market's development has been complicated, involving a series of high-level Irish and European court cases, highly visible exits from the market and other structural changes. In addition, its role has changed over time, as entitlements to publicly financed health care have also changed. However, one of the most distinctive aspects of the Irish experience comes from the complex interaction between publicly and privately financed health care and the impact of private health insurance on the distribution of resources in the wider health system. The chapter unpicks these complexities, highlighting critical issues around equity and efficiency.

The Irish health system

Overview of financing

The Irish health system is financed by a mix of public and private resources. Public resources have consistently accounted for the largest share (approximately 66% in 2014) of total spending on health, mainly funded from the government budget. Private spending includes direct out-of-pocket payments by households (50% of private spending and 15% of all current spending on health) and claims expenditure (41% and 12%, respectively) by private insurers on behalf of their members (WHO, 2018). The share of health spending coming from private sources has increased in recent years, from 21% in 2008 to 31% in 2014 (Turner, 2016).[1]

Access to Irish health care services

There are two broad categories of eligibility to public health care services, with each group facing different sets of prices for health care:

– *Category I ("Full" Medical Card holders)*

Category I beneficiaries [nearly 1.74 million people or 38% of the population in 2015 (HSE, 2016)] are granted a Medical Card (labelled here as a "full Medical Card" for clarity). Full Medical Card holders (individuals and dependants) have access to the following services that are free at the point of use: general practitioner (GP) care, approved prescribed drugs and medicines,[2] inpatient and day-case treatment in public beds in public hospitals, outpatient services in public hospitals, medical and midwifery care for mothers and infants, maternity cash grant for each child born, and dental, ophthalmic and aural services and some personal and social care services (for example, public health nursing, social work services, other community services) (Expert Panel on Medical Need for Medical Card Eligibility, 2014; HSE, 2015a).

---

[1] It should be noted that comparisons of health care financing data between Ireland and other countries remain problematic given the challenges in distinguishing between social and health care spending in the Irish context and it is acknowledged that health care has been over-stated to some degree in Irish expenditure data (www.cso.ie/en/releasesandpublications/er/sha/systemofhealthaccounts2014/ last accessed 23/12/2016).

[2] Prescription charges are now levied (€2.50 per item dispensed, subject to a maximum of €25 a month for an individual or a family) (Expert Panel on Medical Need for Medical Card Eligibility, 2014). However, it was announced in Budget 2016 that these charges will be reduced in 2017 to €2.00 per item subject to a maximum of €20 per month for those aged over 70 in possession of medical cards.

As outlined by the Health Service Executive (HSE, 2015b) the three main groups of people entitled to a full Medical Card include:

- Applicants (and their dependants) whose assessable income comes within a set of income guidelines.[3] The majority of full Medical Cards are granted on the basis of this means test, which takes into account both income and allowances for specified living expenses (for example, childcare costs) so that an individual's overall financial situation is assessed (Expert Panel on Medical Need for Medical Card Eligibility, 2014).[4]
- Applicants (and their dependants) whose assessable income exceeds the income guidelines but where it is considered that refusal of a Medical Card would cause "undue hardship" (HSE, 2015b: p.6).
- Applicants who are exempt from the means test including individuals with EU entitlement,[5] individuals with retention entitlement under Government schemes (for example, retention of Medical Card for specified period after return to work), individuals affected by the drug Thalidomide, and survivors of symphysiotomy.[6]

Between 2001 and 2008, people aged 70 and over were automatically entitled to a full Medical Card, but automatic entitlement

---

[3] Applicants whose weekly incomes are derived solely from Social Welfare or Health Service Executive allowances are entitled to a Medical Card (HSE, 2015b).

[4] For individuals aged 70 and over, the means test is based on gross income at higher thresholds and expenditure is not taken into account but these individuals can also apply under the general medical card scheme (Expert Panel on Medical Need for Medical Card Eligibility, 2014).

[5] This applies to, among others, people receiving social security pension from another EU/EEA country or Switzerland, or working and paying social insurance in one of these countries, if they are ordinarily resident in Ireland. (www.citizensinformation.ie/en/health/medical_cards_and_gp_visit_cards/medical_card.html).

[6] People who contracted Hepatitis C/HIV from the use of Human Immunoglobulin anti-D blood products qualify for a Health Amendment Act Card. This card entitles the holder to a range of services that are free at the point of use, including general practitioner care, prescribed drugs and medicines, home nursing and home help services, and others (HSE, 2015b).

was replaced by means-tested eligibility in 2009 (to save money) (Government of Ireland, 2001, 2008).

– *Category II (Other)*

People in Category II are entitled to public hospital care, subject to inpatient and outpatient charges, and to maternity and infant services.[7] They can apply for the Drugs Payment Scheme, which covers the cost of prescribed drugs, medicines and certain appliances above a threshold of €144 per month.[8,9,10] However, for claimants under this scheme (less than 6% of the population in 2015), the state covered less than half of the total cost of medicines over the period 2011–2015 (PCRS, 2015). This is down from 63% in the period 2003–2007 (PCRS, 2007), and is indicative of a shifting of the burden of payment over that period, arising from increases in the monthly threshold.

Entitlements for individuals in Category II to community and social services (for example, public health nursing, home help, physiotherapy) are difficult to ascertain. The overall pattern of entitlement to community services has been described as "complex and confusing" (Ruane, 2010: p.45). In practice, access to community services can vary depending on availability in each area (Citizens Information, 2015a) and in some cases priority may

---

[7] Inpatient charges are levied at €75 per night up to a maximum of €750 in any 12 consecutive months, and Emergency Department visits without referral letter are charged at €100 per visit, although certain exemptions apply. (www.hse.ie/eng/services/list/3/hospitals/Hospitalcharges.html last accessed 26/11/2015).

[8] www.hse.ie/eng/services/list/1/schemes/drugspaymentscheme/last accessed 26/11/2015.

[9] Medicines prescribed to inpatients are covered under hospital costs.

[10] Additional public assistance schemes include the Long-Term Illness Scheme, which covers the costs of prescription medicines, medical and surgical appliances directly related to the treatment of the illness for certain specified conditions (for example, diabetes). The High-Tech Drugs Scheme covers the cost of very expensive high-technology medicines that are usually only prescribed/initiated in hospital (for example, anti-rejection drugs for transplant patients or medicines used in conjunction with chemotherapy or growth hormones).

be given to Medical Card holders.[11] In particular, lack of clear eligibility criteria in home care (that is, home help, home care packages) has been criticized for giving rise to "uneven provision and hence glaring inequity in access to services throughout the country" (Timonen, Doyle & O'Dwyer, 2012: p.316). Tax relief at the standard tax rate (20%) is available for all medical expenses that are not otherwise reimbursed by public funding or by private health insurance (Nolan & Smith, 2012).

Individuals in Category II who are not eligible for a GP Visit Card (see below) are required to pay privately for GP care (Citizens Information, 2015a) with the exception of maternity and infant GP services, which are provided free of charge for a specific number of visits (Nolan & Smith, 2012). These services can be expensive, with the average charge for visiting a GP estimated to be €52.50 (Burke et al., 2015). There is no high-cost protection from the state (for example, no annual cap on out-of-pocket payments) for GP visits for individuals in Category II.

– *GP Visit Medical Card*

Over time, the above two categories have become more complicated with the introduction of the GP Visit Card. The GP Visit Card was introduced in 2005, granting access to GP visits free at the point of use. GP Visit Card holders fall under Category I for GP care, but under Category II for all other health care services.

Eligibility for a GP Visit Card is based on a means test whereby the income thresholds are approximately 50% higher than those set for the Full Medical Card (Expert Panel on Medical Need for Medical Card Eligibility, 2014). As with full Medical Cards, discretionary GP Visit Cards may be issued where the assessed means of the applicant exceed the income guidelines but the absence of the GP Visit Card would cause undue hardship.

However, since July 2015, all children under the age of 6, and since August 2015, all individuals aged 70 and over, are granted

[11] For example, access to physiotherapy in a primary care team in Dublin South is prioritized for Medical Card holders and for clients living in the catchment area of the health centre (www.hse.ie/eng/services/list/2/PrimaryCare/pcteams/dublinsouthpcts/blackrockpct/physio.html last accessed 15/04/2016).

a GP Visit Card regardless of means[12,13] and there are long-term plans to roll out free at the point of use GP care to the rest of the population (Government of Ireland, 2014), although this is dependent on the successful negotiation of a new GP contract. In 2015 there were over 431 000 people with a GP Visit Card (HSE, 2016).

Many people in Category II, and a small proportion of those in Category I, purchase supplementary private health insurance. Thus, the population can be categorized into four entitlement groups: full/ GP Visit Medical Card only with no supplementary insurance (30%); privately insured only with no medical card (41%); individuals with both medical card and private health insurance (6%); individuals with neither medical card nor private health insurance (23%) (CSO, 2011). Based on descriptive survey data, these entitlement groups can be broadly ranked in terms of socioeconomic status from the medical card only group (lowest) to the privately insured only group (highest), but overlaps in the various measures of deprivation and socioeconomic status suggest that these do not describe mutually exclusive socioeconomic categories (Smith & Normand, 2009). The higher socioeconomic status of privately insured individuals has been a consistent feature of consumer surveys, with those in higher social classes more likely to have private health insurance than those in lower social classes (see, for example, HIA, 2016a). As discussed by Brick et al. (2010), given the links between low socioeconomic status, older age and poor health status, these patterns suggest poorer health status among the medical card groups (with and without private health insurance) relative to the non-medical card groups and there is survey evidence to support this.

Health care delivery structures

Primary care delivery

Primary care is delivered by GPs and other health professionals in the community including public health nurses, community registered nurses,

---

[12] www.hse.ie/eng/services/list/1/schemes/mc/gpvc/GPVisitCards.html last accessed 24/11/2015.
[13] www.hse.ie/eng/services/list/1/schemes/mc/over70s/ last accessed 24/11/2015.

physiotherapists, occupational therapists, and speech and language therapists. There is a also a range of other primary and social care services provided in a community setting including home help, day care and respite care. These services are provided by the HSE or by voluntary organizations operating in conjunction with, or on behalf of, the HSE (Citizens Information, 2015b). It is well-documented that there is a wide variation in the level of services available in different parts of the country (Citizens Information, 2015b).

General practitioners in Ireland are self-employed private practitioners, although a large proportion hold a state General Medical Services contract to provide GP care that is free at the point of use to Medical Card and GP Visit Card holders (HSE, 2015c). A small number of GPs who do not hold a General Medical Services contract are registered to provide services under alternative state-funded programmes (for example, Primary Childhood Immunization Scheme, Heartwatch, Methadone Treatment Scheme) (HSE, 2015c). GPs are mainly paid on a capitation basis for Medical Card and GP Visit Card patients and on a fee-for-service basis by non-Medical Card patients.

Long-term care delivery

Approximately 75% of non-acute long-term care beds are provided by private nursing homes (Health Information and Quality Authority, 2014), 20% are provided by the HSE (mostly in extended care units, and a small number in welfare homes), and the remaining 5% are provided by non-statutory/voluntary agencies (for example, voluntary homes or hospitals for older people, and a small number of beds in voluntary welfare homes) (Health Information and Quality Authority, 2014).

Acute care delivery

Acute hospital services are delivered by public and private hospitals (Brick et al., 2010). Public hospitals are either owned and directly managed by the HSE, or owned by voluntary organizations but for many years have received most of their funding from the Government (Brick et al., 2010). There are 50 acute care public hospitals in the Republic of Ireland, managed by voluntary organizations or directly by the HSE (HSE, 2015d). In addition there are 19 independent hospitals (providing acute and mental health care services) registered with the Private

Hospitals Association.[14] Private hospitals operate in parallel with public hospitals, and some now offer limited emergency department services (for example, office hours only),[15] but there are some complex treatments that are not available in the private sector (Brick et al., 2010).

Specialists (known as "consultants"), working in public hospitals are paid according to a common contract which was revised in 2008 and now includes a new public-only contract. Type A contracts are for public-only consultants who are not permitted to earn private income from the treatment of private patients. Type B contracts allow consultants to treat private patients in public hospitals. Type C contracts allow consultants to treat private patients outside the public hospital campus (that is, in private hospitals). Consultants are paid on a salary basis for treating public patients and can earn additional income on a fee-for-service basis when treating private patients.

Public/private interaction in the Irish health care system

Despite its relatively small financial contribution to total health care resources, private health insurance plays an important role in the health system. To understand its influence requires knowledge of the complex interactions between the public and private sectors within the system. In both primary and acute hospital care, publicly and privately financed care is very often administered by the same staff, using the same facilities. The main structural difference is in the method of reimbursement. Care for private patients is reimbursed on a fee-for-service basis whereas care for public patients is largely reimbursed on a fixed payment basis (for example, salary, capitation).

The overlap between public and private care in the public hospital system was, in the past, explicitly supported in government policy. It was defended in terms of permitting public hospitals to retain the services of top medical specialists and therefore to have them available to care for public patients. The 2001 national strategy for the Irish health care system stated that the public/private mix of beds in the public hospital

---

[14] http://privatehospitals.ie/members/ last accessed 26/11/2016.

[15] For example, the Emergency Department at the Beacon Hospital in Dublin is open 10am to 7pm Monday to Friday, 10am to 6pm Saturdays, closed Sundays and Bank Holidays (www.beaconhospital.ie/emergency-department/ last accessed 23/11/2015).

system was intentional, to ensure that the two sectors could share resources, clinical knowledge, skills and technology (DoHC, 2001). However, the overlap also gave rise to complicated incentive patterns and concerns about equity within the system, discussed in more detail below.

Government policy on this overlap of public and private care in hospitals has since shifted. For example, private bed charges are now levied on the use of any bed in public hospitals by privately insured patients from 1 January 2014 (previously, only those accommodated in designated private beds were charged), and tax relief on private health insurance premiums has been capped (Turner, 2015).

These changes reflect a broader shift in government health care policy aimed at reforming the delivery and financing of the health care system (DOH, 2012). In particular, a White Paper outlining a plan to introduce a system of universal health insurance with mandatory coverage of the whole population provided by competing private insurers was produced in 2014 (DOH, 2014). Under these proposals, the goal was to develop a single-tier health service that promotes equitable access to health care. For example, private health insurers would no longer be able to offer faster access to hospital care, but would still be able to provide better amenities in hospital. However, there is debate as to what would be the most efficient financing mechanism to achieve the reform goals. For example, analysis by Wren, Connolly & Cunningham (2015) indicated that the costs of the chosen model of a multi-payer universal health system could be significant, and there is need to examine alternative mechanisms. Plans to introduce the proposed model have been shelved for now and the Government elected in 2016 established a cross-party parliamentary Committee on the Future of Healthcare tasked with recommending a consensus approach to the future direction of health policy in Ireland over the next 10 years.[16] Part of the Committee's remit is to work towards a universal single-tier health system where access is based on need rather than ability to pay.

Overview of the market for private health insurance

Market structure

Four insurers currently operate in the unrestricted market for private health insurance: a non-profit insurer, Vhi Healthcare, and three

---

[16] For full details of the Committee, including its role, see www.oireachtas.ie/parliament/oireachtasbusiness/committees_list/future-of-healthcare/.

for-profit (commercial) insurers, Laya Healthcare, Irish Life Health and GloHealth. Seven undertakings restrict membership to specific (mostly vocational) groups and they therefore do not compete to any great extent with the other insurers (HIA, 2016b). The largest of these are operated by, or on behalf of, the Irish police force, the country's prison officers and employees of the state-owned Electricity Supply Board. Recent figures suggest that Vhi Healthcare has a 51% market share, Laya Healthcare a 26% share, AVIVA Health (now Irish Life Health) 14% and GloHealth 5%, with the remaining 4% accounted for by the restricted membership undertakings (HIA, 2016c).

Hospital plans account for the vast majority of private health insurance and provide access to semi-private[17] or private rooms in public hospitals,[18] and access to private hospitals (in a semi-private or private room) depending on the level of cover. Most hospital plans provide limited cover for ancillary (non-hospital) services, such as visits to GPs, physiotherapists, dentists and other health care practitioners. However, in recent years, an increasing number of hospital plans with significant ancillary cover have been introduced. Ancillary plans have also been introduced, some of which may be purchased on a stand-alone basis, whereas others can be combined with hospital plans. The ancillary plans are primarily complementary, while the hospital plans (the ones with limited ancillary cover) are primarily supplementary. The combined hospital and ancillary plans are both complementary and supplementary.

A concern expressed about private health insurance markets in general is that product differentiation can restrict competition if consumers find it difficult to compare price and quality across a wide range of products (see, for example, Thomson & Mossialos, 2007). This is of relevance in the Irish context given the increase in the number of plans available in recent years. The Health Insurance Authority (HIA) has commissioned a number of surveys to assess consumer behaviour and

---

[17] A semi-private room may contain up to five beds.

[18] As mentioned above, there was a change to bed designation in public acute hospitals on 1 January 2014. Insured patients are now charged the private bed rate for the use of any bed in a public hospital. Previously, privately insured patients occupying designated private beds were charged the private bed rate but private patients occupying public or non-designated beds were only charged the statutory bed rate (currently €75 per night up to a 12-month maximum of €750). This is despite the fact that consultants were being paid for seeing all of these insured patients as private patients. It should also be noted that private or semi-private accommodation was subject to availability.

attitudes towards the market. The first survey (HIA, 2003a) showed that only 30% of consumers had a full understanding of the cover provided by their plan. As a result of evidence that consumers had difficulty understanding the cover provided by different plans, the HIA engaged in an information campaign, publishing a guide on consumers' rights in relation to health insurance, a guide to switching plans and a comparison table outlining the key elements of cover offered by the main plans available in the market. Recent survey evidence (HIA, 2016a) shows a large majority of consumers (85%) being satisfied or very satisfied with their level of understanding of their cover. However, only a third of all consumers (34%) felt that there was adequate information available to compare plans from different insurers, compared with 46% in 2009 (HIA, 2016a). This may be related to the increasing number of plans available in the market, with 360 plans available at the end of 2015 (HIA, 2016b).

Although insurers are not obliged to contract with all providers, in practice all insurers cover most public and private hospitals and have fully participating agreements with most consultants, although some lower-cost plans in recent years have restricted the number of hospitals covered. Consultants who have signed up to these agreements accept the insurers' payments in full and do not balance-bill the customers of those insurers. Claims account for the majority of insurers' costs, and these have been rising in recent years. Reasons include advances in medical technology, the ageing population and increases in the charges for private beds in public hospitals, an issue to which we shall return (see, for example, Turner, 2013).

In the last two decades, inflation in the health insurance element of the consumer price index (CPI) has tended to exceed inflation in the CPI's Health category which, in turn, has tended to exceed the overall level of inflation. Figures from the Central Statistics Office show that, between January 1997 (when BUPA Ireland began selling plans) and September 2016, the overall CPI increased by 49%, while the Health category of the index rose by 120% and the health insurance sub-index rose by 520% (source: Central Statistics Office database, available at www.cso.ie).

Demand for private health insurance

The initial aim of private health insurance (in the 1950s) was to provide cover for the wealthiest proportion of the population (approximately

15%), who, at the time, were required to pay inpatient bed charges, consultant treatment costs for inpatient care and outpatient charges in public hospitals. Demand was buoyant and the share of the population covered grew from 4% in 1960 to 35% by 1987 and further to a peak in late 2008 of almost 51%, before falling back during the economic crisis, and now stands at 46% (Nolan, 2004; HIA, 2016d). Total premium income in the open (unrestricted) market in 2015 was just over €2.33 billion (HIA, 2016c). This increase in the popularity of private health insurance is not fully understood. Growth occurred in spite of substantial increases in premiums, a reduction in tax relief on premiums[19] and enhanced access to publicly financed health care (eligibility for public hospital accommodation was extended to all Irish residents in 1979 and for treatment by public hospital consultants in 1991).

Econometric analysis has indicated that a large part of the increase in demand remains unexplained, even after controlling for income and price changes (Nolan, 2004). Attention has turned to attitudinal surveys, particularly those commissioned by the HIA (see, for example, HIA, 2016a). Figure 7.1 shows the level of agreement with a number of statements among HIA survey respondents (both with and without health insurance). Overall majorities of consumers in these surveys agreed that private health insurance is a necessity rather than a luxury.[20] There was also broad agreement that having private health insurance enables people to access better health care services and allows faster access. Most consumers disagreed with a statement suggesting that there is no need for private health insurance in Ireland because public services are adequate. These findings mirror those of earlier studies (Nolan & Wiley, 2000; Harmon & Nolan, 2001; Nolan, 2004), which found

[19] Tax relief was granted on private health insurance premiums from the time the market was established. The relief was originally available at the individual's marginal tax rate, but reduced to the standard rate (currently 20%) over two tax years in the mid-1990s, to make it less regressive. Since 2001 tax relief has been deducted at source. The insurer deducts the tax relief from the premium charged to the individual before the premium is paid. Tax relief operates more as a tax credit and is available to anyone whether or not they are a taxpayer (DoHC, 2005). However, in October 2013, the premium subject to tax relief was capped at €1000 per adult and €500 per child (Turner, 2015).

[20] Although a minority of those without insurance agreed with this statement in the most recent survey, it was nonetheless a sizeable minority).

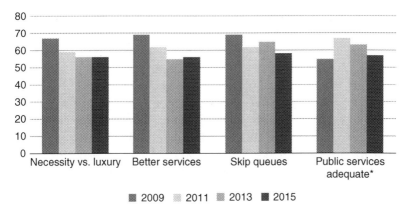

Figure 7.1 Consumer attitudes to private health insurance in Ireland, 2009–2015 (selected years)

Sources: HIA (2010a, 2012, 2014, 2016a).

Note: * Percentage disagreeing.

that perceptions of greater access to hospitals and greater quality of private versus public care were the key drivers underpinning demand for health insurance with other reasons including ensuring good treatment, receiving direct consultant care and avoiding large hospital bills (Nolan & Wiley, 2000).

Market development and public policy

Government objectives

As discussed above, private health insurance has previously been actively supported by the government. The 2001 national health strategy described it as a "strong complement to the publicly funded system" and a vital part of the "overall resourcing of health care in this country" (DoHC, 2001: p.111). As well as providing additional resources, the market was expected to relieve the publicly financed system of demand for care. Tax relief on premiums was justified on the basis "that those who opt for private cover effectively forgo a statutory entitlement while continuing to contribute to the funding of the public health service through taxation" (DoHC, 1999: p.24). However, as noted earlier, more recent government policies have been aimed at unwinding the State subsidy of private health insurance (Turner, 2015) and increasing equity in the Irish health system, although plans for universal health insurance are currently in abeyance.

Objectives for the market have changed over time. Initially, it was envisaged that private health insurance would play a substitutive role for the top 15% of earners in the country (those who were not entitled to free care in public hospitals). However, enrolment was not limited to this group. For some, private health insurance offered the option of better accommodation or choice of consultant, while it gave the option of treatment in private hospitals to many subscribers, irrespective of their entitlements to public hospital treatment. Therefore, it also played a supplementary role, even in the early days of the market. However, since entitlements to publicly financed health care were extended in 1979 and 1991, private health insurance no longer plays a substitutive role. It now plays primarily a supplementary role, with elements of a complementary system.

Legislative background

The market in its current form was established in 1957 with the passing of the Voluntary Health Insurance Act, 1957, which set up the Voluntary Health Insurance Board (VHI, now trading as Vhi Healthcare) as a statutory body. The Minister for Health at the time was advised that such a scheme would have a wider appeal to the public if administered by a non-profit company rather than a state department (O'Morain, 2007). Before 1957, there had been a number of attempts to establish private health insurance, but none of these was successful for a variety of reasons, including a lack of public interest, the cost of meeting claims for pre-existing conditions and large premium increases (see O'Morain, 2007 for further details).

In 1992, the introduction of the European Third Non-Life Insurance Directive[21] required European Union (EU) Member States to open their non-life insurance markets to competition. The Directive was reflected in the Irish Health Insurance Act 1994 which, with associated regulations brought forward in 1996, gave legislative foundation to a number of principles that private health insurance had adhered to on a de facto basis. In particular, the 1994 Act enshrined in legislation what have become known as the three "pillars" of the Irish market: community

[21] Council Directive 92/49/EEC of 18 June 1992.

rating, open enrolment and lifetime cover. The 1999 White Paper on private health insurance states that these three principles "have played a crucial role in making private health insurance cover accessible to a substantial proportion of the Irish population and, in particular, to higher risk groups such as the elderly and the chronically ill" (DoHC, 1999: p.8).

Community rating prohibits insurers from varying premiums or benefits between individuals with the same health insurance contract, subject to some exceptions.[22] Until 2015, this was operated under a system of single-rate community rating, meaning that a person's age at entry did not affect the premium they paid. However, from 1 May 2015, lifetime community rating has operated in the market. Open enrolment requires insurers to accept any applicant,[23,24] although insurers may impose waiting periods, which are age-related. Three types of waiting periods are permitted – an initial waiting period (for a first-time applicant or an applicant who has had a break in cover of 13 weeks or more), one for pre-existing conditions and one for upgrades in cover. The maximum permitted waiting periods for each of these categories, before 1 May 2015, are outlined in Table 7.1. Since that date, the maximum waiting periods have been standardized at the lowest level, that is, 26 weeks for the initial waiting period (except for maternity benefits, for which the waiting period is still 52 weeks), 5 years for the pre-existing condition waiting period and 2 years for the upgrade in cover waiting period. Even during the initial waiting period, however, insured people are eligible for minimum payments for health services provided as a result of

---

[22] The exceptions were children under the age of 18 and full-time dependent students aged 18–23, for whom premiums may be reduced such that any reduced premium was no greater than 50% of the adult premium; and members of a group scheme, for whom premiums may be reduced by up to 10%. However, premiums may not be varied among insured people falling into these categories. Since 1st May 2015, premiums may still be reduced for children and members of group schemes, but the student discount has been replaced by a discount for young adults, aged between 18 and 25 inclusive, on a sliding scale.

[23] Unless the person has committed fraud that caused, or could have caused, financial loss to an insurer.

[24] The original regulations from 1996 specified that this applied only to those aged under 65 when first applying for health insurance, or applying after a break in cover of thirteen weeks or more, but this stipulation was removed in 2005.

Table 7.1 *Maximum permitted waiting periods for private health insurance benefits in Ireland before 2015*

Age (years)	Under 55	55–59	60–64	65 plus
Initial waiting period	26 weeks	52 weeks	52 weeks	104 weeks
Pre-existing condition	5 years	7 years	10 years	10 years
Upgrade in cover	2 years	2 years	2 years	5 years

Source: Health Insurance Act 2001; (Open Enrolment) Regulations 2005.

Note: Maternity benefits are not covered for the first 52 weeks.

accident or injury. During the waiting period for an upgrade in cover, insured people will still be covered at the lower level of cover, subject to any initial or pre-existing condition waiting periods that they may be serving. Lifetime cover means insurers may not refuse to renew cover for any insured person.[25]

In addition to these three pillars, regulations introduced in 1996 specified a set of minimum benefits that any eligible health insurance contract must provide. The regulations were designed "to ensure that individuals do not significantly under-insure due to lack of proper understanding of the restrictions which, in the absence of a specified minimum entitlement, could apply to some types of policies" (DoHC, 1999: p.54). Monetary amounts specified in these regulations were not inflation-linked and are now significantly out of date, given the rate of medical inflation. In practice, however, cover provided by all insurers is significantly greater than the minimum required under the regulations.

The same regulations specified a risk equalization scheme to "equitably neutralize differences in insurers' claim costs that arise due to variations in the health status of their members" (HIA, 2010b: p.8) by transferring money from insurers with relatively low-risk membership profiles to a risk equalization fund, from which money is received by insurers with relatively high-risk membership profiles. These regulations were revoked in 1999 during a period of consultation on the future of private health insurance, which led to the publication of the White Paper (DoHC, 1999). In 2001, the Health Insurance (Amendment) Act allowed

[25] Unless the person has committed fraud or the insurer ceases to carry on health insurance business in the country.

the Minister for Health and Children to specify a new risk equalization scheme, introduced in 2003. It also established a new independent statutory body, the HIA, to regulate the private health insurance market.[26] The HIA's role was initially primarily one of monitoring and advising the Minister for Health and Children, and it did not have widespread powers to impose sanctions on insurers in the event of noncompliance with legislation. The Health Insurance (Miscellaneous Provisions) Act, 2009 gave it greater powers of enforcement.

Development of competition

For 40 years from its establishment in 1957, Vhi Healthcare had a monopoly position in the market. Since the passing of the 1994 Act (to comply with EU law) there have been a number of entries into the market and changes of ownership of these new entrants.

- The first entrant into the market was the British United Provident Association (BUPA), which set up BUPA Ireland in 1996. Following an unsuccessful challenge against the Risk Equalization Scheme, 2003 in the Irish High Court, BUPA Ireland announced its withdrawal from the market in December 2006. BUPA Ireland's business was subsequently acquired by Quinn Insurance Limited, which already sold other forms of non-life insurance in Ireland, and was re-branded Quinn Healthcare in April 2007. After a management-led buyout in 2012 the company was renamed Laya Healthcare.
- VIVAS Health was established in 2004 and was the third provider in the market. In early 2008, Hibernian Insurance Limited, part of the AVIVA group, which already sold both life and non-life insurance in Ireland, acquired a majority stake in VIVAS Health, which was subsequently re-branded as AVIVA Health. In 2016, Irish Life acquired AVIVA Health, which has now been renamed Irish Life Health.
- GloHealth was established in 2012. In 2016, as well as acquiring AVIVA Health, Irish Life also acquired the stake in GloHealth that

---

[26] Before the establishment of the HIA, the Department of Health and Children regulated the market. The HIA can be regarded as the regulator for the market, whereas the Department of Health and Children is the legislator for the market.

it did not already own, although GloHealth has so far been maintained as a separate brand.

The relatively low number of insurers has been an issue of concern since the market opened up to competition. An early report on competition and risk equalization commissioned by the HIA and carried out by the York Health Economics Consortium identified the prospect of risk equalization and the status of Vhi Healthcare as a state-backed dominant player, combined with uncertainty at the time over its future status, as key factors contributing to the low level of existing competition and limited scope for future competition (York Health Economics Consortium, 2003). The report suggested that, even if risk equalization payments were implemented, the Irish market would still be likely to attract some new entrants, but fewer than if payments were not implemented. The report also concluded that, in the absence of risk equalization, the benefits to consumers of new entrants might be limited, as "lower prices and higher profits for insurers could be achieved for some but older people with health insurance, less inclined to move between insurers, would lose from the absence of full risk equalization" (York Health Economics Consortium, 2003: p.97).

Evidence from HIA surveys indicates that, by late 2002, only 6% of respondents who had health insurance had ever switched health insurer. This increased to 10% by 2005, levelled off by 2007, increased to 16% in 2009 and 23% in 2011, before dropping back to 20% in 2013 and increasing again to 24% in 2015 (HIA, 2016a). The main reason for switching is to achieve cost savings, while the main reason for non-switching is satisfaction with current insurer. Most of the surveys also show that fewer than one in seven of those who have not switched have seriously considered switching, although this figure increased to 20% in 2013 and 2015 (HIA, 2016a). Furthermore, recent evidence suggests that switching and price sensitivity are lower among older consumers (Keegan et al., 2016).

These findings suggest that competition among insurers is primarily for first-time purchasers of health insurance, who tend to be younger than the average age of existing consumers, which would work to the disadvantage of Vhi Healthcare, as the longest-established insurer in the market. They are consistent with the idea of adverse retention: the tendency for people who do not switch plans to magnify cost differentials between plans (Altman, Cutler & Zeckhauser, 1998). One of the factors that Altman, Cutler & Zeckhauser (1998) suggested will affect the extent of adverse retention is the length of time for which the plans have been offered; in other words, if people do not switch plans to any great extent, adverse retention will drive up the costs of older plans relative to newer ones. Price & Mays (1985) also suggested that older plans may have an older mix of consumers.

Another issue relevant to competition in the market is risk selection, whereby insurers attempt to cherry-pick low-risk individuals in order to reduce claim costs and increase profits. Community rating accentuates incentives to risk select, and while open enrolment and lifetime cover reduce the opportunities for cherry-picking, they do not eliminate them, as risk selection may occur in subtle forms, such as marketing or plan design – as noted by York Health Economics Consortium (2003), among others. While the effects of adverse retention and risk selection are difficult to disentangle, Turner & Shinnick (2008) find evidence suggesting that risk selection might be present in the Irish market, while Keegan et al. (2017) find that incentives to engage in risk selection may exist even in the face of a risk equalization scheme.

Following BUPA Ireland's withdrawal from the market, the Minister for Health and Children requested the HIA and the Competition Authority to report on competition in the market. Both reports (Competition Authority, 2007; HIA, 2007) recommended the normalization of Vhi Healthcare's regulatory position (see below), an increase in the powers available to the HIA, measures to facilitate switching by consumers (including the implementation of a switching code and the provision of information to consumers at the point of sale and with renewal notices), and updating of the minimum benefit regulations. Similar recommendations were made in a third report commissioned by the Minister (Private Health Insurance Advisory Group, 2007). This report led to a number of policy changes by government, including the reduction of risk equalization payments by 20% (although this was never realized – the Risk Equalization Scheme, 2003 was set aside by the Supreme Court before payments were made under the Scheme; see below).

Sources of controversy

Developments in the private health insurance market have attracted much media and political attention in recent years, particularly in relation to the introduction of risk equalization. The issues are not straightforward and much of the discussion is confused with wider complications around the role played by private health insurance in the health system. Here, we discuss key sources of controversy around the structure of the private health insurance market in some detail to clarify issues that have been confused in popular debate. The complications arising from the interaction between public and private care are discussed separately in subsequent sections.

Prudential regulation

In addition to the regulation of health insurance business, health insurers must comply with prudential regulatory requirements. This has been a source of controversy due to a different prudential regulatory regimen being applied to Vhi Healthcare from that applying to its competitors. Under the 1957 Act, Vhi Healthcare was not subject to the Insurance Acts in Ireland, and it also received a derogation from the EU's First Non-Life Insurance Directive. In particular, it was not required to maintain the same level of solvency reserves as its competitors. However, in contrast to its competitors, Vhi Healthcare has to seek ministerial approval for premium increases.

Before BUPA Ireland's withdrawal from the market, all three insurers at the time had different prudential regulatory accountability. Vhi Healthcare, as a statutory body, reported to the Minister for Health and Children; BUPA Ireland, as a subsidiary of BUPA Insurance Limited, was regulated by the Financial Services Authority in the United Kingdom, while VIVAS Health was regulated by the Financial Regulator (responsible for regulating all financial services firms in Ireland). The different prudential regimen applied to Vhi Healthcare attracted opposition from its competitors. Following a formal complaint from VIVAS Health, the European Commission (EC) deemed that Vhi Healthcare's derogation from solvency requirements should be removed. Legislation was drafted to normalize Vhi Healthcare's status, but not implemented, and in 2011 the European Court of Justice ruled against the Irish government. Following the completion of a funding arrangement with Berkshire Hathaway, Vhi was authorized by the Central Bank of Ireland in July 2015.

Under the Voluntary Health Insurance (Amendment) Act passed in 2008, Vhi Healthcare was required to set up subsidiary companies to undertake non-health insurance business – another source of controversy relating to its statutory status. Previously it had been able to diversify into other business areas, with the permission of the Minister for Health and Children, without having to establish subsidiary companies (unlike its competitors), and had begun selling travel and dental insurance, set up an online health shop and become involved in minor injury clinics. The 2008 Act imposed the same subsidiary requirement on Vhi Healthcare.

Risk equalization

The main source of controversy in the market has been risk equalization. Although a risk equalization scheme was in place when it entered the market, BUPA Ireland was always opposed to the scheme on the basis that it would, in its view, be forced to subsidize the state-backed dominant insurer. Monetary transfers under the 1996 scheme were never made and the regulations governing the scheme were revoked in 1999 as part of a review of the market.

The Health Insurance (Amendment) Act, 2001 made provision for another risk equalization scheme and this was introduced as the Risk Equalization Scheme, 2003. Under the scheme, the HIA had a role in advising the Minister for Health and Children on whether or not to commence risk equalization payments. This depended on the market equalization percentage, which is an indicator of the risk differential between insurers in the market measured by the proportion of equalized benefits that insurers would be liable to pay to the risk equalization fund in order to ensure that their risk profile matched that of the market overall. If market equalization percentage was below 2%, no transfers would be made. If it was between 2% and 10%, the HIA would be required to make a recommendation to the Minister on whether or not payments should be triggered, while if it were above 10% then the Minister would commence payments, unless, having consulted with the HIA the Minister felt that the commencement of risk equalization payments would not be in the best overall interests of health insurance consumers (see HIA, 2003b and 2008b for further details).

For each of the 6-monthly periods from July 2003 to June 2005, the market equalization percentage was found to lie between 2% and 10% (see HIA, 2005b). For the third of these periods, the HIA recommended that payments should be commenced. However, having reviewed representations from the insurers (as allowed for under legislation), the Minister decided not to commence payments, noting that such a move would be premature in advance of a government decision on the commercial status of Vhi Healthcare. For the fourth of these periods, the HIA again recommended that payments should be commenced. This time the Minister decided to commence payments from 1 January 2006, as by then the government had approved legislation regarding the commercial status of Vhi Healthcare.[27]

As soon as payments under the scheme were triggered, BUPA Ireland challenged the scheme through the Irish courts. It had already complained to the EC that the scheme constituted illegal state aid, but the EC ruled that this was not the case in 2003 (European Commission, 2003). BUPA Ireland then took the EC to the European Court of First Instance, but in 2008 this Court dismissed BUPA Ireland's challenge to the EC's decision (European Court of Justice, 2008: p.25). A national High Court ruling in November 2006 (Courts Service, 2006) also dismissed BUPA Ireland's challenge, but BUPA Ireland appealed to the Supreme Court. Following the High Court judgement, BUPA Ireland announced that it was withdrawing from the market and its business was taken over and re-branded as Quinn Healthcare in April 2007. In July 2008, the Supreme Court overturned the High Court decision and set aside the Risk Equalization Scheme, 2003 (Courts Service, 2008). Its decision was taken on the basis of the definition of community rating in the 1994 Act, as amended. The decision did not, however, question the validity of, or need for, risk equalization in a community-rated health insurance market.

Section 7 of the 1994 Act, as amended, specifies that insurers may not vary premiums or benefits among people on the same health insurance contract. It goes on to state that "a health insurance contract that complies with [the conditions outlined in an earlier paragraph within that Section] shall be known as a community-rated health insurance

---

[27] The decision of the Minister to commence risk equalization payments was based on analysis of the figures for the 1 January to 30 June 2005 period, but there was a lag between the end of the period and the Minister's decision to trigger payments, as the HIA had to analyse the returns from insurers and make its recommendations and the Minister had to allow the insurers to make representations. For the next 6-monthly period, that is, 1 July to 31 December 2005, the market equalization percentage was also calculated as lying between 2% and 10% (see HIA, 2007).

contract and 'community rating' shall be construed accordingly". The Risk Equalization Scheme, 2003 was brought forward under the terms of Section 12 of the 1994 Act, as amended. This Section noted that, in forming its decision on whether to recommend to the Minister for Health and Children that payments be triggered, the HIA needed to take into account "the best overall interests of health insurance consumers" and it went on to note that this "includes a reference to the need to maintain the application of community rating across the market for health insurance and to facilitate competition between undertakings".

BUPA Ireland argued that the only valid definition of community rating is that given in Section 7, which defines community rating within plans, and that therefore the Section 12 definition was essentially invalid, which would invalidate the entire scheme. The High Court noted that the definition of community rating was central to the case, but ruled that the Section 12 definition was valid. The Supreme Court agreed that the definition of community rating was central to the case, but decided that the Section 12 definition could not be construed so differently from the Section 7 definition. The Chief Justice, in the judgement, suggested that, if the *Oireachtas* (parliament) had wanted such a different interpretation to be given to the Section 12 definition then it would have made that clear. Therefore, it was the Supreme Court's view that Section 12 could only be interpreted as referring to the maintenance of community-rated plans across the market (or, in other words, community rating within plans). On this basis, the Court ruled that the Risk Equalization Scheme, 2003, as adopted by the Minister, "was founded on an erroneous interpretation of subsection 10(iii) in Section 12" and therefore determined that the 2003 scheme was ultra vires and should be set aside. The Health Insurance (Miscellaneous Provisions) Act, 2009 further amended the definition of community rating in the 1994 Act, reflecting the issues highlighted in the Supreme Court judgement and in line with Section 7(1) of the 1994 Act (Government of Ireland, 2009).

A stay on payments under the Risk Equalization Scheme, 2003 had been put in place subject to the outcome of the legal challenge. By early 2008, before the Supreme Court set aside the scheme, BUPA Ireland would have been liable to pay over €33 million into the risk equalization fund, and Quinn Healthcare would have been liable to pay just over €1 million, while Vhi Healthcare was set to receive over €32 million from the fund, with over €2 million being due to the Electricity Supply Board

Staff Medical Provident Fund, the only one of the restricted membership undertakings participating in the scheme.[28,29]

Following the setting aside of the Risk Equalization Scheme, 2003 by the Supreme Court, the Minister for Health and Children announced two interim measures which were initially put in place for 3 years (2009–2011), but were extended for another year to 2012, while work was carried out on a new risk equalization scheme. These comprised a community rating levy on health insurers for each person they insured and increased tax relief for older health insurance consumers. All insured people continued to benefit from the 20% tax relief at source, but older consumers received additional tax relief. The measures were designed to be revenue neutral to the Exchequer. Since tax relief on health insurance premiums is deductible at source, consumers pay the net premiums (net of the tax relief), and the insurers then claim back the tax relief for all of their members from the Revenue Commissioners. The additional tax relief was therefore claimed back by the insurers.

A new risk equalization scheme was introduced on 1 January 2013 and has been in operation since then with relatively little controversy compared with previous proposed risk equalization schemes. The scheme pays credits to insurers for older members, increasing by age band and differentiated by gender and level of cover (advanced or non-advanced). Risk adjusters are included in the form of credits for inpatient nights and day-case admissions. This scheme is funded by stamp duty on premiums, which vary for adults and children and also by the level of cover (advanced or non-advanced) offered on the plan. However, research has suggested that this scheme does not fully compensate insurers for cost differentials and therefore incentives remain for risk selection (Keegan et al., 2017).

The considerable controversy generated in the Irish private health insurance market stems from the market's origins, which saw the establishment of a state-backed non-profit monopoly provider that was not subject to the same prudential regulation as other financial services organizations. This arrangement survived until the passing

[28] These figures relate to the periods January–June 2006, July–December 2006 and January–June 2007. For details see HIA (2008a).
[29] When the Risk Equalization Scheme, 2003 was brought forward, the restricted membership undertakings were given an opportunity to opt out of the scheme. Electricity Supply Board Staff Medical Provident Fund was the only one that did not avail itself of this option.

of the European Third Non-Life Insurance Directive in 1992, which obliged the market to open up to competition. To ensure that competition did not adversely affect the principles on which the market was then operating, these principles were given legislative foundation under the Health Insurance Act, 1994 and associated regulations. One of the main principles, community rating, was underpinned by a risk equalization scheme, which was opposed by new entrants to the market, but had cross-party political support. As part of attempts to stabilize the private health insurance market following a contraction due to the economic downturn, lifetime community rating was introduced from 1 May 2015. Attempts by the Government in power from 2011 to 2016 to introduce universal health insurance have been halted but as noted earlier, work is underway to design a single-tier health system where access is based on need rather than ability to pay.

Impact of the private health insurance market on the Irish health system

Private health insurance affects a number of health policy goals in the Irish system. In the context of the complexities that characterize the system, identifying the influence of private health insurance on equity and other goals requires more detailed and multi-dimensional analysis than has been applied in other systems.

Equity and related issues

Equity is a central goal in Irish health policy (DoHC, 2001; Department of the Taoiseach, 2011; DOH, 2012). Despite the complexities in defining equity and interpreting the goals of Irish policy statements on equity (see Smith & Normand, 2011) it is possible to identify commitment to a general egalitarian objective in which there is a separation between payment for and use of health services.

Studies on equity in the Irish context have focused on socioeconomic-related equity in health outcomes (Layte et al., 2015), health care utilization (Layte & Nolan, 2004) and health care financing (Smith & Normand, 2009; Smith, 2010a). Much of the analysis of equity in health care financing has examined measures of progressivity in health care payments. Analysis of private health insurance premium payments in Ireland using data from 1999–2000 and 2004–2005 found a regressive pattern, with premium payments falling as a proportion of income as income rises within the privately insured population (Smith, 2010a). This is consistent with community rating in the market, with flat rate, community-rated premiums imposing a relatively greater burden on those with relatively lower incomes. This regressive pattern could also be attributed to the purchase by lower-income, and possibly less healthy, people of more expensive (and comprehensive) insurance packages.

However, relying on progressivity indices to analyse equity in health care financing overlooks complexities that need to be taken into account when considering the impact of private health insurance on equity (Smith & Normand, 2009). First, payment for private health insurance includes not just premium payments made by individuals (or their employers) but also public resources in the form of tax relief on premiums (described earlier). Tax relief might be expected to increase demand for health insurance. However, its impact seems to have been relatively limited given the strong growth in demand for private health insurance over time in spite of reductions in the level of tax relief (for example, from marginal to standard tax rate in 1995,[30] and the more recent cap on the premium on which tax relief is available). Nevertheless, it is a substantial subsidy on the cost of private health insurance and there have been repeated calls for its abolition (see, for example, Commission on Health Funding, 1989; Ruane, 2010).

Second, the state also subsidizes the private health insurance market indirectly via the provision of education and training for medical professionals. Some of the treatment of privately insured individuals takes place in public hospitals, and some hospital consultants work in both public and private practice, so the training of these medical professionals, which is subsidized by the state, benefits both public and private patients.

Third, when analysing equity in private sources of health care financing it is important to consider what is happening in health care delivery. Private spending is directly linked to use of or entitlement to services (see Smith & Normand, 2009). In the Irish case, purchase of private health insurance can bring with it entitlements and patterns of health care use that have negative equity implications within the health sector. In particular, analysis of health care financing and delivery

---

[30] Motivated by concerns to improve the progressivity of the relief since relief granted at the marginal tax rate disproportionately benefited those on higher incomes who paid tax at a higher marginal rate.

together shows that public subsidization of privately insured care is not necessarily limited to tax relief on insurance premiums and training of medical professionals.

In practice, a proportion of privately insured care is delivered in public hospitals.[31] Charges for privately insured care[32] in public hospitals do not cover the full economic cost of that care, leading to additional subsidies. Identifying the full economic cost is not straightforward and analysis in this area has been ongoing (Brick et al., 2010). Earlier estimates indicated that the level of subsidization could be as high as 50–60% of the cost of privately insured care (Nolan & Wiley, 2000; Smith, 2008). More recent evidence is not available and would need to take into account the impact of levying private bed charges on all beds occupied by privately insured patients in public hospitals from 1 January, 2014.

In addition to the subsidization of private care in public hospitals, there are concerns about two-tier access to care within the public hospital system, with privately insured patients receiving priority over, and crowding out, public patients. Before the changes to the common consultant contract in 2008, public hospitals were required to implement a bed designation system intended to safeguard the access of publicly financed patients to public hospital care. Approximately 20% of inpatient non-emergency hospital beds were designated for private patients, with the rest nominally restricted to public patients. However, data on inpatient admissions and discharges indicated that this system was violated and private practice exceeded permitted levels in some hospitals (Wiley, 2001; Brick et al., 2010). The increase in day-case

[31] Published data on the proportion of privately insured care that takes place in public hospitals are limited. The 2003 Vhi annual report indicated that 50% of bed capacity used by its members was provided in public hospitals (Vhi, 2003). The 2009 Vhi report forecast that 70% of the members' health care needs in 2010 would be delivered in private hospitals/facilities (Vhi, 2009). These two measures, although not fully consistent, indicate that a large proportion of privately insured care is delivered in public hospitals but that this has been declining over time. Available survey data on health care utilization indicates that 60% of adults with private health insurance who were admitted as inpatients over a 12-month period were admitted to public hospitals, compared with 90% of those with medical cards and 97% of those with neither form of cover (CSO, 2011).

[32] It is possible to receive private care without holding private health insurance but this is expected to refer to a small proportion of the population.

activity in public hospitals further confused the situation and internal reports by the Department of Health and Children acknowledged that the bed designation system had not succeeded in controlling the level of private activity within public hospitals (Tussing & Wren, 2006). On the demand side, as noted earlier, available data indicate that greater access to hospital care and other non-financial factors have been cited as key reasons for purchasing private health insurance in Ireland.

Moreover, the two-tiered nature of the Irish health care system has been explicitly acknowledged in a number of recent health policy documents. The White Paper on Universal Health Insurance cites the Government's commitment to "ending the unfair, unequal and inefficient two-tier health system" (DOH, 2014: p.5) while the Strategic Framework for Reform of the Health Service outlines the proposed steps to achieve a "single-tier health service" (DOH, 2012: p.1). Concerns about two-tier access and quality are not new. The Commission on Health Funding (1989) recommended the introduction of a common waiting list for public hospital admission, such that cases would be taken in order of medical priority regardless of public/private status (Nolan & Wiley, 2000). Measures to restrict the number of private patients treated within the public hospital system also feature in the revised 2008 consultant contract. For newly appointed Type B consultants, the permitted ratio of public to private workload is 80 : 20. The new consultant contract contains improved measures for monitoring agreed levels of public and private activity relative to the previous contract. However, it is not clear to what extent the revised working arrangements are being adhered to or sanctioned.[33]

These patterns illustrate how the level of resources generated by private health insurance is not commensurate with the leverage within the health system enjoyed by those with private cover (Nolan, 2006). Observed negative repercussions include long waiting times for publicly financed patients. Waiting times have been central to political and policy debates in the health sector, with particular focus on the large gap in

---

[33] Limited available evidence indicates that the agreed levels of public and private activity for those on a Type B consultant contract are not being adhered to (Brick et al., 2010; *The Irish Times*, 2016, www.irishtimes.com/news/health/rules-limiting-private-practice-in-hospitals-a-farce-hse-chief-1.2490156 last accessed 29/11/2016).

waiting times between public and private patients (Tussing & Wren, 2006). The most recent health policy documents directly acknowledge the challenges of "long waiting lists and inequitable access to care" (DOH, 2012: p.2) and various waiting list initiatives have been introduced by the government over the years.[34]

Previous analysis of health care financing and delivery structures in Ireland have identified complicated and inequitable flows of resources through the system (Smith & Normand, 2009) and many of these inequitable structures persist. The purchase of private health insurance is subsidized, via tax relief on premiums, by all individuals in the tax net. As outlined earlier, private health insurance is concentrated among higher-income groups in the population. There is no clear equity principle that would allow lower-income groups to subsidize the purchase of private insurance by higher-income groups, which would subsequently allow those higher-income groups preferential access to a bed in a public hospital, yet this is observed in the Irish system.[35]

---

[34] In 2002, the National Treatment Purchase Fund (NTPF) was established to purchase private care (in Ireland and abroad) on behalf of public patients waiting extended periods of time for care. As a result, the problem of long public waiting times led to further demands on public resources. While the NTPF was successful in reducing waiting lists (Ruane, 2010), it gave rise to a complex flow of resources in the system. In 2011, the NTPF was subsumed into the Special Delivery Unit, and its role in arranging private treatment for patients was suspended. However, funds were made available in Budget 2017 (announced in October 2016) for the NTPF to again arrange treatment in an effort to reduce waiting lists.

[35] The National Treatment Purchase Fund (NTPF) set up another pattern of potentially inequitable cross-subsidization effects. Public resources (generated by all tax payers) were used to purchase private care for public patients (via the NTPF) at the same time as there was evidence that public resources were used to subsidize the treatment of private patients within public hospitals. This anomaly was taken up by the Expert Group on Resource Allocation and Financing in the Health Sector in 2010 (Ruane, 2010). The Group recommended that when appropriate measures are taken to improve resource allocation in the system (for example, treatment protocols and frameworks, a prospective funding mechanism), there would no longer be a need for the NTPF to continue its role in relation to purchasing services to reduce waiting lists, as this role will be mainstreamed into the rest of the system (Ruane, 2010).

Incentives and policy responses

Supply-side financial incentive structures in acute care[36] also support the leverage of private health insurance within the system, with implications for the behaviour of hospital consultants, hospital managers and insurers. As noted earlier, hospital consultants permitted to treat both public and private patients may have a financial incentive to treat private patients.[37]

Acute public hospitals receive income from statutory public inpatient charges (€75 per day) and from maintenance charges for private patients treated in public hospitals (€659 to €1000 per night and from €329 to €407 for day cases, depending on the type of hospital) (Turner, 2015). The private maintenance charge is payable in addition to the public hospital inpatient bed charge. Thus, public hospitals have an incentive to ensure that their private beds are filled to maximum capacity by private patients (private maintenance charges are not recouped where private beds are occupied by public patients) and an incentive to earn additional income by filling public beds with private patients.[38].

Insurers cover the costs of hospital maintenance and consultant treatment for care provided to privately insured patients. In previous years, charges for treatment were generally higher in private than in public hospitals (Brick et al., 2010), particularly where a private patient was treated in a public bed in a public hospital.[39] Policy decisions to increase the private and semi-private bed charges in public hospitals over time [for example, between 2005 and 2013, private and semi-private

[36] See Brick et al. (2012) for further discussion of incentives in acute care services.

[37] Fee-for-service payments are directly tied to the amount of services provided and therefore encourage greater activity relative to salary-based payment mechanisms. However, there are other complicating factors also at play, which may conflict with the incentive to favour the treatment of private patients, outlined in more detail by Brick et al. (2012).

[38] Once a private patient is admitted, the public hospital has a financial incentive to maximize length of stay but to minimize treatment intensity because the per diem payment is independent of the type of treatment received. In contrast, the Type B consultant may have a financial incentive to increase treatment intensity, which could increase his/her income (Brick et al., 2012).

[39] One review of public hospital accounts showed that 45% of private patients were not charged for maintenance because they occupied a public bed (see Brick et al., 2010), whereas around 5% were treated in non-designated beds (Comptroller and Auditor General, 2009).

maintenance charges for large acute public hospitals increased by more than 200% (Turner, 2015)], and to charge private rates for any bed occupied by private patients in public hospitals (since 1 January, 2014) reduce the incentive facing the insurer to favour the treatment of private patients within public rather than private hospitals.

However, focusing on one incentive without addressing others can have limited impact on actual behaviour. Consultants are directly paid by insurers for care delivered to privately insured patients. With regard to decisions on treating private patients in public or private hospitals it is interesting to note that the consultants receive those resources regardless of where the care is provided. For convenience, consultants might prefer to conduct most of their private and public work from one location. From the perspective of an individual public hospital, privately insured patients provide a source of income.[40] The influence of these incentives persists despite the changes to the structure of private maintenance charges.

Overall, the structure of the Irish health financing system is complex and the role of private health insurance within that system is no less complicated. Despite accounting for a relatively small proportion of total health care resources, private health insurance has important leverage on how resources in the public hospital system are allocated, giving rise to complicated incentive structures and inequitable patterns of access and use of services within the system.

Quality and efficiency

The way in which privately insured care interacts with the public system has negative implications for the efficiency with which public resources are used in the system and for the quality of care received by public patients. With regard to the care received by privately insured patients, there is limited evidence that private insurers actively implement disease management initiatives in the Irish context or take other steps to promote efficiency.[41] They do not set treatment protocols or

---

[40] Treatment of privately insured patients in a public hospital also means that consultants are more likely to be on site and are therefore potentially more available to treat public patients.

[41] Earlier commentary indicated that private insurers negotiated contracts with health care providers to contain costs rather than to promote specific health practices (Colombo & Tapay, 2004).

medical guidelines to increase the appropriateness of care or efficiency of resource allocation. However, some insurers are becoming more involved in health-promoting activities (for example, sponsoring health-related events, electronic newsletters, etc., and Vhi Healthcare has begun a screening programme for diabetes), which may be related to the growth in insurance products that cover primary care services.

Administrative efficiency

Operating expenses of Vhi Healthcare accounted for 7.7% of gross earned premium in 2014, having been just over 6% in four previous years (Vhi, 2015). In the period following the opening of the market to competition, the administrative cost percentage steadily increased to reach a peak of more than 11% in 2001, but after that the rate declined (Colombo & Tapay, 2004; Vhi, 2007, 2008). Vhi Healthcare cites investment in the development of appropriate information technology as an important contributing factor to operational efficiency (Vhi, 2008).

Financial protection

As outlined earlier, avoiding large hospital bills is one of the reasons, but not the main reason, cited for purchasing private health insurance. Financial protection may have been a more important factor when private health insurance was first introduced and targeted at individuals who at the time were not entitled to free care in public hospitals. Even then, these individuals were among the top 15% of earners in the pop-ulation and their risk of falling into poverty as a result of medical bills is assumed to have been low. Fig. 7.2 shows the financial mix of health care resources allocated to four different entitlement groups based on data from 2004 (Smith & Normand, 2009). The entitlement groups (outlined earlier) are broadly ranked in increasing order of socioeco-nomic/health status. Most of the health care services received by the group with a Medical Card only are financed from public sources, while private sources play a more important role in the financing of health care services for the other three groups. The group without cover from a Medical Card or private health insurance relies to a relatively large extent on out-of-pocket payments to supplement public resources. The group with private health insurance only can offset some of the out-of-pocket payments (that is, hospital charges) that face non-medical card

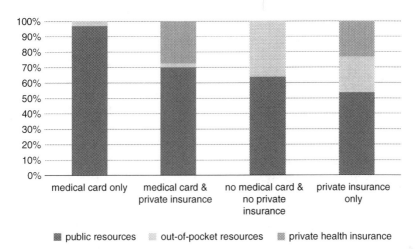

Figure 7.2 Composition of health care resource allocation for different entitlement groups in Ireland, 2004

Source: Extracted from Smith & Normand (2009).

holders in the system. However, while out-of-pocket payments make up a smaller proportion of total resources allocated to the group with private health insurance relative to the group with no cover, they do not disappear completely. This is because the former group still has to pay out of pocket for primary care. The limited financial protection by the state for primary care for the non-medical card groups is a distinguishing feature of the Irish health system (Smith, 2010b; Burke et al., 2015). Further work is needed to incorporate changes in eligibility and financing structures since then (for example, GP Visit Cards, increasing cover of primary care by private health insurance companies). Nevertheless the general health care financing structure underpinning each eligibility group still holds (for example, Medical Card holders: mainly public resources with a small proportion of out-of-pocket financing for prescription charges; Privately insured: mainly private health insurance for acute care and out-of-pocket payments for primary care; No Medical Card or private health insurance: mainly out-of-pocket payments).

The future of private health insurance in Ireland

Given the complicated interaction between privately insured care and the rest of the health system, future developments around private health insurance are difficult to predict. Changes in the private health insurance market can occur in terms of the size and structure of the market, and the interaction with and the impact on the wider health system. Each of these is affected by a wide range of factors, as evidenced by the recent economic downturn.

With regard to the structure of the private health insurance market, the introduction of risk equalization from January 2013 has brought an end to the long-running uncertainty surrounding this measure, although as noted earlier, it has not entirely eliminated the incentives for risk selection and some possible changes have been suggested (Keegan et al., 2017).

The recent entry of general insurers into the market for private health insurance, and the normalization of Vhi Healthcare as an authorized non-life insurer in 2015, may lead to bundling of private health insurance with other forms of insurance. In past years, the Quinn Group (before the buyout that led to Quinn Healthcare becoming Laya Healthcare) offered free household insurance to the value of €200 and free travel insurance to customers holding motor and health insurance with the Quinn Group (Quinn Healthcare, 2008). Hibernian AVIVA Health also ran a "match more, make more" promotion, offering cash back to customers who had multiple policies with the group, including health and motor insurance. There is currently some degree of product bundling between private health insurance and travel insurance, with Vhi Healthcare's travel insurance plan paying for medical care while on holiday only after the limit on the overseas-cover element of the insured person's private health insurance plan has been exceeded. As the market for private health insurance is possibly close to saturation (although HIA, 2016a showed that 38% of those who did not already have private health insurance said they were likely to take it out at some point in the future), diversification into other insurance – and non-insurance – areas may be a logical step for insurers.

Further increases in private health insurance premiums, in both nominal and real terms, are also likely to feature in the future. Factors affecting these increases will include the ageing population, advances in medical technology and possible increases in bed charges for privately insured patients in public hospitals, which are set unilaterally by the Minister for Health. Expansion in the supply of public facilities could also dampen demand for private health insurance, although given restricted budgets it is questionable whether this will happen to any great extent in the short- to medium-term. Consumer surveys (HIA, 2003a, 2005a, 2008c, 2010a) have shown a general satisfaction with health insurance, but the level of agreement that it represents value for money decreased during the economic downturn (HIA, 2016a), although the market has now seen a modest increase in demand again, even after the once-off effect of the introduction of lifetime community rating. The fact that the market contracted by only 12% from peak to trough, despite like-for-like premium increases of over 120% during the same period, suggests significant resilience in demand for health insurance in Ireland.

In terms of the wider implications of private health insurance on health equity and efficiency goals, the recent adjustments to tax relief on premiums, and the equity implications of the lifetime community rating and risk equalization, outlined earlier, will need to be assessed. It is also important to note that without further changes to the incentive structures that favour the treatment of private patients in the public health system, and without full enforcement of the new consultant contract requirements on the ratio of public/private activity, private health insurance will continue to have a distorting effect on the allocation of health care resources within the public hospital system. Any decline in demand for private insurance induced by price rises or improvements in the public health system will not remove these inequitable distortions, but it may make them less visible.

It is also important to look at the future of private health insurance in the broader policy context of health care financing and delivery in Ireland. Much of the discussion in recent years has focused on options for changing the financing mechanism for health care. The Adelaide Hospital Society investigated options for a contributions-based "social health insurance" system to replace the current government-budget-financed system (Thomas, Normand & Smith, 2008). However, a shift to a contributions-based system is not a necessary condition for achieving improvements in resource allocation and equity in the Irish health system. Many of the desirable features identified with a contributions-based system (for example, potential improvements in transparency, a greater degree of prepayment in the system and increasing incentives to provide services efficiently and in the appropriate locations) can be achieved under the current system (Ruane, 2010).

Subsequently, the Programme for Government issued by the coalition government elected in 2011 (Department of the Taoiseach, 2011) outlined a plan to introduce a system of universal health insurance involving mandatory coverage of the whole population provided by competing private insurers, which could selectively contract with providers. Under these proposals, the State would pay for cover on behalf of those on low incomes and partially subsidize the cost for those on middle incomes, whereas those on higher incomes would pay the full cost. Under the plans, voluntary health insurance would no longer be able to offer faster access to hospital care, but may still be able to provide better amenities in hospital. A primary objective was to tackle unequal access to hospital care. The White Paper on universal health insurance was published in April 2014 (DoHC, 2014) and the consultation process that followed demonstrated considerable concerns about the proposed model (Crowe Horwath, 2014). These included concerns in relation to cost and cost containment, and the ability of individuals – particularly those who currently do not have voluntary health insurance or a Medical Card – to pay for mandatory health insurance (Turner, 2014) and the ability of insurers to engage in selective contracting, given the relatively low density of facilities in many parts of the country (Mikkers & Ryan, 2014).

More recently, following a review of the potential costs of universal health insurance (Wren, Connolly & Cunningham, 2015), the proposals in that reform were effectively shelved. A recent report noted a number of challenges in achieving universal health care, and explored some potential routes to advancing towards universality (for example, extension of tax-financed primary care system; addressing two-tier access to hospital care by introducing a new public purchaser of hospital care, or some modified model of compulsory private insurance for elective hospital care only) (Wren & Connolly, 2016).

The Committee on the Future of Healthcare was established in June 2016 with the task of developing a consensus-driven 10-year plan for health policy in Ireland. The Committee has appraised various funding model options for moving to a universal single-tier system, and considered a number of options when looking at what the position of private health insurance would be in this system. Its plan (Sláintecare Report), published in May 2017, recommends a model where private insurance will no longer confer faster access to health care in the public sector, but is limited to covering private care in private hospitals (private care in public hospitals will be eliminated) (Houses of the Oireachtais, 2017).

Concluding comments

This chapter has shown how the development and functioning of the private health insurance market in Ireland has been complicated and controversial. One of the most complex issues concerns the role of privately insured care within the health system. Although private health insurance accounts for a relatively small proportion of total health care financing, it has substantial leverage in terms of how resources are allocated, particularly for acute care. A key reason behind strong demand for private health insurance is to ensure faster access to hospital care, very often in a public hospital. This close interaction between publicly and privately financed care is key to understanding the impact private health insurance has on equity and efficiency in the Irish health system.

References

Altman D, Cutler D, Zeckhauser R (1998). Adverse selection and adverse retention. Papers and Proceedings of the Hundred and Tenth Annual Meeting of the American Economic Association (May). *American Economic Review*, 88(2):122–6.

Brick A et al. (2010). *Resource allocation, financing and sustainability in health care: evidence for the Expert Group on Resource Allocation and Financing in the Health Sector.* Dublin, Department of Health and Children and Economic and Social Research Institute.

Brick A et al. (2012). Conflicting financial incentives in the Irish health-care system. *The Economic and Social Review*, 43(2):273–301.

Burke S et al. (2015). From universal health insurance to universal healthcare? The shifting health policy landscape in Ireland since the economic crisis. *Health Policy*, 120(3):235–40.

Citizens Information (2015a). Entitlement to health services: www.citizens information.ie/en/health/entitlement_to_health_services/entitlement_to_public_health_services.html; accessed on 17/12/2015.

Citizens Information (2015b). Community care services: www.citizens information.ie/en/health/care_in_your_community/community_care_services.html; accessed on 17/12/2015.

Colombo F, Tapay N (2004). *Private health insurance in Ireland: a case study. OECD Health Working Paper* 10. Paris, OECD.

Commission on Health Funding (1989). *Report of the Commission on Health Funding*. Dublin, Stationery Office.

Competition Authority (2007). *Competition in the Irish private health insurance market*. Dublin, The Competition Authority.

Comptroller and Auditor General (2009). *Accounts of the Public Services 2008: Comptroller and Auditor General Annual Report*. Dublin, Office of the Comptroller and Auditor General.

Courts Service (2006). *Case IEHC 431. BUPA Ireland Ltd & Anor* v. *Health Insurance Authority & Ors*. Dublin, Courts Service.

Courts Service (2008). *Case IESC 42. BUPA Ireland Ltd & Anor* v. *Health Insurance Authority & Ors*. Dublin, Courts Service.

Crowe Horwath (2014). *Final Report to Department of Health: Thematic Analysis of Submissions in Response to a Public Consultation on the White Paper for Universal Health Insurance*. Dublin, Department of Health.

CSO (2011). *Health status and health service utilisation: quarterly national household survey. Quarter 3 2010*. Dublin, Central Statistics Office.

Department of the Taoiseach (2011). Programme for Government 2011: www.taoiseach.gov.ie/eng/Publications/Publications_2011/Programme_for_Government_2011.pdf; accessed on 31/08/2011.

DOH (2012). Future Health. A Strategic Framework for Reform of the Health Service 2012–2015. Dublin, Department of Health: http://health.gov.ie/blog/publications/future-health-a-strategic-framework-for-reform-of-the-health-service-2012-2015/; accessed on 20/11/2015.

DOH (2014). The Path to Universal Healthcare. White Paper on Universal Health Insurance. Dublin: Department of Health: http://health.gov.ie/future-health/universal-health-insurance/the-white-paper-on-uhi/; accessed on 22/11/2015.

DoHC (1999). *Private health insurance*. White Paper. Dublin, Stationery Office.

DoHC (2001). *Quality and fairness for all. A health system for you*. Dublin, Stationery Office.

DoHC (2005). *Taxation and medical expenses*. Dublin, Department of Health and Children: www.dohc.ie/public/information/taxation_and_medical_expenses.html; accessed on 24/03/2005.

DoHC (2014). *The Path to Universal Healthcare: White Paper on Universal Health Insurance*. Dublin, Department of Health and Children.

European Commission (2003). *State Aid N46/2003 – Ireland. Risk equalisation scheme in the Irish health insurance market*. Brussels, European Commission, Directorate General for Competition.

European Court of Justice (2008). *Case T-289/03. British United Provident Association Limited (BUPA) and Others v. Commission of European Communities*. Luxemburg, European Court of Justice.

Expert Panel on Medical Need for Medical Card Eligibility (2014). Report of the Expert Panel on Medical Need for Medical Card Eligibility. Dublin: Health Service Executive: www.hse.ie/eng/services/publications/corporate/expertpanelmedicalneed.pdf; accessed on 24/11/2015.

Government of Ireland (2001). Health (Miscellaneous Provisions) Act 2001: www.irishstatutebook.ie/pdf/2001/en.act.2001.0014.pdf; accessed on 26/08/2011.

Government of Ireland (2008). Health Act 2008: www.irishstatutebook.ie/2008/en/act/pub/0021/index.html; accessed on 26/08/2011.

Government of Ireland (2009). Health Insurance (Miscellaneous Provisions) Act 2009: www.irishstatutebook.ie/2009/en/act/pub/0024/index.html; accessed on 12/09/2011.

Government of Ireland (2014). Statement of Government Priorities 2014–2016: www.taoiseach.gov.ie/eng/Publications/Publications_2014/Statement-of-Government-Priorities-2014-2016.pdf; accessed on 17/12/2015.

Harmon C, Nolan B (2001). Health insurance and health services utilization in Ireland. *Health Economics*, 10(2):135–45.

Health Information and Quality Authority (2014). Annual overview report on the regulation of designated centres for older people – 2013. Dublin, Health Information and Quality Authority: www.hiqa.ie/publications/annual-overview-report-regulation-designated-centres-older-people-%E2%80%93-2013-0; accessed on 16/12/2015.

HIA (The Health Insurance Authority) (2003a). *The private health insurance market in Ireland*. Report prepared by Amárach Consulting for the Health Insurance Authority, March 2003. Dublin, The Health Insurance Authority.

HIA (2003b). *Risk equalisation: guide to the Risk Equalisation Scheme, 2003 as prescribed in Statutory Instrument No. 261 of 2003*. Dublin, The Health Insurance Authority.

HIA (2005a). *The private health insurance market in Ireland: a market review*. Report prepared by Insight Statistical Consulting for the Health Insurance Authority, September 2005. Dublin, The Health Insurance Authority.

HIA (2005b). *Staff report to the members of the Health Insurance Authority in relation to its statutory functions and duties regarding risk equalisation*. Dublin, The Health Insurance Authority.

HIA (2007). *Competition in the Irish private health insurance market: A report to the Minister for Health and Children*. Dublin, The Health Insurance Authority.

HIA (2008a). *Summary of amounts due under Risk Equalisation Scheme.* Dublin: The Health Insurance Authority: www.hia.ie/assets/files/publications/Risk_Equalisation/Payments-due-under-the-RE-Scheme.pdf; accessed on 7/08/2008.

HIA (2008b). *Risk equalisation: updated guide to the Risk Equalisation Scheme, 2003 as prescribed in Statutory Instruments No. 261 of 2003, No. 710 of 2003, No. 334 of 2005 and No. 220 of 2007.* Dublin, The Health Insurance Authority.

HIA (2008c). *The private health insurance market in Ireland: a market review.* Report prepared by Insight Statistical Consulting, March 2008. Dublin, The Health Insurance Authority.

HIA (2010a). *The private health insurance market in Ireland.* Report prepared by Red C Research & Marketing Limited, May. Dublin, The Health Insurance Authority.

HIA (2010b). *Annual report and accounts 2009.* Dublin, The Health Insurance Authority.

HIA (2012). *Report on the Health Insurance Market.* Report prepared by Millward Brown Landsdowne. Dublin, The Health Insurance Authority.

HIA (2014). *Report on the Health Insurance Market.* Report prepared by Millward Brown. Dublin, The Health Insurance Authority.

HIA (2016a). *A review of private health insurance in Ireland.* Report by Millward Brown. Dublin, The Health Insurance Authority.

HIA (2016b). *Annual report and accounts 2015.* Dublin, The Health Insurance Authority.

HIA (2016c). *Market statistics 2015.* Dublin, The Health Insurance Authority.

HIA (2016d). *Newsletter, August 2016 edition.* Dublin, The Health Insurance Authority.

Houses of the Oireachtas (2017). *Committee on the Future of Healthcare Sláintecare Report.* Dublin, Houses of the Oireachtas, May 2017.

HSE (Health Service Executive) (2015a). Your guide to medical cards: www.hse.ie/eng/services/list/1/schemes/mc/focuson/aboutmedicalcards.205700.shortcut.html; accessed on 17/12/2015.

HSE (2015b). Medical Card/G.P. Visit card national assessment guidelines. Dublin, Health Service Executive: www.hse.ie/eng/services/list/1/schemes/mc/forms/medicalcardguidelines2015.pdf; accessed on 26/11/2015.

HSE (2015c). Medical workforce planning. Future demand for general practitioners 2015–2025. Dublin, National Doctor Training and Planning, HR Directorate, Health Service Executive: www.hse.ie/portal/eng/staff/Leadership_Education_Development/MET/plan/

reports/Medical_Workforce_Planning_Future_Demand_for_General_
Practitioners_2015-2025.pdf; accessed on 26/11/2015.

HSE (2015d). Public hospitals in Ireland. Dublin, Health Service Executive:
www.hse.ie/eng/services/list/3/hospitals/; accessed on 22/11/2015.

HSE (2016). *Annual report and financial statements 2015*. Naas, Health
Service Executive.

Keegan C et al. (2016). Switching insurer in the Irish voluntary health insurance
market: determinants, incentives, and risk equalization. *European Journal
of Health Economics*, 17(7):823–31.

Keegan C et al. (2017). Addressing market segmentation and incentives for
risk selection: How well does risk equalisation in the Irish private health
insurance market work? *The Economic and Social Review*, 48 (1): 61-84.

Layte R, Nolan B (2004). Equity in the utilisation of health care in Ireland.
The Economic and Social Review, 35(2):111–34.

Layte R et al. (2015). Trends in socio-economic inequalities in mortality
by sex in Ireland from the 1980s to the 2000s. *Irish Journal of Medical
Science*, 184(3):613–21.

Mikkers M, Ryan P (2014). "Managed Competition" for Ireland? The single
versus multiple payer debate. *BMC Health Services Research*, 14(1):442.

Nolan A, Smith S (2012). The effect of differential eligibility for free
GP services on GP utilisation in Ireland. *Social Science and Medicine*,
74(10):1644–51.

Nolan B (2004). Health insurance in Ireland: issues and challenges. *Economie
Publique*, 14(1):55–62.

Nolan B (2006). The interaction of public and private health insurance: Ireland
as a case study. *Geneva Papers on Risk and Insurance*, 31(4):633–49.

Nolan B, Wiley M (2000). *Private practice in Irish public hospitals*. Dublin,
Oak Tree Press.

O'Morain P (2007). *The health of the nation: the Irish healthcare system
1957–2007*. Dublin, Gill and Macmillan.

PCRS (Primary care reimbursement service) (2007). *Finance shared services
primary care reimbursement service: statistical analysis of claims and
payments 2007*. Dublin, Health Service Executive.

PCRS (2015). *Primary care reimbursement service: statistical analysis of
claims and payments 2015*. Dublin, Health Service Executive.

Price J, Mays J (1985). Selection and the competitive standing of health plans
in a multiple-choice, multiple-insurer market. In: Scheffler R, Rossiter L,
eds. *Advances in health economics and health services research*, vol. 6.
Greenwich, CT, JAI Press.

Private Health Insurance Advisory Group (2007). *A business appraisal of private medical insurance in Ireland*. Report for the Minister for Health and Children. Dublin, Department of Health and Children.

Quinn Healthcare (2008). Quinn Healthcare reduces prices, introduces new schemes and benefits, and offers free travel insurance proving competition is good for your health, Press release, 27 May: www.quinn-healthcare.com/press_and_media/pressrelease280508.htm; accessed on 15/12/2016.

Ruane F (2010). *Report of the Expert Group on Resource Allocation and Financing in the Health Sector.* Dublin, Department of Health and Children.

Smith S (2008). Equity in Irish health care financing [thesis]. Dublin, Trinity College.

Smith S (2010a). Equity in Irish health care financing: measurement issues. *Health Economics, Policy and Law,* 5(2):149–69.

Smith S (2010b). The Irish 'health basket': a basket case? *European Journal of Health Economics,* 11(3):343–50.

Smith S, Normand C (2009). Analysing equity in health care financing: a flow of funds approach. *Social Science & Medicine,* 69(3):379–86.

Smith S, Normand C (2011). Equity in health care: the Irish perspective. *Health Economics, Policy and Law,* 6:205–17.

Thomas S, Normand C, Smith S (2008). *Social health insurance: further options for Ireland*. Dublin, The Adelaide Hospital Society.

Thomson S, Mossialos E (2007). Regulating private health insurance in the European Union: the implications of single market legislation and competition policy. *Journal of European Integration,* 29(1):89–107.

Timonen V, Doyle M, O'Dwyer C (2012). Expanded, but not regulated: ambiguity in home-care policy in Ireland. *Health and Social Care in the Community,* 20(3):310–18.

Turner B (2013). Premium inflation in the Irish private health insurance market: drivers and consequences. *Irish Journal of Medical Science,* 182(4):545–50.

Turner B (2014). The path to universal health care: White paper, red flags. *Administration,* 62(3):39–61.

Turner B (2015). Unwinding the State subsidisation of private health insurance in Ireland. *Health Policy,* 119(10):1349–57.

Turner B (2016). The new system of health accounts in Ireland: what does it all mean? *Irish Journal of Medical Science,* 186(3):533–40.

Turner B, Shinnick E (2008). *The development of the Irish private health insurance market and evidence of selection effects therein. Working Paper* No. 08-02. Cork, University College Cork, Department of Economics.

Tussing D, Wren M-A (2006). *How Ireland cares: the case for health care reform*. Dublin, New Island.

Vhi (2003). *Annual report and accounts, 2003*. Dublin, Voluntary Health Insurance Board.

Vhi (2007). *Annual report and accounts 2007*. Dublin,Voluntary Health Insurance Board.

Vhi (2008). *Annual report and accounts, 2008*. Dublin, Voluntary Health Insurance Board.

Vhi (2009). *Annual report and accounts, 2009*. Dublin, Voluntary Health Insurance Board.

Vhi (2015). *Annual Report and Accounts 2014*. Dublin, Voluntary Health Insurance Board.

WHO (2018). *Global health expenditure database* (GHED) [online database]. Geneva, WHO: www.who.int/health-accounts/ghed/en/; accessed on 15/01/2018.

Wiley MM (2001). Reform and renewal of the Irish health care system: policy and practice. In: Callan T, McCoy D, eds. *Budget perspectives: proceedings of a conference held on 9 October 2001*. Dublin, ESRI.

Wren M-A, Connolly S (2016). *Challenges in achieving universal healthcare in Ireland*. Dublin, ESRI.

Wren M-A, Connolly S, Cunningham N (2015). *An examination of the potential costs of universal health insurance in Ireland*. Dublin, ESRI.

York Health Economics Consortium (2003). *Assessment of risk equalisation and competition in the Irish health insurance market – final report*. York, York Health Economics Consortium: www.hia.ie/sec3_reports/AppendixIII .pdf; accessed on 15/12/2016.

8 Integrating public and private insurance in the Israeli health system: an attempt to reconcile conflicting values

SHULI BRAMMLI-GREENBERG AND RUTH WAITZBERG*

The private health insurance market in Israel offers two voluntary products: the first, offered by the non-profit health plans (HPs), is referred to as supplemental insurance (SI); the second, provided by for-profit insurers, is known as commercial insurance (CI). Both types of cover play a complementary role, covering benefits excluded from the National Health Insurance (NHI) scheme such as dental health care for adults. They also play a supplementary role, providing faster access to care, greater choice of provider and improved amenities (in the private sector), and extended cover of services included in the NHI, such as more physiotherapy or psychotherapy sessions compared with what the NHI offers. The Israeli private health insurance market's main distinctive feature is the very high levels of population coverage and dual coverage (almost all people who own CI also own SI).

We observe two trends in the health care market: (i) the decrease in the public share of health spending in the last two decades, followed by a sharp growth in private activity and private health insurance coverage; and (ii) the growth of the private health insurance market accompanied by various negative impacts on the public system's financial sustainability, accessibility and availability of services and quality of care.

Analysis of the Israeli case highlights the complexity of integrating statutory and broad private (voluntary) health insurance. Integration efforts have created a range of, sometimes conflicting, incentives and disincentives, which have implications for achieving public policy goals such as choice, extended coverage, equity, solidarity and curbing government spending while maintaining a strong publicly financed health system.

---

*This chapter is dedicated to the memory of Revital Gross, one of the leading health policy researchers in Israel, who contributed to the conception of this work.

Key features of the health system
Historical background

The structure of the Israeli health system was put in place before the establishment of the State of Israel (1948). Four non-profit HPs,[1] established between 1920 and 1940 by political parties or trade unions, insured their members and provided medical services. In 1948, the Ministry of Health took on the role of planning, regulation and supervision of the HPs, and began to provide selected health services and run hospitals (Gross & Anson, 2002). Although health insurance was voluntary, by 1995 almost all citizens (96%) were insured, mainly by Clalit, which had a 62% share of the market. The HPs were only loosely regulated by the Ministries of Health and Finance, and could set their own benefits and premiums and reject applicants.

Between 1948 and 1995, the structure of the health system was repeatedly debated by government committees, but major stakeholders opposed reform, fearing nationalization of the health system and loss of power[2] (Yishai, 1982; Gross & Anson, 2002; Schwartz, Doron & Davidovitch, 2006). In the 1980s, high inflation rates and economic recession led to a policy of reduced government spending, which affected Clalit in particular, as it had been highly dependent on the financial aid allocated by earlier Labour coalition governments. By 1988, Clalit had accumulated a deficit of US$700 million, which was endangering the stability of the health system (Chernichovsky & Chinitz, 1995). Consequently, the government appointed a commission of inquiry into the financial crisis facing Clalit, inequality in service provision, labour unrest and public dissatisfaction with HPs' services (Gross, 2003; Rosen & Bin Nun, 2006). The commission's recommendations[3] included:

[1] Clalit Health Care Services, Maccabi Health Services, Leumit Health Services and Meuhedet.
[2] A major source of opposition was the Histadrut (the Israeli General Federation of Labor), which opposed the separation of Clalit from the Histadrut, since it provided substantial funding and a powerful organizational base (Rosen, Waitzberg & Merkur, 2015).
[3] Dissension within the Commission of Inquiry over the essence of the proposed reforms, particularly the NHI Law, resulted in separate reports by the majority and minority of members (see State of Israel, 1990). The minority recommended less sweeping structural changes and proposed focusing on a few potent

NHI legislation to regulate competition among the HPs and increase the financial stability of Clalit; transforming hospitals into competing self-financed autonomous non-profit entities; and reorganizing the Ministry of Health to reduce its involvement in service delivery and strengthen its policy-making, planning and monitoring functions (Gross & Anson, 2002).

The development of NHI

The NHI Law came into effect in January 1995, adopting many elements of Enthoven's (1993) managed competition model (Chinitz, 1995; Gross, Rosen & Shirom, 2001; Gross & Anson, 2002; Gross, 2003). It stipulates that all Israeli residents[4] are entitled to a specified package of benefits[5] that includes primary, secondary and tertiary care, emergency and preventive care, listed medications, diagnostic procedures and medical technologies. The Ministries of Health and Finance update the benefits package annually.[6] All residents must register with one of the competing non-profit HPs, which are forbidden by law to reject applicants, and six times a year they may choose to change HP (it is possible to make up to two switches over a period of 1 year). In 2013, Clalit had the largest market share (52.2%), followed by Maccabi (24.8%), Meuhedet (13.6%) and Leumit (9.0%) (Horev & Keidar, 2014). Within the public system, HPs provide care (listed in the NHI benefits package) in the community and purchase inpatient and outpatient care from hospitals (about 80% of hospitals' revenues come from services sold to HPs). Within the private system there are two types of private health insurance, with a broad coverage and a significant overlap (see Fig. 8.1).

Alongside the Ministry of Health, the Ministry of Finance plays a major role and must approve all Ministry of Health decisions that

so-called change levers to make the system more effective (Chinitz, 1995; Shirom, 1995).

[4] The status of resident is granted according to the stipulations of the NHI Law. Tourists, foreign workers and non-Jewish residents of the West Bank and Gaza are not defined as residents of Israel (Gross & Harrison, 2001).

[5] Called the Health Basket.

[6] In 1997 the government established a formal priority-setting process for the addition of new services to the benefits package (Rosen, Waitzberg & Merkur, 2015). For a detailed description of this process, see Shani et al., (2000).

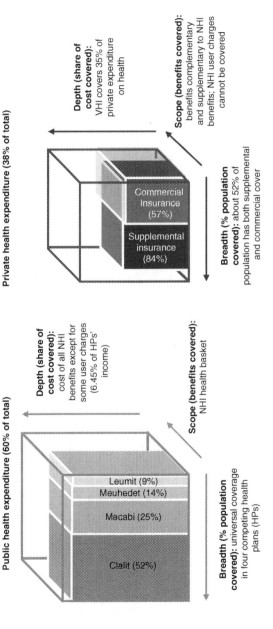

Public health expenditure (60% of total)

Depth (share of cost covered): cost of all NHI benefits except for some user charges (6.45% of HPs' income)

Scope (benefits covered): NHI health basket

Breadth (% population covered): universal coverage in four competing health plans (HPs)

Leumit (9%)
Meuhedet (14%)
Macabi (25%)
Clalit (52%)

Private health expenditure (38% of total)

Depth (share of cost covered): VHI covers 35% of private expenditure on health

Scope (benefits covered): benefits complementary and supplementary to NHI benefits; NHI user charges cannot be covered

Breadth (% population covered): about 52% of population has both supplemental and commercial cover

Commercial insurance (57%)

Supplemental insurance (84%)

Figure 8.1 Public and private health insurance coverage in Israel, 2016.

Sources: Brammli-Greenberg et al. (2014) and Brammli-Greenberg et al. (2019).

have budgetary implications. The two ministries share responsibility for monitoring the HPs' financial performance (Gross & Harrison, 2001; Gross & Anson, 2002); setting the NHI annual budget, setting official price lists and physicians' salaries and so on (Brammli-Greenberg et al., 2016). Other powerful players with considerable influence over national policy-making include the Israel Medical Association and hospital managers.

NHI revenue collection, pooling of funds and allocation to HPs

The government determines the level of funding for the NHI benefits package, adjusting the previous year's budget to take account of demographic changes, inflation and new health technologies. Most (88%) of the NHI budget is divided among HPs prospectively through a capitation formula that takes into account the insured members' age, gender and place of residence (periphery or centre of the country). Another 5.5% of the funds are allocated to the HPs based on the number of members with one of five severe illnesses.[7] The remaining 6.45% is raised by the HPs retrospectively through user charges for outpatient medications and specialist consultations (Ministry of Health, 2014a).

Purchasing services and payment mechanisms

Tertiary care: Of the 45 general hospitals[8] in Israel, 18 are publicly owned and account for 57% of Israel's acute-care hospital beds. Another 40% of beds (16 general hospitals) are operated by non-profit organizations. The remaining 11 are for-profit hospitals, are smaller and operate only 3% of the beds. Hence, non-profit hospitals account for approximately 97% of the acute beds and 92% of acute admissions (Ministry of Health, 2014b). HPs pay for outpatient clinics and emergency departments in hospitals on a fee-for-service basis and for inpatient care via length of stay and activity-based payments. Prices are set by the government by a joint Ministry of Health and Ministry of Finance committee that

---

[7] Thalassaemia, Gaucher disease, terminal renal disease, haemophilia and AIDS.
[8] Israel adopts the OECD definition of "general hospital".

sets maximum price lists for all hospital services (Brammli-Greenberg et al., 2016). HPs contract with other providers (for example, diagnostic centres) predominantly on the basis of negotiated fee-for-service arrangements.

Primary and secondary care: The salaries of primary care physicians employed at HPs' clinics and of hospital physicians and other professionals in the public sector (for example, nurses, pharmacists) are mainly determined through collective bargaining with the Ministry of Finance and Ministry of Health. Contracts are used to remunerate independent physicians on a capitation basis. Payment methods of HPs for community-based specialists may also include a fee-for-service per procedure or a flat rate per shift. Some physicians take on private work on a fee-for-service basis. Most dentists work independently and set their own fee-for-service rates (Rosen, Waitzberg & Merkur, 2015).

Health expenditure

The proportion of GDP devoted to health care has fallen from 8.4% in 2001 to 7.4% in 2015, mainly due to cost control and rationing mechanisms. For example, in the area of outpatient care, HPs negotiate prices with pharmaceutical and medical technologies companies, negotiate salaries with contracted physicians and other professionals, and also control regional supply of workforce and services and can use waiting times as a rationing mechanism (Brammli-Greenberg & Waitzberg, 2017). HPs also negotiate price discounts with hospitals.

Rationing in the area of inpatient care includes supply-side restraints (for example, on workforce, number of hospital beds) employed by the Ministries of Health and Finance and cost containment measures such as maximum price-lists set by the government, caps on hospitals' annual revenues from each HP and stringent control of salaries. The public share of health care funding decreased from 75% of total spending on health in 1996 to 60% in 2015 (see Fig. 8.2) and it is one of the lowest among OECD countries.

From Fig. 8.2 we can see that the dedicated income-related health tax funds only account for a quarter of total spending on health in Israel. The remaining public funding comes from government funds, the amounts of which are decided every year, therefore making this source somewhat volatile. Private spending is significant, especially the out-of-pocket component, described below.

Table 8.1 *Breakdown of private health care expenditure in Israel, 2013*

	Total (NIS million)	Share of total spending on health	Breakdown of private spending on health	Breakdown of out-of-pocket payments
Total spending on health (7.6% of GDP)	79 251			
Private spending on health	31 463	39.70%		
Out-of-pocket payments	20 605	26.00%	65.50%	
Co-payments	5 199	6.56%	10.00%	13.48%
Dental and other care [a]	8 987	11.34%	30.50%	50.82%
Medications	6 316	7.97%	16.50%	35.70%
Commercial premiums	3 963	5.00%	13.00%	
Supplemental premiums	6 895	8.70%	22.00%	

Sources: Horev & Keidar (2014); Chernichovsky et al. (2016); Rosen, Waitzberg & Merkur (2015); CBS (2016).

Notes: NIS: New Israeli Shekel.

[a] Glasses, medical accessories, etc.

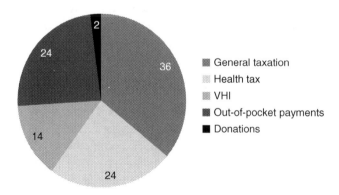

Figure 8.2 Sources of health care funding in Israel (% of total), 2015
Source: CBS (2016).

Out-of-pocket payments

Out-of-pocket payments in Israel consist of user charges paid to HPs for visits to specialists and coinsurance for medications; and spending on services not included in the health basket. For example, households pay privately for dental care for people aged 12 and over, prostheses, hearing aids, medications not included in the medications basket, and services in the private sector such as private hospitals and private physicians (see Table 8.1 for a detailed breakdown of the private spending on health). Although private health insurance does not cover user charges, it covers services provided in the private market. Survey data from 2012 indicate that 35% of households' health spending[9] was for private health insurance premiums, 25% for dental care, 16% for medications and 24% for other services (Horev & Keidar 2014).

Overview of the private health insurance market

Market role, size and regulation

Supplemental insurance

The NHI Law (State of Israel, 1994: Clause 10) allows the HPs to offer SI in addition to the mandatory NHI benefits package, and these are supervised by the Division for Regulating HPs at the Ministry of Health (see Table 8.2).

The Ministry of Health oversees benefits, premiums and user charges, as well as the financial stability of SI, approving their annual budgets and actuarial reports. The Ministry also regulates the interface with NHI benefits: first, to ensure that HPs do not give preference to SI members (for example, SI cannot cover shorter waiting times or offer an extended choice of provider at HP facilities; however, this is allowed in private clinics); and second, to ensure that SI compensates the NHI budget for use of HP facilities and staff.

Commercial Insurance

Commercial insurance is offered by private insurers and is regulated by the Insurance Commissioner at the Ministry of Finance. As for other insurance types, the Commissioner oversees policies to ensure the financial stability of insurers and protect consumer rights (through fair pricing and proper disclosure). Since the NHI legislation in 1995 and the subsequent growth of the commercial market, the Insurance Commissioner has strengthened regulation to protect consumer rights for this type of health insurance (see below).

[9] Health care represents about 5.5% of households' expenditures.

Table 8.2 *Key features of the National Health Insurance and private health insurance in Israel, 2017*

	NHI	Supplemental insurance	Commercial insurance
Provider	Four non-profit health plans (public entities)	Non-profit health plans	For-profit private insurance companies
Enrolment	Mandatory	Voluntary	Voluntary
Role	• Universal statutory health insurance	• Complementary, supplementary health insurance	• Complementary and supplementary health insurance
Coverage	• A comprehensive uniform benefits package including prevention, primary, secondary and tertiary care, mental health and medications • Yearly structured process of review and prioritization of new technologies (adding on average 0.5–1.5% to the budget) • HPs not responsible for providing long-term care or preventive care in schools	• Uniform benefits (within a health plan) • Regulation restricts benefits that can be covered • Extends services included in the NHI cover (e.g. more visits to physiotherapy [a]); covers services excluded from NHI cover (dental care and alternative medicine); provides choice of provider in private facilities; included in the NHI; provides faster access to care in private facilities • Does not cover lifesaving medications not covered by the NHI or NHI user charges.	• Tailored policies and premiums, with some restrictions since 2015 [b] • Extends services included in the NHI cover (e.g. more visits to physiotherapy [a]); covers services excluded from NHI cover (dental care and alternative medicine); provides choice of provider in private facilities; provides faster access to care in private facilities • Does not cover NHI user charges but covers medications not covered by the NHI or medications that are included in the NHI cover but for other indications (mainly for cancer and other severe illnesses)

Terms and premiums	• Compulsory entitlement • Progressive health tax of up to 5% of wages (with ceiling); flat rate for older people and poor people	• Open enrolment • Premium determined by age only • Collective policies	• Medical underwriting with exclusion of pre-existing conditions and application of waiting periods • Premiums determined by risk level; for the standard policy, premiums are mainly determined by age and gender (with possible exemptions due to health conditions) • Individual and collective policies
Regulation	Ministry of Health and Ministry of Finance	Ministry of Health • Aims: to minimize its undesirable effects on equality and safeguard the public system	Insurance Commissioner • Aims: to protect consumer rights and safeguard financial stability

Notes: HP: health plan; NHI: national health insurance

[a] These services are provided in private facilities. Services included in the NHI cover can also be provided in the private sector (for example, a private physiotherapist working under contract with an HP) or in HP facilities (for example, a physiotherapist directly employed in an HP facility).

[b] These restrictions include the requirement on commercial insurers to offer a so-called standard policy (since 2015) and charge mandatory user charges (since 2016).

A reform initiated in 2015 aims to increase transparency and enhance market competition, and recently additional regulation was set to limit the growth of the private provision and private insurance sectors. For example, a law stipulates that a physician who has started treating a publicly funded patient cannot provide that patient with a privately funded service during a period of at least 4–6 months (although, the physician can refer the patient to another doctor in the private system). Another law created a "standard policy" in the CI market with uniform coverage and uniform premiums by age groups for surgeries and specialists consultations only. For a detailed description of the reform see Table 8.4 and HSPM (2015, 2016).

Market structure

Residents can purchase SI from their HP only. Coverage rates[10] are generally high, rising from 37% of the adult population in 1998 to 65% in 2001 and reaching 84% in 2016 (Gross, Brammli-Greenberg & Waitzberg, 2008; Brammli-Greenberg et al., 2019,). Coverage is also high among vulnerable population groups, with the exception of low-income individuals and Arabs.[11]

Commercial insurance is offered mainly by five insurers, who account for 95% of commercial premiums. There are two types of policy-owners in the commercial market: (i) people who buy their policies directly from an insurer for a risk-rated premium based on age, gender and pre-existing conditions; (ii) organizations (for example, employers, labour unions) who purchase group policies for their members for a community-rated premium, reflecting the risk level of the group. The CI group policies have recently gained market share and are concentrated in the hands of two companies.[12,13] In 2016, 57% of the adult

[10] SI coverage rates vary significantly by health plan: 89% of Maccabi's members, 83% of Clalit's, 78% of Meuhedet's and 80% of Leumit's members.

[11] In 2016 SI coverage rates among vulnerable populations were: 87% among chronically ill people, 90% among older people, 84% among immigrants from the former Soviet Union, 66% among the lowest income quintile and 63% among Israel's Arab citizens (Brammli-Greenberg et al., 2019).

[12] Premiums from commercial group policies for medical expenses grew by 329% between 2003 and 2016 and premiums from policies for severe diseases increased by 199% in the same period. The increase for individual policies was 306% and 180%, respectively (Ministry of Finance, 2016).

[13] Harel Group and Haphenix cover 76% of the market.

Table 8.3 *Share of the adult population (22+) with private health insurance in Israel, 1999–2016*

	1999	2001	2003	2005	2007	2009	2012	2014	2016
Supplemental insurance	51	64	73	79	80	81	81	87	84
Supplemental insurance basic layer				70	64	65	40	62	54
Supplemental insurance extended layer				30	36	35	60	37	43
Commercial insurance	24	26	35	34	32	35	43	53	57
Supplemental and commercial insurance[a]	13	20	28	31	28	32	39	50	52

Source: Brammli-Greenberg et al. (2019).

Notes: Self-reported data.

[a] The share of adult population with supplemental insurance reflects ownership of at least one supplemental layer (basic or extended plan).

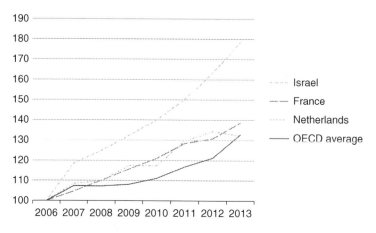

Figure 8.3 Expenditure on private health insurance in Israel in per capita purchasing power parity US$ (2006 = 100), 2006–2013

Source: OECD (2017).

population had CI. However, only 5% had CI alone; 52% had both SI and CI (see Table 8.3). The shares of adult populations owning CI are lower among vulnerable groups, especially lower-income individuals[14]. Multivariate analysis reveals that the likelihood of having both types of cover is higher among younger people, highly educated people, those with high incomes and Hebrew speakers. Over half (53%) of those who have CI have a group policy (Brammli-Greenberg et al., 2019)

The share of the Israeli population with private health insurance coverage has grown rapidly in the last decade. This growth was the major driver of growth in private spending on health: between 2002 and 2011 household monthly spending on SI and CI as a percentage of total household expenditure increased by, respectively 70% and 90% (Ministry of Health, 2012). Payments for private health insurance premiums (both supplemental and commercial) increased by more than 100% between 2005 and 2013, compared with an average increase of 18% in other insurance sectors. Per person spending on health funded by private health insurance skyrocketed by 50% between 2006 and

---

[14] CI coverage rates are 49% among chronically-ill people, 38% among older people, 45% among immigrants from the former Soviet Union, 26% among the lowest income quintile and 48% among Israel's Arab citizens (Brammli-Greenberg et al., 2019).

2011, increasing much faster than the average growth of 15% among OECD countries (see Fig. 8.3). Israel ranks third among OECD countries according to the share of population covered by private health insurance (after France and the Netherlands) (Ministry of Health, 2014d). Israel has also one of the highest shares of private spending in total spending on health among OECD countries (40% in Israel compared with 28% for OECD countries on average; OECD, 2017). In 2014, private health insurance represented about 35% of household expenditures on health, growing from 17% in 2000 (see Fig. 8.4).

According to the Ministry of Health, the private health insurance market is not achieving the goal of financing health care privately while reducing out-of-pocket payments: household spending on health has not changed over the last decade except for the sharp increase in spending on private health insurance premiums (Ministry of Health, 2012). Along with the increase in the share of private health insurance policy-holders in the adult population in the last decades, we have witnessed an expansion of dual coverage: 52% of the adult population own the two types of private health insurance; 92% of those who own CI own also SI, and 62% of those who own SI own also CI (Brammli-Greenberg

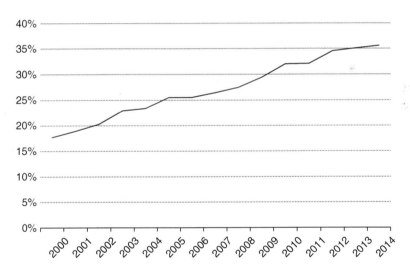

Figure 8.4 Household expenditure on private health insurance in Israel (premiums and co-payments) as a share of total household expenditure on health, 2000–2014

Source: CBS (2014).

et al., 2019). It is worth noting that 100% of private health insurance owners are covered also by the NHI.

Private health insurance policy terms

Supplemental insurance

Since 1998, HPs have been forbidden to reject any applicants for SI, or limit coverage due to pre-existing conditions. Each HP may decide which services to include in its supplemental plan and determines its premium rates, which can differ only by age. Changes in the terms of SI policies are approved by the Ministry of Health and apply to all members. Premiums are based on yearly actuarial calculations, taking into account the benefits covered and the risk profile of members. Cover is provided for as long as the member pays the premium (those who have ceased paying can re-enrol, but will then face waiting times for services).

Health plans offer their members a choice of two SI layers: a basic plan and an extended plan with a higher premium. They also offer a group long-term care insurance (LTCI) policy, for which they contract with commercial insurers, who set premiums based on actuarial calculations (Brammli-Greenberg, Gross & Matzliach, 2007). SI plays a complementary and a supplementary role in the health system. To date, it can provide: (i) services that are not included in the NHI benefits package (for example, adult dental care or alternative medicine); (ii) services that are covered by NHI, but only to a limited extent (for example, in vitro fertilization (IVF) and physiotherapy); (iii) care purchased from private providers that enhance choice and provide faster access or improved facilities.

Health plans use selective contracting to lower costs. They also impose user charges and waiting periods for SI benefits. Charges vary by service and may reach thousands of new Israeli shekels for major procedures (surgery, transplants, treatment abroad and fertility treatment). Waiting periods also vary by service up to a maximum of 24 months. Comparison of the SI benefits offered by each of the HPs reveals that they are similar in terms of the scope of services covered (Brammli-Greenberg, Gross & Matzliach, 2007).

Commercial insurance

Commercial insurance also plays a complementary and a supplementary role in the health system; insurers are free to cover any medical service and offer several coverage options, including coverage for: (i) medical expenses such as surgeries and visits to specialists in Israel; implants and special procedures overseas; medicines (35% of CI health premiums in 2015), compensation for severe diseases[15] (for example, receipt of a fixed sum, set at the insurer's discretion, if the insured develops a severe illness such as cancer) (9%), (ii) LTC (39%) and (iii) dental care (6%). Each insurer offers several policies for each of these options (Ministry of Finance, 2015a).

Enrolment in CI is dependent on medical underwriting and, in individual policies, premiums are fully adjusted for risk (age, gender and health status) and pre-existing conditions. The exception is the standard policy for medical expenses introduced in 2015, in which premiums are standardized for age and sex groups, but insurers can also exclude individuals with medical conditions. Group premiums are lower than individual premiums for the same level of coverage, and usually less profitable. CIs offer access to private providers who are in the insurance network. Mandatory user charges for CI were stipulated by the Ministry of Finance since 2016 to reduce moral hazard.[16] Plans may involve qualifying periods and waiting times for receipt of service. Commercial insurers may offer customers incentives to use their SI cover first so that CIs only pay part of the cost, even though premiums were calculated for the full cost.

Market development and public policy

Development of the SI market

In the mid-1980s, the HPs responded to growing consumer dissatisfaction and the decline in government financial support by providing compulsory SI cover for an additional nominal premium (see Table 8.4). SI included a uniform package for all members, offering indemnity cover (rather than benefits in kind) for expensive new technologies

---

[15] Until 2015 each insurer could determine the illnesses covered and amount and type of diagnosis that defined each illness. In 2015, the Ministry of Finance issued a circular that sets a (minimum) list of illnesses that this type of insurance must cover and their definition.

[16] At the same time, commercial insurers were required to pay providers directly rather than reimburse payments made by policy-holders. This ended physicians' practice of balance-billing.

(for example, transplants, life-saving surgery abroad, IVF) (Cohen & Barnea, 1992; Gross & Brammli-Greenberg, 1996). Maccabi, which had offered voluntary as well as compulsory SI for decades,[17] extended its voluntary cover to include LTC, consultations with private physicians, private surgery and discounts for dental care (Kaye & Roter, 2001). In 1994, Meuhedet also introduced a voluntary plan covering LTC in addition to its compulsory plan.

The enactment of the 1995 NHI Law led to a significant expansion of the SI market. Under the new law, the HPs could offer only voluntary SI, for services not included in the NHI benefits package. The law stipulated that the NHI benefits package would include all the services provided by Clalit in both its core and compulsory SI covers, requiring Clalit to develop an entirely new voluntary SI. The other HPs made their compulsory SI voluntary and automatically transferred their members from the compulsory to the voluntary plan. Those who did not want SI had to notify the HP to dropout of the plan. This default registration resulted in very high rates of SI take-up (89% in Maccabi, 82% in Meuhedet and 50% in Leumit, compared with only 16% in Clalit's plan in 1995) (Gross & Brammli-Greenberg, 1996).

Policy-makers allowed the HPs to sell SI cover alongside NHI in response to pressure from Maccabi and Meuhedet in the run-up to the NHI Law, to compensate them for an anticipated fall in revenue. Maccabi and Meuhedet's membership base was relatively young and wealthy, their revenue from the new capitation formula would have been lower than it had been before the introduction of the NHI Law. Allowing them to sell SI reduced their opposition and facilitated parliamentary approval of the NHI Law (Gross, 2003).

From 1995 to 1997, the structure of the private health insurance market became the focus of intense public debate over whether the HPs should be allowed to manage voluntary cover themselves or whether it should be provided by commercial insurers only, forcing the HPs to contract with them for their SI. Commercial insurers lobbied for this option, which was also supported by the Insurance Commissioner, who was concerned about the financial viability of SI managed by HPs (who had accrued large deficits in the past). The Ministry of Health

---

[17] The voluntary plan was originally introduced in 1950 to cover hospitalization for tourists and temporary residents. By 1991, 33% of Maccabi members held voluntary SI.

and some academic shapers of public opinion also thought SI should be separated from the HPs, emphasizing its potential to compromise equality. Conversely, the HPs argued that SI would enhance equality by making better services accessible to a large share of the population (Gross & Brammli-Greenberg, 2001).

The regulations governing Israel's SI market were drafted in 1998 (State of Israel, 1998). They aimed to design SI to gain from integrating private funding into the public system, while minimizing any negative impact on solidarity and equality, and to find an arrangement that would benefit the HPs and commercial insurers. As a result, the HPs were permitted to manage SI as separate financial entities with balanced accounts; SI would only provide benefits in kind and HPs must offer open enrolment and community-rated premiums (differentiated by age only); and LTCI would be provided exclusively by commercial insurers, who had the capacity to manage actuarial reserves, thereby safeguarding commercial market share. One of the most important changes brought about by the 1998 regulations was to allow SI plans to offer supplementary cover of services covered by the NHI by using private providers, that is, private consultation, private surgery, which meant enhanced choice of provider and reduced waiting times.

Despite the regulations in place, public debate over the structure of the SI market continued. Debate focused mainly on equality; on the separation of the financial management of SI and NHI benefits so that NHI funds would not indirectly subsidize supplemental business, and on the fact that eligibility waiting periods for supplemental cover might limit consumers' ability to change HP (switching rates are low, at around 1.5% annually) (State of Israel, 2002; Israel National Institute for Health Policy and Health Services Research, 2003, 2007). Regulation of SI has evolved in response to these concerns.

A 2002 regulation stipulated that income from SI would compensate the HPs' NHI budget retroactively for the use of infrastructure and staff, so that NHI would not subsidize supplemental business. The Ministry of Health rules (Ministry of Health, 2005) include the following provisions: (i) SI annual expenses should not exceed annual revenue and premiums may be adjusted to that end without prior Ministry of Health approval; (ii) transfer of funds from the NHI budget to the SI budget is prohibited; (iii) there should be a strict separation in accounting and financial management of NHI and SI budgets; (iv) if SI benefits from administrative or other services charged to the NHI budget, it should compensate NHI for its share of the expenses (each HP has discretion to define these rates); (v) temporary SI excess revenue can be transferred to cover NHI deficits as a loan. A regulation introduced in 2010 abolished eligibility waiting periods for those who change HP. This was initiated by the Ministry of Health in response to the State Comptroller's annual report, which criticized SI as a barrier to inter-plan mobility (State Comptroller, 2007).

The debate on the inclusion of life-saving medications

An ongoing debate that remains a central concern is whether the SI should cover life-saving medications. In 2007, the Ministry of Health approved new supplemental policies covering life-saving and life-extending medications.[18] These benefits were added to the extended layer of the SI plans, triggering intense public debate (Gross & Brammli-Greenberg, 2007). Due to Israel's priority-setting process for medications, based on cost-effectiveness analysis, some of these medications cannot be included in the NHI benefits package and are only available on a private basis (Shani et al., 2000; Shemer, Abadi-Korek & Seifan, 2005).[19]

The proponents of the inclusion of these medications in the SI cover claim that it can provide access to important medications that the public budget would not cover to a broad range of individuals; and it can increase the attractiveness of SI. The opponents of this policy argue that the vulnerable population that does not own SI will have no access to those medications, and it is a regressive way of funding. Moreover, once a medication is offered by the SI, the government may consider it less important to provide it through the NHI health basket.

Moreover, adding these benefits to SI cover put the HPs in direct competition with commercial insurers, particularly as they could offer cover more cheaply than commercial insurers. The latter therefore lobbied against the benefit extension. The Ministry of Health and the Knesset (Israeli parliament) also opposed it on the grounds that it would: (i) lead to inequality in access to health care; (ii) bind members to their HPs due to the relatively long waiting periods for eligibility;

---

[18] These were issued by Clalit and Maccabi. In 2004, Meuhedet had introduced coverage for life-saving/extending medications for cancer patients only and Leumit contracted with a commercial insurer to offer this cover to its members.

[19] For example, Herceptin for breast cancer and Avastin for colon cancer were not approved by the NHI committee at first, and were added only in subsequent years following public pressure.

and (iii) weaken public pressure on the Ministry of Finance to add new medications to the NHI benefits package. The Ministry of Finance also feared that the change would increase total spending on health (Gross & Brammli-Greenberg, 2007).

Following this public debate, in 2008 the HPs were forbidden to include life-saving and life-extending medications in SI plans and the approval previously granted by the Ministry of Health was rescinded (State of Israel, 2008). After further heated debate, the Knesset's Welfare and Health Committee approved the legislation. However, it ruled that the prohibition should be conditional on a substantial increase in public funding for NHI benefits over a 3-year period to compensate people for being unable to access these medications through SI.

The debate came back to the public agenda in 2015 when the Minister of Health declared that it is willing to allow the inclusion of such medications in the SI cover.

Development of the commercial market

The CI market was established in Mandatory Palestine in 1933. A single insurance company (Shiloach) marketed substitutive health policies chiefly as an alternative to HP services for the wealthy, providing indemnity coverage for primary, secondary and tertiary care purchased from private providers (Kaye & Roter, 2001). In the 1980s, the perceived deterioration in services provided by the HPs was accompanied by a proliferation of insurers entering the health market. By the early 1990s, a large number of firms (relative to the population's size) were active (43 Israeli and 23 foreign insurance companies), although about 75% of the market was in the hands of six Israeli insurance groups, which provided more than 20 different health products (Cohen & Barnea, 1992).

A 1990 survey indicated that 0.5% of the population had commercial substitutive cover and 13% had CI in addition to their HP membership. The CI market expanded significantly after the introduction of NHI, alongside the expansion of the supplemental market, which had raised consumers' awareness of the benefits of purchasing additional cover. Commercial insurers understood the market's potential – their health cover is extremely profitable[20] – and invested resources in marketing their own competing products.

[20] The loss ratio has been stable from 2004 to 2010 at around 40% for individual CI and 75% for group CI, and has increased significantly since then. The loss

Since 1995 there have been significant changes in the basic features of CIs, partly due to restrictions in the NHI benefits package and regulation of SI; partly due to direct competition with SI; and partly due to regulation of the commercial market. Insurers have developed new policies and new companies have entered the market. The health insurance share of total CI premium income has grown from under 5% in 1986 to 14% in 2006. The scope of benefits offered has also expanded. In 1991, most policies insured against terminal diseases and transplants (catastrophic risk) and only two companies covered private surgery and hospitalization in Israel and abroad. By 1996, most policies offered all of these things as well as LTC cover, other services covered by NHI or supplemental benefits (for example, IVF, ambulatory procedures, alternative medicine), and some services not covered by NHI or SI (for example, cosmetic surgery) (Gross & Brammli-Greenberg, 1996).

More recently, there has been a decrease in marketing of CI as an alternative to SI cover and an increase in marketing of CI as a supplement to SI, including through financial incentives. The prevalence of dual coverage has therefore risen from 5% in 1995 to 22% in 2001 and 52% in 2016 (Brammli-Greenberg et al., 2019). CI has become an additional layer of insurance (with almost all of those who have CI having SI as well; see Table 8.2) rather than an alternative to SI, resulting in less direct competition between the two parts of the market.

Over time the commercial insurers' marketing strategy shifted from selling health policies as part of life insurance packages to selling independent health policies with individually tailored benefits. Insurers also developed uniform policies, similar to the HPs' supplemental plans, to attract group sales among trade unions and large employers (Gross & Brammli-Greenberg, 1996). These changes in marketing strategy combined with changes in the regulation of SI led to increased diffusion of CI in the Israeli population.

Commercial insurance is a very profitable product, with claims ratio of 58% in 2015 (46% for individual policies and 93% for group policies) and an annual (average) increase of 15% in premiums payments (Ministry of Finance, 2016). With people claiming SI coverage first (and having difficulties claiming CI coverage), it seems that CI is not being useful for those who have it (Brammli-Greenberg et al., 2014; Ministry

ratio for individual CI was 49% and 93% for group CI in 2015 (Ministry of Finance, 2016).

Table 8.4 *Development of supplemental and commercial insurance markets in Israel, 1933–2017*

Year	Supplemental insurance	Commercial insurance
1933		• Shiloach offers commercial insurance as an alternative to health plans
1950	• Maccabi offers voluntary supplemental cover	
Mid-1980s	• All health plans institute compulsory supplemental cover • Maccabi extends voluntary supplemental cover to include LTC and other benefits	• Proliferation of insurers entering the health care market
1998	• For the sick funds group LTCI: sick funds could not oblige members to purchase their group LTCI; LTCI and supplemental insurance must be purchased separately	
2001		Regulation on: • Proper disclosure of policy terms for individual policies • Annual reporting to health insurance policy-holders
2002	• Supplemental insurance excess revenue compensates NHI budget (retroactively) for use of infrastructure and staff	Regulation on: • Proper disclosure of policy terms for group policies • Actuarial appendix to be submitted with new/revised policies • Regulation of LTC individual policies
2003		• Definition of the types of terminal illnesses covered by commercial policies • LTC insurance coverage extended to include mental health and care for mentally frail people

Table 8.4 (cont.)

Year	Supplemental insurance	Commercial insurance
2004		• Minimal standards for major medical procedures • Regulation of LTC group policies
2005	• Supplemental annual expenses should not exceed annual revenue and premiums may be adjusted to that end without prior Ministry of Health approval • Transfer of funds from NHI budget to supplemental budget prohibited • There should be a strict separation in accounting and financial management of NHI and supplemental insurance budgets • If supplemental insurance benefits from administrative or other services charged to the NHI budget, supplemental insurance should compensate NHI for its share of the expenses • Temporary supplemental insurance excess revenue can be transferred to cover NHI deficits as a loan	• Regulations for approving increases in premiums and appointment of an actuary for health policies
2007	• Supplemental insurance allowed to cover life-saving/extending medications (reversed in 2008)	• Regulation of terms of policies covering life-saving/extending medications • Mandatory for commercial insurers to offer policies covering only additional expenses not covered by supplemental insurance
2010	• Bill to abolish eligibility waiting periods for new supplemental applicants transferring from another sick fund	

| 2015–2017 | • Payments for surgeries (including physicians' fees) to be made to hospitals, with no direct payment to physicians
• HPs allowed to offer indemnity only for services provided by doctors with whom they have a contractual agreement; choice of physician for the insured limited to physicians within the networks of SI physicians of the HPs | • Commercial insurers allowed to offer indemnity only for services provided by doctors with whom they have a contractual agreement; choice of physician for the insured limited to physicians within the insurers' network of physicians
• Changes in CI coverage and premiums allowed only once every two years
• Every CI policy to include a document detailing services and entitlements
• Unbundling of insurance products: insurers must market policies for the different services separately and not as a bundle; and provide consumers with transparent information on the cost of each type of coverage (severe diseases, surgeries and physicians visits, medications not included in the NHI basket, and transplant abroad)
• Cover of mandatory NHI user charges is prohibited
• Introduction of a standard policy (2015) for surgeries and specialist consultations in the CI market with uniform coverage and uniform premiums by age groups for surgeries and specialist consultations
• CI plans to cover a minimum list of illnesses |

Sources: Kaye & Roter (2001); Cohen & Barnea (1992); Gross & Brammli-Greenberg (1996); State of Israel (1994: Clause 21a, Clause 10); State of Israel (1998, 2002); Ministry of Health (2005, 2014c); Ministry of Finance (2001a, b; 2002a, b, c; 2003a, b; 2004a, b; 2005a, b, c; 2007a, b; 2014a, b; 2015b, c, d, e, f); Brammli-Greenberg & Gross (2006).

Note: CI, commercial insurance; HP, health plan; LTCI, long-term care insurance; NHI, national health insurance; SI, supplementary insurance.

of Health, 2014d). Yet, CI coverage (and dual CI and SI coverage) has increased sharply in the last decade (see section on dual coverage below). The latest regulations from 2015 and 2016 (see Table 8.4) have attempted to limit dual coverage, curb growth in private health insurance coverage and reverse the trend of increasing private spending on health.

Dual coverage and attempts to reduce this phenomenon

A major consequence of the private health insurance market complexity and inability of consumers to wisely choose coverage is the dual coverage phenomenon (see Table 8.3).

Besides the lack of information regarding private health insurance coverage and how to claim it, the insureds also face administrative barriers, such as the requirement to obtain pre-approval before accessing care and a time lag between payment for treatment and reimbursement. SI will only reimburse policy-holders for listed operations, medical implants and medications provided by listed providers selected by the HP. In practice, it is not easy to obtain lists of services and providers. Some are available at HP clinics, but members may not know this. Also, in spite of regulations for proper disclosure, supplemental and commercial policies may not be accessible to a lay person due to the use of legal jargon and unfamiliar concepts and the overwhelming amount of detail they contain. There is a large diversity in private health insurance products, with complex policies and a wide range of services offered. The policies vary in their contents and prices, and some insurance companies used to market different services (that is, coverage for medications/surgeries/ severe diseases) as one bundled package, instead of allowing the purchase of separate coverage for each type of service. As a result, consumers may not have been able to compare among insurers and products, choose the most suitable coverage or take the full advantage of their benefit entitlements (Brammli-Greenberg, Gross & Matzliach, 2007; Brammli-Greenberg et al., 2014).

To keep up with the growth in the supplemental and commercial markets and with the growing competition between them, and to protect consumers from problems caused by double cover, the Insurance Commissioner intensified its regulation of commercial health policies. New regulations required proper disclosure of policy terms in individual (Ministry of Finance, 2001a) and collective (Ministry of Finance 2002a, 2005a) policies, which were to be set out in concise, user-friendly forms, using lay terms; annual reporting to policy-holders (Ministry of Finance, 2001b); an actuarial appendix to be submitted with new or revised policies (Ministry of Finance, 2002b); definition of the types of terminal illnesses covered (Ministry of Finance, 2003a); minimum standards for major medical procedures (Ministry of Finance, 2004a); regulations for approving premium increases (Ministry of Finance, 2005b); and the appointment of an actuary for health policies (Ministry of Finance, 2005c; Brammli-Greenberg & Gross, 2006).

Recent regulation further attempted to tackle CI complexity and dual coverage. In 2015 the Ministry of Finance approved several changes aiming to improve transparency regarding coverage and prices, improve simplicity of insurance products so as to ease consumer choice of policy, thus enhancing competition among commercial insurers. Among others, the Ministry of Finance created a standard policy for health expenses, with set coverage of services (surgeries and specialist consultations), co-payments and premiums.

In order to tackle the lack of information on the part of consumers, in 2014 the Ministry of Health introduced a website that gives access to transparent information about the coverage of the NHI and private health insurance benefits packages. The idea is to empower insured individuals with knowledge and awareness of their rights and eligibility to benefits, so they can demand them from the HPs and/or private insurers; and if refused, they can refer the case to the supervisor (the Ministry of Health). This policy instrument addresses market failures related to information asymmetry and can potentially improve competition among the HPs and within the private health insurance market (Brammli-Greenberg et al., 2014). The driving forces behind it were growth in the market and increased media exposure of evidence of information asymmetry and consumer confusion over the differences between CI and SI. It was also part of a broader effort by the Ministry of Finance to regulate the insurance and capital markets (Antebi, 2005, 2006, 2007 oral presentations).

Another reason for the high level of double coverage in Israel was the fact that until 2014 the CI fully reimbursed the insured for surgeries from the first shekel, even if they were already paid for by the NHI or the SI. This means that the insured earned the cost of the surgery akin to a cash benefit.

In 2007, the Insurance Commissioner obliged insurers to offer new policies for private surgery that cover only those expenses that are not covered by supplemental plans (that is, supplementary to SI cover) (Ministry of Finance, 2007b). This was intended to safeguard consumers' rights by preventing them from purchasing an expensive CI policy, which is difficult to claim, and preventing insureds from undergoing (unnecessary) surgeries based on economic considerations. Despite the greater economic viability of this type of policy, only 13% of the insured with individual CI and 18% of the insured with collective CI have such a policy.

In 2014 the Insurance Commissioner prohibited CI from reimbursing the insured for surgeries covered by the NHI or by the SI. This change is expected to lower dual coverage but it is too early to see its effects in the uptake of private health insurance.

Impact of the private health insurance market on national health spending

During the last decade, Israel has seen a steady growth in national spending on health in per capita terms. In 2005, national per person spending on health increased from US$1769 in 2005 to US$2822 in 2016 (current PPP prices). The main driver of that increase was the growth in private spending on health, which rose from US$672 per capita in 2005 to US$1120 in 2016 (OECD, 2017).

Private health insurance (supplemental and commercial) accounted for a significant share of the increase in private health spending. Both the price of private health insurance premiums and the number of insureds have increased significantly in recent decades. Premium receipts for SI increased by almost 200% between 2007 and 2014 (from NIS2.1 billion to NIS4.1 billion) and total income from payments for CI premiums for illness and hospitalization policies increased from NIS2.1 billion in 2003 to NIS5 billion in 2014 (a total increase of 240%) (Ministry of Health, 2014d; Ministry of Finance, 2015a).

Private health insurance is one of the main sources of funding for private health care providers, who contribute to the increase in demand for more private health care and consequently to the increase in private spending (Ministry of Health, 2014d). In recent years, policy-makers have been concerned with possible spill-over effects over the public health system derived from the sharp increase in private spending. In 2014 the Ministry of Health appointed an Advisory Committee to Strengthen the Public Health Care System, which gathered evidence regarding the exogenous negative effects of the private health insurance on the public health system and recommended diverse policy changes attempting to strengthen the public system (Ministry of Health, 2014d). Some of these recommendations were implemented in the 2015 reform, including efforts to improve information and transparency and reduce the dual coverage phenomenon (see above and also Brammli-Greenberg et al., 2014).

It is also claimed that private health insurance promotes the policy goal of curbing government spending on health, thereby averting the need to raise taxes to cover the NHI budget. There are three arguments here. First, private health insurance reduces pressure on the government to increase the NHI budget because it provides people with access to benefits not covered by the NHI. Second, it provides access to private providers, apparently reducing the public workload and helping HPs to stay within their NHI budget. Third, the 2005 Ministry of Health rules oblige HPs to transfer profits from SI to cover deficits in their NHI budget, theoretically mandating private resources to fund the NHI. For example, in 2015 the HPs received NIS4.3 million from SI surpluses, which represented 8.7% of their total revenues[21] (Ministry of Health, 2016).

However, evidence shows that private health insurance not only does not reduce public spending on health, but actually increases it. For example, because of cream-skimming by the private sector, public sector treats the most severe and complicated cases, including re-admissions and complications from surgeries performed in the private sector (Tuohy, Colleen & Stabile, 2004; Paolucci, 2012). Another adverse exogenous effect of the growing private sector (funded mainly by private health insurance) is the brain drain from the public to private sector. Most physicians in Israel practice in both sectors. Physicians in the private sector are paid more so they have strong incentives to reduce their public sector hours. Indeed, it seems that many senior physicians have reduced their public sector activity in favour of private practice, which has led to increasing waiting times in the public sector (Ministry of Health, 2014d). Finally, private health insurance and other types of private funding are a regressive way of funding health care, which entails problems of access to care among vulnerable populations.

---

[21] The remaining revenues come from the government (79.4%), individuals' co-payments and coinsurance (8.3%) and additional 3.6% from other sources.

Discussion and conclusion

National health insurance is the main tool for achieving most health-financing policy goals, including universal financial protection, equity in financing, equity of access to health care, incentives for quality and efficiency in care delivery and administrative efficiency. Supplemental and commercial private health insurance contribute to achieving some of these goals, but compromise others (Zwanziger & Brammli-Greenberg, 2011).

Private health insurance contributes partially to financial protection by enhancing access to services, including a range of catastrophic and routine items. This in particular applies to SI, which is open to every resident for relatively inexpensive premiums (priced between €1.5 per month for a basic plan for members aged 0–17 years to €43 per month for an extended plan for people aged over 80 years). However, both supplemental and commercial cover undermine vertical equity because premiums are not income related and cover is lower among the most vulnerable population groups such as those with low incomes, Arabs and elderly. CI further compromises access by excluding policy-holders from benefits related to pre-existing conditions. They also lower horizontal equity by creating a two-tiered system of access to health care. For example, private health insurance owners wait less time to receive care, and have more choice of providers.

Reasons for expansion of the private health insurance market

Historical and political factors have played a prominent role in shaping the structure of the Israeli private health insurance market, in which private health insurance is offered both by commercial insurers and the non-profit HPs. When they were established, HPs could define their own benefits and premiums. In the 1980s they offered compulsory supplemental cover to increase revenue and improve quality, and two of them also offered voluntary supplemental cover. Following political pressure from those two HPs, the 1995 NHI reform allowed them to continue offering voluntary benefits, and the other two HPs subsequently introduced voluntary cover. Thus, the government adopted a structure integrating private and public insurance, in spite of the problems associated with the provision of both types of insurance by the same entity (Gross & Brammli-Greenberg, 2004).

Subsequent regulations reflect the policy importance placed on equality as well as political interest in responding to public opinion. The new rules introduced in 1998 were aimed at redesigning SI as a social insurance plan by prohibiting risk selection, defining premiums in a way that would make the healthy subsidize the ill, and by authorizing the Ministry of Health to regulate all future changes in policies and premiums. The strict regulation of SI is particularly striking in comparison to the loose regulation of other aspects of HPs' conduct, such as quality of care[22] (Gross & Harrison, 2001), and can be attributed to political desire to minimize the inequality resulting from supplemental cover.

Analysis of the growth of the CI market since 1995 underscores the role of market forces as well as the interests and power of the insurance companies. The expansion of the supplemental market raised consumer awareness of private health insurance and motivated commercial insurers to increase activity in this area, which enjoys relatively high profits. To gain a competitive edge, commercial insurers market their cover as a third layer on top of NHI and supplemental benefits (which they present as inexpensive and nonprestigious health insurance)[23], thus encouraging double cover. In addition, commercial insurers' strong position in the Israeli capital markets and, consequently, in the economy, has enabled them to lobby for exclusive rights to cover two major risks not covered by NHI (LTC and life-saving/extending medications), leading to regulations that safeguard and may even increase commercial market share. Here, the support of the powerful Budget Division of the Ministry of Finance undoubtedly influenced the policy outcome (Gross & Brammli-Greenberg, 2007). However, as commercial market share has grown, regulatory intervention has intensified, mainly to protect consumers.

Cultural factors have also contributed to the growth of the private health insurance market. These include declining confidence in the scope and quality of public services and the growing importance of free choice

---

[22] Since 2008 the Ministry of Health has published an annual report providing detailed information on each supplemental plan, including its financial status, use of services, claims ratio and other issues that are sensitive in a competitive market.

[23] Commercial insurers suggest that many individuals would prefer CI if they could afford it. However, this may not necessarily be the case as some individuals may prefer to purchase SI for reasons such as their trust in HPs and ease of access to SI.

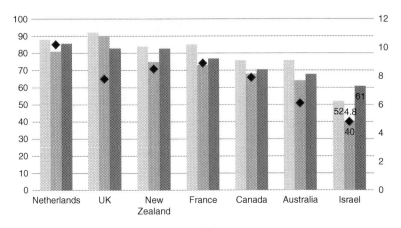

Confident that will receive best treatment

Confident that can afford needed care

Public expenditure on health in 2011 as share (%) of total spending on health

Public expenditure on health in 2011 as share (%) of GDP

Figure 8.5 Public expenditure on health and confidence in the health system in Israel and selected OECD countries, 2012

Sources: Based on survey data from Israel (Waitzberg & Brammli-Greenberg, 2014; Brammli-Greenberg & Medina-Artom, 2015) and selected OECD countries (Schoen et al., 2010); health expenditure data from OECD (2012).

of provider. The growing importance of choice appears to have replaced the pre-state, pioneering value of equality, not only in health care, but also in other public services, such as education and civilian security. This change is reflected in growing income inequality as measured by the Gini coefficient, which rose from 0.233 in 1950, to 0.376 in 2012. In a population survey conducted in 2014, 37% of respondents reported being confident that they would receive the best and most effective treatment within the NHI for a serious illness and 29% were confident that they would be able to afford treatment for a serious illness. These figures are low compared with high-income countries (see Fig. 8.5) and had declined compared with 2012 (Brammli-Greenberg & Medina-Artom, 2015). The declining confidence of the Israeli population in the public health system is also related to the declining share of public funding, which places Israel among the countries with the lowest share of public funds in total spending on health (60% compared with an average of 72% among OECD countries).

The interaction between the private health insurance and the NHI system

The debate on the inclusion of life-saving medications in private health insurance cover highlights the close interaction between SI and the NHI system. Since the introduction of NHI, the supplemental market has been shaped by a combination of competitive forces and government intervention.[24] The latter has significantly altered the features of SI and the size and characteristics of the population it covers. This, in turn, has had indirect effects on the CI market.

The interactions between public and private cover are complex and the effects of these interactions are not always easy to establish. Private health insurance may distort incentives and resource allocation in the wider health system in different ways. For example, it covers benefits that people are willing to pay for but that are not necessarily cost-effective, which may not be the best use of the resources from a health system perspective. However, some cost-effective services – such as Herceptin for breast cancer and drug-coated stents – that were originally only provided in supplemental plans, have subsequently been added to the NHI benefits package. Yet, it is not clear whether private health insurance may serve as a tool to create public pressure to expand the publicly financed benefits package, or alternatively, it allows the government to exempt itself from the responsibility and duty of including certain services in the health basket once they are provided by private health insurance.

This interaction and the concerns that it creates have been vigorously debated in public and policy circles. Initially, there were pressures to curb the growth of private health insurance by forbidding HPs from offering supplemental plans. Today, in view of its market size, the possibility of doing so is less realistic and SI is accepted as an integral part of the health system. CI is also encouraged and given exclusive rights to cover services excluded from NHI, such as long-term care. The Advisory Committee to Strengthen the Public Health Care System has suggested that the close relationship between the private health insurance market and the NHI system is one of the reasons for the expansion of the former (Ministry of Health, 2014d). Nevertheless, the government is aware of the undesirable effects of private health insurance and therefore makes

---

[24] Intervention through tax benefits has not been perceived as necessary because universal coverage is secured through the NHI legislation and therefore a high private health insurance membership rate is not a policy goal.

increasing use of regulatory tools to safeguard consumer interests and protect the public health system.

Future directions for the market and public policy towards it

Although many regard SI as compromising important social values, an issue that is frequently debated, the system endures. The HPs have exerted pressure to allow them to continue to cover private services, which are valued by their members and strengthen their competitive position in relation to commercial insurers, who also cover private services. Physicians and for-profit hospitals also benefit from the ensuing proliferation of private services, since it provides them with an opportunity to earn extra income. However, given that access to supplemental benefits is lower among the vulnerable population, and that SI has some adverse effects on the public system, the latest regulations attempted to improve the supplemental model to maximize its advantages and overcome its disadvantages, and also to limit the growth of private health insurance, particularly to curb dual coverage.

Observed trends suggest that growth in the supplemental market has reached a ceiling. However, although total coverage rates have stabilized, take-up is still relatively low among lower socioeconomic groups and minorities (the Arab population and immigrants from the former Soviet Union), so there might be potential for market growth, especially in the SI segment, which has lower premiums and is considered part of the public system. Other potential market growth is the creation of new layers of SI plans. Simultaneously, the CI may also create new health insurance products, although the coverage rate is already high compared with other countries.

Analysis of commercial insurers' strategies shows that they are innovative and active in seeking opportunities to expand coverage to niches not covered by SI or to exploit weaknesses of the NHI. The CI market may therefore grow in future if commercial insurers succeed in preventing major changes to the SI, as they have done in the past, or if they manage to take further advantage of limits to public coverage and quality. Yet, this might be mitigated if the 2015–2017 reform succeeds in attaining its goal of limiting dual coverage.

Other factors that may strengthen the private health insurance market include population ageing and growth of chronic comorbidities (implying increased health care need and use), accelerated technological advances, and reductions in government spending leading to lower public spending on health care and greater privatization of care delivery. All this is accompanied by the growing trend of distrust of the population in the public system (Ministry of Health, 2014d).

In Israel, as in other countries, private health insurance is seen by policy-makers as a second-best option that enables the government to respond to public expectations for expanded health coverage without increasing public spending on health. However, the market's effects are ambiguous. The alternative to reconciling the two insurance markets (public and private) without negative spillover effects on the public sector is to strengthen the NHI and make it more competitive towards private health insurance.

References

Antebi Y (2005). *Comparisons and trends in the health insurance market.* The Insurance Commissioner's presentation. Jerusalem Israel: http://ozar .mof.gov.il/hon/2001/general/memos/gen_pres200509.pps (in Hebrew); accessed on 26/06/2017.

Antebi Y (2006). *Health and long-term care insurance.* The Insurance Commissioner's presentation. Jerusalem Israel: http://ozar.mof.gov.il/ hon/2001/general/memos/gen_pres200609.pps (in Hebrew); accessed on 26/06/2017.

Antebi Y (2007). *Health and long-term care insurance.* The Insurance Commissioner's presentation. Jerusalem Israel: http://ozar.mof.gov.il/ hon/2001/general/memos/gen_pres200709.pps (in Hebrew); accessed on 26/06/2017.

Brammli-Greenberg S, Gross R (2006). The private insurance health care market: policy issues. In: Bin Nun G, Ofer G, eds. *Ten years of National Health Insurance 1995–2005.* Tel Hashomer, Israel National Institute for Health Policy and Health Services Research (in Hebrew).

Brammli-Greenberg S, Medina-Artom T (2015). *Public opinion on the level of service and performance of the healthcare system in 2014 and in comparison with previous years.* Research report 15-672. Jerusalem, Myers-JDC-Brookdale Institute (in Hebrew).

Brammli-Greenberg S, Waitzberg R (2017). *Waiting times for outpatient specialists as a strategy for rationing care by Health Plans.* Presented at the International Health Economics Association World Congress, Boston USA, 10 July 2017.

Brammli-Greenberg S, Gross R, Matzliach R (2007). *Supplemental insurance plans offered by the health plans: analysis and comparison of baskets of services in 2006.* Research report RR-495-07. Jerusalem, Myers-JDC-Brookdale Institute (in Hebrew).

Brammli-Greenberg S et al. (2014). Low-budget policy tool to empower Israeli insureds to demand their rights in the healthcare system. *Health Policy*, 118:279–84.

Brammli-Greenberg S et al. (2016). How Israel reimburses hospitals based on activity: the procedure-related group (PRG) incremental reform. In OECD (2016), *Better ways to pay for health care.* Paris, OECD Publishing: www .oecd.org/publications/better-ways-to-pay-for-health-care-9789264258211-en.htm; accessed on 21/09/2016.

Brammli-Greenberg S et al. (2019) Eleventh survey of public opinion on the level of service and performance of the healthcare system in Israel: 2016. Jerusalem, Myers-JDC-Brookdale Institute Research Report 19-790.

CBS (Central Bureau of Statistics) (2016). Statistical Abstract of Israel: www .cbs.gov.il/reader/shnatonenew_site.htm; accessed on 26/06/2017.

CBS (2014). Survey on household monthly income and consumption expenditure: www.cbs.gov.il/webpub/pub/text_page.html?publ=25& CYear=2014&CMonth=1; accessed on 24/07/2017.

Chernichovsky D, Chinitz D (1995). The political economy of health system reform in Israel. *Health Economics*, 4:127–41.

Chernichovsky D et.al, 2016. "Private Expenditure on Healthcare in Israel", Jerusalem: Taub Center for Social Policy Studies in Israel. Available at: http://taubcenter.org.il/wp-content/files_mf/privateexpenditureon healthcareinisrael.pdf, accessed on 07/03/2020.

Chinitz D (1995). Israel's health policy breakthrough: the politics of reform and the reform of politics. *Journal of Health Politics, Policy and Law*, 20(4):909–32.

Cohen M, Barnea T (1992). Private outlets for public limitations: the rise of commercial health insurance in Israel. *Journal of Health Politics, Policy and Law*, 17(4):783–811.

Enthoven A (1993). The history and principles of managed competition. *Health Affairs*, 12:24–48.

Gross R (2003). Implementing health care reform in Israel: organizational response to perceived incentives. *Journal of Health Politics, Policy and Law*, 28(4):659–92.

Gross R, Anson O (2002). Health care reform in Israel. In: Twaddle A, ed. *Health care reform efforts around the world.* Westport CT, Greenwood Publishing Group.

Gross R, Brammli-Greenberg S (1996). *Supplemental and commercial health insurance in Israel – 1996.* Research report: RR-272-96. Jerusalem, Myers-JDC-Brookdale Institute (in Hebrew).

Gross R, Brammli-Greenberg S (2001). Supplemental insurance in Israel: changes in policy and consumer behavior. *Social Security*, 61:154–71 (in Hebrew).

Gross R, Brammli-Greenberg S (2004). Evaluating the effect of regulatory prohibitions against risk selection by health status on supplemental insurance ownership in Israel. *Social Science & Medicine*, 58(9):1609–22.

Gross R, Brammli-Greenberg S (2007) Restricting supplemental insurance services. *Health Policy Monitor,* October: www.hpm.org/survey/is/a10/5; accessed on 22/09/2011.

Gross R, Brammli-Greenberg S, Waitzberg R (2008). *Public opinion on the level of services and functioning of the health care system in 2007.* Research report: RR-541-09. Jerusalem, Myers-JDC-Brookdale Institute (in Hebrew).

Gross R, Harrison M (2001). Implementing managed competition in Israel. *Social Science & Medicine*, 52(8):1219–31.

Gross R, Rosen B, Shirom A (2001). Reforming the Israeli health system: findings of a three-year evaluation. *Health Policy*, 56:1–20.

Health System and Policy Monitor, Israel web page (2015). Changes to Improve the Commercial VHI Market: www.hspm.org/countries/israel25062012/countrypage.aspx; accessed on 19/02/2017.

Health System and Policy Monitor, Israel web page (2016). Limiting the diversion of patients to the private sector: www.hspm.org/countries/israel 25062012/countrypage.aspx; accessed on 19/02/2017.

Horev T, Keidar N (2014). National Health Insurance 1995–2013, statistical data. Jerusalem, Ministry of Health (in Hebrew): www.health.gov.il/PublicationsFiles/Stat1995_2013.pdf; accessed on 25/02/2015.

Israel National Institute for Health Policy and Health Services Research (2003). *Gaps and Inequalities in the Healthcare System.* The Fourth Annual Dead-Sea Conference report 2003 (in Hebrew).

Israel National Institute for Health Policy and Health Services Research (2007). *The HMOs' Corporate Governance, Boundaries and Baskets of Services.* The Eighth Annual Dead-Sea Conference report, 2007 (in Hebrew).

Kaye R, Roter R (2001). *Complementary health insurance in Europe and the West: dilemmas and directions.* Research report: RR-366-01. Jerusalem, Myers-JDC-Brookdale Institute (in Hebrew).

Ministry of Finance (2001a). *Fair disclosure to the insured at time of purchase of health insurance policies,* Insurance directive 2001/9. Jerusalem, Ministry of Finance, Capital Market, Insurance and Savings Division.

300   *Private Health Insurance: History, Politics and Performance*

Ministry of Finance (2001b). *Annual reporting to health insurance policy holders*, Insurance directive 2001/10. Jerusalem, Ministry of Finance, Capital Market, Insurance and Savings Division.

Ministry of Finance (2002a). *Fair disclosure in group health insurance*, Insurance directive 2002/3. Jerusalem, Ministry of Finance, Capital Market, Insurance and Savings Division.

Ministry of Finance (2002b). *Actuarial appendix in health insurance*, Insurance directive 2002/10. Jerusalem, Ministry of Finance, Capital Market, Insurance and Savings Division.

Ministry of Finance (2002c). *Individual long-term care insurance*, Insurance directive 2002/6. Jerusalem, Ministry of Finance, Capital Market, Insurance and Savings Division.

Ministry of Finance (2003a). *Definitions of illnesses for terminal illness insurance*, Insurance directive 2003/16. Jerusalem, Ministry of Finance, Capital Market, Insurance and Savings Division.

Ministry of Finance (2003b). *Definition of insurance case in LTC insurance*, Insurance directive 2003/9. Jerusalem, Ministry of Finance, Capital Market, Insurance and Savings Division.

Ministry of Finance (2004a). *Definition of medical procedures in health insurance*, Insurance directive 2004/20. Jerusalem, Ministry of Finance, Capital Market, Insurance and Savings Division.

Ministry of Finance (2004b). *Group LTC insurance*, Insurance directive 2004/11. Jerusalem, Ministry of Finance, Capital Market, Insurance and Savings Division.

Ministry of Finance (2005a). *Fair disclosure in group personal accident insurance – clarification*, Insurance directive 2005-1-36. Jerusalem, Ministry of Finance, Capital Market, Insurance and Savings Division.

Ministry of Finance (2005b). *Requirements for changing health insurance tariffs for existing policy holders*, Insurance directive 2005-1-29. Jerusalem, Ministry of Finance, Capital Market, Insurance and Savings Division.

Ministry of Finance (2005c). *Actuarial assessment in health insurance*, Insurance directive 2005/10. Jerusalem, Ministry of Finance, Capital Market, Insurance and Savings Division.

Ministry of Finance (2007a). *Directives regarding insurance coverage in medication insurance plans*, Insurance directive 2007-1-12. Jerusalem, Ministry of Finance, Capital Market, Insurance and Savings Division.

Ministry of Finance (2007b). *The Insurance Commissioner's annual report*. Jerusalem, Ministry of Finance.

Ministry of Finance (2014a). *Insurance Commissioner directive number 107-2014*: http://mof.gov.il/hon/documents/הרדסה-יקק-הרי 1/insurance/memos/ t2014-107.pdf; accessed on 02/03/2015.

Ministry of Finance (2014b). *Insurance Commissioner regulation on financial services (insurance) for private surgeries, alternative treatments, and consultations with specialist physicians*: http://mof.gov.il/hon/documents/ הרדסה-יקק 1/insurance/memos/tl_2014-43142.pdf; accessed on 26/10/2016.

Ministry of Finance (2015a). *The Insurance Commissioner's annual report*. Jerusalem: http://mof.gov.il/hon/documents/chapter3_report2014.pdf; accessed 26/10/2016.

Ministry of Finance (2015b). *Regulations for Supervision of Financial Services (Insurance): contract terms for surgeries and treatments that replace surgeries in Israel*. Regulations file 7551 dated from 7 September 2015: www .nevo.co.il/Law_word/law06/tak-7551.pdf; accessed on 06/11/2016.

Ministry of Finance (2015c). *Insurance circular no. 17-1-2015 from the 24.9.2015* – CI (individual and group) – regulation of insurance for severe diseases and severe procedures. Jerusalem, Ministry of Finance.

Ministry of Finance (2015d). *Insurance circular no. 20-1-2015 from the 24.9.2015*. CI (individual) – independency of services offered in the health insurance. Jerusalem, Ministry of Finance.

Ministry of Finance (2015e). *Insurance circular no. 18-1-2015 from the 24.9.2015*. Regulation of insurance for medications not included in the health basket (HB) (or included for other indications). Jerusalem, Ministry of Finance.

Ministry of Finance (2015f). *Insurance circular no. 19-1-2015 from the 24.9.2015*. Regulation of updates of coverage and premium of health insurance, for severe diseases and hospitalization. Jerusalem, Ministry of Finance.

Ministry of Finance (2016). *The Insurance Commissioner's annual report*. Jerusalem: http://mof.gov.il/hon/documents/chapter2_report2015.pdf; accessed on 26/10/2016.

Ministry of Health (2005). *Rules for supplemental insurance plans*. Jerusalem, Ministry of Health (in Hebrew).

Ministry of Health (2012). Issues on policy and regulation of private health insurance (in Hebrew): www.health.gov.il/PublicationsFiles/ 281112_11122012.pdf; accessed on 02/12/14.

Ministry of Health (2014a). The 2013 Public summary report on HP activities. Jerusalem: Ministry of Health (in Hebrew): www.health.gov .il/PublicationsFiles/dochHashvaatui2013.pdf; accessed on 25/02/2015.

Ministry of Health (2014b). Financial Report 2012 – the general government medical centers (in Hebrew): www.health.gov.il/PublicationsFiles/finance2012_feb2014.pdf; accessed on 02/12/14.

Ministry of Health (2014c). Directive of HPs supervision department: www.health.gov.il/hozer/sbn05_2014.pdf; accessed on 12/01/2015.

Ministry of Health (2014d). Final Report of the Advisory Committee to Strengthen the Public Healthcare System: www.health.gov.il/PublicationsFiles/publichealth2014.pdf, accessed on 03/03/2015.

Ministry of Health (2016). The 2015 Public summary report on HP activities. Jerusalem, Ministry of Health (in Hebrew): www.health.gov.il/publicationsfiles/dochhashvaatui2015.pdf; accessed on 19/02/2017.

OECD (2012). Health Statistics: www.oecd.org/health/health-statistics.htm; accessed on 01/12/2016.

OECD (2017). Health expenditure and financing: Health expenditure indicators, OECD Health Statistics (database): http://dx.doi.org/10.1787/data-00349-en; accessed on 30/11/2017.

Paolucci F (2012). The Interface between voluntary private health insurance & mandatory public health insurance: challenges, opportunities and options for national policy design, lecture presented at the Joint conference of the OECD and the Ministry of Health *Israel financing models of healthcare systems*, Tel-Aviv, October 22–23, 2012.

Rosen B, Bin Nun G (2006). Legislation of the National Health Insurance Law – why in 1994? In: Bin Nun G, Ofer G, eds. *Ten years of National Health Insurance 1995–2005*. Tel Hashomer, Israel National Institute for Health Policy and Health Services Research (in Hebrew).

Rosen B, Waitzberg R, Merkur S (2015). Israel: health system review. *Health Systems in Transition* 17(6):1–212: www.euro.who.int/__data/assets/pdf_file/0009/302967/Israel-HiT.pdf?ua=1; accessed on 21/09/2016.

Schoen C et al. (2010). How health insurance design affects access to care and costs, by income, in eleven countries. *Health affairs*, 12:2323–34.

Schwartz S, Doron H, Davidovitch N (2006). Between vision and deficit – the historical political struggle for National Health Insurance legislation. In: Bin Nun G, Ofer G, eds. *Ten years of National Health Insurance 1995–2005*. Tel Hashomer, Israel National Institute for Health Policy and Health Services Research (in Hebrew).

Shani S et al. (2000). Setting priorities for the adoption of health technologies on a national level – the Israeli experience. *Health Policy*, 54:169–85.

Shemer J, Abadi-Korek I, Seifan A (2005). Medical technology management: bridging the gap between theory and practice. *Israel Medical Association Journal*, 7(4):211–15.

Shirom A (1995). The Israeli health care reform: a study on an evolutionary major change. *International Journal of Health Planning and Management*, 10: 5–22.

State Comptroller (2007). *State Comptroller's annual report 2007*. Tel Aviv, State of Israel.

State of Israel (1990). *Commission of Inquiry into the functioning and efficiency of the health system in Israel. Majority and minority reports*. Jerusalem, Government Printing Office.

State of Israel (1994). *National Health Insurance Law 1994, Statute Book, Law No. 1469*. Jerusalem, Government Printing Office.

State of Israel (1998). *Budget Reconciliation Law 1998, Statute Book*. Jerusalem, Government Printing Office.

State of Israel (2002). *Report of the Public Commission on the Publicly Financed Health Care System and the Status of Physicians (Amorai Commission)*. Tel Aviv, State of Israel.

State of Israel (2008). *Budget Reconciliation Law 2008, Statute Book*. Jerusalem, Government Printing Office.

Tuohy C, Colleen FM, Stabile M (2004). How Does Private Finance Affect Public Health Care Systems? Marshaling the Evidence from OECD Nations. *Journal of Health Politics, Policy and Law*, 29(3):359–96.

Waitzberg R, Brammli-Greenberg S (2014). *The integration of private funding and services in the public health system and the implications for quality of the service*, lesson presented at the 30th Annual Conference of the Israel Economic Association, in Tel Aviv on 20 May 2014 (in Hebrew).

Yishai Y (1982). Politics and medicine: the case of Israeli NHI. *Social Science & Medicine* 16:285–91.

Zwanziger J, Brammli-Greenberg S (2011). Strong government influence over the Israeli health care system has led to low rates of spending growth. *Health Affairs*, 30(9):1–7.

9 Private health insurance in Japan, Republic of Korea and Taiwan, China

SOONMAN KWON, NAOKI IKEGAMI AND
YUE-CHUNE LEE

Japan, the Republic of Korea and Taiwan, China are neighbouring high-income countries with some similarities in health systems policy. All three have historically organized publicly financed health coverage around the labour market, with the government paying for some or all of the costs of self-employed, retired or poorer people, but Japan has a much higher share of public spending on health and a much lower share of out-of-pocket payments than the other two. All three rely heavily on the private sector to deliver health services. And in all three, private health insurance plays a supplementary role, offering subscribers daily cash benefits in case of hospitalization or lump sum payments in case of severe illness such as cancer. Although private health insurance markets in these countries are marginal in terms of spending on health, they cover relatively large shares of the population.

This chapter reviews the origins and development of private health insurance in the three countries and considers why the market is not larger in terms of health spending, especially given the relatively high share of out-of-pocket payments in the Republic of Korea and Taiwan, China and the widespread use of cost sharing for publicly financed health services in all three countries.

Country case studies: Japan, Republic of Korea, Taiwan, China

Public spending on health accounts for 84% of total spending on health in Japan and close to 60% in the other two countries (see Table 9.1). Consequently, the out-of-pocket share of total spending is lowest in Japan (13%) and significantly higher in the Republic of Korea (37%) and Taiwan, China (34.7%) (MOHW, 2016a; WHO, 2018), although in the latter two countries its share has fallen over time. Private health

Table 9.1 *Health financing indicators in Japan, Republic of Korea and Taiwan, China, 2015*

	Japan	Republic of Korea	Taiwan, China
Private spending as a share of total spending on health (%)	15.3[a]	42.9[a]	40.6[c, f]
Private health insurance as a share of private spending on health (%)[d]	14.4[a]	14.2[a]	23.4[c, f]
Private health insurance as a share of total spending on health (%)[d]	2.2[a]	6.1[a]	9.5[c, f]
Share of population covered by private health insurance (%)[e]	62 (2013)	72[b] (2013)	72.3 (2004)[c]

Sources: Country case studies; [a] WHO (2018); [b] Korea Statistics (2016) (based on 2014 Korea Welfare Panel); [c] Lin (2006), MOHW (2016a) and Taiwan Insurance Institute (2016).

Notes: [d] Private health insurance expenditure data should be interpreted with caution because private health insurance seldom pays directly for health care. The cash benefits that it provides may not bear much relation to the actual health care costs incurred.

[e] Various years (see text). For Japan, the share of those having private health insurance has been calculated as 74% of the 84% who have life insurance policies (based on Association of Life Insurance, 2016).

[f] Because most private health insurance plans only provide cash benefits, only administrative costs (5.7 billion New Taiwan dollars or about 0.58% of total spending on health in 2014) of private health insurance are included in national health spending statistics. The share of private health insurance in total spending on health is calculated as the ratio of private health insurance benefit payments and total spending on health.

insurance accounts for less than 3% of total spending on health in Japan, around 7% in the Republic of Korea and almost 10% in Taiwan, China.

Publicly financed health coverage has historically been organized around employment, with substantial use of government transfers to cover the non-employed part of the population (see Table 9.2). While Japan uses multiple noncompeting health insurance funds to purchase publicly financed benefits, the Republic of Korea and Taiwan, China use a single, national health insurance fund. The private sector plays an

Table 9.2 *Organization of the health systems in Japan, Republic of Korea and Taiwan, China, 2016*

	Japan	Republic of Korea	Taiwan, China[c]
Purchasing market structure	Multiple noncompeting funds	Single fund	Single fund
Relations with providers	Contracting	Contracting (mandatory for all providers)	Contracting
Mix of providers	30% of beds public (2014)[a]	12% of beds public (2012)[b]	34% of beds public (2014)[c]
Gatekeeping to secondary care	No	No (higher cost sharing without referral)	No (higher cost sharing without referral)
Cost sharing (user charges) for publicly financed benefits	30% (10% for people aged 72+ with incomes below the average wage), lower rates for conditions such as renal failure requiring renal dialysis); 1% if the coinsurance for the amount exceeds the monthly ceiling which is determined by the income level	20% (inpatient care; 5% for cancer patients; 30–60% (outpatient care[d]); exemptions for the poor, people under 18 years old and for catastrophic illnesses; income-dependent ceilings on out-of-pocket payments in a 6-month period	5% (home care); 10% (inpatient care with a ceiling; about 20% (outpatient care medications); exemptions for the poor, for catastrophic illness, for childbirth and for people living in remote areas

Sources: [a] MHLW (2016); [b] data from MOHW (2013), adapted from Kwon, Lee & Kim (2015); [c] data for Taiwan, China are from MOHW (2016b).

Notes: [d] Depending on the type of health care facility: 30% for health clinics; 40% for hospitals; 50% for general hospitals; and 60% for high-level (tertiary-care teaching) general hospitals.

important role in delivering health services. There is little gatekeeping by primary care physicians and fee-for-service is the most common form of provider payment.

Private health insurance is sold as a supplement to life insurance or a stand-alone product. Plans typically cover inpatient services (including surgery) for cancer and other potentially high-cost conditions. Accident insurance also covers health care. Benefits are in the form of cash (see Table 9.3), usually lump sum payments in case of cancer or for a surgical procedure, per diem payments for hospital admission or per visit payments for follow up after hospital discharge or surgery. Cash benefits are seldom related to the cost of care and are usually lower than the actual cost incurred. Some private health insurance contracts are multi-year, investment-linked or interest-sensitive products, allowing subscribers to earn interest on their contributions; so they are used as financial instruments, not just for health protection.

Japan

Publicly financed health coverage

The current system was established in 1922 with the Health Insurance Act (*Kenkou Hokenhou*), which secured health services for employees – mainly blue-collar workers – and gradually expanded to cover other groups (Campbell & Ikegami, 1998; Ikegami & Campbell, 2004). Self-employed people began to be covered in 1938 through the Citizens' Health Insurance Act (*Kokumin Kenko Hokenhou*, officially translated as the National Health Insurance Act), which gave munici-palities the power to establish coverage for their residents. At its peak in 1943, 70% of the population was covered by municipal schemes. As the economy recovered after the Second World War, the major political parties worked to establish a welfare state, the Ministry of Health[1] increased its funding for municipal schemes and the whole population was eventually covered by national health insurance (NHI) in 1961.

---

[1] Health was originally under the Ministry of Internal Affairs until the Ministry of Health and Welfare was established in 1938. In 2001, the Ministry of Health and Welfare merged with the Ministry of Labour to become the Ministry of Health, Labour and Welfare. However, for convenience, it will be referred to as the Ministry of Health in this chapter.

Table 9.3 *Key features of the private health insurance markets in Japan, Republic of Korea and Taiwan, China, 2016*

	Japan	Republic of Korea	Taiwan, China
Eligibility	No restrictions	No restrictions	Population under 65 years
Benefits covered	Mainly cash benefits	Mainly cash benefits	Mainly cash benefits
Contract period	Life or annual	Life or annual	Life or annual
Premium setting	Based on age, sex and extent of benefits	Based on age and sex	Based on age, sex and risk factors (for example, smoking)
Pre-existing conditions excluded?	Yes, but some can be included for a higher premium	Yes	Yes
Regulator	Finance Agency	Financial Supervisory Service	Financial Supervisory Commission
What is regulated?	Adherence to stated policy	Price, product, policy conditions	Price, product, policy conditions
Tax incentives	Premiums tax deductible up to 50 000 Yen per year[c]	Premiums tax deductible up to 1 000 000 Korean Won per year[c]	Premiums tax deductible up to 24 000 New Taiwan dollars per year[c]
Market share of nondomestic private health insurance	Not available[d]	16.4% (2013)[a]	4.11% (2014)[b]

Sources: Country case studies; [a] Korea Insurance Research Institute (2014); [b] Taiwan Insurance Institute (2016).

Notes: [c] Applies for the sum of premiums of all types of private insurance, that is, not only for private health insurance.

[d] Over 80% if restricted to cancer products.

Enrolment in NHI is mandatory for all legal residents, including foreigners, except recipients of public assistance and short-term visitors. Around 60% of the population is covered by a health plan provided by their employer and the remaining 40% (the self-employed or retired) are insured by their municipality. Dependants are covered by the scheme of their head of household. For those employed, contributions are deducted from salaries and the employer pays about half of the contribution.[2] Health plans fall into four categories according to the degree to which they rely on tax funding from the central government. Thanks to these transfers from the central government, everybody pays about the same share of their income for health coverage, up to a gross annual income of 14.4 million Yen for the employment-based plans.[3]

A new plan for people aged 75 and over was established in 2008. Managed by a coalition of municipalities in each prefecture, it is financed by contributions from all other plans, and allocations from the government budget. To equalize the cost for people aged between 65 and 74, all plans (except the plan for people aged 75 and over) must contribute on an equal basis. As a result of these two cross-subsidies, over 40% of the revenue of plans in the first category is allocated to pay for the care of older people.

In terms of health service delivery, over two thirds of all beds are in the private sector, mainly in physician-owned hospitals, and the remaining are publicly owned by the local government, or by established public organizations, such as the Red Cross. There is mutual animosity between the two groups as the publicly owned hospitals are the key beneficiary of the government's subsidies and, as a result, can invest in high-tech care and hire more staff.

The national fee schedule set by the government plays a key role in linking financing and delivery by controlling the amount of money that flows from health plans to providers. Plans provide essentially the same benefits, including unrestricted access to virtually all health care providers and to services and medicines on a positive list. Excluded items include surcharges for private hospitals beds, eyeglasses and contact lenses, and new technologies and medicines not yet in the fee

---

[2] Employers must pay at least half and no more than 80% of the premiums. For example, for Society-Managed Health Insurance, the average proportion paid by the employers is 55%.

[3] In 2016, the exchange rate was approximately 100 Yen per US$1.

schedule. Some restrictions are also applied to dental care in terms
of what materials can be used (Tatara & Okamoto, 2009). Items not
listed in the fee schedule cannot be provided in combination with listed
items in the same episode of care administered by the same doctor in
the same setting. Should they be included, all costs, including staff and
facility costs, and not only the costs of the uncovered item, must be
paid for out of pocket. The only exception to this rule is services listed
under the Specified Medical Costs of the national fee schedule, such as
hospital rooms with more amenities and new technologies still under
development, for which extra-billing is allowed (Ikegami, 2006).

In the past there have been major differences in the extent of cost
sharing for different population groups, with initially free care for the
employed and high cost sharing for dependants and those covered by
municipal schemes. Following various changes in policy, all pay 30% of
the cost of covered health services out of pocket, except for more than
90% of the people aged 72 and over who pay 10%, and children whose
co-payment rate depends on the municipality, but this rate declines to
1% for payments beyond the catastrophic amount (Ikegami, 2014).

Private health insurance

Cash benefits for hospitalizations resulting from traffic accidents began
to be sold as an accident insurance option in 1963 and a life insurance
option in 1964. They gradually expanded to cover illnesses and, by 1976,
all life insurance companies offered them. Independently, in 1974, Aflac
Japan[4] offered cancer insurance as a third type of stand-alone insurance
product. In 1995, regulation was passed stipulating that foreign accident
and life insurance companies could freely introduce this third type of
insurance. To protect the interests of foreign companies and allow them
to gain a foothold in a market dominated by domestic companies, the
major domestic companies were only given unrestricted access to this
market in 2001 (Miyaji, 2006). The third type of insurance became
popular because cost sharing for publicly covered health services for
employees was introduced at a rate of 10% in 1984, rising to 20%
in 1997 and 30% in 2003. Private health insurance benefits from tax

---

[4] According to its website, "Aflac Japan is the number one insurance company
in Japan in terms of individual policies in force and the largest foreign insurer
in Japan in terms of premium income" (Aflac, n.d.).

subsidies; up to 50 000 Yen (about US$500) per year can be deducted from gross income for premiums paid for any type of insurance product.

As competition in the insurance market intensified, commercial life insurance companies strove to develop ever more comprehensive products such as plans for cancer patients offering cash benefits for every outpatient visit after hospital discharge or plans including the early stages of cancer (carcinoma in situ). However, an investigation by the Finance Agency revealed that benefits were often not paid out as stipulated in the contract. Many clients took out insurance without having a full understanding of the contractual terms and did not submit their claims. Legitimate claims were also rejected by front-line staff who lacked sufficient knowledge of the contracts. Penalties were imposed on companies that breached contractual obligations and new rules were introduced so that companies had to inform clients about their benefit entitlement at the time of signing the contract and at the point of meeting front-line staff (*Asahi Shinbun*, 2007a).

The Ministry of Health had historically abstained from overseeing the private health insurance market but in 2006 it issued a directive stipulating that the extent of catastrophic coverage (coverage provided when coinsurance exceeds a defined amount) should be clearly stated when private health insurance is advertised, although it stopped short of obliging insurers to provide detailed information on the amount of coinsurance that patients are at risk of paying under public coverage (*Asahi Shinbun*, 2007b). In 2007 the Ministry of Health introduced a further protection for consumers so that eligible subscribers only have to pay coinsurance to the extent not covered by catastrophic illness insurance, instead of paying the whole amount up-front and being reimbursed later. Insurers have to notify eligible subscribers of this entitlement.

In 2001 the Regulatory Reform Council of the Prime Minister's Office started a campaign to remove restrictions on extra-billing.[5] The Council drew attention to areas where such restrictions were both unfair and inappropriate, such as limiting the eradication therapy of

---

[5] The Council was given a broad mandate to put forward proposals on deregulation in all sectors of the economy. In 2004, a new Council for the Promotion of Regulatory Reform was created and it was elevated to Regulation Reform and Opening to Private Sector Council. (www.cao.go.jp/en/reform/milestone.html)

Helicobacter pylori to two regimens.[6] However, removal of restrictions on extra-billing was opposed by the Ministry of Health and the Japan Medical Association on grounds of safety and equity. In December 2004, a political compromise was reached and it was agreed that extra-billing could be applied to services listed under the Specified Medical Costs. Although the prohibition on extra-billing remained essentially unchanged, the momentum for deregulation was lost after political compromises had been made (Ikegami, 2006).

It is worth noting that the Regulatory Reform Council did not mention the possibility of private health insurance complementing NHI coverage. Rather, the Council emphasized the importance of the patient as an informed consumer who should be able to make decisions based on benefits and costs, and of physicians providing full and impartial information. One reason for this omission is that, as economists, the conceptual thinking of the Council's members was focused on ensuring individual choice. A more practical reason is that companies venturing into indemnity-type insurance for extra-billed services would be faced with adverse selection. Another consideration may have been that the Chair of the Regulatory Reform Council was the CEO of a life insurance company and therefore could not openly advocate private health insurance.

The debate on private health insurance is by no means closed. Per person spending on health is the third lowest among G7 countries in purchasing power parity terms (WHO, 2018), three decades of low economic growth have led to a national debt more than twice the size of the gross domestic product and the Ministry of Health has intensified its efforts to contain health care costs. Cuts to the national fee schedule may make the system unsustainable from the perspective of providers, which may remove structural barriers to expanding private health insurance in the future (Ikegami, 2014).

Republic of Korea

Publicly financed health coverage

National health insurance was established in 1977 for the employees of large firms and gradually expanded to cover the whole population

---

[6]   In fact, a third course of treatment is rarely needed and, if administered, it is likely to be counter-productive because the drug used increases the incidence of lung cancer (Fukioka et al., 2006). Nevertheless, the Council thought that patients should have the freedom to obtain more than two regimens.

by 1989. In 2000, over 350 quasi-public health insurance societies were merged to create the single, national National Health Insurance Service (NHIS) (Kwon, 2003a). There is a separate programme for the poor (Medicaid) financed from general central and local government revenues. NHIS contributions are proportional to wages and shared equally by employer and employee, with government providing some subsidy for self-employed people.

The NHI services are subject to cost sharing in the form of coinsurance (see Table 9.2). There is no coinsurance for Medicaid beneficiaries. In 2004, the government introduced a cap on out-of-pocket payments for covered services, which now has seven ceilings depending on income levels: Korean won (KRW) 1.2 million (per 6 months) for the lowest decile, KRW1.5 million for the second and third deciles, KRW2 million for the fourth and fifth deciles, KRW2.5 million for the sixth and seventh deciles, KRW3 million for the eighth decile, KRW4 million for the ninth decile, and KRW5 million for the highest decile.

Patients pay fully out of pocket for non-covered services such as new tests and materials or private rooms and may pay extra for consulting experienced specialists in tertiary care hospitals. On average, out-of-pocket payments can amount to as much as 40% of the total cost of care (OECD, 2016). Extra-billing for services that are not covered enables a private market in which providers can charge their own unregulated prices. By allowing providers to mix covered and excluded services in the same episode of care, extra-billing has contributed to an increase in the provision of services not covered by NHI (Kwon, 2003b).

Health care providers are legally required to participate in the NHI system and treat any NHI-covered person, even if they are not satisfied with the fees paid by the NHIS. However, physicians have considerable power in the market for private services that are not covered by NHI. More than 90% of acute care hospitals and 85% of acute care beds are private. Private hospitals are, in most cases, de facto owned and managed by physicians. There is service overlap and competition among physician clinics and hospitals because physician clinics also have (small) inpatient facilities, mostly for surgery and obstetric care. Specialist clinics compete with hospitals, which have large outpatient clinics as well as beds. The role of gatekeeping by primary care physicians is very limited. Service overlap and fee-for-service payment of providers contribute to inefficiencies in the health system.

Private health insurance

Enrolment in private health insurance plans seems to be high. Different estimates suggest that private health insurance covered 38% of the urban population in 2001 (Korea Labor Institute, 2002), 53% of the total population in 2006 (Lee et al., 2006) and 70% in 2008 (Jeon & Kwon, 2013). High coverage may reflect the fact that private health insurance is often sold as a package with life insurance, which has high take-up rates. However, as a result of the bundling of insurance products, it is difficult to find accurate statistics regarding the size of private health insurance alone.

Survey data suggest that females and economically active groups (especially 35- to 49-year-olds) are more likely to purchase private health insurance (Yoon et al., 2005). Income, education and health status are positively associated with the probability of purchasing private health insurance, which means adverse selection is not a major concern. Analysis of the impact of having private health insurance on health service use and spending found that, among cancer patients in a tertiary care hospital, those with private health insurance used more health care (measured in terms of length of stay for inpatient care and number of visits for outpatient care) (Kang, Kwon & You, 2005). It also found that the outpatient spending of those with private health insurance was greater than those without private health insurance, but there was no difference for inpatient spending. Another study found that people with private health insurance use more outpatient care, resulting in greater spending (Jeon & Kwon, 2010).

Deregulation of the private health insurance market in 2007 allowed private insurers to develop health insurance products that link benefits to actual medical expenses (rather than just providing fixed cash benefits). This was part of a move by the government, driven by the Ministry of Strategy and Finance, to strengthen the competitiveness of the health care industry, encourage more innovation, boost exports in the areas of medical technology and pharmaceuticals and increase medical tourism. The Ministry of Strategy and Finance also supports the introduction of for-profit hospitals, which would be allowed to opt out of the NHI and contract with private insurers. It believes that an expanded role for private health insurance will relieve fiscal pressure on the government.

The Korean Medical Association and the Korean Hospital Association have in the past been strong supporters of private health insurance, but the former is now ambivalent. Initially, it thought that private health insurance would give its members more opportunities to gain financially. However, it has realized that private insurers can be tough negotiators when setting fees and reviewing claims. There is a split in the Korean Hospital Association's position between small and large hospitals, depending on their negotiating power in contracting with private insurers.

Private insurers would like to be allowed to cover NHI cost sharing, but the Ministry of Health and Welfare and the NHIS maintain that private health insurance should be limited to services that are not covered by NHI. They fear that the use of NHI services and spending would increase if NHI co-payments were to be covered by private insurers. Although private insurers argue that their market is small because they are limited to covering non-NHI services, out-of-pocket payments for such services account for as much as 24–33% of patient costs (and even more if a patient requires care at a tertiary hospital) (Kim & Chung, 2005); the relative share of out-of-pocket payment for insured services and direct payment for uninsured services (not in the benefits package) was 54.5% and 45.5% of total out-of-pocket payment in 2011 (Seo et al., 2013). So in fact their potential market is already relatively large. Private insurers have also lobbied to lift the ban on for-profit hospitals and to remove the requirement for all providers to contract with the NHIS. If these changes were implemented, for-profit hospitals might opt out of the NHI and cater exclusively for privately insured patients.

So far there has been little regulation of the non-financial aspects of private health insurance, which is overseen by the Financial Supervisory Service supervised by the Ministry of Strategy and Finance. If the market is to expand and play a larger role, the Ministry of Health and Welfare will need to exercise some regulatory power to ensure complementarity between NHI and private health insurance and to ensure private health insurance does not undermine national health system goals.

Taiwan, China

Publicly financed health coverage

Taiwan, China launched employment-based insurance schemes in 1950 and 1958 and covered 57% of the population by 1994. Coverage was extended to previously uninsured groups (mainly women, children, older people, pensioners, casual workers and unemployed people) through NHI introduced in 1995. In 2015, 99.6% of the population was covered by NHI (NHIA, 2015). Most NHI revenues come from income-related (mainly salary-based) contributions and supplementary premiums (paid on incomes other than salary) collected by the NHI Administration (NHIA) and general taxes collected by central government. Contributions are shared between beneficiaries, their employers and the government – 35.45%, 36.26% and 28.28%, respectively in 2014 (MOHW, 2016a).

The NHI offers comprehensive benefits. Cost sharing in the form of coinsurance is imposed on all patients except for poor people, disabled people, veterans and their dependants, children under 3 years old, those living in remote areas, those suffering from expensive diseases, and for maternity care. The coinsurance rate is 10% for inpatient care subject to a ceiling per hospital admission or annual cumulative ceilings of, respectively, 6% and 10% of the national average income per person. The mandatory coinsurance rate for outpatient care is 20%. Hospital patients without a referral are subject to higher coinsurance rates, but because of political and feasibility considerations, the NHIA tends to set the co-payment amounts at levels which are lower than the mandatory rates. The co-payment for outpatient medications is about 20% of the costs (up to a maximum of 500 New Taiwan dollars (NT$)[7] per visit), except for patients whose medicine costs are lower than NT$100 per visit or for those refilling prescriptions, who do not have to pay the co-payment for medicines. The coinsurance rate for home care is 5%. There is no ceiling on maximum payments for outpatient and home care (NHIA, 2015). In general, extra-billing is prohibited by law except for costs associated with private or upgraded hospital beds, private nurses, designated physicians and medical devices or materials of higher quality, such as drug-coated stents, orthopaedic joints and any other items designated by the Ministry of Health and Welfare.

Health care delivery is a mixture of public and private. In addition to public health stations, most clinics and two thirds of hospital beds are private (MOHW, 2016b) and most hospitals (93%) are contracted by NHI (NHIA, 2015). The market is highly competitive and patients usually have free choice of provider. Payment is mainly on a fee-for-service basis, although fees for 98% of services were capped by the

[7]   The average exchange rate in 2016 was approximately NT$32 for US$1.

national global budget programme in 2002 (Cheng, 2003; Lee et al., 2006). Diagnosis-related groups were introduced in 2010. As of 2016, 401 out of 1017 DRGs have been implemented.

Private health insurance

In 2004 private health insurance covered 72% of the population (Lin, 2006). Survey data indicate that in 2006, among those who had private health insurance, 70%, 80% and 90% had catastrophic, cancer and inpatient cover, respectively (Tsai, 2007). Most had more than one type of cover. Cover was positively associated with income and was highest among those aged 25–44 (about two thirds of this age group had private health insurance), followed by those aged 45–54 (53%) and those aged below 25 (32%). People over 55 had the lowest coverage rate (17%), possibly due to age restrictions set by private insurers (the maximum eligible age for cover is around 75). Overall, private health insurance coverage is highly selective and more likely to favour so-called 'good' risks.

Private health insurance accounted for 9.5% of total spending on health in 2014 (Taiwan Insurance Institute, 2016). Its share of private spending on health grew rapidly from 1.8% in 1991 to 23.4% in 2014. Total income from private health insurance premiums, at about NT$306.5 billion in 2014, was higher than the total income from household NHI contributions, which stood at NT$151 billion. However, private health insurance spending accounted for only 0.6% of gross domestic product in 2014, which was much lower than that of NHI payments (3.2%) in that year. The ratio of income to claims in private health insurance is very low (30.9%), partly due to favourable risk selection and partly because many private health insurance products are multi-year products or investment insurance products, so it may be meaningless to calculate claims ratios on an annual basis. Private health insurance premiums below NT$24 000 per year are tax-deductible.

As the NHIA's global budgets have tightened, providers have become more enthusiastic about developing services not covered by NHI and extra-billing has become more common. The NHIA has also introduced new measures to contain costs by reducing coverage – for example, it has increased co-payments, excluded nonprescription drugs from coverage, introduced selective coverage for some extremely expensive but less cost-effective drugs and expanded the list of services (mainly medical devices) for which extra-billing is allowed. All of these strategies leave more room for the development of complementary private health insurance.

Changes to hospital management also create new opportunities for the private health insurance market. To control spending, since 2003, the NHIA has introduced self-governing strategies (equivalent to individual hospital budgets) for some hospitals that are able to meet set utilization and quality criteria. Although this arrangement provides strong incentives for hospitals to control costs, it could increase the likelihood of waiting times, cream-skimming or lower quality of care, potentially creating more demand for private health insurance. It has also shifted costs to households. Out-of-pocket payments have risen as a share of total spending on health from 32.7% in 2004 to 34.7% in 2014 (MOHW, 2016a).

However, private health insurance has not developed enough products to meet the changing needs of NHI beneficiaries. Currently, it offers coverage that is focused more on the less-prevalent high-loss inpatient care or catastrophic costs, rather than on more prevalent outpatient care for chronic conditions or long-term care, for which people have to pay significant co-payments without any cap. Furthermore, private health insurance reimbursement principles encourage patients to try to obtain more payment, for example, by selecting more expensive inpatient care over outpatient care, or through longer hospital stays. These practices undermine the NHIA efforts to improve efficiency.

Part of the market's lack of responsiveness to changing circumstances may have been due to regulatory constraints. In 2006 the Bureau of Insurance (BOI) loosened its regulation of private health insurance product review. While pre-approval is still required for certain products, the previous pre-filing system has been replaced by a post-filing system. Since 2015, to meet the emerging needs of an ageing population, BOI has been encouraging provision of private health insurance plans offering in-kind benefits for medical care, health management and long-term care (Financial Supervisory Commission, 2016).

A newly amended NHI Act, implemented in 2013, introduced additional NHI contributions from nonsalary income to relieve fiscal pressure. It allows extra-billing for expensive new medical devices and will establish a priority-setting mechanism, to apply health technology assessment to the coverage decisions of new medications/procedures/technologies (DOH, 2011). These policies, except the first one, will increase the need for complementary private health insurance. However, as some civic and welfare groups argue, the extra-billing bill is pro-rich and will increase the allocation of NHI resources to the wealthy who can afford private health insurance. The introduction of Ten-Year Long-Term Care Development Plans in 2008 (The Executive Yuan, 2007) and its amendment in 2016, providing free long-term community and home services with 16–30% coinsurance to all citizens may increase the demand for long-term care and so benefit the private health insurance industry.

Overall, there would seem to be more opportunities than threats for the development of private health insurance playing an enhanced supplementary and complementary role. However, fierce competition in the insurance market has driven insurers into a price war. The majority of life insurance profits come from financial investment income rather than from underwriting profits (Fang, 2006). In a climate of slow gross domestic product growth, private health insurance needs to develop more innovative products so that it is better able to fill gaps in NHI coverage.

Discussion

Private health insurance has not developed beyond cash payments in the three countries and, in spite of relatively high rates of population coverage, its share of total spending remains quite low. This reflects the fact that private health insurance tends to cover younger and healthier people – people who may not need additional cover at all – and may indicate some lack of understanding of the benefits offered by NHI. It could also indicate a high degree of risk aversion, especially among people who can afford to over-insure themselves – an Asian "save for a rainy day" attitude. Some may also be swayed by the investment opportunities that private health insurance offers.

Under NHI, the development of a substitutive role for private health insurance is unlikely. During the 1990s the government in Taiwan, China proposed moving towards a privatized, market-based multi-insurer system that would have facilitated the development of substitutive private health insurance. Although the reform proposal was supported by private insurers and some academics, the society of medical professionals was divided and the reform bill failed, due in part to the inability of political party leaders to reach consensus

(Wong, 2003) but also due to heavy opposition from a social movement to save the NHI involving over 200 groups, primary care physician associations and academics.

Benefits of NHI tend to be comprehensive, limiting the scope for private health insurance to play a complementary role covering excluded services. In addition, private health insurance plans pay out regardless of the actual cost of care and are in fact usually lower than the actual cost incurred, especially for expensive care. Private insurers also set rigorous restrictions on insurance claims and often deny them.

Private health insurance has probably benefited from the high coinsurance rates for NHI coverage in all three countries, although for various reasons insurers have not developed specific products aimed at covering NHI co-payments. First, insurers may have feared adverse selection in offering coverage of co-payments. Second, although coinsurance rates can be high, NHI exempts or caps out-of-pocket payments for some groups of people or types of care in all three countries. Third, in Japan, rich companies sometimes offer much lower coinsurance rates than NHI, lowering demand for additional cover.

Supplementary private health insurance has not developed to offer faster access to health care due to the absence of waiting times or recognized groups of elite specialists. Patients generally have direct access to secondary or tertiary care without referral and are usually seen promptly. The fee-for-service payment of providers also ensures that productivity is high. In the context of growing financial pressure on NHI in all three countries, the role of private health insurance may increase in the future. The loosening of regulation of the private health insurance market in the second half of the 2000s may also lead to the development of new products, which could increase the linkages between NHI and private health insurance. For example, private insurers in the Republic of Korea (and also in Taiwan, China) have begun to sell products that reimburse medical costs instead of simply paying lump-sum benefits (although they can only reimburse up to 90% of NHI out-of-pocket payments). The extent to which private health insurance grows will depend on the political and regulatory context in each country, including the relative powers of the ministries of health and other government ministries responsible for the economy and industry; it will also depend on the willingness of the private health insurance industry to develop new products.

Conclusions

So far, private health insurance in Japan, the Republic of Korea and Taiwan, China has played a relatively minor supplementary role and has had little interaction with publicly financed health coverage, providing mainly lump-sum cash benefits for hospitalization or severe illness rather than covering actual health care costs. However, take-up of private health insurance is quite high, largely due to products being sold alongside or as part of life insurance.

Private health insurance has generated debate in all three countries, especially as fiscal pressures on NHI have grown, and the industry is a powerful interest group in policy discussions about NHI. Over time, regulation of private health insurance has been loosened, which may encourage private insurers to develop new products more closely linked to NHI coverage gaps in terms of excluded services, co-payments and extra-billing.

References

Aflac (n.d.) 'Aflac Japan' (company website): www.aflac.com/aboutaflac/corporateoverview/aflacjapan.aspx; accessed on 05/31/2011.

2007a. Thirty-eight life insurance companies have not paid benefits amounting to 28.4 billion yen. *Asahi Shinbun*, 14 April (newspaper article in Japanese).

2007b. PHI [private health insurance] finally discloses SHI [social health insurance] catastrophic coverage. *Asahi Shinbun*, 29 April (newspaper article in Japanese).

Association of Life Insurance (2016). *Statistics of life insurance business in Japan*. Tokyo, Hoken Kenkyujo; www.seiho.or.jp/data/statistics/trend/pdf/all.pdf; accessed on 9/11/2016.

Campbell JC, Ikegami N (1998). *The art of balance in health policy: maintaining Japan's low-cost, egalitarian system*. Cambridge, Cambridge University Press.

Cheng TM (2003). Taiwan's new National Health Insurance program: genesis and experience so far. *Health Affairs*, 22(3):61–76.

DOH (Department of Health) (2011). *The amendment of the National Health Insurance Act*. Taipei, Taiwan, China, Department of Health, Executive Yuan, R.O.C. (in Chinese).

Fang MW (2006). *Taiwan life insurance market 2004 annual report*. Taipei, Taiwan, China, Taiwan Insurance Institute.

Financial Supervisory Commission (2016). *2015 Annual report.* Financial Supervisory Commission, Executive Yuan, Taiwan, China (in Chinese).

Fukioka T et al. (2006). Guidelines for the management of *Helicobacter pylori* infection I Japan: current status and future prospects. *Journal of Gastroentology*, 42[Suppl XVII]:3–6.

Ikegami N (2006). Should providers be allowed to extra bill for uncovered services? Debate, resolution and sequel in Japan. *Journal of Health Politics, Policy and Law*, 31(6):1129–49.

Ikegami N (2014). Universal health coverage for inclusive and sustainable development, lessons from Japan. A World Bank study. Washington, DC, World Bank Group: http://documents.worldbank.org/curated/en/2014/09/20278271/universal-health-coverage-inclusive-sustainable-development-lessons-japan; accessed on 9/11/2016.

Ikegami N, Campbell JC (2004) Japan's health care system: containing costs and attempting reform. *Health Affairs*, 23(3):26–36.

Jeon B, Kwon S (2010). Impact of private health insurance on health care utilization and expenditure. In: *Proceedings of the First Health Care Panel Conference.* Seoul, Korea (in Korean).

Jeon B, Kwon S (2013). Effect of private health insurance on health care utilization in a universal public insurance system: a case of South Korea. *Health Policy,* 113:69–76.

Kang SW, Kwon YD, You CH (2005). Effects of supplemental insurance on health care utilization and expenditures among cancer patients in Korea. *Korean Journal of Health Policy and Administration*, 15(4):65–80 (in Korean).

Kim J, Chung J (2005). Current status of out-of-pocket payment for health care. *Health Insurance Forum*, 4(1) (in Korean).

Korea Insurance Research Institute (2014). *Evaluation and Recommendation on Korea Insurers' Overseas Business.* Seoul, Korea Insurance Research Institute (in Korean).

Korea Labor Institute (2002). Korean Labor and Income Panel Study 4th wave. www.kli.re.kr/klips/index.do; accessed on 10/11/2016.

Korea Statistics (2016). *Share of population covered by private health insurance*: http://kostat.go.kr/wnsearch/search.jsp; accessed on 10/11/2016 (in Korean).

Kwon S (2003a). Health care financing reform and the new single payer system in the Republic of Korea: social solidarity or efficiency? *International Social Security Review*, 56(1):75–94.

Kwon S (2003b). Payment system reform for health care providers in Korea. *Health Policy and Planning*, 18(1):84–92.

Kwon S, Lee T, Kim C (2015). *Republic of Korea Health System Reveiw*. In: Kwon S, vol. 5, *Health Systems in Transition*. Manila, World Health Organization Regional Office for the Western Pacific.

Lee YC et al. (2006). Impacts of the cost-containment strategies on pharmaceutical expenditures of the National Health Insurance in Taiwan 1997–2003. *Journal of PharmacoEconomics*, 24(9):891–902.

Lin CY (2006). The role of private health insurance under Taiwan's NHI: a social policy perspective. In: Bureau of National Health Insurance, ed. *Proceedings of the Second National Taiwan–Korea NHI international symposium*, 25–26 May. Taipei, Taiwan, China, Bureau of National Health Insurance, The Department of Health.

Ministry of Health, Labour and Welfare (Japan) (2016). *Survey of Medical Institutions Report from Hospitals*. Tokyo, Kousei Roudou Tokei Kyokai.

MOHW (Ministry of Health and Welfare) (2013). *Statistical Yearbook 2013*. Seoul, Ministry of Health and Welfare.

MOHW (2016a). *2014 National Health Expenditures*. Taipei, Taiwan: Ministry of Health and Welfare, Executive Yuan, China (in Chinese).

MOHW (2016b). *Hospital and clinics statistics in Taiwan*: www.mohw .gov.tw/CHT/DOS/Statistic.aspx?f_list_no=312&fod_list_no=6219; accessed on 9/11/2016 (in Chinese).

Miyaji T (2006). Trends in product development in health insurance. In: Hotta K, ed. *Strategies and issues in private health insurance*. Tokyo, Keiso Shobo (in Japanese).

NHIA (National Health Insurance Administration) (2015). *2015–2016 National Health Insurance Annual Report*. National Health Insurance Administration, Ministry of Health and Welfare, Executive Yuan, China (in Chinese).

OECD (2016). *OECD health data 2016*. Paris, Organization for Economic Co-operation and Development: http://stats.oecd.org/index .aspx?DataSetCode=HEALTH_STAT; accessed on 10/11/2016.

Seo NK et al. (2013). *Analysis of out-of-pocket payment in health insurance*, National Health Insurance Service, 2013 (in Korean).

Taiwan Insurance Institute (2016). *Key indicator in the insurance market in Taiwan*: www. Tii.org.tw/opencms/information/information1/000001 .html/; accessed on 9/11/2016 (in Chinese).

Tatara K, Okamoto E (2009). Japan: health system review. *Health Systems in Transition*, 11(5):1–164.

The Executive Yuan (2007). *Ten-year long-term care development plan*. Taipei, Taiwan, China, The Executive Yuan, China (in Chinese).

Tsai YW (2007). *Preliminary report of a national survey on private health insurance in Taiwan*. Taiwan, China, National Health Research Institutes, Miaoli, Taiwan (in Chinese).

WHO (2018). Global health expenditure database (GHED) [online database]. Geneva, WHO: www.who.int/health-accounts/ghed/en/; accessed on 15/01/2018.

Wong J (2003). Resisting reform: the politics of health care in democratizing Taiwan. *American Asian Review*, 21(2):57–90.

Yoon TH et al. (2005). The determinants of private health insurance purchasing decisions under the National Health Insurance system in Korea. *Korean Journal of Health Policy and Administration*, 15(4):161–75 (in Korean).

10 The role of private health insurance in financing health care in Kenya

DAVID MUTHAKA

Kenya has a pluralistic health system, with the government, private actors and donors involved in the financing and provision of health care. Since the late 1980s, the government has encouraged private investment in health care and there is now a large and diverse private health care delivery sector comprising for-profit and non-profit facilities. The growth of private provision has in turn created demand for private health insurance. Private health insurance cover is mainly purchased by higher-income employees in urban areas and only covered under 2% of the population in 2013 (Ministry of Health, 2014). It is beyond the financial reach of most of the population in a country plagued by poverty and income inequality, where access to affordable health care depends not just on the availability of funds but also on the availability of health workers and facilities. Until 2006, health insurers operated in an unregulated environment and there have been issues with fraud. The chapter begins with an overview of health financing policy in Kenya, then outlines the nature of the private health insurance market, the regulatory framework and barriers to market expansion.

Health financing policy

The public–private mix in financing and delivery

Health financing policy has undergone several changes since Kenya gained independence in 1963. Health care was virtually free in the 1960s and 1970s, but a severe economic decline forced the government to initiate a cost-sharing programme for health services and education in 1989 as part of the conditionality imposed by Structural Adjustment Programmes in return for loans from the World Bank and the International Monetary Fund. The new programme substantially expanded the modest fees that had been charged in government hospitals and health centres. Alongside reforms to relax licensing and other regulatory requirements, the programme was intended to create an environment conducive to greater private sector involvement (Muthaka et al., 2004).

Limited government resources led to deterioration in public health care services. Households turned to private clinics, pharmacies and traditional healers to obtain health care and private provision began to grow. In 1999, private health facilities accounted for 48% of all health facilities, but by 2006 their share had risen to 59%, falling to 49% in 2014 (Ministry of Health, 2007, 2013; Government of Kenya, 2010). Nevertheless, bed capacity is still higher in the public sector, because public facilities are on average larger than private ones. In early 2010, about 60% of all beds were in the public sector.

In 2012/2013, public spending on health accounted for 34% of total health expenditure, donor funding for 19% and households (out-of-pocket payments) for 29% (Ministry of Health, 2015a). Public funding comes from government budget allocations to the Ministry of Health and related government organizations such as the National AIDS Control Council. However, given the economic situation and other factors, budget transfers have not been an adequate source of health financing. Privately provided services are financed through out-of-pocket payments and private health insurance premiums. Out-of-pocket payments are the second largest single source of health care financing after government spending.

Between 2001/2002 and 2012/2013, total expenditure on health accounted for well below 10% of gross domestic product (see Table 10.1). Government expenditure on health averaged around 6% of total government expenditure over the same decade, much less than the Abuja commitment of 15% and despite the various challenges Kenya faces, such as poor health indicators and increasing high burden of noncommunicable and emerging diseases. However, owing to sustained levels of financing coming from households and development partners, total per person health expenditure rose from US$45 in 2001/2002 to US$67 in 2012/2013 (Ministry of Health, 2015b).

Cost-sharing revenues

The cost-sharing programme introduced in 1989 was devised as a way of generating more revenue for the health sector (Kimalu et al., 2004). However, funds raised through this programme are usually retained

Table 10.1 *Total expenditure on health in Kenya, 2001/2002 to 2012/2013*

Indicators	2001/2002	2005/2006	2009/2010	2012/2013
Total government expenditure (KES billion)	405.2	769.1	1 013	1 282
(US$ billion)	(5.2)	(10.5)	(13.4)	(15.0)
Government health expenditure as a % of total government expenditure	8.0%	5.2%	4.6%	6.1%
Total expenditure on health as % of nominal GDP	5.1%	4.7%	5.4%	6.8%
Total expenditure on health (KES billion)	109.4	135.6	163.4	234.0
(US$ billion)	(1.4)	(1.8)	(2.2)	(2.7)
Total per capita expenditure on health (KES)	3 506.4	3 805.7	4 231.9	5 679.5
(US$)	(44.6)	(51.8)	(55.8)	(66.6)

Source: Ministry of Health (2015b).

Note: GDP: gross domestic product; KES: Kenyan Shilling.

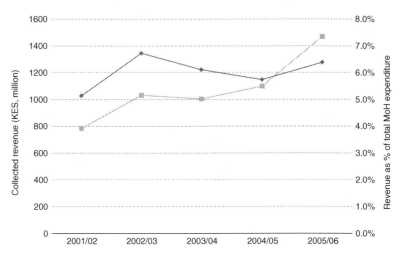

Figure 10.1 Cost-sharing revenue as a share (%) of total expenditure of Kenyan Ministry of Health, 2001/2002 to 2008/2009

Source: Author's compilation based on data from the Ministry of Health (2007) and the Government of Kenya (2010).

by health facilities to boost their recurrent budgets and, as a result, they account for less than 10% of Ministry of Health expenditure (see Fig. 10.1). The decline in cost sharing as a share of Ministry of Health spending observed after 2002/2003 can be attributed to growth in the Ministry's budget and changes in cost-sharing policy, which also coincided with a change in political leadership in the country. In 2004, in response to growing poverty levels[1] (Kenya National Bureau of Statistics, 2007), the Ministry adopted a 10/20 policy, according to which dispensaries and health centres were to forfeit fees for curative health care and instead only charge a registration fee of 10 Kenyan

[1] According to the 2005/2006 Kenya Integrated Household and Budget Survey, which is the latest household survey in Kenya, the absolute poverty level in the rural population was estimated to be 49.1% and the national poverty level for the extremely poor (whose income does not suffice to buy the required daily calorific intake even if it was entirely devoted to purchasing food) was estimated to be 21.9% (Kenya National Bureau of Statistics, 2007). The Kenya Economic Report (2010) published by the government think tank, Kenya Institute for Public Policy Research and Analysis (KIPPRA) projected an increase in the rural poverty level to 53.4% in 2012 (KIPPRA, 2010).

shillings (KES) (US$0.15) and KES20 (US$0.30) respectively, payable on every visit. However, many facilities charged more than these token fees citing inadequate government funding and the resulting inability to cover their financial needs (Onsomu et al., 2014). After health care was fully devolved to county (regional) governments in 2013, the Kenya Health Policy 2014–2030 abolished all user charges in dispensaries and health centres.

National Hospital Insurance Fund contributions

Besides using tax revenues and cost sharing, the Ministry of Health has continued to promote the National Hospital Insurance Fund (NHIF), with plans to turn it into a universal health insurance scheme. The NHIF was established in 1966 under Chapter 255 of the Laws of Kenya to be run by an advisory council appointed by the Minister of Health. In 1998, the 1966 Act was repealed and replaced by the NHIF Act of 1998, which established the fund as an autonomous state corporation "to provide for a national contributory hospital insurance scheme for all residents", replacing the then existing racial insurance schemes. Enrolment in the NHIF is mandatory for all formally employed workers and voluntary for the self-employed, unemployed and those working in the informal sector. In 2015, the NHIF replaced the monthly flat rate contributions for those in formal employment with income-dependent contributions based on gross salary. Contributions range from KES150 to KES1700 per month (NHIF, 2016). At the same time, and for the first time since its establishment, the NHIF also introduced coverage for outpatient benefits, thereby offering comprehensive medical cover.[2] The NHIF-covered services can be accessed in the majority of accredited government facilities, mission health care providers and in some low-cost private health care providers across the country (together, over 400 facilities). No additional user charges are levied on these services. The NHIF cover also includes inpatient services in high-cost private hospitals, but patients using these facilities face user charges due to the high level of fees charged (the NHIF cover does not suffice).

---

[2] The NHIF cover also includes a comprehensive maternity package. Such care can be accessed in government hospitals, in the majority of mission hospitals and in some private hospitals.

Before 2008, almost half of the funds collected by the NHIF (on average 48%) were used to cover administrative expenses, with only a third (on average 33.5%) being used to reimburse health care costs. This improved between 2008/2009 and 2014/2015, with more funds from contributions used for provision of benefits in that period (Table 10.2). Nevertheless, various challenges prevent the NHIF from becoming a successful risk-sharing scheme, including poor governance and management, lack of control over lengths of stay and uncontrolled growth in the number of facilities. The latter has led to a rapid expansion of both legitimate and fraudulent claims, but the number of accredited facilities is still limited and unevenly distributed, which means access to health care may be difficult, particularly in rural areas.

In light of the challenges faced by the NHIF since its establishment, in the early 2000s the government proposed transforming the NHIF into a National Social Health Insurance Scheme (NSHIS) that would be compulsory for all Kenyans and permanent residents and involve a government subsidy for the poor. In addition to correcting the failures of the NHIF, the proposed scheme would address fundamental concerns regarding equity, access, affordability and quality in the provision of health services to the poor. However, the proposed scheme was opposed by health insurance companies, private health care providers and development partners, including the World Bank and the International Monetary Fund. Health insurers feared they would lose business if the scheme was successfully implemented and private providers, including health management organizations (HMOs), feared they would lose customers if public health facilities were improved. Development partners were against the scheme on the basis that it would require more resources than a country of Kenya's economic status could sustain (Consumer Information Network, 2006). The reliability of NSHIS funding was questioned given that the country's formal sector was very small (about two million people out of 39.4 million) and 45.9% of the population was below the national poverty line. This meant that not enough resources could be generated by taxing those in formal employment. Also, the proposed 2.9% earmarked income tax for employees, matched by the same amount paid by employers, was viewed as too high a burden to both. Employees who benefited from private health insurance financed by employers feared that the latter would cease

Table 10.2 *National Hospital Insurance Fund revenues from contributions and benefits paid out in Kenya, 2008/2009 to 2014/2015*

(in KES million)	2008/2009	2009/2010	2010/2011	2011/2012	2012/2013	2013/2014	2014/2015
Contributions	5 079.0	6 025.7	6 765.8	9 595.6	12 054.9	13 629.1	15 826.2
Benefits	2 813.0	3 110.0	3 677.4	5 999.8	8 236.2	9 401.1	10 891.1
(% of contributions)	(55%)	(52%)	(54%)	(63%)	(68%)	(69%)	(69%)
Contributions net of benefits	2 266.0	2 915.7	3 088.4	3 595.8	3 818.7	4 228.0	4 935.10
(% of contributions)	(45%)	(48%)	(46%)	(37%)	(32%)	(31%)	(31%)

Source: Ministry of Health (2015b).

offering private cover[3] when faced with extra NSHIS charges, and that if the costs to employers were too high, they would lower wages or reduce employment. The Ministry of Finance was concerned that the government, as the key employer in the formal sector, would be forced to bear most of the financing burden by paying contributions for civil servants. Thus, meeting the proposed scheme's estimated cost of between KES40 billion to KES70 billion[4] was viewed as unrealistic. Other fundamental issues concerned the scheme's ability to improve access, quality and affordability of care. It was acknowledged that improved access to health care could not be achieved unless the Ministry of Health ensured expansion of health infrastructure to rural areas, where 75% of the population lives.[5] As a result, the proposal was first watered down from a mandatory scheme to a voluntary one and eventually never implemented.

According to WHO estimates, as of 2015, 55% of private health expenditure was paid out of pocket, while 16% was attributable to private health insurance. The remaining 30% was financed from other sources such as non-profit institutions (Fig. 10.2). Expenditure on private health insurance has been relatively stagnant for a long time. In 1995, it accounted for 4.4% of total health expenditure and 7.6% of private sector expenditure. It then declined to 6.8% of private health expenditure in 2002. In that year, 74% of premiums were paid by households, 24% by private employers and the remaining 2% by government agencies (Ministry of Health, 2005). Since then there has been some growth in private health insurance expenditures as shown in Fig. 10.2.

The role and growth of private health insurance

Market origins and expansion

Private health insurance first emerged following the government's call for private sector participation in health care provision in the 1980s and

---

[3] Compared to the NHIF, private health insurance is more expensive but offers better quality of services.

[4] This is approximately US$394 million to US$690 million at an exchange rate of US$1 to KES101.5 in 2016.

[5] The same argument could be applied to health workers, who are also concentrated in urban areas.

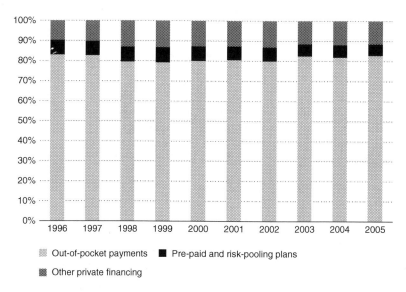

Figure 10.2 Breakdown of private expenditure on health in Kenya, 2004–2015.

Source: WHO (2018).

1990s and the market's expansion was initially closely associated with the development of private health facilities. The government relaxed regulations governing private practice, allowed health professionals to work in both the public and the private sectors and granted them permission to set up their own clinics. The government's cost-sharing policy, introduced at the same time, prompted people to seek care in the private sector as the quality of care in public facilities deteriorated due to limited funding. Demand for private health insurance was further stimulated by employers offering private health insurance as an employee benefit to attract better workers, reduce absenteeism and increase productivity.

In response to this rising demand, general insurance companies developed policies covering medical benefits, initially only selling them to companies as corporate or group cover because individuals were not regarded as reliable customers. In 1999, about 87% of private health insurance policies were purchased by companies for their employees (Ministry of Health, 1999). Other types of insurers also emerged, notably HMOs and medical insurance providers. For example, the Africa Air

Rescue Health Services, a privately owned Kenyan HMO, was established in 1984 as an emergency rescue company and began to provide comprehensive health services in 1991 (Chee & Tharmaratnam, 1997), while MediPlus, a privately owned medical insurance provider, was founded in 1996 through a network of independently owned health service providers operating throughout the country (McCord & Osinde, 2002). Increased competition within the insurance industry contributed to growth in the private health insurance market.

Take-up of private health insurance

According to Ministry of Health data (Ministry of Health, 2003), 9.7% of the population had some form of health insurance in 2003. The NHIF was the largest single provider of health insurance (88.1% of the insured population), followed by group private health insurance (6.3%), individual private health insurance (5.0%) and other sources, including community insurance (0.6%). This means that in 2003 only about 1.1% of the population (353 000 people) was covered by private health insurance. By 2007, NHIF coverage had declined to 83.8% of the insured, group private health insurance increased to 12.0%, individual private health insurance to 7.9% and other sources to 1.1% (Ministry of Health, 2009). By 2013, the share of those insured through NHIF increased to 88.4%; private health insurance covered 9.4%;[6] community-based insurance 1.3%; and other forms of insurance 1.0% (Ministry of Health, 2014). The increase in NHIF's coverage can be associated with improvements in NHIF's functioning, including enhanced benefits coverage, and successful campaigns promoting public awareness of NHIF benefits, which increased coverage in the informal sector.

Private health insurance is mainly purchased by the non-poor, the employed and urban residents. Health insurers tend to be based in or focus on urban areas; most urban residents have regular incomes from employment or self-employment (including small-scale or informal

---

[6] It has to be noted that contrary to earlier household surveys, the 2013 survey did not include the question about the possession of group insurance (it only asked whether the respondent had private health insurance cover, without distinguishing between individual and group cover). This means that there may have been some double counting for people who had both individual and group covers in the previous surveys.

Table 10.3 *Distribution of insured people by the type of health insurance coverage and region in Kenya, 2013*

	NHIF	Private health insurance	Community insurance	Other
Nairobi	76.60	22.20	0.30	0.80
Central	85.80	8.94	3.68	1.62
Coast	92.03	6.83	0.38	0.77
Eastern	93.29	4.44	1.53	0.76
Nyanza	96.10	2.75	0.47	0.70
Rift Valley	93.16	5.74	0.61	0.51
Western	92.25	5.43	1.33	1.00

Source: Ministry of Health (2014).

Notes: Figures show percentages of total population in a given region. NHIF: National Hospital Insurance Fund.

businesses); they are generally better educated than rural residents and therefore have access to more information on private health insurance. Having private health insurance is regarded as a symbol of higher social status. Household survey data from 2013 indicate that private health insurance take-up is 26.6% among urban residents, 12.1% among rural residents, 16% among those in the highest income quintile, 3.3% in the middle quintile and 3.6% in the lowest quintile (Ministry of Health, 2014). It is therefore evident that the number of rural poor people with private cover is very small. What is more, even this small number may in fact represent the dependants of those who are employed and privately insured or those who are covered through the NHIF.

As shown in Table 10.3, the government's NHIF has the widest coverage in all regions among the insured population. This is not surprising given that it is mandatory for formal employees and covers their dependants as well.[7] Population coverage of private health insurance is very low in all regions and stands at less than 10% across the country (see above). The exception is Nairobi, where roughly one in every four

[7] The average household size for Kenya is about six people. With 2 million people in formal employment, this means that around 12 million people were covered for inpatient care through the NHIF (NHIF's cover was only extended to outpatient care in 2015).

citizens has private health insurance cover. Individual private health insurance has very low penetration rates in all regions, with some regions having less than 2% of their populations covered by this type of insurance.

Types of private health insurance provider

In 2015, there were 51 general and life insurance companies, 22 medical insurance providers (MIPs). There were also 144 insurance brokers and 6428 insurance agents (AKI, 2016). Nineteen of the 51 general insurers offer health insurance policies (see Table 10.4). Before the amendment of the Insurance Act in 2006, some MIPs provided health care through their own facilities (the HMOs) or through third-party facilities. As the HMOs only used their own doctors and facilities, their premiums were often low in comparison with other private insurers and this made them especially popular with employers who offered private health insurance cover to their employees.[8] When the 2006 amendment came into force, the MIPs restructured their operations to separate medical insurance and health care provision. As a result, there are no more HMOs operating in the market and the MIPs are exclusively focused on health insurance business, contracting health service provision from private doctors and hospitals.

Types of private health insurance cover

There are two main types of cover: individual cover and group cover. For both sorts of cover, contracts are normally renewed annually and premiums are paid once a year. Only a few insurers offer individual cover. People can choose from varying levels of cover and premiums are usually age related. Some insurers have discontinued individual cover due to moral hazard issues and cases of fraudulent behaviour in which enrollees would falsify information in order to obtain medical treatment for friends and family members who were not covered. However, as the health insurance market opens up and becomes more competitive, the scenario is changing and insurers have introduced measures to

---

[8] However, the geographical coverage of their service providers was not as wide as it was for other insurers, so access to health care was probably lower for HMO members.

protect themselves from fraud and moral hazard. For example, some use biometric measures to verify membership (for example, Resolution Health and UAP Insurance). Others have introduced cost sharing and restrictions regarding pre-existing conditions (waiting periods); most enrol children only after a 1-month waiting period; some require annual medical examinations from enrollees above 60 years old and do not enrol new members over 60 years old.

Most insurers offer cover to corporate and non-corporate groups (including families) of at least 10 individuals, usually tailored to the specific needs of a group. Employers who offer cover to their employees often work closely with insurers to develop plans and set annual uniform limits for each employee. Some of them opt to cover inpatient care only (basic cover), while others develop more comprehensive plans, covering both inpatient and outpatient care and other supplementary benefits, such as dental and optical care. Most corporate plans cover employees' dependants as well. Employees sometimes negotiate private health insurance cover for themselves and their dependants.

The most common methods of paying providers are so-called credit facilities and fee-for-service (see Table 10.4). The former is offered by most medical insurance providers, which makes health care services more accessible (enrollees receive benefits-in-kind). General insurers typically require that enrollees pay providers up front on a fee-for-service basis and claim reimbursement by submitting claims. Reimbursement policies are not popular among corporate clients.

Public policy towards private health insurance

The government is mandated to facilitate and regulate the provision of health care to all citizens. The legal framework covering general and health insurance can be found in the 2006 Insurance Amendment Act, the National Hospital Insurance Fund Act (No. 9 of 1998), which affects private providers because the NHIF contracts them to provide services to its members, and the Medical Practitioners and Dentists Act, Chapter 253 of the Laws of Kenya.

Before 2006, the Insurance Act had no provisions relating to health insurance. At the same time, there was a large number of health insurance providers operating in the private sector whose operations were not regulated by the law. For instance, HMOs were not required to register

Table 10.4 *Private health insurance market structure and regulation in Kenya, 2016*

Type of insurer	Examples	Type of cover	Relationship with providers	Regulatory framework
General insurance companies	Jubilee Insurance Company, Heritage Insurance Company (only corporate cover), Britam General Insurance, and UAP Insurance	Group and individual	Contracts with providers; providers are either paid on a fee-for-service basis (and the insured are later reimbursed by the insurer) or via credit facilities[a]	Insurance Act (Chapter 487) (enacted in 1986 and in force since 1 January 1987)
Medical insurance providers	BUPA International, Health Management Services and Health First International	Group and individual	Contract with providers: using credit facilities[a] (mostly) or fee-for-service	2006 Insurance Amendment Act which requires medical insurance providers to be registered
Medical service providers (HMOs before the 2006 amendment of Insurance Act)	AAR Health Services, Avenue Healthcare Ltd, Comprehensive Medical Services, Health Plan Services	Group and individual	Provide medical services in their in-house clinics that are prepaid with the premiums[b]	2006 Insurance Amendment Act which requires medical service providers (and previously HMOs) to register as insurance brokers; Medical Practitioners and Dentist Board

Source: Author's own compilation.

Note: [a] Health care providers are paid by the insurer after providing health care services. The insured thus receive benefits-in-kind, without an upfront payment (unless cost sharing applies).

[b] If a medical service provider cannot render a particular service, the patient must look for another provider.

with the Commissioner of Insurance as medical insurance providers (and their operations were therefore not controlled) and the medical insurance providers were not insurance brokers under the Insurance Act. Also, the professional qualifications of the insurance brokers were not considered important or not considered at all during registration and the brokers were not required to register with the Insurance Office of the Commissioner of Insurance (companies registered under the Company's Act, Chapter 486 of the Laws of Kenya could provide insurance if this was stated in their memorandum of association).

Before 2006, there was no regulation for specialist medical insurance companies. Consequently, MIPs did not come under general insurance regulations and only had to register as private companies under the Companies Act (Chapter 486 of the Laws of Kenya). In the 1990s, some MIPs collapsed due to challenges such as weak management structures, moral hazard and financial liquidity problems resulting from the absence of capital requirements (solvency margins). Research into one MIP, MediPlus, before it ceased operations in 2003 concluded that between 2000 and 2001 its so-called trade payables (payments to clinics and hospitals) had increased by 308% but its total premiums had only increased by 98% (McCord & Osinde, 2002: p.11). One possible cause of this liquidity problem was the lack of provisions to minimize adverse selection; for example, MediPlus did not require whole families to enrol (McCord & Osinde, 2002). HMOs also operated in an unregulated environment for a number of years (Muthaka et al., 2004) and were only required to register under the Companies Act and the Medical Practitioners and Dentists Act (Chapter 253).

The Insurance Amendment Act of 2006 aimed to strengthen the regulatory framework for MIPs. The Insurance Regulatory Authority was established and MIPs were required to register with it and meet certain capital requirements, and capital requirements for insurance companies were increased. To avoid any conflict of interests, medical insurance providers were no longer allowed to provide medical care services but instead had to rely on third-party providers.

The Insurance Amendment Act, the main law regulating the insurance market, applies to general insurance companies, MIPs and medical services providers (also known as HMOs). Only people or bodies registered under the Act can participate in the insurance market and do so only for the class or classes of insurance products indicated in their Articles and Memoranda of Association at the point of registration as corporate entities (under the Companies Act, Chapter 486 of the Laws of Kenya). Applicants have to meet requirements regarding adequacy of assets, capital, reinsurance arrangements and staff. To protect consumers against high premiums and insolvency, the government requires insurance companies to present to the registration board indications of their premiums and methods of calculation as well as examples of policy forms, terms and conditions.

The Insurance Amendment Act (2006) of the Laws of Kenya also transformed the Department of Insurance into an autonomous supervisory authority through the creation of an independent Insurance Regulatory Authority that replaced the Office of the Commissioner of Insurance. The function of the Insurance Regulatory Authority is to supervise and regulate the insurance sector by formulating and enforcing standards of conduct, protecting the interests of the insured and advising the government on policies to protect the sector (Section 3A, Insurance Amendment Act 2006). The Commissioner of Insurance has the right to inspect the activities of insurance companies, which acts as a deterrent to unscrupulous or unethical practices.

The HMOs used to be registered as companies under the Companies Act, Chapter 486 of the Laws of Kenya. From 2006, however, they also had to register with and apply the provisions of the Insurance Amendment Act, which classified them as brokers.[9] Because HMOs ran their own health facilities and employed health practitioners, they were subject to additional legal requirements set out in the Medical Practitioners and Dentists Act (Chapter 253 of the Laws of Kenya) and had to be licensed both by the Commissioner of Insurance and the Medical Practitioners and Dentist Board.

The impact of private health insurance

The impact of private health insurance is assessed in light of the government's goal to provide affordable, accessible and equitable health care of good quality to all citizens. These dimensions, as well as the

---

[9] Brokers are defined as "an intermediary concerned with the placing of insurance business with an insurer or reinsurer for or in expectation of payment by way of brokerage, commission for or on behalf of an insurer, policy-holder or proposer for insurance or reinsurance and includes a health management organization ...". See Section 2(1), Insurance Amendment Act 2006.

externalities of the private health insurance sector, are explored in the following sections.

Timely access to health care

Access to health care is problematic for many people due to the lack of adequate health facilities and equipment and the poor road network and infrastructure. It is questionable whether private health insurance can address these access barriers, especially for people living in rural areas. Moreover, because private health facilities are not evenly distributed throughout the country, private health insurance cannot guarantee the insured equitable access to health care services.

Improving financial protection

Given Kenya's low per person income (about US$1410 a year in 2015; Government of Kenya, 2016) and high poverty levels, particularly among people living in rural areas, the majority of the population cannot afford to buy private health insurance. Annual premiums range from US$524 (UAP insurance) to US$894 (Avenue Healthcare) for a comprehensive family policy (covering principal, spouse and child) with defined benefits (see Table 10.5), putting it well beyond the reach of all but the richest households. The fact that private health insurance requires lump-sum annual payments rather than smaller monthly payments makes it even less affordable for the poor. It is only the NHIF and a few community-based insurance schemes (for example, *Kinga ya Mkulima* insurance cover for small-scale tea farmers) that allow monthly payments of their premiums.

Improved revenues to health facilities

Patients with private health insurance do not leave hospital without paying their hospital bill, which allows health facilities to recuperate costs. Musau (1999) confirms that all health facilities accredited to treat privately insured patients experienced improved revenues compared with those that are not accredited to do so. Health facilities are also used more effectively when they partner with private health insurance providers, especially those that were formerly under-used. However, anecdotal evidence provides examples of fraudulent behaviour, where health facilities collude with policy-holders against insurance companies,

Table 10.5 *Range of premiums for private health insurance charged by selected insurance companies in Kenya, 2016*

Insurer	Member	Annual premium (KES[a])		Benefits limits (KES[a])		Additional charges
		Inpatient	Outpatient	Inpatient (per family)	Outpatient (per member)	
Jubilee Insurance Company	Principal (18–30 years)	13 600 (US$134)	18 800 (US$185)			
	Spouse	11 400 (US$112)	18 800 (US$185)			
	Child (1–17 years)	7 200 (US$71)	18 800 (US$185)			
UAP Insurance Company	Principal (19–29 years)	9 757 (US$96)	10 239 (US$101)			Co-payment KES100 (US$1) for all consultations
	Spouse	8 170 (US$80)	10 239 (US$101)			
	Child (0–18 years)	4 537 (US$45)	10 239 (US$101)			

Resolution Health Insurance	Principal (19–34 years)	16 915 (US$167)	23 394 (US$230)	500,000 (US$4,926)	50,000 (US$493)	Co-payment between KES500 and KES1000 (US$5 to US$10) depending on health facility visited
	Principal +1	21 099 (US$208)	34 398 (US$339)			
	Principal +2	25 093 (US$247)	37 945 (US$374)			
Avenue Healthcare	Principal (19–34 years)	53 370 (US$526)	Included in inpatient			
	Principal +1	74 100 (US$730)	Included in inpatient			
	Principal +2	90 770 (US$894)	Included in inpatient			

Source: Respective websites of insurers listed in the table (accessed in November 2016).

Note: [a] According to average exchange rate of US$1 to KES101.5 in 2016.

or where accredited facilities lodge fake reimbursement claims causing revenue losses to the insurance company.

The impact of private health insurance on the publicly financed health system

The growth of the private health care market is thought to have exacerbated inequalities in access to health care. After the introduction of the cost-sharing programme in 1989 the private sector became an alternative for people able to pay higher fees for a better quality of care. As the private health insurance market has grown, there has been a migration of health professionals from public to private facilities, eroding human resources in the public sector and contributing to the poor quality of services in public facilities. Private providers contracted by private health insurance companies have been able to attract good health workers by offering better pay and a good working environment. This trend has been a major cause for concern due to its negative impact on quality in public facilities and on health care inequalities. It is estimated that only 600 out of 5000 registered doctors work in public health facilities, with the rest working in private establishments at home or abroad (Siringi, 2001). Given that most health professionals work in urban centres, this adds to the urban–rural divide in terms of access to private health insurance and quality health services.

Barriers to the expansion of private health insurance

The private health insurance market is very small in Kenya, both in terms of contribution to total and private spending on health and in terms of population coverage. The vast majority of private spending on health comes from out-of-pocket payments (WHO, 2018). Uptake of private health insurance is low because the population is poor, most health professionals and facilities are located in urban areas (Kimani, Muthaka & Manda, 2004) and health insurance schemes usually target urban centres and the formal sector. In 2015, employment in the formal sector accounted for only about 17.2% of total employment (Government of Kenya, 2016). Private health insurance companies tend to focus their marketing efforts on low-risk individuals (Kimani, Muthaka & Manda, 2004), so private health insurance is often regarded as a service for the middle or upper classes. Finally, the credibility of private health insurance companies has been low in recent years, with illegal practices and poor financial management leading to the closure of several medical insurance companies; fraudulent activities have also been carried out by the insured.

In spite of these significant barriers to expansion, the private health insurance industry has some potential to grow in future, especially if mechanisms are put in place to ensure quality and affordability. Private insurers could reduce premium prices by encouraging groups to enrol or by paying more attention to how providers deliver health services – for example, specifying the use of generic medicines and adherence to clinical guidelines. Fraud and mismanagement could be minimized through improved regulation and oversight. To address the issue of affordability for individuals, premiums could be made payable in monthly instalments rather than in annual lump-sum payments (see Box 10.1).

Box 10.1 Affordable private health insurance scheme by Kenya Women Finance Trust

In 2008, the Kenya Women Finance Trust launched a cheap health insurance product that targets members of cooperative societies, social clubs and investment groups. The scheme offers inpatient care, personal accident and funeral cover for KES3600 per year (approximately US$35) and allows monthly payments. It also uses a health identity card and offers family rather than individual cover to address concerns about fraud and adverse selection.

The Kenya Women Finance Trust is a large national microfinance institution that provides microfinance to low-income female entrepreneurs. Information about the organization and its health insurance cover is available at www.kwft.org.

Conclusions

The promotion of affordable and equitable access to health care is a major challenge in Kenya. The government, development partners and the private sector all play significant roles in addressing this challenge. Private health insurance supplements publicly financed coverage, but mainly focuses on households living in urban centres, where most quality health facilities are concentrated, exacerbating inequalities in access. However, even if health care facilities were more evenly distributed across the country, the expansion of private health insurance would still be limited by the high levels of poverty in rural areas. Thus, the pace with which private health insurance can expand in future is likely to be dictated by the speed with which poverty is reduced.

At the same time, health insurers need to design products that are more affordable to the poor and do more to raise public awareness of and confidence in the sector and to educate people about the benefits of health insurance. This is especially important because many Kenyans either do not understand the idea of insuring against risks or believe insurance is a service reserved for the rich.

Fraud and financial mismanagement have been major challenges for private insurers. Better use of information technology and smart card technology might help to reduce fraud, although information technology infrastructure is lacking in many rural areas, so this could only be used effectively in urban centres. The government also needs to ensure that there is adequate regulation in place to provide consumers with effective protection. Public policies used to be inadequate and poorly enforced, but current policy on insurance seems to be conducive to the expansion of private health insurance and to promoting government goals for the health sector. Care is needed, however, to ensure that the health insurance system is designed in a way that promotes equitable access to health care and does not undermine quality and accessibility for those who rely on publicly financed services.

References

AKI (2016). *Insurance industry annual report 2015*. Nairobi, Association of Kenya Insurers.

Chee G, Tharmaratnam V (1997). *AAR Health Services – Kenya: final evaluation report, July 1995–July 1997*. Arlington, VA, Promoting Financial Investments and Transfers to Involve the Commercial Sector in Family Planning (PROFIT) (submitted to USAID/Office of Population Family Planning Services Division).

Consumer Information Network (2006). *Bridging the health financing gap in Kenya: tough choices for a struggling nation*. CIN Briefing Paper No. 8/2006. Nairobi, Consumer Information Network.

Government of Kenya (2010). *Facts and Figures 2010*. Nairobi, Ministry of Medical Services.

Government of Kenya (2016). *Economic survey 2016*. Nairobi, Kenya National Bureau of Statistics, Government Printer.

Kenya National Bureau of Statistics (2007). *Basic report on well-being in Kenya, based on Kenya Integrated Household Budget Survey 2005/06*. Nairobi, Kenya National Bureau of Statistics.

Kimalu PK et al. (2004). *A review of the health sector in Kenya. Working Paper Series 11/2004*. Nairobi, Kenya Institute for Public Policy Research Analysis.

Kimani DN, Muthaka DI, Manda DK (2004). *Healthcare financing though health insurance in Kenya: the shift to a National Social Health Insurance Fund. Kenya Institute for Public Policy Research and Analysis Discussion Paper No. 42*. Nairobi, Kenya Institute for Public Policy Research and Analysis.

KIPPRA (Kenya Institute for Public Policy Research and Analysis) (2010) *Kenya Economic Report 2010: Enhancing sectoral contribution towards reducing Poverty, unemployment and inequality in Kenya*. Nairobi, Kenya Institute for Public Policy Research and Analysis.

McCord MJ, Osinde S (2002). *MediPlus health services: notes from a visit July 2002*. Memphis, TN, The Microinsurance Centre.

Ministry of Health (1999). *Kenya National Health Accounts 1994*. Nairobi, Ministry of Health, Department of Planning, and Ministry of Health, Partnerships for Health Reform.

Ministry of Health (2003). *Kenya Household Expenditure and Utilization Survey report 2003*. Nairobi, Ministry of Health.

Ministry of Health (2005). *Kenya National Health Accounts (2001–2002)*. Nairobi, Ministry of Health.

Ministry of Health (2007). *Facts and figures at a glance: health and health-related indicators 2006*. Nairobi, Ministry of Health, Division of Planning.

Ministry of Health (2009). *Kenya Household Expenditure and Utilization Survey report 2007*. Nairobi, Ministry of Health.

Ministry of Health (2013). *Transforming Health: Accelerating Attainment of Universal Health Coverage: The Kenya Health Sector Strategic and Investment Plan (KHSSP) July 2014–June 2018*. Nairobi: Ministry of Health.

Ministry of Health (2014). *2013 Kenya Household Health Expenditure and Utilization Survey*. Nairobi, Ministry of Health.

Ministry of Health (2015a). *Kenya National Health Accounts 2012/13*. Nairobi, Ministry of Health.

Ministry of Health (2015b). *Health Facts and Figures 2014*. Nairobi, Ministry of Health.

Musau SN (1999). *Community-based health insurance: experience and lessons learned from East Africa*. Technical Report No. 34. Partnerships for Health Reform Project. Bethesda, MD, Abt Associates, Inc.

Muthaka DI, Kimani DN, Mwaura S, Manda DK (2004). A review of the regulatory framework for private healthcare services in Kenya. *Discussion Paper Series* 35/2004. Nairobi, Kenya Institute for Public Policy Research Analysis (KIPPRA).

National Hospital Insurance Fund (2016). Customers: www.nhif.or.ke/healthinsurance/customers; accessed on 14/11/2016.

Onsomu E, Muthaka D, Mwabu G, Nyanjom O, Dutta A, Maina TM, Barker C, and Muchiri S (2014). *Public Expenditure Tracking Survey in Kenya*, 2012 (PETS-Plus). Washington, DC: Futures Group, Health Policy Project; and Nairobi, Kenya: Kenya Institute for Public Policy Research and Analysis.

Siringi S (2001). Kenya government promised to increase doctor's salaries to curb brain drain. *Lancet*, 358(9278):307.

WHO (2018). Global Health Expenditure Database; http://apps.who.int/nha/database/Select/Indicators/en; accessed on 15/01/2018.

11 | *Private health insurance in the Netherlands*

HANS MAARSE AND PATRICK JEURISSEN

Private health insurance has been a constituent part of the Dutch health system since the early 20th century. Before the major reform in 2006, almost a quarter of the population held so-called pure private health insurance cover as a substitute for sickness fund cover. The 2006 Health Insurance Act created a single, mandatory health insurance scheme covering the whole population under private law. One of its most important consequences was the abolition of the traditional division between statutory health insurance operated by sickness funds and all other insurance schemes including substitutive private health insurance with experience-based underwriting. However, the newly created scheme is not a pure private arrangement (the term 'pure' will be explained later in this chapter) but one extensively regulated by the state to protect public interests including, among others, solidarity in health care financing and access to health care.

This chapter starts with a brief overview of the history of private health insurance in the Netherlands and its structure in the 1990s and early 2000s. The focus in the second part is on the 2006 reform and its consequences for the health insurance market. Developments in long-term care insurance are beyond the scope of the chapter.

Private health insurance before the 2006 reform

Historical origins

The history of health insurance in the Netherlands dates back to the 19th century and is closely related to the rise of the medical profession and the advance of modern medicine. At that time, many workers could not afford to pay for health care and were dependent on charities or local governments in case of illness. Another problem was the absence of income protection in case of illness. To improve social protection, labour unions, guilds, employers, and municipalities established voluntary sickness funds (*ziekenfondsen*) covering only a few medical

349

services including family medicine, some specialist care, maternity care and pharmaceuticals. By the beginning of the 20th century, about 10% of the population was affiliated with a sickness fund. This percentage had climbed to about 38% at the eve of World War Two (Veraghtert & Widdershoven, 2002; Kompanje, 2008).

Under strong pressure from the Medical Association (established in 1840) sickness funds only accepted people with low incomes. People who did not qualify for a sickness fund cover could purchase private cover on a voluntary basis. These voluntary schemes can be regarded as the precursors of private health insurance. Notice however that, strictly speaking, sickness funds too operated as private insurers in the early days of health insurance. In the absence of any state regulation they could set their own premium and benefits package. Furthermore, they were fully risk-bearing (no risk pooling). Nevertheless, there were also some differences between sickness funds and voluntary schemes. The former fulfilled a primarily social function and offered their clients a benefits-in-kind plan with community rating, whereas the latter used the cost-reimbursement model and experience-based rating (De Bruine & Schut, 1990).

The first government intervention was the 1901 Law on Accidents (*Ongevallenwet*), which offered workers some financial protection against accidents in the workplace. Attempts to introduce legislation on health insurance and sickness leave aroused significant controversy, not only for economic reasons (for example, the financial crisis of the late 1920s), but also as the result of political factors. Employers were sceptical about the introduction of statutory health insurance because of their fear of high costs and its impact on the overall economy. Neither was the National Medical Association, the best-organized interest group at the time, in strong favour of statutory health insurance. Physicians were particularly afraid that it would jeopardize their professional and economic autonomy. The Association would only accept a public arrangement if each of the following conditions were met: there was free choice of physician; half of the seats in the sickness funds' boards were reserved for physicians; and enrolment in sickness funds was limited to people with low incomes. Stimulated by the National Association, many physicians established sickness funds of their own. These physician funds proved successful and soon had more subscribers than other sickness funds (De Bruine & Schut, 1990).

Health insurance legislation was not passed until 1941. Ironically, it was introduced by the German occupying forces. The Sickness Funds

Decree (*Ziekenfondsenbesluit*) established compulsory cover for workers with incomes under a state-determined threshold. Others (such as self-employed or older people) could join a sickness fund on a voluntary basis. The rest of the population was excluded from sickness fund cover and had to rely on (voluntary) private health insurance cover (Kroneman et al., 2016). The key elements of the Decree were as follows: employers and employees paid an equal share of income-related contributions; the benefits package was substantially extended to include hospital care, nursing care in a sanatorium and dental care; full risk pooling among the funds was introduced; competition between the sickness funds was abolished; and the national government was placed at the top of the health insurance pyramid (De Bruine & Schut, 1990).

The 1941 Decree marked the beginning of an era of centralization in health insurance, putting an end to the self-regulatory governance structure of the sickness funds in the pre-war period. However, it did not fundamentally alter the role of private health insurance. In fact, by introducing an income threshold, the Decree institutionalized the pre-existing division between the sickness funds and private health insurance. This separation would remain a constituent element of the structure of health insurance in the Netherlands until 2006 (Kompanje, 2008).

Policy developments from the end of the Second World War to the late 1980s

After the Second World War there was broad consensus that the German arrangement needed to be replaced with new legislation on statutory health insurance. This again appeared politically troublesome, just as in the pre-war period. The workers' associations and the Labour Party demanded a single national scheme, whereas the Medical Association, the confessional (religion-affiliated) parties and the liberals fought for voluntary arrangements combined with a mandatory scheme for workers with an income under a state-set threshold. The latter proposal was also supported by employers who feared the adverse effects of a single national scheme on the fragile post-war economy. The political conflict was eventually settled by the enactment of the Sickness Fund Act (*Ziekenfondswet*) in 1964, which in most respects codified the earlier Sickness Fund Decree of 1941. As it only provided compulsory coverage for workers with incomes below a defined income threshold, it preserved the pre-existing division between the sickness fund scheme and private health insurance (Kompanje, 2008).

Another post-war event was the establishment, in 1957, of a specific sickness fund for older people with incomes under a state-set threshold. The (income-related) contribution rate and benefits package were set by the state, which also covered, together with the sickness funds, the yearly deficit between premium revenues and spending. A specific sickness fund scheme for self-employed people, known as the voluntary sickness fund scheme, had already been established during World War Two. Both specific schemes would later become a matter of financial concern.

In the pre-war period the market for private health insurance was heterogeneous. In the 1930s, there had been a rapid growth in the number of commercial and noncommercial insurers offering coverage of a number of health services or fixed lump sum pay-outs in case of hospitalization. After the war, many sickness funds, usually in collaboration with other funds, set up subsidiaries to penetrate the private market. The subsidiary funds offered benefits similar to those covered by the private funds, targeting former enrollees with incomes above the threshold who could no longer be affiliated with a sickness fund. They proved very successful because of their policy of open enrolment, lifetime cover and community rating. These arrangements radically differed from the principles of actuarial fairness applied by the so-called pure private insurers. It was not until 1947 that a private insurer guaranteed lifetime cover for its subscribers (De Bruine & Schut, 1990).

The success of the subsidiary funds motivated commercial insurers to adapt their products by reducing the number of exclusions and introducing full cost reimbursement. The universal application of lifetime cover and the creation of a common risk pool for private high-risk subscribers in 1957 were further illustrations of the evolutionary convergence between the sickness fund scheme and private health insurance. However, the mix of open enrolment, unlimited cover and low premium rates did not prove to be a sustainable business model. After a few bankruptcies, the state introduced public regulatory oversight of all private insurers, including private health insurers, to protect consumer interests.

In the 1960s and 1970s, commercial insurers started to offer health plans with high deductibles, age-related deductibles and age-related premium increases. They also introduced a maximum enrolment age. In the early 1980s, they began to attract young self-employed people (until then mainly covered on a voluntary basis by the sickness funds) by offering age-related premiums, deductibles and other attractive arrangements.

This aggressive marketing strategy of private insurers further undermined the already weak financial position of the voluntary sickness fund scheme for the self-employed and prompted the state to intervene in the private health insurance market by the passing of the Access to Health Insurance Act (*Wet op de Toegang tot de Ziektekostenverzekeringen*, WTZ) in 1986 to be implemented by private insurers. The Act introduced a safety net by securing private cover for people who were not eligible for the mandatory sickness fund scheme and who could not purchase private health insurance cover for medical (pre-existing conditions) or financial (high premiums) reasons. Among other things, the Act included a government-defined benefits package and a flat-rate premium as well as open enrolment and full risk pooling. As the premium revenues did not cover all WTZ spending, people with private health insurance cover had to pay an annual surcharge to cover the deficit. The Act also enabled private insurers to transfer anyone aged over 64 years to the WTZ scheme. As a result, private insurers – the champions of the free market – were able to avoid incurring any financial risk for high-risk subscribers (Schut, 1995).

Another state intervention was to abolish the scheme for older people in 1986 because of increasing financial deficits (the share of expenditure covered by contributions declined from 39.4% in 1970 to 18.6% in 1985). All subscribers were transferred to the mandatory sickness fund scheme. To compensate sickness funds for the resulting over-representation of older people among their members, the government adopted a law that obliged private health insurers to pay a solidarity contribution to the sickness fund scheme (Schut, 1995).

The policy measures taken in the mid-1980s mark an important development in the health insurance market: private health insurance had gradually become the target of state intervention. Yet, many policy-makers felt that a more fundamental reform was still required. They considered the new legislation to be an emergency measure that only tackled some urgent financial problems but did not offer any structural solution. It was not until 2006 that a fundamental reform came into force. Before discussing this reform, first an overview of the private insurance market between 1990 and 2005 will be given.

The health insurance market between 1990 and 2005

Following the 1986 reform, there were three types of substitutive health insurance plans. First, a broad range of pure private health insurance plans. These were voluntary individual or group plans offering a variety of benefits packages, deductibles and eligibility criteria for people who could not enter the sickness fund scheme because their income was higher than the state-set income threshold. Premiums were flat but, to some degree, age-related. Insurers were permitted to reject applicants and exclude pre-existing conditions. Second was the WTZ scheme offering open enrolment and a standard benefits package for those not eligible for the sickness fund scheme. Third, there were a number of public health schemes covering local and regional government employees, the police force and fire brigade. The first public scheme dated from 1926. Public health schemes resembled the sickness fund scheme in many respects, in particular in terms of mandatory participation, income-related contributions and benefits package. However, as they fell beyond the scope of the Sickness Fund Act, they were seen as belonging to the private insurance market, which was of course highly confusing if not misleading terminology. The heterogeneous structure of the private insurance market explains the introduction of the term pure private insurance in the introductory section. Pure private insurance is a distinct category to be discerned from other substitutive so-called private schemes.

Between 1990 and 2005 the population shares of different health insurance schemes remained stable (Table 11.1), largely due to yearly adjustments of the income threshold for sickness fund eligibility. During the political debate on the Sickness Fund Act the government

Table 11.1 *Health insurance population shares in the Netherlands (%), 1990–2005 (selected years)*

Insurance scheme	1990	1995	2000	2005
Sickness funds	61	63	65	62
Pure private health insurance	27	25	24	24
The WTZ scheme	5	5	4	5
Schemes for public employees	5	5	5	5
Other[a]	2	2	2	2

Source: Vektis (2006).

Notes: WTZ: Access to Health Insurance Act (*Wet op de Toegang tot de Ziektekostenverzekeringen*.

[a] Sector-specific governmental arrangements (e.g. covering the military).

had appeased opposition from the private health insurance sector by promising to keep the share of the population covered by the sickness fund scheme constant. This agreement, known as the peace borderline agreement, remained in place until the 2006 reform.

Private insurers operated either as non-profit mutual funds or as for-profit companies. Private health insurers were precluded from involvement in the sickness fund scheme, but sickness funds were allowed to offer both substitutive and complementary private health insurance, but had to establish separate organizational forms for that purpose. The Sickness Funds Act prohibited any form of cross-subsidization from the statutory to the private sector.

Many employers contracted with a private insurer to offer a group plan to their employees. In 2005, 52% of those who were privately insured belonged to a group plan (Vektis, 2006). The private market was also characterized by higher switching rates than in the sickness fund scheme (15.4% of the privately insured switched in 2005 compared with 7.5% of sickness fund members) (Laske-Aldershof & Schut, 2005).

Per person annual health care spending was significantly lower among people with voluntary private insurance than among sickness fund members (€1357 in 2005 versus €1946), mainly due to the favourable risk profile of the former. However, administrative costs were higher for private health insurers (10.9% in 2005) than for sickness funds (4%) due to their smaller size, higher marketing costs and claim filing costs (Vektis, 2006).

With regard to provider payment, the key difference between private insurers and sickness funds was that the former paid general practitioners on a fee-for-service basis, whereas the latter applied capitation-based payment. Both types of insurers paid self-employed specialists on a fee-for-service basis. Traditionally, pure private insurers paid higher fees than sickness funds, but since the mid-1990s fees were similar due to central regulation (Lieverdink, 1999).

Gradually, private insurers also became closely involved in health policy-making. Following the corporatist tradition in Dutch health policy, their national association (set up in 1961) acquired a privileged status in health care price negotiations, alongside the National Association of Sickness Funds. In 1995, both associations merged to form a single national association, named Health Insurers Netherlands (*Zorgverzekeraars Nederland*), signifying the convergence of interests between sickness funds and private insurers.

Steps towards regulated competition

The Dekker Plan and its aftermath

The first steps towards the 2006 reform were made in 1986 with the establishment of the Dekker Commission, named after its chairman Dr W. Dekker, a former CEO of Philips. In 1987, it published its report *Willingness to Change (Bereidheid tot Verandering)*, containing the outline of a new model for health care based on the principles of what was termed regulated competition. The report contained several radical proposals, including the abolition of the traditional division between statutory and private health insurance by integrating both types of insurance into a single mandatory scheme under public law covering the entire population. According to the Commission, the fragmented structure of health care financing proved to be an important source of inefficiencies and inequities. Central state planning was viewed as another source of inefficiency. To enhance efficiency, the Commission proposed a complex institutional framework in which market competition was to be strictly regulated by the state to prevent market failures and preserve solidarity in health care financing (Kroneman et al., 2016).

The Dekker Report received only a lukewarm reception and it took over a year before the government sent its proposal for new health insurance legislation – known as the Simons Plan, named after the then Deputy Minister of Health – to the parliament. This proposal, which deviated in several respects from the recommendations of the Dekker Commission, met with growing political resistance. Sceptical opinions were voiced not only in parliament but also by the national associations of insurers, providers, employers and other stakeholders. The unions embraced the idea of a single scheme but rejected the introduction of competition. It soon became evident that the reform lacked political momentum and political support for it rapidly crumbled (Okma, 1997). The Plan was declared politically dead in 1993 when the government did not receive parliamentary approval for some steps essential to the reform.

With hindsight, the political failure of market reform in the early 1990s can be seen as the result of two closely connected factors. First, there were many unresolved substantive policy questions. Would competition work? How would it affect access to health care and the distribution of health financing? Would it be technically possible to design a system of risk equalization that would adequately compensate insurers for differences in the risk profiles of their members? Was the implementation schedule realistic? Second, and on a deeper level, ideological convictions and political motives played an important role. The national associations of employers, unions, insurers, providers and other stakeholders denounced the Simons Plan as conflicting with the interests of their constituencies. For private insurers, acceptance of the Simons Plan would even mean the end of their business. A parliamentary evaluation of the failure of political decision-making concluded that the government had been unable to break through the so-called clay layer of interests. Another conclusion was that there had never been a sense of urgency (Willems Commission, 1994).

The new government (in place since 1994) declared that it would abstain from fundamental reform. Instead, it opted to move forward by means of incremental changes (see Table 11.2). Although the practical implications of these policy changes should not be overstated, each of them can be seen as a small but important step towards the 2006 reform, illustrating the evolutionary nature of the reform (Helderman et al., 2005; Van der Grinten, 2007).

Introduction of the 2006 reform

With the publication of its policy document *A Question of Demand* (*Vraag aan Bod*) in 2000, the government resumed the reform process. Its analysis was largely similar to that of the Dekker Report. It identified the strong supply orientation in health care as the key cause of inefficiencies, the absence of entrepreneurship and insufficient focus on consumer demand and health care quality. The dual structure of statutory and private arrangements was viewed as a source of inequity in financing health care and inefficiency. Like the Dekker Committee 14 years earlier, the government argued for the introduction of regulated competition. In 2004, after a few more years of debate, a new government (in place since 2003) sent its proposal for health insurance reform to the Dutch Parliament.

In this proposal the government opted for what may be termed a private model. The new health insurance scheme was construed under private law (an idea also supported by most sickness funds), to be operated by private insurers, to underscore the new roles and responsibilities of the state and the private sector in the post-reform health system. Following the new governance philosophy, health care had to be

Table 11.2 *Overview of policy changes in the 1990s introducing some competition in statutory health insurance in the Netherlands*

Year	Policy change
1991	Sickness funds were allowed to set their flat-rate (nominal) premiums. This measure created some room for premium competition between the funds. Nominal premiums had already been introduced in 1989 and had been set by the government until 1991. In 2004, annual flat-rate premiums averaged around €250 per subscriber.
1992	Sickness funds were permitted to operate nationwide, thereby losing their regional monopoly position. Subscribers were allowed to switch to another fund every 2 years (every year from 1997).
1992	With the introduction of maximum fees for medical care, sickness funds and private insurers were given the option to negotiate lower fees with providers.
1993	To encourage efficiency, a prospective reimbursement scheme for sickness funds was introduced by means of risk-adjusted capitation payments. This scheme put an end to the principle of full retrospective cost reimbursement. The average risk that the funds incurred increased from 3% of their spending in 1995 to approximately 50% in 2004. Since its inception, the risk equalization scheme has become ever more sophisticated.
1994	Sickness funds were given the option to selectively contract with physicians, physiotherapists and pharmacists.
1995	Start of the development of a case-mix financing system for hospital care to replace the fixed budget system based on capacity.
1998	As a consequence of the new Competition Act (*Mededingingswet*) mergers of provider organizations or health insurers required pre-authorization by the Netherlands Competition Authority.

Source: Authors.

"given back" to the private sector after years of increasing state interference. Acknowledging serious market failures in health care and health insurance, the role of the state would be to create optimal conditions for competition and define public constraints to competition or public interests to preserve solidarity, universal access and affordability. A private scheme with public constraints could resolve the conflict between competition and public interests in health care. A private model was seen as the best way to stimulate entrepreneurial behaviour in health care and health insurers were therefore to be permitted to operate on a for-profit basis, although with a 10-year moratorium on the distribution of any profits. It also defined the market role of consumers in health care: the relationship between insurers and subscribers was to be based on an annual contractual arrangement that the subscribers could choose to renew or terminate. With this strategic choice, the government took a different route from Dekker and the 2000 report. The latter had opted for a universal scheme under public law with a leading role for the state to reflect the tradition and social nature of health insurance in the Netherlands.

Opting for a private model not only reflected a neoliberal trend in Dutch public policy-making at the time, it was also necessary in order to overcome opposition from private insurers, many of whom were negative about the reform. Whereas many sickness funds were sceptical about competition, private insurers feared that a single scheme would deprive them of their business and lead to a further increase in regulation. The private model was therefore a political instrument to temper their concerns. It was also a heavily contested choice and an important reason for the Labour Party to vote against the new legislation, even though it supported the idea of a universal scheme.

Health insurance post 2006

The 2006 Health Insurance Act (*Zorgverzekeringswet*) put an end to the traditional distinction between sickness funds and private insurers, introducing a single scheme covering all legal residents. The scheme is known as the basic health insurance scheme to be distinguished from the many complementary insurance schemes covering extra services not included in the benefits package of the basic scheme. The basic scheme was seen as significantly improving solidarity in health insurance. Implemented by private insurers, including former sickness funds, the new health insurance legislation created an institutional setting intended to encourage competition between insurers which, in turn, was expected to increase efficiency, to make health care more demand-driven and to improve its quality. It was also an attempt to upgrade the insurers' role in health care. They were positioned as a countervailing power to providers. Their new role was to negotiate on behalf of their customers with providers on the costs, volume and quality of care within an institutional structure set by the state.

To stimulate consumer choice and competition the new legislation gives residents the right to terminate their contract at the end of the year and switch to another insurer or type of health plan. However, consumer choice is not unrestricted. Every resident is obliged to purchase a basic health plan (to be distinguished from complementary plans). Any person who fails to do so is uninsured. Insurers must offer open enrolment and cannot terminate contracts (ban on risk selection). A standard benefits package, similar to the benefits previously covered by sickness funds, is determined by government to prevent consumers from under-insuring themselves, to facilitate competition by enabling value-for-money comparison across insurers and to prevent risk selection through product differentiation. All adults pay an income-related contribution set by the government (see Fig. 11.1). These contributions flow into a central risk equalization fund, which compensates insurers for differences in the risk profile of their subscribers by means of a sophisticated risk-adjustment formula. The government pays contributions for children aged under 18 (Van de Ven & Schut, 2008).

To foster competition, subscribers pay a flat-rate premium (known as a nominal premium) directly to their insurer. Each insurer is allowed

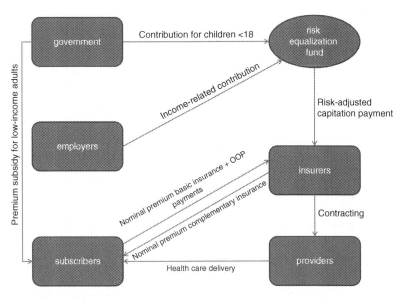

Figure 11.1 Health insurance in the Netherlands after the 2006 reform

Source: Adapted from Maarse (2009).

to set its own nominal premium, which may vary depending on the nature of benefits selected by subscribers (for example, benefits in kind versus reimbursement, lower premiums for preferred-provider networks or higher voluntary deductibles), but cannot vary according to age, sex or pre-existing medical conditions.

The Health Care Allowance Act (*Wet op de Zorgtoeslag*) compensates subscribers with low incomes for the cost of their nominal premium by means of an income-related cash subsidy (health care allowance). Competition is also stimulated by allowing insurers to negotiate with providers on health care prices, care volumes, service levels and also quality of care. To reinforce their negotiating power, the new legislation permits selective contracting of preferred providers. At the same time, insurers are obliged to guarantee their subscribers access to all types of care covered by the basic health plan (Van de Ven & Schut, 2008)

To make people more aware of the costs of health care and motivate them to abstain from unnecessary care, the reform introduced a no-claims arrangement under which each subscriber had to pay a government-set annual charge of €255 on top of the nominal premium. Subscribers who incurred no health care costs in a given year received a refund of this premium (those who spent less than €255 received the difference). Because the refund did not prove to be cost-effective (Goudriaan et al., 2006), it was replaced in 2008 with a mandatory annual deductible of €150. Children under 18, maternity care and general practitioner consultations are exempt from the mandatory deductible. Since then the mandatory deductible has been elevated every year to €395 in 2016 with a jump from €220 to €350 in 2013. The deductible has always been controversial in Dutch health care politics, particularly after some compensation programmes (health care allowances) ended in 2014 (see for example Section 3.3.1 in Kroneman et al., 2016). Municipalities have been made responsible for tailor-made compensation for which they receive a limited grant from the government. The Health Insurance Act also permits insurers to offer their subscribers a lower deductible under certain conditions. Opponents frame the mandatory deductible as a so-called penalty for disease and claim that it causes people to forgo care. There is some evidence for this adverse effect but evidence of its magnitude is missing (Van Esch et al. 2015).

The new scheme builds upon the traditional division between basic and complementary health insurance. Although the purchase of the basic plan is mandatory, taking out a complementary plan is voluntary. In fact, one may consider complementary health insurance as pure private health insurers: insurers are free to set their own policy conditions and benefits.

In 2015, revenues from nominal premiums accounted for 36.6% of total health insurance revenues (excluding complementary private health insurance cover), revenues from income-related contributions for 50%, state grant for children for 5.9% and out-of-pocket payments for 7.5% (Ministry of Health, 2016).

The many regulations, mainly aimed at protecting the general good, make the new scheme different from pure private schemes, which usually feature a high degree of voluntary action, differentiated products, risk-related premiums and medical underwriting. In fact, debate about whether or not the new scheme is seen as public or private is to some extent semantic and depends on the perspective taken. The fact that the new scheme is mandatory and includes many legal provisions to protect the general good may be used to argue that it is a public rather than private scheme. This is also reflected in health care statistics: between 2004 and 2006 the share of public financing in current expenditure on health jumped from 65.6% to 85.7% (OECD, 2016). However, from the subscriber and insurer perspectives (annual contracts; private insurers, some commercial) it is clearly a private scheme.

The mixed public–private nature of the new scheme raised a debate about the compatibility of the new scheme, presented as a private scheme, with the third non-life Insurance Directive of the European Economic Community. The Directive permits governments to set rules to protect the general good, but these rules must be necessary and proportional. Communication with the European Commission on this issue established that the regulations were indeed necessary and proportional.

Effects of the 2006 reform

Effects on consumer behaviour

Table 11.3 summarizes some trends in consumer behaviour after the enactment of the Health Insurance Act.

After an unexpected 18% of subscribers switched in 2006, consumer mobility dropped significantly. In 2010–2015 it was hovering at around 6–7%, still suggesting a competitive health insurance market. Only 1.5% of consumers switched four times or more to another insurer

Table 11.3 *Trends in consumer behaviour in the Netherlands, 2006–2015*

	2006	2007	2008	2009	2010	2011	2012	2013	2014	2015
Consumer mobility (% subscribers[a])	18	3.5	3.5	3.9	5.5	6.0	6.0	8.2	7.0	6.3
Subscribers in collective plan (% all subscribers)	52	58	59	60	64	65	67	68	70	69
Subscribers without complementary insurance (% all subscribers)	7	7	8	10	11	11	12.2	14.2	15.8	15.9
Subscribers with voluntary deductible (% all subscribers)	n.a.	n.a.	n.a.	n.a.	5.9	5.9	6.9	9.5	10.8	11.7
Subscribers with budget plan[b] (% all subscribers)	0.	0	0	0	0	1.0	1.7	3.3	4.4	7.3

Source: Vektis (2016).

Notes: n.a.: not available.

[a] Subscribers switching to another insurer in a given year.

[b] Budget plans are lower-priced plans with preselected providers for planned care.

in 2006–2016; 73% had never switched (Vektis, 2016). Consumer mobility was highest among younger, more educated people, people who perceived their health to be good, people living in large cities and adults with a partner and one or more children. The most important reason for switching was to benefit from a lower premium.

The new scheme allows employers or other groups (for example, members of a sports club, patient associations) to negotiate a collective contract in return for a discounted nominal premium. Legislation limits the maximum premium discount to 10%. Before the 2006 reform, employer-based contracts were common in private health insurance. After the reform, the market for collective contracts became very competitive because insurers sought opportunities for expansion in this market segment. Currently, collective contracts account for more than two thirds of the market. More than two thirds of collective contracts are employer-based. Collective contracts have always been controversial, because they undermine solidarity (see below). There are also questions about their added value for employers and subscribers.

Complementary plans have long been popular in Dutch health care. However, Table 11.3 shows a steady decline of the percentage of subscribers with such a plan. The drop is probably due to the substantial increase in the premiums of complementary plans as well as some declines in benefit levels (see Table 11.4); decreases in premiums observed since 2012 do not seem to have affected this negative trend.

The low percentage of subscribers with a voluntary deductible on top of the mandatory deductible suggests a widespread attitude of risk aversion in health insurance. Nevertheless, the percentage of subscribers with a voluntary deductible doubled to 12% between 2010 and 2015. Of these subscribers 71% opted for a maximum voluntary deductible of €500 (Vektis, 2016).

Freedom of choice

The 2006 reform was, among others, intended to give consumers more choice. Under the new legislation they can switch to another insurer by the end of the year and to another type of health insurance plan. There is a choice between benefit-in-kind plans, cost-reimbursement plans and a combination of both. Insurers also offer lower-priced plans with preselected providers for planned care (budget plans), lower reimbursement percentages for noncontracted care and on-line communication between insurer and subscriber. The number of these budget plans grew from 5 in 2011 to 17 in 2015. The total number of insurance plans was 71 in 2015 (NZa, 2016). Opponents of competition in health insurance often criticize this number. In their view it is a source of waste and many customers are not able to compare plans and make an informed choice.

Customers may also be deceived by the complexity of insurance plans. For instance, it may be unclear to them which providers have been contracted by their insurer, although insurers are requested to list the contracted providers on their websites.

Premium and contributions

Table 11.4 shows the development of the average nominal premium rate for individual subscribers and subscribers with a collective insurance plan since 2008. The percentages demonstrate that individual subscribers pay a higher nominal premium than subscribers with a collective plan do. As the cost to premium ratios of individual and group plans do not differ much it seems evident that subscribers with an individual plan pay for the premium discounts in collective plans.

Between 2008 and 2012 the average nominal premium rose by 16.3%. The remarkable drop in 2014 is attributable to the insurers' decision to use their financial reserves to lower premiums. Insurers claim that they did so voluntarily, but political pressure also played a role (in its calculation of the expected premium, the government assumed that insurance companies would transfer €500 million from their reserves to lower subscriber premiums; Maarse, Jeurissen & Ruwaard, 2016). The lower premium was a one-off event; further increases are expected in the future. However, the average premium in 2015 was still less than the average premium in 2011. There is a large variation in premium rates. For example, in 2014, the difference between the highest-priced and lowest-priced nominal premiums was 30% (Vektis, 2016). The maximum income-related contribution has risen by 60.6% since 2008, but this is less visible because it is part of income tax.

Non-insured and defaulters

Under the Health Insurance Act each person aged 18 years and older is requested to purchase a basic health insurance plan. A person who fails to do so is uninsured. The number of people without insurance

Table 11.4 *The development of nominal premium and income-related contribution rates in the Netherlands, 2008–2015*

Average annual premium and contribution rates	2008	2009	2010	2011	2012	2013	2014	2015
Nominal premium paid by individual subscribers	1081	1088	1127	1226	1241	1230	1111	1164
Nominal premium paid by subscribers with collective plans	1010	1033	1055	1168	1195	1188	1060	1120
Average nominal premium (individual and collective subscribers)	1040	1056	1082	1188	1210	1201	1076	1133
Premium for complementary plans	263	278	288	308	322	314	308	n.a.
State-set income-related contribution rate (%)	7.2	6.9	7.05	7.75	7.1	7.75	7.5	6.95
Maximum income-related contribution (€)	2249	2233	2340	2591	3535	3941	3856	3612

Sources: Vektis (2016); www.zorginstituutnederland.nl.

is estimated at 0.1% (NZa, 2016). This low percentage is attributable to a joint campaign conducted by the government, municipalities and insurers to track uninsured people. A more serious problem is the number of defaulters, defined as people who failed to pay their insurance premium over an uninterrupted period of 6 months. The latest estimate of the number of defaulters showed a decline from 325 000 in 2014 to 280 000 in 2015 (2.1% of insured people aged 18 or older) (Ministry of Health, 2016). This reduction is attributable to a new legislation which enables insurers to make tailor-made arrangements with defaulters on repayment schedule.

Effects on the insurer market

The number of insurers had already seen a steady decline in the pre-reform period (see Fig. 11.2). Consolidation was driven by the need to reduce administrative costs and enhance risk pooling. In 2006 the total number of insurers fell by a further 42% (from 75 to 53) due to mergers between sickness funds and private insurers. In 2015, there were 25 health insurers, grouped into nine business companies. The four largest companies each had a market share of between 13% and 32%; together the so-called big four covered about 90% of the market. In 2006–2016 no new insurance company managed to enter the market; one company tried to do so but failed. The oligopolistic and, in some regions, even semi-monopolistic, structure of the health insurance market has given rise to concerns because of the danger of cartel formation

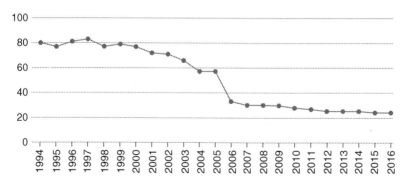

Figure 11.2 Number of insurers in the Netherlands, 1994–2016

Source: Vektis (2016).

and the erosion of consumer choice. It also explains why providers, in particular providers working in private practices, complain about the strong power position of health insurers. They perceive the insurers' contract as a dictate. Insurers on their side argue that their power position is grossly overstated, particularly in relation to hospitals (Maarse, Jeurissen & Ruwaard, 2016). The latter conclusion was recently also drawn in a report on the newly established power balance in Dutch health care. There is a great deal of mutual dependence between insurers and providers: insurers feel compelled to contract almost all providers, especially hospitals and primary care offices (Loozen, Varkevisser & Schut, 2016).

Another aspect of the insurer market is administrative costs. In 2005 these costs were 4.2% for sickness funds and 10.7% for private insurers. Total administrative costs decreased to 3.0% in 2015. Hence, the reform has resulted in lower administrative costs. Administrative costs also include the costs of marketing (and commissioning) which critics of competition see as waste of public money. Administrative costs of complementary health insurance plans are significantly higher (12.4%) (Vektis, 2016).

The financial position of insurers is sound. After incurring deficits in the 2006–2008 period, insurers have achieved surpluses since 2009. For instance, in 2013 their legally required solvency rate was more than twice the officially required rate of 11% (Vektis, 2016). These results have prompted a political discussion on the insurers' surplus, mostly framed as high profits.

Contracting

The cornerstone of the 2006 reform was to transform health insurers from relatively passive bureaucratic reimbursement agencies into active health care purchasers who negotiate with providers to obtain high-quality health care at low cost for their subscribers. Under the new legislation they are no longer obliged to contract with each provider. For a long period of time negotiations on prices, volume and quality were barely possible. Insurers simply had no reliable information on costs and quality of care. The market structure in some regions and fear of reputation damage were also not conducive to insurers engaging in hard negotiations. Furthermore, there was a temporary safety-net in place, which compensated insurers for a deficit.

This situation has changed. More information is now available on quality and prices. Whether quality is really an important topic in the negotiations is disputed. Insurers say that they focus on quality, but, according to anecdotal evidence, providers often claim that quality of care is not the key subject in negotiations. Nevertheless, hospitals are no longer automatically contracted for all types of care. In 2010, a large insurer announced that it would no longer contract four hospitals for breast cancer surgery, because the quality of their breast cancer care, measured in terms of capacity, volume (number of operations) and patient satisfaction, did not meet minimum standards. This initiative has been followed by other insurers, mostly for some forms of elective surgery. Some insurers have also set up insurance plans with pre-selected providers. Most contracting currently comes down to negotiating an annual-budget and a predetermined volume level. In 2015, for the first time since the 2006 reform, a contract between a health insurer and a hospital explicitly concerned improved quality. The cardiology department of the Catherina Hospital and insurer CZ have developed a method to measure quality. If quality improves, the hospital receives an extra amount of money. Another new development is for insurers to agree on multi-year hospital budgets. This gives the hospitals more leeway in the use of their resources, especially when patient volumes decline. One large insurer (VGZ) had 10 such agreements in 2017 (www.nu.nl).

To influence patient decisions about choice of provider, insurers have so far mainly used soft instruments, such as providing them with information on waiting times for different hospitals. Some insurers use positive incentives, such as waiving the mandatory deductible if patients visit a preferred hospital; others require patients to visit preferred providers for non-emergency care. However, the use of such incentives by insurers and patients is still marginal.

Impact on solidarity

As discussed before, one of the objectives of the reform was to strengthen solidarity by putting an end to the traditional dual structure of health insurance and introducing a single and mandatory scheme for all legal residents in the Netherlands. What is the impact of the reform on solidarity?

Let us first look at income solidarity by analysing income-related contributions. Two points are important here. First, it should be mentioned that there is a cap on the income-related contribution. As a result, people with low incomes pay proportionally more than people whose income is higher than the maximum threshold set by the state. The second point relates to the nominal premium subsidy for people with low incomes. In 2013, 62% of households qualified for a subsidy. The government's policy has been to rein in spending, not only by reducing the number of people qualifying for a subsidy but also by reducing the level of compensation (people with the lowest incomes were exempted from this measure). A rough analysis by Vermeend & van Boxtel (2010) concluded that health care financing was still regressive after the reform, even when taking into account the state-paid compensation.

To guarantee risk solidarity, the Health Insurance Act obliges insurers to accept each applicant (open enrolment). Furthermore, insurers are forbidden to differentiate their premiums according to medical risk; instead, they must apply a community rating (ban on premium differentiation). Offering differentiated benefits packages to their customers is also restricted because the basic benefit package is set by the Minister of Health. Furthermore, a sophisticated risk equalization scheme is in place to compensate insurers for differences in risk profile. According to the theory of regulated competition, variation in nominal premium rates should predominantly reflect differences in efficiency (Van de Ven et al., 2013).

Despite the formal ban, risk selection cannot be ruled out (Duijmelinck et al., 2013). The main cause for this is that the risk equalization scheme is imperfect (if it is ever possible to construct a perfect scheme). The following example serves as an illustration. If one singles out the group of subscribers with the worst score on health, insurers would make a predictable loss of €2275 if risk compensation was absent. Risk-adjusted payments from the equalization fund reduce this loss, whereby sophisticated models with several parameters reduce it by more than simple models. However, even with the most sophisticated model the predictable loss for this group of subscribers is still estimated at €646 a year (Van Kleef, Van Vliet & van de Ven, 2012). The loss makes it attractive for insurers to look for loopholes in the legislation to circumvent the ban on risk selection. There are several strategies for this, including targeting young people with higher incomes (although this is officially forbidden) or offering a significant discount in exchange for a voluntary deductible. Indeed, people with more favourable risk profiles switch more between plans and more often choose a voluntary deductible (NZa, 2016).

Impact on health care spending

One of the objectives of the reform was to foster competition and, in that way, curb annual growth in health spending. Is there evidence for this effect? To answer this question, it should first be emphasized that the introduction of the reform was an expensive affair, with the implementation of the scheme to compensate people with low incomes for the nominal premium costing around €2.5 billion. One can argue that the reform would not have been feasible in times of austerity (between 2004 and 2006 the national economy flourished). Also note in this respect that the reform, contrary to the reform of long-term care in 2015, did not at the time explicitly seek any significant expenditure cuts (Maarse & Jeurissen, 2016).

Fig. 11.3 presents the average annual percentage growth of health care expenditure in three consecutive periods. The percentages clearly exhibit a declining trend. The high percentage in 2000–2005 is largely

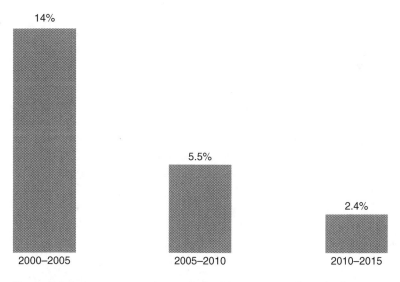

Figure 11.3 Average growth rates in health care expenditure in the Netherlands, 2000–2015

Source: www.zorginstituutnederland.nl.

attributable to the government's policy of removing waiting lists. The lower percentages in 2005–2010 and particularly 2010–2015 are often used in the political debate to argue that the new system is effective in curtailing health care expenditure growth (since 2012, health care spending has been lower than the maximum growth rate set by the government). However, there is limited evidence for this claim. Although price negotiations may have had some effect, it seems more plausible that the low growth rate in 2010–2015 was largely the result of an agreement in 2012 between the government and the national associations of hospitals and insurers to cap the annual growth of hospital expenditure to 2.5% in the 2012–2015 period. In a renewed agreement in 2013 the percentage was further reduced to 1% in the 2015–2017 period. The agreement nicely fits in the tradition of shared responsibility of the government and the national associations in health care policy-making (and many other policy sectors) (Maarse, Jeurissen & Ruwaard, 2016). However, it seems antithetical to competition to set maximum growth rates. The agreement also demonstrates that the scope for market competition in the Netherlands should not be overstated.

One area where competition seems to work is the market of outpatient generic drugs. Health insurers have managed to negotiate significant price cuts, as a result of which total spending on prescription medicines has been flat in nominal terms over the last decade (www.farminform.nl).

Trust

As explained before, the reform has always been controversial. An important aspect of this controversy is trust (or lack of trust) in health insurers. According to a recent survey, 57% of respondents said that they were satisfied with their insurer. However, when asked about the role of insurers in general, one can observe a serious lack of trust: only 31% of the respondents said they trusted health insurers. For GPs and hospitals these figures were, respectively, 87% and 73%. Insurers often tend to be seen as money-driven organizations making 'too high profits' (Brabers, Reitsma-van Rooijen & De Jong, 2014). One may speak of a problem of trust: patients seem to trust their doctor, but not so much their insurance company (Boonen & Schut, 2011). Over time this may undermine efforts to increase efficiency through the use of selective purchasing (see also Discussion).

The low level of trust motivated insurers to start a campaign in the media in 2015 to explain what they were doing and how they defined their role in the new system. The effect of this campaign on public opinion is unclear.

Discussion and conclusions

Private health insurance has always been a constituent element of health insurance in the Netherlands. The traditional distinction between the sickness funds and private insurers that developed in the pre-war period was legally institutionalized in the Sickness Fund Decree of 1941 and later by the Sickness Funds Act of 1964, which introduced compulsory insurance for a section of the Dutch population (employees earning below a threshold). Those not entitled to join sickness funds had to rely (voluntarily) on private health insurance to be protected against the costs of ill health. As a result, about 35% of the population had private cover, although this figure is misleading because it includes people covered by arrangements for specific categories of public servants and people covered by the WTZ. The share of the population with pure private health insurance was estimated at 24% in 2005.

The 2006 reform had major implications for private health insurance. Substitutive cover was integrated with the sickness fund scheme to form a single, mandatory scheme covering the whole population. This should be understood as a major achievement, putting an end to decades of political discussions. The new scheme is operated by private insurers, many of them former sickness funds. From a legal perspective, the new scheme is private. However, the legislation contains many provisions – termed public constraints – to preserve the general good. As a result, it may be concluded that the new scheme is an attempt to combine private structure and social purpose – an arrangement that could be called a private social health insurance scheme. The scheme's hybrid status is important from the perspective of European Union competition and single market rules.

The health insurance reform triggered a change that can be best described as gradual transformation. On the one hand it implied a significant alteration of the health insurance landscape with the introduction of a single mandatory scheme operated by private insurers under private law as the most significant institutional changes. At the same time, many elements of the former sickness fund scheme were continued. The Health Insurance Act includes numerous public constraints to preserve the legacy of the past and avoid the adverse consequences of an unregulated private health insurance market for solidarity and universal access.

From the very beginning the reform has been controversial. It took, for instance, almost 20 years between the publication of the report *Willingness to Change* (1987), which recommended a reform based upon the principles of regulated competition, and the year the Health Insurance Act came into force (2006). This long period indicates that the need for and direction of reform were not self-evident. Controversy has not weakened since 2006. This is perhaps best illustrated by an event in 2013 when the government's legislative proposal to stimulate selective contracting by relieving insurers from an unofficial obligation to reimburse 75–80% of the costs of noncontracted care was defeated in the Upper Chamber. The government's proposal was rejected on the grounds that it would restrict free choice of physician.

Currently, health insurance is still the subject of a political struggle. There is much debate on the size of the mandatory deductible, which is seen as an unfair obstacle to accessing medical care. Left-wing political parties argue for a lowering or even full abolition of the deductible, which would require significantly higher premiums or income-related contributions. Another hot issue is the presumed power of insurers. The election programme of the Socialist Party included a proposal for a radical overhaul of the present health insurance landscape by introducing what is called a National Health Fund, the elimination of all insurers, the replacement of nominal premiums with only income-related contributions and the abolition of any mandatory deductible. The probability of acceptance of this plan seems low, not only because it would be very costly, but also because it would trigger a new ideological debate on the structure of health care. Many practical problems would remain unsolved for years. There is also little enthusiasm for the introduction of a National Health Fund among most other parties. The proposal signifies the contested structure of the current form of health insurance arrangements, but there is no good reason to believe that this will alter in the near future.

References

Boonen L, Schut F (2011). Preferred providers and the credible commitment problem in health insurance: first experiences with the implementation of managed competition in the Dutch health care system. *Health Economics, Policy and Law*, 6:219–35.

Brabers A, Reitsma-van Rooijen M, De Jong J (2014). *Barometer Vertrouwen in de gezondheidszorg* (Barometer trust in health care). Utrecht, NIVEL: www.nivel.nl/consumentenpane; accessed on 11/12/2016.

De Bruine M, Schut F (1990). Overheidsbeleid en ziektekostenverzekering (Public policy and health insurance). In: Maarse J, Mur-Veeman I, eds). *Beleid en beheer in de gezondheidszorg* (Policy and administration in health care). Assen/Maastricht: Van Gorcum, 114–49.

Duijmelinck D et al. (2013). *Overstapgedrag en risicoselectie op de zorgverzekeringsmarkt* (Switching behaviour and risk selection on the health insurance market), report iBMG. Rotterdam, Erasmus University.

Goudriaan R et al. (2006). *Evaluatie van de no-claimteruggaveregeling* (Evaluation of the no-claim refund arrangement). The Hague, Aarts De Jong Wilms Goudriaan Public Economics bv (APE).

Helderman J et al. (2005) Market-oriented health care reforms and policy learning in the Netherlands. *Journal of Health Politics, Policy and Law*, 30(1–2):189–210.

Kompanje KP, ed. (2008). *Tussen volksverzekering en vrije markt* (Between statutory insurance and free market). Amsterdam, Aksant.

Kroneman M et al. (2016). The Netherlands: health system review. *Health Systems in Transition*, 18(2):1–239.

Laske-Aldershof T, Schut F (2005). *Monitor verzekerdenmobiliteit* (Monitor consumer mobility in health insurance). Rotterdam, Erasmus University/ iBMG.

Lieverdink H (1999). Collectieve besluiten, belangen en wetgeving. De totstandkoming van tarieven voor medisch specialisten in Nederland tussen 1986 en 1992 (Collective decisions, interests and legislation. The establishment of tariffs for medical specialists in the Netherlands between 1986 and 1992) [thesis]. Maastricht, Datawyse.

Loozen E, Varkevisser M, Schut F (2016). *Goede zorginkoop vergt gezonde machtsverhoudingen. Het belang van markt- en mededingingstoezicht binnen het Nederlandse zorgstelsel* (Good purchasing requires sound power relations. The importance of market and competition oversight in Dutch health care). Rotterdam, Instituut Beleid & Management Gezondheidszorg.

Maarse H (2009). The Netherlands. In: Thomson S, Mossialos E, eds. *Private health insurance in the European Union*. London, European Commission by the London School of Economic and Political Science.

Maarse H, Jeurissen P (2016). The policy and politics of the 2015 long-term care reform in the Netherlands. Health Policy, 20(3):241–5.

Maarse H, Jeurissen P, Ruwaard D (2016). Results of the market-oriented reform in the Netherlands: a review. *Health Economics, Policy and Law*, 11(2):161–78.

Ministry of Health, Welfare and Sports (2016). *Begroting 2017* (Budget Estimate 2017). The Hague, MOHW.

NZa (2016). *Marktscan zorgverzekeringsmarkt 2016* (Marketscan Health Insurance 2016). Utrecht, the Netherlands, Nederlandse Zorgautoriteit (NZa).

OECD (2016). OECD Health Statistics. www.oecd.org/els/health-systems/health-data.htm.

Okma K (1997). Studies on Dutch health policies, politics and law [thesis]. Rijswijk.

Schut F (1995). Competition in the Dutch health care sector [thesis]. Rotterdam, Erasmus University.

Van der Grinten T (2007). *Zorgen om beleid. Over blijvende afhankelijkheden en veranderende Bestuurlijke verhoudingen* (On lasting dependencies and changing administrative relations in health care). Rotterdam, Erasmus University/iBMG.

Van Esch T et al. (2015). *Inzicht in zorgmijden. Aard, omvang, redenen en achtergrondkenmerken (Insights in avoiding healthcare* (Typicalities, extent, reasons and background characteristics). Utrecht, Nivel.

Van Kleef R, Van Vliet R, van de Ven W (2012). *Risicoverevening. Een analyse van voorspelbare winsten en verliezen op subgroepniveau* (Risk equalisation. An analysis of predictable gains and losses on subgroup level). Rotterdam, Erasmus University/iBMG.

Van de Ven W, Schut F (2008). Universal mandatory health insurance in the Netherlands: a model for the United States? *Health Affairs*, 27(3):771–81.

Van de Ven W et al. (2013). Preconditions for efficiency and affordability in competitive healthcare markets: are they fulfilled in Belgium, Germany, Israel, the Netherlands and Switzerland. *Health Policy*, 109(3):226–45.

Vektis (2006). *Zorgmonitor 2006* (Health care monitor). Driebergen/Zeist, Vektis.

Vektis (2016). *Zorgthermometer. Verzekerden in beweging 2016* (Care thermometer. Mobility in health insurance). Zeist, the Vektis.

Veraghtert K, Widdershoven B (2002). *Twee eeuwen solidariteit. De Nederlandse, Belgische en Duitse ziekenfondsen tijdens de negentiende en de twintigste eeuw* (Two centuries of solidarity: the Dutch, Belgian and German sickness funds in the nineteenth and twentieth century). Amsterdam/Zeist, Aksant.

Vermeend W, van Boxtel R (2010). *Uitdagingen voor een gezonde zorg* (Challenges to a healthy health care). Amsterdam, Lebowski Publishers.

Willems Commission (1994). Parlementair onderzoek besluitvorming volksgezondheid (*Parliamentary Investigation On Decision-making in Public Health*. The Hague, Willems Commission.

12 The challenges of pursuing private health insurance in low- and middle-income countries: lessons from South Africa

DI MCINTYRE AND HEATHER MCLEOD

South Africa's apartheid history of legislated discrimination on the basis of race has left a legacy of massive income inequalities – with, at 0.63 in 2011, one of the highest Gini coefficients in the world (World Bank, 2017) – and inequalities in access to social services. It has also left an indelible imprint on the health sector, where private health insurance was developed to serve white workers, whereas the public health sector served the majority black population and lower-income whites.[1] Since the first democratic elections in 1994, there has been considerable commitment to addressing these inequalities. However, progress has been limited: income inequalities have in fact been growing and inequalities within the health sector are increasingly related to class rather than race.

The development of private health insurance, and policy related to it, has been heavily influenced by the social and political context. Medical schemes (the name given to private health insurance organizations in South Africa) were introduced at the turn of the 20th century, under British rule, for white mineworkers, and restricted to white South Africans until the 1970s. The number of schemes grew rapidly from the 1940s, alongside the growth of private providers. The apartheid government actively promoted privatization of health care financing and provision during the 1980s, deregulating medical schemes in 1988. Following transition to a democratic government in 1994, there were concerted efforts to re-regulate medical schemes, but in spite of

---

[1] The use of the terms African, Coloured, Indian (and the combined group black) and white indicates a statutory stratification of the South African population in terms of the former Population Registration Act. The use of these terms does not imply the legitimacy of this racist terminology, but is necessary for highlighting the impact of former apartheid policies on the health system.

these reforms, medical schemes still reflect inequities in South African society. Only the wealthiest are able to afford medical scheme cover and they are often supported by their employers and by a substantial government subsidy through tax deductions for contributions. There have been ongoing debates about introducing some form of mandatory prepayment system to address inequities in the public–private health sector mix. Although a Green Paper on introducing a so-called National Health Insurance system was released in 2011 (Department of Health, 2011), followed by a White Paper in 2015 (Department of Health, 2015), policy proposals are yet to be finalized. This chapter explores health system inequalities, the substantial inefficiencies that plague the system and the role of private health insurance within the system.

Health system context and the role of private health insurance

South Africa has a dual health system. The private sector serves the higher-income minority and the public sector serves the vast majority of the population. Before 1994, the public health sector was very fragmented, with separate health departments for each race group and for each of the four former provinces and 10 former homelands.[2] In addition, curative and preventive primary care services were provided in separate facilities and administered by different health authorities and, until the late 1980s, there were separate hospitals and other public sector health care facilities for blacks and whites. Distribution of facilities was biased towards historically white areas, while certain geographic areas (rural areas, particularly former homeland areas, township areas and informal settlements) were systematically underfunded as a result of apartheid policies (McIntyre & Gilson, 2002). The public health sector was also biased towards hospital-based, curative care.

After 1994, a single Department of Health was created at the national level and one in each of the nine newly created provinces. A district health system has also been instituted and considerable emphasis placed on improving primary care, with an extensive clinic upgrading and building programme and a redistribution of financial resources to the primary

---

[2] The 1913 'Natives Land Act' confined Africans to living in ten 'homelands', which were established along 'tribal lines'. They were highly fragmented geographic areas scattered throughout South Africa and comprised less than 14% of the total surface area of the country.

care level. In addition, there have been efforts to redistribute public health care funds between provinces to redress historical inequities.

Medical schemes (non-profit organizations initially known as Friendly Societies) have existed since 1889. At first they were only open to whites; membership for groups other than whites began in the late 1970s (McIntyre & Dorrington, 1990). Historically, there has also been significant private provision of health care, including general practitioners (GPs) in solo or group practice, a limited number of primary care clinics run by nongovernmental organizations and some commercial health maintenance-type organizations. Initially, private hospitals were limited to non-profit mission hospitals in rural areas and industry-specific facilities such as on-site hospitals at large mines. For-profit hospitals developed later and have experienced particularly rapid growth since the 1980s, promoted by an explicit government policy of privatization and deregulation. This rapid growth has continued. By the end of the 1990s, as many as 73% of doctors worked in the private sector (van Rensburg & van Rensburg, 1999). Private hospital beds have been increasingly concentrated in three large hospital groups – Netcare, Life and Medi-Clinic (who together own 84% of all private hospital beds) (van den Heever, 2007). With the exception of nongovernmental organizations, most private providers are heavily concentrated in the metropolitan and other large urban areas.

Health care expenditure was approximately US$30.78 billion in 2013/14, equivalent to 8.6% of gross domestic product in that financial year (Department of Health, 2015). About 48% of total health care expenditure is channelled via public financing entities (including the national, provincial and local Departments of Health, the Departments of Defence, Correctional Services and Education as well as statutory funds for workers' compensation and road accidents). Private expenditure accounts for 50% of total funds. Medical schemes and provincial health departments each account for nearly 42% of total health spending. However, while medical schemes covered only 16% of the population in 2013, 84% of the population depends on provincial health department services, particularly for specialist and inpatient care. Direct out-of-pocket payments to providers account for nearly 7% of all health care funds.

Box 12.1 provides an overview of the health system. It is evident that one of the greatest challenges facing the health system is the inequitable public–private mix in health care financing and provision – the private

---

Box 12.1 Overview of the South African health system

Revenue collection

Sources of funds

- Burden of funding placed both on companies and individuals, but households ultimately bear most of the burden of funding health care services (through tax, insurance contributions and out-of-pocket payments). Employers increasingly offer their employees integrated cost-to-company packages and medical scheme contributions are effectively borne by the individuals because increased contribution levels reduce other elements of remuneration.

- Some population groups are not expected to contribute (for example, the lowest income groups do not have to pay income tax but do pay other forms of tax such as value added tax (VAT); pregnant women, children under six, the disabled, the elderly and the poor are exempt from user fees at government hospitals).

- Very little donor funding in South Africa (less than 2% of total health care funding).

Contribution mechanisms

General tax revenue

- Generated from personal income tax (35.8% of total tax revenue); VAT (26.5%); company tax (20.9%) and a range of customs, excise and other taxes and levies (16.8%).

- Personal income tax is structured progressively with exemptions for low-income earners and the marginal tax rate ranging from 26% to 41%.

- Company tax is charged at a flat rate of 28%.

- VAT is charged at 15%, but many basic foods are exempt from tax.

Private voluntary health insurance: medical schemes

- Community-rated contributions.

- Very few medical schemes relate contributions to income level; contributions are generally at a flat rate linked to a specific benefits package. A few company-based schemes provide income cross-subsidies.

Box 12.1 (cont.)

- Government offers a significant tax break to those with private medical scheme membership. Although partially reformed over the past decade (where total scheme contributions are now a taxable fringe benefit in the hands of the employee, with a generous amount of US$233 per person for the first two family members and US$157 per person[a] thereafter in the 2016/2017 tax year being regarded as a tax deductible allowance), those with the highest incomes benefit most from the subsidy, whereas those below the tax threshold receive no benefits.

Out-of-pocket payments

- User fees at public sector hospitals (there are no fees for primary care services) are differentiated according to income levels – the poor are exempt from fees (but there are difficulties in proving eligibility for exemptions). There are three additional income categories with very low fees for the lowest-income groups.
- Some low-income workers, who are not members of medical schemes, use private general practitioners (GPs) and retail pharmacies and pay on an out-of-pocket basis.
- The biggest share of out-of-pocket payments is attributable to medical scheme members, either in the form of cost sharing or payments for services that are not covered under the benefits package. Cost sharing is either in the form of flat amounts (co-payments) or percentage shares of the total bill (coinsurance).

Collecting organizations

- Tax is collected by the South African Revenue Service. The South African Revenue Service improved its tax collection mechanisms in the 2000s (through initially offering an amnesty to those who had not been tax compliant previously and then actively investigating noncompliance and imposing heavy fines) and, as a result, tax revenue has increased dramatically.
- Health insurance contributions are collected directly from members (often employer and employee payroll contributions) by the medical schemes. Each scheme has a Board of Trustees, which oversees the scheme's activities.

Box 12.1 (cont.)

Risk pooling

Coverage and composition of risk pools

- Medical schemes cover only 16% of the population and include high- and some middle-income formal sector workers and their immediate dependants. There is risk pooling within individual schemes in relation to the Prescribed Minimum Benefits (PMB) package (see section on Recent developments), but most schemes have individual medical savings accounts for primary care services. There are 83 medical schemes (2015) that compete with each other for members, and each scheme has a number of benefits packages (known as options), so there is a considerable fragmentation into some 300 small risk pools.

- The remaining 84% of the population is largely dependent on tax-funded health services, and comprises low-income formal sector workers, informal sector workers, the unemployed and the poor. A small part of this population pays out of pocket to purchase primary care services in the private sector, but is entirely dependent on the public sector for specialist and inpatient services. Therefore, there is a very large risk pool and anyone who needs care and is unable to pay will receive a user fee exemption (the exemption policy is liberally applied).

- There is no risk pooling between the tax funded pool and the medical schemes. The public–private mix is therefore the main challenge to equity: while medical schemes cover only 16% of the population, 50% of funds are in the private sector (the 42% funded through medical schemes and most of the 7% of out-of-pocket payments are made by scheme members).

Allocation mechanisms

- At present, there is no risk equalization between individual medical schemes; although risk equalization was proposed, which would have increased pooling between individual schemes, this has never been introduced. Even if it were introduced, this will not address the lack of pooling between the tax-funded pool and medical schemes environments unless there is explicit risk pooling across the sectors (McLeod, 2012b).

Box 12.1 (cont.)

- Tax funds are centrally collected. Funds are allocated from the central government to provinces (for all sectors) using a needs-based formula and then each province has the autonomy to decide how to allocate these funds to individual sectors (for example, health and education); that is, South Africa has a fiscal federal system.

Purchasing

Benefits package

- Those using tax-funded health services have a relatively comprehensive benefits package. No set of services is specified; instead South Africans have access to a full range of health services from those provided at primary care clinics through to those provided at highly specialized hospitals. Certain very expensive services (such as dialysis and organ transplantation) are implicitly rationed through resource constraints.
- All medical schemes have to cover services in the PMB package, which includes inpatient care, certain specialist services and care for common chronic conditions. Each scheme offers different benefits options, which include the PMB and various other services. Although schemes are not permitted to impose financial limits or charge co-payments for services in the PMB, there are considerable limits and co-payments for other services and large out-of-pocket payments for care outside the PMB package. The PMB package accounts for just over 50% of risk benefit expenditure in medical schemes, that is, excluding benefit expenditure paid from medical savings accounts. Some schemes (or benefits options within a scheme) specify the service providers that can be used (for example, a specific chain of private primary care clinics or a specific private hospital group or sometimes public hospitals) while others permit free choice of provider. Scheme members may choose to use public sector hospitals, for which their scheme will be expected to pay (although fees charged at public hospitals are the highest for medical scheme members, they are nevertheless lower than at private hospitals). There is an incentive for scheme members to declare their insurance status at public hospitals as the scheme will cover the entire bill. However, submission of bills by public hospitals to schemes is notoriously poor, not least because hospitals do not retain user fee revenues but instead remit them to the provincial Treasury.

Box 12.1 (cont.)

Purchaser–provider relationship and provider payment mechanisms

- Public sector facilities are allocated budgets from the provincial Department of Health, via districts, which are expected to develop plans and budgets that reflect the health needs of the local populations. All public sector staff are paid salaries.

- Medical schemes are the largest purchaser of private sector services (although some individuals purchase services directly from these providers). Medical schemes have not been very active in their purchasing activities and private providers have relatively more power in the process of purchasing and agreeing reimbursement mechanisms and rates (for example, the three large private hospital groups dominate these processes relative to the 83 schemes). Despite attempts at reform, private providers are still often paid on a fee-for-service basis. Some general practitioners have accepted capitation payments from medical schemes that serve lower-income groups. There are also a few private primary health care clinics that employ salaried staff. Private hospitals prefer to bill on a fee-for-service basis, but have agreed to per diem payments and case rate reimbursement for common operations with some schemes.

Provision

- There is an extensive and well-distributed network of public sector primary health care facilities. The hospital network is less well developed and hospital distribution is uneven (there is an average of 458 people per public hospital bed), with specialist services being heavily concentrated in certain provinces. The number of health professionals working in the public health sector is very low relative to the population it serves. There is considerable controversy at present about staff to population ratios in South Africa due to the poor quality of human resource data. However, according to the most recent estimates there were approximately 27 doctors per 100 000 inhabitants and 10.7 medical specialists per 100 000 inhabitants in the public sector in 2010 (Day & Gray, 2010).

Box 12.1 (cont.)

- The private health sector is very well developed but is heavily concentrated in the large metropolitan areas. There are three large private hospital groups (there is an average of 266 people per private hospital bed). The majority of health care professionals work in the private sector, despite serving a minority of the population. The most recent estimates indicate that there were 37 general practitioners per 100 000 inhabitants and 57 medical specialists per 100 000 inhabitants in the private sector in 2010 (Day & Gray, 2010).

- There is growing interest in complementary medicine among higher-income groups and 11 healing modalities (such as homeopathy) are formally recognized (Gqaleni et al., 2007). It is estimated that there are over 185 000 traditional healers in South Africa (Gqaleni et al., 2007) (that is, about 230 people per traditional healer) and these are in the process of becoming registered.[b] Payment for complementary and traditional medicine is almost entirely on an out-of-pocket basis.

Sources: Authors; all medical scheme information in this box is taken from CMS (2016).

Notes: [a] Average exchange rate in 2016: US$1 = 14.7 South African Rand.

[b] The Traditional Health Practitioners Act of 2007 was signed into law in 2008. The Interim Traditional Health Practitioners Council was inaugurated in 2013 (Sabinet, 2013).

---

health sector has the majority of financial and human resources, which are used to serve a minority of the population.[3]

Private health insurance market development and trends

Brief historical overview

The early history of private health insurance saw the unregulated formation of company-based health care funds, which were subsequently formalized under the Friendly Societies Act (1956) and later under the

---

[3] Medical scheme members are the major users of private sector services. By 2010, 'whites' made up only 35.7% of medical scheme beneficiaries (McLeod, 2012a). Hence, the minority using private services is now based on class or income level, rather than race.

Medical Schemes Act (1967) (see Box 12.2). Medical schemes were initially subject to community rating and minimum benefits requirements, and different schemes provided very similar benefits. Reforms implemented during the 1980s and early 1990s led to increasing use of private insurance principles (McLeod, 2005). The 1986 Browne Commission supported the application of risk and experience rating of contributions, as well as more individualized benefits (Department of Health, 2002). It also argued that there would be significant cost savings if members paid small claims themselves and only claimed from pooled funds after paying an initial amount. These measures would substantially reduce the size of risk pools and the degree of cross-subsidy between young, old, healthy and sick people.

Before 1989, a medical scheme could only vary its contribution rates based on income and number of dependants. After 1989, contributions could also be based on age, geographic area, extent of cover provided, length of membership, size of group and actual claims experience. Schemes were therefore able to reduce existing cross-subsidies in line with the view prevailing among insurance companies that cross-subsidies within health insurance were unfair. Hence, in 1994, the first democratic government inherited a medical scheme system characterized by risk rating. The same year, a leading scheme introduced personal medical savings accounts (MSAs), with no intervention from the regulator, and other schemes rapidly followed suit (see Chapter 13 in this volume).

Aggressive competition among medical schemes for low-risk members (risk selection) in the 1990s had adverse consequences in terms of health care equity and access, with older people and those with chronic diseases particularly affected. Throughout the 1990s, benefits declined and vulnerable groups were increasingly excluded from coverage. By 1999, no open scheme[4] permitted anyone over the age of 55 to join as an individual member and almost all open schemes applied lifetime exclusions for pre-existing conditions and used experience rating without restriction (Department of Health, 2002). Since 1994, policy formulation and legislation have turned back to solidarity principles, although medical schemes still operate in a voluntary membership environment. The substantially revised Medical Schemes Act No. 131 (1998) (the Act) has applied since 1 January 2000.

---

[4] Schemes may choose to restrict their membership if they are attached to a large employer, union or other defined group. In contrast, open schemes must freely admit anyone who applies.

Box 12.2 Key developments in the market for private health insurance in South Africa, 1889–2015

1880s to 1950s: Before regulation

- First employer-based private health insurance scheme, De Beers Consolidated Mines Ltd Benefit Society, set up (1889). Seven such schemes develop (1910)
- Public Health Act to coordinate health care (1919)
- Private practitioners develop. Rapid growth in unregulated medical schemes (48 schemes in 1940)
- Gluckman Commission proposes national health service similar to the British model but the political landscape shifts and the proposal is not implemented (1944) (Gluckman, 1944)
- Change of government and the beginning of the formal apartheid years (1948)
- Advisory Council for Medical Fund Societies formed (1950) to act as a representative in negotiations with organized doctors

1950s to 1970s: Early regulation and tariff conflict

- Financial control of schemes imposed by the Friendly Societies Act (1956). This included the need to maintain financial accounts, appoint an auditor, impose restrictions on loans to members, follow a certain process for mergers and submit annual accounts to the regulator. No legislated control of solvency margins
- Continued rapid growth in the number of schemes (to 169 schemes in 1960). These only serve the needs of the urban white middle class, for which membership is de facto mandatory via employment
- Calls for more regulation, but not mandatory membership, by Reinach Committee of the Snyman Commission (1962) (Reinach Committee, 1962)
- First Medical Schemes Act (No. 72 of 1967) creates Central Council for Medical Schemes to look after the interests of schemes with a registrar to oversee their activities. Minimum benefits for members and community rating formalized
- Remuneration Committee established to deal with fee-setting conflict between schemes and the medical profession (1969)
- Continued growth of medical schemes, which reach their highest number of 305 (1974)

Box 12.2 (cont.)

- Conflict between providers and schemes on tariffs escalates. Remuneration Committee is abolished and fees to be set by statutory medical council provided that doctors no longer contract out of tariff schedule (1978)
- Contracted-in doctors can send bills directly to medical schemes rather than to patients for payment (1980)

1984 to 1994: Free market reforms and risk rating

- Medical Schemes Amendment Act No. 59 of 1984 aims "to prevent the socialization of health services" and introduces a series of market reforms. Contracting-in is abolished. Each profession and supplier group to determine their own tariffs through their own statutory control bodies. Representative Association of Medical Schemes to determine the scale of fees for schemes after consultation with providers. If provider charges are equal to or less than the scale of benefits, the scheme must pay the provider directly (1984)
- Browne Commission (1986) argues that the public interest is served through the gradual privatization of public health services with the state responsible only for indigent patients. Recommends removal of minimum benefits, freedom in benefit design, risk rating for specific member groups (for example, age categories) and making consumers financially responsible for the cost of low-cost, high-frequency doctor claims
- Amendment to Regulation 8 of the Medical Schemes Act No. 72 of 1967 allows the market to determine the number of schemes and risk rate contributions (1989)
- Medical Schemes Amendment Act, No. 23, introduces further far-reaching changes, abolishing statutory guaranteed minimum benefits package and guaranteed payment for claims. The statutory role of the Representative Association of Medical Schemes in fee-setting also abolished. Schemes allowed to exclude or limit cover, risk rate to a greater extent and supply health care directly to members through their own facilities and by employing health professionals (1993)
- Melamet Commission established and reports just before transition to democratic government (Melamet Commission, 1994).

Box 12.2 (cont.)

Further deregulation recommended and insurance (underwriting at enrolment, freedom in benefit design, risk-rated premiums) argued to be the best way of providing health cover. Recommendations also include allowing brokers to charge commission, using a statutory actuary, investing in listed companies' shares and removing protections for retired persons. Insurance products provide non-indemnity cover, typically a fixed amount paid on occurrence of an event regardless of the actual spending. In contrast, medical schemes provide indemnity cover (the amount reimbursed is linked to actual spending). Insurance products to compete with medical schemes and both to be governed by a single piece of legislation. Scheme supervision and the role of trustees to be strengthened while the schemes to be given more autonomy: freedom with disclosure. Supervision of the industry and the regulator's office to be significantly strengthened with an independent statutory body (1993–1994)

1994 to 2000: Return to solidarity under democratic government

- African National Congress elected in the first democratic elections. Key African National Congress Health Plan published. Role of medical schemes to be further investigated, but principles already established for social health insurance (1994)
- Philosophical direction recommended by the Melamet Commission rejected and replaced by the strategic direction from the National Health Insurance Committee of Inquiry (1995) (South Africa (Republic), 1995)
- Completely revised Medical Schemes Act No. 131 (1998) prepares medical schemes for future social health insurance. Core principles of open enrolment, community rating and PMB re-established. Supervision of the industry substantially strengthened by the establishment of the Council for Medical Schemes (CMS) and the Registrar as an independent statutory regulator (1998, implemented from January 2000)
- Indemnity business (Medical Schemes Act) demarcated and legitimate health insurance (Long-term and Short-term Insurance Acts) clarified (1998). In effect, all indemnity cover (that is, related to actual spending) can only be offered by medical

Box 12.2 (cont.)

schemes. Health insurance products supplied by long- and short-term insurers can only provide non-indemnity cover and must not allow for payments directly to health care providers

2000 to 2008: Preparation for social health insurance

- Taylor Committee reports on a comprehensive social security framework, proposing to change retirement and health care funding from voluntary to mandatory for formally employed people (2002) (Department of Social Development 2002)
- Long-awaited National Health Act establishes the framework for the health system consisting of public, private and nongovernment components. The Department of Health to act as the steward of the whole health system, with responsibility for regulating the private sector to achieve national health objectives (2003)
- Competition Commission rules that collective fee-setting by the organizations representing medical schemes, health care providers and hospitals is not lawful. Temporary measures put in place for the CMS to determine national reference prices on behalf of the Department of Health. These used in negotiations between individual schemes and providers. Reimbursement levels typically expressed as a percentage of the National Health Reference Price List (NHRPL), although very large schemes also develop their own fee schedules (2004)
- Formula Consultative Task Team designs and obtains industry consensus on formula for risk equalization between schemes (McLeod et al., 2004). International Review Panel supports its findings and calls for urgent implementation (Armstrong et al., 2004). Task Team dealing with income cross-subsidies reports but does not obtain consensus or approval (2004)
- Extension of minimum benefits in medical schemes to cover diagnosis, treatment and medicine according to therapeutic algorithms for 25 common chronic conditions (2004)
- Introduction of regulations on medicine pricing (at the level of manufacturers, logistics service providers and dispensing fees for pharmacists and doctors). Spending on medicines, previously the main cost driver in medical schemes, now lower than spending on hospitals or specialists (2004)

Box 12.2 (cont.)

- Low Income Medical Schemes stakeholder consultative process reports on ways of extending cover to low-income workers (Broomberg, 2006), but no formal acceptance by the government (2006)
- Medical Schemes Amendment Bill No. 58 of 2008 provides for the establishment of a Risk Equalization Fund to be managed by the CMS to set up a framework for paying risk-adjusted amounts to medical schemes (2007, but not passed)
- Retirement reform accelerated as plans for a mandatory social retirement system are explored by an Inter-Ministerial Task Team (Ministerial Task Team on SHI, 2005). Health reforms lag behind (2007)
- Regulatory framework for NHRPL, to be managed by the Department of Health, established after delays. Some providers charge 300% of NHRPL and conflict in fee-setting escalates with members of medical schemes bearing the brunt of escalations. Industry concerned about hospital costs and calls for a central bargaining chamber for fee-setting (2007)
- Department of Health prepares NHRPL, but this is challenged in court by private provider groups. No effective regulation or guidance on private provider fees in place (2008–2011)

2008-present: Efforts to move towards universal health coverage

- The 52nd National Conference of the African National Congress (ruling party), held in Polokwane in mid-December 2007, commits to pursuing what is termed a National Health Insurance System. Substantive reform of medical scheme environment put on hold
- Green Paper on the National Health Insurance released in August 2011; suggests medical scheme cover could be restricted to top-up insurance
- The Competition Commission began a Market Inquiry into the Private Healthcare Sector in January 2014. The brief is to enquire into the state, nature and form of competition in the private health sector
- White Paper on the National Health Insurance released in December 2015; similar implications for medical scheme cover as Green Paper

The 1998 Medical Schemes Act

Since 1998, medical schemes have been clearly demarcated as the only vehicles providing for the reimbursement of actual spending on health (known as indemnity cover). Hence, any funding arrangement that is intended to assist in meeting the actual costs of medical services must satisfy the requirements of the Medical Schemes Act. These requirements include being registered under the jurisdiction of the Council for Medical Schemes (CMS), having financial guarantees, maintaining prescribed solvency levels, having at least 6000 principal members,[5] adhering to product design requirements and regular reporting to the Registrar of Medical Schemes, who is the chief executive of the CMS.

Crucially, the Act re-introduced three key principles to enhance risk pooling within schemes (Doherty & McLeod, 2003):

- *open enrolment*: open schemes have to accept anyone who wants to become a member at standard rates;
- *community rating*: everyone must be charged the same standard rate, regardless of age or state of health. Community rating currently applies to each benefits option in each medical scheme rather than for the industry as a whole;
- *prescribed minimum benefits*: a minimum benefits package as regulated by the CMS must be offered by all schemes. Beneficiaries must be covered in full for the specified conditions[6] with no financial limits or cost sharing. Schemes may insist on the use of a contracted network of preferred providers and drug formularies to manage care.

As the Act came into force, some schemes attempted to create hybrid products combining a medical scheme plan with high deductibles (no

---

[5] That is, members who pay contributions. Beneficiaries are all those covered by the medical scheme, including the families of principal members.

[6] The PMB package is a list of some 270 diagnosis and treatment pairs primarily offered in hospital (introduced on 1 January 2000); all emergency medical conditions (clarified from 1 January 2003); diagnosis, treatment and medicine according to therapeutic algorithms for 25 defined chronic conditions on the Chronic Disease List (introduced on 1 January 2004). The goal of introducing PMB was to cover potentially catastrophic costs and the costs of the most common chronic diseases.

underwriting, community rating, low commission) with a health insurance policy that exactly met the deductible (underwriting, risk rating, very high commission). The net effect was essentially to continue to offer risk-rated cover. Another challenge to the new environment included the excessive use of reinsurance contracts to transfer all of the risk from the non-profit medical scheme to a registered long-term insurer in the same financial group. These activities required decisive action by the new regulator. Despite considerable opposition over several years, the regulator prevailed and the industry settled down to the new legislative environment.

The Medical Schemes Act of 1998 provided for much stronger governance of medical schemes and the industry as a whole. Each scheme is now governed by a board of trustees, of which half are elected by members, and their duties are codified by the Act. The Act also tasked the CMS with the protection of beneficiaries, rather than with the protection of the industry, as was previously the case. Its executive arm, the office of the Registrar of Medical Schemes, has grown substantially from being a small deputy directorate within the Department of Health to being a statutory body with expanded regulatory powers. Funded by a levy on medical scheme members, the office is staffed by a professional team including accountants, lawyers, health economists and health professionals. In addition to regulation, the CMS is responsible for accrediting organizations that provide services to medical schemes.

Trends in private health insurance

Medical schemes have steadily declined in number from 305 in 1974 to 83 schemes in 2015 (CMS, 2016), and further consolidation is expected. In 1994, open and restricted schemes had approximately equal numbers of members. Open medical schemes, under the direction of aggressive insurance companies, began to use brokers to attract business with favourable risk profiles and gradually the entire open scheme market followed. Brokers were only legally recognized from 2000, by which time nearly 70% of all medical schemes members belonged to open schemes. Brokers' costs incurred by open schemes constituted 1.2% of gross contribution income and 14% of non-health care spending by these schemes in 2015 (CMS, 2016). This cost is of concern because it mostly relates to members being 'churned' from one open scheme to another, rather than to acquisition of new members. By 2007 there were more individual health brokers accredited with the CMS (over 9700)[7] than there were GPs (approximately 7000; Econex, 2009).

Member numbers have increased steadily from 1.4 million in 1974 to 3.95 million in 2015, and the number of beneficiaries grew from 3.5 million to 8.8 million over the same period (CMS, 2016). In the mid-2000s, there were an estimated 1.5 million people without cover who live in households in which somebody has cover (McLeod, 2007). Although these numbers are somewhat dated, they highlight that some families do not register all their children with schemes. While there are age restrictions whereby children cannot be covered when they reach 21 years, a key issue influencing coverage is that contributions must be paid for each dependant (even though the contribution rate per child is lower than that for adults), suggesting that some families struggle to afford medical scheme cover.

Based on the available information, the distribution of health coverage is as follows. Over 84% of the population is entirely dependent on tax-funded hospital-based services (inpatient care and specialist outpatient care). About 20% of this population uses private sector primary care services (mainly GPs and retail pharmacies) on an out-of-pocket basis while the remaining 80% use public sector primary care services. Just over 16% of the population is covered by medical schemes. About 45% of medical scheme beneficiaries belong to schemes with an MSA component.

The problem of medical scheme affordability is considered to be the greatest obstacle to growth in the industry. At higher income levels, some 75–85% of the employed are already members. This share falls rapidly for lower-income groups so that, among those with earnings just above the tax threshold, only one third are members (McLeod, 2010). Less than 10% of workers with earnings below the tax threshold can afford medical scheme cover. This drop in affordability is compounded by the inability of many lower-income families to cover all of their family members, even with an employer subsidy.

---

[7] From Council for Medical Schemes schedules of brokers, available at: www.medicalschemes.com.

Changes in relation to key actors [8]

Although medical schemes are non-profit entities, they are surrounded by a number of for-profit entities that provide administration, marketing, managed care, consulting and advisory services. Consumers can therefore confuse the non-profit medical schemes and the high-profile listed companies that act as third-party administrators. Since 2000, scheme administrators and managed-care companies have been required to be accredited by the CMS. There has been some consolidation among the largest administrators, but many small administrators have been set up to profit from this lucrative business. In 2015, there were 16 third-party administrations, down from 23 in 2009 (CMS, 2016). The market is highly concentrated and the largest three administrators provide services for 80% of beneficiaries. Less than 7% of beneficiaries belong to schemes that are self-administered. In 2015, there were 25 accredited managed-care organizations; there are some concerns about the risk-taking role of some of these organizations. As indicated earlier, the increasing and substantive involvement of brokers over the past decade and a half is also of concern.

The role of employers in medical schemes has been declining for some time. Over the past decade, a growing number of employers have chosen to limit their involvement with medical schemes to paying

---

[8] A small market for nonindemnity health insurance (allowing for underwriting and risk rating and characterized by high rates of commission), provided by short-term and life insurance companies supervised by the Financial Services Board, accounts for about 1.1% of private health expenditure. According to the Long-term Insurance Act (Act 52, 1998) and Short-term Insurance Act (Act 53, 1998), health insurance policies may not indemnify policy-holders against actual medical expenses, but instead must offer a sum that is assured and defined in advance of any health care provision and may not directly reimburse health care providers. However, the insurance industry, and in particular short-term insurers, continued to sell indemnity products in defiance of the 1998 legislation. A landmark judgement in December 2006 that would have terminated this practice was appealed. The initial judgement was overturned and an appeal by the regulator to the Constitutional Court was turned down. The Minister of Health produced revised wording for the definition of the business of a medical scheme in the Medical Schemes Amendment Bill, which was introduced to parliament in mid-2008 but subsequently withdrawn in an attempt to enforce the original intention of the 1998 legislation. As these products have very limited coverage, they are not dealt with further in this chapter.

contributions to open medical schemes. This is partly due to the changing nature of employment, with people no longer spending their entire working life with one employer. In the 1970s, it was typical for an employer to provide medical cover and other employee benefits over and above a cash salary. In the 1980s and 1990s there was a growing move to so-called cost-to-company remuneration; as employers became concerned about the total cost of an employee (cash salary plus benefits), they fixed the total remuneration level, but also gave employees more flexibility in choosing cash or benefits. Medical scheme membership is seldom offered as an additional benefit but included as part of an employee's total remuneration. Moreover, the presence of brokers and the incentives offered to them to direct members to open schemes has exacerbated the declining role of employers.

Trends in relation to income and risk cross-subsidies

Medical schemes are not permitted to differentiate contributions by age, gender or state of health, but they can use income-related contributions as a factor to build in a deliberate cross-subsidy from high-income to low-income workers. The proportion of options within restricted schemes making use of income-related contributions has declined significantly over time, from 83.9% in 2004 to 61.0% in 2006. Nevertheless, restricted schemes make greater use of income-related contributions than open schemes. Open schemes struggle to obtain reliable income information and have largely moved away from any internal income cross-subsidies, not least because they fear attracting low-income older people instead of more desirable low-income, young workers.

Since 1994, surveys have documented a significant movement towards excluding pensioners from company funding for health care, which reduces risk cross-subsidies within medical schemes. The full effect of transferring investment risk and medical inflation risk to older people and future pensioners will take some time to unfold. McLeod et al. (2003) described the issue as "a future affordability time bomb", warning that it will affect the industry when those joining companies from around 2000 onwards reach retirement age. The issue has been receiving some attention from the Department of Social Development as part of the evaluation of retirement reform proposals (McLeod, 2007) that postulate setting up a mandatory social security system for retirement.

Developments over the last decade

A very positive development over the last decade has been the government's re-establishment of a restricted scheme for public sector workers. In the apartheid years, the public sector had a restricted scheme for each racial group, but during the 1990s public sector workers were allocated an employer subsidy for medical schemes and could use this to join any open medical scheme of their choice. This approach fuelled the growth of the role of brokers in the 1990s. A review of remuneration for public sector employees identified major shortcomings in relation to medical scheme cover, including inequality in access to cover, affordability concerns, lack of value for money, spending inefficiencies and little integration with public sector health care (McLeod & Ramjee, 2007). Despite a relatively generous medical scheme subsidy, less than half of the 1 million state employees were using the subsidy, and those that did so were using open schemes.

In 2002, the cabinet approved a framework policy for a new restricted medical scheme for public sector employees only, centred on the principles of equity (equal access to basic benefits), efficiency (with respect to costs and delivery of benefits) and choice of benefits (employees could choose more expensive cover and pay for it themselves). The Government Employees Medical Scheme was registered in January 2005 and became operational in January 2006. Government attracted potential members by offering a higher medical scheme subsidy within the Government Employees Medical Scheme and making it the only option available for new employees. The scheme grew rapidly and by December 2009 it had over 400 000 principal members or over 1.1 million beneficiaries. It has since grown more slowly, reaching a peak of 1.85 million beneficiaries in 2013 and declining to 1.77 million beneficiaries in 2015 (CMS, 2016). (The evolution of the number of beneficiaries of open and restricted schemes is shown in Fig. 13.2 in Chapter 13.) It is the largest restricted scheme, accounting for over 45% of all restricted scheme beneficiaries, and the second-largest medical scheme in South Africa. The high subsidies, income-related contributions and strong purchasing power of the new scheme proved successful in many respects. In particular, a low-wage-earning civil servant and his or her family are able to join the lowest cost option without contributing (that is, the government pays the full contribution). The implementation of the Government Employees Medical Scheme sets an example to other employers by demonstrating that it is possible to develop benefits packages that are affordable to all employees.

There were also efforts to promote risk pooling across individual schemes and across benefits options within schemes. A proposed amendment to the Medical Schemes Act in 2008 would have given the CMS responsibility for the operation of a Risk Equalization Fund. However, this amendment was never passed by parliament; efforts to introduce a range of new regulations of medical schemes were overtaken by the ruling party's decision to rather pursue a tax-funded, single purchaser system (see below). The purpose of the Risk Equalization Fund that was proposed was to protect open enrolment and community rating by ensuring that risk selection (deliberately attracting the young and healthy) was penalized. The Risk Equalization Fund would have created an industry-wide risk pool for those covered by medical schemes, and ensured an industry-wide community rate for the PMB, regardless of the age and disease profile of each option.

Policy-makers also signalled a desire to reduce the number of benefit options. In 2004, an International Review Panel argued that only a limited number of supplementary benefits options should be allowed above the PMB (Armstrong et al., 2004). The 2008 Medical Schemes Amendment Bill took a different line, suggesting that all hospital events should be covered in a single basic pool and that benefits above that level must also be pooled across all members in the scheme that choose an extension of cover. In essence, this would have changed benefit design from a series of vertical silos, each with its own community rate, to a series of horizontal pools and non-overlapping benefits pools, each with a community rate. Members would then have been able to choose which benefits they wanted and the contribution rate would have been determined by summing the prices of components of the benefits package. There was a strong negative reaction to this proposal from the schemes and the bill was not passed. Benefit package reform has largely stalled; the only change, introduced in 2008, was to allow efficiency-discounted options (EDOs) (CMS, 2016: p.27). There is no difference in benefit coverage between EDOs and non-EDOs; EDOs are simply more restrictive in the network of service providers that members can use. By 2016, only eight open schemes had introduced an EDO (CMS, 2016).

Assessment of market performance

This section critically assesses the effects of voluntary private health insurance (in the form of medical schemes) on financial protection, equity in financing, equity in the use of health care, efficiency and quality of care; it also analyses its effects on the overall health system.

Financial protection

The extent to which medical schemes have contributed to ensuring universal protection against the financial risks of ill health has changed considerably over time. In colonial times, South Africa had a strong public health sector that covered almost all citizens. Mission hospitals served some rural populations where there were no public facilities, but over time these hospitals were integrated into the public health sector. During the apartheid era, separate public health services were provided for white and black people (for example, there were always at least two public hospitals in large towns). Token user fees were charged at public facilities and as there was no incentive for facilities to generate user fee revenue, given that all revenue was transferred to the Treasury, fee exemptions were applied liberally. Generous exemptions constituted substantial protection from direct health care costs, although many patients, particularly in rural areas, had to incur considerable transport costs due to the relatively limited provision of services in rural areas.

Medical schemes initially developed to cover the costs of privately provided primary care (particularly GP visits, retail pharmacy services and some specialist care), essentially a response to the rising expectations of wealthier, particularly white, people. In this way, they provided financial protection for those who wished to spend more on health care. However, the costs that were covered, mainly for routine primary care, were relatively small, and medical scheme members are now expected to cover these costs on an out-of-pocket basis or through MSAs.

In the 1980s, there was an explicit government policy of promoting the growth of the private sector (Working Group on Privatization and Deregulation, 1986; South Africa (Republic) 1987). As noted by a policy-maker at that time: "Health authorities must not be seen as an infinite source of health facilities and medical care. More people should be able to make use of private health facilities" (Ross, 1982). As a result, by 1990, 62% of general doctors and 66% of specialists worked in private practice (Rispel & Behr, 1992), compared with about 40% of doctors in the early 1980s (Naylor, 1988), and the number of for-profit general hospital beds nearly doubled from around 9900 beds in 1988 to over 18 400 in 1993 (McIntyre et al., 1995). Public facilities were racially desegregated in 1988 and the use of public hospitals by medical scheme members began to decline very rapidly, with an equally rapid growth in the use of private hospitals. During this period, medical scheme membership among the black population grew particularly fast, largely as a result of trade union demands for employers to provide medical scheme cover to black staff and as part of the government's efforts aimed at "the co-option of certain groups of urban blacks by improving their immediate living environment and welfare services, and by offering them a stake in the capitalist system" (Price, 1989).

These developments made out-of-pocket payments for privately pro-vided health care unaffordable, particularly in relation to the growing use of private specialist and hospital care. Consequently, medical schemes are now an important mechanism for providing protection from poten-tially catastrophic costs for those who choose to use private facilities. However, medical schemes also provide less financial protection than previously because of rapidly rising health care costs and reductions in benefits (increasing cost sharing and growing exclusion of services from cover). Many scheme members cover these costs out of pocket. By the late 1990s, two thirds of all out-of-pocket payments for health care were made by medical scheme members (Cornell et al., 2001). The most significant development in recent years has been the introduction of PMBs in 2000. These have been critical to providing financial protection for those choosing to use privately provided health care.

Equity in financing

Contributions to medical schemes are community rated and so not explicitly linked to age or health status. However, given that each scheme has a number of different benefit options, it is possible that there is an element of self-selection into more comprehensive and higher-cost benefits options by higher-risk members, if they have sufficiently high incomes to afford these options. The most recent financing incidence study found that the incidence of medical scheme contributions is regressive across members. Contributions by the lowest-income 40% of members are equivalent to 14% of household consumption expenditure, whereas contributions by the richest quintile of members are less than 6% (McIntyre, 2010). This is largely due to most contributions being charged as a flat monetary amount. Higher-income individuals tend to choose more comprehensive benefits packages and thus, in general, pay higher contributions than lower-income groups, but the regressivity of contributions indicates that the differentiation of the flat contribution ráte across benefits packages is not as great as the differences in income levels across members.

When considering the overall incidence of health financing across all South Africans, medical scheme contributions are strongly progressive for two main reasons (Ataguba & McIntyre, 2012). First, the highest-income groups belong to medical schemes and, second, the contributions these groups make to schemes are very high. However, the fact that the magnitude of the contributions is related to inefficiencies and poor cost containment within this environment (see below) detracts from this so-called progressivity: a far greater proportion of the population could benefit from the funds in medical schemes if the schemes operated more efficiently. Also, although the higher-income groups that belong to medical schemes bear the greatest burden for financing health care, they also derive all the benefits provided by the schemes.

Evaluation of the impact of medical schemes on equity in financing also needs to take into account the substantial subsidy provided by the government in the form of tax relief for contributions. According to the most recent estimates, these tax credits amounted to 16 billion South African Rand in the 2014/2015 financial year (Department of Health, 2015). In addition, the government devotes a considerable amount of general tax revenue to pay medical scheme contributions on behalf of civil servants, estimated to exceed 20 billion South African Rand in 2014/2015 for the largest civil servant schemes. These tax credits and contributions to medical schemes reduce the amount of tax resources available for those who rely on publicly funded health services. The magnitude of this subsidy has been repeatedly criticized by health sector analysts, especially since the tax deductions particularly benefit those with the highest incomes and do not benefit employees who fall below the income tax threshold. Partly as a result of these criticisms, the Treasury revised tax concessions for medical schemes in 2005, spreading the subsidy more equitably across tax payers; nevertheless substantial public funds are directed to supporting medical schemes.

Equity in provision and use

Private providers are heavily concentrated in urban areas; this does not create too many barriers to accessing services for medical scheme members because most of them live and work in urban areas, although as service provision is relatively biased towards the wealthiest localities within urban areas, it is the lowest income scheme members who face limitations in access. Nevertheless, given the overall magnitude of private provision relative to the population served, there are very few barriers to service access for medical scheme members.

In terms of use of health services, an analysis of data from the only household survey that permits the calculation of utilization rates indicate greater utilization rates among medical scheme members (an average of 5.5 outpatient visits per beneficiary per year and 144 inpatient admissions per 1000 beneficiaries per year) in 2008 than among those who are not members (4.1 outpatient visits per person and 92 inpatient admissions per 1000 people per year) (Harris et al., 2011). Use of services by medical scheme members occurs largely in the private sector (85% of outpatient and 82% of inpatient care), with very limited use of private providers by those not covered by medical schemes (17% of outpatient and 4% of inpatient care).

Medical schemes have played an important role in removing financial barriers to using health care when needed for those with cover. However, in terms of the overall health system, they have entrenched inequities in access to health care between those with private cover and those relying on publicly funded health care. Developments since 1995 may have changed this pattern. Severe reductions in medical scheme cover of routine health care spending may have led to differences in rates of service use by socioeconomic status[9] among medical scheme members. The introduction of free primary care at public facilities in 1996 has also reduced financial barriers to health care for those without medical scheme cover. Unfortunately, recent data on utilization rates that could demonstrate these likely changes are not available.

---

[9] This may not be the case for PMB-covered services, to which all medical scheme members are entitled, irrespective of socioeconomic status.

Quality of care and efficiency in the delivery of services

There are almost no data that would allow evaluation of the quality of care or efficiency of service delivery. There is no routine assessment of the quality of care purchased by the medical schemes, and patients have limited recourse when they receive poor quality of care. They may report providers to the Health Professions' Council of South Africa, but experience has shown that this institution seldom takes action. A Hospital Rating Index developed by the largest medical scheme administrator (Discovery), which took into account cost, quality and value for money, was scuttled due to vociferous opposition from private hospitals. The reality is that scheme members often have no real choice of hospital. Almost all private specialist practices are based in private hospitals and thus the specialist to whom one is referred automatically determines the hospital of admission. In addition, choice of hospital for specific procedures is usually limited outside the largest metropolitan areas.

Although data on efficiency are limited, it is evident that medical schemes have few incentives to operate efficiently. Evidence on the rate of spending increases, particularly in the periods 1981–1993 and 1996–2004 (McIntyre et al., 1995, 2007), indicates that schemes have paid very little attention to ensuring that services are provided at the lowest possible cost. This appears to have continued over the last decade. Medical schemes use the standard set of managed-care practices, such as pre-admission certification and drug utilization review, but it is not clear that these have been effective. One initiative aimed at enhancing technical efficiency is the promotion of generic medicine use through user charges for prescriptions, but this is a relatively passive approach on the part of the schemes. Government legislation and regulation, such as enabling generic substitution by pharmacists and medicine-pricing regulations, have been far more effective in controlling the costs of medicines than actions by medical schemes.

Medical schemes have very limited purchasing power and are unable to effectively negotiate reimbursement rates with providers, either in terms of the form of payment mechanism or the level of the reimbursement rate. This is particularly true in relation to private hospitals (which account for the largest portion of medical scheme spending), given how concentrated the market has become, with three groups owning over 80% of all private hospital beds (van den Heever, 2007).

A few of the largest medical schemes have succeeded in negotiating a per diem rate with certain private hospital groups, and a few schemes serving low-income employees pay GPs on a capitation basis, but fee-for-service is by far the dominant payment mechanism. As indicated in Box 12.2, former statutory mechanisms for establishing provider reimbursement rates are no longer in place. There has been discussion since 2007 about establishing a central bargaining chamber, and in 2014 the Competition Commission initiated a Market Inquiry into the Private Healthcare Sector to address growing concerns about the high costs of private health care.

In terms of allocative efficiency, there is potential for medical schemes to change their benefits packages as health care priorities change, but there is no evidence that they have adapted benefits on this basis. Once again, it is regulatory intervention that has promoted allocative efficiency goals. For example, the PMBs have focused on chronic diseases and hospital care to address the major burden of disease among scheme members, including adding AIDS to the list of chronic diseases, a clear demonstration of allocative efficiency concerns. The PMBs have also been involved in the development of very detailed treatment protocols, to enhance cost-effectiveness. However, medical schemes have undermined allocative efficiency by reducing cover of primary care, which must be paid for via MSAs or out of pocket, whereas specialist visits are still usually covered. This has promoted a relative reduction in the use of GPs and an increase in the use of specialists.

The existence of 83 schemes and some 300 benefit options does not contribute to administrative efficiency. The rate of increase in non-health care spending within medical schemes, particularly in the late 1990s and early 2000s, was dramatic. This spending, which includes administrative costs, managed-care management services, reinsurance costs and broker fees, accounted for only 8.4% of total scheme spending in 1997 but had increased to 16.2% by 2006 (CMS, 2008). This was of considerable concern, especially given that managed-care efforts do not seem to be particularly effective and brokers are not introducing new members but simply juggling existing members between different schemes. The Council for Medical Schemes consistently interrogated these costs in their annual reports. By 2015, non-health care spending had been reduced to 8.6% of medical scheme spending (CMS, 2016).

Impact on the health system

The existence of voluntary private health insurance has had a profound and largely negative impact on the overall health system. First, it has seriously limited the potential for income and risk cross-subsidies, separating 16% of the population (the highest earners) from the rest of the population. At present, there is no risk pooling between schemes, or between different benefit options within schemes. Of more concern is the fact that the wealthy minority belong to schemes that dispose of 42% of the financial resources in the health sector. This disproportionate spending highlights the system's deficiency in relation to income cross-subsidies.

Second, voluntary private health insurance has been the main contributor to high and rapidly increasing health care spending, which is not translated into commensurate improvement in health status. Public spending on health care flatlined in real per person terms from the mid-1990s to 2003, whereas the spending spiral in medical schemes continued unabated, with real contribution rates per beneficiary increasing by over 6% per year between 1996 and 2006. However, real public spending on health care has been increasing over the past decade, while medical scheme contributions have continued to grow at rates well above the consumer price index. Real per person spending on medical scheme beneficiaries was 3.6 times greater than the government's per person spending on nonbeneficiaries in 1996. This differential rose rapidly to 7.6 times by 2003, but has since declined to 4.8 times in the early 2010s.

Third, private provision could not have grown as rapidly in the absence of voluntary private health insurance. Prepayment to schemes (as opposed to out-of-pocket payments to private providers) and the fee-for-service provider payment mechanism have induced a migration of health professionals from the public to the private sector. This has created a vicious cycle of health professional incomes becoming far higher in the private sector (with the possible exception of nurses), resulting in a further exodus of staff to the private sector; a growing number of professionals serving a stagnant pool of medical scheme beneficiaries, leading to increases in the fees charged by these professionals as well as supplier-induced demand and uncontrolled growth in medical scheme spending; and medical scheme cover becoming increasingly unaffordable at the same time as schemes being unable to expand cover to lower-income workers. All of this leaves the public sector with a limited number of health professionals attempting to serve the needs of the vast majority of the population in the context of growing health needs, particularly those related to the HIV/AIDS epidemic, contributing substantially to a decline in the quality of publicly provided care.

Proposed mandatory prepayment for universal coverage

The possibility of introducing some form of mandatory (social or national) health insurance has been a subject of considerable debate since the late 1980s. The objectives of all proposals to date have been to address problems in the medical scheme environment and the public–private mix by promoting social solidarity in health care funding (McIntyre & van den Heever, 2007).

Initially, the focus was on introducing a social health insurance scheme with mandatory contributions and membership for formal sector workers and their dependants, or at least those formal sector workers above the income tax threshold. The Treasury opposed such proposals, viewing social health insurance contributions merely as another tax that would increase the tax-to-gross domestic product ratio above the level it deems desirable and place a burden on what is believed to be an already over-taxed middle-income group (McIntyre, Doherty & Gilson, 2003). The Treasury was also concerned about the potential impact on employment levels if mandatory contributions were to increase the cost of labour, a concern shared by employer groups.

Although initially anxious about the potential implications of social health insurance, medical schemes were generally supportive of these proposals, given that it was envisaged that medical schemes would serve as financial intermediaries or insurers under social health insurance (as in the Dutch health system). Not only would this secure their future within the health system, it would also expand their membership base to include all formal sector workers and their dependants. Private for-profit providers were of a similar view; they anticipated that extending insurance coverage through social health insurance would translate into a larger group of patients being able to use their services.

However, the reform direction changed when, in December 2007, the African National Congress (the ruling political party) adopted a resolution at its policy conference to implement what was termed National Health Insurance (NHI). At first it appeared that this would mean that efforts would be made to create a more integrated funding pool, with formal sector workers making mandatory insurance contributions and government contributing on behalf of the rest of the population. It was unclear what the role of medical schemes would be, but the Government Employees Medical Scheme was seen as the foundation of the proposed NHI.

The Minister of Health released a Green Paper on NHI in August 2011 (Department of Health, 2011), which proposed more extensive reforms than those envisaged previously. This document indicated that the NHI reforms would be phased in, and that the focus of the first phase was to create the conditions for the efficient and equitable provision of quality services within the public health system. Ten health districts were designated as NHI pilot sites in 2012, where concerted efforts were made to address deficiencies in facility and equipment infrastructure and improve service quality. Although the first phase was envisaged as lasting 5 years, there remains much work to be done to improve health service quality in the public sector. This is critical as the public health sector has the greatest infrastructure, serves the majority of the population and would continue to be the backbone of health service delivery in future.

In the second phase of reforms, the emphasis would be on establishing an NHI fund. Although termed insurance, the NHI fund is not envisaged as a contributory insurance scheme with benefits tied to contributions. Instead it would be a tax-funded public institution, whose primary role would be that of a strategic purchaser of health services from both public and private providers. Together, the two phases of reforms are intended to ensure universal entitlements to comprehensive health services for which there would be no user fees at the point of service delivery. The role of medical schemes is seen as that of providing top-up insurance.

A White Paper on the NHI was released in December 2015 (Department of Health, 2015). This reiterated the proposed approach outlined in the Green Paper. It also discussed potential sources of funding for the NHI fund, namely a combination of continued allocations to the health sector from general tax revenue as well as possibly a surcharge on personal income tax, increases in value added tax and/or other tax increases. There was a call for public comment on the White Paper; the revised White Paper has yet to be released.

Although neither the Green nor the White Paper clearly states the reasons for the shift in reform direction, several likely motivations are apparent. The emphasis in these reforms is on moving towards universal health coverage with a universal entitlement to financial protection from the costs of health care and access to quality health services. Pursuing social health insurance for the benefit of formal sector workers and their families would likely entrench inequalities in health service access across socioeconomic groups, whereas a single funding pool would dramatically improve both income and risk cross-subsidies in the overall health system. A monopsony purchaser could use its financial power to ensure that the cost of health services is affordable and sustainable and to pay providers in a way that creates the appropriate incentives to promote efficient delivery of quality care and an equitable distribution of services across the country (McIntyre, Brijlal & Nkosi, 2015), something that medical schemes have been unable to achieve.

Although there is potential for the NHI proposals to move the South African health system towards a universal health system, many challenges would need to be overcome. There are widespread concerns that there has been little progress in finalizing a policy and detailed implementation plans for health care financing reforms almost a decade after the ruling party's commitment to the NHI approach. At the same time, any substantive legislation or regulation of medical schemes has been put on hold. This policy hiatus not only contributes to uncertainty for all health sector actors and the public, but also means that existing health system challenges remain unaddressed.

Conclusions

South Africa provides an excellent example of the dangers of pursuing voluntary private health insurance and serves as a stark warning for other low- and middle-income countries not to follow that path. None of the arguments presented in favour of private insurance coverage are upheld in the South African context. There is no evidence that medical schemes have promoted efficiency and, in fact, their track record on technical and administrative efficiency has been dismal. Medical schemes are unable to control rapid increases in health care spending and non-health care spending grew particularly dramatically until placed under relentless scrutiny by the CMS. Although there are no accurate data on technical quality of care in the public and private sectors, there is undoubtedly a perception among South Africans that the private sector offers better quality of care than the public sector. This is in no small part due to the disparities in staff-to-population ratios (particularly in relation to specialists) in the two sectors. Thus, voluntary private health insurance has not led to higher quality of care; it has simply contributed to rising quality differentials that did not exist in the past.

There is no doubt that considerable additional financial resources have been drawn into the health system through the development of medical schemes. However, these resources only benefit the 16% of the population covered by medical schemes. Most importantly, these schemes have not significantly relieved pressure on government budgets. Instead, considerable government resources are used to sustain them, both through tax relief on medical scheme contributions and through government contributions to very costly medical scheme cover for civil servants. In the context of the disproportionate share of people with HIV/AIDS who rely on publicly financed and provided care, it is the public sector that bears the major burden of meeting the health needs of South Africans.

Finally, while medical schemes in their early years of development provided a prepayment option for those who were paying out of pocket for privately provided health care, this has not been the case for some time now. Medical scheme members face considerable out-of-pocket payments due to cost sharing and coverage exclusions. Schemes have been unable to expand coverage to low-income workers who use private primary care providers on an out-of-pocket basis; indeed, coverage declined relatively dramatically as a percentage of the population, from about 17% of the population in the early 1990s to under 15% in 2003, and only began increasing again with the introduction of Government Employees Medical Scheme in 2006.

The South African health system has reached a critical point. On the one hand, the public sector has seen an exodus of health professionals and received no real per person funding increase for the decade up to 2003, despite growing health needs arising from the HIV/AIDS epidemic and an epidemiological transition. Over this period, staff morale and quality of care declined at alarming rates in the public sector. Although government funding for the health sector has increased over the last decade, the task of rebuilding a deeply undermined public health system is enormous. On the other hand, the voluntary private health insurance environment is faced with spending increases that have spiralled out of control. Government regulatory efforts have been helpful in some respects, but they do not tackle the fundamental issues of the quantity and distribution of private providers or the price of private sector services. For these and related reasons, South Africa is seriously considering pursuing a more integrated funding system to achieve universal coverage to address existing income and risk cross-subsidy problems. However, excessive delays in finalizing proposed reforms have created a policy vacuum and challenges facing the South African health system are mounting by the day.

Postscript

Since this Chapter was drafted, the Competition Commission's Health Market Inquiry released its final report in late 2019 (http://www.compcom.co.za/wp-content/uploads/2020/01/Final-Findings-and-recommendations-report-Health-Market-Inquiry.pdf). The findings are in line with the analysis presented in this Chapter. In addition, the National Health Insurance Bill was submitted to parliament in 2019, and is undergoing public comment (https://www.gov.za/sites/default/files/gcis_document/201908/national-health-insurance-bill-b-11-2019.pdf). The Bill is in line with the policy direction laid out in the White Paper.

References

Armstrong J et al. (2004). *International Review Panel report to the South African Risk Equalization Fund Task Group*. Pretoria, Department of Health.

Ataguba JE, McIntyre D (2012). Paying for and receiving benefits from health services in South Africa: Is the health system equitable? *Health Policy and Planning*, March, 27 Suppl 1: i35–45.

Broomberg J (2006). *Consultative investigation into low income medical schemes*. Johannesburg, LIMS.

Browne Commission (1986). *Final report of the Commission of Inquiry into Health Services*, RP 67/1986. Pretoria, Government Printer.

CMS (Council for Medical Schemes) (2008). *Evaluation of medical schemes' cost increases: findings and recommendations*. Pretoria, Council for Medical Schemes.

CMS (2016). *Council for Medical Schemes Annual Report 2015/16*. Pretoria, Council for Medical Schemes.

Cornell J et al. (2001). *South African National Health Accounts: the private sector*. Pretoria, National Department of Health.

Day C, Gray A (2010). Health and related indicators. In: Fonn S, Padarath A, eds. *South African health review: 2010*. Durban, Health Systems Trust.

Department of Health (2002). *Inquiry into the various social security aspects of the South African health system. Policy options for the future.* Pretoria, Department of Health.

Department of Health (2011). *National Health Act (61/2003): Policy on National Health Insurance. Government Gazette 34523.* Pretoria, Department of Health.

Department of Health (2015). *National Health Act (61/2003): White Paper on National Health Insurance. Government Gazette 39506.* Pretoria, Department of Health.

Department of Social Development (2002). *Transforming the present – protecting the future: consolidated report.* Report of the Committee of Inquiry into a Comprehensive System of Social Security for South Africa. Pretoria, Department of Social Development.

Doherty J, McLeod H (2003). Medical schemes. In: Health Systems Trust, ed. *South African health review 2002.* Durban, Health Systems Trust.

Econex (2009). NHI note 4: supply constraints, November. Stellenbosch: www .econex.co.za/index.php?option=com_docman&task=cat_view&gid= 904&Itemid=60; accessed on 08/09/2011.

Gluckman H (1944). *The provision of an organized national health service for all sections of the people of the Union of South Africa, 1942–1944.* Report of the National Health Services Commission, Chair Dr Henry Gluckman. Pretoria, Government Printer.

Gqaleni N et al. (2007). Traditional and complementary medicine. In: Harrison S, Bhana R, Ntuli A, eds. *South African health review 2007.* Durban, Health Systems Trust.

Harris B et al. (2011). Inequities in access to health care in South Africa: a national household survey. *Journal of Public Health Policy*, 32 Suppl 1:S102–23.

McIntyre D (2010). Private sector involvement in funding and providing health services in South Africa: implications for equity and access to health care. EQUINET Discussion Paper 84. Harare, Regional Network for Equity in Health in Southern Africa: www.equinetafrica.org/bibl/docs/ DIS84privfin%20mcintyre.pdf; accessed on 08/09/2011.

McIntyre D, Dorrington RE (1990). Trends in the distribution of South African health care expenditure. *South African Medical Journal*, 78:125–9.

McIntyre D, Gilson L (2002). Putting equity in health back onto the social policy agenda: experience from South Africa. *Social Science & Medicine*, 54:1637–56.

McIntyre D, van den Heever A (2007). Mandatory health insurance. In: Harrison S, Bhana R, Ntuli A, eds. *South African health review 2007.* Durban, Health Systems Trust.

McIntyre D, Brijlal V, Nkosi M (2015). Health systems financing. In: Fryatt B, Matsoso MP, Andrews G. *The South African health reforms 2009–2014: Moving towards universal coverage.* Cape Town, Juta.

McIntyre D, Doherty J, Gilson L (2003). A tale of two visions: the changing fortunes of social health insurance in South Africa. *Health Policy and Planning,* 18:47–58.

McIntyre D et al. (1995). *Health expenditure and finance in South Africa.* Durban, Health Systems Trust and the World Bank.

McIntyre D et al. (2007). *A critical analysis of the current South African health system.* Cape Town, Health Economics Unit, University of Cape Town and Centre for Health Policy, University of the Witwatersrand.

McLeod H (2005). Mutuality and solidarity in healthcare in South Africa. *South African Actuarial Journal,* 5:135–67.

McLeod H (2007). *Framework for post-retirement protection in respect of medical scheme contributions. Reform of retirement provisions feasibility studies.* Pretoria, Department of Social Development.

McLeod H (2010). Affordability of health insurance: national health insurance. Policy Brief 9, Innovative Medicines South Africa: www.innovativemedicines .co.za/national_health_insurance_library.html; accessed on 08/09/2011.

McLeod H (2012a). Myths about medical schemes. National Health Insurance Policy Brief 21: Innovative Medicines South Africa (IMSA): www .heathermcleodnz.com/#/imsa-nhi-policy-briefs/4580334234; accessed on 17/06/2017.

McLeod H (2012b). The role of risk adjustment in the equitable financing of national health insurance in South Africa. *Development Southern Africa,* 29(5):636–56.

McLeod H, Ramjee S (2007). Medical schemes. In: Harrison S, Bhana R, Ntuli A, eds. *South African health review 2007.* Durban, Health Systems Trust.

McLeod H et al. (2003). *The impact of prescribed minimum benefits on the affordability of contributions.* Pretoria, Council for Medical Schemes.

McLeod H et al. (2004). *The determination of the formula for the Risk Equalisation Fund in South Africa.* Prepared for the Risk Equalisation Fund Task Group on behalf of the Formula Consultative Task Team. Pretoria, Council for Medical Schemes.

Melamet Commission (1994). *Commission of Inquiry into the manner of providing for medical expenses.* Pretoria, Government Printer.

Ministerial Task Team on SHI (2005). *Social health insurance options: financial and fiscal impact assessment.* Unpublished technical report to the Department of Health.

Naylor CD (1988). Private medicine and the privatisation of health care in South Africa. *Social Science & Medicine,* 27:1153–70.

Price M (1989). Explaining trends in the privatization of health services in South Africa. *Health Policy and Planning*, 4:121–30.

Reinach Committee (1962). *Reinach Departmental Committee regarding medical benefit, friendly and assurance schemes*. Pretoria, Government Printer.

Rispel L, Behr G (1992). *Health indicators: policy implications*. Johannesburg, Centre for Health Policy, University of the Witwatersrand.

Ross MH (1982). Future provision of health services in the RSA. *RSA*, 2000(4):32.

Sabinet (2013). Interim Traditional Health Council Inaugurated. Department of Health, 15 February 2013: www.sabinetlaw.co.za/health/articles/interim-traditional-health-council-inaugurated; accessed on 14/06/2017.

South Africa (Republic) (1987). *White Paper on privatisation and deregulation in the Republic of South Africa*. Pretoria, Government Printer.

South Africa (Republic) (1995). *Restructuring the national health system for universal primary heath care: report of the Committee of Inquiry into a National Health Insurance system*. Pretoria, Department of Health.

van den Heever AM (2007). *Evaluation of the merger between Network Healthcare Holdings and Community Healthcare*. Pretoria, Council for Medical Schemes.

van Rensburg D, van Rensburg N (1999). Distribution of human resources. In: Health Systems Trust, ed. *South African health review 1999*. Durban, Health Systems Trust.

Working Group on Privatisation and Deregulation (1986). *Privatisation and deregulation of health care in South Africa*. Pretoria, National Department of Health and Population Development.

World Bank (2017). World Development Indicators. GINI index (World Bank estimate) [Data file]: http://data.worldbank.org/data-catalog/world-development-indicators; accessed on 13/06/2017.

13 | Undermining risk pooling by individualizing benefits: the use of medical savings accounts in South Africa

HEATHER MCLEOD AND DI MCINTYRE

South Africa has a dual health system in which the majority of the population is covered by the public health care sector and 16% of the population with higher incomes is covered by voluntary private health insurance delivered through medical schemes. Medical savings accounts (MSAs) were first introduced by medical schemes in 1994 and their usage grew rapidly in the first decade but declined in the second decade. By 2005, MSAs covered 88% of open scheme beneficiaries and 49% of restricted[1] scheme beneficiaries but by December 2014 MSA coverage had declined to 67% of open scheme beneficiaries and 18% of restricted scheme beneficiaries. This chapter focuses on MSAs, but more information on medical schemes and private health insurance can be found in Chapter 12 in this volume.

Factors that fostered the development of MSAs

The increasing involvement of insurers in the health care market in the late 1980s resulted in calls for greater individualization of health care expenditure. This was in line with life insurance and retirement designs, which at the time moved towards individualized accounts and away from pooled risk. Chapter 12 deals in more detail with the free-market reforms of the private health insurance market in the late 1980s that culminated in the abolition of community-rated premiums in 1989 and the abolition of minimum benefits in 1993. The democratic government, newly elected in 1994, therefore inherited a system that had turned

---

[1] Open schemes must admit all applicants under the principle of open enrolment. Restricted schemes are typically employer or union based, or may be set up for a professional body or other defined group with restricted membership.

substantially in the direction of private insurance principles, with members being charged premiums based on their age and state of health.

In 1993, immediately before South Africa's transformation to democracy, the Melamet Commission reported on the status of medical scheme regulation. The Commission warned that the industry's regulator was woefully inadequate to supervise it appropriately. At that time, the office of the regulator consisted of the Registrar and seven staff, one of whom was the secretary and none of whom had any tertiary academic qualifications. This group was supposed to supervise an industry with some 230 different schemes and multiple options within them.

The history of personal MSAs dates from this period of lack of regulation. MSAs were first introduced by Discovery Health Medical Scheme[2] in 1994.[3] There was no intervention from the regulator and other schemes rapidly followed suit. The 1990s were a period of rapid innovation by insurers and the role of savings accounts and their influence on benefit design and risk selection is discussed here in more detail.

From a policy perspective, the 1990s was a period of regulatory efforts leading to a completely revised Medical Schemes Act, No. 131 of 1998, which came into effect in January 2000. The Act allowed for the formation of a new independent regulatory body, funded by the industry and with access to legal, accounting and actuarial expertise. The Act also began to substantially roll back the freedom to operate that insurers and the MSA movement had seized in 1994.

The key elements of the Medical Schemes Act of 1998 were the introduction of open enrolment and the re-introduction of community rating and minimum benefits. There was increased protection for members changing schemes, but schemes were also given some protection

---

[2] Discovery Health was originally registered as Momentum Health Medical Scheme on 8 October 1971 and changed its name to Discovery Health Medical Scheme on 1 September 1998. It was however known in the market as Discovery Health (personal email correspondence, Danie Kolver, 26 October 2016).

[3] According to the Registrar of Medical Schemes at the time (personal email correspondence, Danie Kolver, 26 October 2016), there seems to have been a savings-like component to an earlier scheme administered by Docmed. Members had been transferred to a medical scheme from a Friendly Society benefit fund, recognized in terms of the Income Tax Act, and the scheme attempted to retain the benefits previously available. The philosophical development and market introduction of MSAs is generally credited to Discovery Health.

against adverse selection as they were allowed to apply waiting periods to members switching schemes. The Act significantly strengthened the governance of the industry through the introduction of the new Council for Medical Schemes, which was tasked with looking after the interests of beneficiaries of medical schemes (the first Medical Schemes Act of 1967 required the Council to look after the interests of the schemes, see Chapter 12). The Council began to operate in 2000 with the appointment of a new Registrar and senior staff. The governance of schemes was also strengthened with provisions for increased independence of the Board of Trustees from the administrator and other advisors.

The introduction of MSAs in the 1990s

A paper setting out the basic tenets of MSAs was written in 1993 by Adrian Gore, an actuary and the entrepreneurial founder of a leading health insurance group, Discovery Health.[4] Gore argued that with the planned deregulation, the environment was about to be freed up "to test virtually every known cost containment technique in the financing of health care" (Gore, 2003). He argued strongly in favour of individuals becoming the principal buyers of health care with opportunities to compare options and prices in order to facilitate their decisions. Gore described a conceptual framework for personal MSAs under which members would make deposits to their personal accounts, which would be used to pay for smaller day-to-day medical expenses such as consultations, medicine and spectacles. Rather than a "use-it-or-lose-it" mentality, these savings accounts would encourage careful purchasing and unused balances would be rolled over to future years. Major and

[4]   Discovery Health Limited is a health care administrator and a managed care company that described itself initially as a health insurer. Subsequently, a separate insurer, Discovery Life was established. Both Discovery Health Limited and Discovery Life are part of Discovery Holdings Limited, a company that was listed on the Johannesburg Stock Exchange in 1999. Its non-profit medical scheme is confusingly also known as Discovery Health, although the legal name is Discovery Health Medical Scheme. Disentangling the relationships between these entities was the subject of a public conflict with the regulator of medical schemes in the period from 2000 to 2003. Health care consumers were understandably confused by the naming of the entities.

catastrophic medical expenses like hospitalization would still be paid from the risk pool.

Gore (1993: p.147) argued that the establishment of MSAs "is a movement in the direction of a worthwhile social goal: making all employee benefits personal and portable". In his opinion, MSAs would lower the cost of health care (Gore, 1993: p.145): "The use of Medical Savings Accounts institutes the only cost containment system that has ever worked – members avoiding waste because they have a financial interest in doing so. When members are spending money on medical goods and services, in effect they are spending their own money, not someone else's – an excellent incentive to buy prudently." He concluded by saying that: "In our opinion, the results will be better if we follow the individualistic vision of health care wherein people bear the costs of their bad decisions and reap the benefits of their good ones. A choice must be made between health care and other uses of money; as often as possible these choices should be made by individuals." (Gore, 1993: p.156).

Jost (2005) found that the development of MSAs in South Africa was encouraged by John Goodman, president of a United States MSA advocacy group, the National Center for Policy Analysis, who worked with Discovery Health in developing the concept. Subsequent papers by Discovery Health executives on the experience of savings accounts in South Africa were published by the National Center for Policy Analysis (Matisonn, 2000, 2002). Attempts by Discovery to export the savings account concept to the Unites States through a subsidiary, Destiny Health, have been less successful than at home. Discovery Health and its associated medical scheme have been perceived as market leaders in benefit design and industry practice since their launch in 1993. The market-oriented reforms of 1993 were among the last actions of the apartheid government. Discovery Health Medical Scheme took advantage of the new freedom to design benefits and introduced personal MSAs in 1994. This innovation was rapidly copied by other schemes, particularly those in the very competitive open schemes market.[5]

The South African private health insurance environment is highly competitive and, with the lack of regulatory oversight, a number of

---

[5] Open medical schemes have to accept all applicants.

practices emerged in the 1990s that caused concern to researchers and policy-makers. The use of brokers and reinsurance was encouraged by the prevailing insurance mentality of the 1990s, and aggressive underwriting of entrants and claims became widespread.

The Department of Health (2002) found that by 1999 no open scheme was permitting anyone over the age of 55 to join as an individual member. Lifetime exclusions for pre-existing conditions as well as age rating and experience rating occurred without restriction. Thus the majority of medical scheme members were in an environment that excluded vulnerable groups from cover, where medical costs continued to rise (because fee-for-service reimbursement was maintained) and where non-health care costs were driven up (through profit-taking and hidden commission costs).

At the time of the conceptual development of MSAs, Gore (1993) had noted that medical expenses paid by employers provided benefits effectively paid with pre-tax money, whereas expenses paid by members themselves were paid from after-tax money. He argued that "properly structured Medical Savings Accounts provide the perfect solution in that members effectively pay for their own medical expenses with pre-tax money" (Gore, 1993: p.147).

Brokers and employers rapidly used the new structures to create tax breaks for employees and more money flowed to medical schemes. Initially there was no limit as to the amount an employer or employee could contribute to the MSA. Employees could opt to take part of their salary increase in the form of pre-tax payments to the MSA. Some employees took their entire salary increase in this form and were able to build up significant MSA balances.

Reining in MSAs from 2000 onwards

The Medical Schemes Act of 1998, implemented from January 2000 onwards, closed the tax loophole by limiting the amount that could be paid to MSAs to 25% of annual medical scheme contributions. The newly strengthened Council for Medical Schemes was able to moderate increases in non-health care costs and dampen the excesses of benefit design by introducing regulations that would enhance, rather than reduce, the pooling of health expenditure (for these and other key developments in the MSA market, see Box 13.1).

Box 13.1 Key developments in benefit design and the market for medical savings accounts in South Africa, 1986–2016

This box should be read in conjunction with Chapter 12, which describes key developments in the broader South African health care market.

1986 to 1994: Free market reforms

- Browne Commission supports the application of risk rating and experience rating by medical schemes, as well as the individualization of health care expenditure. Differentiation of benefit packages is encouraged, allowing people to choose according to their needs and permitting the schemes to charge according to the risk of those choosing the package. Insurers argue and the Commission concurs, that there would be significant cost savings if members paid small claims themselves and only claimed from pooled funds thereafter (1986).
- Amendment to Regulation 8 of the Medical Schemes Act of 1967 allows contributions to be determined according to risk (1989).
- Medical Schemes Amendment Act, No. 23 abolishes guaranteed minimum benefits (1993).
- Actuarial Society of South Africa publishes key paper by Adrian Gore on the rationale for MSAs (1993).
- Melamet Commission is established under the old political regimen and reports immediately before transition to a democratic government. Dismal state of regulatory supervision is highlighted and recommendations are made for an independent statutory regulatory body (1993–1994).

1994 to 2000: Preparation for re-regulation under the democratic government

- Discovery Health creates first health plan with personal MSAs (1994).
- African National Congress Health Plan of 1994 is published and principles are established for moving to social health insurance (1994).
- The philosophical direction that was recommended by the Melamet Commission is rejected and replaced by a strategic

Box 13.1 (cont.)

direction from the 1995 National Health Insurance Committee of Inquiry (1995).

- Completely revised Medical Schemes Act, No. 131, of 1998 reinstates open enrolment, community rating and prescribed minimum benefits. Substantially strengthened regulatory supervision is enacted. Contributions to MSAs are limited to 25% of total medical scheme contributions (1998, implemented from January 2000).

2000 to 2008: Preparation for social/national health insurance

- Legislative amendments are made to clarify savings account legislation: accumulation of unexpended benefits can only be done under savings account regulations; minimum benefits must be covered from risk pool and not from savings accounts; credit balances can be transferred to another option within the same medical scheme or another scheme if the new option or scheme has an MSA; if the new option or scheme does not have an MSA, the balance can be paid out but will be subject to tax (2002, effective January 2003).
- Formula Consultative Task Team designs and obtains industry consensus on the formula for risk equalization between schemes (2004).
- International Review Panel argues that benefit designs should be standardized and simplified to improve competition (2004).
- Minimum benefits in medical schemes are extended to cover diagnosis, treatment and medicine for 25 common chronic conditions (2004).
- Circular 8 from the Council for Medical Schemes argues that common benefits should in the future be paid from a single risk pool. Due to the lack of industry agreement these ideas have not yet been implemented (2006).
- Council for Medical Schemes applies to the High Court for a declaration on status of savings account balances. There had been concerns that savings account balances could be seized by creditors in case of insolvency. However, the courts confirmed that these balances belong to members in the event that a scheme is wound up or liquidated, that is, individual MSAs are protected in case of the medical scheme's bankruptcy (2006).

Box 13.1 (cont.)

- Medical Schemes Amendment Bill of 2008 provides for establishment of a Risk Equalization Fund to be managed by the Council for Medical Schemes in order to set up a framework for paying risk-adjusted amounts to medical schemes (Republic of South Africa, 2008). Legislation prepared for Parliament in 2008 but allowed to lapse and not re-submitted. The possibility of a new national health insurance system that might impact on the medical schemes' environment was the cause of the legislation not being dealt with in 2008, after a resolution to introduce national health insurance was taken in December 2007 by the ruling party.

2008 to 2016: Reform at the margins and waiting for national health insurance

- South African government publishes a Green Paper in 2011 outlining proposals for a single-payer national health insurance arrangement as a means to achieve universal health coverage, followed by a White Paper in 2015 (van den Heever, 2016). All financing and purchasing would occur nationally through a new National Health Insurance Authority and medical schemes would no longer provide substitutive cover, although some voluntary supplementary cover may be allowed to continue. Arguments between the Department of Health and National Treasury on the affordability of the proposals have not yet been resolved but the lack of progress on NHI and the lack of a clear proposal for the future role of medical schemes means that further medical scheme legislation has been stalled since 2008. Plans to introduce risk equalization between schemes and to allow some form of low-cost option are therefore stalled.
- Council for Medical Schemes allows efficiency-discounted options to be created from 2008 onwards. Efficiency-discounted options are benefit options with network arrangements for health care provision. They allow medical scheme contributions to be differentiated on the basis of the health care providers that are used to provide benefits. Rather than create new legislation, the Council allows schemes to be exempted from Section 29(1)(n) of the

Box 13.1 (cont.)

Medical Schemes Act, which stipulates that contributions may be differentiated only on the basis of income or family size, or both.

- Council for Medical Schemes issues two circulars on the accounting treatment of MSAs and interest earned on MSAs (Circular 38 of 2011 and Circular 5 of 2012). The schemes were forced to pay interest at the rate earned on the underlying funds. Previously most schemes did not charge interest on any upfront MSA provided but also did not pay interest on positive balances or paid a very low rate. As interest could still not be charged on the upfront MSA, MSAs in effect became a cost to schemes. Schemes also have to invest the MSA balances separately and account for MSAs more transparently than before.

- Council for Medical Schemes rejects (2013) the Genesis Medical Scheme's 2012 annual financial statements on the basis that these statements understated the scheme's financial position by excluding the members' personal MSAs from its liability. In the view of the Council, this money belonged to the members and not to the scheme. Genesis took the matter to the High Court which subsequently ruled in its favour. Later, the Supreme Court of Appeal ruled in the Council's favour (2015), but on further appeal, the Constitutional Court ruled in favour of Genesis (2017). This judgement overturns the understanding that MSA balances belong to members and are protected in the event of the scheme becoming insolvent.

Highly competitive medical schemes reacted to the re-introduction of community rating, open enrolment and minimum benefits in 2000 by attempting to find ways to continue risk rating. Early attempts by some of them to combine medical schemes with insurance products[6]

---

[6] Medical schemes provide indemnity cover, in other words they can reimburse in whole or in part the actual expenditure following a health event. Health insurance in South Africa has a very narrow definition in that it covers only nonindemnity cover. Health insurance products need to be designed to pay a predetermined amount unrelated to the actual expenditure and they may not reimburse health care providers directly. The demarcation between medical schemes and health insurance has been the source of some heated debate

(sold under different legislation with high commissions, underwriting and risk rating allowed) were rapidly dealt with by the new regulator in 2000. Other abuses, such as paying brokers to attract only young members, were also quickly made illegal.

More subtle were the attempts to get around the community rating through benefit design and marketing practices. Discovery Health again led the market in creating incentive and wellness programmes similar to the frequent-flyer programmes used by airlines. Points were initially earned for gym visits and preventive care but later could also be earned from loyalty programmes, for example by using the Discovery group credit card. Points can be redeemed for low-cost airline tickets and other shopping rewards. Although this wellness programme (called Vitality) was technically outside the non-profit medical scheme, many consumers saw this as a medical scheme initiative. Many other medical schemes have followed their lead but a few have begun to make a feature out of being involved only in purchasing health care for their members, refraining from offering incentive and wellness programmes.

To escape the provisions limiting contributions to MSAs to 25% of total medical scheme contributions, schemes developed innovative new structures. One example of such a structure was to pay the benefits from the risk pool but to create an entitlement to the rollover of unexpended benefits to the next year. A legislative amendment effective from 2003 ensured that individualization of benefits could only be done under the provisions for MSAs. Other aspects of savings account administration were also clarified.

Of particular concern was the fact that minimum benefits (prescribed by regulations) were being paid from savings in some cases and the revised legislation made it clear that minimum benefits were to be paid from the risk pool. The design of the Risk Equalization Fund will further entrench the use of the risk pool to pay minimum benefits. Only amounts paid from the risk pool will count towards proving that a person meets the treated patient criteria for a chronic disease.

Fig. 13.1 illustrates generic benefit design by the end of the first decade of MSAs in South Africa. Initially, MSAs were used to pay almost all of the day-to-day benefits. Above-threshold benefits were introduced to

and disagreement between the government and the insurance industry. A further attempt to clarify the "business of a medical scheme" was tabled in the Medical Schemes Amendment Bill of 2008 but was not enacted.

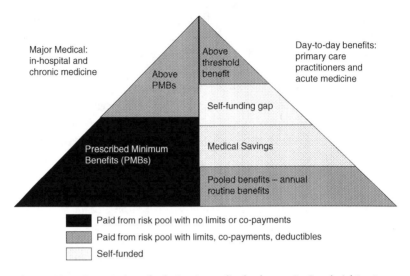

Figure 13.1 Generic benefit design in medical schemes in South Africa in the mid-2000s

Source: Drawn by the lead author, based on teaching material used by the lead author and Shivani Ranchod.

assist those members who had higher day-to-day expenditure than their annual savings allocation. Access to pooled benefits required that the MSA was exhausted and that expenditure had been on items deemed by the medical scheme to be allowable.[7] When the size of MSAs was restricted in the Medical Schemes Act of 1998, many schemes developed a pooled lower tier such as the annual routine benefits. Some schemes require a self-funding gap between the MSA and the above-threshold benefit. Increasing this gap is a way to mask increases in the price of medical scheme contributions as the larger the gap, the lower the cost of the above-threshold pooled benefit.

Variations in the generic benefit design continued to emerge as schemes attempted to evade the regulatory restrictions. As the

---

[7] Members have an incentive to exhaust their own savings accounts if they have access to a pooled benefit when personal savings run out. Medical scheme benefits therefore typically list what expenditure is allowable for counting towards reaching the pooled benefit. For example, expenditure on expensive frames for glasses would not be counted but expenditure on equivalent standard frames would be. Each medical scheme makes its own rules in this regard.

amount that could be paid to the savings schemes was decreased by legislation, annual routine benefits were introduced. This was legally a portion of the pool but created a notional amount available for expenditure by the family at the discretion of the member, as if it were a balance on a savings account. Unused money at year's end reverted to the pool, although some variations initially attempted to hold this amount over for the member, contravening the legislation. Variable savings accounts had become widespread in the early 2000s as schemes allowed members to determine how much they wanted to put in savings themselves, so creating an almost infinite variety of contribution levels for the same option. The regulator saw them as a means of risk rating members because part of the contribution paid by members reflected their health needs. The Medical Schemes Act specifically prohibits contributions being set according to the state of health of the beneficiaries.

While medical schemes tried ever-more innovative ways to attract members, the regulator, the Council for Medical Schemes, argued for simplification and standardization of benefit structures (CMS, 2005). The regulator increasingly tightened the annual process of registering benefit design changes. A directive was sent to the medical schemes in 2005 on the use of annual routine benefits[8] and variable savings accounts. Over several years, annual routine benefits disappeared from medical scheme designs, as the Registrar insisted that schemes must start payment of day-to-day benefits from the MSA first before using any benefits from the risk portion. From 2006, the Council for Medical Schemes insisted that variable savings account levels needed to be registered as separate options. As a result, medical schemes rationalized their savings account plans, typically by creating one option with an MSA and another without.

---

[8] A small defined portion of the risk pool is isolated for the effective use as a savings account for each member. The member can choose which practitioner or service to use, subject only to the overall limit of the savings account. However, at the end of the benefit year the notional balance is not rolled over but reverts to the risk pool. Some schemes used annual routine benefits together with conventional savings accounts to attempt to exceed the restriction that the contribution to the savings account must not exceed 25% of the total contribution.

Government Employee Medical Schemes with an alternative to MSAs from 2006 onwards

The period from the introduction of MSAs in 1994 through to the end of 2005 was one in which Discovery Health Medical Scheme dominated the South African medical scheme market, both in terms of innovation and in growth of the numbers of beneficiaries. Fig. 13.2 shows the split between the numbers on open and restricted schemes in South Africa and the rising dominance of Discovery Health Medical Scheme.

A major disrupter to the MSA market was the registration of the Government Employees Medical Scheme (GEMS) in January 2005, which became operational in January 2006 (see Chapter 12 for the rationale on the introduction of GEMS).

As shown in Fig. 13.2, GEMS grew rapidly from 2006 at the expense of open schemes other than Discovery Health. Government employees that had previously used their medical scheme subsidy in the open market increasingly moved to GEMS, and new public sector employees were required to move to GEMS. In a short space of time, GEMS became a role model for other medical schemes in terms of benefit design (McLeod & Ramjee, 2007). GEMS did not develop any MSA options but rather focused on provider network restriction and using the bargaining power of the scheme.

While MSAs are still available in South Africa, the competition provided by GEMS was a significant factor in reining in the use of MSAs to attract members. Although MSAs are described as a benefit in medical scheme marketing material, it has always been the case that members pay for MSAs from their own money (Kaplan & Ranchod, 2015).

In a study in 2013 on open scheme benefit design, Kaplan and Ranchod found a very wide distribution of the size of MSAs marketed, with the maximum per annum savings level for a one adult, one child family to be 54 times that of the minimum savings level offered (Kaplan & Ranchod, 2015).

Contribution increases in medical schemes continue to be at levels in excess of wage inflation, adding to the unaffordability of private health insurance for many. MSAs have at times been used as a buffer in presenting increases to the highly-competitive open market. An overall increase to the member can be artificially made to seem smaller by not increasing the MSA portion at the same pace as the risk pool contribution.[9]

[9] For example, a 10% increase in risk contributions can be positioned as a 3.1% overall increase to the member if the MSA portion is reduced from 25%

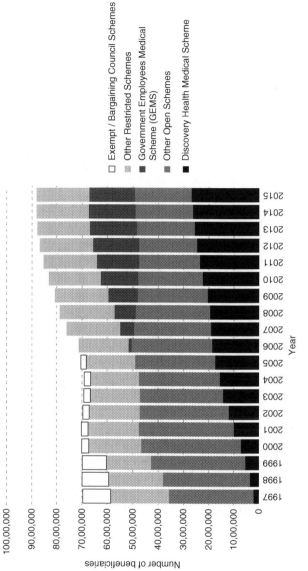

Figure 13.2 Number of beneficiaries in open and restricted medical schemes in South Africa, 1997–2015

Source: Based on data from the Annual Reports of the Registrar of Medical Schemes and the Council for Medical Schemes.

Over time, this means that the total proportion of medical scheme benefits paid from savings has declined from the peaks of the mid-2000s. In 2005, MSAs accounted for 11.7% of total benefits (CMS, 2006a, 2014, 2016) but by 2013 the proportion had declined to 9.7%. By the year 2015 with restrictions on the size of risk pool increases and a reversal in the growth of GEMS, MSAs accounted for 10.1% of total medical scheme benefits paid.

Given the greater use of MSAs in open scheme design, 14.5% of benefit expenditure in open schemes was from MSAs, compared with 4.0% in restricted schemes.

Benefit design and MSAs as a tool for risk selection

McLeod & Ramjee (2007) explain that benefit design fulfils three (sometimes conflicting) functions for a medical scheme. Benefit design decisions influence the marketability and competitiveness of a scheme, the extent of risk pooling within a scheme, and the manner in which benefits are rationed and delivered. The emphasis differs considerably between open schemes and restricted membership schemes, largely due to the differences in competitive dynamics. In a community-rated environment without a Risk Equalization Fund, open schemes with a lower risk profile will be more competitive. There is therefore a strong incentive to use benefit design to "cherry-pick" healthy members.

In the absence of risk equalization mechanisms, the regulatory challenge shifts to limiting the extent to which schemes can use benefit design to select members and influence their risk pool. The minimum benefit package defined for use in 2000 was interpreted by many schemes to exclude out-of-hospital coverage of chronic conditions. Some schemes substantially reduced chronic medicine benefits to be less attractive to older and less healthy members. The minimum benefit package was revised with effect from January 2004 to include diagnosis, treatment and medicine for 25 defined Chronic Disease List conditions.

In 2014, more than 60% of all restricted schemes have only one option whereas all open schemes, in attempting to provide a wider choice for competitive reasons, have multiple options. Open schemes

to 20% of total contributions. It has the further positive effect of increasing solvency (defined pooled assets over total contributions) as the denominator has not increased as much as the pooled portion.

typically offer four to six options but some offer many more, with Discovery Health Medical Scheme offering 15 options in 2014, 12 of which have MSAs. Open schemes use the higher number of options to steer members with similar risk profiles to particular options, which negates risk pooling.

Benefits for chronic conditions remain an effective tool for differentiating between the options and hence for risk selection. Schemes have moved away from providing chronic cover in excess of the Chronic Disease List, with even comprehensive options moving away from completely open disease lists. Some schemes use a higher level of self-funding through MSAs for non-Chronic Disease List diseases.

Without the competitive pressures that open schemes are subject to, restricted schemes have historically been able to provide more generous chronic benefits. Restricted schemes make more use of the cross-subsidies between young and old members in the same option and in this way can offer more extensive benefits for chronic conditions for the same community rate contribution.

There has been a long-term shift in medical schemes away from funding primary care towards funding major medical benefits (hospitals and specialists, together with the Chronic Disease List chronic diseases). Major medical expenditure accounted for only 42.5% of pooled funds in 1974 but it had risen to 71.4% by 2005. This shift has been driven partly by the strong increases in hospital expenditure and the shifting of out-of-hospital expenses to MSAs, and is underpinned by the minimum package emphasis on major medical benefits from the implementation of the Medical Schemes Act of 1998.

The increases in hospital expenditure have led to an increasing use of deductibles by schemes as a means of discouraging elective hospital admissions and some expensive diagnostic procedures. Deductibles are inherently regressive in nature and have an adverse effect on affordability for low-income members.

Operation of MSAs

While the terminology medical savings accounts has been applied to examples from Singapore, China, South Africa and the USA, the details of how the accounts function are often subtly different. Matisonn (2000) explains the US model as a single deductible across all benefits with a savings account to cover expenditures below this deductible. In South

Africa, Prescribed Minimum Benefits (PMBs) have an important impact on the use of MSAs. Treatment falling under the PMBs (about half of all expenditure) must be covered in full with no co-payments (similar to the so-called first-dollar coverage in the USA).

The MSAs in South Africa are typically used for day-to-day benefits like doctors' visits, basic radiology and pathology. The initial design suggested that all prescription medicines could be included but subsequent changes to competitive designs and legislation have meant that only acute prescription medicines are typically covered with chronic prescription medicines and other major medical expenses covered in the risk pool. MSAs are used almost exclusively for outpatient care but could be used to pay for inpatient care not covered as a minimum benefit (PMBs) or by the risk pool. Spending from an MSA is not restricted but if the option has an above-threshold benefit (see Fig. 13.1), there will be restrictions on what savings expenditure is counted towards reaching the threshold. The distinction between actual MSA expenditure and allowed expenditure adds a further layer of administrative complexity and is confusing to members.

Regarding the benefits of the medical schemes, to the extent that a person does not use the designated service provider, network or drug formulary, they may be liable for the difference in cost compared with the PMBs. Initially this could be paid out of pocket, or the MSA was used to pay the difference. However a strict interpretation of the Medical Schemes Act requires that PMBs may not be paid from savings and the Council for Medical Schemes has taken a stricter line on this since the early 2000s. Members may no longer use their MSAs to pay for any shortfall on a PMB event as the Council wants PMBs to be fully covered by pooled funds. PMBs typically cover about 55% to 60% of all in-hospital expenditure. MSAs can be used to cover benefits not covered by the health plan, such as complementary health practitioners, nonformulary medicines, corrective eye surgery or cosmetic surgery.

The MSAs are set up at the member level, that is, the principal member that joins the scheme. This means that the account can be used freely across any covered family member. The schemes quote the total contribution needed but some members may be supported by an employer. The split between employer and employee is the subject of negotiation in the workplace and is of no consequence to the medical scheme. Hence the total contribution, irrespective of how it is split between employer and employee, is credited to the member. The amount for the savings account is then allocated and there is no cognisance of whether the amount came from the employer or employee.

Contributions to the MSA are payable monthly, usually at a fixed level set at the beginning of the year by the medical scheme for each benefit option. Many medical schemes allowed members to draw up to 12 times that level at any time during the year, effectively making a loan to the member. If interest is paid on balances, it should also be charged on the loans. Interest rates paid on balances were usually less than commercial rates and the difference was kept by the scheme until regulation in 2011 and 2012 (see Box 13.1). Some schemes had opted to simplify administration by neither paying nor charging interest; some levied a specific MSA administration fee but it was more likely to be hidden in the overall administration fee for that option.

The MSAs form part of the medical scheme's pool of investment funds. A large part of schemes' investments are in cash and near-cash instruments and the funds are rarely invested separately from the MSAs. In general the administration of savings account balances had been poor and the regulator introduced changes in 2011 and 2012 (see Box 13.1). Solvency is calculated as a fixed percentage of the gross contributions (risk pool and MSA portion). This makes for inequity between schemes as if there are two identical schemes in all regards, except that the one has an additional MSA, they have to hold different reserve levels. Both these schemes have the same underlying risk but require different levels of reserves to be held for solvency. The introduction of some form of risk-based capital could improve this but discussions have been underway with the industry since 2004.

In accounting terms, the MSA balances had been viewed as a liability rather than an asset as the understanding was that they belonged to the members and not to the scheme. The status of members' savings account balances has been subject to legal disputes since 2013 (see Box 13.1). In 2017, the Constitutional Court ruled that funds in medical scheme members' personal MSAs can be treated as assets of a medical scheme, rather than as liability. The implications of this ruling have not yet been worked through in terms of solvency calculations. It seems likely that the ruling may result in reduced attractiveness of MSAs to members and hence to lower use of MSAs in future. The Council for Medical Schemes may need to introduce new regulations to cover the preferred treatment of savings as belonging to members.

Table 13.1 *Benefit expenditure by registered medical schemes in South Africa, 2014*

Benefit description		Total benefits (% total)	Pooled benefits (% pooled)	MSAs (% MSAs)	MSAs as % of total benefits
Facilities	Private hospitals	35.8	39.7	0.5	0.1
	Public hospitals	0.1	0.2	0.0	0.2
	Day clinics/unattached operating theatres	0.6	0.7	0.0	0.5
	Mental health and substance abuse	0.6	0.7	0.0	0.0
	Step-down, rehabilitation and hospice	0.4	0.4	0.0	0.0
Practitioners	General practitioners	6.6	5.7	15.1	22.5
	Medical specialists	6.6	6.7	6.1	9.1
	Surgical specialists	5.2	5.5	2.8	5.3
	Anaesthetists	2.1	2.3	0.2	0.8
	Radiology	4.3	4.3	4.0	9.2
	Pathology	5.3	5.2	6.6	12.2
	Dentists and dental specialists	3.2	2.3	11.0	34.1
	Allied health professionals	7.5	6.5	16.7	22.0
	Complementary practitioners	0.1	0.1	0.7	53.0
	Managed care out-of-hospital	2.0	2.2	0.0	0.0

Medicines	Medicines dispensed by pharmacists	14.7	12.7	33.1	22.2
	Medicines dispensed by all practitioners	1.9	1.8	2.7	14.5
Other	Ambulance	0.5	0.5	0.0	0.1
	Blood, oxygen and technology	0.9	1.0	0.0	0.4
	Other benefits	1.4	1.6	0.5	3.2
	Ex gratia payments	0.0	0.1	0.0	0.0
Total		**100%**	**100%**	**100%**	**9.9%**

Source: Based on CMS (2016).

The balance on the MSAs is carried over from year to year and can only be withdrawn when a person leaves the medical scheme to join a scheme without an MSA or moves to another option that does not have an MSA. The withdrawal of the MSA balance is taxed as income in the hands of the member. On death, the balance will be transferred to the surviving spouse or child who becomes the new principal member. If there are no dependants, the balance will form part of the deceased member's estate.

Payments are made from the MSA directly to the health care practitioner who submits a bill to the medical scheme for the service rendered. Health care practitioners have found MSAs to be problematic in terms of their cash flow as they might render a service only to find out that the MSA had been exhausted when they submit the bill. Schemes responded by providing doctors and pharmacists with access to information on MSA balances via electronic terminals, allowing them in some cases to immediately reserve a portion of it for future claims. This gave doctors and pharmacists the certainty that the savings account was in positive balance at the time the service was purchased and that they would receive payment for the service rendered. Some schemes have experimented with smart cards that hold details of the MSA balance, others have linked up with banks to provide card facilities similar to a debit card. Discovery Health Limited at one stage offered credit at First National Bank, a bank in the same financial group, when the MSA was exhausted. MSAs have increasingly fallen out of favour with the health authorities and the medical schemes regulator, who see MSAs as resembling banking accounts.

Benefit expenditure from savings accounts

Table 13.1 shows the total expenditure by medical schemes in 2014 on various services, split into pooled benefits and MSAs. Expenditure from MSAs is concentrated on out-of-hospital care. While MSAs are used for less than 0.5% of private hospital expenditure, nearly a third of visits to dentists and dental specialists are paid from MSAs. Some 20–25% of visits to general or family practitioners and medicines are paid from MSAs. This understates the amount of out-of-pocket expenditure as the doctor may be paid directly rather than by submitting the bill to the medical scheme to be paid from the savings account. In total, 9.9% of benefit expenditure in 2014 was from MSAs (Fig. 13.3).

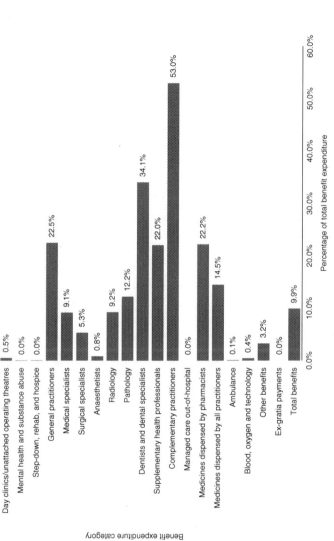

Figure 13.3 Personal medical savings account expenditures in South Africa by benefit category, 2014

Source: Based on CMS (2016).

The savings balances held on behalf of members and carried over from 2015 to 2016 amounted to 11.1% of total assets of medical schemes in 2015. To put this in context, the savings balances carried over were equivalent to 51.3% of total MSA contributions in 2015.

Policy concerns about MSAs

The Department of Health does not view MSAs in a positive light; it has long argued that the justification for MSAs is very limited and that all evidence suggests that they are counter-productive (Department of Health, 2002). A major concern is the effect on reducing risk pooling in medical schemes. The Department of Health found no objective evidence that self-insurance reduces the cost trends of necessary medical services and argues that costs will only be contained by strategic purchasing of services covered by the risk pool. Services paid for from MSAs are effectively purchased by individuals, further fragmenting purchasing power and potentially allowing providers to charge even higher fees for such services. This could ultimately translate into greater financial access barriers to health care.

Although high administration fees have been under scrutiny by the regulator, additional charges of more than 10% of the saved amounts were at times levied for managing the savings accounts. The reconciliation of individual entitlements and interest accrued and charged was not transparent before regulatory changes in 2011 and 2012 (see Box 13.1). The Department of Health is of the view that as MSAs are essentially personal savings of an individual, many individuals are likely to be financially worse off by putting their money into an MSA rather than placing them in their own personal bank account. The ruling that MSA balances belong to the scheme and not the members (see Box 13.1) would make MSAs even less attractive.

The Department of Health (2002) concluded in 2002 that:

> "Medical savings accounts are clearly problematic in a number of important policy goals and from the consumer protection perspective. It is therefore recommended that the current policy be revisited with a view to phasing them out of medical schemes, or at least substantially diminishing their impact on risk pools and contribution costs. The focus of health policy needs to be on risk-sharing and cost containment and none of these key health policy objectives can be achieved through medical savings accounts."

The Council for Medical Schemes (2006b, 2007) expressed concern about the increased risk-shifting to members through the use of savings accounts. However, while the environment remains voluntary, there is a delicate cross-subsidy from the young to the old in private insurance schemes. There has therefore been a reluctance to remove MSAs completely because that might encourage the young and healthy to leave the system. This may be changed following the 2017 ruling (see Box 13.1).

Evidence for risk selection by MSA plans

The MSA issue generates heated arguments and it is difficult to find objective and independent evidence on the impact of MSAs. Jost (2005) found that most of the material available in Europe and the USA on the South African experience was written by one executive from Discovery Health. These documents, used for lobbying for consumer-driven health care in the USA, deliberately imply a high level of government support for the MSAs,[10] whereas South African government policy has in fact been completely the opposite.

A major independent study of risk in South African medical schemes (RETAP, 2007) was carried out using 2005 data from the four largest administrators, who provide services to 63.4% of the private health fund beneficiaries in the country. The risk factors used were those identified for use with the Risk Equalization Fund, namely age, gender, maternity events, chronic diseases[11] and multiple chronic conditions.[12] It was found that there were substantial differences in age profile between different

---

[10] In Matisonn (2000): "For most of the last decade – under the leadership of Nelson Mandela – South Africa enjoyed what was probably the freest market for health insurance anywhere in the world," and "Under Nelson Mandela's regimen, the popularity of Medical Savings Accounts soared."

[11] The 25 common chronic conditions that must be covered by PMBs are: Addison's disease, asthma, bronchiectasis, bipolar mood disorder, cardiomyopathy, chronic obstructive pulmonary disease, chronic renal disease, Crohn's disease, diabetes insipidus, diabetes mellitus type 1 and type 2, dysrhythmias, epilepsy, glaucoma, haemophilia, hyperlipidaemia, hypertension, ulcerative colitis, coronary artery disease, multiple sclerosis, Parkinson's disease, rheumatoid arthritis, schizophrenia, systemic lupus erythematosus, hypothyroidism and HIV/AIDS.

[12] It was found that some people have up to 11 simultaneous chronic conditions from the list of 25 common conditions covered by the PMBs. The risk in schemes is measured as having two, three and four or more simultaneous conditions.

product types in open schemes. Network plans that require the member to obtain all primary care through a network of capitated providers were, at the time, a recent initiative and were marketed primarily to low-income workers. Plans with network options covered only had a very young age profile whereas those members who had a choice of benefit design and chose a non-MSA option were found to have an older age profile. The surprising finding in the study was that all benefit types had a similar rate of incidence per 1000 of chronic disease and multiple chronic diseases by age band. In other words, there was no evidence that choice of a savings account leads to the selection of more healthy members, after adjusting for the effects of age.

Assessment of market performance

Financial protection

Although the motivation for introducing MSAs explicitly stated by the medical schemes was to reduce moral hazard and to promote more restrained use of health care by members, MSAs were seen by members as a desirable development due to declining benefit packages. Medical schemes have over time moved towards covering the potentially catastrophic costs of hospitalization, with declining coverage of routine health care (such as general practitioner and dental services and acute prescription medicines). Initially, benefit restrictions took the form of increasing co-payments and deductibles but later they took the form of removing such services from the risk-pooled benefit package altogether. This meant that medical scheme members were incurring increasing out-of-pocket payments. By the late 1990s, although medical schemes only covered about 16% of the population, two thirds of all out-of-pocket payments for health care were attributable to medical scheme members (Cornell et al., 2001).

Within this context, many medical scheme members were persuaded, through intensive marketing by the schemes advocating MSAs and by brokers, that MSAs were necessary for financial protection. Anecdotal evidence suggests that there seems to be very little awareness among medical scheme members that "you get only what you pay for" in MSAs and that in fact they were simply spending their own money. Members may be better off placing the money that they contribute to MSAs in a savings account in a financial institution where they can earn interest on these funds (given that few medical schemes offer interest on MSA balances). They would not only benefit from earning interest on these funds, but would also avoid having to go through the inconvenience and cost of paying a provider up front (given that many providers will not directly claim from MSAs), submitting the account to the scheme and sometimes waiting a considerable time for reimbursement. The only benefit to members of an MSA is that it is a form of enforced savings, when many individuals may not be sufficiently disciplined to establish a personal account and routinely deposit savings for health care costs not covered by their scheme, and that they may have access to the value of a full year of savings at any point in the year.[13]

What is of concern is that the introduction of MSAs appears to have contributed to a vicious cycle. Declining benefit packages created a perceived need among members for MSAs, but, in turn, the existence of MSAs has allowed schemes to reduce risk-pooled benefit packages even further. A study by the Council for Medical Schemes (2007), showed that while risk pool contributions and claims had increased by 43.9% and 39.9%, respectively, since 1997 in real terms, MSA contributions and claims increased by 185.6% and 250% respectively in this period.

Equity in financing

Although there is no comprehensive empirical evidence for this at present, it is likely that MSAs do not promote equity in health care financing. This is based on the fact that those who are younger are more likely to choose a benefit option that has an MSA for day-to-day expenses rather than have these expenses covered through a risk pool. This is confirmed by the earlier finding that non-MSA options have an older age profile among schemes that offer both MSA and non-MSA options. This means that contributions to MSAs will be influenced by the member's perceived risk of requiring health services rather than being income-related. Hence, it is unlikely that contributions to MSAs are such that higher-income members contribute more than lower-income members and MSAs therefore represent a regressive financing mechanism within the insured population. Nevertheless, as it is only higher-income people who are covered by medical schemes, medical

---

[13] There is also some benefit from the tax exemption associated with contributions to MSAs but also out-of-pocket payments are tax deductible within certain limits. For more information see www.sars.gov.za/TaxTypes/ PIT/Pages/Medical-Credits.aspx and www.sars.gov.za/TaxTypes/PIT/Pages/ Additional-Medical-Expenses-Tax-Credit.aspx.

scheme contributions (including those with MSAs) are progressive in terms of overall health care financing, that is, the burden of contributing to MSAs does not fall on the poorest households.

Equity in service provision and use

As noted in Chapter 12, although there are no substantial inequities in service provision affecting medical scheme members, there are service provision inequities that favour medical scheme members relative to those not covered by medical schemes. In relation to the use of health services, MSAs undoubtedly contribute to inequities in service use, if defined as the use of health services being distributed according to the need for care. Although the review of risk differentials between MSA and non-MSA members found that there was no significant difference in the incidence of chronic illnesses between the two groups, it did find that MSA options had a membership base with a younger age profile. As most of the common chronic conditions are covered under the risk-pooled PMBs, and as MSAs are primarily used for services such as acute prescription medicines (33% of MSA expenditure in Table 13.1), general practice services (15%), dental care (11%) and allied health professionals (17%), there will be relatively less need for such services among young adults. Older medical scheme members tend to choose benefit options that cover these day-to-day expenses from a risk pool, but the only contributors to this risk pool are members who tend to be equally old and/or with equally high health care needs. By definition, MSAs do not allow risk cross-subsidies, except for within an individual family.

Quality of care and efficiency in the delivery and use of services

While the introduction of MSAs was explicitly viewed as a mechanism for promoting efficiency in health service use, by encouraging individual members to take more responsibility for managing their own health service use and expenses, there is no evidence that MSAs have in fact promoted efficient use of health care. If the introduction of MSAs had promoted efficiency in use, one could reasonably expect that there would have been some slowing down in the rate of annual contribution increases, which has not occurred.

While many factors have contributed to this rapid scheme contribution and expenditure spiral, the lack of improvement in affordability, together with the widespread availability of MSA plans by 2005, casts doubt on the claim by Gore (1993) that MSAs are "the only cost containment system that has ever worked." The temporary reversal of the real cost spiral (in 2005 and 2006) is ascribed to the introduction of the GEMS in January 2006, which is able to achieve cost containment through active purchasing for a very large risk pool,[14] and through a growing number of medical scheme members buying down to lower-cost scheme options due to the increasing unaffordability of medical scheme cover.

A key issue is that members of medical schemes appear to make little distinction between their risk-pooled and MSA benefits; anecdotal evidence implies that an attitude of wishing to benefit from any contributions made, which is central to moral hazard, appears to prevail. Another issue that militates against MSAs achieving efficiency gains is that there is very limited purchasing power in the MSA context. Each individual is the purchaser of services, and while a health insurance organization could negotiate rates with providers for benefits covered under a risk pool, it has little incentive to do so for services covered under the MSAs, not least of all because members can use their MSAs for a very wide range of service providers.

The one area that has seen a slowdown in real expenditure, and in fact real decreases in expenditure for some years, is that of medicines. Medicine pricing regulations introduced in 2004 have been particularly important in contributing to real decreases in pharmaceutical spending, but increased generic substitution has also been critical in constraining spending on medicines.[15] The legislative requirement for retail pharmacists to offer individual patients a less expensive generic equivalent to the prescribed medicine is likely to have contributed to efficiency gains in the case of medicines paid for from MSAs. However, much of the efficiency gains from the generic substitution relate to the use of formularies for the treatment of chronic conditions covered by the PMBs.

---

[14] By the end of the first year of its operation, that is, December 2006, it was the 15th biggest scheme (out of 120 schemes). By November 2007 GEMS had reached nearly 190 000 principal members and 500 000 beneficiaries, making it the largest restricted (employer-based) medical scheme and the third largest scheme in South Africa.

[15] Generics as a proportion of total medicines dispensed to medical scheme members increased from 35% in 2003 to 40% in 2004 and 44% in 2005 (Bester & Hammann, 2005; Bester, Brews & Hammann, 2006).

In terms of quality of care, MSAs could contribute at least to improvements in perceived quality of care. Before MSAs were introduced, the benefit packages covered by medical schemes were relatively restrictive in that they did not cover many providers. Hence, the fact that MSAs can be used to cover the costs of a very wide range of health services (for example, chiropractors, homeopaths and many nonbiomedical healers) has allowed members to consult practitioners of their choice.

Likely impact of proposed mandatory health insurance on MSAs

As indicated in Chapter 12, introduction of some form of mandatory health insurance is planned. This is likely to significantly impact on the MSAs because their major role is to cover day-to-day expenses and the benefit package under a mandatory health insurance is anticipated to cover at least some primary care services. This would weaken the rationale for MSAs. Further, the key goal of the proposed mandatory health insurance is to promote social solidarity through improved income and risk cross-subsidies in the overall health system. As MSAs would not contribute to achieving this goal, they are unlikely to be permitted in the mandatory insurance regulatory context, and possibly even within the top-up insurance (covering treatments not available in the minimum package) environment.

Conclusion

The development of MSAs in South Africa was closely linked with the increasing involvement of insurance companies in health care funding in the late 1980s, which translated into a move away from risk pooling and towards the individualization of risk. Insurers introducing MSAs argued that this development was necessary to promote cost containment through making individuals the main buyers of health care. At the time, medical schemes were faced with rapid cost escalation.

The MSAs have been a successful strategy for highly competitive open medical schemes to grow their businesses. Discovery Health grew from a start-up in early 1993 to being the largest medical scheme, with 2 692 million beneficiaries by December 2015, equivalent to nearly one third of the total number of beneficiaries in private health insurance. Schemes with MSAs have also been somewhat successful in the voluntary environment in keeping some of the younger members in the system, as can be seen from their age profiles submitted to the Risk Equalization Fund.

MSAs have brought some benefits for individuals in the sense that they were introduced at a time when benefit packages were being reduced and co-payments increased. Funds in MSAs could be used to cover the increasing burden of these out-of-pocket payments. In addition, MSA contributions are paid from pre-tax incomes whereas direct out-of-pocket payments are paid from after-tax disposable income. However, a vicious cycle has developed with schemes using the existence of MSAs as a means to further reduce day-to-day benefits and/or increase co-payments on services outside the PMBs package. MSAs have not increased financial protection in reality, as individuals can only benefit to the extent that they contribute, except in the case of scheme members who would otherwise not have saved funds independently to cover unexpected out-of-pocket payments.

In addition, MSAs have the effect of shifting some of the rationing decisions from health care funders to individuals and their families. This has meant that funders avoid the more difficult work of negotiating cost-effective and quality delivery of care with health care providers but can instead concentrate on benefit design and cream-skimming. MSAs have not had the desired effect of dampening moral hazard; in the South African context, there is an urgent need to actively engage in supply-side controls to address spiralling costs rather than continue to further shift the cost and rationing burden to individuals.

Chapter 12 outlined in considerable detail how private health insurance has had a profoundly negative impact on the overall health system in South Africa, particularly in relation to:

- its contribution to rapidly spiralling health care expenditure;
- its contribution to growing disparities in the public–private mix and undermining the public sector through diverting health professionals away from the public health sector, which serves the vast majority of South Africans; and
- severely limiting the potential for income and risk cross-subsidies in the overall health system.

Because they are personalized for the individual members and their dependants, MSAs undermine income and risk cross-subsidies even more than risk-pooled private insurance. On this basis, MSAs can be said to be even more detrimental to the overall South African health system than other components of the private health insurance system, both in terms of allowing funders to avoid their responsibility for strategic purchasing and through undermining risk pooling. While private health care funders raised serious concerns about the 2007 decision by the ruling political party to introduce a system of national health insurance, it is precisely their actions in systematically undermining risk pooling that have created the rationale for the introduction of these reforms. The competition provided by GEMS was a significant factor in reining in the use of MSAs to attract members and the 2017 ruling of the Constitutional Court may accelerate the demise of MSAs in medical schemes.

Postscript

Since this Chapter was drafted, the Competition Commission's Health Market Inquiry released its final report in late 2019 (http://www .compcom.co.za/wp-content/uploads/2020/01/Final-Findings-and-recommendations-report-Health-Market-Inquiry.pdf). The findings are in line with the analysis presented in this Chapter. In addition, the National Health Insurance Bill was submitted to parliament in 2019, and is undergoing public comment (https://www.gov.za/sites/default/files/ gcis_document/201908/national-health-insurance-bill-b-11-2019.pdf). The Bill is in line with the policy direction laid out in the White Paper.

References

Bester M, Hammann E (2005). *Mediscor medicines review – 2004*. Centurion, Mediscor Pharmaceutical Benefit Management.

Bester M, Brews M, Hammann E (2006). *Mediscor medicines review – 2005*. Centurion, Mediscor Pharmaceutical Benefit Management.

Cornell J et al. (2001). *South African National Health Accounts: the private sector*. Pretoria, National Department of Health.

Council for Medical Schemes (2005). Regulating in the public interest: taking stock and looking to the future. A five-year review of the Council for Medical Schemes. Pretoria: www.medicalschemes.com/Publications .aspx; accessed on 15/02/2011.

Council for Medical Schemes (2006a). Annual Report 2005/2006. Pretoria: www.medicalschemes.com/publications/publications.aspx?catid=7; accessed on 15/02/2011.

Council for Medical Schemes (2006b). Report of the Registrar of Medical Schemes, 2005/2006. Pretoria: www.medicalschemes.com/Publications .aspx; accessed on 15/02/2011.

Council for Medical Schemes (2007). Report of the Registrar of Medical Schemes, 2006/2007. Pretoria. URL: www.medicalschemes.com/Publications .aspx, accessed on 15/02/2011.

Council for Medical Schemes (2014). Annual Report 2013/2014. Pretoria: www.medicalschemes.com/publications/publications.aspx?catid=7; accessed on 15/12/2016.

Council for Medical Schemes (2016). Annual Report 2015/2016. Pretoria: www.medicalschemes.com/publications/publications.aspx?catid=7; accessed on 18/12/2017.

Department of Health (2002). Inquiry into the various social security aspects of the South African health system. Policy options for the future: www .medicalschemes.com/Publications.aspx; accessed on 15/02/2011.

Gore A (1993). The search for successful health insurance principles in a changing South African health care environment. *Transactions of the Actuarial Society of South Africa*, IX(III):123–56.

Jost TS (2005). Consumer-driven health care in South Africa: lessons from comparative health policy studies. *Washington and Lee Legal Studies Paper No. 05-08, Journal of Health and Biomedical Law*, 1(2):83–109.

Kaplan J, Ranchod S (2015). An actuarial perspective on medical scheme benefit design. Paper presented at the Actuarial Society of South Africa 2015 Convention Sandton, South Africa: http://actuarialsocietyconvention. org.za/convention2015/wp-content/uploads/2015/11/2015-Convention-David-Kirk.pdf; accessed on 15/12/2017.

Matisonn S (2000). Medical savings accounts in South Africa, National Center for Policy Analysis, Policy Report No. 234: www.ncpa.org/studies/s234/ st234.pdf; accessed on 04/10/2005.

Matisonn S (2002). Medical savings accounts and prescription drugs: evidence from South Africa, National Center for Policy Analysis Policy Report No. 254: www.ncpa.org/pub/st/st254/st254.pdf; accessed on 14/01/2008.

McLeod H, Ramjee S (2007). Medical schemes. In: Harrison S, Bhana R, Ntuli A, eds. *South African health review 2007*. Durban, Health Systems Trust: www.hst.org.za/publications/711; accessed on 07/12/2007.

RETAP (2007). Methodology for the determination of the Risk Equalisation Fund contribution table 2007 [Base 2005, Use 2007]. Recommendations by the Risk Equalisation Technical Advisory Panel to the Council for Medical Schemes. Recommendations Report No. 9: www.medicalschemes .com/Publications.aspx; accessed on 15/02/2011.

Republic of South Africa (2008). Medical Schemes Amendment Bill (as introduced in the National Assembly (proposed section 75) by Minister of Health). Government Gazette No. 31114 of 2 June 2008: www .pmg.org.za/bill/20080623-medical-schemes-amendment-bill-b58-2008; accessed on 08/09/2011.

van den Heever AM (2016). South Africa's universal health coverage reforms in the post-apartheid period. *Health Policy*: www.ncbi.nlm.nih.gov/ pubmed/27450773; accessed on 15/12/2017.

14 Consumer-driven health insurance in Switzerland, where politics is governed by federalism and direct democracy

LUCA CRIVELLI[1]

When compared with the other case studies analysed in this book, the role played by private health insurance in Switzerland may seem peculiar and perhaps corresponds only with the Netherlands post-2006 (see Chapter 11). The crux of the Swiss health sector is a system of federally established universal health insurance coverage with atypical characteristics lying somewhere between private and social insurance (OECD 2006; Leu et al., 2007).

Swiss statutory health insurance is run by competing private institutions called sickness funds. It is strongly reliant on consumer choice and mainly financed through non-income-related premiums. Consumers (not employers or the government) buy health insurance plans, pay the bulk of health care costs through insurance premiums, co-payments and out-of-pocket payments, and choose the size of the deductible and other characteristics of the plan according to their own needs and preferences. Health insurers, whose business providing basic coverage is framed by social law, are also entitled to make profits by selling voluntary supplementary and complementary coverage governed by private law.[2] From this perspective, health insurance in Switzerland conceptually belongs within the scope of private insurance.

---

[1] The author is very grateful to Iva Bolgiani and Massimo Filippini for their suggestions regarding a previous version of the chapter. My thanks also go to Mary Ries and Rebecca Tekula for their assistance in proofreading the English text. Responsibility for any remaining errors lies solely with the author.

[2] Insurers are only allowed to generate profits in the voluntary insurance sector. Within mandatory insurance, if the premium revenues of a sickness fund exceed the amount paid for health care services and administrative costs, the money left over must be used to increase the stock of actuarial reserves or to decrease premiums in the following year.

446

However, many features distinguish the Swiss case from classic private health insurance: since 1996 Swiss citizens have been mandated to purchase a comprehensive package of health care benefits; insurer activity in the domain of mandatory health insurance is managed in accordance with non-profit regulations; risks are adjusted between sickness funds by means of a risk equalization mechanism; premiums and enrolment are highly regulated by the state; and earmarked subsidies are designed to help people with a low income to pay their health insurance premiums. From this perspective the characteristics of the sector are similar to those of social insurance (Thomson et al., 2013).

The ambiguity of the Swiss health insurance system was highlighted in two articles published in the same issue of the *Journal of the American Medical Association* (Herzlinger & Parsa-Parsi, 2004; Reinhardt, 2004). Although considering the same set of facts, the two articles proposed radically different hypotheses and explanations of the (alleged) superior performance achieved by the health care sector in Switzerland when compared with the United States. According to Herzlinger and Parsa-Parsi, Switzerland's good performance is supposedly rooted in the significant role consumers play in paying for health care and the resulting high cost transparency, which leads to effective cost control and enables citizens to obtain what they consider to be good value for money. The interpretation offered by Reinhardt is diametrically opposite: he argues that the performance of the Swiss health care system must be ascribed to pervasive government regulation. Both articles, however, underestimate the importance of the particular political and social context in which the health sector in Switzerland is embedded.

This chapter aims to illustrate how the institutional peculiarities of the Swiss political system, combined with the hybrid health insurance model, result in a weakened role for both health insurance competition and state regulation. The organization of the Swiss health sector reflects at least three fundamental factors (Achtermann & Berset, 2006: 20): (i) a strongly decentralized political system, based on federalism, subsidiarity and the institutions of direct democracy; (ii) a liberal economic culture, which emphasizes freedom of choice and consumer-driven economic decisions; and (iii) a unique historical path for social security, in which non-profit institutions[3] led to the creation of a voluntary insurance sector and continue to influence the current system of universal coverage.

---

[3] On the role of private non-profit organizations in the Swiss social security system, see Rossini & Martignoni (2000).

The Swiss health insurance sector relies on the principles of regulated competition, which plays out within a national regulatory framework, but mostly at the cantonal (decentralized) level.

To better understand this puzzle, the chapter is organized as follows: the second section presents some discussion of the history of the Swiss health insurance system; the third section describes the principal changes introduced by the 1996 Federal Health Insurance Act [*Krankenversicherungsgesetz* (KVG)]. The fourth section assesses the performance of the present system, focusing on market structure, premium growth, financial sustainability, risk pooling, switching behaviour, risk selection and innovation. The chapter ends with analysis of the role played by direct democracy in defining the particular dynamics of reform pursued by the health insurance sector in Switzerland and outlines future scenarios.

Historical development of statutory health insurance in Switzerland

In order to understand why the Swiss model of health insurance is so different from the global pattern it is necessary to consider the particular role played by Swiss social culture and political institutions since the 19th century. In this context the relevance of federalism[4] and the significance of the institutions of direct democracy[5] and a solid tradition

[4] Switzerland is a small federal state (8.4 million inhabitants in 2016) of 26 cantons. Article 3 of the Swiss Constitution grants a high degree of autonomy to the cantons, stating that "The cantons are sovereign insofar as their sovereignty is not limited by the Federal Constitution; they shall exercise all rights which are not transferred to the Confederation." The precept of Swiss decentralization is that public policies and their implementation should be assigned to the lowest level of government capable of achieving the objectives.

[5] In the Swiss political system (both at cantonal and federal level) the citizen has the chance to participate directly in every state decision by means of direct democracy. For example, federal laws and generally binding decisions of the Confederation are subject to an optional referendum; in this case, a popular ballot is held if 50 000 citizens so request. The referendum is similar to a veto and has the effect of delaying and safeguarding the political process by blocking amendments adopted by parliament or the government or delaying their effect. The referendum is therefore often described as a brake applied by the people. A second way for citizens to induce a change is called popular initiative. If at least 100 000 signatures are collected within 18 months to

of mutual benefit organizations in civil society must be borne in mind. From the beginning of the 19th century various examples of mutuality and cooperation among citizens sprang up, leading to the spontaneous formation of numerous mutual support groups. The assessment of these initiatives by social scientists is not conclusive. In similar initiatives all over the world many authors see the principles of reciprocity and solidarity of the cooperative movement and civil economy at work (Bruni & Zamagni, 2007), with citizens organizing themselves from the bottom up to face emerging problems of unemployment, disability and sickness collectively. However, other authors interpret these initiatives as the adulteration of what began as an instrument of political and trade union struggle into a powerful means of promoting "a pedagogy of providence able to guarantee the integrity of an economically liberal social order" (Muheim, 2003: p.22). What is not contested is that the existence of these mutual support groups strongly conditioned the fundamental choices of the Swiss welfare system, which was coming into being (Gilliand, 1986: pp.247–60).

At the beginning of the 20th century four kinds of mutual support groups could be clearly distinguished in Switzerland, and their origins are still recognizable in the names of some of today's sickness funds:

- *professional funds*, linked to the trade union world and therefore limited to trade union members;
- *company funds (Betriebskrankenkassen)*, realized by the initiatives of philanthropic capitalists, intended for the employees of a given firm;
- *confessional funds*, promoted within Catholic confraternities and inspired by the social doctrine of the Church;
- *public funds* (the *öffentliche Krankenkasse*), created by a canton, a regional district or a municipality (*Dorfkrankenkassen, Bezirkskrankenkassen*).

While membership of the first three types of funds was restricted to people belonging to a particular category, in public funds affiliation was theoretically open and linked only to place of residence. However, even in the public funds, membership was often subordinated to the

propose a constitutional amendment, then a popular ballot must be held. The outcome will be binding, provided a majority of voters and cantons support the proposal.

moral integrity of the person and to his/her favourable personal situation (good health status, not too old).

A census held in 1903 counted 2006 mutual support groups, to which 14% of the population were affiliated (about 500 000 people).[6] Half of the groups had fewer than 100 members and grouped together the inhabitants of one municipality. The risks they attempted to guard against were not limited to sickness (nine mutual groups out of ten offered cover against health risk, usually in the form of a daily cash benefit),[7] but also included death (assistance to widows and orphans) and long-term unemployment. Years earlier, in 1899, the federal assembly had approved a draft bill (Lex Forrer) which envisaged setting up a decentralized system of public funds, jointly financed by the insured and employers and organized on a territorial basis starting from a minimum number of 1500 insured (Knüsel & Zurita, 1979; Gilliand, 1990). Undoubtedly it was a more modern and rational system of health insurance, following the Bismarck model. However, a referendum was launched against it and it was clearly rejected in a popular ballot in May 1900.

From the ashes of that ballot, the first federal Law on Sickness and Accident Insurance (*Kranken- und Unfallversicherungsgesetz* (KUVG)) developed a decade later. It was accepted by parliament in 1911 and approved by the people in 1912. The legislature realized that to overcome the obstacle of direct democracy and introduce a federal law on the subject of health insurance it was necessary to leave the management of the sector in the hands of private institutions and respect the cantonal autonomy that is particular to federalism. This lesson, as we will see below, lasted throughout the entire 20th century and still casts its shadow on present-day political choices.

Unlike the model set up by Bismarck in Germany, with the KUVG the Swiss legislature relinquished the idea of making health insurance compulsory on a national scale, leaving the cantons to decide whether to make it compulsory at cantonal level.[8] Instead, they opted for

---

[6] These mutual support groups were not uniformly spread throughout the territory. They reached greater levels of concentration in the urban, industrialized areas of the German-speaking cantons and were less prevalent in the Latin cantons (Muheim, 2003).

[7] The total coverage of expenses for medical care and medicines was guaranteed only in a few cases. In many cases benefits were interrupted after 3 or 6 months.

[8] It is important to point out that six cantons made affiliation to a sickness

voluntary individual affiliation by citizens and flat-rate premiums not related to income, whose values were established by each sickness fund and adjusted for age and gender. To reduce the financial fragility of the sickness funds and to stimulate voluntary affiliation the state decided to participate in the financing of premiums with public money, by transferring a lump-sum per person subsidy to the sickness funds.[9] In order to qualify for subsidies, sickness funds had to: accept any national below a certain age limit (usually 55 years), regardless of health status and sex; allow a change of sickness fund if justified (for example, by marriage or change of domicile); and limit the premium surcharge for female members (compared with males of the same age) to 25%[10] (Zweifel, 1990: p.80). Finally, to encourage the early enrolment of the young, the KUVG obliged sickness funds to rate premiums on the basis of member age at the time of enrolment. Those who joined the fund at the age of 25, and thus contributed to the insurance fund from an early age, would continue to pay the premiums reserved for this age class for the rest of their lives provided they did not switch funds. The earliest statistics available show that about half the population was insured in 1945, while nearly universal coverage was achieved between 1985 and 1990. By this time premiums had lost any reference whatsoever to the actual age and risk profile of the insured, making switching to another insurer somewhat expensive for older people who had joined the sickness fund when young.[11]

The strong corporative organization of sickness funds[12] led to the adoption of important restrictions to market competition in the health

---

fund compulsory for the whole population before 1994; twelve cantons made affiliation compulsory for special social groups such as people with a low income and foreigners; and four cantons delegated the decision for a mandate to each municipality (Alber and Bernardi-Schenkluhn 1992: 210).

[9] Despite these subsidies the financial status of sickness funds remained precarious until the partial revision of the law in 1964 (Alber and Bernardi-Schenkluhn, 1992: 184–91).

[10] This was 10% after the 1964 partial revision of the law.

[11] For newly enrolled people the KUVG permitted health insurers not to cover known pre-existing diseases at the time of enrolment for a maximum of five years, making a change of sickness funds even more costly for sicker and older people.

[12] The history of the Swiss Sickness Funds Association (*Konkordat der Schweizerischen Krankenkassen*) goes back to 1891. In 1985 the Swiss-German *Konkordat* was merged with the Swiss-French and Swiss-Italian

insurance sector (Swiss Antitrust Commission, 1993: pp.77–85). Explicit comparisons of benefits and premiums among insurers, as well as poaching customers from other members of the Sickness Funds Association, were forbidden. Moreover, provider fees were established by collective contracting as a result of bargaining at cantonal level between the medical association and the federation of sickness funds. As sickness funds could not differ in the set of contracted doctors and hospitals nor in the level of fees, there were limited opportunities for a single sickness fund to widen its own market. Just one strategy was left open to them: to compete on the basis of the size of the benefit package. Because the benefit package was not defined in the form of a positive list, insurers started to enlarge the range of covered services beyond the minimum standard established by the 1964 revision of the law (Sommer, 1987: pp.51–3; Alber & Bernardi-Schenkluhn, 1992: pp.213–17). Another form of competition was the promotion of collective insurance contracts for members of specific organizations, particularly companies employing low-risk workers.[13]

Competition among insurers became particularly pernicious at the beginning of the 1990s, when some new companies began to attract younger cohorts by exploiting the premium-setting regulations. Seventy-five years after the introduction of the KUVG a large portion of the clientele of the old sickness funds consisted of people who had been paying contributions for decades (Sommer, 1987: pp.54–7). New companies began to cream-skim through full-scale promotion of their own products at particularly convenient youth-oriented premiums.[14] Not all

federations and in 2002 the national association and the different cantonal federations were merged into a new body called *santésuisse*. In 2013, four large health insurers, which together account for about 41% of all insured, left *santésuisse* and founded *curafutura*. The reason of the divorce was a substantial disagreement with respect to the governance of *santésuisse*, which was (and is today) strongly in the hands of the emerging health insurer *Group Mutuel*.

[13] Between 1979 and 1989 the diffusion of collective insurance contracts rose from 13% to 18% (Swiss Antitrust Commission, 1993: p.66). In 2015 the Swiss Financial Market Supervisory Authority introduced a more binding regulation of discounts offered by means of collective insurance contracts. Starting from 2017, a formal approval of the authority, based on actuarial data, will be necessary if the offered discount exceeds 10%.

[14] The most prominent example of successful cream-skimming was that of Artisana. The expansion of this company was abruptly stopped by the

younger citizens could resist the temptation of fleeing the burdensome solidarity required by the old sickness funds, in which they were required to subsidize the health care cost of older people. Following this exodus of the young, the average risk profile in the historical funds worsened, forcing administrators to increase premiums generally, so pushing more and more low-risk individuals out of these funds (Sommer, 1987: pp.55–9; Beck & Zweifel, 1998). In 1993, acting with the right of emergency powers, the federal government took remedial action to prevent an insurance death spiral, which would have completely segregated the high-risk insured. These new regulations mandated the sickness funds' participation in a risk-adjustment mechanism based on age, gender and canton of residence (Beck, 2000; Beck et al., 2003), thus halting the segmentation of risks.[15]

The Federal Health Insurance Act (KVG) was approved following a referendum in 1994[16] and came into force in January 1996. The next section describes this new legal framework.

Organization of health insurance in the 1996 Federal Health Insurance Act

The introduction of the KVG in 1996 marked a turning point for the Swiss health care system; not only was this the first radical reform at federal level after more than 80 years of immobilization (Table 14.1), but the Act also had enormous implications in terms of both intergovernmental task-allocation and the role of competition in the Swiss health insurance sector. The reform objectives, laid out in the Federal Council's bill of 8 November 1991, could be grouped into four broad categories: (i) strengthening solidarity (in relation to the previous legal framework); (ii) enhancing healthy competition among sickness funds; (iii) filling existing gaps in the benefit package by guaranteeing

introduction of risk adjustment in 1993, which forced it to merge with one of the largest sickness funds in Switzerland (Helvetia) a few years later to avoid insolvency.

[15] Risk compensation was anchored in the federal law on sickness insurance in 1996, but for a limited time (10 years). The regulation had been prolonged until the end of 2011 and then prolonged again until the end of 2017, with a substantial improvement in the risk equalization formula starting from 2012.

[16] Only a narrow majority of 51.8% voted in favour of the new law.

Private Health Insurance: History, Politics and Performance

high-quality services; and (iv) containing health spending.[17] These objectives were pursued with a mixed strategy, strengthening the role of competition and giving major recourse to planning and regulatory interventions by virtue of a bill that underwent several adjustments to overcome the obstacle of a referendum.[18]

Table 14.1 *History of popular ballots and legislative reforms in the field of federal health insurance in Switzerland, 1900–2014*

Year	Ballots and legislation
1900	Law Forrer rejected in referendum (by 70% of voters) Participation rate: 66.7%
1912	**Federal law of Sickness and Accident Insurance (KUVG) accepted in referendum (by 54.5% of voters)** Participation rate: 64.3%
1964	**Partial revision of the KUVG (the minor changes were accepted without popular ballot)**
1974	Failure of the popular initiative social health insurance (rejected by 70% of voting people and all cantons) and rejection of the counter-proposal (by 61% of voting people and all cantons) Main aim: to make health insurance (limited to hospital treatments and costly interventions) compulsory and to fund the coverage through wage-dependent premiums and State contributions Participation rate: 39.2%
1987	Law amendment rejected in referendum (by 71% of voters) Main aim: to enable a better control of health insurance spending (for example, by means of a stronger price control and a more binding planning of hospital capacity) and to expand the coverage of maternity insurance Participation rate: 47.6% Start of the preparatory work for the KVG

[17] In 1996 Switzerland experienced concurrently the three classical reform waves identified by Cutler (2002): (i) universal coverage and equal access; (ii) control, rationing and expenditure caps; and (iii) incentives and competition.
[18] See OECD (2006, 2011), Leu et al. (2007) and De Pietro et al. (2015), for an exhaustive presentation of the Swiss system.

Table 14.1 *(cont.)*

Year	Ballots and legislation
1992	Failure of the popular initiative "for a financially bearable health insurance" (rejected by 60% of voting people and all but one of the cantons) Main aim: to establish cantonal earmarked premium subsidies on top of the general federal contribution to health insurance funding Participation rate: 44.4%
1993	**Urgent federal decree accepted in referendum (by 80% of voters)** Main aims: to freeze health care tariffs and prices on the one hand, and premiums on the other until the planned complete revision of the Health Insurance Act comes into force; to set equal premiums for men and women; to slim down the benefit basket and further strengthen cantonal planning Participation rate: 39.8%
1994	Failure of the popular initiative "for a healthy health insurance" (rejected by 76% of voting people and all cantons) Main aim: to make premiums wage-dependent (equal contribution of employer and employee) **KVG accepted in referendum by 51.8% of voters** Participation rate: 43.8%
2000	Failure of the popular initiative "for lower hospital costs" (rejected by 82% of voting people and all cantons) Main aim: to limit mandatory health insurance entitlement to hospital costs Participation rate: 41.7%
2001	First revision of the KVG (no popular ballot requested)
2003	Failure of the popular initiative "health care has to remain payable" (rejected by 73% of voting people and all cantons) Main aim: to establish a new funding mechanism for mandatory health insurance, using value added tax and income-dependent as well as wealth-dependent premiums. Participation rate: 49.7% Failure in the parliament of the second revision of the KVG
2004	Start in the parliament of a new approach to the second revision of the KVG (unbundling strategy)
2007	Failure of the popular initiative "for a single, social sickness fund" (rejected by 72% of voting people and 21 cantons) Main aim: to establish a single health insurer and to introduce income-dependent premiums Participation rate: 45.9%

Table 14.1 *(cont.)*

Year	Ballots and legislation
2008	Failure of the referendum on the counter-proposal to the withdrawn popular initiative "for lower insurance premiums" (rejected by 69.5% of voting people and all cantons) Participation rate: 43.7%
2009	**Accepted referendum on the counter-proposal to the withdrawn popular initiative "yes to complementary medicine"** (accepted by 67% of voting people and all cantons) Main aim: to include specific alternative medicines in the mandatory health insurance coverage – previously only covered by voluntary health insurance Participation rate: 38.8%
2012	Failure of the referendum on an amendment of the KVG (rejected by 76% of voting people and all cantons) Main aim: to promote integrated networks of care with budget responsibilities by means of financial incentives for the insured, such as lower co-payment rate Participation rate: 38.7% Start of the new hospital financing and of the improved risk adjustment formula (hospitalization of three or more days in the previous year was added as a new criterion, next to the previous factors of age and sex)
2014	**Accepted referendum on the counter-project to the withdrawn popular initiative "yes to a family doctor medicine"** (accepted by 88% of voting people and all cantons) Main aim: to commit both cantons and the federal government to promote high-quality primary care that is easily accessible to all Swiss citizens Failure of the popular initiative "for a public health insurer" (rejected by 61.8% of voting people and 21 cantons) Main aim: to replace the current pluralistic system, based on health insurer competition, with a single, public health insurer Participation rate: 47.2% Federal Law on the Supervision of Mandatory Health Insurance (KVAG/LSAMal), which came into force without popular ballot and introduced a stronger control by the Federal Office of Public Health on premiums proposed by insurers and a clearer separation between the mandatory and voluntary health insurance schemes issued by the same insurer

Source: Author.

Note: Initiatives and referendums passed are in bold.

Strengthening competition among health insurers

With the aim of strengthening competition, the Swiss legislature drew inspiration from the model of managed competition.[19] To enforce such a system, the role of the exit reaction mechanism[20] was reinforced by making the switch from one health insurer to another even easier than it has been in the past. One of the major changes introduced in 1996 was the establishment of a uniform statutory health insurance contract at national level. The contract obliged each health insurer to:

- guarantee the same benefit package (quite comprehensive in comparison to other OECD countries)[21] to all people living in Switzerland;[22]
- openly enrol anyone unconditionally and define premiums based on community rating at the regional level (all people aged more than 25, living in a given region and insured by a given sickness fund would pay the same premium);
- establish the same minimum amount of financial risk to be borne by the insured; since 2004 there has been a minimum annual deductible of 300 Swiss francs (Sw.fr.) (around €275)[23] and, for yearly health expenditure exceeding the deductible there is coinsurance of 10% up to a maximum amount of Sw.fr.700 (around €640) per year;[24]
- offer homogeneous quality of health care services because the law (as in the previous legislation) forces each health insurer to contract with all hospitals and physicians operating in the market (compulsory contracting).[25]

As a result of contract standardization, basic health insurance offered by each sickness fund can be assumed to be completely homogeneous,

[19] This concept defines the mechanism of restricted competitive regulation proposed for the first time by Enthoven (1993, 2003). See also Zweifel (2000).

[20] This terminology stems from Hirschman (1970).

[21] See Polikowski & Santos-Eggimann (2002).

[22] Since the benefit package is established by federal law, no differences can exist in the coverage offered by the different competing sickness funds or for people living in different cantons.

[23] We consistently use the 2016 average annual exchange rate of Sw.fr.1 = €0.91.

[24] In other words, for people with the minimum deductible the maximum co-payment per year totals Sw.fr.1000 (€915).

[25] There are some exceptions, such as the voluntarily chosen managed care plans, which are based on selective contracting.

458   *Private Health Insurance: History, Politics and Performance*

such that competition between health insurers should play out at the level of the quality of administrative services provided (time taken to reimburse bills, client support, etc.) and based on the price of the policy (the flat-rate premium established by each insurer in a particular canton). In order to facilitate switching between sickness funds, the insured have the opportunity to change insurer twice a year (on 1 January and 1 July).[26]

Beside this form of radical exit (that is, switching between sickness funds), the federal law also facilitates two methods of partial exit (Gerlinger, 2003; Crivelli & Bolgiani, 2009). First, the insured can choose to bear a higher amount of risk, by selecting a higher deductible, in exchange for a premium discount. Choice of deductible is considered to be an instrument to limit moral hazard and increase individual responsibility. To reduce risk selection, the Swiss law establishes a maximum annual deductible of Sw.fr.2500 (about €2288) and maximum premium discounts associated with different deductible levels. Second, insurers can complement the ordinary policy by designing alternative managed-care-style insurance contracts, which limit choice of provider: Health Maintenance Organizations (HMO), Preferred-Provider Organizations (PPO) and Independent Practice Associations (IPA), which are networks of family doctors.[27] In exchange for a discount on the flat-rate premium, insured people can exit from the classic contract and select a managed-care insurance contract. In theory these alternative forms of insurance, while reimbursing the same range of services, should contribute to bringing health care costs under control through instruments such as selective contracting, gatekeeping, the use of guidelines, the introduction of bonus–malus systems,[28] and disease

---

[26] Some restrictions on changing insurers exist for special forms of insurance. For example, those who have chosen a higher deductible than the compulsory one may change sickness fund only once a year (1 January), whereas those who have opted for the no claims bonus model (Zweifel, 1992) only every 5 years.

[27] For more about the organization of managed care in Switzerland see Zweifel (1998). Beck (2000), Lehmann (2003), Baur (2004), Berchtold & Peytremann-Bridevaux (2011) and Berchtold & Peier (2012). To know more about the impact of such contracts on efficiency, see Lehmann & Zweifel (2004), Grandchamp & Gardiol (2011), Reich, Rapold & Flatscher-Thöni (2012) and Trottmann, Zweifel & Beck (2012).

[28] That is, a system that adjusts the premium paid by insured clients according to their individual claim histories.

and case management programmes. The 1996 reform was based on the assumption that over time the insured would become more sensitive to differences in premiums and, therefore, more mobile. It also expected that greater use of the exit mechanism would encourage insurers to invest more in controlling moral hazard by developing and advertising these new insurance products.

Separation of two realms of activity: social (statutory) versus private (voluntary) insurance

From the beginning of health insurance in Switzerland statutory cover by the sickness funds was offered alongside private insurance policies. Sickness fund cover was governed by the Social Insurance Law, within the framework of the KUVG, and controlled by the Federal Social Insurance Office, while private insurance policies were sold by companies operating in the life or non-life insurance sectors, governed by private law and subject to less strict control by the Federal Office of Private Insurance.

Historically, two types of quite distinct institutions operated within the field of health insurance: one of a non-profit nature (with the benefit of direct public subsidies and tightly controlled) and the other of a for-profit nature with decidedly less rigid legal constraints. Under KUVG regulation the legal status of most of the sickness funds was that of an association, foundation or cooperative, or they were local public institutions.[29] The enactment of the KVG in 1996 brought about a profound change in this traditional distinction. Instead of distinguishing institutions on the basis of legal status (non-profit versus for-profit), the new system differentiates two realms of activity: social insurance and private insurance. Accordingly, since 1996 social insurance (which includes statutory health insurance and voluntary cash benefit insurance) can be provided by any institutional form. All institutions operating in the compulsory social insurance sector come under the tight control of the Federal Office of Public Health and are obliged to comply with

---

[29] In 1966, 215 of the circa 900 existing sickness funds were public bodies integrated into local or cantonal public administration or managed as independent institutions of public law. The last public insurer was transformed into a stock company in 2009.

the more restrictive regulations of the KVG.[30] Conversely, institutions offering voluntary insurance products are rooted in the private Law on Insurance Contracts (*Versicherunsgvertragsgesetz*) and supervised today by the Swiss Financial Markets Supervisory Authority.

As of 1996, therefore, sickness funds have been authorized to operate in the profit-oriented voluntary insurance sector as well. In the meantime, several mandatory health insurers created independent branches to operate with more leeway in the market for voluntary health insurance. In 2016, 30 mandatory health insurance companies (party directly, partly through independent branches) offered supplementary voluntary health insurance, whereas the number of insurance companies exclusively offering voluntary health insurance was 26. The possibility given to so-called social insurers to offer contracts under private law creates major problems in terms of patient mobility and risk selection, particularly for those who have or wish to buy voluntary insurance.[31] According to a comprehensive analysis of the sector (Hefti & Frey, 2008), in 2007 about 70% of the sickness funds (mainly small and operating at the regional level) had maintained their initial legal status. The remainder had become stock companies;[32] these are mostly active across the whole country and together cover two thirds of the population.[33] Table 14.2 summarizes the most important differences between compulsory social and voluntary private insurance contracts.

[30] Since 1996 only one private insurer has moved into the realm of social insurance (Winterthur in 1997). However, in 2005 it left the KVG sector as it was sold to a non-profit private health insurer.

[31] Although tie-in practices are forbidden and voluntary health insurance is offered by independent branches, the ambivalent character of contractual relations with the health insurer (who offers, alongside statutory insurance, private voluntary cover in a less regulated market) raises serious difficulties for the insured in understanding the distinction between the two types of contract. If, in the mind of insured people, the two types of contract cannot be clearly separated, the contents of voluntary insurance may influence the choice of basic insurance.

[32] These are not public companies listed on the stock exchange. With just one exception, the owners of the stocks are not private individuals but the foundations or associations who historically started running social health insurance in Switzerland. As of 2007, 96% of the population was covered by a sickness fund owned by an association or a foundation (Hefti & Frey, 2008: pp.18–21).

[33] The exact market composition as of 1 January 2016 was (own computation based on FOPH, 2016b): four co-operatives and 14 associations (mostly regional or cantonal, with 11 500 members on average); nine foundations

Table 14.2 *Main differences between statutory health insurance and private voluntary insurance in Switzerland*

Statutory health insurance (KVG)	Voluntary health insurance (VVG)
Compulsory insurance with open enrolment	Free contract between insurer and insured
Fixed benefit basket	Freedom in the definition of the services included (beyond the basic benefit basket)
Community rating	Risk-adjusted premiums (at individual or group level)
Unlimited duration of the contract	Possibility to limit the duration of the contract
No coverage restriction to people entering the contract or switching health insurer	Possibility to restrict coverage and waive payment of care related to diseases existing at the time of enrolment

Source: Brunner, Cueni & Januth (2007).

The domain of voluntary insurance can be divided into three distinct product lines, each one accounting for about one third of premium revenues:

- supplementary hospital insurance, which offers free choice of hospital across all cantons,[34] free choice of physician in public hospitals and higher standards of hotel comfort in private and semi-private wards
- cover of services not included in the compulsory benefit package (for example, complementary medicine performed by (non-physician) therapists, dental care and home care beyond the standard covered by compulsory social insurance)
- daily cash benefits insurance.

(four of which operate at the national level, with 33 000 members on average); 31 stock companies (all nationally active, with 250 000 members on average).
[34] In 2012, free hospital choice across cantons was introduced in mandatory health insurance plans. However, because inpatient care in other cantons is covered by mandatory health insurance only up to the diagnosis-related group tariff applying in the canton of residence, this voluntary health insurance product line continues to have some value for patients, although it is far less than in the period before 2012 (for this reason the Swiss Financial Markets Supervisory Authority recently forced companies to reduce premiums for this voluntary health insurance product line).

As far as supplementary hospital insurance is concerned, in 2014 12% of the population owned a policy sold by a sickness fund operating in the mandatory health insurance sector and covering access to private or semi-private wards.[35] The first two product lines are dominated by sickness funds, whereas private insurers have a significant market share in the more complex daily cash benefits and voluntary group insurance sectors (that is, employer-driven contracts).

Overall, two distinct trends can be seen in the voluntary health insurance market. First, voluntary health insurance revenues have grown more slowly than for mandatory health insurance. Between 2000 and 2014 premium revenues increased by Sw.fr.1.2 billion for the first two product lines and by Sw.fr.1 billion for cash benefits, whereas mandatory health insurance premiums grew by Sw.fr.12.4 billion. During the same period voluntary health insurance premiums declined as a proportion of total health insurance revenues, from 34% to 27%. Many companies today are not willing to offer voluntary cover to older people, while the young, who are faced with the heavy burden of mandatory insurance, increasingly choose not to take out voluntary cover for hospital care as long as they are in good health. The consequence of this trend is a worsening of risk pooling.

Second, the sickness funds' share of the voluntary insurance sector has fallen. In 1997, 89% of those with voluntary cover for private or semi-private wards in hospital had a policy with a sickness fund. By 2006 this proportion had declined to 43%. The market shares of sickness funds in terms of voluntary health insurance premium revenues declined between 2000 and 2014 from 57% to 16% (own computation based on FOPH, 2016a: table 911b). These data conceal a very specific strategic choice: many sickness funds have decided to give up the voluntary insurance sector and have set up separate companies to which they have transferred their private portfolios. In this way, organizations that manage private insurance contracts can avoid being monitored by both agencies regulating health insurance, making themselves subject only to the less severe of the two.[36]

---

[35] Since 2008 the Swiss Financial Markets Supervisory Authority stopped the publication of the figures for private insurers.

[36] Konstantin Beck, CSS Insurance, Switzerland, oral communication, 9 July 2008. Hefti & Frey (2008: pp.23–5) have shown a surprising result with respect to profit distribution. From a survey conducted in 65 funds it emerges that only one company has distributed part of its profits to the holding company.

Devolution of competences to the federal government

Historically, the organization of the health system has come under the control of the cantons. Over time, decentralization of competences, ample autonomy of the cantonal governments in public spending decisions and fiscal federalism have created significant differences among cantons with respect to per person health care spending, regulatory setting, the role of the private versus public sector and the level of production capacity (Vatter & Rüefli, 2003; Crivelli, Filippini & Mosca, 2006). Instead of a single health care system, Switzerland is composed of 26 subsystems, connected to each other by the KVG. However, although each canton is formally responsible for ensuring access to good quality health services, the KVG has shifted the balance of power from the cantons to the Confederation. Health insurance is now compulsory at the federal level and the Confederation defines the benefit package guaranteed to each resident.[37] In effect, health insurance is a public service institutionalized at national level to which all citizens have universal access. The public service is financed by two instruments: compulsory insurance supplied by private sickness funds within the framework of the KVG and the public spending of the cantonal and municipal authorities. The latter is financed by general local government taxation and used to subsidize providers who offer services included in the compulsory benefit package (for example, hospitals of public interest, public nursing homes, public and non-profit home care institutions). Furthermore, both federal and cantonal contributions are used to subsidize health insurance premiums for households with modest incomes.

The KVG forced a reduction in cantonal autonomy on decisions regarding public spending, leading to several important changes in the distribution of tasks between the Confederation and cantons.[38] In 2013,

Therefore, the empirical evidence shows that the profits of the voluntary sector are generally kept within the companies, to increase reserves, to further develop the business (for example, marketing campaigns to attract good risk profiles) or reduce premiums.

[37] Social insurance is not automatic but it is compulsory. The cantons are responsible for the surveillance of this mandatory insurance and check the membership status of each citizen. It is impossible to leave one sickness fund without having a contract with another insurer and fines are imposed on those who are caught without coverage (Brunner, Cueni & Januth, 2007: pp.151–2; Cheng, 2010: p.1443).

[38] Switzerland is moving in the direction hoped for by the theory of fiscal

the federal health minister issued, for the first time in Switzerland's history, a strategic plan (called *Gesundheit2020*) that sets priorities for health policy action in four areas and defines 36 measures to be implemented in the coming 8 years.[39] The reactions of stakeholders and cantonal authorities to this initiative were mixed. Nevertheless, this initiative of the federal government demonstrates that even federal states with a longstanding tradition of decentralization need, at a certain point in their history, to overcome fragmentation and weak health policy leadership, and start to increasingly rely on central power interventions (Crivelli & Salari, 2014b). The essence of the problem lies at a different level: such a transfer of new tasks to the Confederation cannot take place without an amendment of the Federal Constitution (Schaffhauser, Locher & Poledna, 2006) and must be accompanied by a corresponding adjustment of the public spending share borne by the federal government (Crivelli & Filippini, 2003). The absence of these adjustments would result in a violation of the principle of "who decides, pays", as the bulk of public spending on health is still financed by the cantons, even though the Confederation plays an increasingly important role in health policy decisions. Accordingly, it is not surprising that in the last 20 years cantons have been unwilling to accept radical reforms of the system aimed at transferring additional responsibilities and decision-making power to the central government and to health insurers without an equivalent transfer of financial responsibilities. Several times in the last two decades cantons have been the main opponents of the federal government's roadmap of reform, and hence the search for consensus on fundamental changes continues to be slow and complex (Bolgiani, Crivelli & Domenighetti, 2006).

Assessing the performance of health insurance

The contribution of statutory health insurance to health care finance

Switzerland is distinct, among high-income countries, in its highly regressive health care financing system (Wagstaff & van Doorslaer, 1992;

federalism, according to which the central government should have responsibility for income redistribution (and therefore also for financing the basic stock of merit goods), whereas cantons should be responsible for the organization and production of health services (Oates, 1999).

[39] See www.bag.admin.ch/gesundheit2020/index.html?lang=en.

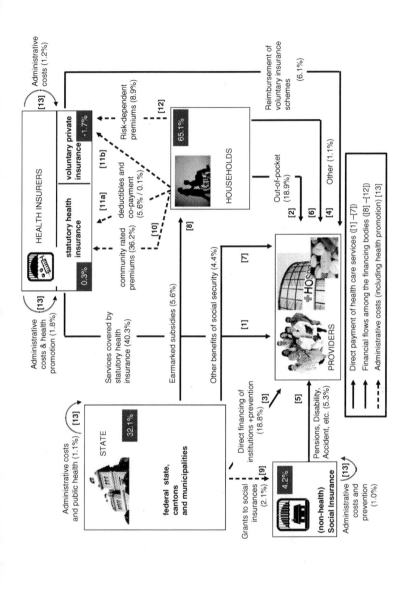

Figure 14.1 Health care financing in Switzerland in 2014

Sources: FSO (2016); FOPH (2016a).

Note: In 2014 total health care financing amounted to Sw.fr.71.3 billion.

Wagstaff et al., 1999; Bilger, 2008; Iten et al., 2009; Ecoplan, 2013; Crivelli & Salari, 2014a). This is due to two factors: first, compulsory health insurance premiums are established independently of citizens' ability to pay; and, second, citizens are called on to pay a considerable share of the health care costs (approximately 31%) out of pocket or through voluntary insurance. This share is high compared with other OECD countries, illustrating how a combination of fiscal federalism, direct democracy[40] and a private insurance system can lead to low achievement with respect to the objectives of redistribution and vertical equity (Banting & Corbett, 2002).

The Swiss health care system is also characterized by a multiplicity of actors who finance health services: the three levels of government (federal, cantonal and municipal); approximately 60 sickness funds; private insurers and other social insurance bodies; and, finally, every Swiss household. Direct payments for health services are indicated in Fig. 14.1 by the solid arrows with the numbers [1] to [7]; in addition to which several financial transfers take place between the financing bodies, shown by the dashed arrows from [8] to [12]. Finally, the dotted lines [13] indicate administrative costs (which include spending on prevention and health promotion).

Total spending on health care is therefore distributed in the following manner:

- The share borne by the state (Confederation, cantons and municipalities) is about 32%, financed by Swiss residents in a generally progressive way by means of taxation. The bulk of the state share comes from cantons and is used to finance hospitals. A significant but smaller portion of this share is used to subsidize premiums (56% from federal government, 44% from the cantons in 2014).
- The net share borne by non-health social insurance funds (accident, invalidity and pensions) is about 4.2%.[41] This share comes from

---

[40] Fiscal federalism and direct democracy are jointly responsible for the significantly lower level of public spending on health care (Feld & Kirchgässner, 2005).

[41] In general, the main goal of such social insurance is to provide cash benefits. However, premium revenues finance in-kind benefits too. For example, health care delivered to an employed person due to an accident is financed by accident insurance rather than mandatory health insurance.

contributions proportional to income and is jointly financed by employers and employees.

- The share of expenditure borne by households accounts for 65.1%.[42] This spending, whose main feature is the absence of any relation to citizens' ability to pay, comes in four distinct forms, with different redistributive effects:

- net community-rated premiums for mandatory health insurance,[43] which amount to 30.6% of total spending (36.2% less 5.6% of premium subsidies) and reflect solidarity between the healthy and the sick, and between generations
- voluntary private insurance premiums, which are risk-rated but still defined ex ante and therefore represent a way of financing health care based on mutuality (8.9% of total spending)
- contributions depending ex post on each individual's health care consumption, net of the public contributions in various regimens of social protection such as social aid, allowance, etc. (24.5%); this category includes direct out-of-pocket payments as well as coinsurance and deductibles for services covered by mandatory health insurance
- private donations to non-profit institutions represent 1.1% of health spending.

In a nutshell, approximately one third of Swiss health care financing is linked to citizens' income and ability to pay (federal, cantonal and municipal tax financing, with the exception of value added tax, non-health social insurance contributions). The second third reflects each citizen's risk profile and individual health care consumption (voluntary private insurance and out-of-pocket payments). The last third allows for a high degree of solidarity between the sick and the healthy (the community-rated premiums). As a result, the middle class bear a disproportionately heavy share of the financial burden in the interests of solidarity.

---

[42] The total of the three shares exceeds 100%, since it includes the deficit of statutory health insurance (0.6% in 2013) and the surplus of voluntary insurance (2.1% in 2013).

[43] Mandatory health insurance is for individuals, with every family member having a separate contract. Premiums are paid directly to the sickness funds, generally on a monthly basis.

Unsustainable health insurance premiums for the middle class

Overall, Swiss health care is characterized by good equity of access[44] and substantial and widespread public approval – in spite of high levels of out-of-pocket expenditure – by virtue of the high degree of responsiveness to patients' desires, the large benefit package and ample freedom of choice. However, beyond these positive performance scores, emphasized in several international analyses (WHO, 2000; OECD, 2006; van Doorslaer, Kollman & Puffer, 2002; van Doorslaer, Masseria & Koolman, 2006; Schoen et al., 2010), there is little pressure to enhance efficiency in the Swiss health care system.

Retrospective (fee-for-service) provider payment for outpatient care, collective negotiations at the association level and ineffective risk adjustment by health insurers are not the best way to prevent monopoly rents in income distribution (Zweifel, 2004). The explosion of health care costs experienced in Switzerland is reflected in constant increases in health insurance premiums over the last 10 years. Between 1996 and 2016 the average national annual premium for adults has grown by 147% from Sw.fr.2077 (about €1900) to Sw.fr.5138 (about €4700).[45] The increase may have been more pronounced without the concurrent transfer of risk from the health insurers to the insured; from 1996 to 2005 the minimum deductible doubled from Sw.fr.150 to Sw.fr.300. The ongoing reduction in statutory reserve standards since 1998 has also contributed to containing the size of actual premium inflation.[46]

---

[44] Although financial barriers might be a problem for lower social classes [EU-SILC data show that in 2014 almost 10% of the poorest income quintile reported having an unmet need for dental care due to cost; Eurostat (2016)], horizontal inequity scores for Switzerland are not significantly different from zero with respect to the probability of visiting a doctor and the mean number of visits, whereas the probability and number of general pracitioner visits are pro-poor and those of specialist visits are pro-rich (van Doorslaer, Masseria & Koolman, 2006; De Pietro et al., 2015: p.238). However, according to some evidence of supply-induced demand in Switzerland (Domenighetti et al., 1993; Crivelli, Filippini & Mosca, 2006), we cannot exclude the possibility that poorer households obtain the appropriate quantity of specialist visits whereas richer households over-consume specialist care.

[45] There is significant variation across cantons. From 1996 to 2014, the largest growth was noted in Argovia (+182%) and the lowest in Vaud (+71%). In absolute terms, the annual premium increased from a minimum of Sw.fr.2049 (in Wallis) to a maximum of Sw.fr.3775 (in Basle-Town); see FOPH (2016a).

[46] By law, sickness funds have to withhold a fixed percentage of premium

As a result of cost and premium inflation, combined with increased cost shifting to consumers, the economic burden of health insurance has become unsustainable for a large number of citizens (Kilchenmann, 2014; Frey & Neumann, 2015).[47] Although premium subsidies for households with modest incomes (provided jointly by the Confederation and cantons) have increased by 64% between 1998 and 2014, the impact of the net premium on disposable income for many households has also increased greatly, in many cases exceeding the 8% threshold to which the Federal Council committed itself when presenting the KVG draft bill in 1991 (Kägi et al., 2012; Frey & Neumann, 2015). Fig. 14.2(a) shows the evolution of net premium incidence (as a percentage of disposable income) for two typical households (a family of four and a retired single person) from 1998 to 2014. The graph highlights the Swiss average as well as the situation in the cantons with the lowest and highest incidence. Fig. 14.2(a) illustrates two facts. First, a general growth in incidence over time; the almost flat development for the retired person between 2004 and 2007 is due to a change in the economic

revenues to lower the risk of insolvency. The total amount of reserves decreased from 25.7% in 1996 to 15.7% in 2011, reflecting the significant reduction in the statutory solvency requirements (for the largest funds with more than 250 000 insured the minimum reserve ratio decreased from 20% to 10%). The freed reserves have been used by insurers partly to absorb cost inflation and smooth out premium increases. Since 2012, a new method has been used to compute the solvency ratio of Swiss sickness funds. The new solvency ratio declined from 172% in 2012 to 155% in 2014 (FOPH, 2016a).

[47] In Switzerland, a growing number of the insured (on average, young people in socially and economically weak situations, who are still in good health or do not have significant health problems) no longer pay their premiums. In 2006, the parliament strengthened the sanctions these people face, giving the sickness funds the opportunity to suspend coverage until all unpaid invoices have been settled. Since 2012, if individuals fail to pay their premiums, mandatory health insurance companies can request cantons to pay 85% of the unpaid bills on behalf of the insured. This change was introduced to ensure that all residents have valid insurance coverage and can receive care. However, cantons can keep a black list of individuals with frequent arrears. These lists are sent to public (cantonal) providers, and mandatory health insurance companies have to reimburse only emergency care provided to them. According to data of the FOPH (2016a), more than 350 000 people had arrears on their premiums in 2014, whereas 23 000 people were registered on the black lists due to repeated arrears in paying their premiums.

situation of the underlying reference household,[48] which masks the real development of the situation. Second, the strong horizontal inequity of financing across the cantons; the distance between the lowest and the highest canton remains constant over time for the retired person, but it increases for the family. This variation can be explained by the different levels of cantonal spending on health as well as the cantons' diverging strategies in earmarking subsidies for low-income households; some cantons distribute small allowances to a large share of the population, whereas others prefer to target smaller groups of citizens and give them larger amounts of money (Preuck & Bandi, 2008).[49] Moreover, the large reform of the fiscal equalization scheme in 2008 provided cantons with more leeway to react to budgetary pressures by cutting their spending for earmarked premium subsidies (Gerritzen, Martinez & Ramsden, 2016). As a result, heterogeneity of incidence across cantons could even further increase in the coming years.

As would be expected from the system's design, those bearing the greatest share of the financing burden belong to the middle class, the group that no longer benefits from premium subsidies or receives only a marginal contribution from the state. Fig. 14.2(b) illustrates a typical ratio of net insurance premium incidence on household disposable income in Switzerland, computed for a couple living in Ticino canton in 2011.[50] The highest level of incidence, in this particular case 17.5% of disposable income, corresponds to the middle class (an income of Sw.fr.53 000 for a couple). Moreover, for many insured people whose income is slightly above the poverty line, small increases in income are to a large extent eroded by the immediate stopping of means-tested social aid and by the quick reduction in the subsidies provided, resulting in significant threshold effects (the almost vertical line between Sw.fr.44 000 and Sw.fr.53 000 in Fig. 14.2b).

---

[48] The income of the retired person was changed from Sw.fr.30 000 to Sw.fr.45 000 between 2004 and 2006.

[49] See Gilardi & Füglister (2008) for an empirical analysis of the diffusion of health insurance subsidy policies across cantons, using a dyadic approach.

[50] Although the system of premium subsidies differs greatly from one canton to another (Crivelli et al., 2007), the final outcome in terms of incidence is very similar to that illustrated in Fig. 14.2(b). This can easily be demonstrated by looking at the new on-line monitoring of premium incidence in the different cantons, set up in 2008 by the Swiss Office of Public Health (see www .bag.admin.ch/praemienverbilligung/index.html?lang=de).

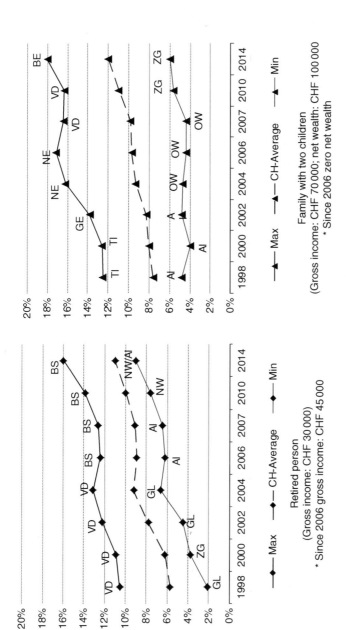

Figure 14.2 (a) Change in net premiums as a percentage of disposable income (Swiss average and cantons with lowest and highest incidence), 1998–2014

Source: Balthasar, Bieri & Gysin (2008).

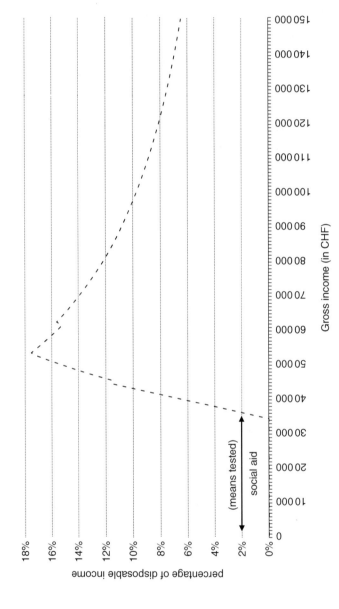

Figure 14.2 (b) Shape of the 2011 net insurance premium incidence for a couple living in Ticino

Source: Crivelli et al. (2015).

Victor Fuchs foresaw this problem in his presidential address to the American Economics Association in 1996, although Fuchs himself may have been unaware that only a few days earlier Switzerland had adopted this system. He noted that:

"There are only two ways to achieve systematic universal coverage: a broad-based general tax with implicit subsidies for the poor and the sick, or a system of mandates with explicit subsidies based on income. I prefer the former because the latter are extremely expensive to administer and seriously distort incentives; they result in the near-poor facing marginal tax rates that would be regarded as confiscatory if levied on the affluent." (Fuchs, 1996: p.17).

Evolution of health insurance market structure

Throughout the first half of the 20th century (Fig. 14.3a) the number of sickness funds doubled from about 500 in 1915 to over 1100 in 1950. This was followed by a phase of progressive concentration in the market, largely through mergers and acquisitions (Frei, 2007),[51] marked by a dramatic fall in the number of sickness funds (from 984 in 1965 to 58 in 2015) and an increasing degree of professionalism and range of operation.[52] Nevertheless, the administrative costs of mandatory health insurance remain moderate (compared with United States standards), amounting to 4.9% of total operating costs in 2014.

Over time the change in numbers of sickness funds has been accompanied by other profound changes. Once-local mutual support groups were transformed into modern insurance companies – global players[53] – losing their local vocation and their link to particular population groups such as employees in a given firm, members of a trade union, special professional categories and inhabitants of a given area. The Herfindahl–Hirschman Index (HHI) computed for each individual

---

[51] At the same time, there was an increase in the degree of population coverage.
[52] Although there was an overall decrease in the number of insurers nationally, the average number of companies operating in each canton (that is, the choice set from the insured's point of view) increased from an average of 40 sickness funds per canton in 1997 to 56 in 2004 (Frank & Lamiraud, 2008) and then decreased again to reach an average of 45 in 2015.
[53] In 1980 the global players made up just 1.8% of total number of sickness funds (Alber & Bernardi-Schenkluhn, 1992: p.241), while in 2016 most health insurers (83%) operated on a national scale.

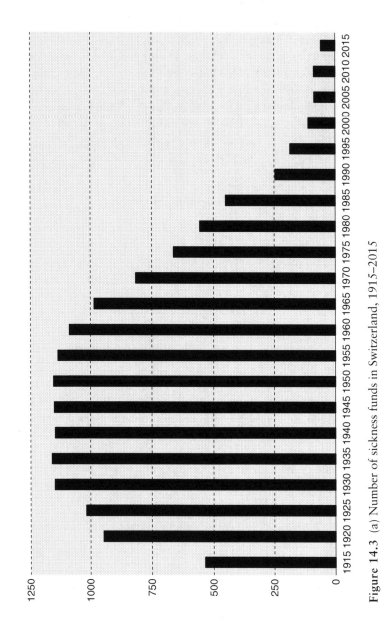

Figure 14.3 (a) Number of sickness funds in Switzerland, 1915–2015

Sources: Alber & Bernardi-Schenkluhn (1992), FOPH (2016b).

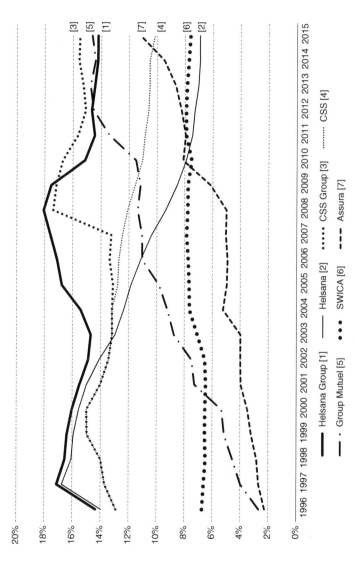

Figure. 14.3 (b) Market share of the largest insurers and holdings in Switzerland, 1996–2015

Source: FOPH (2016b).

health insurer shows a weak reduction in market concentration (the HHI declined from about 0.0757 in 1996 to 0.0545 in 2015). In fact, the largest sickness funds (Helvetia/Helsana, CSS and Visana) have increasingly lost clients, to the benefit of average-sized companies investing in risk selection, in particular Assura and sickness funds belonging to the insurance holding Group Mutuel, which in 2003/2004 included 17 different companies and was very successful at segmenting its clientele into risk groups. Starting from 2003 even the largest sickness funds have tried to imitate this strategy, transforming themselves into holding companies and grouping sickness funds, which maintain their own company names (as well as their independent legal status) but are managed according to a common strategic orientation.[54] By acquiring small funds and creating new companies CSS and Helsana have managed to stop the loss of affiliated members observed since 1997 and reverse the trend (see Fig. 14.3b). Another successful sickness fund, that managed to maintain its market share without creating a holding structure, was Swica. The competitive advantage of Swica has been its strong investment from the very beginning in the development of HMOs. Hence, when considering the market share of the holding companies that exist today, instead of individual sickness funds, we observe a significant increase in market concentration between 1996 and 2015 (the HHI increases from 0.0763 to 0.1008). The regional markets are much more concentrated. In five cantons (Geneva, Jura, Obwalden, Basel City and Graubünden) the 2006 HHI was higher than 0.1800 (which corresponds to the usual threshold indicating a highly concentrated market) (Hefti & Frey, 2008: p.46). The improvement of the risk adjustment formula, which was implemented in 2012 with the aim of making cream-skimming strategies less attractive, had the expected positive effect. Already in 2011, Group Mutuel decided to slim down its structure by reducing the number of companies from 15 to four, significantly enhancing market transparency.

Risk pooling and switching behaviour

Hirschman (1970) argues that in order to judge the functioning of the exit-reaction mechanism one must evaluate switching behaviour in

---

[54] People are generally not aware of the holding structure of the health insurers and still regard each sickness fund as if it were a completely different company.

relation to differences in price and quality. As explained previously, collective contracting for the compulsory benefit package removes differences in the quality of covered health services. Disparities exist, however, in the quality of administrative services and the price of community-rated premiums. The latter reflects the average profile of an insurer's risks (and is therefore susceptible to cream-skimming strategies) and the insurer's ability to control consumers' invoices, limiting the consequences of moral hazard. Although there are tangible differences between insurers in terms of administrative service quality,[55] these are difficult to quantify. It is even more difficult to determine elasticity of demand with respect to administrative quality. What can be hypothesized is that these differences are more evident to those with frequent relations with their insurers – for example, people with chronic conditions who often require information or regularly submit invoices and can better assess speed of reimbursement.[56]

Despite large differences in premiums (Leu at al., 2007) and low switching costs, for many years only a small fraction of policy-holders (between 2% and 3%) switched insurer.[57] However, the situation has changed significantly in recent years, due to continuous premium growth, which makes health insurance more and more unaffordable for the middle class (households not eligible for subsidies). The percentage of people switching to a cheaper health insurer between 2009 and 2010 exceeded 15% and has since then remained consistently above 6.5%. According to Diserens (2002), quoted in Beck (2004a), price elasticity for mandatory health insurance (estimated from aggregate market-share data) is approximately −0.5 in Switzerland, higher than is seen in the Netherlands, but much lower than in Germany (Schut, Gress & Wasem, 2003). However, using individual data Beck & Gelpe (2002) obtained much higher estimates (average value −1.09) and elasticity estimates calculated by Rütschi (2006) are even higher. In other words,

---

[55] See the Comparis survey (www.comparis.ch).

[56] For this reason, from a theoretical viewpoint, increased competition among health insurers to acquire good risks and avoid bad risks can contribute to a general decline in the quality of client support services, so vitiating signals from dissatisfied enrollees or (exiting) people to the sickness fund management.

[57] The percentage of individuals switching funds (which includes movement between companies of the same insurance group) was, for example, 3.3% in 2005, 2.7% in 2006, 2.3% in 2007 and 2% in 2008; see the Comparis survey (www.comparis.ch).

Swiss consumers seem to be less responsive to changes in the price of premiums than German consumers, but recent data highlights a new trend leading to the expectation of higher switching rates in the future. Empirical evidence shows that those willing to change sickness fund frequently come under the category of good risks: young, healthy and higher educated enrollees (see Strombom, Buchmueller & Feldstein, 2002; Beck et al., 2003).

What emerges from this picture is that most insured people do not exit but stay with their sickness fund, even if their premiums are 40% higher than the least expensive on offer. There are many ways of interpreting this limited degree of switching. The insured may regard the transaction costs of switching to be very high, particularly if they are older or sicker and have voluntary insurance coverage.[58] Alternatively, low mobility could be explained by asymmetric information (people underestimate the potential gain of switching health insurer), the limited rationality of individuals and their status quo bias. Moreover, even though the premium is higher, many insured may be unwilling to switch out of loyalty to their own sickness fund. Finally, there are risk-averse individuals who prefer to remain faithful to a company whose faults and merits they know rather than face the uncertainty of a new insurer. Or perhaps, more simply, they hold on to the hope that in future their current insurer will offer the compulsory benefit package cover at a more competitive rate.

According to Laske-Aldershof et al. (2004), the reasons for increased premium variation in Switzerland include a risk-adjustment formula with poor predictive power before 2011,[59] the low-risk profile of switchers,

[58] Customer mobility is limited for voluntary insurance contracts (which are governed by private law) because when taking out such a policy, the insurer may request a medical examination and use the information obtained to calculate risk-adjusted premiums and introduce limits to coverage. Some people fear that by changing their basic insurer they might lose their voluntary cover.

[59] Technically, risk adjustment is calculated as follows: sickness funds with an age structure that compares favourably with that of the general population (many younger and male, few female and older) must contribute to a risk equalization fund, whereas those showing a competitive disadvantage in this regard will receive a subsidy from it. On the shortcomings of the Swiss risk-adjustment formula, based only on sex and age, and on the reform proposals see Spycher (2002), Holly et al. (2004), Beck (2004a, 2004b), Beck et al. (2006). Since 2012 the formula considers a new factor: hospitalization in the previous year and this change is considered as a major improvement

the success of risk-selection strategies adopted by the most aggressive sickness funds and the relative share of people choosing higher deductible levels in the population enrolled in the different sickness funds. As a result, risk-pooling has become less efficient over time. As shown by Frank & Lamiraud (2008), the broadening choice set facing the insured in most cantons (see footnote 255) brought about, ceteris paribus, a significant decrease in the frequency of switching.[60] All these data suggest that further liberalization of the health insurance market, if accompanied by an increase in insurers, could have negative outcomes such as lower efficacy in the exit decisions of the insured and, indirectly, increased risk of transferring so-called rent to insurers.

Risk selection versus moral hazard control

For people who do not switch insurer, the opportunity for partial exit remains an option through the choice of a higher optional deductible or a managed care contract. The number of adult insurees opting for an optional deductible rose between 1996 and 2014 from 32% to 56%.[61] The diffusion of higher deductibles may have both a positive and a negative impact. The positive consequence is an increase in individual responsibility and a reduction in the use of unnecessary health services. Some authors concur that high deductibles have significantly reduced moral hazard in Switzerland (see Werblow, 2002; Felder & Werblow, 2003; Werblow & Felder, 2003), whereas other studies estimate the positive impact of high deductibles to be modest (Schellhorn, 2002). The negative effect is the process of self-selection that determines deductible choice. Geoffard, Gardiol & Grandchamp (2006) have observed, from a representative sample of clients, that the mortality rate of the insured selecting the minimum deductible is 200% greater than that of those selecting a medium deductible. On the other hand, the insured choosing

[60] in mitigating cream-skimming (Beck, Trottman & Zweifel, 2010; Eugster, Sennhauser & Zweifel, 2010).

[60] These results were obtained through a complex econometric model that controlled for variables such as the potential saving achieved by switching fund, the existence of voluntary cover, the degree of satisfaction towards one's own insurer, the duration of the contract, and sex, age and self-reported health status.

[61] In 2005 the maximum deductible rose from Sw.fr.1500 (about €1370) in 1996 to the present Sw.fr.2500 (about €2290).

a high deductible had a 30% lower mortality rate than those choosing a medium deductible when the data were standardized by age and sex.

The exit of Swiss insurees towards managed care contracts has been less common than the choice of optional deductibles up to 2012. After an initial burst of enthusiasm,[62] a period of stagnation ensued. A possible explanation for the limited diffusion of managed care, which many experts believe is not yet capable of introducing competitive pressure on health care providers, is that discounts for these particular insurance forms are regulated to values far below the actual cost savings achieved and lower than the compensation generally necessary to overcome consumer resistance to managed care restrictions (Zweifel, Telser & Vaterlaus, 2006). Since 2004 another upsurge in the popularity of managed care contracts has been observed. The 2008 market share of these alternative insurance forms was 24.3% of the adult population and rose in the last 6 years up to 62% in 2014. The new possibility to combine a managed care contract with an optional deductible (and to benefit from both discounts) certainly helped to increase the popularity of these contracts. Instead of switching health insurer, a growing number of policy-holders are opting for these alternative models in an attempt to avoid raising premiums in the classic form of cover. Lehmann & Zweifel (2004) have attempted to evaluate risk-adjusted expenditure differentials for clients who are members of the three most widespread forms of managed care (HMO, PPO, IPA) compared with the expenditure of clients selecting the traditional contract form. Overall, observed costs are 62% below average in HMO contracts, 39% below with PPO and 34% below with IPA. Yet the maximum premium discount allowed by law is 20%. After controlling for the effects of risk selection, the true savings account for two thirds of the cost reductions recorded by HMOs, half of those by PPOs and one third of savings made by IPAs. A more recent study (see Reich, Rapold & Flatscher-Thöni, 2012) estimates efficiency gains of 21.2% for HMO, of 15.5% for IPA and of 3.7% for the so-called Telmed contracts,[63] whereas the risk selection effects account for 8.5%, 5.6% and 22.5%, respectively. Given that only a part of the savings made can be retransferred to the client in the form of a premium discount, particularly in HMOs, it is quite probable that

[62] Between 1996 and 1997 membership of alternative insurance models quadrupled to reach 8%.

[63] The insured who sign such a contract are obliged to consult a medical call centre, before turning to other medical providers.

the people who have opted for these systems did so due to their inability to pay the ordinary premium and are therefore mainly people in good health but with a relatively low income.

The central role of direct democracy in past and future health insurance reforms

Direct democracy and federalism are at the origins of the very slow pace of radical reforms in the Swiss health insurance system. Referenda and popular initiatives allow Swiss citizens to intervene directly in the decision-making process, approving or rejecting each reform through a popular ballot. Because unbalanced and radical revisions have a high likelihood of rejection in popular ballots, bills are generally amended early on in a pre-parliamentary phase involving negotiation ex ante with opponents of reforms originating in government or parliament and incorporating the demands of the most powerful lobbies (Cheng, 2010: p.1450).[64] In addition, federalism encourages the proliferation of organizational models and spending levels that vary across cantons (Crivelli & Salari, 2014b). Although these variations should reflect citizens' preferences, they create inevitable tensions in maintaining a universal system. Between 1974 and 2014 the Swiss population was called to the ballot box no less than 14 times[65] to deliberate on reforms in the health insurance sector (two urgent federal decrees, three reforms of the federal law proposed by parliament and put to referendum, seven popular initiatives and four counter-proposals). With the exception of the referendum on the KVG in 1994, of two referendums on counter-proposals and of those regarding the two urgent federal decrees accepted by the people, the remaining 11 popular ballots failed (see Table 14.1).

A recurring topic during these years of health insurance reform is the enhancement of equity in financing through more extensive use of general

---

[64] In some cases, when recourse to direct democracy cannot be prevented, negotiating ex post is possible. This occurs when the demands of an initiative's promoters can be partially met in a formal counter-project (a more moderate constitutional amendment) or, more frequently, in legislative amendments that will not necessitate a popular vote.

[65] On two occasions (1974 and 1994) the Swiss people were called to vote on two proposals in the same ballot round.

taxation[66] or by changing from community-rated to income-dependent health insurance premiums.[67] What can be considered a potentially radical change to the system was rejected five times with a sweeping majority of between 60% and 76% of the population, but each time with a participation rate of less than 50% of citizens (ranging from 39.7% in 1974 to 49.7% in 2003). The 2003 popular ballot is particularly illustrative. Two surveys conducted during the second half of 2002 showed a substantial majority of citizens (63%) declaring themselves willing to pay income-related health insurance premiums (Crivelli, Domenighetti & Filippini, 2007). However, 6 months later, in May 2003, 73% of the electorate rejected the popular initiative "Health at Accessible Prices", which proposed a mixed financing system including income-related premiums alongside an increase in value added tax. Undoubtedly, there were substantial differences between the (generic) question asked of the sample interviewed in the 2002 surveys and the specific model proposed by the promoters of the initiative. The media campaign launched at the end of 2002 (see, for example, Credit Suisse, 2003) also persuaded many citizens that it was in their interest to maintain the status quo. There were similar results in the popular ballot held in March 2007 concerning the creation of a single sickness fund with income-related premiums. Two months after the clear No to the initiative (72% of the votes), a survey undertaken for the health insurers showed that 60% of the population favoured the change to income-related premiums. Finally, the impact of the ballot campaign in shifting opinions towards the status quo has been assessed also in the latest ballot of September 2014 (initiative "for a public health insurer"). In a poll carried out in June 2013, 65% of respondents declared themselves in favour of a single, public health insurer. The opponents' campaign kicked off in 2013 and strengthened in June 2014. As a result, the percentage of those supporting the initiative fell constantly over time. This decline in supporters, observed in the polls, shows again how a majority in favour of the initiative (until June 2014) can be gradually transformed into a majority against it (De Pietro & Crivelli, 2015), with 61.8% of voting people finally rejecting the initiative.

[66] The popular initiative voted on in 1992 suggested anchoring sufficient premium reductions in the Constitution, financed by the Confederation and cantons, to the benefit of people with modest income.
[67] With four popular ballots in 1974, 1994, 2003 and 2007.

Yet there is another explanation which invokes Hirschman's theory: the opportunity of exit (towards sickness funds with lower premiums, higher deductibles or managed care contracts) takes strength away from voice.[68] Many people (especially good risks and those with modest income) who, in the absence of this exit opportunity, would vote in favour of radical reforms of the system, either do not participate in popular ballots or vote in favour of the status quo. When it is a question of voting on reforms to the health system, natural tensions occur within each individual, as interests as patient and tax payer[69] diverge from preferences about being insured.[70]

Following the rejection of the single sickness fund proposal in March 2007, which would have strengthened the role of voice[71] in the governance of health insurance and suppressed the possibility of switching insurer, in June 2008 the Swiss people were called on again to make an important decision, which could have caused the fragile compromise between market and state regulation in the present legislation to break down. Right-wing groups blame the state-constrained Swiss health care system for preventing competition between sickness funds, and the existence of (in their view) an overly comprehensive benefit package for encouraging over-consumption and moral hazard on the part of many patients. The Swiss People's Party therefore launched an initiative based on two fundamental pillars: the transfer of part of the health services presently included in the compulsory benefit package to voluntary private insurance[72] and the strengthening of competition and market logic (by abolishing compulsory contracting, accepting liberalization of provider

---

[68] Following Hirschman (1970: ch.4), the opportunity to resort simultaneously to the reaction mechanisms of "exit" and "voice" can cause strong tensions that can result in weak governance of the system.

[69] These interests include maintaining maximum freedom of choice of physician, not closing hospitals in one's own region, keeping the bundle of insured services as comprehensive as possible and paying fewer taxes.

[70] These preferences include avoiding continuous premium increases by means of a better redistribution of the premium burden.

[71] This would be achieved through the opportunity for the insured to be represented on the boards of directors and through surveillance of the single sickness fund.

[72] According to their proposals the compulsory benefit package should only cover the costs of medical care needed to alleviate pain and cure and rehabilitate the patient that are also cost-effective. As a result, maternity and preventive care would have been excluded from the compulsory benefit package.

fees and granting the insurers the status of single purchasers of health services).[73] In particular, market mechanisms would be reinforced in the relations between insurers and the insured, and in the relations between insurers and providers.

Parliament drew up a counter-project to this initiative (called "For a More Effective and Better Quality Health Care System Thanks to Greater Competition"), with the aim of anchoring the most important principles of the initiative within the Federal Constitution and increasing the probability of acceptance.[74] The most significant amendment to the initiative's text was to remove the shrinking of the compulsory benefit package from the proposal. In January 2008, the Swiss People's Party withdrew their initiative in support of parliament's counter-project. Two months previously, surveys undertaken by Swiss Television had outlined a fairly clear picture of the ballot's potential outcome: 60% claimed to be in favour of the counter-project, 20% were against it and 20% undecided. In the following 2 months an extremely fierce campaign (cantonal authorities were strongly opposed to the counter-project, as were doctors' and patients' associations and the centre-left parties) succeeded in bringing about a sensational reversal in the outcome of the vote; in fact on 1 June 2008, 69.5% of voters rejected the counter-project, opting once again for the status quo.

As shown in Fig. 14.4, the results of these two consecutive popular ballots bear witness to a clear negative correlation between the preferences of the population of the 26 cantons. Both reform projects were far from obtaining the required dual majority (of the people and of the cantons), but they had the merit of pushing the debate on reforms towards a well-defined strategic choice. This in turn would have the advantage of clarifying not only the role given to market mechanisms and state regulation, but also whose stake (citizens, patients or insured

---

[73] Recall that until 2011 the cantons had to cover at least 50% of the operating costs and 100% of investment in public-interest hospitals through local taxes. Since 2012, they have to pay 55% of the diagnosis-related group prices in all (public and private) hospitals that are included in the cantons' hospital lists (https://en.comparis.ch/krankenkassen/info/glossar/kantonale-spitalliste). In the promoters' proposal this money would be transferred (through capitation) to the insurers, who at this point would become the single purchasers of all health services and would be liable to cover the entire cost.

[74] The health insurance lobby in the Swiss parliament is powerful. A significant number of members of parliament sit on the executive boards of sickness funds.

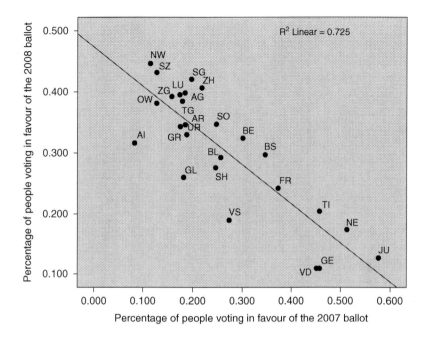

Figure 14.4 Correlation of cantonal results in the 2007 and 2008 popular ballots in Switzerland

Source: Own illustration based on the popular ballots data at the cantonal level.[75]

people) would ensure governance of the Swiss health system. It is not easy to see how a compromise can be found between two antithetical reform strategies in a ballot system that requires a dual majority.

What does seem certain is a slow but inexorable cultural change among citizens and the insured. The obligation to insure themselves combined with (radical and partial) exit options has modified citizens' perceptions of what is acquired by paying the health insurance premium. As Ostrom (2005) well emphasizes, some policies can crowd out reciprocity and collective action. The irrevocability of regressive premium payments has prompted many citizens to view health insurance as a socially unjust tax, and there is an alarming increase in the number of citizens who no longer pay their compulsory premiums regularly (with a prevalence that in some cantons reaches 5% – see Egloff, 2016). At

[75] See www.parlament.ch/de/services/volksabstimmungen/fruehere-volksabstimmungen.

the same time, the possibility of frequently switching insurer makes the typical social insurance values of solidarity and mutuality less obvious. In recent years, a growing number of citizens seem driven to consider cover against the risk of ill health as a commodity; a premium is paid in exchange for health services (and not for the right to transfer financial risk to third parties in case illness strikes). The inflationary incentives inherent in the Swiss fee-for-service payment of ambulatory care (provided both in hospitals and private medical practices) with only weak referral systems (Schwenkglenks et al., 2006) encourage the use of inappropriate diagnostic and therapeutic services by people who are in fact in good health. Hence, the perception of a welfare state in which "abuses are the order of the day" infects the population and raises questions about the legitimacy of proposals intended to maintain and strengthen solidarity among the healthy and sick, young and old, rich and poor,[76] giving rise to the danger of undermining the foundation upon which the Swiss system of universal health insurance is based.

References

Achtermann W, Berset C (2006). *Gesundheitspolitiken in der Schweiz – Potential für eine nationale Gesundheitspolitik. Band 1: Analyse und Perspektiven*. Bern, Bundesamt für Gesundheit.

Alber J, Bernardi-Schenkluhn B (1992). *Westeuropäische Gesundheitssysteme im Vergleich: Bundesrepublik Deutschland, Schweiz, Frankreich, Italien, Grossbritannien*. Frankfurt/Main, Campus Verlag.

Balthasar A, Bieri O, Gysin B (2008). *Monitoring 2007. Die sozialpolitische Wirksamkeit der Prämienverbilligung in den Kantonen*. Bern, Bundesamt für Gesundheit.

Banting G, Corbett S (2002). *Health policy and federalism: a comparative perspective on multi-level governance*. Montreal and Kingston, McGill-Queen's University Press.

Baur R (2004). *Managed Care-Modelle Bestandesaufnahme 2004*. Bern, Bundesamt für Gesundheit.

Beck K (2000). Growing importance of capitation in Switzerland. *Health Care Management Science*, 32:111–19.

---

[76] As illustrated by Fong, Bowles & Gintis (2005).

Beck K (2004a). *Risiko Krankenversicherung – Risikomanagement in einem regulierten Krankenversicherungsmarkt.* Bern, Paul Haupt Verlag.

Beck K, ed. (2004b). *Reformstau beim Risikoausgleich? Internationale Erfahrungen und konkrete Lösungen für die Schweiz.* Luzern, Risk Adjustment Network (RAN).

Beck K, Gelpe V (2002). Mobility in the Swiss health insurance market, *paper presented at the RAN Conference in Leuven* (28–29 June 2002). Luzern, CSS health insurance mimeo.

Beck K, Zweifel P (1998). Cream skimming in deregulated social health insurance: evidence from Switzerland. In: Zweifel P, ed. *Health, the medical profession and regulation. Developments in Health Economics and Public Policy series*, vol. 6. Dordrecht and Boston, Kluwer Academic.

Beck K, Trottmann M, Zweifel P (2010). Risk adjustment in health insurance and its long-term effectiveness. *Journal of Health Economics*, 29(4):489–98.

Beck K et al. (2003). Risk adjustment in Switzerland. *Health Policy*, 65(1):63–74.

Beck K et al. (2006). *Nachhaltige Gestaltung des Risikoausgleichs in der Schweizerischen Krankenversicherung.* Bern, Ott Verlag.

Berchtold P, Peier C (2012). Ärztenetze in der Schweiz 2012: Eindrückliches Wachstum. *Care Management*, 5(3).

Berchtold P, Peytremann-Bridevaux I (2011). Integrated care organizations in Switzerland. *International Journal of Integrated Care*, 11(special edn):e010.

Bilger M (2008). Progressivity, horizontal inequality and reranking caused by health system financing: a decomposition analysis for Switzerland. *Journal of Health Economics*, 27(6):1582–93.

Bolgiani I, Crivelli L, Domenighetti G (2006). The role of health insurance in regulating the Swiss health care system. *Revue française des affaires sociales*, 60(2–3):227–49.

Bruni L, Zamagni S (2007). *Civil economy.* Oxford, Peter Lang.

Brunner HH, Cueni S, Januth R (2007). Krankenversicherung. In: Kocher G, Oggier W, eds. *Gesundheitswesen Schweiz 2007–2009. Eine aktuelle Übersicht.* Bern, Verlag Hans Huber.

Cheng T-M (2010). Understanding the 'Swiss Watch' Function of Switzerland's Health System. Interview with Thomas Zeltner. *Health Affairs*, 29(8):1442–51.

Credit Suisse (2003). *Spotlight: risques et effets secondaires de l'initiative-santé du PS.* Zurich, Economics and Policy Consulting.

Crivelli L, Bolgiani I (2009). Consumer-Driven Versus Regulated Health Insurance in Switzerland. In: Okma K, Crivelli L, eds. *Seven countries, seven reform models: the health care reform experience of Chile, Israel, The Netherlands, New Zealand, Singapore, Switzerland and Taiwan.* Singapore, World Scientific Publishers.

Crivelli L, Filippini M (2003). Il federalismo nel settore sanitario. In: Ghiringhelli A, ed. *Il Ticino nella Svizzera*. Locarno, Dadò.

Crivelli L, Salari P (2014a). The inequity of the Swiss health care system financing from a federal state perspective. *International Journal for Equity in Health*, 13(17):1–13.

Crivelli L, Salari P (2014b). The impact of federalism on the healthcare system in terms of efficiency, equity, and cost containment: the case of Switzerland. In: Levaggi R, Montefiori M, eds. *Health Care Provision and Patient Mobility. Health Integration in the European Union*. Developments in Health Economics and Public Policy 12. Milan, Springer.

Crivelli L, Domenighetti G, Filippini M (2007). Federalism versus social citizenship: investigating the preference for equity in health care. In: Porta PL, Bruni L, eds. *Handbook on the Economics of Happiness*. Cheltenham, Edward Elgar.

Crivelli L, Filippini M, Mosca I (2006). Federalism and regional health care expenditures: an empirical analysis for the Swiss cantons. *Health Economics*, 15(5):535–41.

Crivelli L et al. (2007). *I costi dell'assicurazione malattia nel Cantone Ticino*. Rapporto finale per il Consiglio degli Anziani del Cantone Ticino.

Crivelli L et al. (2015). *Valutazione del sistema RIPAM. Rapporto finale*. Bellinzona: IAS: http://m4.ti.ch/user_librerie/php/GC/caricaAllegato .php?allid=88902; accessed on 15/11/2016.

Cutler D (2002). Equality, efficiency, and market fundamentals: the dynamics of international medical care reform. *Journal of Economic Literature*, 40(3):881–906.

De Pietro C et al. (2015). Switzerland: Health system review. *Health Systems in Transition*, 17(4):1–288.

De Pietro C, Crivelli L (2015). Swiss popular initiative for a single health insurer ... once again! *Health Policy*, 119(7):851–5.

Diserens D (2002). *Die Prämienbudgetierung – ein Kernprozess von Lrankenversicherungen*. Büblikon/Wohlenschwil: mimeo.

Domenighetti G et al. (1993). Revisiting the most informed consumer of surgical service: the physician patient. *International Journal of Technology Assessment in Health Care*, 9(4):505–13.

Ecoplan (2013). Umverteilungseffekte in der obligatorischen Krankenversicherung: Mikrosimulation für die Schweizer Bevölkerung auf Basis der SILC-Erhebung unter Berücksichtigung der kantonalen Strukturen. Bern, Federal Office of Public Health: www.bag.admin .ch/themen/krankenversicherung/06392/06517/index.html?lang=de; accessed on 17/10/2016.

Egloff M (2016). Assicurati morosi, sospesi e insolventi in Ticino. Valutazione dell'applicazione cantonale dell'art. 64a LAMal cpv. 7 entrato in vigore il 1° gennaio 2012: www4.ti.ch/user_librerie/php/GC/caricaAllegato .php?allid=114800; accessed on 11/11/2016.

Enthoven AC (1993). Managed competition: history and principles. *Health Affairs*, 12(suppl.):24–48.

Enthoven AC (2003). Employment-based health insurance is failing: now what? *Health Affairs* Web Exclusives 28 May: http://content.healthaffairs .org/cgi/content/full/hlthaff.w3.237v1/DC1; accessed on 11/02/2010.

Eugster P, Sennhauser M, Zweifel P (2010). Capping risk adjustment? *Journal of Health Economics*, 29(4):499–507.

Eurostat (2016). Self-reported unmet needs for dental examination by sex, age, detailed reason and income quintile [hlth_silc_09]: http:// ec.europa.eu/eurostat/web/health/health-care/data/database; accessed on 25/11/2016.

Feld LP, Kirchgässner G (2005). Sustainable fiscal policy in a federal system: Switzerland as an example. In: Kriesi H et al., eds. *Contemporary Switzerland: revisiting the special case*. New York, Palgrave Macmillan.

Felder S, Werblow A (2003). Swiss social health insurance: co-payments work. *CESifo DICE report*, 1(3):43–6.

Fong CM, Bowles S, Gintis H (2005). Reciprocity and the welfare state. In: Gintis H, Boyd S, Fehr E, eds. *Moral sentiments and material interests*. Cambridge, MA, MIT Press.

FOPH (Federal Office of Public Health) (2016a). *Statistik der obligatorischen Krankenversicherungen 2014*. Bern, Bundesamt für Gesundheit.

FOPH (2016b). Verzeichnis der zugelassenen Krankenversicherer (1.1.2016) [Register of the licenced health insurers]: www.bag.admin.ch/bag/de/ home/themen/versicherungen/krankenversicherung/krankenversicherung- versicherer-aufsicht.html; accessed on 25/11/2016.

Frank RG, Lamiraud K (2008). *Choice, price competition and complexity in markets for health insurance*. NBER Working Papers No. 13817. Cambridge, MA, National Bureau of Economic Research.

Frei W (2007). Krankenversicherer. In: Kocher G, Oggier W, eds. *Gesundheitswesen Schweiz 2007–2009. Eine aktuelle Übersicht*. Bern, Verlag Hans Huber.

Frey M, Neumann R (2015). *Wirksamkeit der Prämienverbilligung – Monitoring 2014*. Bern: Bundesamt für Gesundheit: www.bag-anw.admin .ch/kuv/praemienverbilligung/data/download/Monitoring%202014%20 -%20Schlussbericht.pdf?webgrab=ignore; accessed on 15/11/2016.

FSO (Federal Statistical Office) (2016). *Coût et financement du système de santé en 2014*. Neuchâtel, Office fédéral de la statistique.

Fuchs V (1996). Economics, values and health care reform. *American Economic Review*, 86(1):1–24.

Geoffard PY, Gardiol L, Grandchamp C (2006). Separating selection and incentive effects: an econometric study of Swiss health insurance claims data. In: Chiappori P-A, Gollier C, eds. *Competitive failures in insurance markets*. Cambridge, MA, MIT Press.

Gerlinger T (2003). Gesundheitsreform in der Schweiz - ein Modell für die Reform der gesetzlichen Krankenversicherung? *Jahrbuch für Kritische Medizin*, 38:10–30.

Gerritzen BC, Martinez IZ, Ramsden A (2016). Saving on a tight budget: cantonal health care financing and health care expenditure burdens for low-income households in Switzerland. Working Paper: https://sites.google T.com/site/isabelzenaidamartinez/research; accessed on 15/11/2016.

Gilardi F, Füglister K (2008). Empirical modeling of policy diffusion in federal states: the dyadic approach. *Swiss Political Science Review*, 14(3):413–50.

Gilliand P, ed. (1986). *Les Coûts et l'assurance*. Lausanne, Éditions Réalités Sociales.

Gilliand P, ed. (1990). *Assurance-maladie – Quelle révision?* Lausanne, Éditions Réalités Sociales.

Grandchamp C, Gardiol L (2011). 'Does a mandatory telemedicine call prior to visiting a physician reduce costs or simply attract good risks?', *Health Economics*, 20(10):1257–67.

Hefti C, Frey M (2008). *Die Entwicklung der Versicherungslandschaft in der Krankenversicherung 1996–2006*. Neuchâtel: Schweizerisches Gesundheitsobservatorium: www.obsan.admin.ch/bfs/obsan/de/index/05/ publikationsdatenbank.Document.113391.pdf; accessed on 15/11/2016.

Herzlinger RE, Parsa-Parsi R (2004). Consumer-driven health care: lessons from Switzerland. *Journal of the American Medical Association*, 292:1213–20.

Hirschman A (1970). *Exit, voice and loyalty: responses to decline in firms, organizations, and states*. Cambridge, MA, Harvard University Press.

Holly A et al. (2004). *Health-based risk adjustment in Switzerland: an exploration using medical information from prior hospitalization*, revised version of the final report on research financed by the Swiss National Fund (National Research Program 45). Lausanne, Institut d'économie et management de la santé (IEMS), University of Lausanne.

Iten R et al. (2009). Volkswirtschaftliche Wirkungen steigender Gesundheitsausgaben. Zuerich: INFRAS: www.vips.ch/dok_download .cfm?dokID=1446; accessed 17/10/2016.

Kägi W et al. (2012). *Monitoring 2010: Wirksamkeit der Prämienverbilligung*. Bern, Federal Office of Public Health: www.bag.admin.ch/themen/

krankenversicherung/01156/01159/index.html?lang=de; accessed 15/11/2016.

Kilchenmann C (2014). Krankenversicherung: Wer bezahlt, wer bekommt? *Soziale Sicherheit*, 3/2014:184–5.

Knüsel R, Zurita F (1979). *Assurances sociales: une sécurité pour qui? La loi Forrer et les origines de l'état social en Suisse*. Lausanne, Institut de science politique.

Laske-Aldershof T et al. (2004). Consumer mobility in social health insurance markets: a five-country comparison. *Applied Health Economics and Health Policy*, 3(4):229–41.

Lehmann H (2003). *Managed care: Kosten senken mit alternativen Krankenversicherungsformen*. Zürich/Chur, Verlag Rüegger.

Lehmann H, Zweifel P (2004). Innovation and risk selection in regulated social health insurance. *Journal of Health Economics*, 23(5):997–1012.

Leu R et al. (2007). *A tale of two systems: the Swiss and the Dutch health care systems compared*. Baden-Baden, Nomos Verlagsgesellschaft.

Muheim D (2003). Caisses privées et assurances sociales: retour sur les premiers projets d'assurance-maladie (1893–1912). In: Fédération suisse des employés en assurances sociales (FEAS) (ed). *Aspect de la sécurité sociale: dossiers problèmes non résolus*. Lausanne, FEAS.

Oates W (1999). An essay on fiscal federalism. *Journal of Economic Literature*, 37(3):1120–49.

OECD (2006). *OECD Reviews of Health Systems: Switzerland*. Paris, OECD

OECD (2011). *OECD Reviews of Health Systems: Switzerland*. Paris, OECD

Ostrom E (2005). Policies that crowd out reciprocity and collective action. In: Gintis H, Boyd S, Fehr E, eds. *Moral sentiments and material interests*. Cambridge, MA, MIT Press.

Polikowski M, Santos-Eggimann B (2002). How comprehensive are the benefit packages of health services? An international comparison of six health-insurance systems. *Journal of Health Services Research and Policy*, 7(3):133–42.

Preuck R, Bandi T (2008). Prämienverbilligung – zwischen wünschbaren Zielen und finanziellen Rahmenbedingungen. *Soziale Sicherheit*, 3:178–81.

Reich O, Rapold R, Flatscher-Thöni M (2012). An empirical investigation of the efficiency effects of integrated care models in Switzerland. *International Journal of Integrated Care*, 12:1–12.

Reinhardt UE (2004). The Swiss health system: regulated competition without managed care. *Journal of the American Medical Association*, 292:1227–31.

Rossini S, Martignoni Y-L (2000). *L'importance des institutions privées sans but lucratif dans la protection sociale en Suisse.* Neuchâtel, Office fédéral de la statistique.

Rütschi C (2006). *Who cares about prices? An empirical analysis of basic health insurance choice in Switzerland.* Technical report, University of Bern.

Schaffhauser R, Locher H, Poledna T, eds. (2006). *Das Gesundheitswesen – Motor von Wohlbefinden und Wohlstand. Radikale Denkanstösse für das Schweizer Gesundheitswesen.* St Gallen, Institut für Rechtswissenschaft und Rechtspraxis.

Schellhorn M (2002). Auswirkungen wählbarer Selbstbehalte in der Krankenversicherung: Lehren aus der Schweiz? *Vierteljahrshefte zur Wirtschaftsforschung*, 71(4):411–26.

Schoen C et al. (2010). How Health Insurance Design Affects Access To Care And Costs, By Income, In Eleven Countries. *Health Affairs*, 29(12):2323–34.

Schut FT, Gress S, Wasem J (2003). Consumer price sensitivity and social health insurer choice in Germany and the Netherlands. *International Journal of Health Care Finance and Economics*, 3(2):117–38.

Schwenkglenks M et al. (2006). Economic efficiency of gatekeeping compared with fee for service plans: a Swiss example. *Journal of Epidemiology & Community Health*, 60:24–30.

Sommer JH (1987). *Das Malaise im Gesundheitswesen. Diagnose und Therapievorschläge.* Zürich, Orell Füssli.

Spycher S (2002). *Compensation des risques et pools possibles (pools de hauts risques) dans l'assurance maladie obligatoire.* Rapport de recherche No. 19/03. Bern, Office fédéral des assurances sociales.

Strombom BA, Buchmueller TC, Feldstein PJ (2002). Switching costs, price sensitivity and health plan choice. *Journal of Health Economics*, 21(1):89–116.

Swiss Antitrust Commission (1993). *Krankenkassen und Tarifverträge.* Bern, Veröffentlichungen der Schweizerischen Kartellkommission und des Preisüberwachers, Vol. 2/1993.

Thomson S et al. (2013). Statutory health insurance competition in Europe: a four-country comparison. *Health Policy*, 109(3):209–25.

Trottmann M, Zweifel P, Beck K (2012). Supply-side and demand-side cost sharing in deregulated social health insurance: Which is more effective? *Journal of Health Economics*, 31(1):231–42.

van Doorslaer E, Masseria C, Koolman X (2006). Inequalities in access to medical care by income in developed countries. *Canadian Medical Association Journal*, 174(2):177–83.

van Doorslaer E, Koolman X, Puffer F (2002). Equity in the use of physicians in the OECD countries: has equal treatment for equal need been achieved?

In: OECD, ed. *Measuring up: health systems performance in OECD countries*. Paris, OECD.

Vatter A, Rüefli C (2003). Do political factors matter for health care expenditure? A comparative study of Swiss cantons. *Journal of Public Policy*, 23(3):301–23.

Wagstaff A, van Doorslaer E (1992). Equity in the finance of health care: some international comparisons. *Journal of Health Economics*, 11(4):361–87.

Wagstaff A et al. (1999). Equity in the finance of health care: some further international comparisons. *Journal of Health Economics*, 18(3):263–90.

Werblow A (2002). Alles nur Selektion? Der Einfluss von Selbstbehalten in der Gesetzlichen Krankenversicherung. *Vierteljahreshefte zur Wirtschaftsforschung*, 71(4):427–36.

Werblow A, Felder S (2003). Der Einfluss von freiwilligen Selbstbehalten in der gesetzlichen Krankenkasse: Evidenz aus der Schweiz. *Schmollers Jahrbuch*, 123(2):235–64.

WHO (World Health Organization) (2000). *The world health report 2000. Health systems: improving performance*. Geneva, World Health Organization.

Zweifel P (1990). Comparative health systems: Switzerland. In: Scheffler RM, Rossiter LF, Rosa J-J, eds. *Comparative health systems: The future of national health care systems and economic analysis. Advances in Health Economics and Health Services Research*. London, JAI Press.

Zweifel P (1992). *Bonus options in health insurance*. Dordrecht, Kluwer Academic.

Zweifel P (1998) Managed care in Germany and in Switzerland: Two approaches to a common problem. *Pharmacoeconomics*, 14(0):1–8.

Zweifel P (2000). Switzerland. Special section: reconsidering the role of competition in health care markets. *Journal of Health Politics, Policy and Law*, 25(5):937–44.

Zweifel P (2004). Competition in health care – the Swiss experience. *Économie Publique*, 14(1):3–12.

Zweifel P, Telser H, Vaterlaus S (2006). Consumer resistance against regulation: the case of health care. *Journal of Regulatory Economics*, 29(3):319–32.

15 Regression to the increasingly mean? Private health insurance in the United States of America

LAWRENCE D. BROWN AND SHERRY A. GLIED

Life can be a tale of woe so people contrive arrangements that insulate them from the consequences of some familiar feared mishaps. Insurance – a small present payment in promise of larger compensation in the event of future losses – is one such arrangement. Insurance contracts recompense policy-holders for, for instance, loss of or damage to their home in a fire or their car in an accident, or the death of a benefactor who took out life insurance. People may also buy insurance that will cover some (maybe most) of their medical costs if they or members of their family fall ill and need care.

In health policy parlance the options for insurance are often dichotomized between private and public but both terms are partly misnomers. In theory, an individual called an insurer might bet (gamble) on the continued good health of another individual called the insured, but in practice those in the insurance game insure pools of people and rely on the law of large numbers to turn the profits that make it worth their while playing that game in the first place. So-called private health insurance, then, has an inescapably social character. Public health insurance, meanwhile, is an entitlement to care (or anyway, to have most medical bills covered) conferred by the state on its citizens by law. The contract in question is social/political/legal, a right of citizenship, not the product of decisions made by consumers.

Private health insurance is socialized risk pooling and risk sharing managed by non-public entities, which might be so-called private organizations with a public charter (European sickness funds, for example) or for-profit or voluntary insurance firms operating under public rules of greater or lesser scope and specificity. In most Western nations private insurance has a complementary or supplementary role: it covers co-payments (as in France), for instance, or services that the basic public plan does not (as in Canada) or that are delivered in ways that

494

are distinct from those of the public plan (access to the private sector in the United Kingdom). In some societies private insurers sell coverage within a set of government rules that regulate what they offer and how (for instance, Switzerland and – since 2006 – the Netherlands). And in one country (the United States of America) private carriers supply the preponderance of health coverage within government constraints that leave purchasers and insurers considerable discretion as to who gets covered for what, on what terms and at what price. However, since the passing of the Affordable Care Act in 2010, comprehensive health reforms have been implemented to protect consumers from the exclusionary practices of the insurance industry (US Department of Health and Human Services, 2015).

Health insurance of whatever type rests on two axioms. First, everyone is vulnerable to illness, perishable and mortal (a sameness principle, so to speak). Second, illness strikes different people differently (the difference principle). Most nations emphasize the sameness principle and pay little policy attention to the differences. The United States does the reverse. Most nations ponder what particularistic accent marks to paint on their broad universalist canvas. The United States wonders how its particular parts can be made to sum to something closer to a universalist whole. The United States is, then, as everyone knows, an international outlier, an exceptional case in its reliance on weakly regulated private health insurance as its basic source of basic coverage. This chapter reviews how and why this happened, why the pattern endures, and what it means for such evaluative criteria as adequacy and equity of coverage. It also looks at how the arrival of the Patient Protection and Affordable Care Act (ACA), passed in March 2010 but now under threat of repeal, has changed and may continue to change the privatist picture.

Emergence of private health insurance

Before the early 20th century, the demand for health insurance was weak because health care was rarely efficacious or costly. The main concern – impoverishment when illness cost workers their wages or jobs – was addressed mainly by fraternal associations and unions (Starr, 1982; Hacker, 2002: p.53), which also occasionally contracted with medical providers to care for their members for prepaid sums. As the quality and cost of medical care began rising, European and American paths diverged. Germany launched public health coverage for workers in 1883 and Britain did likewise in 1911, for example. In the United States Theodore Roosevelt, though a surpassingly rugged individualist, called for something similar, as did the American Association for Labor Legislation, but physicians and business groups protested vigorously, and then the First World War and the Russian Revolution rendered anything German or socialized unfit for mention in polite society. A handful of large commercial insurers began to apply the practices of the life insurance trade to health coverage (Starr, 1982; Hacker, 2002; Klein, 2003), but such products achieved very low penetration. And so matters stood when the Depression struck in 1929 and raised a number of questions about health coverage.

Economic collapse damaged both consumers (who were less inclined to seek medical care) and providers (whose bills were less inclined to get paid). Leftist reformers within and around the New Deal programmes of President Franklin D. Roosevelt detected a window of opportunity and pushed Roosevelt to include national health insurance (NHI) alongside other welfare state staples such as social security, public assistance and unemployment compensation, which he was in the process of pushing through Congress. Various political streams (Kingdon, 2003) converged, however, to slam the window shut: strident antipathy from physicians roused to active opposition by the broad reform agenda of the Committee on the Cost of Medical Care (Fox, 1986: pp.50–1); whispers in Roosevelt's ear by trusted physicians about the alleged miseries of Germany's health system (Swenson, 2008); and the unwillingness of the president and his aides to spend large amounts of political capital in a battle with doubtful prospects when so many other conflicts beset the New Deal (Hacker, 2002). Roosevelt would revisit the issue rhetorically by including universal health coverage in the Economic Bill of Rights that he sketched in 1944, but by then the nation was at war and the providers, perhaps sensing that the best defence against NHI was a good offence, had concocted a seemingly feasible alternative – Blue Cross and Blue Shield.

The third sector

From a historical and social point of view it is misleading to portray so-called private health insurance as roaring out of the Depression to conquer the field of coverage. This view discounts the inestimable importance, then and still, of the third sector, that is, health insurance institutions designed to mirror the character of voluntary hospitals and physicians (whose presentation of self to themselves and the public highlighted their commitment to professionalism, not profit). Voluntary hospitals held a position of special virtue in between the politics of the public sector and the profit seeking of the private sector. Graced with a community-service mission and unpaid boards of trustees drawn from community elites, they stood alone, aloof and above the tainted preserves of politics and profit. (In this they also resembled the philanthropic foundations that then supplied much of their capital.) Blue Cross was essentially a financing arm for the voluntary hospitals, and built in their normative image. The comparative oddity of the origins of private health coverage in the United States – the insurance system was invented by and for providers themselves – should not obscure the nuanced nature of a private system that rested on three pillars – voluntarism (the third sector), cooperation (insurance would be marketed to local purchasers who could accept, reject or bargain over it as they pleased) and community (these private insurers elevated service and benefits for the community above the profits they formally did not accrue). [For more on Blue Cross see Law (1974), Anderson (1975), Brown (1991) and Chapin (2015).]

As so often happens in American life, these assertions of special virtue were accompanied by claims to special advantage. In recognition of the benefits the so-called Blues conferred on their communities and their charitable contributions, state after state and then the federal government exempted them from taxes, a competitive edge that tilted the playing field against their commercial competitors. Adorned with a moral halo, official sponsorship of the American Hospital Association, and special public status – which helped the American Hospital Association to achieve "a virtual monopoly over health pricing in most communities" (Quadagno, 2005: pp.23–4) – Blue Cross and Blue Shield (which formed its first plan with that name and the shield logo in 1939) rapidly gained subscribers.

By showing that this distinctively American gambit in voluntary, cooperative and community-based coverage could work, the growth of Blue Cross illuminated, and in some measure tamed, the terrain for commercial insurers. Voluntary health insurance thus begat private counterparts – or at any rate, encouraged these latter carriers to be fruitful and multiply. This they did partly by checkmating the Blues' tampering with the playing field via tax advantages with an innovation of their own, imported from the life insurance field – experience rating, which helped the commercials to gain market share by offering purchasers rates tailored to the particular demographics and use patterns of their workforces and union memberships. The Blues' community rating (one family rate across the community regardless of age, health status and the like) had been a circumscribed voluntarist exercise in solidarity. Experience rating signalled the arrival of hard-nosed private "actuarial fairness" (Stone, 1993), the feature that most powerfully gave the private US health insurance industry its industrial strength – and societal weakness.

During the 1930s the contest among the Blues, their small but gaining commercial competitors and reformers dreaming of a public health insurance regimen remained unresolved. Blue plans grew steadily and commercial plans nipped at their heels but, Roosevelt's silence notwithstanding, providers read the introduction of the Wagner–Murray–Dingell bill in Congress in 1943[1] as a worrisome sign that NHI might really happen. The entry of the United States into the Second World War changed the political and economic landscapes, however. The Stabilization Act of 1942, which exempted fringe benefits from federal wartime control on increases in wages, and an administrative tax court ruling in 1943 that employers' contributions to the purchase of workers' health insurance were excluded from the taxable income of employees, gave a boost to enrolment in voluntary (and, increasingly, commercial) plans (Thomasson, 2003).[2]

In Britain, wartime decimation of the health system and the egalitarian agenda of the Beveridge Commission paved the way for the post-war National Health Service. In the United States, the war years saw the flowering of private health coverage, and their end brought the Cold War and a resurgent conservatism resolved to fight fiercely

---

[1] Named for its sponsors, Democratic Senators Robert Wagner of New York and James Murray of Montana and Democratic Representative John Dingell of Michigan, the bill aimed to add health coverage to the social security system through employer and worker contributions to a trust fund that would pay for physician services and up to 30 days of hospital care.

[2] *Pace* conservatives who fixate on these rulings as the evil genius behind the spread of health insurance, they were a boost, not a lease on life. Employer-based health insurance had been growing steadily before the rulings were promulgated (Hacker, 2002; Glied, 2005).

against communism, socialism and, of course, socialized medicine, as lately incarnated in the National Health Service. When President Harry Truman renewed the fight for NHI in the late 1940s he was opposed not only by the two usual suspects – organized medicine and the business community (congenitally allergic to so-called big government interventions except those of benefit to themselves, and increasingly integral to private health coverage) – but also by a new one, a formidable lobby of Blue and commercial plans that argued, not implausibly, that the United States was proudly in process of meeting the citizenry's coverage needs with voluntary and private arrangements that honoured American *mores* and values. Meanwhile, proposals for a universal public plan, which had never enjoyed serious organizational support outside segments of the labour movement, lost much of the little that it had as unions, ever protective of their private collective bargaining prerogatives, increasingly joined the private club by creating their own Taft–Hartley health insurance plans[3] (Gottschalk, 2000). As the ranks of Americans with health coverage skyrocketed from 10% in 1940 to 76% in 1957 (Mayes, 2005: p.48), NHI was ceasing to be "culturally conceivable" (Dobbin, 1994: p.228).

Medicare and Medicaid

During the Eisenhower years (1952–1960) proponents of universal coverage shifted ground from insistence that NHI was the one right way, to reiteration that the voluntary/private health insurance system could not feasibly cover sizeable swaths of the population, especially older people, who, having retired from the workforce, stood outside the reach of employer-based insurance, and the unemployed. Various small federal programmes offered grants to induce the states to pay some of the medical bills of lower-income older people, but results were disappointing. Both the benefits and the costs of medical care for older people were growing steadily and, in a surge of mini-solidarity,

---

[3] Named after Republican Senator Robert Taft of Ohio and Republican Representative Fred A. Hartley Jr of New Jersey, these created, in 1947 legislation, multi-employer health and welfare trusts, jointly managed by labour and management representatives, that held their assets in a trust fund, bargained collectively with each participating employer and enabled workers to keep their health coverage if they changed jobs among employers in the fund.

public opinion duly noted that neither the aged nor their expectant heirs deserved to see their savings and assets depleted by medical bills. Organized medicine had concerns about the savings and assets of its own members but – although new paying customers would have been nice, if these came at the price of greater federal regulation of fees and practices, charity care was the lesser evil – its aggressive opposition stalemated legislation until the national elections of 1964 gave liberal Democratic President Lyndon B. Johnson a landside victory, accompanied by the arrival of a large new contingent of liberal Democrats in both houses of Congress. The next year the famous three-layer cake – Medicare Part A for hospital care of older people, Medicare Part B for their physicians' services and Medicaid for some of the poor (including indigent older people) – became law. As Hacker (2002) notes, this enormous public breakthrough was not a repudiation of the voluntary/private system but rather (in effect) an endorsement of its basic premise: the non-public status quo worked well for most of the population but inevitably left gaps in coverage, which it was the government's role to patch and fill.

The implementation of Medicare and Medicaid in 1966 set the mould that endures today. Data from 2015 show that 20% and 14% of the US population are covered by Medicaid and Medicare, respectively (Henry J. Kaiser Family Foundation, 2015).

For 3 years after enactment of the new federal programmes, liberals surmised that this long-sought breaching of the barricades against a major federal role in funding coverage and care presaged incremental slicing of the "salami" until universal coverage was achieved. By 1968, these hopes were gone. The nation was in political turmoil over conflicts domestic (race tensions, urban riots) and foreign (the Vietnam War), the costs of Medicare and Medicaid far exceeded projections, and the election of Richard Nixon, a Republican, to the White House signalled a rightward shift that pushed NHI off the public agenda. Attention turned to two questions: how to contain health care costs, which were rising fast enough to prompt talk of a cost crisis (Hackey, 2012), and how to design health coverage for those outside the employer and public systems. The two questions connected less symbiotically than parasitically: efforts to solve one drained energy from attempts to address the other, leaving another round of policy stalemate and frustration that proved to be long-lived.

The managed care era: rescue and miscue

Costs dominated the federal agenda partly because medical progress is impressive but not cheap (technology and medical innovation are a clinical blessing and fiscal curse to public and private purchasers alike) and partly because a single federal purchaser/payer (plus the 51 single Medicaid purchasers/payers in the states and Washington, DC) were now directly and heavily implicated in the problem. Policy-makers spent countless hours worrying about health care policy and sought advice from all the best minds whose views fitted their ideological predilections. The Nixonites soon learned that the cost problem had two fundamental sources – moral hazard and provider dominance – both of which were aggravated by (indeed institutionalized in) the synthesis of third party insurance and fee-for-service medical practice that characterized the US system. The correction, the policy-makers were pleased to hear, need not disrupt the voluntarism and privatism of that system – rather it mainly served to perfect and expand it by introducing new measures of consumer choice, correct incentives and competition – in a word market forces. Health Maintenance Organizations (HMOs; of which prepaid group practice plans such as Kaiser Permanente were an example but by no means a blueprint) would let consumers choose plans that ran efficiently because they combined the financing and delivery of care within an integrated organizational framework and subjected providers to fiscal and managerial discipline. When obliged to compete with HMOs that offered good access and quality at lower premiums, lax Blue and commercial plans would have to shape up or cede market share. A few federal grant and loan dollars would give entrepreneurs the incentives to build HMOs whose correct incentives would in turn beam into the whole system further incentives to change its wanton ways. Gatekeeping and other tools to channel access would smite moral hazard while organizational controls would dethrone sovereign providers (Brown, 1983).

The Nixon administration also proposed a Comprehensive Health Insurance Plan, thoroughly grounded in the private system, which would have required most employers to cover their workers. Though a far cry from the NHI templates that were still alive and well (at least rhetorically) in the early 1970s, the plan was not absurd prima facie: the great majority of uninsured Americans were (then as now) workers (or dependants), mainly in lower-paid jobs in small firms. For better or worse, negotiations among the administration and the two key Democratic legislators (Representative Wilbur Mills and Senator Edward Kennedy) collapsed in 1974, even as the newly minted measure to promote HMOs began to be implemented (Blumenthal & Morone, 2009: pp.242–6).

The story of HMOs (soon to be known as managed care organizations) has had a fairly clear beginning, middle and end. Because this new organizational form challenged the standard practices of all those involved in making it work – consumers, employers, insurers, providers and government itself – HMOs diffused and gained enrolment slowly between 1975 and 1985. By the mid-1980s, however, three factors – unabated increases in health costs, lack of consensus on what system-wide regulatory strategies (if any) to adopt and (probably most important) myriad organizational innovations that made HMOs less rigorous (and also less effective) controllers of care and cost – prompted a fresh and increasingly favourable look at these plans by all the players noted above. By 1990, managed care plans had conquered the private sector and replaced old-fashioned insurance as the mainstream model. (The public sector's own ventures in managed care, meanwhile, were a study in contrast: in Medicare, which deferred to the rights of beneficiaries on the free choice of provider, penetration hovered around a meagre 10%. In Medicaid, which permitted the states to put beneficiaries into managed care, enrolment exceeded 50%.) The dominant institutional form managed care assumed was the preferred-provider organization – in which insurers contracted with providers who essentially added their names to a list of those willing to accept a measure of utilization review and some withholding of revenues to keep the plan reliably afloat but otherwise practised much as before – was a far cry from the integrated prepaid group practices such as Kaiser Permanente that launched visions of health maintenance organizations in 1970.

During the 1990s it gradually dawned on all but the most fervid aficionados of managed care both that the dilution of organizational controls so crucial to the diffusion of managed care plans had severely weakened their power to contain costs and that a backlash by consumers and providers was reducing the number of cost-containing arrows that remained in the controllers' quivers. In the latter half of the 1990s, the growth of health costs slowed impressively, though how much credit goes to managed care, to insurance cycles and to lingering caution among insurers and providers, traumatized by the prospect of health reform (which in the early 1990s had been widely viewed as imminent before it collapsed in 1994 and could presumably return from the dead), into holding the line on prices is impossible to say. In any case, after 2000, managed care no longer looked like much of an answer to the cost problem and weary policy-makers wondered what to do for an encore.

Why not manage competition?

To some on the left (then three decades out of office and public favour) the managed care episode proved that the nation's employer-based private health insurance system was hopeless, and that wisdom lay in emulating the NHI systems of other, wiser western nations with all deliberate speed. One strategic variant on market forces however, which would impose public management on otherwise unmanaged competition among managed care plans, both enjoyed high-level consideration in Washington and ran parallel to reform projects unfolding in Switzerland, the Netherlands, Israel and the internal market in the United Kingdom. The theory of managed competition saw managed care as a step in the right direction but also a potential source of market failure. Left alone, HMOs might seek profits and market share by misrepresenting the nature of their providers and products, segmenting markets, under-serving enrollees and selecting preferred risks. Incentives could not be truly correct without a framework of pro-competitive regulations crafted and enforced by government (Enthoven, 1980). In his health reform proposals of 1993/1994, President Bill Clinton sought to harmonize the public and private sectors, an employer mandate and managed care into a seamless legislative package designed to satisfy both the left and right of the political spectrum and key interest groups. Alas, a public hand visible and vigorous enough to rationalize the unwieldy US health system attracted boundless derision and negligible political support (see Johnson & Broder, 1996; Glied, 1997; Hacker, 1997; Skopol 1997).

The demise of the Clinton plan in 1994 tossed the system back onto unmanaged competition among managed care plans, and a few years later the collapse of confidence in managed care left policy-makers facing their old nemeses: moral hazard and provider dominance. The administration of George W. Bush got back to basics: costs ran high because consumers paid too little for their health care, and health savings accounts (known euphemistically as consumer-driven health plans and accurately as high-deductible health plans) would give consumers the latest model of correct incentives to avoid using too much care and to shop for cheaper providers. Critics panned this strategy as a reductio ad absurdum of 30 years of policy regression, social unlearning and unintelligent design.

Though the trend went largely unheralded, during the administrations of Clinton and Bush, public insurance plans increasingly became dominated by private insurers. In Medicare, the Medicare Advantage programme gave beneficiaries extra benefits and reduced out-of-pocket payments if they chose private managed care plans rather than fee-for-service Medicare. State governments, seeking stability in health care prices, increasingly contracted with private insurers for their Medicaid programmes. Today, nearly a third of Medicare enrollees are enrolled in private health plans (Henry J. Kaiser Family Foundation, 2016c). Similarly, the vast majority of Medicaid enrollees are enrolled in private health plans.

The Affordable Care Act

During the national elections of 2008, health care scored high on lists of the public's concerns and all the leading presidential contenders issued reform proposals of greater or lesser detail. As usual, the employer-based system of coverage, now intimately intertwined with the private health insurance industry, came under fire. Single-payer advocates, citing Canada as a model, would have done away with work-based coverage and private health insurance in one fell swoop. Some reformers argued for retaining employer coverage but mandating it for all but the smallest firms, while others sought to make the system less employer-centric but more private by encouraging health savings accounts; by mandating that each individual citizen acquire health insurance through employment or otherwise, with the assistance of public subsidies for those who could not afford to do so with their own (or their employers') funds; or by expanding tax credits or deductions to spur the voluntary purchase of private coverage.

The ACA of 2010 altered the roles and prerogatives of private health insurance in ways that are less than fundamental but more than merely marginal. In elections in November 2008, buoyed by multiplying Republican misadventures and misfortunes (capped in September 2008 by a severe economic downturn) the Democrats won the White House and achieved sizable majorities in both congressional chambers.

President Obama and congressional leaders wanted to enact health reform legislation, believed that they had political support sufficient to bring it off, and quickly set about crafting measures that aimed to reconfigure the private/public mix with due respect for political reality. Despite intense controversy and intractable Republican opposition, the Democrats' stratagems worked: party unity held, congressional draftmanship was constructive, the legislative package (closely modelled on reforms enacted in Massachusetts in 2006) proved serviceable, and cost containment conundrums did not derail consensus (Beaussier, 2012). Not least important, the traditional forces of opposition splintered. Business groups, notably the Chamber of Commerce, resisted the reform plan, but organized medicine lent support in exchange for the promise of political leaders to fix a Medicare formula that annually threatened reductions in their payments (Laugesen, 2011), and leaders of the private health insurance industry agreed that the protections against adverse selection that accompanied a federal mandate that almost all citizens buy health coverage, made newly tolerable the restrictions on their rating and enrolment practices that reformers were bent on imposing (Brown, 2011).

The law that emerged in March 2010 changed the rules of the game for private insurance in several ways. By the end of 2010, new protections allowed consumers to compare health insurance coverage options, prohibited insurance companies from denying coverage of children based on pre-existing conditions, prohibited insurance companies from rescinding coverage, and eliminated lifetime limits on insurance coverage. In 2014, consumer protection laws were further expanded under the ACA. Insurance companies were prohibited from discriminating on the basis of pre-existing conditions or gender, and annual limits on insurance coverage were eliminated (US Department of Health and Human Services, 2015). Insurers are now required to take all comers, and, within a region and market segment (individual versus small group) can charge higher rates only to a limited extent based on age and tobacco use.

The law created a national health insurance exchange – marketplace – for the highly regulated sale of private insurance, but also allowed states to set up their own exchange for all or some of the activities involved in such sales. By 2016, 12 states had their own exchange, 28 deferred to the federal version, and the rest had exchanges that shared some functions with the federal exchange. Each exchange operates a system of risk adjustment, transferring money from insurers who cover healthier people to those who cover sicker people. Low- and moderate-income consumers who purchase through these marketplaces are eligible for tax credits. The existing Medicaid programme has been expanded; in most states, this programme uses private insurance plans. Since the beginning of 2014, the law has mandated that all but the poorest citizens buy health insurance or face a financial penalty, although this penalty has since been eliminated. By 2015, companies with 100 or more full-time workers were required to insure a minimum of 70% of their full-time employees. Companies with 100 or more full-time employees were required to have 95% of full-time staff insured, and small businesses with 50 or more full-time employees were required to start insuring full-time workers by 2016. Depending on average annual wages, employers with 10 or fewer full-time employees qualify for employer tax credits through the ACA's Small Business Health Options Program.

The law also regulates, to some extent, the content of insurance and the nature of the industry. Health insurers must devote at least 80% (85% in the case of large group insurers) of their revenues to clinical care; are no longer allowed to impose co-payments and deductibles on preventive measures such as immunizations, check-ups and screenings for a range of conditions; must market policies on a guaranteed issue and renewal basis; must limit waiting periods for the onset of coverage to no more than 90 days; and must justify unreasonable premium increases to public authorities.

These innovations in the ACA leave the character of the US system closer to, but still well distant from, other western models of affordable universal coverage (Rodwin, 2011). The sustainability (indeed the survival) of these reforms is far from assured. The court of public opinion has been slow to embrace the reform. In 2016, the Kaiser Health Tracking Poll found that Americans' opinion of the ACA was split down the middle – 45% favourable and 45% unfavourable. Most Democrats (76%) favoured the ACA while a majority of Republicans (83%) did not. Among Independents, 52% were unfavourable to the health care law (Kirzinger, Sugarman & Brodie, 2016)

Meanwhile, electoral politics portend further uncertainties since the Republicans captured control of the White House and both chambers of Congress in the elections of November 2016. Throughout the campaign,

President Donald Trump repeatedly declared that the Affordable Care Act would be repealed – and replaced with something better – once he took office. Additionally, during his presidential campaign, Trump also proposed a series of measures that would allow people to obtain affordable health insurance policies outside exchanges established by the ACA (Jost, 2016). These measures include helping people save money to pay for tax-free health saving accounts, allowing individuals to deduct premium costs on their personal income tax returns, and permitting insurance companies to sell policies across state lines, to increase competition. One of the biggest hurdles to repealing the ACA is that approximately 20 million people have gained health insurance under it. Depending on the alternatives put in place if the law were repealed, some 25–32 million more Americans would likely become uninsured (Kodjak, 2016; Congressional Budget Office, 2017).

Since the implementation of the ACA, about 12.7 million people have found coverage in the marketplaces, and approximately 20 million people overall have been insured by the Marketplaces, Medicaid expansion, young adults remaining on their parents' plan, and other provisions of the law such as requiring plans to cover people with pre-existing conditions (US Department of Health and Human Services, 2016). The Centers of Disease Control and Census data show that the uninsurance rate decreased from 15.7% to 8.6% since the ACA began.

For some groups within the US population the increase in coverage has been especially striking. For the 18–64 demographic, the uninsured rate fell to 11.9% from 22.3% when the ACA was signed in 2010 (ObamaCare Facts, 2016b). The law has also had a significant impact on the immigrant population. States that decided to expand Medicaid after the beginning of 2014 now offer the programme to US citizens and lawfully present immigrants whose incomes are at or below 138% of the federal poverty level and who have been residing in the United States for more than 5 years (National Alliance of State and Territorial AIDS Directors, 2014). By contrast, undocumented immigrants have not become eligible for new coverage under the ACA (ObamaCare Facts, 2016a).

Private health insurance Pre-ACA

Pre-ACA, private health insurance in the United States occupied three distinct markets. First, there were voluntary or compulsory options in public insurance plans. For example, in 2010, 24% of Medicare beneficiaries chose to enrol in private Medicare advantage managed care plans. Two thirds of these enrollees were in HMOs, the rest were in preferred-provider organizations or hybrid plans. (The other 75% or so of beneficiaries remained in traditional Medicare, the nation's last remaining island of freedom of choice and fee-for-service payment.) And in 2010, 71% of Medicaid beneficiaries were enrolled (most of them mandatorily) in mainly private managed care plans before the ACA (Centers for Medicare and Medicaid Services, 2016).

Second, private coverage supplements public insurance in Medicare. Roughly two thirds of the Medicare population had private coverage over and above the programme's benefits for physician and hospital care. The prescription drug benefits added to Medicare in 2003, moreover, were allocated entirely via private plans. About 39% of beneficiaries received this coverage in stand-alone drug plans, another 23% were in employer-sponsored plans, and 18% more benefited from drug coverage through Medicare Advantage plans that also supplied the programme's physician and hospital benefits. Employers also opted to give retirees health coverage of greater or lesser scope in private plans (Henry J. Kaiser Family Foundation, 2016d).

Third, most of the US population that was neither in Medicare, Medicaid or military health systems nor uninsured received coverage from a private market segment, of which the most important are group health insurance sponsored by employers (about one third of the population under 65); coverage supplied by means of self-insured employer plans (the employer assumes financial risk for workers and contracts with a private health insurer or third party administrator for so-called administrative services only); individual, nongroup coverage (about 7% of the under-65 population); and a few multi-employer plans and assorted hybrids (Henry J. Kaiser Family Foundation, 2015).

The private health insurance firms in question show a pronounced trend toward concentration. Before 1975, the industry split among multiple commercial insurers and Blue Cross/Blue Shield (which did not allow for-profit plans within its ranks until 1994), most of which had small market shares. In 2015, there were 5926 insurance companies offering health insurance in the United States and territories. Of these, 2544 were property and casualty companies (which primarily sell auto, home, and commercial coverage), 872 sold life/annuities policies, and 859 issued health insurance (Insurance Information Institute, 2015). By contrast, the group market is highly concentrated. In 2008 the five largest of the 30 top health insurance companies (United Health Group, WellPoint, Aetna, Health Care Service Corporation and CIGNA) accounted for about 55% of total medical enrolment (Austin & Hungerford, 2009: p.10, table 1).

There has been an increase in industry concentration over the past decade. Between 2006 and 2014, the market shares of the four largest insurers (Blue Cross Blue Shield, Anthem, United and Aetna) have seen a nine-percentage-point increase (74% to 83%) in the four-firm concentration ratio for the sale of private insurance. Between 2011 and 2015, insurer concentration also increased in the Medicare market, with a 13% increase in the combined market shares of the four leading Medicare Advantage insurers (Dafny, 2015).

In 2010, the annual report of the American Medical Association detailed market share data for the top two insurers, showing that the average degree of concentration in insurance markets is higher within metropolitan statistical areas than in the nation as a whole. In 313 metropolitan areas examined, 99% of HMO and preferred-provider organization markets were highly concentrated (up from 94% a year earlier). The percentage of these markets in which one insurer had at least 50% of the market had risen from 40% in 2009 and 2010 to 50% in 2010. In 24 of 43 states studied, the two largest insurers held a combined market share of 70% (up from 18 states of 42 studied the year before) (Emmons, Guardado & Kane, 2010). Although some non-profit and mutual insurers remain, for-profit firms have been the most common form of ownership in the industry since the 1990s (Viswanathan & Cummins, 2003). Adding for-profit Blue Cross Blue Shield plans raises the market share of the Blues to 44% from the 31% covered by their non-profit plans (Robinson, 2004). Providing medical coverage to about 104 million members, Blues plans and affiliates commanded more than 60% of the market share for health insurance in nine states in 2015 (Mark Farrah Associates, 2015).

Public regulation of private health insurance takes myriad arcane forms that are opaque to many policy-holders and policy-makers alike. The Medicare and Medicaid programmes regulate private health insurance policies that enrol their beneficiaries. Insurance that supplements Medicare is regulated partly by the federal government (which allows only certain standardized policies to be sold) and by the states (excepting Medicare Part D plans, state regulation of which is partly pre-empted by the federal government). Outside public programmes, before the ACA, states had primary responsibility for regulating private insurance, although the Health Insurance Accountability and Portability Act of 1996, a wide-ranging law that aims (among other things) to improve the portability of coverage for workers who lose or change jobs, gave the federal government new regulatory powers (for example, limiting the use of pre-existing conditions by health plans as a basis for restricting benefits). Federal rules on the enrolment and pricing practices of private insurers were expanded by the ACA in 2010 and largely overrode these state rules.

States seek to assure the solvency of insurers (lest carriers be unable to pay as promised) and have set special rules for small groups (those with fifty or fewer workers). Well before ACA, all but three states required that policies be guaranteed as renewable[4] at the average rates charged to other members of the rating class (Patel & Pauly, 2002). A few states mandated that plans also practise guaranteed issue (insurers must take all comers, without underwriting, though perhaps subject to pre-existing condition clauses) and community rating in the small group or individual markets (Pauly & Herring, 2007). About 35 operated high-risk pools that made it somewhat (though seldom markedly) easier for individuals at high risk to buy coverage (Chollet, 2002; http://naschip.org/portal/) and all states regulated the content of health insurance sold within their borders. They might specify the providers whose services must be covered (for example, chiropractors); the benefits that must be provided (for example, mental health care) and the populations that must be included in insurance offerings (for example, children). Insurers and small business lobbies have long complained that these accumulating mandates are a reason – some say the main reason – why the cost of coverage is high and have urged state governments to prune them to a bare minimum.

A federal law – the Employee Retirement Income Security Act of 1974 (ERISA), which aimed to stop corruption in pension plans but also acquired a regulatory role over health plans in their capacity as employee welfare benefit plans – exempts employer-funded (self-insured) plans

[4] Insurers must reissue guaranteed renewal policies to individual subscribers and do so without regard to changes in the health of individuals, although insurers may limit these policies to fixed terms and may – and usually do – change premiums for the entire group covered by that specific policy.

from state regulation, even if they buy commercial reinsurance (as most do) above a plausible stop-loss level. After ERISA passed, the fraction of firms opting to self-insure rose from about 25% (pre-1980) to 60% in the mid-1990s, and then settled at about 50%.[5] In 2009, 82.1% of firms with 500 or more workers offered at least one self-insured plan, but only 25.7% of firms with 100–499 workers and 13.5% of those with fewer than 100 workers did so (US Department of Health and Human Services, 2011: p.3). Beyond reporting requirements and delineation of the fiduciary duties of plan administrators, ERISA rules were, until 2010, remarkably few. In principle, an ERISA plan could choose not to cover a disease (HIV, for instance), decline to insure children, require a 1-year waiting period before coverage commences, contract only with Christian Science doctors or require employees to pay the whole premium. Nor are such plans subject to managed care malpractice laws.

Other important pieces of the pre-ACA regulatory picture include provisions of the federal Consolidated Omnibus Budget Reconciliation Act of 1985, which required that all plans, self-insured included, allow workers in firms of 20 or more who leave a job (whatever the reason) to continue their health coverage for up to 18 months by paying the full premium themselves. The 1996 Health Insurance Accountability and Portability Act mandated that all insurers (including self-insured plans) enrol anyone who had been previously insured without regard to pre-existing conditions – albeit without restriction on the size of the premiums plans choose to set for this coverage. In 1996 the federal government also gave self-insured plans a taste of the detailed mandating that is so controversial at the state level by obliging plans that offer maternity benefits to cover a 48-hour maternity stay in a hospital. The same year also brought mental health parity legislation: plans that offer mental health benefits cannot impose more stringent annual dollar limits on those services than on general health care; this restriction was further expanded in 2008. In 1998 national legislation required that all plans cover reconstructive surgery for mastectomy patients.

The ACA partially ended laissez faire for self-insured plans. Where and how these plans fit within the catalogue of group health plans caused

---

[5] The decline may reflect the complexities of self-insurance in managed care plans, which merge the risks and costs of corporate customers, whereas under a straightforward fee-for-service indemnity arrangement, services are used by the firm's employees, claims come in and money goes out, perhaps through an administrative services entity.

the law's authors no small vexation, and the resolution predictably embodied complex compromises, several of which continue to require regulatory or judicial explanation. On the one hand, ACA imposes "a significant number of requirements regarding both the eligibility for plan membership and the scope of the benefits that self-insured plans must provide." So-called musts include timely notification of "material" changes in employee coverage, coverage without cost sharing of a range of preventive services, payment of fees to help support the Patient-Centred Outcomes Research Fund, and direct access of women to a gynaecologist or obstetrician without referral by a primary care physician. Among the cannots are prohibitions against: imposition of annual limits on essential health benefits after 2014, rescission of employee coverage except in cases of fraud or misrepresentation, and discrimination based on health status, including pre-existing conditions. All the same, self-insured plans are "not nearly as comprehensively regulated... as insured plans are." For example, they remain exempt from offering certain benefits, from limitations on annual limits on deductibles, and from requirements that guarantee the issue and renewal of coverage (Temchine, 2010: p.2). In practice, the benefits, premiums and other features of self-insured firms look very similar to, and indeed perhaps somewhat more generous than, those found in insured firms. This is not surprising: self-insured firms tend to be larger and to have higher-paid workers than their non-self-insured counterparts (Acs et al., 1996).

Group markets, large and small

The many inequities and complexities of private, employer-based coverage in the United States have moved critics to contend that these arrangements are an anachronism the expiry date of which should have long since passed, and that any reform worthy of the name must radically reconfigure that system if not junk it outright. The employer role is more subtle than these categorical indictments acknowledge, however. All health care financing systems are employer-based in at least one of two senses. First, corporate and other taxes on business firms enrich the base of general revenues that fund health care even in single-payer nations without insurers (private or other) for basic coverage. Second, countries with social insurance systems are overtly employer-based. Payroll taxes on employers and workers are the mainstay of the trust funds on which sickness funds draw to pay providers. These taxes have at least two salient limits, however: they are vulnerable to the declining ratio of worker-contributors to beneficiaries over time, and they leave untapped sources of wealth (capital gains, real estate and so on) that have gained prominence since Bismarck unveiled social insurance for health care in 1883. As birth rates decline while the ranks of retirees grow, these extractive limits are much on the minds of policy-makers in (for example) France, Germany and US Medicare, who have responded by infusing larger sums of general revenue into their health systems, thus adulterating Bismarck with Beveridge.

Before the ACA was passed, employers had the freedom to offer health insurance voluntarily for recruitment, retention and improvement of the health and productivity of staff. They were also free to determine the contents and financial terms of coverage – or to decline to cover workers (and dependants) at all. Provisions of the ACA have had a significant impact on employer-based coverage. Its Employer Mandate (a component of the Employer Shared Responsibility Provision), requires all employers with 50 or more full-time equivalent employees to offer health insurance for a minimum of 95% of their full-time employees (and offer it to their dependants), or face penalties (for example, US$2000 per full-time employee after the first 30 employees if no workers are covered). Employees, however, do not have to accept the employer-offered coverage (ObamaCare Facts, 2015).

Employer-based though it be, the US health system accepts government mandates on employers uneasily if at all. Before the ACA, federal government declined to enact a national employer mandate (plans to do so in the Clinton reform infuriated small business lobbies and won little support from big businesses, one of many cautionary tales on the minds of the Democrats who designed the ACA in 2009/2010). Meanwhile the national ERISA statute prohibits the states from passing mandates of their own. (Hawaii, for reasons of no great importance here, is the sole exception.) No wonder that American reformers (not to mention foreign observers) often contend that employer-based private health coverage should be thrown out of the next open window of opportunity.

The case against the US version of employer-based coverage is far from airtight however. Between 2001 and 2011 97–99% of large firms (those with 200 or more workers) offered health benefits and, complaints about high cost notwithstanding, these larger firms show little inclination to stop doing so. The much-noted decline in the share of business offering health benefits from 68% in 2001 to 56% in 2016 occurred almost entirely among small and mid-sized firms (Henry J. Kaiser Family Foundation, 2016a). The large-group sector of employer coverage remains reasonably stable because health benefits help firms to attract and retain the workers they want, because some executives believe that offering coverage is the right thing for paragons of private enterprise to do and because they can shift some of the rising costs of health insurance to their workers by requiring them to contribute more to premiums, by raising wages more slowly, or by increasing cost sharing in health plans. The average worker contribution to the total cost of family coverage stayed fairly steady – around 28% – between 2001 and 2016. Cost sharing, however, has increased 2.5-fold since 2006. On average, workers with family coverage contribute US$5277 annually toward their health insurance premiums, whereas workers with single coverage spend approximately US$1129 annually (Henry J. Kaiser Family Foundation, 2016a). Employers that represent big books of business wield clout as they bargain for better deals with competing insurers, enjoy some flexibility in seeking a larger, better or different mix of benefits or providers, and have pursued their purchasing largely without the benefit (or handicap) of public regulation. Rising costs have eroded coverage among larger groups, but not very much, and certainly not enough to validate alarms about the collapse of employer-based coverage (Glied, 2005).

The small group and individual insurance market is another world, however, one in which the employer-based system falters badly. In 2001 58% of firms with fewer than 10 workers offered coverage, but by 2005 that proportion had fallen to 47%, and still had not recovered (46%) in 2016 (Henry J. Kaiser Family Foundation, 2016a). Workers whose "employment situation does not readily lend itself to employment-based coverage", for example, "new economy" workers with contingent employment contracts, multiple jobs and part-year employment; people who change jobs often; and those in firms of 25 or fewer workers – account for "just under half of the active US labour force" (Glied, 2005: p.45).

Self-employed individuals and small firms suffer from limited bargaining leverage, few economies of scale for insurance brokers and agents, relatively little money to spend on coverage, unappealing risk pools and (at least in insurance lore) workers who are in poorer health and more inclined to use care than those in larger groups. As noted above, about three quarters of the uninsured were in the workforce, usually though not always in small firms, before the ACA. Unsurprisingly, the uninsured tended to be poorer; and, workers who are younger, non-white, foreign-born and employed part-time disproportionately lacked coverage (Clemans-Cope & Garrett, 2006). Before the Employer Mandate, the percentage of workers with employer-sponsored coverage descended from 81.3% of those who earned above 300% of the federal poverty level, to 41.4% of those who made 150–199% of that level, to a meagre 12.6% for those who were in the 0–99% category (Fronstin, 2010: p.19, fig. 18).

For years, philanthropic innovators, most notably the Robert Wood Johnson Foundation, sought to fill this market niche by funding grantees to develop deeply discounted insurance products that small firms would agree to offer and their workers to take-up. These programmes repeatedly came up short: very few firms and workers have discretionary cash they are prepared to spend even for lower-cost health insurance, nor do they clamour to trade off relatively low worker wages (or increases in them) for health coverage that these predominantly young employees hope not to use anyway (McLaughlin, 1993; Brown & Stevens, 2006). Moreover, given the high perceived risks and costs insurers faced by cultivating these markets, such affordable policies as they offered might be sharply restricted by medical underwriting and related stratagems designed to limit insurers' exposure to bad risks. Before the ACA, insurers could require that workers have a medical examination as a precondition of coverage; deny coverage outright or for pre-existing conditions; impose waiting periods for coverage; or tailor group or individual rates to the health status of the group or any of its members. It was of course precisely on this score that private health insurance in the United States departed most drastically from cross-national norms and most readily evoked hoots and jeers. No other nation allows health insurers to compete for profits/revenues on basic coverage by selecting preferred risks and rejecting or heavily penalizing undesirable applicants. In the United States, notes Deborah Stone (1993), solidarity has struggled vainly with actuarial fairness for the soul of health insurance. Rarefied exceptions aside, such scraps of solidarity as open enrolment and community rating failed to gain much ground in an unmanaged competitive market milieu – as early as 1959, little more than a quarter (28.2%) of Blue Cross plans relied solely on community rating in group markets; most combined community and experience rating (Thomasson, 2004). The health insurance industry long successfully fought proposals to curtail experience rating and exclusions for pre-existing conditions, but the federal Health Insurance Portability and Accountabiltiy Act of 1996 "sealed some cracks", as noted above. That law, however, did little to constrain their pricing behaviour, yielding a pyrrhic victory – easier access by poor risks to coverage they could not begin to afford (Quadagno, 2005: pp.196–7). In short, the genius of the US health insurance system made it hardest for those who most needed coverage to get it, and thereby triggered demands for the tougher regulations that are now incorporated in ACA.

Even post-ACA, the proposition that equity precludes the expression of invidious distinctions in the enrolment and pricing practices of insurers had not entirely carried the day in the US system. It is not even clear that workers in the large-group sector of the system have stood as immune from exclusionary expedients as conventional wisdom contends. The ever increasing popularity of workplace wellness programmes, which charge higher premiums to workers who engage in unhealthy behaviours, for example, belies solidarity within these pools.

Coverage and culture

Arguably everyone would be better off if the phrase "national health insurance" were traded for "affordable universal coverage", thus acknowledging that the issue is not individual contracts and prepayments in return for indemnification should illness strike, but rather government's willingly undertaken obligation to pay providers for rendering a very wide range of health services to people within its jurisdiction. The word "insurance", in short, serves mainly to confuse matters. Arguably too, in a sensible system of affordable universal coverage, government would raise from multiple sources the money needed for the health care budget, and define the services to be covered and the terms on which providers will be paid for delivering them – tasks that leave no logically necessary role for insurance and insurers. It is hard to find much social utility in health insurance organizations that have traditionally competed by selecting healthier risks. This private competitive system in the United States has been a major problem per se, working as it has to make coverage least attainable for those who need it most. All the same, social utility is a matter not of logic but of cultural preferences, which vary among and within societies. Bismarckian systems may find it comforting to have sickness funds mediating between citizens and a state that stages and bankrolls, but does not entirely run, the show. Some, perhaps many, Americans find in the nation's insurance industry assurance that a half-hearted socialization of risks is not a slippery slope to socialized medicine.

Some citizens might want more services than, or services delivered differently from, what the public plan of basic universal coverage offers – private hospital rooms, dental care, faster access to specialists, for example. So long as basic benefits are adequate and equitable, these preferences can be addressed by a system of complementary or supplemental coverage – perhaps one like the French, in which mutual, non-profit and for-profit insurers compete for subscribers who pay for the extra benefits out of pocket or with contributions by employers or (for the poor) the state.

The United States could adopt such a system only if it were willing radically to revise the roles now played by the business, provider and insurance sectors well beyond the innovations introduced in ACA. Business would participate in funding the system, perhaps by means of payroll taxes, surely through extractions via corporate taxes, but only supplementary coverage would be offered at the discretion and on the terms of employers. Providers (physicians, hospitals and others) would be paid fees (or salaries or capitated sums and so on) set in negotiation with government agencies (or perhaps intermediary agents such as sickness funds). Health insurance might survive institutionally (sickness funds that could compete, if at all, only within rules that proscribed selection of preferred risks), but the US health insurance industry would disappear – except, again, in markets for extra coverage or as carriers for public programmes.

Considerations of profit and power stand high on the list of obstacles to such a transformation, but cultural factors should not be discounted. The American allegiance to actuarial fairness in private health insurance is no mere accident of omission by policy-makers and a public that somehow fail to notice the cruelties this doctrine inflicts. Rather it reflects deep and culturally distinct images of equity and justice. Other western nations recognize health care (hence coverage for it) as some kind of right (metaphysical, natural, human, constitutional, whatever) that it is a duty of the state to secure and assure. Some Americans may high-mindedly call health care a right but when confronted with the corollary – a right is something the state must realize for all citizens (and legal residents) – they tend to demur. In American-ese health care is less a right than a very special "good" – a good of such surpassing importance that society should do everything possible (including the crafting of sizeable public subsidies) to spread it around privately, at which point – and only at this point – one might (perhaps) extend public coverage to those – and only to those – who deserve it but cannot feasibly acquire it privately.

This world view has still deeper roots of its own. Other western nations tend to honour redistribution and cross-subsidies between haves and have-nots (in this case, the sick and the poor) as the equitable essence of social justice. In the United States, redistribution and cross-subsidies from above to below are eternally problematic and contested – and most certainly so in the health sphere, wherein "good risks deserve good rates" is deemed only fair although (perhaps indeed because) it inverts European notions. This mind-set seems to be an amorphous amalgam of the importation of principles of life-insurance pricing into health coverage, the triumph of experience rating over community rating, the growing legitimacy of invidious distinctions between fat and lean Americans (and more generally, among lifestyles of varying degrees of self-discipline), and a settled scepticism about the wisdom and fairness of sharing with and shoring up the disadvantaged. In this context, a private health insurance industry engaged in risk selection is a virtue not a vice. That roughly 45% of the population viewed ACA unfavourably 6 years after its passage suggests that a sharp cultural sea-change toward support for affordable universal coverage has yet to transpire (Kirzinger, Sugarman & Brodie, 2016).

Americans might of course be expected to lament the plight of approximately 28.5 million cohabitants who lack health coverage, and so they do. This uninsured population are mostly (75%) US citizens and 21% are non-citizens (Henry J Kaiser Family Foundation, 2016b). The nation stands little risk of protesting too much, however, because another distinctive American institution – the safety net – ensures that those who lack coverage can still get some care. Conservatives (including eminences such as George W. Bush and Mitt Romney) have long averred that in America anyone who needs medical care can go to the emergency room. The uninsured can indeed get care – so long as the care they need can be supplied in those emergency rooms or by primary care providers in community health centres, public health clinics, free clinics and public hospitals, and does not entail much by way of referrals to specialists, long inpatient stays, expensive technological treatments or prescription drugs. Such advanced interventions may – or may not – get an uninsured patient qualified for Medicaid and may – or may not – be provided and then billed to public uncompensated care accounts or written off as bad debt, the incurrers of which may or may not be hounded by bill collectors seeking to recover part of the cost of the care the safety net delivered. Whether such rationing of care tips the scales for or against the interests of uninsured patients, and whether positive interventions come in time to save or improve their health, is an almost entirely implicit matter – that is, at the behest of providers themselves. Whether the public understands that the safety net glass is at best half full is unclear. Be that as it may, the ironic and dependable success of the safety net in draining moral urgency from health reform has been perhaps the most conspicuously efficient feature of the US health system.

Whatever its eventual fate, the ACA episode can be read as the latest, and probably the clearest, source of evidence of the institutionalized ambivalence that governs the US approach to health care coverage. Private health insurance in the United States is nothing if not resilient. Widely attacked in the mid-1990s as public enemy number one, less favoured even than tobacco companies, the industry rebounded and by the end of the decade had, as Quadagno (2005: pp.163,170) notes, "vanquished any public sector alternative". Another decade on, ACA left that industry more tightly regulated but also contemplating 16 million adverse-selection-free customers thanks to the individual mandate plus financial return on those of the millions more who may enter Medicaid-managed care plans run by private insurers. Given the entrenchment of private insurance, its malingering conflation with all-American voluntarist virtues, the raw political power of the insurance industry, the strength it might yet again display in alliance with providers and business lobbies in opposing unpalatable reforms, chronic popular suspicion that a government take-over of the system will only make things worse, and the absence of evidence that all (indeed any) of this is changing much, prospects are dim that private health insurance in the United States will soon be reformed into something resembling a European configuration.

On the other hand, the steady growth of gap-filling by the public sector will likely continue to be essential to save the private system from itself, as has happened with Medicare and Medicaid. Well before the ACA, gap-filling was incrementally transforming the public–private mix.

When the ACA passed, Medicare covered about 44 million Americans, Medicaid around 49 million, and the Children's Health Insurance Program roughly 8 million – together, almost a third of the population. Add the nearly 50 million uninsured, who depended heavily on public institutions and funds for care, and the public share rose to around half the population. Add millions more who receive employer-based health coverage through government jobs at the local, county, state and federal levels and the proverbial tipping point was already a *fait accompli*. In 2016, dollars told the same tale as the count of covered lives: about 48% of the money in the system came from government programmes. The figure rose to around 64% if one factored in so-called tax expenditures (business deductions for employers for the money they spend to buy health coverage for workers and exclusion of the health benefits thus purchased from workers' taxable incomes amount to more than US$200 billion in federal revenue foregone annually) and funds spent to cover public employees (Himmelstein & Woolhandler, 2016). The subsidies and Medicaid expansions in the ACA push the system somewhat farther and faster down this well-travelled road. Which, then – public or private – is centre and which periphery?

The familiar cultural and structural advantages that private insurance enjoys in the United States remain largely intact, and beholders are free to read the ACA as a major step toward contriving new public coverage and authority or as a lamentable capitulation to constraints that leave the system little more coherent than before. The trio of propositions that has long governed US health care policy – diffuse health coverage as widely as possible in private markets, bring government in to fill gaps in those markets, and fund local safety nets to serve those who fall through any remaining cracks – shows little sign of succumbing to solidaristic appeals, and it remains to be seen whether public sensibilities, political leaders and judicial solons will accept the progressive and redistributive policy departures encoded in the ACA. Solidarity remains an effete force in American political life. Health reform in the United States, like the private health insurance system itself, is always about the money, but never only about the money.

References

Acs G et al. (1996). Self-insured employer health plans: prevalence, profile, provisions, and premiums. *Health Affairs*, 15(2):266–78.

Anderson OW (1975). *Blue Cross since 1929: accountability and the public trust*. Cambridge, MA, Ballinger.

Austin DA, Hungerford TL (2009). *The Market Structure of the Health Insurance Industry*. Washington DC, Congressional Research Service.

Beaussier A-L (2012). The patient protection and affordable care act: the victory of unorthodox lawmaking, *Journal of Health Politics, Policy and Law*, 37(2012):741–78.

Blumenthal D, Morone JA (2009). The heart of power: health and politics in the Oval Office. Berkeley, CA, University of California Press.

Brown LD (1983). *Politics and health care organisation: HMOs as federal policy*. Washington DC, Brookings Institution.

Brown LD (1991). Capture and culture: organizational identity in New York Blue Cross, *Journal of Health Politics, Policy and Law*, 16(1991):651–70.

Brown LD, Stevens B (2006). Charge of the right brigade? Communities, coverage, and care for the uninsured. *Health Affairs*, 25(3):W150–W161.

Brown LD (2011). The Elements of Surprise: How health reform happened, *Journal of Health Politics, Policy and Law*, 36(3):419–27.

Chapin CF (2015). *Ensuring American's health: the public creation of the corporate health care system*. New York, Cambridge University Press.

Chollet D (2002). Perspective: expanding individual health insurance coverage: are high-risk pools the answer? *Health Affairs*, Web exclusive (23 October):W349–W352.

Centers for Medicare and Medicaid Services (2016). *Medicaid Managed Care Enrollment and Program Characteristics, 2014*. Baltimore, MD, Centers for Medicare & Medicaid Services, with assistance from Mathematica Policy Research.

Clemans-Cope L, Garrett B (2006). *Changes in employer-sponsored health insurance sponsorship, eligibility, and participation: 2003 to 2005*. Washington DC, Commission on Medicaid and the Uninsured.

Congressional Budget Office (2017). *How Repealing Portions of the Affordable Care Act Would Affect Health Insurance Coverage and Premiums*. Washington, DC: https://www.cbo.gov/sites/default/files/115th-congress-2017-2018/reports/52371-coverageandpremiums.pdf; accessed on 15/12/2017.

Dafny LS (2015). Evaluating the Impact of Health Insurance Industry Consolidation: Learning from Experience. New York City, The Commonwealth Fund.

Dobbin F (1994). *Forging industrial policy: the United States, Britain, and France in the railway age*. New York, Cambridge University Press.

Emmons DW, Guardado JR, Kane CK (2010). *Competition in HealthInsurance: A comprehensive study of U.S. markets, 2010 update*. Chicago, American Medical Association.

Enthoven A (1980). *Health plan: the only practical solution to the soaring cost of medical care.* Reading, MA, Addison-Wesley.

Fox D (1986). *Health politics, health policy: the British and American experience 1911–1965.* Princeton, NJ, Princeton University Press.

Fronstin P (2010). *Survey of health insurance and characteristics of the uninsured: analysis of the March 2010 current population survey,* Issue Brief 347. Washington DC, Employee Benefit Research Institute.

Glied S (1997). *Chronic condition: why health reform fails.* Cambridge, MA, Harvard University Press.

Glied S (2005). The employer-based health insurance system: mistake or cornerstone? In: Mechanic D et al., eds. *Policy challenges in modern health care.* New Brunswick, NJ, Rutgers University Press.

Gottschalk M (2000). *The shadow welfare state: labor, business, and the politics of health care in the United States.* Ithaca, NY, ILR Press.

Hacker J (1997). *The road to nowhere: the genesis of President Clinton's plan for health security.* Princeton, NJ, Princeton University Press.

Hacker J (2002). *The divided welfare state: the battle over public and private social benefits in the United States.* Cambridge, Cambridge University Press.

Hackey R (2012). *Cries of crisis: rethinking the health care debate.* Reno, University of Nevada Press.

Henry J. Kaiser Family Foundation (2015). Health Insurance Coverage of the Total Population: http://kff.org/other/state-indicator/total-population/?currentTimeframe=0&sortModel=%7B%22colId%22:%22Location%22,%22sort%22:%22asc%22%7D; accessed on 15/12/2017.

Henry J. Kaiser Family Foundation (2016a). *2016 employer health benefits: an annual survey.* San Francisco, CA, Henry J. Kaiser Family Foundation.

Henry J. Kaiser Family Foundation (2016b). *Key facts about the uninsured population.* San Francisco, CA, Henry J. Kaiser Family Foundation.

Henry J. Kaiser Family Foundation (2016c). Medicare advantage: http://kff.org/medicare/fact-sheet/medicare-advantage/; accessed on 15/12/2017.

Henry J. Kaiser Family Foundation (2016d). The Medicare Part D Prescription Drug Benefit. (2016b). The Henry J. Kaiser Family Foundation: http://kff.org/medicare/fact-sheet/the-medicare-prescription-drug-benefit-fact-sheet/; accessed on 15/12/2017.

Himmelstein DU, Woolhandler S (2016). The current and projected taxpayer shares of U.S. health costs. *American Journal of Public Health,* 106:449–52.

Insurance Information Institute (2015). Insurance Industry at a Glance: http://www.iii.org/fact-statistic/industry-overview; accessed on 15/12/2017.

Johnson H, Broder DS (1996). *The system: the American way of politics at the breaking point.* Boston, MA, Little Brown.

Jost T (2016). Day one and beyond: what Trump's election means for the ACA. *Health Affairs Blog,* November 9, 2016, http://healthaffairs.org/

blog/2016/11/09/day-one-and-beyond-what-trumps-election-means-for-the-aca/; accessed on 15/12/2017.

Kingdon J (2003). *Agendas, alternatives and public policy.* New York, Longman.

Kirzinger A, Sugarman E, Brodie M (2016). *Data Note: Americans' Opinions of the Affordable Care Act.* San Francisco, CA, The Henry J. Kaiser Family Foundation.

Klein J (2003). *For all these rights: business, labor, and the shaping of America's public–private welfare state.* Princeton NJ, Princeton University Press.

Kodjak A (2016). Trump can kill Obamacare with or without help from Congress. *National Public Radio*; retrieved from http://www.npr.org/

Law S (1974). *Blue Cross: what went wrong?* New Haven, CT, Yale University Press.

Laugesen MJ (2011). Civilized medicine: physicians and health care reform. *Journal of Health Politics, Policy and Law*, 36(3):507–12.

Mark Farrah Associates (2015). Blue Cross and Blue Shield still leads in many markets: http://www.markfarrah.com/healthcare-business-strategy/Blue-Cross-and-Blue-Shield-Still-Leads-in-Many-Markets.aspx; accessed on 15/12/2017.

Mayes R (2005). *Universal coverage: the elusive quest for national health insurance.* Ann Arbor, University of Michigan Press.

McLaughlin C (1993). The dilemma of affordability: health insurance for small business. In: Helms R, ed. *American health policy: critical issues for reform.* Washington DC, AEI Press.

National Alliance of State and Territorial AIDS Directors (2014). Health Reform Issue Brief: Immigrants and the Affordable Care Act: https://www.nastad.org/sites/default/files/Immigrant-ACA-IB-March-2014.pdf; accessed on 15/12/2017.

ObamaCare Facts (2016a). ObamaCare Facts: ObamaCare and immigrants: http://obamacarefacts.com/obamacare-immigrants/; accessed on 15/12/2017.

ObamaCare Facts (2016b). ObamaCare Facts: uninsured rates: http://obamacarefacts.com/uninsured-rates/; accessed on 15/12/2017.

ObamaCare Facts (2015). The employer mandate / employer penalty delayed until 2015/2016. ObamaCare Facts: http://obamacarefacts.com/obamacare-employer-mandate/; accessed on 15/12/2017.

Patel V, Pauly M (2002). Guaranteed renewability and the problem of risk variation in individual health insurance markets. *Health Affairs* Web exclusive (28 August): W280–W289.

Pauly M, Herring B (2007). Risk pooling and regulation: policy and reality in today's individual health insurance market. *Health Affairs*, 26:770–9.

Quadagno J (2005). *One nation, uninsured: why the United States has no national health insurance.* New York, Oxford University Press.

Robinson JC (2004). Consolidation and the transformation of competition in health insurance. *Health Affairs*, 23(6):11–24.

Rodwin MA (2011). Why we need health care reform now. *Journal of Health Politics, Policy and Law*, 36(3):597–601.

Skopol T (1997). *Boomerang: health care reform and the turn against government*. New York, W.W. Norton.

Starr P (1982). *The social transformation of American medicine*. New York, Basic Books.

Stone D (1993). The struggle for the soul of health insurance. *Journal of Health Politics, Policy and Law*, 18:287–317.

Swenson P (2008). Good distribution, bad delivery, and ugly politics: the traumatic beginnings of Germany's health care system. In: Shapiro I, Donno D, Swenson P, eds. *Divide and deal: the politics of distribution in democracies*. New York, New York University Press.

Temchine DDE (2010). *The impact of the patient protection and affordable care act on self-insured ERISA health and welfare benefit plans: a guide for administrators of self-insured plans*. Washington DC, Epstein, Becker and Green, P.C.

Thomasson MA (2003). The importance of group coverage: how tax policy shaped US health insurance. *American Economic Review*, 93(September):1873–84.

Thomasson MA (2004). Early evidence of an adverse selection death spiral? The case of Blue Cross and Blue Shield. *Explorations in Economic History*, 41(October):313–28.

U.S. Department of Health and Human Services (2011). Report to the Congress on a study of the large group market: http:// aspe.hhs.gov/health/reports/2011/LGHP study/; accessed on 15/12/2017.

U.S. Department of Health and Human Services (2015). Key Features of the Affordable Care Act by year: https://www.hhs.gov/healthcare/facts-and-features/key-features-of-aca-by-year/index.htmlfeatures-of-aca-by-year/index.html; accessed on 15/12/2017.

U.S. Department of Health and Human Services (2016). 20 mllion people have gained health insurance coverage because of the Affordable Care Act, new estimates show: https://www.hhs.gov/about/news/2016/03/03/20-million-people-have-gained-health-insurance-coverage-because-affordable-care-act-new-estimates; accessed on 15/12/2017.

Viswanathan K, Cummins J (2003). Ownership structure changes in the insurance industry: an analysis of demutualization. *Journal of Risk and Insurance*, 70:401–37.

16 | *Health savings accounts in the United States of America*

SHERRY A. GLIED, DAN P. LY AND LAWRENCE D. BROWN

The medical savings account model of health insurance in the United States combines a high-deductible health insurance plan[1] with a dedicated savings account used to pay expenses incurred below the deductible. Savings in the plan can roll over from one year to the next and, after some predefined period during which they are dedicated to health spending, can be used for non-health-related expenses.[2] In principle, this model combines the incentives for frugal use of health services that exist in high-deductible health insurance with assurance that the funds required in the event of true medical need will be available.

In the United States, interest in and experimentation with this model began, on a very small scale, in the mid-1970s. Beginning in 1996, the use of this model in private, voluntary health insurance in the United States was promoted through a series of tax incentives. The first of these incentives, a limited demonstration project (capped at a maximum of 750 000 enrollees), was passed as part of the Health Insurance Portability and Accountability Act of 1996, which allowed self-employed individuals and businesses with fewer than 50 employees who were covered under qualified high-deductible health plans to make tax-exempt contributions to medical savings accounts.

When the demonstration project ended enrolment in 2000, about 100 000 individuals had signed up. Next, in 2002, the Treasury Department, which directs the Internal Revenue Service, issued a notice indicating that an employer's contribution to an account set aside for

[1] A high-deductible health plan is an insurance plan under which the beneficiary is responsible for a substantial amount of expense (the deductible) before the insurer begins paying benefits. US federal law as of 2015 requires a deductible of at least US$1300 for single coverage and US$2600 for family coverage for health saving account-qualified high-deductible health plans (Dolan, 2016).
[2] Use of savings for non-health expenses before this predefined period (age 65 under current law), incurs a tax and 20% penalty.

health care is not taxable income to the employee and that any unused funds in such an account can be rolled forward from year to year (Newhouse, 2004). The resulting Health Reimbursement Accounts can be, but need not be – and often are not – coupled with high-deductible health plans. Health Reimbursement Accounts are similar to Health Savings Account, but are funded entirely by employers and are generally not portable between jobs.[3]

The following year, Title XII of the 2003 Medicare Prescription Drug, Improvement and Modernization Act provided a tax incentive for the establishment of Health Savings Accounts (HSAs) coupled with qualified high-deductible health plans. Under this legislation, contributions to HSAs are tax exempt, as is interest on savings that accumulate within HSAs, and disbursements from HSAs are also tax exempt if they are used for qualified medical expenses (Grudzien, 2006). HSA plans are owned by the insured individual and can be transferred from one job to another. The provisions governing HSAs were made somewhat more generous under the Tax Relief and Health Care Act of 2006. The Affordable Care Act enacted in 2010 set binding minimum medical loss ratios (percentage of premiums spent on health care claims and quality-improving expenses) for all plans, including HSA-qualified high-deductible health plans. The reform also raised the penalty for premature withdrawals from HSAs, limited their use in paying for over-the-counter pharmaceuticals, and required all plans, including HSA-qualified plans, to cover a set of preventive services without cost sharing (so making them exempt from the deductible) (Kaiser Family Foundation, 2013; Dolan, 2016).

In addition to these tax incentives, which apply to the private health insurance market, the medical savings account model has been incorporated into public health insurance programmes – Medicaid and Medicare (see Chapter 15 in this volume). Medicaid, which is funded jointly by the federal and state governments and operates under state jurisdiction in compliance with federal regulations, serves low-income

[3] Health Reimbursement Accounts (HRAs) are funded and owned by employers. Because of this, when an employee with an HRA changes or loses his or her job, the remaining amount in the HRA defaults to the employer. Health Savings Accounts (HSAs) may be funded by both employers and employees. As a result, an employee may take unused amounts with him or her when changing jobs. More firms offer HSAs than HRAs (Kaiser Family Foundation, 2015).

Americans who meet various categorical eligibility criteria. Before the Affordable Care Act, several states had incorporated health savings accounts into their Medicaid programme (Andrews, 2014). Two states currently have waivers allowing them to incorporate HSA-like features in their Medicaid expansions for people with incomes between 100% and 138% of the Federal Poverty Level (Musumeci & Rudowitz, 2015).

Medicare is a federal programme that provides health insurance to older (aged 65 years and over) and disabled Americans, regardless of income. The Centers for Medicare and Medicaid Services is the federal agency that operates the traditional Medicare health insurance programme and also subcontracts with private insurers to offer a variety of alternative plans. Medicare beneficiaries can select medical savings account model plans as an alternative to traditional Medicare (Centers for Medicare and Medicaid Services, 2012). The plans involve a high-deductible insurance product and a savings account, into which Centers for Medicare and Medicaid Services will make an annual lump-sum deposit. Funds will be tax exempt as long as they are used to pay for qualified medical expenses.

These policy initiatives have generated considerable interest. In 2014, about 35 million Americans were enrolled in health insurance plans with deductibles above the HSA threshold (see footnote 285). Of these, just over a third had an HSA (Cohen & Martinez, 2015). In this chapter, we review the history and motivation behind the introduction of HSAs. We then describe the regulation of the HSA market, the structure of this market and its performance to date. We conclude by discussing the implications of HSAs for the US health insurance system.

History and current status

The adoption of public policies promoting the use of medical savings accounts in the United States occurred through the confluence of three distinct developments: a line of academic research; a set of entrepreneurial lobbying and marketing efforts; and a market vacuum.

Academic research

Beginning in the late 1960s, academic economists turned their attention to the structure of prevailing voluntary health insurance plans. Economic theory suggested that the plans that were most frequently selected were excessively generous in their cost-sharing requirements and benefits and, correspondingly, charged excessively costly premiums (Pauly, 1968; Feldstein, 1973). The logic of this argument was based on a general theoretical point in conjunction with observation of the marketplace. Economic theory suggests that, given the choice between the cash value of medical services and the medical services themselves, many people would prefer the cash. However, under health insurance, which effectively subsidizes the cost of medical services to the consumer, they would tend to use the medical services. Moreover, in a purely private and voluntary market, they would pay for these low (subjective) value services through their premiums, leaving them with less cash and more low subjective value medical services than they would prefer. The RAND experiment, conducted in the late 1970s and early 1980s, provided empirical confirmation of the expected theoretical result, showing that people who faced higher cost sharing used fewer medical services, even though they were compensated by the study sponsors for the higher out-of-pocket costs by lump-sum cash transfers (Newhouse, 2004).

This excess medical service use induced by the presence of insurance, or so-called moral hazard, which diminishes individual welfare, is the inevitable consequence of the economically valuable risk reduction implicit in health insurance (Feldstein, 2006). Thus, the existence of moral hazard, alone, called for no particular policy response. In a series of simulation studies based on estimates of willingness to pay to avoid risk, however, several economists concluded that the most common voluntarily selected insurance plans generated much more welfare loss in the form of moral hazard than the gains in welfare that they induced through reduced risk bearing. The prevailing plans appeared to be economically inefficient choices (Feldman & Dowd, 1991; Manning & Marquis, 1996).

Economists concluded that the leading factor inducing these apparently inefficient choices was the favourable tax treatment of employer-sponsored health insurance. At the time of the introduction of private employer-sponsored health insurance, in the early 1930s, the tax authorities had, in practice, ignored the value of employer insurance payments on behalf of employees in computing income taxes owed. This practice was ratified in the 1954 Internal Revenue Code that formally exempted employer contributions to insurance plans from income taxation (Blumenthal, 2006). Employer contributions for health insurance are also exempt from Medicare and Social Security payroll taxation and, in general, from state income taxes. In effect, these exemptions can generate a subsidy of over 40% (for high-income workers who face high marginal tax rates) toward health insurance premiums.

The effect of this substantial subsidy, economists argue, is to induce people, especially those with higher incomes, to choose health insurance plans with higher than optimal premiums (because the premiums are so heavily subsidized) and correspondingly lower cost sharing (because payments made for cost sharing are not subsidized at all) (Pauly, 1986). These generous health insurance plans then induce the excess use of medical services. A public policy – the tax treatment of health insurance – can explain the apparently irrational health insurance choices prevailing in the private market.

The obvious policy response to this argument would be to withdraw the favourable tax treatment of employer-sponsored coverage. Although the economic logic for such a move is impeccable, and withdrawing the subsidy would be progressive over much of the population, it is politically challenging.[4] Instead, advocates sought a policy that would undo the effects of the tax treatment without withdrawing the tax treatment itself. One such option is to extend the favourable tax treatment to include not only premiums, but also out-of-pocket payments made to cover coinsurance and deductibles. The effect of this further tax exemption would be to neutralize the distortion between premiums and cost sharing induced by the existing tax treatment and lead people to choose less generous health insurance policies (Jack & Sheiner, 1997; Cogan, Hubbard & Kessler, 2005). Medical savings accounts, which provide a tax exemption to funds saved for cost sharing and other medical expenses, offer one vehicle for providing this additional, off-setting tax subsidy (Bunce, 2001).

Entrepreneurial lobbying

The academic research arguing that conventional health insurance plans led to welfare losses spurred the development of insurance plans that

[4] The recent health care reform law included a provision that would, starting in 2018, implement a 40% excise tax on plans with annual premiums over a certain amount. The tax would apply to the portion exceeding this amount, and it would not be deductible. The provision has been delayed until 2020 and there have been sustained efforts to repeal it.

would not have these negative effects. The first of these options, the so-called health bank, was proposed in the mid-1970s by economists Jesse Hixson and Paul Worthington, working in the Social Security Administration (Hixson & Worthington, 1978). Under this proposal, employers would deposit money for health care directly into the savings accounts of employees and employees could draw on these accounts to pay for routine expenses. In 1979, the Office of Education in Mendocino County adopted a stay-well plan in which employees' first-dollar coverage plan was replaced with a US$500 deductible policy from the same insurer, and the annual premium savings of about US$480 per worker were used to establish a side fund. Unused balances remaining in the side fund would be remitted to the employee when he or she quit or retired (Heffley & Miceli, 1998; Bogetic & Heffley, 2007).

In the early 1980s, conservative think-tanks began to popularize the health bank idea, and developed the notion of a medical savings account (Bunce, 2001). The chair of one small insurance company, Golden Rule Insurance, decided to move ahead with the idea, offering a combination high-deductible and savings plan initially to his own employees and, later, more broadly (Bunce, 2001). The market for this coverage was small, however, and proponents and promoters of the plan argued that the lack of interest could be attributed to the existing tax subsidy.

During the 1990s, opponents of the tax subsidy and a coalition of small insurers, led by Golden Rule, lobbied very aggressively for changes in the tax code that would promote the development of medical savings accounts (Dreyfuss & Stone, 1996; Pear, 1996). Their efforts were successful in achieving passage of the medical savings account demonstration project as part of the 1996 Health Insurance Accountability and Portability Act legislation, and then in the inclusion of the HSA provisions in the Medicare Modernization Act (2003).

Market vacuum

The third impetus for the introduction of HSAs was growing disenchantment with managed care (see Chapter 15 in this volume). Enrolment in managed care plans had soared during the 1990s and, between 1993 and 1999, this form of insurance slowed the growth of costs quite effectively (Glied, 2003a; Gratzer, 2005). Cost containment in managed care, however, came at the expense of patient and provider autonomy (Blendon et al., 1998). In the latter half of the 1990s, critical media coverage, provider resistance, negative legal decisions, and legislation in the states to protect subscribers and providers ate away at the ability of managed care plans to control costs (Bloche & Studdert, 2004; Brodie, Brady & Altman, 1997). By the end of the decade, health care cost growth had returned to customary levels, and managed care was becoming increasingly unpopular.

In this environment, employers (who make most private health insurance purchasing decisions in the United States), the brokers, agents and consultants who advised them and the insurers selling plans, all sought an alternative cost containment option. In response, market proponents advocated a model of consumer-driven health care (Reinhardt, 1998). The consumer-driven model, promulgated by a group of new technology-savvy insurance companies funded through venture capital, was designed to exploit new information and communications technologies so as to provide patients with information and decision tools, allowing them to weigh the costs and quality of the care they chose. Implicit in this model was the use of a high-deductible health plan and a related medical savings account.

High-deductible health plans had always been available, but the combination of these innovative information tools and the HSA tax subsidy made them a more attractive choice for employers. The lack of an attractive managed care-style alternative further cemented their appeal. By the early 2000s, consumer-directed health plans were a highly prominent focus of health insurance industry marketing attention.

Current status

As the discussion above suggests, the public policy treatment of the medical savings account model continues to evolve. For the private sector, policy-makers have promoted the model exclusively through a tax subsidy to savings accounts held in combination with qualified high-deductible health plans. The current (2016) tax subsidy, provided through the provisions of the 2003 Medicare Modernization Act, offers three benefits to holding an HSA. First, money contributed to the account by individuals or by employers on their behalf is not subject to tax; individual buyers, including the self-employed, may deduct these contributions from their taxable income; and employer contributions are excludable from income and wage taxes. Second, money can accumulate interest in the account tax-free and may be invested at the account holder's discretion. Lastly, the money may be used tax-free for qualified medical expenses (other than insurance premiums). Spending on things other than qualified medical expenses can be included in an individual's gross income and is subject to an additional 20% tax penalty (Grudzien, 2006; Dolan, 2016).

Under existing law, a person may only make contributions to an HSA as long as he or she is covered by a qualified high-deductible health plan. A health plan qualifies under this law if the annual deductible is not less than US$1300 for individuals or US$2600 for family coverage, and the maximum out-of-pocket costs[5] do not exceed US$6550 for individuals and US$13 100 for families (Dolan, 2016). Most Affordable Care Act-compliant bronze level plans sold in the marketplaces could, therefore, be paired with an HSA, though in practice, few such plans are sold in combination with savings accounts (Federal Register, 2016).

The maximum annual contribution to an HSA is also defined in law. For 2017, individuals may make contributions of up to US$3400 for individuals and US$6750 for families (Internal Revenue Service, 2016). Contributions to HSAs may be made by individuals or by employers on their behalf. The account, however, belongs to the individual, and all contributions, whatever their source, remain in the ownership and control of the individual. Payments for premiums for high-deductible plans made in conjunction with HSAs are subject to the same tax rules that govern other insurance plans. For employed people, employer contributions toward premiums are excludable from taxable income. For self-employed people, premium payments are deductible from taxable income.

Lower-income people who purchase health insurance in the Affordable Care Act marketplaces may receive subsidies toward their premiums. Those who purchase nongroup coverage through the exchanges have access to two types of subsidies: premium tax credits, which reduce monthly payments for insurance coverage, and cost-sharing subsidies, which reduce enrollees' out-of-pocket costs for medical care. Enrollees are eligible for premium tax credits if their income is between 100% and 400% of the federal poverty level; they do not have access to affordable coverage through an employer; and they are not eligible for public assistance programmes like Medicare, Medicaid, or the Children's

---

[5] Out-of-pocket costs include the deductible and other forms of cost sharing but not premiums.

Health Insurance Program. They are eligible for a cost-sharing subsidy if they purchase a silver plan; meet all criteria for receiving a premium tax credit; and have household incomes between 100% and 250% of the federal poverty level (Kaiser Family Foundation, 2013). People with incomes above the subsidy level, who do not obtain coverage through an employer receive no tax advantages – they must pay for premiums from after-tax income.

Regulation of medical savings account model plans

The federal legislation that enabled the creation of tax-exempt HSAs regulates only the deductible and out-of-pocket maximum requirements of the corresponding high-deductible health plans. Other tax-related regulations governing HSAs and other employer-provided benefit pro-grammes focus on ensuring that benefit plans are not used to shield highly compensated employees from taxation.

At the federal level, the Internal Revenue Service requires that employers make "comparable contributions" under benefit plans for all "comparable participating employees". This requirement implies that employers must make the same contribution to the accounts of all employees who select the same type of plan (Moran & Farmer, 2007). In the HSA context, this comparability requirement has been modified to permit employers to make larger HSA contributions on behalf of non-highly compensated employees (those in the lower 80% of the compensation distribution within the firm; Joint Committee on Taxation, 2006; Internal Revenue Service, 2017). Both the favourable tax treatment of HSAs (which varies positively with marginal tax rates) and the tax-free savings component of these plans make them inher-ently more attractive to higher-paid employees. This provision allows employers to sweeten an HSA-qualified plan for lower-paid employees by making larger contributions into their accounts.

States also have the option of extending their own tax preferences toward HSAs. Twenty-seven states use the federal definition of taxable income and therefore recognize all deductions and exclusions under federal law for state income tax filers, while another nine states do not have a state income tax. The remainder of the states, however, need a specific law singling out HSAs for favourable tax treatment and, although many have passed such laws, several have not. Many of the states that have not given HSAs tax subsidies have done so because of budgetary concerns, whereas others question HSAs on policy grounds (Jost & Hall, 2006).

The substantive regulation of private insurance largely falls under the authority of the 50 states. The law authorizing HSAs requires nothing of health insurers or the states and it does not free insurers from any existing state requirements (Jost & Hall, 2006). The law does not compel states to require insurers to offer such policies nor does it force states to allow policies conforming to HSA requirements to be sold.

In practice, although most states quickly paved the way for the establishment of HSA-compatible plans, some did not. At the time that the HSA law was passed, several states mandated coverage of specific nonpreventive services with no or a low deductible. These mandates would disqualify any plan in that state from being HSA-qualified. For example, Florida had a law prohibiting insurers from charging insurance deductibles or co-payments to victims of violent crime while Maryland and Pennsylvania prohibited the application of a deductible for certain home health visits for recently delivered mothers and newborns (Jost & Hall, 2006). HSA compliant plans are now offered in all 50 states.

Finally, about 80% of employers with 500 or more employees, and about a third of all employers, currently offer at least one self-insured health plan – plans where the employer, rather than an insurance company, bears the risk of medical expenses (Agency for Healthcare Research and Quality, 2015). These may include HSA-qualified plans. Under the provisions of the federal Employee Retirement Income Security Act (ERISA), these self-insured plans are exempt from all state insurance regulation (and, hence, from virtually all substantive insurance regulation). ERISA does impose fiduciary responsibility on employers, however, and, in the context of HSAs, would make an employer responsible for monitoring the investment performance of such accounts (Moran & Farmer, 2007). Perhaps to encourage employer funding of HSAs without subjecting them to state regulation, the Labor Department, in *Field Assistance Bulletin* 2004–1, declared that an employer would not ordinarily become subject to ERISA's fiduciary requirements if it made contributions to an HSA established or maintained by a third party (see Chapter 15 in this volume; Moran & Farmer, 2007). The provisions of the Affordable Care Act enacted in 2010 do not apply to self-insured plans, so ERISA remains the major piece of federal legislation directly affecting HSA-qualified self-insured plans to date (Jost & Hall, 2012).

As noted at the beginning of this chapter, federal regulation of non-self-insured, HSA-qualified plans increased with the passage of the Affordable Care Act, enacted in 2010. That law set binding minimum medical loss ratios (which limit the allowable share of premiums spent on health care claims and quality-improving expenses) for all plans, including HSA-qualified high-deductible health plans; raised the penalty for premature withdrawals from HSAs; limited their use in paying for over-the-counter pharmaceuticals; and required all plans, including HSA-qualified plans, to cover a set of preventive services without cost sharing (which includes deductibles) (Kaiser Family Foundation, 2013; Dolan, 2016). It also required that all health plans pay at least 60% of the actuarial value of covered benefits. A plan with a 60% actuarial value is a bronze plan on the Affordable Care Act marketplace.

The health savings account market

The market for health plans sold in conjunction with medical savings accounts has matured in the United States. Nonetheless, several issues remain.

Forms of medical savings account plans

The impetus for the development of the medical savings account model has been to allow the market to develop insurance designs that best meet consumer preferences regarding choice, quality and cost. This broad goal meshes uneasily with the need to define the characteristics of plans that will be eligible for tax subsidies (Cannon, 2006).

Regulations interpreting the 2003 HSA legislation permitted some forms of plan design and prohibited others. One important design feature that was permitted is the exemption of preventive health care services from the plan deductible. A series of guidelines issued by the Internal Revenue Service progressively expanded the scope of preventive services exempted. Initially, preventive care was defined to include periodic health evaluations (as well as the tests and procedures used for these evaluations), well-baby and child care, immunizations, tobacco cessation, weight-loss programmes for obesity and certain screenings (Moran & Farmer, 2007). Subsequently, certain additional procedures, such as the removal of polyps during a diagnostic colonoscopy, performed in conjunction with preventive care, were declared as exempt from the deductible requirement (Dotson 2006a). The exemption for preventive care was further extended to include prescription medications provided to prevent the development of a disease in a person who has risk factors for that illness, or to prevent recurrence of a disease (Dotson, 2006b). Two examples given by the Internal Revenue Service were the treatment of high cholesterol with cholesterol-lowering drugs (for example, statins) to prevent heart disease and the treatment of recovered heart attack or stroke victims with angiotensin-converting enzyme inhibitors to prevent a recurrence (Dotson, 2006a).

Insurers took advantage of these provisions by offering HSA-qualified plans that exempt preventive screening. As of 2006, over 80% of workers enrolled in HSA-qualified high-deductible plans were enrolled in ones that did not apply the deductible to preventive benefits (Claxton et al., 2006). At least one major insurer, Aetna, also made several drugs eligible for first-dollar coverage (including anti-hypertensives, anti-diabetic agents, lipid-lowering agents, medications for asthma and osteoporosis, and prenatal and childhood vitamins), within its HSA-qualified high-deductible plan (Robinson, 2005). As noted above, the ACA health care reform law has since standardized preventive care coverage, requiring all plans, included HSA-qualified high-deductible health plans, to cover these preventive services free of cost sharing (Kaiser Family Foundation, 2013; Dolan, 2016).

The exemption of preventive care from deductibles makes eminent sense from a health care delivery perspective – but very little sense in terms of the conventional theory of optimal insurance provision. In theory, insurance, which loads an administrative cost on all covered expenses, should cover unanticipated, catastrophic events – not predictable, more affordable, expenses such as preventive services. The market success of high-deductible health plans that provide first-dollar coverage for preventive care suggests that consumers view health care coverage differently from what basic insurance theory predicts.

A second, unanticipated innovation in HSA-qualified plan design has been the fusion of high-deductible plans with elements of managed care. Several insurers have combined high-deductible plans with preferred-provider arrangements (Scheffler & Felton, 2006). Under these arrangements, the insurer contracts with selected providers to obtain favourable rates for care. The cost of services purchased from in-network providers is then set against the plan's in-network deductible (which must conform to the qualified-plan minima). The cost of services purchased from noncontracted, out-of-network providers are applied to a higher, out-of-network deductible. Federal regulations permit the out-of-pocket limit in the HSA law to be exceeded for these out-of-network services (Moran & Farmer, 2007). These preferred-provider high-deductible plans place limits on the patient's choice of provider – the types of limits that led to concerns about constrained choice under managed care. For many people, however, the advantages of improved bargaining power and price information generated through insurer contracting appear to outweigh these constraints (Hall & Havighurst, 2005).

Some insurance plans have combined other elements of managed care with HSA-qualified plans. For example, Kaiser Permanente, a large, non-profit, group-model health maintenance organization, which provides fully integrated coverage that includes its own hospitals and exclusively contracted clinics, offers an HSA-qualified plan that restricts participants to the services offered by the health maintenance organization (Kaiser Permanente, 2004, 2016). It is likely to be more difficult to integrate high-deductible provisions with capitation payment or pay-for-performance arrangements that do not pay physicians for each service or visit. In such cases, it is not clear what payment would be made from the consumer's HSA (Hall & Havighurst, 2005).

Savings plans

The medical savings account model is most conceptually attractive when funds to pay for medical expenses under the high-deductible plan are readily available within a segregated savings account. Without such an account, policy-holders may fail to use medical services that they do value at full cost because they do not have liquid funds available.

The tax incentives that promote the use of high-deductible health plans coupled with savings accounts in the United States encourage, but do not compel, policy-holders (or their employers) to make contributions to their savings accounts. The tax advantages make fully funding accounts economically attractive, but, in practice, other, similar, tax-favoured savings vehicles, such as retirement accounts, are often underfunded (Burman, Gale & Hall, 2004).

Contributions to plans may be made by employees, employers or both. In calendar year 2015, over half of employers who offered HSAs made no contribution to their employees' savings plans. Among those who did make contributions, the average contribution to a single plan was about US$1000, about half the size of the deductibles in these plans (Kaiser Family Foundation and Health Research and Educational Trust, 2016). One study of the earlier medical savings accounts demonstration project found that about two thirds of account holders saved money in their accounts from one year to the next (Minicozzi, 2006).

The extent of under-saving in HSAs is likely to depend on the form they take. If they are offered as a voluntary option, with the tax-exempt savings provision as the main inducement for participation, they are likely to attract participants who wish to exploit the tax-free savings component. Conversely, if they are offered as the only option to lower-income workers for whom tax-free saving is not an important consideration, by employers who make a modest or no contribution to the HSA, underfunding of HSAs may be a serious problem, leading to under-utilization of valued care. A recent study found that high-income and older tax filers both established HSAs and fully funded their HSAs at least four times as often as did low-income and younger filers (Helmchen et al., 2015).

Market structure

The origins of the medical savings account movement were in small to mid-size health insurance plans, such as Golden Rule, and venture-capital-funded entrepreneurial consumer-directed models. Most of these pioneering firms have now been acquired by large commercial insurers, who can offer HSAs in conjunction with other types of insurance products. Anthem, a for-profit insurer formed through the conversion of several non-profit Blue Cross plans, which is among the leading private insurers in market share, bought a venture-capital funded consumer-driven pioneer, Lumenos, in 2005 (Glabman, 2006). UnitedHealth, another of the largest commercial insurers, acquired Golden Rule in 2003 and another consumer-driven firm, Definity, in 2004. Other large insurers have developed their own HSA products.

The medical savings account model requires health insurance to be paired with a distinctly different product, the tax-favoured savings account that accompanies the requisite high-deductible plan. Some insurers have paired up with financial services corporations, which have expertise in operating tax-favoured retirement savings accounts, to manage the new HSAs. Other insurers have chartered their own banks to operate the accounts (Dash, 2006).

Participation

In 2015, the total number of Americans enrolled in health insurance plans with deductibles above the HSA threshold (see footnote 285) was about 40 million. Of these, over a third had a health saving account (Cohen & Martinez, 2015). People may purchase qualified high-deductible health plans and open HSAs either through their employers or in the nongroup market. In the employer market, employers may elect to offer only HSA-qualified plans, or they may offer a choice of plans, including one or more HSA-qualified high-deductible plans.

The nongroup insurance market in the United States had been small, heavily regulated and, until the introduction of tax-exempt HSAs, not subsidized at all. Coverage offered in this market was (and continues to be) less generous than typical employer-based coverage. Many enrollees in this market already had health coverage that incorporated deductibles and cost sharing exceeding the HSA minima, and for them the HSA legislation was an unmitigated boon because it provided a new tax-exempt savings vehicle to accompany their existing health plans. For this reason, much of the early enrolment in HSA plans came from the nongroup market. Passage of the health reform law significantly increased the level of regulation and standardization in the nongroup market, both for those participating in the health care marketplaces and those buying coverage outside them. The least generous plans currently offered (Bronze plans) in the nongroup market are HSA-eligible. As of 2015, about 2 million nongroup enrollees hold HSA-qualified high-deductible health plans (America's Health Insurance Plans, 2015).

As in the nongroup market, one easy source of new HSA enrolment was in large firms that had always offered a high-deductible, indemnity insurance option. In 2003, immediately before the introduction of HSAs, 5% of American private sector employees worked for firms that offered at least one high-deductible health insurance plan, including 17% of workers in establishments with 5000 or more employees. Building from this base, about a quarter of all firms now offer an HSA-eligible health plan (Kaiser Family Foundation and Health Research and Educational Trust, 2016).

In settings where employers offer a choice between HSA-qualified plans and other forms of insurance, the share of workers choosing HSAs depends on the required employee premium contributions to the various plans, the nature of plans offered and the extent to which the employer contributes to the HSA. On average, the percentage of workers choosing these plans has increased from 2% in 2006 to 19% in 2016 (Kaiser Family Foundation and Health Research and Educational Trust, 2016). Many small employers offer only a single type of plan, but several very large firms have also chosen to offer only an HSA-qualified high-deductible option (Glabman, 2006).

Performance

Future growth in HSAs in the voluntary, private insurance market will depend on the performance of existing plans with respect to cost, outcomes and consumer satisfaction. Here we describe what is known about performance to date.

Costs

The effects of medical savings account plans on spending depend partly on whether these plans are voluntarily selected or imposed on all market participants. Simulation studies based on the RAND health insurance experiment indicate that moving all Americans from the typical preferred-provider organization plan to an HSA-qualified plan with a savings account could reduce health care spending by about 5–15% (Baicker, Dow & Wolfson, 2006; Buntin et al., 2006; Haviland et al., 2012).

If medical savings account participation is voluntary, however, the effect of the high-deductible plan/HSA option will depend on the characteristics of those who select the plans and the nature of the plans that these participants would have held in the absence of this new option. For example, to the extent that early enrollees in HSA plans were drawn primarily from holders of high-deductible plans in the nongroup and large-group markets, the new tax-exempt savings option would not reduce costs and might even lead to cost increases (as cost-sharing payments would now be tax favoured) (Remler & Glied, 2006).

Studies find that prepayment premiums in HSA-qualified high-deductible health plans are generally lower than in other insurance plans (Claxton et al., 2005, 2006, 2015). This finding is not unexpected, as the lower coverage levels of qualified plans both shift costs from premiums to plan participants and discourage the use of services.

Most studies of HSA adopters have found that HSA-qualified plans lead to lower average health care costs than other plans, but the nature and magnitude of the estimated effects are critically dependent on what components of spending the studies measure, what the comparison group is, and how well the studies control for the characteristics of people who choose to participate in these plans (Buntin et al., 2006). Many studies conducted by the industry, for example, measure only effects on premiums, ignoring the increases in consumer spending that follow from shifting expenses from premiums to deductibles. Many studies fail to control for selection. Well-controlled studies of early HSA adopters have found only modest effects on total spending when firms switched from standard preferred-provider organization plans to HSA-eligible plans (Parente, Feldman & Christianson, 2004; Feldman, Parente & Christianson, 2007). A more recent, well-designed study found that in one large self-insured firm, spending was reduced by 12–14% after switching from an insurance plan that provided free health care to a high-deductible health plan (Brot-Goldberg et al., 2015).

Health care utilization and outcomes

A perpetual concern about high-deductible plans, including those associated with HSAs, is that they will lead to reductions in the use of appropriate care, particularly by those with low incomes and by the chronically ill, and therefore lead to worse health outcomes. The RAND health insurance experiment found that differences in cost sharing did not affect the health of most people, but that the health status of some low-income people was compromised by assignment to high cost-sharing plans (Feldstein, 2006). Current versions of HSA-qualified plans, however, differ from the RAND experiment plans in that they provide first-dollar coverage for preventive care, which may mitigate the potential effects of high cost sharing on use of these services.

The existing literature on the effect of HSAs on health utilization shows mixed results (Buntin et al., 2006; Charlton et al., 2011; Reed et al., 2012). Some studies of HSA participants find that their use of preventive services is maintained or even improves, relative to those in traditional plans (Agrawal et al., 2005; Charlton et al., 2011). Other studies find that those in high-deductible plans are more likely to avoid, skip or delay receipt of needed health care (Fronstin & Collins, 2005; Buntin et al., 2006; Reed et al., 2012). A few studies have found that high-deductible plan participants with chronic conditions are more likely than others to follow the appropriate treatment regimen, but these studies did not control for the characteristics of people with chronic conditions who choose to enrol in HSAs (Agrawal et al., 2005). A recent study by Brot-Goldberg et al. (2015) finds reductions in both potentially valuable care (for example, preventive services) and potentially wasteful care (for example, imaging services). Little is known about how HSA-qualified high-deductible health plans will affect outcomes. Overall, it appears unlikely that participating in high-deductible plans with tax-favoured HSAs will harm the health of most of those who voluntarily choose them, but the evidence to date does not rule out problems for low-income participants.

Satisfaction

The final dimension of performance that seems likely to influence the diffusion of medical savings account-style plans in the voluntary private health insurance market is satisfaction. The rhetoric surrounding these plans has emphasized the role of participants as consumers and an important factor in their development has been consumer dissatisfaction with restrictions in managed care.

Perhaps unsurprisingly, the most consistent finding about HSA-style plans to date has been that satisfaction is generally lower among people with these plans than among those with traditional coverage. Fewer than half of participants in the new plans report that they are as satisfied with their current plan as they had been with previous coverage, although this group may be dominated by workers whose employers offered only HSA plans (Agrawal et al., 2005; Fronstin & Collins, 2005; Employee Benefit Research Institute, 2013).

Although much of the dissatisfaction is undoubtedly due to the increased cost sharing, studies have also found that many enrollees are not satisfied with the information available to help them make medical decisions. Plan participants report that they do not have enough information about the prices doctors charge to make sensible cost-conscious choices. Many do not trust information on provider quality provided by their insurance plan and seek information from alternative sources (Agrawal et al., 2005). Information provided is often either too aggregated – describing average costs in a market – or insufficiently aggregated – describing costs for subcomponents of care rather than for an episode of care – to be useful in consumer decision-making (Reden & Anders Ltd, 2005; Rosenthal, Hsuan & Milstein, 2005; Sinaiko, Mehrotra & Sood, 2016). Information on hospital quality and on pharmaceutical options is more readily available than information on physician quality and cost (Regopoulos et al., 2006). Recent research, however, suggests that even when good information is provided, few members make effective use of it (Brot-Goldberg et al., 2015).

The effect of medical savings account-style plans on the US health system

The tax-favoured medical savings account model in the US health system has grown over the past decade. HSA-style plans may continue to grow as employers seek lower costs and consumers become more comfortable with the health care decision-making that these plans demand. That outcome has potentially substantial ramifications for the entire system along three dimensions: risk pooling; vertical equity; and consumer choice.

Market segmentation and risk pooling

The HSA-qualified plans are usually offered as one among several health insurance options. Allowing people to choose these plans can have consequences for the cost of other plans, if HSA-qualified plan enrollees are systematically different in their health care utilization patterns from enrollees in other plans.

Several characteristics of HSA-qualified plans suggest that they attract a distinct group of enrollees. The opportunity to save tax-free through the HSA vehicle is only valuable for those who expect to have funds remaining after paying for their uncovered medical expenses. This feature makes the HSA model more attractive to younger, healthier people than to older, sicker ones. Conversely, people who have health conditions that lead them to spend substantial sums out of pocket each year may find the opportunity to pay for care using pre-tax dollars valuable. To the extent that HSA-qualified plans allow more freedom of choice of provider than conventional plans (this is not always the case), they may also be popular among those with health conditions that benefit from highly specialized care. Studies of enrollees in high-deductible plans generally find that they are somewhat healthier and younger than average, but the pattern is not uniform and, in some contexts, enrollees are more likely to be drawn from middle-aged than younger cohorts (Buntin et al., 2006; Greene et al., 2006; Minicozzi, 2006; America's Health Insurance Plans, 2015).

There is undoubtedly a potential for high-deductible plans to promote risk fragmentation. Most employers do not risk-adjust health insurance premiums and concerns that high-deductible plans will skim off the healthiest members of a group and drive overall costs up may be one impediment to their adoption. The tax treatment of employer-sponsored health insurance favours more costly plans, such as those preferred by sicker people. By undoing the effects of existing tax policy, the HSA tax exemption may drive up relative costs for this sicker group. Although the potential for risk fragmentation due to HSAs is real, the magnitude of this effect remains uncertain.

Equity

The tax exemption for HSA savings is greatest for those in the highest marginal tax brackets and, within this group, for those with the greatest propensity to save. Both features make this benefit most valuable to those with the highest incomes and assets. As noted before, a recent study found that high-income and older tax filers both established HSAs and fully funded them much more frequently than did low-income and younger filers (Helmchen et al., 2015). The tax exemption for HSA contributions also provides a small subsidy for health insurance to those purchasing coverage in the nongroup market, including employed people who are not offered or choose not to take-up employer-sponsored coverage. This subsidy, however, is too small to induce much shifting from the group to the nongroup market.

In its structure, the subsidy offered through the tax exemption for HSAs provides little benefit for most uninsured and low-income people in the United States. About half of uninsured adults do not face any income tax liability, so any plan promoting health insurance through tax exemptions or deductions would not benefit them much. Most uninsured adults who face tax liability are in very low tax brackets and very few have savings, so HSAs are not an attractive option for this group (Glied & Remler, 2005). Moreover, high-deductible plans combined with HSAs may not provide much value to low-income people, who are unlikely to keep sufficient funds in their HSAs to pay for their medical expenses and often have limited disposable income outside these dedicated savings vehicles. Given the choice between contributing towards the premium of an HSA-qualified plan and going without coverage altogether, some lower-income people may prefer to remain uninsured (Glied, 2003b).

Although the promotion of HSA plans does nothing to promote vertical equity in the system, it does not make the system much more regressive, within the context of existing health insurance tax policy. The effect of the HSA tax exemption is largely to counterbalance the equally regressive impact of the existing favourable tax treatment of employer-sponsored health insurance (Cannon, 2006). The Affordable Care Act's high-cost plan tax, known as the Cadillac Tax, which is now scheduled to take effect in 2020, should have a more progressive impact on health insurance tax policy. Designed to maximize revenue and minimize coverage disruptions, this is a 40% excise tax on employer plans with high premiums, including those that are HSA-qualified. Because high earners benefit most from HSAs, the high-cost plan tax should help mitigate the regressive effect of favourable tax treatment (Glied & Striar, 2016).

Consumer choice

Advocates of medical savings account plans in the United States see the empowering of consumer decision-making as one of their most important benefits. A subgroup of Americans is deeply sceptical that any outside authority – whether the medical profession, a private insurer or the government – will make appropriate trade-offs between the cost and quality of medical care. Sceptics recognize that, given the astronomical costs of catastrophic care, insurance is inevitable, but they wish coverage to take a form that allows them as active a part as possible in making decisions about their own health care.

The HSA model is clearly attractive to members of this group. Enrollees in HSA-qualified plans are substantially more likely to ask about health care costs, to independently identify treatment options and to select among treatments than enrollees in conventional insurance plans (Agrawal et al., 2005; Fronstin & Collins, 2005). They are more educated and more comfortable with information technology. Allowing a choice of an HSA-model plan permits people with these authority-challenging preferences to escape the limitations of conventional insurance allocation. To the extent that this subgroup exhibits preferences on other aspects of medical care that differ from those of conventional insurance enrollees, their departure from the pool has little cost. To the extent, however, that this vocal subgroup provides a constraint on quality-reducing cost-cutting in employer, insurer or government behaviour within conventional health plans, their exit to the HSA market may generate a reduction in the overall quality of the health system.

Conclusions

Forty years since the idea of HSAs was first introduced, these accounts have become a routine feature of health insurance debates in the United States. The provision of tax-exempt status to these accounts through the passage of the 2003 Medicare Prescription Drug, Improvement and Modernization Act has effectively entrenched them in the landscape, and HSAs have become a growing feature of the health insurance market.

Developments to date suggest that the HSA market, as it evolves, is not likely to lead to the crises feared by opponents. Plans currently on the market must offer access to preventive care at no charge to the beneficiary and some also exempt medications for the management of chronic illness from the deductible. Enrolment in HSA plans has not been associated with deteriorations in health status (although this might change if enrolment shifts to lower-income groups), nor has it led to significantly increased fragmentation of the insurance market.

At the same time, HSA plans are far from achieving the potential promised by advocates. HSA enrollees do not have adequate information with which to weigh costs and quality. They typically fail to maintain sufficient reserves in their savings accounts. Most report that they are less satisfied with their plans than they had been with previous coverage. Most HSA plans continue to contract with physicians and to review utilization above the deductible, so enrollees have not been freed of the constraints imposed by managed care. Although enrolment will probably continue to grow, it seems unlikely that the HSA model will solve the problems of cost, access and quality that plague the US health insurance market.

References

Agency for Healthcare Research and Quality (2015). *Medical expenditure panel survey*: https://meps.ahrq.gov/data_stats/summ_tables/insr/national/series_1/2015/tia2a.pdf; accessed on 07/10/2016.

Agrawal V et al. (2005). *Consumer-directed health plan report – early evidence is promising*: www.mckinsey.com/client_service/public_sector/people/~/media/a4a25ce45a1344c8bf8b0c1eddbcd1c2.ashx. Accessed on 07/10/2016.

America's Health Insurance Plans (2015). 2015 census of health savings account - high deductible health plans: https://ahip.org/wp-content/uploads/2015/11/HSA_Report.pdf; accessed on 07/10/2016.

Andrews M (2014). States experiment with health savings accounts for Medicaid. National Public Radio (NPR): www.npr.org/sections/health-shots/2014/07/22/333745570/states-experiment-with-health-savings-accounts-for-medicaid; accessed on 07/10/2016.

Baicker K, Dow W, Wolfson J (2006). Health savings accounts: implications for health spending. *National Tax Journal*, 59(3):463–75.

Blendon R et al. (1998). Understanding the managed care backlash. *Health Affairs*, 17(4):80–94.

Bloche G, Studdert D (2004). A quiet revolution: law as an agent of health system change. *Health Affairs*, 23(2):29–42.

Blumenthal D (2006). Employer-sponsored health insurance in the United States – origins and implication. *New England Journal of Medicine*, 355(1):82–8.

Bogetic Z, Heffley D (2007). *Reforming health care: a case for stay-well health insurance*. Policy Research Working Paper Series No. 1181. Washington DC, World Bank.

Brodie M, Brady L, Altman D (1997). Media coverage of managed care: is there a negative bias? *Health Affairs*, 17(1):9–25.

Brot-Goldberg Z et al. (2015). What does a deductible do? The impact of cost-sharing on health care prices, quantities, and spending dynamics. Working paper 21632: www.nber.org/papers/w21632; accessed on 07/10/2016.

Bunce V (2001). Medical savings accounts: progress and problems under HIPAA: http://object.cato.org/sites/cato.org/files/pubs/pdf/pa411.pdf; accessed on 07/10/2016.

Buntin MB et al. (2006). Consumer-directed health care: early evidence about effects on cost and quality. *Health Affairs*, 25(6):W516–30.

Burman L, Gale W, Hall M (2004). Distributional effects of defined contribution plans and individual retirement arrangements. *National Tax Journal*, 57(3):671–701.

Cannon M (2006). *Health savings accounts: do the critics have a point?* Policy Analysis No. 569. Washington DC, Cato Institute.

Centers for Medicare and Medicaid Services (2012). Your guide to Medicare Medical Savings Account (MSA) plans: www.medicare.gov/pubs/pdf/11206.pdf; accessed on 07/10/2016.

Charlton ME et al. (2011). Effects of health savings account-eligible plans on utilization and expenditures. *The American Journal of Managed Care* 17(1):79–86.

Claxton G et al. (2005). What high-deductible plans look like: findings from a National Survey of Employers, 2005: http://content.healthaffairs.org/cgi/content/full/hlthaff.w5.434/DC1; accessed on 08/08/2007.

Claxton G et al. (2006). Health benefits in 2006: premium increases moderate, enrollment in consumer-directed health plans remains modest. *Health Affairs*, Web exclusive (5 August).

Claxton G et al. (2015). Health benefits in 2015: stable trends in the employer market. *Health Affairs*, 34(10):1779–88.

Cogan J, Hubbard G, Kessler D (2005). *Healthy, wealthy, and wise.* Washington DC, AEI Press/Hoover Institution.

Cohen RA, Martinez ME (2015). Health insurance coverage: early release of estimates from the National Health Interview Survey, January–March 2015. National Center for Health Statistics: www.cdc.gov/nchs/data/nhis/earlyrelease/insur201508.pdf; accessed on 15/12/2016.

Dash E (2006). Health savings accounts attract Wall Street. *New York Times* 27 January.

Dolan R (2016). Health policy brief: High-deductible health plans. *Health Affairs*: www.healthaffairs.org/healthpolicybriefs/brief.php?brief_id=152; accessed on 07/10/2016.

Dotson K (2006a). HSAs and preventive care. *Journal of Deferred Compensation*, 11(2):3–8.

Dotson K (2006b). Prescription drug coverage in light of consumerism initiatives. *Journal of Deferred Compensation*, 11(2):9–15.

Dreyfuss R, Stone P (1996). Medikill: www.motherjones.com/news/feature/1996/01/medikill.html; accessed on 07/10/2016.

Employee Benefit Research Institute (2013). Notes: www.shrm.org/ResourcesAndTools/hr-topics/benefits/Documents/EBRI_Notes_08_Aug-13_RetPart-CEHCS1.pdf; accessed on 07/10/2016.

Federal Register (2016). Patient Protection and Affordable Care Act; HHS notice of benefit and payment parameters for 2017.

Feldman R, Dowd B (1991). A new estimate of the welfare loss of excess health insurance. *American Economic Review*, 81(1):297–301.

Feldman R, Parente S, Christianson J (2007). Consumer directed health plans: new evidence on cost and utilization. *Inquiry*, 44(1):26–42.

Feldstein M (1973). The welfare loss of excess health insurance. *Journal of Political Economy*, 81(2):251–80.

Feldstein M (2006). Balancing the goals of health care provision and financing. *Health Affairs*, 25(6):1603–11.

Fronstin P, Collins SR (2005). *Early experience with high-deductible and consumer-driven health plans: findings from the EBRI/Commonwealth Fund Consumerism in Health Care Survey.* New York, Commonwealth Fund.

Glabman M (2006). Taking the pulse of consumer-driven health plans. *Physician Executive*, 32(5):CS-259.

Glied S (2003a). Health care costs: on the rise again. *Journal of Economic Perspectives*, 17(2):125–48.

Glied S (2003b). Health insurance expansions and the content of coverage: is something better than nothing? *Forum for Health Economics and Policy*, 6 (Frontiers in Health Policy Research): Article 4.

Glied S, Remler D (2005). *The effect of health savings accounts on health insurance coverage.* New York, The Commonwealth Fund.

Glied S, Striar A (2016). Looking under the hood of the Cadillac Tax. Washington, DC, The Commonwealth Fund.

Gratzer D (2005). What ails heath care? *Public Interest*, 159:109–24.

Greene J et al. (2006). Which consumers are ready for consumer-directed health plans? *Journal of Consumer Policy*, 29(3):247–62.

Grudzien L (2006). HRAs or HSAs: how does an employer decide? *Journal of Deferred Compensation*, 11(2):27–47.

Hall M, Havighurst C (2005). Reviving managed care with health savings accounts. *Health Affairs*, 24(6):1490–500.

Haviland AM et al. (2012). Growth of consumer-directed health plans to one-half of all employer-sponsored insurance could save $57 billion annually. *Health Affairs*, 31(5):1009–15.

Heffley D, Miceli T (1998). The economics of incentive-based health care plans. *Journal of Risk and Insurance*, 65(3):445–65.

Helmchen L et al. (2015). Health savings accounts: Growth concentrated among high-income households and large employers. *Health Affairs*, 34(9):1594–8.

Hixson J, Worthington P (1978). Alternative prepayment finance for hospital services. *Inquiry*, 15(3).

Internal Revenue Service (2016). Rev. Proc. 2016-28: www.irs.gov/pub/irs-drop/rp-16-28.pdf; accessed on 07/10/2016.

Internal Revenue Service (2017). *Health Savings Accounts and Other Tax-Favored Health Plans.* Washington DC, Internal Revenue Service Department of the Treasury.

Jack W, Sheiner L (1997). Welfare improving health expenditure subsidies. *American Economic Review*, 87(1):206–21.

Joint Committee on Taxation (2006). *Technical explanation of H.R. 6408, the 'Tax Relief and Health Care Act of 2006' as introduced in the House on December 7, 2006*: www.finance.senate.gov/imo/media/doc/prg121206.pdf; accessed on 07/10/2016.

Jost T, Hall M (2006). The role of state regulation in consumer-driven health care. *American Journal of Law & Medicine*, 31(4):395–418.

Jost T, Hall MA (2012). Self-insurance for small employers under the Affordable Care Act: federal and state regulatory options. *New York University Annual Survey of American Law*, 68:539.

Kaiser Family Foundation (2013). Summary of the Affordable Care Act; www.kff.org/health-reform/fact-sheet/summary-of-the-affordable-care-act/; accessed on 20/06/2017.

Kaiser Family Foundation and Health Research and Educational Trust (2015). 2015 employer health benefits survey: http://files.kff.org/attachment/report-2015-employer-health-benefits-survey; accessed on 20/06/2017.

Kaiser Family Foundation and Health Research and Educational Trust (2016). 2016 employer health benefits survey: http://kff.org/health-costs/report/2016-employer-health-benefits-survey/; accessed on 07/10/2016.

Kaiser Permanente (2004). New Kaiser Permanente health plans and health savings accounts (HSA) offer increased access and choice: https://share .kaiserpermanente.org/article/new-kaiser-permanente-health-plans-and-health-savings-accounts-hsa-offer-increased-access-and-choice/; accessed on 07/10/2016.

Kaiser Permanente (2016). Kaiser Permanente: Bronze 60 HSA HMO: http://info.kaiserpermanente.org/healthplans/california/individual/pdfs/2016-ON-Exchange/PLNSBC_CAL_800222_9000_20160101_20120501_en.pdf; accessed on 15/12/2017.

Manning WG, Marquis MS (1996). Health insurance: the tradeoff between risk pooling and moral hazard. *Journal of Health Economics*, 15(5):609–39.

Minicozzi A (2006). Medical savings accounts: what story do the data tell? *Health Affairs*, 25(1) 256–67.

Moran A, Farmer G (2007). Health savings accounts: will new legislative changes increase their use? *Employee Relations Law Journal*, 33(1):87–99.

Musumeci M, Rudowitz R (2015). The ACA and Medicaid Expansion Waivers. Kaiser Family Foundation Issue Brief: http://kff.org/report-section/the-aca-and-medicaid-expansion-waivers-issue-brief/; accessed 09/10/2016.

Newhouse J (2004). Consumer-directed health plans and the RAND Health Insurance Experiment. *Health Affairs*, 23(6):107–13.

Parente S, Feldman R, Christianson J (2004). Evaluation of the effect of a consumer-driven health plan on medical care expenditures and utilization. *Health Services Research*, 39(4 part 2):1189–210.

Pauly M (1968). The economics of moral hazard: comment. *American Economic Review*, 58(3 Part 1):531–7.

Pauly M (1986). Taxation, health insurance, and market failure in the medical economy. *Journal of Economic Literature*, 24(2):629–75.

Pear R (1996). G.O.P. plan would profit insurer with ties to party. *New York Times* 14 April.

Reden & Anders Ltd (2005). *Consumer directed insurance products: survey results. Internal company report* Minneapolis, MN, Reden & Anders Ltd.

Reed ME et al. (2012). In consumer-directed health plans, a majority of patients were unaware of free or low-cost preventive care. *Health Affairs*, 31(12):2641–8.

Regopoulos L et al. (2006). Consumer-directed health insurance products: local-market perspectives. *Health Affairs*, 25(3):766–73.

Reinhardt U (1998). Quality in consumer-driven health systems. *International Journal for Quality in Health Care*, 10(5):385–94.

Remler D, Glied S (2006). How much more cost sharing will health savings accounts bring? HSAs don't appear to be living up to their reputation for increasing consumers' cost sharing. *Health Affairs*, 25(4):1070–8.

Robinson J (2005). Consumer-directed health insurance: the next generation, *Health Affairs* Web exclusive (13 December):W583–W590.

Rosenthal M, Hsuan C, Milstein A (2005). A report card on the Freshman class of consumer-directed health plans. *Health Affairs*, 24(6):1592–600.

Scheffler R, Felton M (2006). Consumer-driven health plans: new developments and the long road ahead. *Business Economics*, 41(3):44–8.

Sinaiko AD, Mehrotra A, Sood N (2016). Cost-sharing obligations, high-deductible health plan growth, and shopping for health care: enrollees with skin in the game. *JAMA Internal Medicine*, 176(3):395–7.

Index

Printed in the United States
By Bookmasters